Price $ 49.95

ISBN: 0-9651186-2-2

Printed in the United States of America

Book of Astrology by LIGIA BALU

ASTROLOGY - HOW TO FIND YOUR SOUL-MATE, STARS, AND DESTINY - ARIES

Visit: www.ligiabalu.com

FORWARD

Astrology means the study of the stars. It is an ancient course of study dating to prehistoric times which concentrates on the correlation between celestial events and human events. *HOW TO FIND YOUR SOUL-MATE, STARS AND DESTINY* is based on traditional research and offers a basic introduction to this age old science. It is important to know how to find one's soul mate and destiny, and one important aspect of that search is a better understanding of one's self. Understanding ourselves and our motivations sets us on a path of better understanding the other persons in our lives and those persons we come in contact with. If you are very careful in your decision making, when you learn to match the signs by hour, days, months, and years with your own sign, you are less likely to make mistakes in choosing your love, soul mate, and destiny for life. This is a unique book designed for the reader to prevent unnecessary mistakes in life: broken hearts, broken families, lost loves, lonely times, crying and screaming over loved ones. Through the study of Astrology, you the reader, may come to a better understanding of the problems you have suffered in life. Perhaps you have found yourself asking why other people appear happy together and why other people appear to have so few problems. Perhaps you have asked yourself, "Why not me? What is wrong with me? Why can't I be happy? I have many good qualities just like other people. Why am I attracted to the wrong person? Why do bad things happen to me?" By thoroughly understanding not only your conscious self but your subconscious reasoning (often referred to in Astrology as the unconscious), you may finally find the answers you have been searching for. Just as effectively, you can study and begin to understand persons born to other signs as well. Why does a person act or behave the way they do, either obstinate, or changeable, or impulsive? Perhaps a basic answer to that question can be found in the nature of the Sun sign.

The Zodiac refers to the "Circle of Animals" or the "Circle of Life" and is the name for the belt of constellations viewed in the celestial heavens. It is made up of twelve signs: Aries, Taurus, Gemini, Cancer, Leo, Virgo, Libra, Scorpio, Sagittarius, Capricorn, Aquarius, and Pisces. These are referred to as the Sun signs or the sign which the Sun was in on the date a person was born. The Sun, as the most important celestial body, is considered the greatest influence in one's personal horoscope. A further understanding of Astrology, however, depends upon an understanding of one's Moon sign, Ascendant, Houses, Planets, and the Aspects these Planets make to one another. Each of these influences the person as well which is why two people with the same Sun sign can be so different. *STARS AND DESTINY* provides the reader with an explanation of each of these influences. And because each person is different, *STARS AND DESTINY* presents both the positive and the negative characteristics of each of these influences. And it is the combination of these positives and negatives that produce the individual. And it is left to each individual to determine how to react to these positives and negatives. In other words,

i

one person may use assertiveness to develop leadership qualities while another becomes aggressive, obstinate, and even hostile. Life is a long road of self-improvement, but the basics remain the same. How one person reacts and relates to another depends to a large degree on each person's security and self-esteem. That is what this book strives to explain: Why we are the way we are.

Over the last twenty years, in my journey through life, many friends, co-workers, acquaintances, and others who chose the wrong soul mate for better or for worse have called me for counseling. Because love can be blind, these situations often change into disaster. I have observed over time that these decisions lead to misunderstandings, disappointments, tragedies, divorce, and loneliness. What suffers the most is the creation of love. The resulting lonely time is not a life to live. Life is short, and this is no way to find happiness or to be content. A broken heart can lead a person to believe that all men and/or women are the same, and it is no use to continue looking for the right one. This attitude can result in the person choosing to be alone for a long time or to attempt to protect themselves and the creations of love: their children. Rather than trying again to find the right partner, they choose to remain alone when it, otherwise, would be possible to be happy and never lonely. It may be difficult to believe, but Astrology can help people learn the lessons they need to know in order never to be lonely. The simple truth comes from God above. God doesn't like to see us alone. He never intended people to go through life by themselves, but instead, He planned for each of us to discover our true soul mates and to go through life - and eternity - together. This is simple logic because the soul mate is the other half of ourselves.

In life, it is easy to make mistakes especially if one is attracted to the wrong person in the wrong place for the wrong reasons. We are all really looking for love rather than to be left lonely and by ourselves. Why have the men and women in your life been mistakes? When thinking about love, remember it is the most powerful force in life. It is nice to have someone to share your life with. Success is an empty bag when you have no one to share it with. You ask yourself, "What is wrong with me?" Nothing is wrong with you. You have just been attracted to the wrong person. It is difficult to find Mr. or Mrs. Right when you are attracted to Mr. or Mrs. Wrong. Once in this relationship, you struggle to make it work. Many times, when we are caught up in these wrong relationships, we miss the opportunity to meet Mr. or Mrs. Right. Why do we struggle so much when there is a way to make life easier and never to be alone again? Take time for yourself. Study not only yourself but the others around you. Of the people you meet, select one for your destiny with whom to share love and life. Astrology provides you with this necessary information. What is required is the time and effort to grasp a fuller understanding of yourself. When you truly understand yourself, you better understand what it is you want, what you are looking for, and what makes you happy. You are a unique individual with a specific combination of characteristics, personality traits, likes, and dislikes. What you must also accept is that others have particular tendencies which you must either accept and learn to live with or make the decision to find that special person with whom you are the most compatible. Love is the magic which propels us all to initiate this search throughout the universe for our true soul mate and love match. I like to see people happy and to see less sorrow and loneliness. Lift is short. Today we are here, and tomorrow we are not. Learn to live each day to its fullest.

HOUSE RULERSHIPS

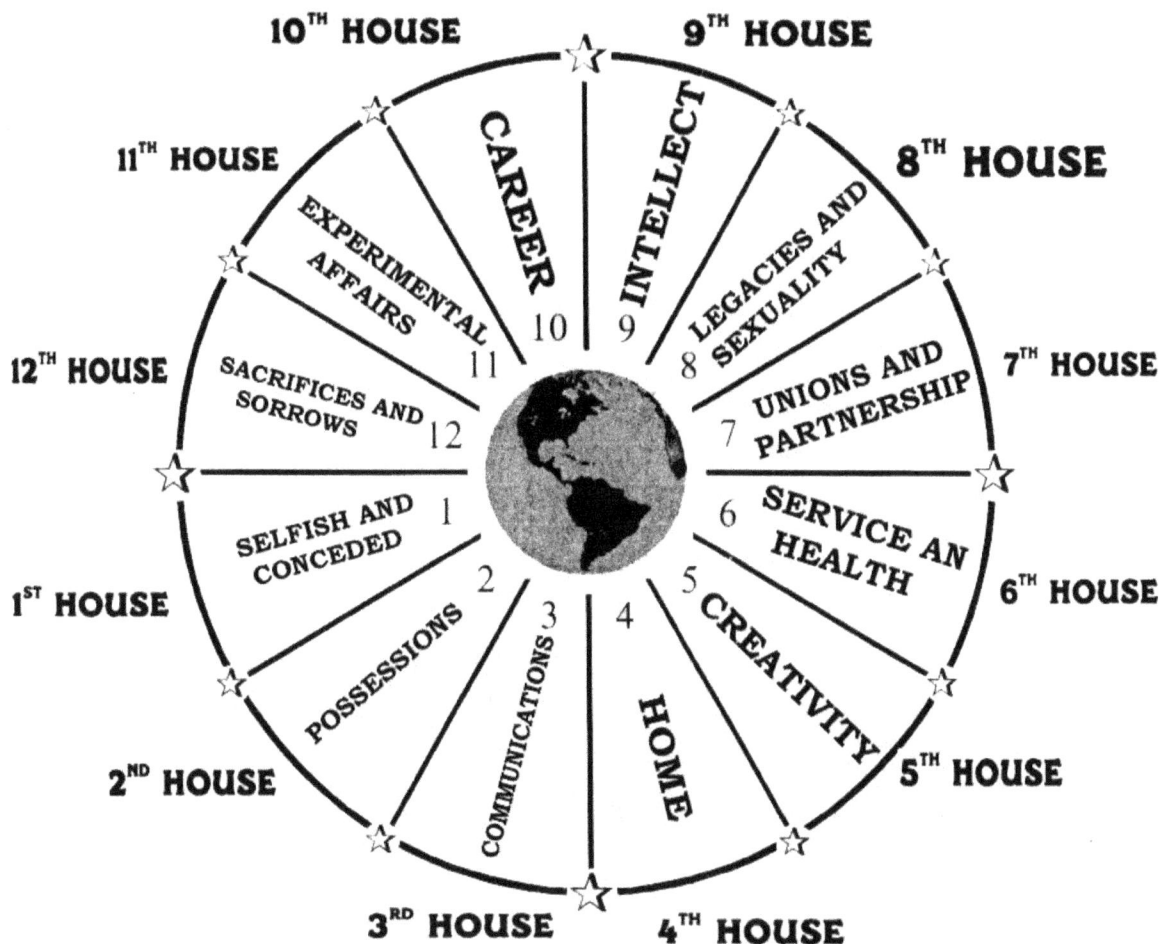

10TH HOUSE   9TH HOUSE

11TH HOUSE   8TH HOUSE

12TH HOUSE   7TH HOUSE

1ST HOUSE   6TH HOUSE

2ND HOUSE   5TH HOUSE

3RD HOUSE   4TH HOUSE

CAREER   INTELLECT

EXPERIMENTAL AFFAIRS 11

LEGACIES AND SEXUALITY 8

SACRIFICES AND SORROWS 12

UNIONS AND PARTNERSHIP 7

SELFISH AND CONCEDED 1

SERVICE AN HEALTH 6

POSSESSIONS 2

CREATIVITY 5

COMMUNICATIONS 3

HOME 4

10   9

COMBINATIONS OF ELEMENTS - OUR MISSION ON THE EARTH

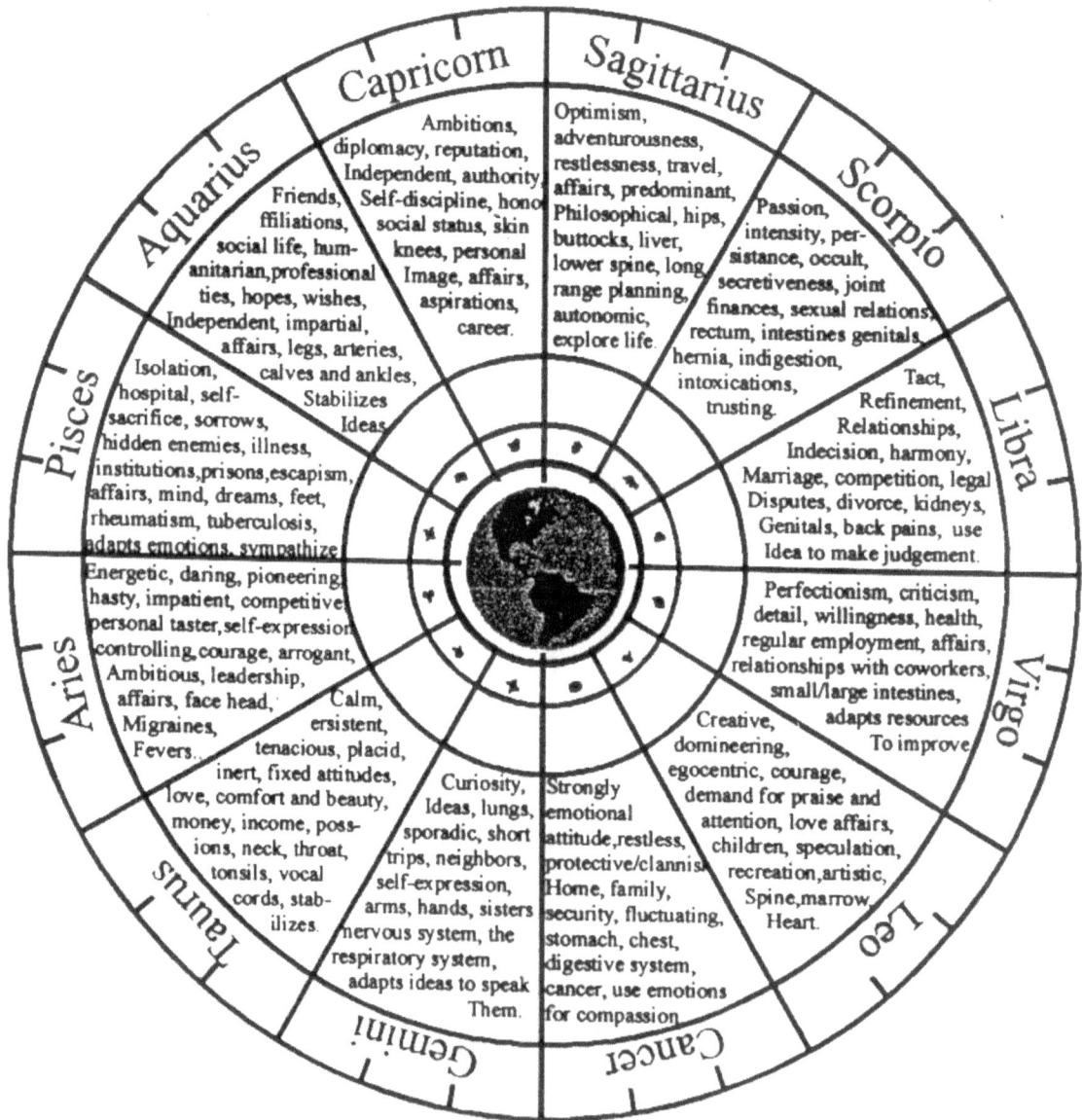

Capricorn — Ambitions, diplomacy, reputation, Independent, authority, Self-discipline, honor, social status, skin, knees, personal Image, affairs, aspirations, career.

Sagittarius — Optimism, adventurousness, restlessness, travel, affairs, predominant, Philosophical, hips, buttocks, liver, lower spine, long range planning, autonomic, explore life.

Aquarius — Friends, ffiliations, social life, humanitarian, professional ties, hopes, wishes, Independent, impartial, affairs, legs, arteries, calves and ankles, Stabilizes Ideas.

Scorpio — Passion, intensity, persistance, occult, secretiveness, joint finances, sexual relations, rectum, intestines genitals, hernia, indigestion, intoxications, trusting.

Pisces — Isolation, hospital, self-sacrifice, sorrows, hidden enemies, illness, institutions, prisons, escapism, affairs, mind, dreams, feet, rheumatism, tuberculosis, adapts emotions, sympathize.

Libra — Tact, Refinement, Relationships, Indecision, harmony, Marriage, competition, legal Disputes, divorce, kidneys, Genitals, back pains, use Idea to make judgement.

Aries — Energetic, daring, pioneering, hasty, impatient, competitive, personal taster, self-expression, controlling, courage, arrogant, Ambitious, leadership, affairs, face head, Migraines, Fevers.

Virgo — Perfectionism, criticism, detail, willingness, health, regular employment, affairs, relationships with coworkers, small/large intestines, adapts resources To improve.

Taurus — Calm, ersistent, tenacious, placid, inert, fixed attitudes, love, comfort and beauty, money, income, possions, neck, throat, tonsils, vocal cords, stabilizes.

Gemini — Curiosity, Ideas, lungs, sporadic, short trips, neighbors, self-expression, arms, hands, sisters, nervous system, the respiratory system, adapts ideas to speak Them.

Cancer — Strongly emotional attitude, restless, protective/clannish, Home, family, security, fluctuating, stomach, chest, digestive system, cancer, use emotions for compassion.

Leo — Creative, domineering, egocentric, courage, demand for praise and attention, love affairs, children, speculation, recreation, artistic, Spine, marrow, Heart.

iv

THE MEANING OF LIFE ON EARTH

THE METEMPSYCHOSIS OR TRANSMIGRATION OF EVERYONE'S SOULS, THEIR SOUL-MATES, STARS, AND DESTINIES

HOW TO FIND YOUR SOUL-MATE, STARS, AND DESTINY

LIGIA BALU, AUTHOR

LIGIA BALU blends the wisdom of the ancient astrologers together with her insight of discovering your *destiny*, fulfilling your *fantasies*, and finding your *soul-mate*. This book provides the stepping stones to unlocking the mysteries of A*strology*.   Through

LIGIA BALU'S sensitivities, the reader comes to understand the influence of the stars on our very lives.

LIGIA BALU explains not only how the stars lead us to our destinies but why we make the decisions we do, why we are attracted to certain people and certain situations, and why we face the challenge in our daily lives of overcoming our individual problems.

LIGIA BALU provides us with an understanding of ourselves and of other people. She explains how to recognize your *soul-mate*, how to become more compatible with others, and most importantly, how to be happier and more content through an understanding of your own destiny. The stars lead us and guide us, influencing us daily, and challenging us with obstacles that mold us into the people we become. Learn to read the future and how to make better decisions through the stars.

LIGIA BALU takes her readers on the grand adventure of inner exploration through an understanding of the vastness of the Universe. Sensitive by nature, she explores with her readers the dilemmas of everyday life that face us all. She brings to her readers the needed information for finding the *soul-mate* of our dreams.   She explains why some Sun signs are compulsively drawn to others even when it is against all logical explanation while other Sun signs seldom waver from a logical course of action and rarely experience spur of the moment activities.

LIGIA BALU takes her readers on a guided tour of the mysteries of the Universe and explains why:

SAGITTARIUS are impulsively drawn to the stubborn ARIES.

LEO and CAPRICORN disagree about money.

CANCER women are patient with GEMINI men.

TAURUS develop either love or hate relationships with SCORPIO.

VIRGO women never approve of how SAGITTARIUS men spend money.

GEMINI may upset the boat for AQUARIUS.

LIBRA can be easily unbalanced by SCORPIO moods.

PISCES women find excitement with ARIES men.

SCORPIO has trouble understanding the flaky AQUARIUS.

ARIES men with an ARIES women spells competition.

SCORPIO can exact retribution from SAGITTARIUS.

CAPRICORN men delight in PISCES women if they can rule the magic.

There is a relationship between the causes and effects, a relationship born of fatalistic attractions in an order established by Ethereal reasoning. The Sun, Moon, Planets, and Stars are celestial bodies adding to and influencing our daily lives and spiritual beings. Through an intangible electromagnetic force this influence rides like waves of energy pulsating and dispensing impending causes and effects and leading us on a journey through life and understanding. This law can appear to be a terrible experience for some people because, quite often, a person is destined to suffer during either part or all of his life. No matter how hard this person attempts to avoid this suffering it seems that whatever is destined will be accomplished. While this law of cause and effect can seem like a terrible injustice, it is respectful and Holy in that it also serves a purpose. In its mystery, this law is superior to our ability to fully understand it or its reason for being. The law precedes our development and in no way fits comfortably into our way of thinking.

The aspects of the sky during our birth, our dreams, and even during our human misgivings, indicate a very strange but real connection between our perception of life and this Ethereal influence which surrounds us. Through the Universe designed by God comes these guides offering us warnings that we are destined for these experiences, and that the suffering serves a purpose in our lives.

Ancient scholars living in remote and desolate areas of the old world studied this phenomena. These scholars devoted their lives to studying God's purpose for man. Their lives were difficult, and they maintained minimum contact with the outside world. They turned their thoughts to studying the mysteries of the Universe and the secrets of the world. From time to time, they shared these secrets with a few chosen people who sought them out. They taught that all of our present lives are linked to our past lives.

This transmigration of the souls, as it iscalled, was studied by Pythagora, the Greek philosopher. Pythagora explained that the visible Universe, the sky with all its stars, are only passing stages of the soul of the whole world. Matter is concentrated then dissolved and seeded in all of the Cosmic and imponderable space. Every solar whirlpool contains a part of the Universal soul which is developing within itself during the millions of centuries and which contains an impressive, impulsive force and measure. When considering these Powers, the species of the live souls, which appear one by one on the stage of our little World, are given by God and descend from the Father. They are coming from an unalterable and superior spiritual order, conforming to a preceding material evolution, and belongs to a dead solar system. Some of these invisible, endless powers are guiding the existence of this World, and others are waiting, in a cosmic divine dream-like sleep. They blossom to re-enter into later generations according to the Divine law.

THE PLANETS ARE THE DAUGHTERS OF THE SUN, born of the

Sun, and each is in tune with the attractive forces with its inherent material rotating. Each possesses a semiconscious soul which rises from the solar heart, and each possesses a specific character relating to its special evolutionary role. As every Planet is a different expression of God's will, it has a specific function in the chain of the Planets and, therefore, in the chain of events. The ancient scholars identified the characteristics associated with each of these Planets and with those of the gods--characteristics which represent divine faculties of the action and reaction in the Universe.

The ancients identified the four elements as the fundamental indicators of the four graduated stages of the material world. The first element, the densest and roughest one, is the most unmanageable to the Spirit while the last element, the finest one, has the closest relationship with the Spirit. Earth represents the solid state, water the liquid state, air the gaseous state, and fire the imponderable state. There is another fifth element, the Ethereal one, which represents such a subtle force that it does not exist in the material state. This is the original Cosmic Fluid, the Astral Light or the Soul of the World.

What is the human soul but a part of the Great Soul of the World, a sparkle from the Divine Spirit--a coin for immortality. Everyone of us has within himself GOD, but to find Him, we need to develop ourselves. We must build a moral foundation upon which we can remain next to Him.

The Creator made man to have His face and to be like Him; however, Man does not accomplish this until after many incarnations. These successive lives are given to man so that he can improve himself and atone for previous sins thus helping him to differentiate the good from the bad and the light from the darkness.

Only these cycles can explain terrible injustices and unfairness which are suffered by some people, great happiness which is given to other people, sudden deaths, twin souls searching for each other all their lives, enemies and friendships, and unexplainable passions. Is there a Director behind the scenes whose existence we cannot explain? Are we not the same actors just performing in different plays? Is it not possible for one to have moments of lucid retrospective, which seems to be reminiscences of a previous life?

And what happens to the soul at the time of death of the body? When death approaches, the soul may have misgivings about separating from the body, and in some instances, pictures of the life flashes before it in rapid succession and frightful clearness. The approaching death disturbs the soul as it slowly loses consciousness.

In a saintly and pure soul, there is a Spiritual Awakening that occurs during this gradual detachment from the body. Through introspection this soul perceives the existence of another world before the body's last dying breath. It hears a remote call and responds to a pale, invisible beam of light. This soul feels happiness when it is at last released from the dying body. There is a feeling of escaping and being caught up in the middle of that great light that takes it to the spiritual world where it will belong from now on.

Most likely this does not happen with the many people whose lives were a fight between the material and any superior aspiration. In these cases, the soul may awake as if in a nightmare with no guiding hand to lead it. With no voice to cry out, this soul remembers the suffering and may exist in fear and darkness. It longs for its earthly body which it may still see and which holds an unbearable attraction to it. This soul was living only by its body and for its body, and at death, it searches through the cold body and the dead brain matter, but it cannot find itself. Whether dead or alive, it does not know, and while it wishes to see and understand, it does not. The darkness is all encompassing as is chaos and obscurity. This soul may cling to the phosphorescence of its mortal remains which is frightening but attracting it at the same time. Then the ugly dream and chaos begins again. This state may continue for several months or years depending upon the forces of the material instincts of the soul. Whether good or bad, this soul becomes, little by little, conscious of the new stage of existence. It leads itself, finally free from the body, to drift and fly between the hollows of the Earth's atmosphere as if it is carried upon electrical rivers and where it will see other lost souls. In this way a journey begins like a dizzy and fiery flight. It will climb higher and higher in an effort to escape the Earth's atmosphere and travel to a region of the solar system where it will find guides who, in some cases, are friends and relatives from the former life. The Earth slowly disappears like in a dream, and a new sleep which is like a delicious swoon wraps the soul like a sweet caress. The soul sees only its flying guide which carries it into the deepest infinity of space. It reawakens on a star where the mountains, flowers, and vegetation provide a sweet embrace. The soul is surrounded by lightening creatures, both men and women, who overlook and initiate it into the mystery of this new life. Here, the aspect of the body does not become the mask of the soul. The transparent soul appears in its true shape as if shining in the daylight. The soul's psyche, led by a sublime wisdom, finds the Divine Country in which it attempts to understand the Symphony of the

Universe. The soul rests on the golden beaches of this star paradise, and it rests under the transparent veil of a dream filled with sublime light, perfumes, and melodies.

This celestial life of the soul can last for hundreds of thousands of years depending upon its scale and impulsive force. Only the most perfect soul or the most sublime; however, can prolong this existence endlessly. Other souls are recalled by the law of reincarnation to suffer new trials in order to forget previous sins. Exactly like the human life, the spiritual life has a beginning, an apogee or culmination, and a decline. When the spiritual life is ending, the soul is trapped in a whirlpool of melancholy, but an undefinable force is attracting it again to the pain and suffering of the Earth. This desire is filled with terrible misgivings of leaving the Earthly life. But the day has arrived, and the law must be accomplished. A veil-like mist covers the face, and the soul can no longer see its companions through this veil which becomes thicker and thicker. The soul hears their sad farewells, and the tears of the people who loved him are penetrating him like a celestial dew, leaving it thirsty for a now unknown happiness. Then the soul solemnly swears and makes promises to remember the truth from a world of love or lies and pain from a world of hate.

When the soul awakens again, it is in the heavy atmosphere of the Earth, in the abyss of birth and death, not having yet lost its heavenly memories. It is here that its guide introduces the soul to its new mother who is carrying the child's seed. Then, the most impenetrable mystery of life on Earth, the mystery of reincarnation and maternity transpires. This mysterous fusion is carried out slowly, organ by organ, fiber by fiber. Step by step, the soul loses its Divine Self-Conscience, and the Light becomes dimmer and dimmer. With birth, that horrible pain pushes the soul, and a bloody convulsion uproots it from the Eternal Soul and places it in a newborn body. The new-baby arrives into this world and is yelling frightfully. The Celestial Memory has entered the deep recesses of the unconsciousness.

The Law of Reincarnation and Deincarnation is the true sense of live and death. This law represents the main mode of the soul's evolution and enables us to watch the past or the future and into the depth of Nature and Divinity. This law shows us the rhythm and the measure, the immortality and the goal. From the Spiritual point of view, it shows us that the correspondence of Devine life and death - as birth on Earth is like a Devine death - and the death is like a revival. The alternation of these two lives is necessary for the development of the soul, and each is the consequence and the explanation of the other. According to this Law, the facts from a specific life have an influence on the next life.

These lives follow one by one, but they do not seem to be alike, and yet they are linked by an undefeatable logic. Each of these lives has his or her own law and his or her different destiny. According to the Law of Repercussion, the events in a specific live have a punishing or rewarding influence on the next life. The individual will be reborn owning the instincts and the talents molded in his previous incarnation, and the quality of his next existence will be determined, in most cases, by the quality of his choices made in his previous life.

Pytagora taught that the apparent injustices of destiny, misery, suffering, and misfortunes, can be explained by the fact that each existence is the reward or punishment for the previous life.

THERE ARE NO WORDS OR ACTIONS WITHOUT AN ECHO IN ETERNITY.

When the soul finally wins over the material, then it finds itself at the beginning and ending of all things. By development of all its Spiritual Faculties, the soul then enters into a Divine Stage and in full agreement with the Holy Will. According to this, when the soul arrives at that progressed state, it does not go back but becomes immortal in a place where there is no pain and no sadness, but only endless love.

A sinful life will only allow a painful next life; an imperfect life will only allow a hardworking next life; and that is the way morality, while imperfect during a single life, can be perfectly achieved in successive lives.

What is the Ultimate Goal of man and of mankind, according to this doctrine? After so many lives, deaths, reincarnations, leisure, and painful awakens is there an end for the infinite soul?

Yes, undoubtedly yes! Only through the development of all his spiritual faculties, will the soul finally matter. He will find within himself the beginning and ending of all things. Only then will he enter into the Divine stage in full agreement with the Holy Will. We know that once the soul has arrived at this Superior Stage, it cannot go back. He will be immortal forever.

The above is an explanation of why some people have "lucky" stars, why some people suffer and why, after a sad or happy time on Earth, nobody will encounter a final death. Then, when our missions on Earth come to an end, and when our souls are lost in the land where:

"THERE IS NO PAIN, NO SADNESS, NO TEARS, BUT ONLY AN ENDLESS HAPPY, LOVING LIFE FOREVER AND EVER." Only then shall we encounter the GREAT GATE, written upon it:

"IDEALS, DREAMS, LOVE, FORGIVENESS, FORGETFULNESS, PEACE"

TABLE OF CONTENTS

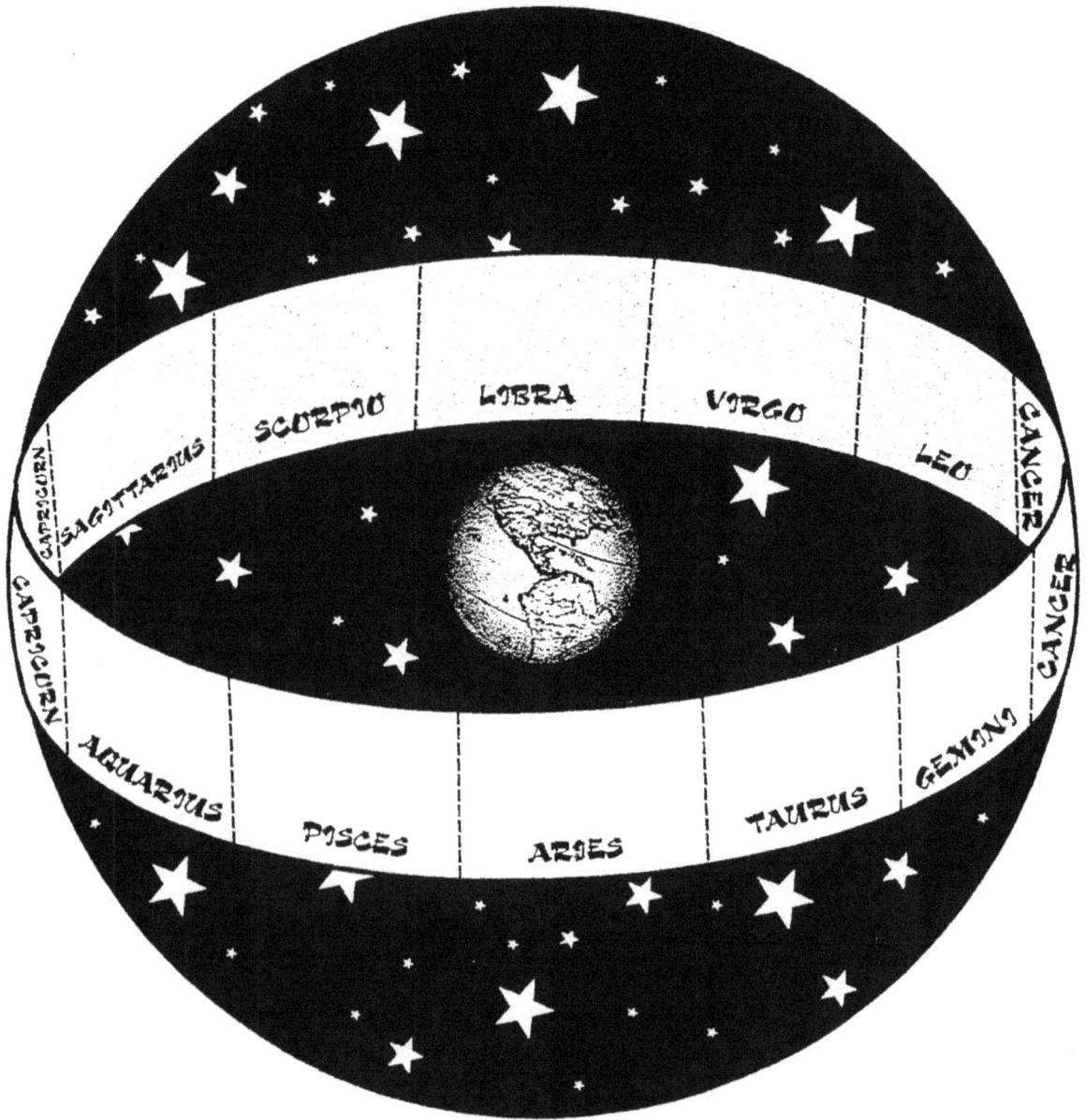

Introduction to Astrology

How to Find Your

Soul-Mate, Stars, and

Destiny

The science of astrology encompasses many precepts of the Universe including the relationship existing between the movements of the Moon, the Sun, the Planets, and the occurrences in the everyday lives of people. Historically, astrology was considered by some a science and by others a pseudo-science, witchcraft, artistic theory, or as a celestial theology. In more recent times, there are those who began to give it more serious consideration, elevating it to the level of pure science. The phenomena of this relationship between the stars and people's lives have even been studied at many well-known universities.

Imagine the primitive civilizations when man faced the challenge of comprehending the tides, the changing Moon and Sun, the eclipses, seasons, and equinoxes. These primitive peoples developed not only the first calendars, but also, the rudiments of astrology and astronomy. The Summerians and the Babylonians, the Maya and the Chinese, developed calendars based on the changing Moon and Sun. They could perform meteorological forecasts or foresee the nebula, the new stars, and the comets.

The early astrologers were the wizards of this science. These wizards were consulted to prevent drought, famines and floods. They foresaw battles, victories, defeats, natural disasters and times of prosperity. Many also played a role in determining the destinies of royal families and of powerful people the world over.

During these early times, the Moon was considered supernatural which gave the new science of astrology a celestial character. The personified divinities of the Moon, the Sun, and stars held specific significance and power. This scientific study intensified ushering in the age of the benevolent astrologer who could foresee atmospheric conditions, good or bad days, and the will of the gods. In many societies, these decisions makers became the high priests whose power influenced the day-to-day activities of others.

The development of astrology was not without its Greek influence. After conquering Chaldeea, Alexander the Great brought magicians and astrologers from Babylon to Greece where

1

they influenced the philosophers who were all ready questioning the origin of the Universe. Astrology was considered a divine science by Empedocle, Plato, and Aristotle. These Greek philosophers were the first to ponder how the stars influenced an individual's date of birth. And from this comes the adage, "To be born under a good star".

The Greek influence reached Rome where astrologers were an elevated class of scientists. Claudius Ptoloemeus, while living in Alexandria during the second century, authored two important books: *Almagestell* and *Tetrabiblonly.*

THE HOROSCOPE

The horoscope is the determination of the position of the stars and planets in relation to time, or an event, at a certain longitudinal and latitudinal point of the Earth. The individual horoscope is represented as a sphere around which all the sky bodies are moving. According to their position at the moment of birth, each individual encounters varying influences. It is important to know the time of birth (even the minutes and seconds) in order to determine the position of the stars.

In addition to providing a philosophical explanation or a scientific theory, we can consider the importance of the stars in the same manner as our ancestors. Consider the affirmation, "The nineteenth century was the progress century: many discoveries allowed humanity to go forward and improve. The twentieth century is the technology century, the time when all the inventions have been applied; the twenty-first century will be magicians' and poets' century." The term magician is used because there will be a rational explanation of what was once thought of as phenomenon. The term poet refers to the hope that future technology will be saved by poetry, that is, it will save people from total alienation. Einstein referred to astrology as a, "science, a source of life for humanity,".

THE ZODIAC

What kind of person are you? Often, we take our own character for granted considering ourselves as normal as the next person until someone has the audacity to criticize us. Whether it's criticism or praise, how helpful is it?

It does help to know our strengths and weaknesses, but our sensitive nature often times does not allow us to find ourselves. Our tired minds and busy schedules just as often prevent or distract us from discovering our inner person, our other intellect, our potentials, and our connection with the Universe.

Everybody has a psychic power or ability, but it depends on how we choose to use it or to ignore it. How does one find this power, connect with it, and utilize it to benefit themselves and the lives of others?

The study of the Zodiac is one of the most popular methods of coming to terms with our complicated lives. Have you ever wondered, "Why did I do that?" By the time the question is asked, it is too late to alter the action or the outcome. The motto, "know thyself", appears obvious, but consider that it was the foundation of the wisdom of the ancient Greek philosophers and was adopted by not only the "mystery religions" of Greece, Rome and the Middle East, but also remains tantamount in all serious schools of mind training or mystical training as, for example, those of India based on yoga and those of the West founded on the Kabala.

Various classification systems of the personality exist. One system divides men into three types according to whether they most often follow the impulses received from their muscles, leading to physical action, or from their digestive organs, resulting in emotion, or from the brain and nerves, resulting in cognitive processes. Another system portrays character as determined by the endocrine glands and gives us such labels as „pituitary', „thyroid', or „hyperthyroid' types. These various systems are not necessarily inclusive or in conflict. Often, they are different methods of saying the same thing. Heredity and environment both contribute to mold our character. And genetics, it is being proven, plays an ever important role in determining our natures.

The disadvantage of these systems of classification is the need to place oneself in a category. For example, a person may be reluctant to admit that he acts to please his emotions. So, he deceives himself for years by attempting to fit into the „best' type. Of course, there is no best. Each category has its strength and weaknesses. But when the classification process is simply guesswork or is done to flatter one's ego, then the result is easily self-deception.

Consider the advantages of the signs of the Zodiac. The problem of deciding the classification is removed. If the date of birth is known, the sign is automatically determined. The only guessing required, in some instances, is the hour.

Can anything be that easy? Can the entire population of the world be divided, uncontroversially, into twelve types? Truthfully, the Zodiac was never designed in that manner. There exists a wide range of personality types within each sign. Why? Because each sign is influenced to some extent by one or two of the other signs.

Consider it this way. A single sign is inadequate to explain the differences between people because very few people are born under only one sign. A horoscope means „a consideration of the

3

hour'. Thus, besides the day and month of birth, the time including the hour and minute down to the nearest five minutes and preferably the exact minute are important.

The birth month determines which sign of the Zodiac was occupied by the Sun. The day and hour determine what sign was occupied by the Moon, and the accurate minute indicates which sign was rising on the eastern horizon. Referred to as the Ascendant, this rising sign is considered one of the most important aspects of the horoscope.

Take for example, if you were born at one in the morning, the Sun is not important so the month of birth will not be important. What is important is the Ascendant and perhaps one or two of the planets. On any given day and hour, the Ascendant is the same at any given place. However, the Moon and the planets are different from day to day, moving at different speeds. Because of this, the planets are noted in an astronomical table referred to as an ephemeris. It is from the information gained from these tables that the inner most nature of a person is determined.

The Sun signifies the heart. The Moon signifies a person's mannerisms, behaviors and even his gestures. For that reason, the Romans referred to the Emperor Augustus as a Capricorn, meaning that he had the Moon in Capricorn. An astrologer might call Disraeli a Scorpio considering that he had Scorpio rising, but others would refer to him as a Sagittarian based on the Sun, while the Romans would have determined that he was a Leo because his Moon was in Leo.

The Sun becomes a principal influence if a person is born near sunrise, sunset, noon or midnight. Therefore, when a person doesn't appear to fit into his sign, perhaps it would be worthwhile to read the other indicators to determine if one of them is rising or occupied by the Moon. It also appears that the influence of the Sun develops as one grows older making it easier to guess the month of birth in people over forty. Younger people are supposedly influenced mainly by their Ascendant which characterizes both the body and the physical personality.

The planets are of importance also. For example, if Mars, the planet of war, was rising at birth, the person will be active and energetic but not necessarily aggressive. Mars in the south is aggressive, and Mars setting is apt to attack in self-defense often without good reason. People influenced by Venus are known to exert charm, Jupiter rising looks for wealth and rank, Mercury talks a lot and likes to make many friends. But each planet can rise in every sign, meaning that the sign of one's birth can be complicated by three or four planets rising or soothing simultaneously, besides being partly canceled out by the signs containing the Sun and Moon.

This illustrates how complicated a horoscope can be and explains the differences in personalities. But does it explain why the signs of the Zodiac would have an effect on a person's character at all? Astrologers describe the physical influence over the Earth such as the Moon's gravitational pull on the tides. This may also hold true of the planets which are physical bodies and have a gravitational pull, but the signs of the Zodiac are not physical bodies and don't have a gravitational field. Therefore, they are more difficult to explain. Stars are arranged in irregular distribution across the sky, and each must have a small gravitation effect as well; but this offers no explanation because the stars are not divided into twelve regions like the signs, nor are they confined to the belt called the Zodiac.

What does appear to be important is the minute of birth. If this matters, it suggests that the signs of the Zodiac do have an influence. But consider the word „influence'. Perhaps in the world of physical bodies the signs of the Zodiac have no influence, but it does not follow that they have no meaning. And what is the definition of „meaning'? But where the Zodiac has meaning and implies knowing, its concept has seeped into the universal consciousness of our minds, and it is there that its influence lies although it has no physical properties. And so the mystery remains.

The Zodiac, this idea in the mind of the human race dating back to the ancient mystics, while not a physical property, is related to a band around the sky wherein lies our destiny. Every person on this planet is born with a star. A star that directs you in your life. With luck, you are born under a good star. Every twenty four hours has seven bad hours. You never know when the seven bad hours appear. If you say something, or make a good or bad decision, or joke around about something, you would be surprised how by accident or mistake you reach the bad hour and it comes true exactly as you said or as you wished in your life or someone else's life. If you don't like what you said, or you don't mean it, the words of the bad hour follow you for the rest of your life. So be careful what you ask for. The stars are the magnet of the destiny, the present, the future, and the past.

The central line of the Zodiac is called the Ecliptic. Along this line the Sun passes taking just under 365 days to complete the circle. It is the same every year and perfectly straight. Its most northerly point is the Summer Solstice, where the Sun is in the longest day, and this is in the constellations of Gemini.

The most suitable method for following the course of the Zodiac is to use the Moon which when full is opposite the Sun. The full Moon at the Summer Solstice marks where the Sun will be at the Winter Solstice and vice versa. However, the Moon does not follow exactly the same path and can be over five degrees north or south of the central line. This means that the Moon passes sometimes below and sometimes above the stars in the Zodiac.

A sign of the Zodiac most definitely appears different with a planet in it as the planet is usually brighter than any of its stars. Planets, like the Moon, vary in brightness from time to time, according to the angle at which they are seen. Mars in the south at midnight is very bright and red because it is opposite the Sun and therefore fully illuminated, just like the full Moon, but two months later it is much dimmer and not so red.

A brilliant planet in the west or southwest after sunset is usually Venus or sometimes Jupiter. Venus is always either the evening star or the morning star, and when very close to the Sun, invisible all together. Mercury is usually invisible except in clear climates and with no city lights.

Saturn is white and appears in the east just before sunrise and, as the months pass, progresses slowly across the sky from east to west, rising roughly four minutes earlier everyday until after a year, it is seen for a week or two in the west at dusk and then is lost in the sunset glow. At that time, it is in conjunction with the Sun and can not be seen.

The twelve constellations of the Zodiac take their turns being visible after sunset in the east and at midnight in the south, but this happens at the time of year when the Sun is in the opposite sign. Aries the Ram, for example, holds this position in October, Taurus in November, and Gemini in December. But a constellation cannot be seen at all when it holds the Sun. It is useless to look for Aries in April and May or for Taurus in May and June. Just after the Sun has passed through it, your constellation is only visible in the early morning.

To find a particular constellation, start with a bright and obvious group. The best known of all constellations is the Wain, Plough or Big Dipper, which is north of the Zodiac and the only sign of the twelve which can be found from it is Leo, or, by passing through Arcturus, Virgo.

Across the equator and a little south of the Zodiac is Orion, under the feet of Taurus and Gemini. This is one of the brightest areas of the sky. The ancient Egyptians used Sirius as the fixed point of their calendar perhaps because it rose in time to announce the annual inundation of the Nile.

Aries, the Ram, is not an obvious constellation. It is most easily found either from Taurus to its left or from the great square of Pegasus on its opposite side. The only noticeable part of it is the three stars of the head marking its eye, nostril and mouth. Aries rises at sunset at the end of October and reaches the south at midnight in the same period.

Taurus does not resemble a bull, but it has two obvious features, the Pleiades and Hyades. The Pleiages is a large but tight cluster of little stars with six being clearly distinguishable. The Hyades follows forming a V of five stars, some of which are double, and the upper one on the left is a large red one called Aldebarin or the Forecaster. There are two other fairly bright stars on the tips of the horns, El Nath and Al Hecka which extend to the northeast between Capella and Orion's head.

The forepart of the Bull is shown on star atlases, the hind part being omitted to leave room for Aries since Greek times. Perhaps this is due to the triangle of the Hyades which could be compared to the Bull's face with the horns rising up as far as El Nath and Al Hecka. But the name is plainly not derived from the shape; for the plowing season in Babylon was marked by the Moon being full in this constellation; and the Babylonian Plough, drawn by an ox, was not the Wain, but our small constellation Triangulum, over the head of Aries. The Pleiades represented a tuft of hair on the shoulder which most bulls do not have. And in any case the Babylonian bull was smaller than ours, otherwise the earliest Babylonian Zodiac could not have contained eighteen signs instead of twelve.

Of the two stars in the upper part of Orion, Betelgeuze, the larger and redder, means „shoulder of the giant', and Bellatrix means „female warrior'. They mark his shoulders and not his face which is the small triangle of stars between and above them. His belt, three equal stars in a straight line, is a very useful reference point. His sword, containing the famous nebula, hangs below it on the left side, and the brighter of his two feet is called Rigel, or Rijl, which is Arabic for foot.

Gemini, the Twins, is one of the few constellations obtaining its name from its shape. It originally consisted of only two stars which were very bright and of equal magnitude. The constellation as a whole now forms an oblong with an extra star (Propus) protruding at the upper right hand corner. The feet extend southward towards Orion's shoulders and the brightest star in the feet is called Alhena.

Cancer, the Crab, the smallest and most inconspicuous constellation in the Zodiac, has as its principal features two Asses eating out of the Manger. The Manger has also been called the Beehive. Its astronomical name is Praesepe. It is a large cluster of dim stars, and the Asses, called the North and South Aselli, are obliquely above it. However, people born under Cancer are no more foolish and selfish than others.

Leo the Lion is a large, obvious constellation with a vague resemblance to a large animal. The Babylonians called it the Great Dog, but it is probably Egyptian in origin. Virgo is positioned on the equator, rising due east and due west.

THE HEAVENLY HOUSES

The sky is gauged by astronomers from the spring equinox of the northern hemisphere. It seems natural that the positions of the Moon and Planets are described in reference to the fixed stars. The proper measuring stars became Spica, Antares, Aldebaran and Regulus. The first guess at the proper way of measuring was used by the Greeks. However, for centuries there was a great deal of confusion and a number of different Zodiacs were used by different astrologers. Thus, the confusion continues with the dates of the twelve signs used in newspapers being different.

Remember, the significant aspect of the horoscope is not the position of the Sun or Moon, but the Ascendant, rising on the eastern horizon at the moment. Before it was noted which sign was rising, the actual stars were of importance. This is complex, considering that it requires either actual observation without clouds at night or a series of complex computations. For example, the stars rising along the eastern half of the horizon vary with every half-degree of latitude. It would appear difficult to analyze the influence of that number of stars. For that reason, perhaps, the signs of the Zodiac were given a similar influence regardless of the number of stars involved.

A guide to designating the characters of the signs of the Zodiac would be the ruling Planets. Mars, for example, is a masculine planet and the god of war, and, therefore, Aries and Scorpio were considered the most positive and aggressive signs. Venus, the feminine Planet, stands for peace, love, beauty, art and friendship, clothes and cosmetics, and these concepts are associated with Libra and Taurus along with natural beauty.

Mercury represents the communication and circulation of ideas (speech, writing, gossip and news) as well as learning, teaching, methods and the circulation of other things such as transport, correspondence, and may include stolen properties.

Jupiter represents growth and ‚the bigger the better' attitude while Sagittarius is associated with ambition, snobbery, aspiration, idealism and/or religious devotion. Pisces may represent self-indulgence but, conversely can also be a kind or tolerant acceptance of everyone, a tendency to think the best.

Saturn, with its principle of contraction, has a disagreeable nature suffering with limitations or restrictions. However, considering that concentration is essentially an abstract form of thinking, Saturn is considered a beneficial Planet to be born under in that it provides the ability to control one's mind.

There are exaltations in certain signs that also affect the character of the sign although not to the same degree as does rulership. Saturn, in this regard, is exalted in Libra, the constellation of justice adding dimension to the Venusian leanings toward art, peace, fine clothes, and sales. Jupiter's exaltation is in Cancer, the sign of the Moon which is feminine and associated with growth. Mercury is exalted in the sign of Virgo, while Venus is in the Fishes, the sign of pleasure. It would appear that the least desirable exaltation is that of Mars in the Saturnian sign of Capricorn because energy under restriction wouldn't be advisable; however, compressed energy achieves a great deal such as a vacuum of air suddenly released.

Medieval astrologers assigned the Twelve Houses of the horoscope which originally were designed to enable astrologers to forecast the sphere of life of a coming event. These are:

1st: Personality, Character, Leadership, Enterprise, Physique, Attitude

2nd: Money, Prosperity, Property, Resources, Peace, Liberty, Emotions

3rd: Family, Relationships, Short Journeys, Messenger, Politics

4th: Home, Parents, Security, Real Estate, Second Half Of Life, Moody

5th: Children, Pleasure, Theaters, Speculation, Love Affairs, Domineering

6th: Health, Servants, Employment, Military Service, Meticulous

7th: Marriage, Other Partners, Enemies, Competition, Tempermental

8th: Death, Inheritance, Sexual Relationships, Proud, Sensual, Scientific

9th: Religion, Long Journeys, Education, Religion, Philosophical Views

10th: Status, Profession, Reputation, Business Dealings, Supervisors

11th: Friends, Helpers, Affiliations, Diplomacy, Social Life, Desires, Flaky, Selfish

12th: Secret Enemies, Imprisonment, Illness, Martyr, Artistic, Indecisive, Sacrifice, Sorrow

There has also been noted a relationship between the signs of the Zodiac and that of human life. Naturally, these phases are not of equal length because change comes more readily during youth. The first phase corresponds to Aries who, like a baby, demands what it wants immediately even if it requires yelling regardless of the effect on others. Consider how many dictators were born under the sign of Aries.

The second phase regards relationships. In this phase, Taurus, the second sign, ruled by Venus, begins to be aware of relationships and love. Gemini, the phase of play, represents family and the age of first friendships outside the home. Cancer, ruled by the Moon, suggests mother, home, and the age of adolescence. It is a changing, emotional phase like the Moon, but like an adolescent is not independent, often reflecting the opinions of others.

Leo, ruled by the Sun, represents the first phase of adulthood, but its desires are not yet achieved. Virgo, the Virgin or the Servingmaid is the youthful, willing helper who is prepared to learn. Libra, the Balance phase enhances finding its proper place in the world, equality, and polarity in marriage. Scorpio, ruled by Mars, works toward achievement with energy and conflict if necessary. Sagittarius is either the ambitious or conversely the religious attempting to find wisdom. Capricorn, the Goat, is the phase of enjoying one's achievements. Aquarius is the phase of understanding. And Pisces, at last, is concerned with pure enjoyment but with ultimate meaning.

Consider, each person is born with a destiny. A destiny determined by the character given to the individual by the stars. Astrology is the study of the stars, and the corresponding effects on individual lives based on an ongoing-compilation of data and research, an ongoing evolution of understanding based upon research first begun by ancient civilizations, and it continues to mystify and influence us.

This destiny is enhanced by cosmic influences projected upon the newly born by a "fixed electromagnetic condenser", the Zodiac, and mobile condensers, the wandering Planets, the Sun, and the Moon. These cosmic influences leave marks on the human body, along the force lines, that are sensitive during the entire life of the individual. This sensitivity develops in each individual becoming the „Destiny'. With harmony between the actual projection of the sky condensers and the imprints created since birth, the events will be happy or lucky; conflict between these events result in unpleasant or dramatic happenings. And these electromagnetic occurrences produce havoc or harmony within the communications of the basic elements of the body.

There is the thought that when God made people, he made them with a little map and a little star. The individual has to follow both. When each person is born, their little star is born too, at the same time. When the person dies, the star dies at the same time. The person becomes the servant to both the star and the map until the end. A person cannot do in life what he or she wants to do but what the star and the map allow him to do. How do you bring God into your heart? By the same method, the ancients brought the Sky closer to the Earth to form an intimate and absolute unity.

The Zodiac was assigned names by the ancients, the old Magi, who imagined the shapes in the night sky of the stars as being similar to the different shapes of people and of animals. Our information today indicates that the twelve signs of the Zodiac were completed hundreds and hundreds of years before the birth of Chirst: Aries, Taurus, Gemini, Cancer, Leo, Virgo, Balance, Scorpio, Sagittarius, Ram, Aquarius, and Pisces.

The Planets, thought of as living creatures in motion in the sky, had weaknesses, like humans, and preferences for certain Zodiac signs. The Sky Houses, however, were different from the Planets and the signs. The Sky Houses consist of six houses above the Earth and six under ground. These six Houses were unconditionally motionless. The old Magi established that the Houses numbered one and eight, were governed by Mars, controlling the temperament and death; the second and the seventh, were governed by Venus, controlling fortune; Mercury governed the third and sixth House with writing and servitude; ninth and twelfth were under Jupiter, taking care of the voyages, ideas, and isolation. The tenth and eleventh, governed by Saturn, controlled social situations. The planets Saturn and Mars were limiting, Jupiter and Venus were good or lucky, and Mercury and the Moon were very moody. The same remains true today for the Planets as well as the Zodiac.

The Planets are very sensitive, like people. They are influenced by the Zodiac. This can be good or bad. According to the Planets' positions in the sky, the ancients arrived at conclusions, made predictions, and gave advice. The Zodiac, a reflection of the Earth, shows how everything is happening on our planet. The ancient people believed that the human body was protected in the Orion Zodiac.

The ancients imagined a huge body with the head corresponding to the first House of the sky, i.e., Aries and the legs corresponding to the last House, number twelve, which is Pisces. The throat and neck are under the sign of Taurus; the fourth House, Cancer, corresponds to the chest and lungs; Leo, the fifth, is the heart and spine; Virgo, the sixth, the internal organs; Balance, the seventh, the kidneys; the eighth is Scorpio with the sexual organs; the ninth is Sagittarius, the hips and upper legs; the tenth is the Goat with knees and joints; the eleventh is Aquarius, the lower legs and feet; and the twelfth is Pisces with the feet. These were the symbols of the ancient astrologers.

Astrology has occupied the minds of kings, Popes, presidents, scholars, and philosophers. No science has been more appreciated or more ridiculed than astrology. The more one learns, the more one becomes enthralled with the mystery of the stars, Planets, and the Zodiac. There are those people born more gifted, with knowledge and sensitivities, who like to practice and to develop the ability and the power of this gift from God. These people are those who appreciate and make the astrologies and horoscopes. This is especially true of people born between January 20 and February 20. The ones born between October 20 and November 20 have an interest in stars in general. Those born under the sign of Aries, between December 20 and January 20, have a speculative interest; and those born under the sign of Pisces are passionate in astrology and psychic ability. Generally, individuals born in Spring or Summer, under the remaining signs, have a curiosity but a selfish nature, like Taurus, April 20 to May 20, taking mostly into consideration their own fate. Gemini, May 20 to June 20, reflect those of an intellectual nature and interest. The Cancer individual, born June 20 to July 20, will always love astrology as they do any science that provides information from the past.

These people who have more abilities, who deal with the cumulative knowledge and mysteries of the Universe, appear to be on another level as compared to more average people. Perhaps this is because they have evolved from successive existences, making them ever more sensitive with powers of the mind.

Psychiatrists have been observing and studying the personalities of not only the genius but also the criminal and the psychotic. They have developed methods and treatments, but the conclusions remain elusive. We're aware that the genius may also exhibit abnormal behavior. This is of a celestial influence, the electromagnetic imprint on the new born. This break in the balance of the Horoscope is completely abnormal. The Moon represents the factor of receptivity that can lead to psychosis, madness, when the factor is dissonant and to genius when the factor is harmonious. If a sector of the sky is under a violent sign or has a large crowd of planets, this indicates a prominent predisposition for a frantic instinctual life. If a break occurs in a particular part of the Horoscope, by a planetary low tide, it will create a blockage in the instinctual flow by sublimation. If the individual cannot achieve through his instincts, he will become a teacher or a great artist. In other words, he will play in public what he cannot play in his intimate life. Women who become nuns always have contradictory instinctual factors.

There are areas of the Zodiac that don't receive as much magnetism. This creates an unbalance. Violent criminals have a few planets, a few Celestial condensers under the violent sign of Aries, in a weak, miserable, isolated House, the secret twelfth House of the Sky. People with double personalities are usually born between two Zodiac signs. Or consider the Horoscopes of two people, victims of a passionate connection, and you'll immediately notice a difference of potential between certain Zodiac signs in a particular area of the Horoscope.

Have you ever tried to understand an attraction or a rejection of another person. Remember, there are those who bring good luck or who bring bad luck. An agreement among good planets leads to good luck, chance and possibilities. When a negative planet influence encounters a positive planet in a particular spot of the Horoscope, it is absolutely fatal resulting in a loss or misery brought on by someone else. These negatively influenced individuals can enter your life and cause trouble without warning.

Like Celestial bodies, people receive and send impulses. People who can heal have the ability to control their own magnetism, and even their presence is pleasant and soothing. In contrast, other people who create confusion, bother us by sending out impulses faster.

In studying the birth skies, it can be seen that the good times in life are the reenacting of an imprint or imprints that occurred at birth. These imprints can arrive at harmony with the stars' movements at some time during life. A series of good or bad events can occur when the planets are grouped in a cluster at a particular time. Some people receive a „chance' during the first part of life, others during the second part of life. The former were born during the day when the majority of the planets were above the horizon while the latter were born at night when the planets were below the horizon. The happiest part of life is the second „chance', particularly for those born at midnight. Later in life, some people become rich, others lose everything. This happens when their Planet changes directions at birth.

When studying the Horoscope, it can be observed that sometimes the majority of the Planets are situated on one side, for example, the East side. This means that the person will live half their normal life expectancy or the second part of their life can become meaningless. Then again, if the Planet Saturn is rising before it is continuously descending, a person has a continuous descending rhythm.

Wise people keep a low profile, perhaps inferior to what they deserve, in order to maintain balance and the best situation over a length of time. Others attain material wealth but also a moral misery, depression and deception with families which have continuous unfortunate events occurring, like a curse, even from generation to generation. A horoscopic genealogy can show a fatal event happening during many generations with some changes and transformations; one person dies, depressed, another one is sick or loses his situation or money, but all the time someone sooner or later dies. In this situation, no one can do anything about it. Some people choose to have children later in life, and if you watch these children's Horoscope, you'll see they were created under a certain influence and constellation in order to correspond to a certain familiar destiny and in order to close the circle of events of their families.

Children born around seven months are destined to create a balance with their brother's life. Many times these children can become very psychic and gifted. Born at nine months, a person's existence corresponds with the one in the sky, under a certain star influence, in conjunction with the Birth-Sky of their parents or ancestors. The children who die at birth, or soon after, cannot adapt to the Celestial heredity.

The combination between different nationalities are interesting because each of the partners comes with his own Celestial possibilities. Combinations between relatives can create birth defects, or even block the possibility of having children because the Celestial possibilities are minimal having been used by the rest of the family.

The movement of the Planets, in their celestial clusters and separate from each other, influence people's rhythm. Some people give and receive good energy, others negative energy. Remember, the good energy can bring good luck, the bad energy bad luck!

Astrology, when understood, makes crystal clear the understanding of the manifestations of Nature through human and mundane affairs. Even ordinary people with average education can benefit and learn astrological insights. Granted, true skill is best acquired by those who have an inborn love of all that is mystical and who possess an active sense of intuition. The temperament of the metaphysically gifted rather than formal schooling is the prerequisite for those wishing to become adept in this science.

Astrology has been garnered from the records of astral phenomena and reduced to a science by observing the effects of Planetary influence, commencing with the history of man. These observations have been compiled and recorded by some of the brightest intellects known, both ancient and modern. Astrology explains the inequalities of humanity shedding light upon the path leading to improvement in living conditions and relations with others. Much pleasure, satisfaction, and knowledge can be gained through the study of astrology. The insights gained provide people with broader views and more tolerant attitudes making them more charitable toward their fellow man.

The study of astrology continues becoming more and more scientific. As the number of serious students increases so does the evidence of its usefulness. Note that no one can claim to possess a proper understanding of astrology until he can cast and delineate the horoscope of birth and design and read a progressed chart.

The word horoscope is a derivative of „hora', an hour, and „scope', to view. It is a view of the heavens at a certain hour as measured by the Sun. Originally the word referred only to the Ascendant, but now it refers to a more general reference to a whole figure or map of the heavens at birth and is some times referred to as a nativity.

Some say that the purpose of astrology is to learn by Planetary indications that were affecting the Earth and its atmosphere at the time of birth and to endeavor to develop in this nature qualities which will insure an exalted expression of life. A well-cast horoscope can become a guide regarding changes, health, marriage, business and important affairs of life and relationships.

Why would any person be interested in Astrology? For starters, the study of astrology pre-dates all the other known sciences as well as present day organized religions. Every prehistoric and ancient culture left behind artifacts and proof that the study of the stars which later developed into astronomy and astrology were important to these societies. Astrology appears to have begun many of thousands of years ago in the very cradle of civilization and has been added to and influenced by scholars of every culture. And a science that was once available only to dignitaries and heads of state is now of use to each and every person. The language of astrology pervades our daily lives from the names of the days of the week to the names of the Planets and stars.

Modern societies put satellites in the sky and those satellites communicate with Earth. In much the same manner, the celestial bodies, the Sun and Moon, the Planets and the stars communicate with Earth. People can't see this happening, but it is accepted, felt intuitively, and proven scientifically that a correlation and an interrelation does exist. There is, in other words, an interaction between all of life, nature and mankind, and the Universe beyond. And whether it is the Moon's pull on the Earth's tides, or the Sun's radiation, or the unseen and unfelt rhythms and waves of the Planets in their transits, this interaction is continuous and pervasive. Our days and nights, our seasons and the weather all depend upon this interaction--this movement of our Planet, Earth, through its course in space and the Earth's correlation to the other rotating bodies.

Astrophysics is a science that applies the principles of physics to many fields of astronomy and which provides the basis for one of the concepts of astrology. Astrophysicists attempt to determine the physical nature and the origin and development of the solar system, stars, galaxies, and the universe. They conduct many studies with optical telescopes which enable them to observe cosmic objects that give off electromagnetic waves in the form of visible and infrared light. Radio telescopes are used to study radio waves that are emitted or reflected by Planets, stars, and galaxies. And various cosmic objects give off gamma rays, X-rays, and ultraviolet light. Other special detectors are used to study electromagnetic waves that are largely absorbed by the Earth's atmosphere and so cannot be detected by telescopes. These scientists estimate the motion of a star or galaxy by measuring the shift in the wavelengths of its light on the spectrum. Cosmic ray research also helps scientists understand the nuclear processes that occur within certain stars.

Research by biologists has proven that any number of Plants and animals respond to the interrelationship of the cycles of the Moon to the Earth and Sun. Worms react to the new Moon and the full Moon as do sea urchins, the fiddler crab, oysters, chickens, and hamsters. Even the migratory pattern of birds in flight appears to be influenced by the stars in the sky. There are natural rhythms which humans respond to as well, as if to some natural and internal clock. Behavioral scientists refer to these natural rhythms as a person's biological clock or bio-rhythms.

This gradual recognition by scientists that there exists a correlation and significant relationship between celestial bodies and life on Earth has helped to bring the study of astrology into proper perspective. The earliest astrologers, however, didn't appear to need this scientific affirmation of their observations and conclusions. They studied not only the heavens but the behavior of people and noted their findings before the advent of written histories. And what was a mystery to these ancient scholars remains in many ways just as much a mystery to modern scientists. The importance of astrology has also been recognized by notable psychologists such as Carl Jung who conducted his own studies into the behavior of people based on a comparison of their Birth Charts.

The earliest thinking people watched the stars, plotted the courses of the Planets and began timing events based upon the patterns of the stars in the sky. By plotting and anticipating the heavens, agrarian cultures knew when to expect flooding, when to plant their crops, and the best time for harvesting. Based on the luminaries, the Sun and the Moon, and the pattern of the Planets and the stars, the first calendars were devised. For centuries, early astrologers found favor with kings, queens, pharaohs, rulers, and leaders and advised them concerning matters of state, decisions, and events of importance. Astrology and astronomy, in those days, were linked for this purpose, and this link produced noted astrologers.

This preoccupation with astrology has had its own history of interest and disinterest, favor and disfavor. First it was accepted and favored by the early churches, numerous Popes, and religious leaders, and then it was suppressed, forbidden, and banned. Then moving almost as if in a cyclical pattern, astrology became once again an accepted study and practice becoming a subject matter which today is offered in many university classes and through astrological societies. And even the most skeptical of people and others who know very little about this science and study will know their Sun signs and the signs of their family members, lovers, and friends. Ancient scholars gazed at the stars and detected the constellations which make a wide belt or arc in the sky. The same ancient scholars named these constellations, and it is from these that the names of the twelve signs of the Zodiac are based. It might seem to many that individual lives make an arc as well, and when a person looks back it seems notable that each event is connected and leads to the next.

These very early astronomers and astrologers based their assumptions and calculations on the then accepted fact that the Sun moved around the Earth. In fact, the early Church and religious leaders considered it heresy to even suggest that the Earth actually moved around the Sun which resulted in it taking a number of years for this concept to be accepted. But for the casting of an individual horoscope or a Birth Chart, this earlier assumption is still practiced. There is a reason for that. The Birth Chart actually represents a picture of time taken at the exact moment of birth of an individual. The picture is taken from Earth and places the luminaries and the planets on the chart in relative degrees of each other. The person's Sun sign correlates with the constellation the Sun is moving through at the time of birth. The Ascendant, or rising sign, is the planet on the horizon at the time of birth. And each of the other planets fall into place around the 360 degree chart. The science of astrology is then the practical use of astronomy which links luminaries and planets with our daily lives. And it is by ascertaining the Birth Chart that an astrologer can give insight to the individual about personality and character traits, strengths, weaknesses, emotions, and predispositions to certain decision making processes and actions. How a person responds and interacts with parents, family, and other people and personal relations is indicated. What makes a person feel most secure and happy is indicated. And, of course, what kind of person this individual is attracted to may well be indicated by the Birth Chart. Has the person's life been filled with good luck or with difficult times and obstacles? Many times, how a person reacts to obstacles determines their luck. What modern astrology attempts to do is give the individual enough information for that person to understand his or her own character traits better. If you understood why you make the decisions you make, would you then make better decisions?

Many people want to know if astrology can predict the future for an individual. This is not the function of astrology. Free will being what it is, each person is free to either succumb to negative traits or to overcome even the harshest of obstacles in order to lead a better life. What astrology can tell a person is when the Planets may be properly aligned for making decisions, taking actions, or holding off on actions. That picture of the sky at the moment of the individuals birth can portray for the person the basic nature inherent in his or her make up. How that person uses this information to live life is still up to that person. The modern interest in astrology is indicative of the fact that people want to know more about themselves and to understand themselves better. And neither does it hurt to know other people better. By comparing Birth Charts, individuals can learn in what areas of life they are compatible with their lover and what other areas may cause stress or tensions. What is of importance to astrologers, then, is the positions of the Planets.

The idea of the arc, or celestial sphere, was first perceived as a dome rising above the flat Earth. This arc appeared to early observers to revolve around the Earth once a day. In drawing up a Birth Chart, the most relevant information is the position of the Planets to this arc or celestial sphere. It is the projection of the Earth's equator to this celestial sphere that marks the celestial equator, and the direction of the Earth's axis indicates the two poles of the sky with the north pole being marked approximately by Polaris. The yearly path of the Sun in the sky is referred to as the ecliptic and may be defined as the projection of the plane of the Earth's orbit to the celestial sphere which intersects at the vernal equinox and the autumnal equinox. The solstices represent those times when the Sun reaches its maximum north or south point on the celestial equator. Presently, those dates are approximately June 22 for the Summer Solstice and December 22 for the Winter Solstice. These dates or times were significant to early astrologers to whom fell the duty of compiling and organizing the first calendar. Because of the Earth's rotation around the Sun, the Sun appears to make one trip around the ecliptic in the same time span passing through each of the signs of the Zodiac in a year's time.

Ancient lore applied to modern life? Does it work? What the modern astrologer attempts to do is utilize the combined knowledge of the past and to apply it to modern precepts. And, yes, for all practical purposes, this application does appear to work. Why else do so many people open an astrology book, read about themselves, and come away with the feeling that the information applies to them and to their lives. Why then, one might ask, are there variations within each Sun sign? Why are so many people within the same Sun sign so different from one another? The Sun sign is indicative of a set of characteristics and personality traits. But it is the entire chart and the positions of the Planets that actually point to the individual differences and make each person unique. As the rising sign changes within a matter of minutes, each Birth Chart is uniquely different as well. Astrology is a complicated but precise science.

It is a study based on centuries old observations combined with modern observations. The basis of this science is numbers. In other words, astrology is a mathematical based science with predictions of future planetary positions determined by astronomy and calculations. Within astrology, the very precepts of the study is a numerical division which starts with the twelve signs of the Zodiac and then enumerates them into further divisions. These twelve signs are first divided into dualities, or two groups of masculine and feminine. They are also divided into four triplicities each representing a different element. Next, the twelve signs are again divided into three groups of four signs each, called quadruplicities, which denote a quality. Last, the twelve signs are divided into six groups containing two signs each and called a polarity.

And like any discipline or field of study, astrology has its own language, that is, certain words pertain to particular concepts. To come to an understanding of even the most basic astrological thoughts means taking the time to become familiar with this special blend of math and language. One significance of these divisions is that no two signs have the same designations which in effect makes each sign distinctive one from the others. Therefore, the Fire signs are different from each other even though they possess the same characteristics of being a Fire sign. The differences become more apparent in the following analysis which delineates each sign into separate groups.

DUALITY

Each of the twelve signs of the Zodiac is designated a duality which is either masculine or feminine, and this distinction was given to the signs by early astrologers some two thousand years ago. Using the language of astrology, a masculine sign is direct and energetic while a feminine sign is receptive and magnetic. In modern terms, the masculine signs are said to be outgoing and active while the feminine signs are thought of as self-controlled with inner strength.

MASCULINE	FEMININE
ARIES	TAURUS
GEMINI	CANCER
LEO	VIRGO
LIBRA	SCORPIO
SAGITTARIUS	CAPRICORN
AQUARIUS	PISCES

TRIPLICITIES

The triplicities denote the elements of Fire, Earth, Air, and Water which symbolizes the fundamental characteristics of the signs. The Fire signs are said to be active, enthusiastic and fiery. The Earth signs are thought of as practical and stable. The Air signs are the intellects and communicators of the Zodiac while the Water signs are more emotional and intuitive. The element of the Sun sign influences how a person reacts to everyday stimulus. Are you fiery and impulsive? Do you intellectualize your feelings? Do you feel deeply and react to the world through your emotions? Or do you apply logic and rationalization to your decisions?

FIRE: ARIES, LEO, SAGITTARIUS

EARTH: TAURUS, VIRGO, CAPRICORN

AIR: GEMINI, LIBRA, AQUARIUS

WATER: CANCER, SCORPIO, PISCES

QUADRUPLICITIES

The three quadruplicities each contain four signs and denote a quality of either Cardinal, Fixed, or Mutable which signify the Sun sign's interrelation and interaction with others. The Cardinal signs possess an inclination to lead others and exhibit initiative and an enterprising, outgoing spirit. The Fixed signs are more fixed in their opinions and resistant to change, and these people follow through and complete projects. The Mutable signs are the most flexible, adaptable, tolerant and versatile and are more easily capable of adjusting to change and to different people, ideas, and situations. Now then, are you resistant to change and like to have your own way, or are you open to the ideas of other people and receptive to different thoughts, opinions and lifestyles?

CARDINAL: ARIES, CANCER, LIBRA, CAPRICORN

FIXED: TAURUS, LEO, SCORPIO, AQUARIUS

MUTABLE: GEMINI, VIRGO, SAGITTARIUS, PISCES

POLARITIES

The polarities which contain two signs each signify the opposites in the Zodiac. Each sign has its opposite on the other side of the Zodiac wheel. This is not a necessarily bad designation because quite often opposites find that they are capable of blending their positive traits in order to overcome their negative traits.

ARIES & LIBRA: Aries, the most personal sign, is very self-oriented while Libra remains interested in partnerships and the other person.

TAURUS & SCORPIO: The sign of Taurus represents personal possessions, while Scorpio represents legacies and shared possessions.

GEMINI & SAGITTARIUS: Gemini is the sign of intellect and self-expression, while Sagittarius is the philosopher with an expansive nature.

CANCER & CAPRICORN: Cancer is interested in home and family, while Capricorn represents public life and ambition.

LEO & AQUARIUS: Leo is powerful with a creative and dramatic flair, while Aquarius is the independent thinker and humanitarian.

VIRGO & PISCES: Virgo is known for hard work, diligent efforts and a critical, analytical mind,. while Pisces is emotional, intuitive, and prone to dreaming.

All of the above is pretty simple math and if that was all there was to astrology, each and everyone of us could follow it quite easily. But these designations comprise only the basics, and just the beginning of the complexities entailed in this remarkable study of humankind based on the observations of the heavens. That brings us back to the subject of the planets and how they influence our daily lives and behavior. For it is the movement of the luminaries, the Sun, the Moon, and the Planets, as observed from Earth, which most influence astrological precepts and concepts.

Each Sun sign in the Zodiac is ruled by a Planet (The Sun and Moon are often included in discussions of the Planets.). Each Planet is associated with particular characteristics which are bestowed upon the individuals of that Sun sign, but that is not the only job of the Planets. Each Planet also rules a House of the Zodiac and there are twelve Houses. Each Planet is also placed on a person's Birth Chart by degrees according to its location in the sky at the moment, of that person's birth. These locations of the Planets on the Birth Chart form aspects, or angles, which are either beneficial or strenuous to each other. The locations of the Planets are determined by astronomy and can be found in an ephemeris which lists their positions for each day of each year. The Planets are also considered to be in detriment, in exaltation, or in fall in particular signs. A Planet is most powerful when in exaltation and loses its power or is less influential when it is in fall or in detriment. Two Planets are in mutual reception when each falls in the sign ruled by the other which strengthens them and allows them to benefit the individual. On the Birth Chart, the Sun is considered the most powerful Planet followed by the Moon, Mercury, Venus, Mars, Jupiter, Saturn, Neptune, and Pluto. The influences of Neptune and Pluto, because of their distances from the Earth, are considered to be generational in effect. Take all of that into consideration and then place the nodes of the Moon on the Birth Chart, and a person will have an overall picture of the information. From all of this, it is quite readily seen why a person would seek out a professional astrologer not only to draw up the chart but also to have it analyzed and interpreted. This has been made easier with the use of computer programs which do just that.

The next step for the professional astrologer would be to progress the Birth Chart which would allow the determination of favorable periods in an individuals life. Also, a comparison of two Birth Charts can provide information regarding the compatibility of two people. The study of astrology is both fascinating and intriguing. It allows for and enhances the uniqueness and individuality of the human experience. And it allows each individual the opportunity for self exploration and understanding as well as for personal growth and development. In essence, it provides the colors with which the Creator painted the skies.

Astrology is, therefore, a math, science, and language based study with very strong cultural inferences. No doubt there are many people who do not consider it a pure science in that it is also closely associated with spiritualism and has been, in one way or another and at one time or another, closely associated with the major religions of the world. And in this respect, astrology is not only spiritual but historical as well, as evidenced by the numerous archeology and anthropology findings which indicate and prove man's earliest interest in the stars and heavens.

It should be mentioned that astrology appears to be influenced by the culture and the period in which it is being studied. In many instances, modern astrology, much like modern translations of the Bible, seem to be watered down versions which are deemed suitable for the acceptance and understanding of the masses (which also makes it more commercial). It is notable that the language becomes richer when reading earlier astrologers just as the language in earlier translations of the Bible is more meaningful and more poetic. In fact, a comparison of the word usage in both earlier astrology writings and older Biblical translations reveal numerous similarities. Words such as afflictions, obstacles, adversities, determination, patience, and endurance are most obvious as are many others. Modern astrologers appear to have a tendency to pointedly down play such words as afflictions and adversities preferring words like stress and tensions. However, in real life there remains more than a fair share of serious problems which each individual must deal with. As well, there are also numerous Biblical references to the stars, Planets, skies and luminaries.

One example of this is found in the modern translations of the Dead Sea Scrolls, which have only recently been made available for translation for the general public. From these translations comes the story of Maskil, leader of a strict Jewish sect known as the Essenes, who in about 30 B.C., left his desert compound to speak to the Sons of Dawn, disciples who were serving a two-year novitiate before being accepted as Sons of Light and allowed to enter the community. Maskil, it seems, was taking a risk because he was carrying with him a doctrine which he didn't want to fall into the hands of the Sons of Darkness. Thus, he wrote his speech in code and encrypted it on a scroll with only the title being readable, "Words of the Sage to the Sons of Dawn". Using a painstaking technique of counting letters and comparing their frequency in the text to known Hebrew texts, this scroll and others has been translated. One, dating to the second century B.C. explains the Book of Moses while another from the same period is a calendar setting out a system for following the phases of the Moon. The calendar appears to have been a draft which attempts to find a pattern between lunar months and the solar year. It seems that a precise calendar was crucial to the Essenes because the regular movement of the heavenly bodies was believed to be a divine sign that, if properly understood, enabled a man to live in step with the designs of the heavens above. The "Words of the Sage", hidden in a desert cave for over 2,000 years only to be found by a Bedouin shepherd, spoke of the creation of the universe, how its branches reach to the heavens and its roots to the abyss below. The Maskil spoke of man, created from the dust of the Earth.

And in like manner, the study of the stars and astrology has been intertwined in one manner or another in the history of all cultures. That it has touched the lives of so many people from great kings to infamous scholars is perhaps the most remarkable story of all. It is all pervasive, and whether anyone likes it or not, it is shrouded in a rich spiritualism and mysticism. For it appears to be our intuitions that draw us to the study of astrology more so even than our intellects. How then did it come to be a science taken less seriously than the other sciences? Again, that question leads one to religion and science. It appears that a few influential and powerful religious leaders decided the study of astrology should be shunned. Then along came the Age of Science and the skeptics who felt they could prove anything that was observable and astrology wasn't observable. All of which brings us to modern times when even famous physicists are attempting to mathematically prove that there is a God. Believers have never needed mathematical proof of a Supreme Being any more than serious students of astrology needed to be told how to think. What free will grants is the ability for each person to make that determination and his or her own decisions.

The test of any great thought has always been its longevity, and astrology has been with humankind throughout the ages. The earliest man and woman gazed at the stars in wonder just as people do to this day. It is little wonder then that we all want to know what is beyond our reach in the heavens above. And it is little wonder that the stars and Planets compel us and draw us to study and observe them. Our probings into the vast unknown of the universe, and the galaxies beyond our own, are only indicative of the curiosity that beset humankind from the very beginnings of time. And this very curiosity is indicative of the influence the Planets and luminaries have upon each and every one of us.

SIDEREAL ASTROLOGY

It needs to be mentioned that, like any science, astrology has branched and formed different areas of study. One branch of astrology is Sidereal. The Sidereal astrologers reflect that the Earth slowly shifts position and the stars slowly shift their positions in relation to Earth. Therefore, dates of the Sun's entrance into each sign should change along with the Earth's shift in position. This concept is seen by the Sidereal astrologers as being more scientific because it is based on the actual positions of the constellations in the Zodiac. They point out that the dates established by Claudius Ptolemy in the second century A.D. have changed by approximately twenty-five days.

Traditional astrologers, however, feel that the Zodiac never actually corresponded to the actual constellations but rather to the movement of the planets. Traditional astrologers continue to use the groupings that have been around for thousands of years. That is, the signs of the Zodiac are divided into twelve equal segments of thirty degrees each.

In studying astrology, the casual reader will also come across various methods for drawing up the Birth Chart. Again this personal preference is left up to the individual person and to the professional astrologer being consulted.

SYNASTRY

Synastry is the practice of comparing two or more Birth Charts for indications of compatibility. While numerous generalizations have been made about compatibility based on Sun signs alone, Synastry offers a more detailed perspective on matters of partnerships, associates, friends, lovers, and spouses. The practice of Synastry provides basic factors and driving forces to the nature of the relationship.

In comparing two Birth Charts, one major indicator is whether one person's Sun sign is the same as the other person's Ascendant sign. Another factor is whether the first person's Sun sign is on the cusp of the Seventh House on the other person's chart. Or, is one person's Sun in the same sign as the other's Midheaven. Another strong indication would be to consider whether the Sun sign is in the opposite sign of the other person's Ascendant. On the other hand, stress can occur within the relationship when the Sun and Ascendant have an aspect which is square, and this square can provide that area of life which the couple either disagree about or that provides obstacles to overcome. A trine or sextile aspect between the Sun and Ascendant produces a pleasant and easy going relationship, but it can also produce a relationship that becomes dull. Negative situations can occur when the Sun and Ascendant are in semi-sextile aspects because signs which are next to each other are so different. This, of course, is strengthened or weakened by other aspects in the two respective Charts, and is also negated in a relationship between Capricorn and Aquarius. Another factor considered negative is a quincunx aspect with the exception of relationships between Aries and Scorpio, Taurus and Libra, and Leo and Pisces.

The next consideration in Synastry is a comparison of the relationship of the Planets and their aspects in the two individual Charts. Traditionally, only the major aspects and quincunx are used for this comparison. Again, what is being examined is the interrelationship of the Planets and no one aspect should be considered out of context with the entire picture. Particularly positive Planetary relationships between two Charts are when the two Suns form a conjunction, the woman's Sun conjuncts with the man's Moon, the woman's Moon conjuncts with the man's Sun, the ruling planets form positive aspects, or ruling planets make strong aspects to the other person's Sun and Moon. Next, comes the comparison of each person's Houses. And, after all that is completed, the two Charts can be progressed (examined) for indications of future compatibility.

Is all of this helpful to the people involved? Evidently enough people think so to keep astrologers busy calculating and drawing up Birth Charts. And this same process can be used for business and even political advice.

Birth Chart

Astronomers have discovered that stars get their energy through the transformation of mass into energy. Humans, comparatively, transform energy into actions. What is it exactly that impels and compels people to decide to take particular actions? Some people act on impulse while others use rational and logical thought. There are those people who intellectualize their actions and others whose actions are a reaction to their emotions or their intuitions. It required centuries for the behavioral scientists and psychologist to be taken seriously, and it may require more time for it to catch up to the precepts of astrology. And even genetics are proving that people are born with certain characteristics.

Astrology addresses the differences in the make-up of individuals which makes each of us unique. Add to that our cultural, economical, social, and familial differences, and there is produced a rich mosaic of people. The fact that each person is an unique individual is reflected in the Birth Chart. A horoscope is a picture of the heavens, referred to as the Zodiac, and can be drawn up for any particular time such as when decisions must be made, when a person is entering a new relationship, at the beginning of a business venture, or a career change. The Birth Chart, as already mentioned, is a picture of the heavens drawn up to represent the time of birth. This is also called a Natal Chart and is somewhat different than a Solar Chart. The Solar Chart, used by many astrologers, can be drawn up if a person doesn't know the exact time of birth. It represents the day a person was born and will be the same for everyone sharing that birth date. The Solar Chart is, of course, less personal than the Natal Chart.

It is the time of birth that allows the astrologer to determine the Ascendant or Rising Sign and this information is a determining factor in the Birth Chart because it falls on the cusp of the First House on the Chart. From there, the Chart is made up of Planets, Signs, and Houses. The Planets represent the forces that act while the Signs determine how the Planets will act, and the Houses represent where in life the Planets will have an influence. Another important factor is the ruling Planet. This is the Planet that rules the Sign in a person's First House. Also of significance, is the Planet, called a dispositor, that rules a person's Sun Sign and strengthens the power of the Sun in the Chart. A person's emotional life may be indicated by the position of the dispositor or ruler of the Moon. Next, the astrologer looks at what Planets fall in the Angles of a Chart which enhances their power and strength. The four Angles are the Ascendant (cusp of the First House), the Nadir (cusp of the Fourth House), the Descendant (cusp of the Seventh House), and the Midheaven (cusp of the Tenth House). Next, it is determined if a person has Planets in their Dominion, that is, Planets that are in the sign that they rule. A Planet in its Home Sign is more powerful especially in relation to the House which it is in. Then too, Planets are considered in mutual reception if each one occupies the Sign that the other one rules. For example, if Mars is in Libra (ruled by Venus) and Venus is in Aries (ruled by Mars). This means that the two Planets are cooperating and each is strengthened. The Planets and the Signs each rules are listed below in order of significance to the Chart.

SUN -- Rules LEO, is exalted in ARIES, is indetriment in AQUARIUS, and is in fall in LIBRA.

MOON -- Rules CANCER, is exalted in TAURUS, is indetriment in CAPRICORN, and in fall in SCORPIO.

MERCURY -- Rules GEMINI and VIRGO, is exalted in VIRGO, is indetriment in SAGITTARIUS, and in fall in PISCES.

VENUS -- Rules TAURUS and LIBRA, is exalted in PISCES, is indetriment in ARIES, is in fall in VIRGO.

MARS -- Rules ARIES (and traditionally SCORPIO), is exalted in CAPRICORN, is indetriment in LIBRA, and in fall in CANCER.

JUPITER -- Rules SAGITTARIUS (and traditionally PISCES), is exalted in CANCER, is indetriment GEMINI, is in fall in CAPRICORN.

SATURN   -- Rules CAPRICORN (and traditionally AQUARIUS), is exalted in LIBRA, is indetriment in CANCER, is in fall in ARIES.

URANUS   -- Rules AQUARIUS, is exalted in SCORPIO, is indetriment in LEO, is in fall in TAURUS.

NEPTUNE -- Rules PISCES, is exalted in LEO, is indetriment in VIRGO, is in fall in AQUARIUS.

PLUTO   -- Rules SCORPIO, and is indetriment in TAURUS.

PREDICTIONS

Serious astrologers do not claim to be able to predict the future. What they do is ascertain the upcoming trends and indicate possible areas of stress and obstacles or possible times when opportunities or changes may present themselves. And while various astrologers put to use different methods for arriving at this information, a reliable astrologer is likely to be familiar with more than one method.

One of the most frequently used methods of determining future trends is the Progressed Chart. Progressed aspects, as mentioned, are indicative of general trends in a person's life. Lunar aspects affect the life for two to three months, and planetary transits last for a few weeks or a few days depending upon the particular planet. Years in which the progressed Sun progresses into the next sign are considered important in the life of the person.

One way to progress a chart is to use the one day for one year system. This involves noting the Birth Date and then counting forward the number of days which corresponds to the year in question. For example, if a person was curious about events to transpire when he or she was age forty, the astrologer would count forward forty days from the date of birth and then cast a new Chart. This system is related to the theory that there exists a relationship in the make up of the person between the Earth's daily rotation on its axis and its annual revolution around the Sun. It is theorized that the days after birth represent the development of the psyche of a person during the corresponding years. Another method to progress the Chart is to use the perpetual noon-date or the date directly related to the date and time of birth. Using this method, the Planetary positions at noon on the day in question are taken to relate to noon on the perpetual noon-date and to conditions for the twelve months afterwards. This is correlated to the amount of time between the birth time and noon on the birth date. The one-degree method of progression involves progressing a Planet from its position at birth, one degree for each year of life.

Followers of horary astrology use a different method altogether. These astrologers cast a Chart for the moment in time when the question is asked. In other words, a person asks the question, and the astrologer believes that when the question is asked is indicative of a relationship of what will happen, i.e., events are felt to take on the nature of the time at which they occur.

Another method is to study the transits of the Planets in comparison to the positions of the Planets in the Birth Chart. Planetary positions can be ascertained by checking an ephemeris for the date in question. Then compare these transits with the Birth Chart to find out what aspects are formed. Positive aspects formed with the transits of Jupiter, for example, are considered beneficial and enjoyable and a good time for action or travel. On the other hand, aspects formed with Saturn would indicate a time to hold off on major decisions. Mars is thought of as adding energy to another Planet (which is good but it can also make the person accident prone) while the transits of Venus bring about an enjoyable social life, and Uranus and Pluto indicate changes.

One other method is the Solar Return Chart. This involves a horoscope which is drawn up for the exact moment that the Sun is passing through the degree of the sign it was in at the moment of a person's birth. The Solar Return Chart is compared with the Birth Chart in order to determine any aspects formed between the two charts. This is considered a most useful method for spotting trends in the upcoming year. Similar to the Solar Return Chart is the Lunar Return Chart which is used to determine trends in the forthcoming month.

Modern astrologers are also observing and analyzing what is referred to as midpoints. This system dates back to the 13th century and focuses on the degree of the ecliptic which falls halfway between any two Planets, the Ascendant, or the Midheaven. This is considered a sensitive area in that it is the point at which the magnetic forces of the two Planets meet and connect. This midpoint, it is felt, is activated by the transits of the Planets or by Planetary progressions. It goes without saying that this system requires a thorough understanding of transits and progressions, but it is useful in that unexpected and often uncharted occurrences happen at these points.

THE STAGES OF LIFE

One of the interesting corollaries often mentioned in astrology texts is the relationship between the signs and the stages of life. These do not form a direct connection to the individual Birth Chart, but as one becomes more familiar with astrology and the descriptions of the Sun signs and how they relate to real people, the Stages of Life Concept gains significance in its applicability.

ARIES - The first stage of life, that of the newborn baby in its cradle, is often used in portraying the characteristics of Aries. The baby is capable of thinking only of itself and its immediate needs, wanting what it wants at once and being quite prepared to yell and to demand what it wants if necessary. The baby is incapable of considering the effects of its demands on other people.

TAURUS - The second stage of life corresponds to Taurus and implies a time in life when the infant is learning to interact with others and to form its first relationships. This child is aware of others and becoming aware of feelings. The child is also learning and discovering the ability to do things for oneself. Thus, Taurus likes to work.

GEMINI - Is considered the playful child who learns to make friendships outside of the home. This is also the time of life when one is learning and developing intelligence.

CANCER - Corresponds to the adolescent who is changeable, susceptible to suggestions, and emotional. He is not quite ready to be independent, and home and mother are important. Often Cancer reflects the opinions of others (peers) rather than the individual.

LEO - Is the first stage in an individuals life when effort is being made to be independent and grown up, and ambitions are becoming important. This person may be overly impressed with himself.

VIRGO - Next is Virgo who is associated with the Serving-maid who is willing to help others and to learn a skill through training and effort.

LIBRA - Is associated with that stage of life when one is attempting to find the proper balance and place in the world through relationships and partnerships.

SCORPIO - Represents the active stage of a persons life which requires applying energy to endeavors and overcoming any obstacles along the way.

SAGITTARIUS - Might be that worldly, ambitious person or the person who strives to achieve wisdom and spirituality.

CAPRICORN - Represents achievements in life and realizing one's ambitions.

AQUARIUS - Is associated with loftier ideals and a person who is no longer striving for achievement but is reflecting on life.

PISCES - Is that stage of life that reflects the ultimate meaning in the previous stages, and it is said that Pisces individuals are old souls who have evolved through the other signs and are ready for rebirth or the beginning of the next wheel or cycle of life.

THESE CHARACTERISTICS, of course, do not apply directly to the signs but are used as references in regard to the general nature of the Sun Signs.

CONCLUSION

That astrology is a complex study should be apparent. An effort has been made to introduce many of the concepts which will be discussed within this book, and, hopefully, this general overview will add to the understanding of the efforts being made within the field of astrology.

Many within this field accept it as part of what is referred to as the collective mind or the collective human experience. And this explanation may go a long way in explaining the lasting interest in astrology which has endured through the ages. There is also discussion of the unconscious aspect of the human experience which alludes to that part of the mind which is unaware of itself and cannot be controlled by conscious effort. The psychologist Carl Jung, with his interest in astrology, offered his own explanation of this collective experience.

Perhaps the most basic concept found within astrology is the idea that nothing exists which is not in some way related or interrelated to some other part of the universe. That is to say that no one part of the universe is ever independent or cut off from the rest of the universe. There is a link, however subtle, between the forces of nature and the dependency that life on Earth has to not only the Sun and the Moon but in some degree to the other Planets as well. And this interrelation ties in most directly with the rhythms, the waves, and the movements of these heavenly bodies through space. Did atoms not exist before they were discovered? Or were quarks some unknown mystery before the physicist learned to quantify them? What leads even the greatest of these scientists and thinkers to want to know more? And what leads everyday people to also want to know more and to discover some explanation for the reasoning behind what makes the world go round?

Astrology, in conclusion, is not an entertainment made up merely for distraction, but rather. But rather considering its age alone, it is a science that has been studied, added to, and evaluated throughout the time of men and women on Earth. It is a fascinating discovery and correlation of events, times, and people. That its scope includes the entire universe as we know it today adds to its fascination. And that it is only as old as our knowledge of the universe adds to its perplexities. It is a field of study which undoubtedly will continue to grow and expand.

Astrological Months

The twelve Zodiac constellations do not correspond with the so-called constellations any more. When we talk about "the Virgo" it does not mean that the respective Planet is in the Virgo constellation. The signs of the Zodiac are astrologically classified (1) according to their nature as: Cardinal, Fixed, and Mutable; (2) according to gender: masculine and feminine; and (3) according to the four fundamental elements as: Earth, Air, Fire and Water.

The Classifications of The Signs According to Their Respective Elements are:

EARTH: TAURUS, VIRGO, CAPRICORN

FIRE: ARIES, LEO, SAGITTARIUS

AIR: GEMINI, LIBRA, AQUARIUS

WATER: CANCER, SCORPIO, PISCES

The Signs Correspond to
The Following Periods of The Year:

ARIES:	MARCH 21 TO APRIL 20
TAURUS:	APRIL 21 TO MAY 20
GEMINI:	MAY 21 TO JUNE 21
CANCER:	JUNE 22 TO JULY 22
LEO:	JULY 23 TO AUGUST 22
VIRGO:	AUGUST 23 TO SEPTEMBER 22
LIBRA:	SEPTEMBER 23 TO OCTOBER 22
SCORPIO:	OCTOBER 23 TO NOVEMBER 21
SAGITTARIUS:	NOVEMBER 22 TO DECEMBER 20
CAPRICORN:	DECEMBER 21 TO JANUARY 19
AQUARIUS:	JANUARY 20 TO FEBRUARY 18
PISCES:	FEBRUARY 19 TO MARCH 20

When referring to a sign, we must first consider the month that sign represents because nature shows the psycho-temperamental characteristic of a respective person and also his evolution. From, the moment of birth, the person follows nature's path. For example, the Sun moves from the Spring equinox towards the Summer Solstice. This is a cosmic impulse of the life giving Plan et. Many writers and poets describe this as the moment of triumph, the awakening of nature.

33

THE PLANETS ARE THE DAUGHTERS OF THE SUN BY SCIENCE, PAIN, LOVE, OR BY DEATH

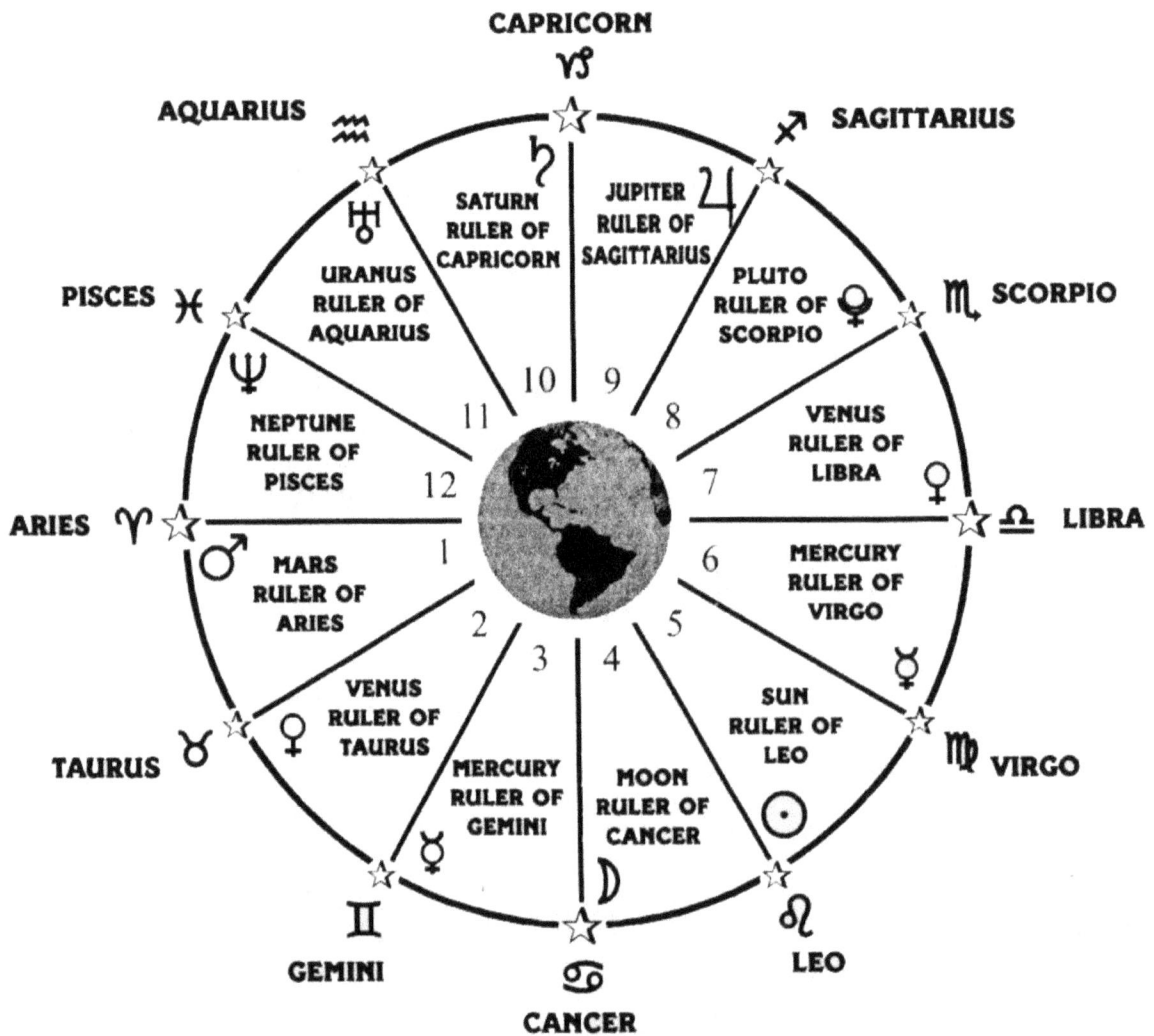

THE TWELVE SUN SIGNS OF THE ZODIAC

ARIES: MARCH 21 -- APRIL 20

Cardinal, Fire sign; Positive; Masculine; Ruled by Mars; Aries rules the head; Symbolized by the Ram; Glyph represents a ram's horns; indicates sandy, hilly, dry or arid settings, fireplaces, ceilings, tools, furnaces; sayings: "the untamed fire of impulse."; keywords: "I AM", representing the birth of awareness; traits: dynamic, ambitious, active, ardent, headstrong, impatient, courageous, enthusiastic, imaginative, energetic, excitable, proud, impulsive, rash, undomestic, hasty, sharp spoken, passionate, quick tempered, self-centered, quick with ideas, aggressive, enterprising, executive, pioneering, confident, independent, ingenious, scientific, explorative, forceful, strong willed, urgent, generous, seeking affirmation and admiration; Color: red; Metal: copper; Stone: diamond.

TAURUS: APRIL 21 -- MAY 20

Fixed, Earth sign; Feminine; Receptive; Ruled by Venus; Taurus rules the throat and cerebellum; symbolized by the Bull; Glyph represents the bull's head and horns; indicates banks, safety deposit boxes, money boxes, jewel cases, stables, dairies, tack rooms, pastures, fields, and round items such as rings, coins, wheels; sayings: "Mad as a bull"; keywords: "I HAVE"; traits: possessive, permanency, artistic, gentle, loyal, domestic, proud, self-indulgent and self-interested, sensual, amorous, patient but hot tempered when angry, persistent, thorough, conservative, retentive, discriminating, determined, can be stubborn and obstinate, materialistic, hard working, diligent, steady, kind, trustworthy, self-reliant, composed, practical, sympathetic, careful, fearless, enduring; Color: pink and pale blue; Metal: copper; Stone: sapphire.

35

GEMINI: MAY 21 -- JUNE 21

Mutable, Air sign; Masculine; Positive; Ruled by Mercury; Gemini rules the hands, shoulders, arms, and lungs; symbolized by the Twins; Glyph represents the two figures of the Twins; indicates letters, communications, messengers, news, newspapers and magazines, neighbors, relatives, short journeys, lecturing, debating, teaching, advertising, reporting, clerical assignments, story telling, merchandising, printing, education; sayings for Gemini: "Here today, but gone tomorrow," "Too many irons in the fire,"; keywords: "I THINK"; traits: communicative, adaptable, versatile, sensitive, eloquent, generous, likes traveling, undomestic, companionable, changeable, congenial, sociable, temperamental, mood-swings, inventive, curious, tricky, dexterous, literary, expressive, intellectual, idealistic, restless, impulsive; Color: yellow; Metal: mercury; Stone: agate.

CANCER: JUNE 22 -- JULY 22

Cardinal, Water sign; Feminine, Receptive; Ruled by the Moon; Cancer rules the breasts and stomach; symbolized by the Crab; Glyph is drawn from the human breasts representing motherhood; indicates lakes, rivers, streams, springs, marshy lands, homes, stables, mangers, taverns, public places, kitchens, water receptacles, cellars; sayings: "The restless tides of the oceans," "Clings like a crab," "By the light of the silvery Moon,"; keywords: "I FEEL"; traits: protective, sensitive, imaginative, sympathetic, kind, emotional, shrewd, active, intuitive, moody, artistic, dreamy, maternal, romantic, domestic, impressionable, psychic, restless, changeable, versatile, receptive, drawn to history and ancestors, cautious, reserved, brooding, self-centered, selfish, possessive, vain; Color: green; Metal: silver; Stone: pearl.

LEO: JULY 23 -- AUGUST 22

Fixed, Fire sign; Masculine, Positive; Ruled by the Sun; Leo rules the back, spine, and heart; symbolized by the Lion; Glyph represents two incomplete circles of the Sun joined by the Moon, i.e., power derived from the intellect and the emotions; indicates rounded hills, wilderness, deserts, forests, forts, palaces, clubs, theaters, playgrounds, ballrooms, amusement parks, sports and games of chance, social gatherings and functions, fireplaces, furnaces, sun porches; sayings: "All is fair in love and war," "Lionhearted," "Fire of the heart,"; keywords: "I WILL"; traits: idealistic, proud, magnetic, loyal, philanthropic, creative, impressive, powerful, ambitious, commanding, generous, fixed opinions, challenging, bold, domineering, autocratic, hopeful, sociable, magnanimous, outspoken, ardent, arrogant, self-centered; Color: gold and orange; Metal: gold; Stone: ruby.

VIRGO: AUGUST 23 -- SEPTEMBER 22

Mutable, Earth sign; Feminine, Receptive; Ruled by Mercury; Virgo rules the nervous system and intestines; symbolized by the Virgin; Glyph represents the Virgin; indicates gardens, fields, grain mills and elevators, pantries, restaurants, storage for fruits and vegetables and grains, file cabinets, shelves, and storage for books, papers, maps, charts and plans; sayings: "He serves most who serves best," "Virtue is its own reward,"; keywords: "I ANALYZE"; traits: kind, domestic, ingenious, witty, studious, intellectual, methodical, detail-oriented, analytical, serious, active, concise, discreet, sensitive, perceptive, intuitive, industrious, calculating, anxious, worries, skeptical, critical, quick-tempered, discontent, fearful of disease and poverty, indecisive, contemplative; Color: blue and gray; Metal: mercury; Stone: sapphire.

LIBRA: SEPTEMBER 23 -- OCTOBER 22

Cardinal, Air sign; Masculine, Positive; Ruled by Venus; Libra rules the lower back, buttocks, and kidneys; symbolized by the Scales; Glyph represents the Scales in perfect balance; indicates windmills, barns, cut wood, harbors, shipyards, mountain tops, hills, trees, hunting grounds, sandy soil, domed buildings, courthouses, lofts, closets, guest rooms, pianos, scales, weights, measures, dresser tops, jewel cases; sayings for Libra: "Tell it to the judge," "Blessed are the peace makers,"; keywords: "I BALANCE"; traits: refined, impartial, diplomatic, thoughtful, gracious, modest, decorous, artistic, adaptable, persuasive, sociable, peace loving, judicial, affectionate, charming, kind, understanding, harmonious, well balanced, romantic, idealistic, tactful, indecisive, reckless, gullible, procrastinating, susceptible, impressionable, illusive, vain; Color: blue and purple; Metal: copper; Stone: opal.

SCORPIO: OCTOBER 23 -- NOVEMBER 21

Fixed, Water sign; Feminine, Receptive; Ruled by Pluto; Scorpio rules the genitals; symbolized by the Scorpion; Glyph represents the Scorpion stinger connected to the reproductive organs; indicates surgeons, chemists, detectives and investigators, researchers, lowlands, gardens, vineyards, slaughter houses, meat markets, laboratories, funeral homes; sayings: "The eye of an eagle,"; keywords: "I DESIRE"; traits: intense, passionate, active, energetic, positive, fearless, tenacious, penetrating, thoughtful, eloquent, devoted, secretive, emotional, subtle, persistent, obstinate, imaginative, possessive, jealous, quick-tempered, revengeful, temperamental, sarcastic, vindictive; Color: crimson and maroon; Metal: Plutonium; Stone: topaz.

SAGITTARIUS: NOVEMBER 22 -- DECEMBER 20

Mutable, Fire sign; Masculine, Positive; Ruled by Jupiter; Sagittarius rules the liver, hips, and thighs; symbolized by the Archer; Glyph represents the arrow of the Archer; indicates high or elevated places, around fire; stables; arrows, spears, swords, needles, obelisks, poles, canes, rope, long tools, race horses, incense burners; sayings for Sagittarius: "For he's a jolly good fellow," "A good sport,"; traits: energetic, optimistic, zealous, proud, lucky, tolerant, open minded, sincere, honest, prophetic, humane, foresight, out spoken, freedom loving, exploratory, jovial, progressive, curious, amiable and friendly, speculative, risk taker, idealistic, daring, impatient, undomestic, self indulgent, charitable, assertive, defiant, stubborn, independent, sport loving; Color: dark blue and purple; Metal: tin; Stone: turquoise.

CAPRICORN: DECEMBER 21 -- JANUARY 19

Cardinal, Earth sign; Feminine, Receptive; Ruled by Saturn; Capricorn rules the bones, joints, and knees; symbolized by the Goat; Glyph represents the beard of the Goat; indicates leather, logs, older trees, lumber, cement, brick, mortar, goats, plaster, bones, skeletons, docks, hemlock, frost, snow, ice; sayings for Capricorn: "Watch and wait," "What is worth doing is worth doing well,"; keywords: "I USE"; traits: prudent, aspiring, steadfast; dignity, cautious, patient, disciplined, determined, practical, well organized, service, leadership, ambitious, forceful, economical, conservative, thrifty, scrupulous, trustworthy, stubborn, domineering, good friends and bad enemies, brooding, egotistical; Color: green and brown; Metal: lead; Stone: garnet.

AQUARIUS: JANUARY 20 -- FEBRUARY 18

Fixed, Air sign; Masculine, Positive; Ruled by Uranus; Aquarius rules the circulatory system, calves and ankles; symbolized by the Waterbearer; Glyph represents waves as in the water pouring between Heaven and the Earth, electrical energy, and universal wisdom; indicates hilly terrain, springs, roofs, highways, cups, vases, pitchers, smoke, steam, vapor, rain, fog, bridges and ferries, railroads, vehicles and airplanes, electricity and electrical engines, telephones, radios, ladders, and stairs; sayings: "The waters of life," "A stranger in a strange land,"; keywords: "I KNOW"; traits: idealistic, truth seeker, humanitarian, sincere, assertive, independent, progressive, analytical, inventive, intellectual, tolerant but fixed in opinion, domestic but changeable, kind, well-liked, gentle, altruistic, anxious, unconventional, temperamental, sociable, considerate, intuitive, scientific, earnest, futuristic, can be radical, irrational, scattered, skeptical, and gullible; Color: aquamarine and sky blue; Metal: Uranium; Stone: amethyst.

PISCES: FEBRUARY 19 -- MARCH 20

Mutable, Water sign; Feminine, Receptive; Ruled by Neptune; Pisces rules the feet; symbolized by the Fish (two fish going in opposite directions); Glyph represents the two fish tied together or two crescent moons--one for emotions and one for reality, i.e., a higher consciousness limited by the restrictions of a physical body and the temptations of the world; indicates: oceans, fish, nets, fishing, boats, canneries, bodies of water, aquariums, under water ventures, oil and petroleum, spiritualism, and churches; sayings for Pisces: "A fish out of water," "Two ships passing in the night,"; keywords: "I Believe,"; traits: idealistic, hospitable, loyal, self-sacrificing, refined, perceptive, emotional, sensitive, romantic, intuitive, mystical, impressionable, changeable, moody, devoted, psychic, secretive, compassionate, versatile, tempted by pleasures, dreamy, submissive; Colors: sea green, lilac, lavender; Metal: platinum, tin; Stone: aquamarine, moonstone.

ZODIAC ANATOMY

SIGNS	PARTS OF THE BODY	ORGANS	GLANDS	SYSTEM
ARIES	Head Face	Blood Brain	Pituitary	Muscular
TAURUS	Neck	Throat	Thyroid	Metabolic
GEMINI	Shoulders Arms, Hands	Lungs, Nerves	Thymus	Central Nervous System
CANCER	Breasts	Stomach, Uterus	Mammary, Salivary	Digestive (Upper)
LEO	Upper Back	Heart, Upper Spine, Blood Marrow	Spleen	Cardiac
VIRGO	Abdomen	Small Intestines	Pancreas	Digestive (Lower)
LIBRA	Small of the Back	Kidneys, Genitalia	Adrenals	Endocrine
SCORPIO	Genitalia, Intestines	Colon, Internal Genitalia	Glands	Reproduction Renal
SAGITTARIUS	Buttocks Hips, Calves	Lower Spine	Liver	Autonomic Nervous System
CAPRICORN	Knees Skin	Joints, Bones, Teeth, Hair	Gallbladder, Sebaceous Glands	Skeletal
AQUARIUS	Ankles Legs	Nerves	Parathyroid	Circulatory
PISCES	Feet	Body Fluids	Lacrimal, Lymph, Pineal	Lymphatic

Date With Destiny

ARIES
MARCH 21-APRIL 20

Share With Me Your Fantasy

Date With Destiny

ARIES
MARCH 21-APRIL 20

Share With Me Your Fantasy

ARIES

MARCH 21 - APRIL 20

MAN - WOMAN - CHILD - CHARACTER - RELATIONSHIPS - COMPATIBILITIES - LOVE SIGNS

The word Aries is taken from the Latin word for Ram and is often depicted as such. But Aries was also the Greek god of war, and many of the personal characteristics of individuals born to this Sun sign resemble this mythological and legendary ruler of war and conflict. Aries was an erotic lover who had numerous affairs. He was both brave and insolent, youthful, and impulsive.

Aries is the first Sun sign of the Zodiac, and because of this, is often referred to as the baby of the Zodiac. Like a baby, Aries can be self-centered, demanding, and delighting in immediate gratification. This is a brave, courageous, and daring person who is unafraid of standing up for personal rights and freedoms. But Aries is at other times considered rash, crude, pushy, and overly aggressive. This is the demanding egotist who is Aries.

The first sign of the Zodiac, Aries, is under the control of Mars. It is the Cardinal sign of Fire, which represents the Earth as it was before Genesis, i.e., during the time when fire, the chaos and other elements were ravishing the Universe. Mars is the sign of force coordinating the other natural forces. It represents action and direction. It begins each year as the Sun reaches the Equator at the Spring Equinox, bringing forth the cosmic impulse of the life-giving planet. Many philosophers and writers refer to this as the moment of triumph, of the awakening of nature. This constellation is divided into two groups: A fixed group of stars forms the shape of the Aries; a part of the head, neck, the right horn and the front legs belong to the Aries area, the Ram, with the rest of the body inside the area of the Taurus.

The symbol of the Ram can represent a battering ram thrusting forward, ever rambunctious and even rampaging on its journeys. Aries rules the head and is noted for its headstrong impulsiveness which may often compel its natives to plunge into endeavors and situations without considering the outcomes or consequences of their actions. Their overpowering self-assertiveness can prevent them from judging well the reactions of other people. If the Ram persistently butts up against too much opposition, losing his energies, he can become as the sheep, losing direction and meandering from place to place.

Aries, being the first Fire sign, represents action, direction, energy, and courage. The Aries individual possesses a strong belief in his or her own value or self-worth. People born under the sign of Aries are known for being dynamic with swiftness of action and thought and with an extremely strong will. They possess an exceptional ability to organize and to coordinate. They rarely lose courage and are gifted with an excellent character. They fight back adversity, retain courage in difficult moments, and reshape their existence, paying with their own life if necessary. However, it is quite possible for the Aries person, at times, to reach their purpose or to obtain their goal, and, as will be explained later in this text, this is not always very favorable to them.

Then too, Aries natives are authoritarian and impulsive. They want everyone else in their lives to shape according to their will, but, at the same time, it can be said that they are capable of making great sacrifices for their loved ones. And even when their finances are moderate, they can also be generous to a fault. They are ready to forgive but not to forget inequities, attempting with all their effort to turn a negative experience into a future profitable one.

The Aries soul wonders toward metaphysical thought, and if this gift is developed through meditation and self-improvement, it can inspire the individual. The clairvoyant and psychic powers often being so phenomenally great that the Aries can readily read the minds and thoughts and know the motives of others without the exchange of a single word. When in a highly developed state, many mysteries of the spirit world are revealed to them. Aries people are surrounded with occult, magnetic and solar forces which, when realized, can be so great that these people have the power to banish the misgivings and doubts of others. Many gifted psychics, mind readers, telepathists and spiritual advisers have been Aries individuals.

However, it must be remembered that the first-sign Aries can be impractical and impulsive, and although his or her moral code may at times be flexible, they are most generally honest, helpful and courageous. Many famous pioneers and explorers were born under this sign. If the individual is involved in a medical career, he becomes scrupulous, careful and very conscientious.

Some astrologers view Aries as having the ability to develop his or her positive traits or submitting and falling prey to their less than positive traits. The individual Aries has the propensity or opportunity to choose either direction. Aries, as the first sign of the Zodiac, has not only the freedom but the strength and youthful energy to walk either path, choosing his directions as he pleases. Aries, representing the cosmic principle of action, evokes the will to begin, to seek, to take the initiative. This sign signifies the drive to expand, ,to be', to experiencing becoming what one all ready is, all that one is, to externalize and explore all possibilities, keeping nothing latent, but, rather, exploring and tasting every emotion, pleasure, sensual sensation, and adventure. Aries is considered a mental sign because an individual must have a strong intellect in order to make decisions and to select a path or to venture into an unknown future. To the Aries individual comes the realization that ideas are the most potent force known to man. This person, preferring words to a sword, can be the inspired thinker who compels others to action. To the Aries individual, words are the most effective implements of his or her will power.

Aries has been called the birthplace of divine ideas. As the first sign, Aries initiates ideologies and causes. Metaphysically, it signifies the entrance into a higher state of increased self-realization and spiritual illumination. Man, as a thinking creature, has over the ages utilized this visionary power of Aries to explore and conquer the Universe. The dynamism, the speed and strong will are the features of the native Aries, influenced by Mars. In certain situations Aries becomes distracted and is just as happy that they passed the difficulties, perhaps not even being curious about the results. There are times when Aries needs others to take over what they started. Aries live for the present. They don't want to worry about the future. Their ideas is, "to try to solve today the problem of the moment." Aries can not wait--they want everything "now".

Aries Personality

Aries are open, outspoken, enthusiastic, and intensely individualistic. Enterprising and ambitious, they are often versatile, but headstrong with a tendency to be impulsive. They have a forceful nature and make determined efforts, but they can also be fiery and quick-tempered. With their strong ambition and drive, their desire to lead is compelling. This is a fiercely independent person who can be the first to take the side of the underdog or to accept unpopular viewpoints.

Aries are outgoing, extroverted, self-assured, active, combative, enterprising and industrious; and they strive to appear self-possessed and self-confident under all conditions. They possess both physical and moral character and a supreme courage that carries them forward in their existence and their survival of all situations both good and bad. They strive to achieve practical goals and tangible rewards and with the influence of Mars are predictably people of swift, expeditious, decisive conduct and movements. This person is most generally concerned with intellectual pursuits rather than spiritual values. Aries are outspoken and frank to a fault, and while they are basically amiable and friendly, they are hasty to jump to conclusions and to make decisions. The keen and alert Aries intellect is swift to grasp and to initiate new ideas. This attribute aids the Aries individual in his or her desire to be noticed and to stand out in a crowd. These desires are also augmented by a quick wit, alluring charm, inspiring conversation, and open generosity. They are well aware of their strong beliefs, and often declaring their superiority, which when coupled with their impatience and enthusiastic desire to lead, can appear arrogant and dogmatic.

They can also appear rash and reckless, qualities that are exhibited in unconscious impulses and compulsive behavior. Sometimes this is the first impression they make on others because Aries has the innate ability to think extremely fast, to grasp ideas and to size up situations, to weigh pros and cons, to estimate chances, and to calculate risks rapidly. Often times, although he appears rash, his plans have been calculated and well planned beforehand. Aries are willing to act independently, initiate plans, take the first step, attempt new methods, innovate, change, and improvise. Any action taken is likely to be direct and forceful, and Aries are often scornful of the slow-moving diplomatic methods, much preferring to plunge into endeavors with eagerness and energy. Little concern is given to obstacles that would prevent others from proceeding, as the Aries sizes up the situation, lays out a plan, and plows around or through any walls, fences, oppositions or rules that he considers made for others and not for him.

The Vernal Equinox, the beginning of the new cycle of seasons, compels Aries to begin, to seek the new, to take the lead, to break new ground and to pioneer by example. There is a fresh but impatient dynamism to Aries. This beginning youthful sign with its boundless and ardent energies also lacks reasoning and maturity. There is an almost childlike innocence, a trusting quality with great appeal and charm, but one which at times works against the individual. This is the underlying cause of major disappointments, disillusionment and failures in the Aries life. These setbacks can often hurt the Aries ego, resulting in deep depression. However, the Aries nature is resilient. It rebounds from defeat, recovers from depression, and turns to new endeavors and enterprises with inspired and renewed enthusiasm, optimism, and energy.

Aries espouses great intensity, even if it is at times short lived. They require recognition and appreciation which fuels their drives, renews their energies, and satisfies their egos. At first, Aries may appear self-centered, striving to increase their self-esteem and improve other people's regard or impression of them. At the same time, the more positive attributes of Aries include generosity, courage, spontaneity and idealism. Aries are extremely generous with their time, effort and money. They are sympathetic, giving advice and listening, and taking steps to help those who are less well off. Aries loves to solve the problems of others, but in return will require recognition for his or her efforts, unquestionable loyalty and ongoing patronage reminiscent of slavery.

The Aries moral and physical courage motivates these individuals to be protective and supportive of those being persecuted or unfairly treated. Aries can act with spontaneity, without premeditation or much thought given to the results of their actions. This leads to their genuine idealism which is unconcerned with spiritual or abstract values. This idealism motivates them to take definite steps to achieve results to benefit themselves and others.

Psychologically, this youthful sign, being the first in the Zodiac and known as the infant of the Zodiac, is innately endowed with deep-seated insecurities and a sense of inadequacy. The fundamental youthfulness of the Aries nature can result in extravagant shows of opinionated knowledge and elaborate exhibitions of self-assurance that displays their arrogance. However, some Aries are unconsciously flawed by anxiety to such a degree that the person will abandon a task or endeavor out of fear of failure and then suddenly direct his or her attention and energies in an entirely new direction. Another anxiety is the fear of rejection. This may be the unconscious motivation behind the Aries tendency to make hasty or critical judgments about other people and to reject those who are not immediately responsive or who don't actively seek acquaintance or friendship. In other words, Aries are likely to reject others first before they are rejected. This is a definite and profound weakness in the Aries personality. There is a pronounced lack of effort to assess human nature and character because this requires patience and reflection rather than quick thinking. Therefore, Aries are not known for always developing their appreciable gifts of insight and often times because of their rash judgments, they make erroneous assessments of others-- either trusting those who flatter them too readily or disregarding altogether those more worthy of their appreciation.

The Aries ego is strong, vital, and robustly healthy in regard to its ability to strike balances through the use of logic, intellect, and reason. But when it is allowed to run freely, the Aries ego, uninhibited by restraint, may over-compensate for anxieties and fears of failure with egotistical convictions that only his or her ideas, concepts and methods have any worth or validity. There may even exist a distortion of the qualities of initiative, independence, and impatience to a degree that causes the individual to act and to react to irrational impulses and compulsions in an oppositional and forceful manner. And oppositional behavior can become a way of life for many Aries. Oppositional behavior can become a way of life for Aries.

The Aries vulnerability arises at several levels, even though they may feel wiser and superior to others. Being quick to reject people, they cannot tolerate rejection themselves and lack any comprehension of why they have been rejected. This conflict is resolved only with an emotional maturity which understands and appreciates the give and take that is necessary in human relations.   Another deep-seated conflict occurs with the inability to reconcile their impulsiveness in romantic affairs and their idealistic concept of love and romance. Males born in the first and second decans manage to resolve this conflict by accepting themselves thus liberating them from anxieties over their behavior. Other Aries develop deep guilt feelings arising from their intense hatred of deceit and duplicity. In extreme cases, the burden of guilt may cause impotence in the male and hysterical frigidity in the female.

Many Aries have a tendency toward extreme jealousies stemming from unconscious fears of inadequacies. These jealousies may be exhibited in sudden, violent outbursts and even physical violence. Only emotional maturity and the development of a sense of security regarding personal adequacy can resolve this particular conflict. Otherwise, many Aries destroy their personal relationships with their extreme jealousies.

Aries' personalities, in many instances, lack a sense of proportion. They have a tendency to exaggerate, to be extravagant, to be over-optimistic, and to allow their enthusiasms to rule the day. Over-optimism, over-estimation, excessive enthusiasm and exaggeration can and do lead to invariably disappointing results in many of their endeavors. This causes painful moments and wounded feelings as Aries may not always be able to comprehend the cause of their problems. Quite obviously, there is a need to acquire a reasonable sense of proportion between exaggerated hopes and aspirations as opposed to reality and fact in order to prevent the possibility of eventual neurotic complications.

When badly aspected, the positive gift of leadership is warped and twisted into a domineering, even tyrannical nature. Dynamism is transformed into ruthless, demanding, slave-driving qualities. Aries should be ever aware of negative tendencies: the failure to follow through and see plans completed because of a lack of determination, perseverance and patience; nervous and emotional instability; arrogance; and a lack of consideration for the feelings of others.

While Aries is endowed with potential leadership abilities, they are often unable to discipline themselves because of their conceitful belief that they are right and consequently others are wrong and should concede and be grateful for the Aries presence. They demand that others, who often the Aries has aided or helped in some manner, should in turn be loyal and willing to unquestioningly follow their ideas and opinions. Aries demands that others contribute to and back their plans faithfully and with enthusiasm. Put simply, to question the plans of an Aries person is to appear disloyal and unfaithful--conduct which can result in the loss of the friendship or relationship or at the least in a healthy tongue lashing.

The otherwise healthy ego of the average Aries exhibit an innate ambition and a desire for achievement and recognition in ways that are constructively productive, aiming for goals that are real and tangible, that can be counted and gauged. The chances are that Aries has little interest in establishing his individuality within himself. His individuality has been established only when he has accomplished a measurable, proven goal, that is, when he has succeeded.

Aries most desire success. When they are defeated, it is many times because they defeat themselves. The seeds of Aries destruction lie within the personality. Their advantage is in the fact that they are capable of controlling their destinies to a far greater extent than most, providing they learn to exercise self-discipline. Remember, the personality of Aries is derived from its „Number One', first-sign position, and from the rulership of Mars. This is the sign of the overbearing dictator, the most political of the constellations, often full of energy and decision, generous but often unreliable, changing strides while vehemently insisting he was right all along.

Thus, Aries, you are not the type to sit quietly in a corner at a party. You prefer to talk and to move around, to work the crowd. Mobility is important to you. Your desire to stand out in the crowd leads you to move from one group to another, learning what others have to say. At the same time, you have difficulty relating to others. This detachment in your personal make-up is due partially to your feelings of superiority and partially to your self-protective defense mechanisms which protect you from rejection and disappointment in others and in yourself. You strive to be the leader in any group even with your friends, to be the best at every skill and competition. This drive to be superior, to be the best, leads to a contempt for familiarity. And you make every effort to illuminate any risk of bruising your ego.

Therefore, you limit your associates, your list of friends, to those you consider your entourage, followers, and confidants, and to those you view worthy of your time and friendship. In other words, people who impress you. These are the chosen people who you trust, judged through the narrow prism of your conscious attitude of superiority, to be worthy of your time. To these people, you are intensely loyal, although often this trust is misguided as you have a tendency to misjudge people.

Self-improvement strategies for any Aries who is interested would require (1) curbing the tendency to be outspoken and opinionated, (2) avoiding arrogance, and (3) forcing themselves to reserve judgments about others, allowing themselves the time to see past their initial first impression.

You are at your best when you are guiding, controlling, governing or commanding yourself and others. You have the ability to shape the outcome of the future and to develop and conceive great plans. You are in your element when you feel the strength and freedom of your independence and determination, the execution of your ideas, the drive of your energies at full force, and the admiration of others who follow and believe in your ideas and plans. You are not easily discouraged nor is your strong will power easily subdued. Those individuals who personify the pioneering spirit of the Aries sign incessantly pursue exercising their powers of decision-making and their independence which makes them self-determined people.

ARIES CHARACTER

Ruling as it does over the brain, the Aries intellectual development can be exceptionally remarkable. This sign can produce the deepest thinkers with marked cognitive abilities who have the capacity to impart knowledge to others. They can be brilliant scholars and excellent conversationalists. It is through their brilliancy and exceptional wit that they charm and attract others to them. The Aries individual with his gifted and vivacious mind and excellent memory can readily converse on numerous subjects, appearing well-read and well-informed. They are never at a loss for words or for a variety of information on various subjects. The spiritually evolved Aries knows that his freedom and independence depend to a great degree on his intellectual and cognitive abilities. You love to be the provider of entertainment, information, assistance, and advice for your friends.

The sign of Aries is the first of the twelve signs of the Zodiac. It is also the Cardinal sign of the Fire Trinity. Mars gives you extraordinary character. You are highly regarded for your executive ability, assertiveness, speedy thoughts and actions, initiative, energy and determination. In these regards, you have no equals among the other signs. You are absolutely fearless when faced with opposition, and you may go through life feeling like you are forever relentlessly pushing through or riding over obstacles placed in your path as you attempt to accomplish your goals. Aries, you desire to be in the lead, feeling it your privilege and duty to command and rule over those around you.

You prefer public life to private life, group activities to individual companionship, and crowds to smaller, more intimate get togethers. While you are well known for being quick in thought and able to give impromptu little speeches, you may at times stammer in your impatience to get your thoughts out first, and may even have two or more ideas running consecutively through your mind. Being capable of appreciating and adapting to many points of view, while holding to your own, you may appear overly opportunistic. Aries, guard against this rash outpouring of words. Others may have difficulty keeping up with your overflowing rush of ideas.

The sign of Aries, influencing those born between March 21 and April 20, represents the Fire elements of energy and courage. It is a masculine sign with a tendency to come to attention. This person, who enjoys new endeavors, craves being exposed to a variety of prospects for enterprising and innovative ideas, schemes, or adventures. You obstinately hold to your personal impression of not only your self-worth but of the superiority of your ideas and plans. The sign of Aries marks the Spring solstice, the change of seasons. It is a Cardinal sign representing a strong determination, a courageous spirit, a power of command and execution, ambition, enterprising spirit, combativity, strong will, independence, activity and most of all the desire to rule. The intellect leads this sign; however, the person should be aware of his energies and take care not to expend them needlessly in too many directions.

Aries' greatest problem is impatience with others, especially those who don't always agree, which can lead to irrational and excessive fury. And while demanding total loyalty from others, fidelity is not a main attribute, thus allowing Aries to be easy going and capable of cheating--and capable of rationalizing such behavior afterward. Remember, Aries is always right. This person is a better friend than spouse, but a friendship before marriage may lead to a successful marriage. This person may have many problems with family members who ask for money but who at the same time are not loyal nor do they generally understand the strong characteristics of the Aries nature. While Aries is a caring person with a good character, they can be controlling to a fault.

Aries individuals possess great courage and an enterprising nature which is coupled with a tendency to change purposes frequently. They generally have many skills and stay busy in a variety of activities. They remain active even as they grow older. They love and appreciate music and can, if so inclined, become talented musicians. If they play an instrument, a powerful one is preferred with which to express the Aries vitality, energy, and passion. If in the military, the Aries person prefers leadership positions. Often a polished public speaker, Aries can gain success in politics or as a comedian.

The most remarkable types of Aries have become dictators. Others use this ability to control their families, and they most generally respect tradition. If someone attempts to change your routine, your life, or your ideas of traditions, you can become depressed. The Aries defect is that you are not a diplomat: if you do not like something, you leave--slamming the door or phone, first, before the other person has the opportunity to do so. And you never admit defeat. You are never wrong. Fault lies with the other person in all instances. Whatever has happened to you, whatever obstacles has held you back, it is someone else's fault. Your superior actions and ideas could not possibly be wrong. In a disagreement, you may become furious and use foul words, apologizing later and expecting all to forgive and forget, to move on. But no one should attempt to cheat or deceive you or even to disagree with you, for you find this unforgivable. The Aries person has a most difficult time trusting other people's advice.

If people are good and fair to you, you are very kind and generous. You are willing to help and to understand, and you go to great lengths to aid others. Aries, you are extroverted, outgoing, witty, and friendly, and you make an excellent companion and confidant. Your supportive, protective nature wants to take care of others, listening to their troubles and solving their problems. This is partially because of your need for praise and to be admired as a tower of strength and wisdom. Your conversation, Aries, is stimulating and amusing, and you radiate a vital energy that is appealing and magnetic. On occasion, you have a tendency to wear out your thought power, your cognitive ability and mental energies, because everything with which you come in contact must be scrutinized by your active mind and intellect. Watch that you don't fill your mind with various facts and opinions all at the same time.

You enjoy being surrounded by people and you stand out in a crowd. While you prefer to have many friends, you also like to think of yourself as a self-sufficient loner. You prefer to suffer alone. This is only another example of your method of compensation for your fear of rejection which causes you to hold people at a distance, secretly afraid that if you trust someone, that person will eventually reject you, or disagree with you, or do you in, or leave you. Learn to accept rejection from others as everyone has to come to terms with this, not just you.

You can be blatantly frank and up front with others when expressing your ideas and thoughts. This lack of subtlety or diplomacy, this preference for straight-forward, honest opinions, can be softened for better effect. And, Aries, is there any help for the person who has strong opinions that differ from yours? Despite your intellect, you have a tendency to use your temper, your natural aggression, to talk louder than your opponent, rather than using reason and patient persuasion to win your point.

The Aries propensity to make quick decisions results in a lack of intuition in judging other people. This can lead you to misjudge people and to place your trust in the wrong people. You base your judgments on superficial impressions that are often misguided. Hence, it is quite possible that you have rejected or chased off those who meant well, but who disagreed with you, while you chose to keep around those who know that if they flatter you, you will be pleased with them.

The artless, guileless Aries does not resort to the kind of strategies frequently used by those individuals of other signs. You have your own form of interpersonal gamesmanship. You steam roll over your opposition. Because you find it difficult to lie, you artfully use bluster, and sound and fury when cornered, hoping to avoid embarrassing, direct questions.

The shrewd Aries capitalizes on the ability to impress and gain points with a winning personality and mannerisms. By using the astute Aries mind, with astounding speed, you hit upon some gesture or point of persuasion that will gain you what you want while all the time appearing to be your usual super-charming, impulsive self. Those who would accuse Aries of fraud and deceit are misinterpreting the Aries ability to simply exploit an innate trait: and only when they are cornered or pressed is it used. This trait manifests itself naturally, effortlessly, and automatically. It hardly requires conscious thought. You use finesse in playing out the scenes in the drama of your own life sometimes to the point of resorting to artifice and stratagem which you manage to apply to your personal and public life. This constant exercise of cunning can build character into an abode where only tragedy can dwell, tragedy for yourself and for others caught up in the drama of your ideas and your life.

With maturity, Aries becomes capable of idealizing and universalizing his love of independence which is derived from his egocentricity. Your vitality and physical energy enhances this independence. You must be first in everything you do. You are a professional, competitive contestant in life. While your interest may appear to be material gain, your actual objective is to win. You never brag about being second. You are most concerned by the person who beats you at your own game. This Aries nature displays itself throughout your daily life. You walk one step ahead of your companions, entering through doorways first (sometimes even before ladies). You have the first word and often the last in any argument. You love a good argument, not so much in order to discover the truth as to demonstrate or prove that you are right. You often win by sheer volume and noise and vitality, forcing your opponent to submit to your ideas.

You are original and frequently novel in your effort to be first. But, consider the difference between novel and originality. When an Aries is original, he or she is a pioneer, an inventor, and a great thinker. When you are merely novel, you are putting forth your egotistical desire to be first, and often times neglecting sound ideas and practical methods. You thus can easily lose the benefit of your energy, genius and ambition. You must be aware of self-centeredness. This trait can make you arrogant, conceited, self-serving, overly aggressive, and in the face of opposition can lead to feelings of persecution and mild or acute self-delusions.

For you to forget the „self‟, and to become cognitively absorbed in intellectual pursuits, to insure that your original and novel ideas are well-grounded, and to be able to consider the other person's point of view, his or her needs, wishes, desires, just as seriously as your own, are the means by which you, Aries, may emphasize and benefit from your strong characteristics and insure that your desire to be first will actually result in you succeeding.

In spite of this natural desire of the Aries to rule and command, you are noble, charming and attractive as well as sympathetic, tender, loving, magnetic and progressive. You are known among your friends for your warm heart and remarkably passionate nature. Success is largely due to personal accomplishments or through a domestic relationship, social standing or influential friends. You have a strong appreciation for literature, science, study, philosophy, travel and all methods which you perceive will better your mind and your social abilities.

Being at your best in social situations and amidst elegant surroundings, you are drawn to luxurious, opulent settings, caring little if you appear ostentatious. You can be a show-off. You are generally considered wealthier than you are, perhaps because of your commanding, well-dressed appearance. You are often thought of as a progressive person who is ambitious and aspiring. At the same time, you can be candid, high-minded, ardent in your beliefs and arguments, and on other occasions, reasonable. You are usually well-respected, and this is important to you as you value the high opinions of your friends and associates.

You are more than willing to fight for your rights. You possess and exhibit strong and pronounced convictions as to what is right and what belongs to you. You would choose to destroy a possession rather than surrender it. In the courts, you will litigate and fight as long as there is anything to fight over. In many instances, it appears that the „fight' is more important than the end result to you. This may often lead you to engage in unnecessary disagreements. Other times, you may enter needlessly into conflicts, offending those who have the power to cause you harm or setbacks. There is a need to beware of depending on unrealistic hopes and to realize that common sense will suffice where luck may fail as wishful thinking may lead to extravagant planning. Difficulties may also arise in living up to promises made in those moments of impulsive generosity.

Aries are determined and set in their own ideas. At their best, they are willing to resort to any honest scheme to prove their point and to accomplish their goals. At their worst, there are those Aries who resort to dishonest means to accomplish their goals. Yet, you are rarely if ever unjust, seldom holding a grudge against even your strongest enemies. But, be careful. Once your confidence is lost, it is very difficult to reclaim it. You are willing to die fighting for a friend or a principle, standing by your friend or friends when it seems the whole world is against them; and while you are forgiving, you never forget transgressions or someone who you feel has done you wrong.

Aries are excellent advisers, often giving others better advice than they follow themselves. Many of your friends have faith in your judgment. You are most capable of sweeping away outmoded ideas from conservative minds and ushering in innovative, new ideas.

Aries Destiny

Optimistic and future-oriented in your thinking, you have a strong prophetic sense and may be inspired to act based on insights which come to you out of the blue. You desire most to be free and unrestrained, and you have the energy to perform that which your mind imagines. You, perhaps more so than any others, dare to go where others fear; dare to attempt what others fail to imagine; dare to strive for the impossible regardless of the obstacles; or of the possible adverse consequences to yourself or others. Often others follow out of sheer willingness to be led and because they are so impressed with your belief in your own plans and abilities. But when others fail to share your enthusiasm, or have the audacity to point out any pitfalls in your thinking, you are sincerely amazed--so strong is your belief in yourself.

Aries can expect a tumultuous life in which they pay for everything they achieve. Obstacles and troubles may appear in the first half of life. The social achievements obtained can be abruptly lost through violent incidents or bankruptcies, etc. Their life is active and athletic, but the end may be violent. Their personable qualities attract many friends who help in the most difficult situations, but they will create envy also. To summarize, a succession of great situations, unstable, never long-term ones, will find the Aries person in perpetual action. You are fond of traveling, of exciting adventures, and independent ventures. You no doubt will make every effort to carve out your own path, becoming the leader of whatever enterprise or endeavor you aspire to or in some way becoming prominent in your sphere of influence.

If well aspected, the Aries individual takes a leading role in the correction of human ills or conditions, or the reform of existing social institutions and there may be an incentive toward a public or political career. This person may feel strongly about mystical experiences and may have strong feelings about religious or spiritual matters. The well-aspected Aries, intensifies the feelings, emotions and senses, softening or elevating the disposition toward sympathy, benevolence, spiritual perception or inner strength and understanding. As Aries matures, there is a tendency to develop a viable philosophy of life.

If afflicted, there is some danger of drowning, trouble with the opposite sex, or changes of occupation and position. The afflicted may also suffer peculiar feelings, aversions, and premonitions in their thought processes. There may be an inclination toward addictive habits for pleasure and the gratification of the senses such as smoking, alcohol, drugs, or sex.

Aries, being at the head of the Zodiac, often initiate plans which aren't always finished or completed. Perhaps this is due to your remarkable quickness in grasping new ideas which leads you to abandon your previous pursuits. You are alert and longing to engage in new and great undertakings even when the results do not live up to your expectations. You become brilliant in everything that you do, especially where action is involved.

In describing any group of people, and endeavoring to describe their astrological paths, it is important to warn them of the inherent elements of discord and evil in their natures. The main defects or shortcomings in the Aries nature are impatience, anger, stubbornness, selfishness, foolish generosity, and fickleness of purpose. You are not revengeful and don't hold a grudge, but you are slow to forgive. Your egotism can lead you to talk too much and to brag about yourself, your possessions and your accomplishments. This can create envy and resentment on the part of your friends or associates. You have a defensive tendency to take everything personally, and you have definite leanings toward the selfish forces also. Jealousy in both Aries men and women often distracts from what would otherwise be a most charming personality.

By cultivating your higher nature and permitting it to dominate your lower nature in every circumstance, you can overcome any and all of your faults. You need to cultivate patience and the ability to wait out the workings of your plans, to see them through to conclusion. You need to become more patient with the weaknesses of others as well as with your own disappointments and shortcomings. This will prevent your fiery outbursts of anger and your intolerance of those who don't readily agree with you. Also, cultivating your spirit of true charity will enable you to do good for others more effectively and to improve your perseverance and patience. You must learn to apply concentration in all that you do. Concentrating your energy on one pursuit at a time will bring success.

While you love an argument, you can be sarcastic, critical and overbearing to a fault. You make enemies because of your forcefulness which you see as a strength of character. You are impulsive, irritable and quick-tempered. Yet, emerging from your passion when the storm has passed, you expect immediate forgiveness of your harsh and bitter words. You expect your opponent to forget your actions without the slightest admission on your part of poor or hasty judgment. You cannot tolerate to be contradicted, teased, or tormented, or told your faults. Your unwillingness to yield a single point in an argument marks you as impetuous, defeating your own best interest. You can be so headstrong and reckless that you plunge into a path or endeavor without any consideration of the obstacles or eventual outcomes. Aries people can never be coerced, driven or forced. You are obstinate and must be left to carry out your plans in your own way because if your plans are interfered with, you will abandon them. You have an innate desire, a compulsion, to direct the endeavors and even the lives of others.

You can never rise to any great height of accomplishment until you have acquired self-control. Do not expect God to grant power to those who have not mastered control of their personal appetites, desires, and passions. Remember, Aries, the physical body is influenced by the magnetic currents and solar forces which to a large degree effect the lower or animalistic nature thus slowing your progress. Aspire, Aries, to live a moral and chaste life and to cultivate the higher qualities of your sign. It is the cultivation of your intellect and the spiritual side of your life that will allow you to attain your highest goals, to amass great wealth, and to achieve high honor and distinction. Beware of your temptation to lead a hedonistic lifestyle or to live only for pleasure. Yes, you can rationalize your reason for doing this while satiating and satisfying your desires, but it slows and impedes personal growth. The argument that everyone else is doing it, does not justify you doing it. You delude yourself, and by so doing what you are actually accomplishing is a manner to distract yourself from your higher abilities. Intellectual pursuits and accomplishments of goals require self-control of the mind and body.

Aries, you should set aside a portion of each day to reflect in silent meditation on the important aspects of life. Search your soul. Make an earnest effort to focus your mind on the purity of your inner spirit which you possess. This effort will result in the ability and power to rise to the lofty height which is yours by right of birth. By cultivating these powers, you may obtain the greatest gains in life. Develop your mystical gifts which will give you a wonderful force and power enabling you to influence and control those with whom you come in contact.

When you strive to eliminate the faults in your nature, and to advance to a higher plane of life and conduct, you are assured of the most powerful assistance. Invoke this assistance by self-communion, by constant efforts to give your better nature dominion, and by contemplation of the great truths of science. If you will assimilate the truths of astrology, resolve to possess yourself of your heaven-sent heritage, and resolutely turn from the weaknesses and faults that threaten you, you can win success beyond measure including limitless honor, esteem, position, power, health and love. Search your own heart for the source of all evil and cast it out so that you can become powerful and magnetic.

If you were to accept advice, Aries, listen to this wisdom: cultivate your mentality and your intuition for with proper self-improvement and development, there is no limit to the greatness and heights you may achieve. Actually, it is next to impossible to conceal anything from the Aries who has recognized his or her power of intuition. Develop these, the natural gifts of the spirit, and then attain and grasp all of what is important in life and spirit. The intellect leads the sign of Aries, but they should always watch their energy level in that it might be used to their disadvantage and go beyond the rational limit. These are the words passed down to us for our knowledge from the great Sages and Seers of ancient times.

Found at his best, Aries implies a strong sense of self-reliance and self-assurance with a keenness for duty which compels the individual to persist indomitably, resolutely, through all vicissitudes. These individuals expect to carve their own niche in life succeeding through their own ability to exert themselves and their ideas and because they possess the courage of their convictions. They pay little attention to their conservative associates. Aries has a strong desire to broaden the scope of his experiences and generally will always have a distinctive philosophy of life, based not on an understanding of others, but on an urge to expand his own consciousness. The forcefulness of Mars found in Aries can produce boundless ambitions and can lead to the person seeking adventure. In fact, this person is often more refreshed by new sensations than by a period of rest. The main need is to slow down, pace yourself, and channel the vitality of Mars into worthwhile projects.

ARIES OCCUPATION

Resolute, determined, and ambitious for success, Aries aspire to be pioneers whether in the intellectual, business, civic, or military world. You have a love for independent thinking and action. You have an intense desire for freedom, positive forces, and impulses which increase your mental vitality. This not only produces but inspires activity, energy, resourcefulness, originality and inventive ability. You desire more than anything else to be recognized as an authority (on a wide range of topics) in order to be able to exercise your ability to organize and administer your affairs without taking orders or obtaining directions from others. You are eager to hold the reins of power in your hands, and with your capacity for sustained physical work, this often makes you the controlling element in complex situations.

Aries are not psychologically well equipped to be drones performing routine, dull, or monotonous tasks. You seldom enjoy coping with details, preferring a position where you can delegate these more tedious chores to others. Aries are known for originality and imagination, great mental and nervous energy, and for preferring work that requires these traits while providing an opportunity for advancement. You require endeavors that challenge your mind and your creative spirit. You become frustrated when working at a job requiring routine, repetitive tasks, even to the point of becoming rebellious and hostile. You perform best when working in a position that allows you to work on your own, directing others, and finding outlets for your talents and boundless energies. You have a strong aversion for all bonds, limitations or restrictions, preferring to be free to explore and pioneer into new areas of thought and activity. Seek these situations out. Don't settle for less than what you can achieve, or you will be unhappy in the long run. Aspire to success in all that you wish to accomplish. Only then can you realize your dreams.

Aries are excellent at communication and persuasion. Others love to listen to you talk, finding inspiration and insight in the energy of your convictions whether well-grounded or not. People believe in what you say, because you believe in yourself. You excel in all activities requiring quick thought, public speaking to groups, and impromptu speeches or conversations. Male or female, you perform well in occupations such as journalism, television and radio broadcasting, advertising, public relations, publishing, or promoting. Because of your strong drive for tangible goals, you excel as financiers and businessmen and in the arts and the entertainment fields as well.

Aries, influenced by Mars, is well-suited for military careers most particularly in the army rather than the navy or air force. But you prefer to be in command or at least in a leadership position. The Mars influence also produces skilled doctors, surgeons, nurses, and mining engineers, as well as persons skilled in refining and handling non-precious metals. Another well-aspected occupational field is law enforcement.

Many Aries are drawn to the field of literature becoming writers of fiction, poets, novelists and essayists. Persons of this sign make excellent lawyers and judges as their sense of justice and equality in many instances outweighs personal prejudices. And, of course, your arguments, being quick and to the point, carry much influence. Lovers of science, art and music, Aries are naturally gifted and may become talented architects and inventors. The self-assertive Aries, being an excellent conversationalist, make fine clerks, traveling salesmen, speculators, bankers, and brokers. You are very enthusiastic and exhibit great determination to win in whatever endeavor that holds your attention.

Real estate is another field in which Aries find successes. Aries consciously feel an advantage to acquiring and owning property. It was this restless search for new land that led many Aries pioneering West into new territories.

While Aries can be impulsive, you are serious about your business affairs and can be hard-headed and conservative in financial matters. You make successful financiers, being fast to grasp opportunities. You may spend money (preferably cash) for tangible assets which add to the value of what you all ready own. Being cunning and shrewd, you have a talent for making money, although, at least early in life, you may not have the talent of saving or spending wisely because you have a pronounced tendency to be rather extravagant and to spend freely. You are appreciative of physical pleasures and will spend money to stay in shape and to keep your body in good health in order to make the most of this adventure called life. The Aries individual has a pronounced fondness for travel, music, painting, sculpture, decorative art, singing, poetry, theater, entertainment, and you may well excel in sports.

You are generously endowed with natural gifts that aid you in your vocation. Learn to use these gifts. You have a keen intellect, initiative, intuition, inventiveness, energy, leadership ability, and enthusiasm. However, the Aries tendency toward impatience, not planning ahead, spending unwisely, and being bossy and domineering can easily offset your strong points. You must make every effort to develop self-constraint in order to succeed. Others will guide you, too, if you will learn to listen to their advice.

The Aries ego requires constant approval, compliments, praise, and attention. Without it, your efficiency and productivity declines. This need for positive reinforcement can be satisfied if you learn the value of intrinsic appreciation. In other words, your achievements become the rewards rather than the rewards being the words or praise from others. This reinforcement comes from within with a job well-done. Do this often enough, and your pride in your accomplishments will become real. And others will recognize and realize your abilities also.

The Aries inclination to boast and exhibit strong self-confidence, making claims to your ability to handle complex, unfamiliar tasks, rather than admitting a lack of knowledge or ability, can eventually result in a failure to produce results. Aries has the ability to convince and impress others with his strong self-confidence. You believe in yourself and what you say and you seldom admit defeat or faults. This is not a bluff or an out-and-out lie. Rather, it's the Aries trait that thrives on challenge; and remember, you are convinced that you can do anything. But sooner or later, you must follow through with your plans and aspirations.

This unconscious drive to compensate for your doubts about your abilities and your insecurities can hurt you in the long run. Strive to eliminate or at least control your penchant to attempt those tasks for which you are inadequately trained, or to bite off more than you can chew. You can do this by acquiring and developing an emotional balance of patience, self-discipline and the perseverance to stay at one task long enough to learn the requisite skills to allow yourself to excel and advance.

When well-positioned at the head of an undertaking, for example in the business world, you display creative drive and energy. Being adventuresome and ambitious, you should strive to associate with more conservative individuals who, while appreciating your strengths, would restrain your impulsive nature to make quick decisions. Benefit from the conservative nature of others. If nothing else, at least take into consideration what they have to say. You and they approach problems differently, but each of you can contribute to the outcome and eventual success of a project or an endeavor.

As a rule, you have an unusual executive ability, but, having great confidence and self-esteem, you tend to overestimate your powers and to become too enthusiastic and even reckless in your desire to succeed. Watch that you don't go down with your own ship. You have a strong dislike for all bonds, limitations and restrictions, preferring to be free to explore and pioneer into new ideas and activities. Your strong self-interest will inspire you to push forward in all your endeavors with very little outside encouragement or stimulus. You are self-motivated.

It is not unusual for Aries to change his pursuits during their lifetime and to have two very different occupations or careers. Aries, be confidant that you can expect prosperity through industry, diligence, hard work and perseverance. But remember also that you require an incentive. You must feel you have a goal you are working toward.

ARIES MARRIAGE

Aries men and women are extremely intense in their love relationships. This is due to Aries being at the head of the Fire sign, and ruled by Mars. They crave affection and sympathy and constant attention and praise. You may be more affectionate than passionate, but you have insatiable sexual desires. If you don't receive the requisite sexual pleasures and attention at home than you have no inhibitions about finding it elsewhere. This combined with your head-strong, impulsive nature provides the setting for the tempest in your many stormy relationships. Although you may be rash, you are most likely to sow your wild oats early in life and then to settle down with a person who you have carefully selected as your perfect mate. But you may find marriage similar to a balancing act, and you must mentally control your frankness and cultivate the art of give-and-take in order to maintain your balance.

Aries, usually so independent and cool, can be unexpectedly sentimental about their feelings for family and traditions. Being deeply rooted in your instincts, you long for a comfortable home and companion so that you can be coddled like a baby. This may be an idealized memory or fond thoughts saved from childhood that continue to plague your thoughts making you yearn to return from your travels and far-flung pursuits to the family hearth and to the warm, open arms of a loving, accepting companion.

The Aries nature infinitely requires great depth and dimension in love and marriage. Your strong opinions and idealism demand total loyalty and sexual fidelity from your partner or mate, even though the male doesn't hold himself to the same standards. You are likely to be extremely jealous, at the same time resenting jealously from the person who you love.

In order to make a total commitment, Aries, both male and female, have their respective criteria. Aries males demand a loyal woman who is submissive, dependent, and preferable one who appears helpless. In fact, a helpless woman attracts this man. And understand, that if he wants a particular woman he is attracted to, he will claim she is helpless. Then, because he is always right, he will go to great lengths to prove to her that, indeed, she is the helpless female in need of him. And he is there to save her. In order to feel successful in a domestic role, the male Aries must be the supportive-protective, dominant man who is in total control. This control must be in all areas of the family life, and most especially over every aspect of his partner's life. After all, this is the helpless female that he saved. She must relinquish all control to him in her appreciation of his attentions. Not only that, but he must receive total admiration, praise and flattery in order to remain the ideal lover or husband. And while he may stay with his wife, the slightest affront will give him the incentive he needs to head out the door looking for another woman to stroke his ego. Quite possibly, the Aries male with his self-doubts, insecurities and anxieties over his own masculinity demands this total submissive-female to soothe his strong ego or to reinforce and prop it up. Of course, to a lesser degree, males of other signs can also be beset by the same fears and negative qualities. In spite of his controlling nature, the Aries male, who strives to be a good provider, is likely to be an excellent, ideal husband in every sense except sexual fidelity. Expect him, generally speaking, to engage in numerous extramarital affairs.

However, don't expect these purely physical, casual affairs to be a threat to the marriage. The Aries male adheres to the double-standard: what is good for the gander is definitely not good for the goose. Intensely jealous, he tolerates no infidelities in sexual behavior from his wife.

However, you, the passionate female Aries, once a commitment is made, and you fall in love and marry, you make a total commitment including sexual fidelity. You too demand certain standards, requirements, and the necessary criteria from your chosen man before your love-life is complete. You are charming, physically attractive, sexy, and desirable, knowing how to use your charms and beauty to enhance your desires and get what you want from your many admirers and later from your husband. You know that you have much to offer a man, and, therefore, you pick and choose carefully, making an effort to find the right man; or unfortunately, all too often, who you think is the right man. (Remember, your tendency to misjudge people.)

The female Aries, with her strong personality, believes she can contribute and help the man she loves. Because of this, you are likely to select a man who is weaker than you, who you can dominate and who will allow you to be the boss. This can lead to domestic tragedy for you cannot be happy for long with a man who you do not respect. Once you realize that you are not merely guiding, but dominating your husband, you lose all respect for him. However, if you take the time to choose carefully rather than making a quick decision, if you marry a man who is right for you, you will make an exceptional wife. For you are a woman who considers marriage a never ending adventure, a complete partnership, in which you fully expect to carry your share of the responsibilities. You exert every effort and energy to work toward a successful marriage going so far as to place your husband's welfare and interests above your own. Your main requirements are to receive expressions of appreciation, love, and affection that make you feel wanted, admired and adored. You also demand to be sexually appreciated and satisfied.

Both Aries men and women may experience difficulties in marriage. You may discover yourself unhappily married because you rarely find partners who truly understand and appreciate your nature and your temperament. If you are not divorced in the first part of life, your marriage will survive throughout your life. Marriage is a precarious venture for Aries individuals. Although you make ideal companions, Aries people know little about domestic affection and tranquillity. The best choice of mates are those born under the sign of Libra and next Gemini. Ideally, such marriages generally produce more happiness. Marriage to another Aries can be good but may produce troublesome children.

THE ARIES MAN

Y ou, the Aries male, possess a very strong determination, a courageous spirit, a power of command and execution, ambition, enterprising spirit, combativity, a love of independence, and an overwhelming desire to be active and to lead. The brave, daring, and adventuresome Aries male is frank and outspoken to a fault, generously extravagant, and possesses a most stubborn, strong will to the point of becoming quarrelsome and petulant. You are well-informed, industrious, and ingenious, but rather limited in your knowledge of human character. You are opinionated in the areas of religion, politics, and social issues and would be the one most likely to rebel or crusade against existing institutions and limiting social constraints. In matters related to religion, you are broad-minded within the bounds of convention; however, you quite probably believe in believing rather than conforming.

In all matters, you may change your viewpoint and perspective, but you adamantly believe in your ideas and beliefs while you hold them. You are most remarkable for your quick thinking and your ability to act quickly. Although you may be somewhat bigoted, you are generally progressive in your thoughts and beliefs.

Aries wants to be first in all areas of his life. He transcends from ideas to action with hardly a backward glance. Your pioneering, adventurous spirit is rarely too discouraged to begin fresh or to start anew. Nor are you likely to outgrow your innate capacity to stake a claim and then move on, seeking ever greener pastures and loftier heights, and leaving the tedious chores of completion to others. As a result, you may find yourself missing out on the results of your own labor. Your reach greedily and avidly for your desires only to abandon them, leaving them by the wayside when unforeseen difficulties arise.

The Aries male remains absolutely confident in himself, his abilities and his present ideas and projects. You have no doubts about your ability to succeed at a plan. Even when shaken to the depths of despair by a crisis or personal setback, you remain self-assured. This attribute above all others, may be what attracts people to you and what gains you admiration from others. It is this confidence in yourself that influences others to believe in your ideas and to follow your lead.

It may appear that people, to you, are no different than things as you have a tendency to consider them in the context in which you deal with them. This makes you seem heartless at times, unless others understand your psychology. And this can be a difficult thought-pattern to follow for it seems that people are expendable; that it's acceptable to forfeit people in order to achieve the completion of the tasks or your success at an endeavor. In order to understand this psychology, consider that you are capable of combining the absolute extreme of freedom from superficial social conditioning. You resent all forms of criticism but you can respond to logic, reason and proof. That is unless you decide to overrule logic and proof believing that your ideas are right and others simply either don't know what they're talking about or are plotting against you.

You crave affection, attention and sympathy, but you may be unhappy in your domestic situation because of an inability to meet a woman who understands your nature. You seldom understand a woman very well and you continue to make mistakes in your dealings with women. Your sexual drive is strong and you prefer a very feminine, kind, soft, romantic, docile, generous and submissive female who is willing to forfeit all control to you. And you are more than willing to go to great lengths to find such a woman.

Your greatest desire is to be the leader, professionally, at home, and socially. Endowed with great mental energy, your greatest happiness seems to come from overcoming obstacles, succeeding at work, and leading others. There is no height to which you cannot succeed providing you keep your head about you. Success, though, in many instances can be your undoing. It can quite easily result in an over-inflated ego which prevents you from assessing your situation correctly. Study the facts and pay less attention to the flattery and praise from others. Remember, others are astute enough to know that flattery will get them everywhere with you. Tactless rejection of those who don't always agree with you, prevents you from attaining insights. Patience, my dear man, is a virtue.

THE ARIES WOMAN

The Aries woman, sensitive, caring, kind and independent, handles responsibilities well in various situations both personally and professionally. Whether at home or on the job, you are not timid about accepting new roles or assignments. You thirst for achievement and success, and are often praised for your enterprising nature. You have a strong desire to outshine others in your field.

You enjoy physical activity and may excel at sports. No sloucher, you are considered to be hardworking. You are both diligent and industrious, and you are known for you ability to organize. You are often wonderfully helpful to your friends and family, offering both advice, time, and lending a hand, even when you'd rather stay uninvolved. You prefer those around you to be active and busy. This is most especially true in your home and with your family. You love art and bright colors and enjoy searching for new and lovely items for your home. Modest and practical, you have few children, but you take excellent care of them, raising them in a loving, caring, and secure environment. If childless, you shower your attention on your nieces and nephews and the children of your friends. You love a good argument, but you never forget your well-polished manners which makes you better, in this respect, than the male Aries. All you really want in regards to your love life, is to find a man stronger than you, capable of dominating your strong, independent nature. As a wife, you are very dedicated, but be very careful in your marriage as you require not only appreciation but abundant affection to be happy.

There is one great obstacle that stands in the way of the Aries woman--that green-eyed creature called jealousy. This one pervasive fault has resulted in more unhappiness and heartache coming into the lives of the female Aries than any other they may possess. The Aries woman is extremely charming, possessing an entertaining and pleasing personality, except for this one negative trait. Jealousy can blind you from enjoying life; and if it were not for jealousy, you would otherwise have a beautiful temperament. You lose too much energy through anger, impatience, and a quick temper. These traits become an emotional drain on your other more remarkable abilities with which you are naturally gifted. To master these negative traits, you must diligently develop self-control or risk never attaining a true peace of mind. This will require a great deal of effort on your part because it won't come quickly or naturally; it goes against your grain not to respond quickly and often sharply. Stop sometimes and think. Practice schooling your mind to master and control your body and your impulses and compulsions. Possessing as you do a great will power, learn to use it to overcome your weaker tendencies by training your higher nature to rule and dominate. When this is accomplished, you will find joy, happiness and tranquillity, and abundant peace and prosperity.

Your intellect underscores your ability to speak effectively, but you have a inclination to recognize only your own viewpoint, your perspective. You may have a tendency to resort too quickly to argumentative or clever remarks thus offending the other person. With effort, you can control your stubbornness and your propensity to out talk others in a conversation. Learning to listen more and to talk a little less will benefit you by giving you insights into the interpersonal relationships with others who you must deal with on a daily basis. Learn to organize your ideas, concentrate your thoughts, and hold your tongue long enough to generate the power which comes from mental control and restraint.

The Aries woman does well in the professional areas of art, design, writing, sales, and management. Any position that requires a quick mind and a person who is unafraid of making decisions. You are highly capable of holding positions of authority, trust and responsibility. Remember, you are impatient and become irritable when criticized or limited by narrow, stifling rules and regulations. It is best that you have a thorough understanding of your undertaking, the task at hand, and then that you are left alone to carry out the task with your own methods.

ARIES LOVE LIFE

The first-sign Aries natives, both male and female, are passionate, possessing a strong sex drive and a healthy appetite that demands variety. They have a strong libido and are headstrong and impetuous in love and romance. For you, sex is a pleasurable, transient pastime requiring only a brief commitment on the physical level rather than a strong emotional commitment. While romance includes sex, you also require an element of companionship and mutual respect, of liking the other person and of sharing an experience beyond the purely physical.

Love, on the other hand, is something entirely different. In your realm, for there to be real love in your life, you require full commitment and acceptance of emotional responsibility. Therefore, there are three distinct categories that fit within your love life. (1) You jump impulsively into an endless series of sexual adventures producing no emotional scars for either partner, or (2) you're less interested in casual romance, and (3) demand more than just passing pleasure or a sexual outlet. Unless Aries individuals learn self-control, numerous troubling situations, inconveniences, problems and annoyances are brought on by their involvement with the opposite sex, to whom they are strongly attracted physically, enjoying the sexual experience almost as much as success in other endeavors.

With the sign of self-expression in the house of pleasures, you gain personal satisfaction in the creation of spectacular effects which often produce dramatic results. You ardently desire praise and approbation, craving applause for what you consider one of your remarkable accomplishments. This urge to outshine, to stand first, may impel you to seek shortcuts perhaps through rash actions, speculation and gambling with chance. However, often these actions are designed for entertainment and, while others may question your actions, they do not jeopardize your basic sense of security. Your tendency to indulge in love affairs is often for the sake of ego-gratification and to gain even more praise and adulation.

The Aries desire is to share life with others. You crave seeing yourself reflected in someone else's affectionate and admiring gaze while at the same time you wish to have an influence over that person's thought process and behavior, right down to how the other person dresses. In your love life, you have a tendency to keep your deeper feelings well hidden and to repress the tender side of your nature. Generally speaking, you are more sensual than sentimental, and even though you have hidden depths of passion, you do not openly discuss your love life. You have the capacity to keep the different aspects of your life in distinct compartments, and you may be unaware of your own unconscious motives. Your active mind has so little time for introspection that you push your feelings into the background to prevent them from interfering with current projects. Then you are surprised, as is everyone else, that these suppressed elements break into the open in the form of sudden impulses and compulsive urges. Aries, attempt to restrain your libido, focusing your energies into socially acceptable channels of expression. You have the ability to renew yourself through sex and physical activity, but you should make an effort to reduce the number of incidental romantic affairs in your life.

The erotic overtones of your life are caused to a large extent by your enthusiasm, your spur of the moment inspirations, and the attraction to you of all things youthful. In love affairs, romance is sustained by this same charming impulsiveness, but often times it is too inconsistent for enduring affection. You not only enjoy but thrive on excitement, and you are known for starting new affairs before the last one is concluded. The excitement and joy you discover in your numerous amorous affairs may fill you with intense passions, but they rapidly lose their appeal. You may be in love with love, and you may find yourself searching throughout your life for new sensations, new romances, replenished love, until you finally come to the realization that continual gratification rarely guarantees real and lasting satisfaction. Aries, you must be careful not to become a slave to your own desires. You can never truly be the master of your own destiny, in control of your own fate, until you master controlling yourself, your whims, and your libido. That your list of accomplishments also includes your long list of sexual conquests only impresses you.

ARIES CHILDREN

The Aries child can be difficult to manage unless there is an understanding of his nature which requires reason, love and kindness. They demand a reason and explanation for everything being stubborn and self-willed. Generally, they excel in school, perhaps because of their ambitions, retentive memories, and quick-thinking abilities. The Aries child is restless, inquisitive and prying. They are seldom content with one thing for any length of time. This child should be left to work out their tasks in their own way in order to develop individuality.

A calm and quiet talk at bedtime is the best method of correction for the Aries child. Physical punishment can be very harmful for them and should seldom if ever be used. An abundance of love and praise is the only influence that can gain control over these children. They should not be coerced, tormented, scolded, abused, or punished corporally. Kindness and gentleness accomplishes much more and they should be protected from excitement and unstable conditions. They do better in loving, secure environments offering a comforting routine which also provides an outlet for their inquisitive natures. Do not interfere with their endeavors or they will quickly lose interest and move on to another activity. Excessive constraint, may force them out of the secure home environment into the world before they are ready, causing them to enter into hasty marriages or in extreme cases to become involved in crime. Their stubbornness and determination results in them insisting upon carrying out their ideas regardless of the cost or consequences to themselves or others. Allow them some leeway, some freedom, in making their own mistakes and learning the hard way because they are not going to listen to a lot of verbal advice. Discover an interest, and encourage it, so that the active Aries mind can stay occupied. And while their interests may jump around from one activity to another, be patient and encourage these various interests. Verbal criticism is a waste of time. Patiently model correct behavior in a loving manner.

These chidden are happy and lively but can also be mischievous, requiring kindness and understanding more than strict authority from their parents. It may appear that they are more accident prone than the average child, and have more incidental, unexplainable accidents; and even little girls are somewhat more active and rebellious. The Aries child may find choosing a career difficult as their active minds jump from one idea to another. They possess an innate vitality and a love for nature and outdoor adventure. They love to discover mysterious places and seem to fear nothing (but watch out for those accidents). They exhibit an interest in animals and the natural environment, loving to learn all they can about not only these subjects but the universe beyond as well. While they may appear insensitive, they are easily hurt if they don't receive adequate attention, love and affection from their parents. The Aries child has the most sensitive nature of all the Zodiac signs.

Relationships with Other Signs

The ardent Aries nature is affectionate, demonstrative, generous in praise and affection, with a preference for love and admiration. You are warm-hearted, passionate and attracted to friends of the opposite sex as well as friendships and associations with the same sex. You excel at group situations, being entertaining and gregarious. You are a natural host, ever attentive to the needs of your guests. You love social functions, entertaining at home and in public, outdoor festivities, sports events, and any occasion or celebration providing the promise of a festive crowd. You have a keen sense of enjoyment, pleasures, fun and adventure.

You may have two types of friends: those with whom you associate in business; and others with whom you feel free to share your broader interests. You are attracted to people intellectually rather than sentimentally, and you may get along well with eccentrics, appreciating their talents and new ideas, and with others who share your strong opinions. Your personal insights and ideas often appear progressive, sometimes too much so to your social groups, and you need to watch that your liberal attitudes don't make you a disruptive element, allowing you to lead your many followers down the wrong path.

An afflicted Saturn in Aries may result in bringing about feelings of inadequacy which effects the personal area of friendship. These people may inadvertently react against strict limitations by becoming disciplinarians and by asserting themselves in aggressively authoritarian actions. And, a driving ambition may often work against harmony in interpersonal relationships. This person may be less sociable than other Aries, being overly dogmatic and exerting a certain aloofness in their desire to exercise control and command over others.

Aries does well with the moderating characteristics of the native Leo. And you can expect to establish positive relations with those born under the sign of Gemini and Aquarius.

Do not entertain high expectations for relations with persons born under the sign of Virgo who have a critical nature which, as has been mentioned, Aries can't tolerate. And relationships with Scorpio can lead to violent encounters while Libra attraction is primarily physical. Cancer and Capricorn relationships are infrequent in that they don't share your perception of life and the world. You may find Taurus and Pisces individuals easier to deal with professionally. Aries may be compatible with each other, but often these relations may become somewhat monotonous and, if romantic, may produce negative sexual attractions.

The many strong attributes of the Aries personality leads to popularity. You have many friends and associates. You may possibly have an early or hasty marriage or marriages and a long string of casual, sexual relationships.

You will find the most enduring and rewarding friendships with those born between July 21 and August 20-27; from November 21 to December 20-27; and also from September 21 to October 20-27. Aries have unusually strong will power and great obstinacy of purpose leading them to form strong and lasting friendships with certain individuals who are endowed with the abilities to admire their strengths while overlooking their strong dispositions.

Beware making enemies. It is not unusual for the arrogant Aries to be subject to exile in a foreign country or to be restrained in forced seclusion necessitating escape and flight from enemies. Enemies are found in the religious, legal and publishing fields, and are numerous but not formidable to the undauntable Aries. However, the most powerful enemies abound in foreign countries or are from foreign countries and will make every effort to harm or molest the Aries individual. It is quite possible that you will be the cause of your own death or downfall if you aspire to martyrdom or fight to boldly for what you perceive as worthy causes.

ARIES SEXUALITY

That subject which interests us all: our own personal sexuality. Why does a person feel the way they do? Why does he or she like a certain person and not another? What arouses a person and why? On some level, these questions influences one and all. Like all aspects of our lives and lifestyles, the public attitude toward sex is ever changing and evolving. From the restrictive taboos of the Victorian Age, through the revitalization of the Industrial Age, to the make love not war of the 1960s to the commercialism of the 1980s and the 1990s, sex is always on our minds. Will the Age of Information or the Age of Aquarius bring new insights?

The American culture is not only influenced by popular trends and thought but by its unique cultural diversity as well. To the newcomer or newly arrived, American society can appear perplexing. What is difficult to understand is that in this freedom-based culture, the individual is literally free to be whoever he or she decides. And the gamut runs from the most traditional, reserved, cautious, and sexually repressed individuals to others who flaunt their sexuality, centering their lives around their sexual habits. Perhaps it is because of this very diversity that our culture makes some attempt not to be overly offensive to the sensitivities of some while giving a tolerant nod to the liberties of others. We are totally free, within the guidelines of laws, to seek divine enlightenment or to destroy ourselves with pleasures. Americans have the freedom to choose, individually, what importance their sexual behavior will play in their lives.

That being the case, sex is recognized by every serious discipline--from psychologists to scientists to astrologers--as being a central focus on individual lives. Freud saw sex as an influence on every aspect of the individual life. And from the sexist boys in the locker room to the most enlightened of intellectuals, sex remains a fundamental part of life that cannot be ignored. Get two friends together and the subject eventually turns to sex, romance, or marriage. One can blame it on the media, but sooner or later discussing the stock market gets boring, but sex never does.

There are those who hold to the theory that the primary function of sex is to have children and any other consideration is secondary. There are others for whom sex is an integral part of life, providing one of the greatest stress relievers ever invented. That all other living species procreate seasonally points to the reasoning of the second theory. But all pleasures (or temptations) in life also promote the possibilities of problems and health concerns unless a little logic is also applied.

Astrologically, the sexual nature has been examined from the Garden of Eden to the lives of contemporary celebrities. And what every serious astrologer will say is that how the individual relates to sexuality is not based on the Sun sign alone. The entire chart must be examined because each person is a unique combination of Sun, Moon, Ascendant, Planets, Houses and aspects. A comparison of two charts often sheds light on compatibility. Compatibility between two people is often found when the Sun sign is in the same sign as their lover's Ascendant, or vice versa. Opposite Sun signs or an opposite Sun sign and Ascendant may also blend well together.

In a woman's chart, the placement of Venus is indicative of her sexuality while the position of Mars and the Sun indicates what kind of man she is attracted to. In a man's chart, the position

69

of Mars tells how he relates to women, and the position of Venus and the Moon indicates what type of woman arouses him. In comparing two charts, look for the aspects of conjunction, sextile, square, trine, and oppositions. Remember that oppositions can blend. The square brings differences but much energy while conjunctions can be beneficial. The sextile and trine bring harmony. When a person's Venus and their lover's Mars are in the same sign, there is a strong attraction even if differences of opinions occur. When Venus and the other person's Ascendant are in the same sign, it adds to the sexual compatibility. Venus in the lover's Sun sign brings a mutual interest while Mars in the lover's Moon sign is emotionally intense.

There is a vast variety of people found within each Sun sign, but basic characteristics and traits do exist. However, generalizations are just that and a fuller picture of the individual is reflected by the complete chart. The following section deals with Sun sign sexuality in a general manner. While the importance of sex remains the same in each Sun sign, the focus and attitudes vary.

ARIES SEXUALITY - MAN

Influenced by Mars, the Aries man has fiery emotions and is driven by strong physical desires. He is aggressive, pioneering and lustful for adventure. Sex is an integral part of life and rates high on the list of experiences and priorities to the Aries man. This man creates excitement and a casual nod or smile aimed at him will be perceived as holding sexual overtones. He can be selfishly ego-driven, thinking that every woman wants him and that every woman is there for his needs.

An Aries man can be brilliantly attentive, flattering, generous, and extremely difficult to resist especially once he sets his mind on a conquest. If he desires a woman sexually, he pursues her tirelessly until she relents. He believes in himself and will in all earnestness tell a woman he is a real man. He thrives on experiences, challenge and novelty, wanting to sample one and all. He wants to be the leader in any endeavor and in any relationship with a woman will think, talk, and expect sex. His sexual appetite is enormous and he is ready at a moments notice to participate.

However macho may be the mask he shows the world, beneath this exterior is found a man who yearns for the embodiment of the perfect female and true, romantic love. He seeks another who will devote her life to him in a selfless, generous manner. And if she fails him in any manner, that is an excuse to continue the hunt for the perfect female for him. This man must have a relationship in his life, however, and he will seek a new one before ending his present affair.

Aries is the infant of the Zodiac, and this man wants to be babied, attended to, and cared for. He can be demanding especially sexually because he must have his gratification, repeatedly and frequently. The very sexual act stimulates him to want more if not from one woman than from another. An if rejected by one woman, he may continue his pursuit of her while actively engaged with another. Sex is an all consuming part of life to this lustful and energetic man.

This is the man who will want to change and recreate the woman in his life into the picture of perfection he holds in his mind. He will want her to have style, class and the kind of looks that turns the heads of other men. But he is intensely emotional, possessive, and jealous, and his woman must be faithful and loyal even though he isn't. As he matures and gains financial security, he may feel as if he has to buy the attentions of women, but this is fine with him as long as he is in control. In fact, he can be so controlling and demanding that he leaves the woman in his life with little time for independent activities. And if he feels neglected in any manner, his behavior can turn childish, producing the temper tantrums for which Aries is infamous. This man can easily allow his passions and his desires to preoccupy his life.

Any woman can entice his interest, but if he finds independent and intelligent women too difficult to pursue, he will turn to one less well educated or a younger woman who is easier to control and dominate. He needs a woman who will allow herself to be molded and who will want to become what he wants in order to please him. Aries is impulsive and impetuous, and wants what he wants when he wants it.

The Aries male is susceptible to attention, praise, adoration, and flattery. He may overlook the more timid types for those who also like attention. And to get his attention, simply ask his opinion or his advice. He loves to talk endlessly and to offer advice and assistance. He also wants to be recognized and thanked for his generosity.

The sign of Aries rules the head and face, and any attention to this part of the body brings results. Gentle caresses, stroking the head or playing with his ears will get his attention. He also loves to have his face massaged as well as his scalp, and if you buy him any kind of facial treatment like a soothing mask, he will know you are in love. Don't forget, however, how important sex is to this man. He doesn't seek unfilled promises, he wants the real thing. And he likes for the center of his sexuality to be admired as well which means that his lover should praise his penis, giving it lots of attention. If he thinks she yearns for him and is addicted to his erection, he will desire her all the more. This man stays where he is made the center of attention and affection by a person who adores him and learns how to make him happy.

ARIES SEXUALITY - WOMAN

The Aries woman can be aggressive and seeks what she wants, but she is also caring, kind and generous. She desires the perfect lover and mate to whom she can devote her loving attention. She is exciting and independent, and she loves sex and her sexuality. She wants to explore the compelling curiosity she possesses regarding her personal sexuality and preferences and will invest in all the literature, tapes, and paraphernalia required to satisfy her interest in this captivating subject. Men fascinate her, and she is drawn to explore as many as possible until she finally decides upon Mr. Right. Once her passions are aroused, this is not a timid or inhibited woman. Her Mars sign brings intense emotions, a fiery nature, and unlimited energy to her love making. One of her greatest challenges in life, in fact, may be finding a man who can keep up with her energetic drive.

She seeks and desires the perfect man to be her true love and soul mate and to fulfill her lust for life. Her lover must be attentive and demonstrative to make her happy. And an unhappy Aries woman can be a miserable person to be around when her frustrations turn to complaining. Her temper is just as fiery as her male counterpart, but remember, Aries soon forgives and forgets. This woman wants to be admired and made the center of attention whether it's in the privacy of her own home or in public. And the more daring a sexual adventure is, the more it will excite her. She seeks change, new experiences, and novelty as well as various forms of erotica. Like the male Aries, she may interpret the most innocent of attentions as being sexually oriented, believing that any and all men desire and want her. And since Aries is never wrong and never makes a mistake, no one could possible convince her otherwise. She can be restless, impatient, and impulsive to satisfy her sexual desires. Uninhibited, she may find it easy to reach a climax, but this woman may be dissatisfied with just one. And, being Aries, she may demand multiply orgasms on a regular basis. In fact, her sexual releases may be the one area of life where she is able to allow herself total freedom and lack of self-control. In other words, she isn't one to hold back. She wants the total experience. Even the most intellectual of Aries women will relent when their sexual nature is aroused.

Being an assertive female isn't the easiest of roles in any society (unfortunately), and this woman who seeks the perfect man to understand, cherish and adore her is often faced with disappointments in love. Men don't seem to understand her. In fact, she can destroy the macho and ego of any man and turn him into her slave. When she does find her mate, she will either negate his faults, praising him and forever offering illustrations of how perfect he is, or she will accept that no one is perfect and she must learn to live with his good points as well as his faults. Because of her outgoing and pleasant nature, she is accustomed to being made the center of attention by adoring male fans, and she will desire that this type of attention continue with her lover. She can devote herself totally to her lover, but she will want his admiration and total attention in return. But let's not forget that she must have sex, and if her lover in any way fails her in this department, she may have no choice but to seek it elsewhere. This is after all, a modern woman who wants all life has to offer.

Many an Aries female will crave to heighten the sexual adventure by seeking new experiences in unusual places. Whether this be the local bar or exotic places, the hint of daring excitement propels her to seek that new experience. She is a relentless explorer, and to experience a passing affair with a newly acquired acquaintance may entice her passions. The active Aries intellect rationalizes away perversity which is a word promoted by the more conventional thinkers. One can't think social mores and new experiences at the same time. And her lover must accept that she needs exploration and innovation in life and especially in sex. This woman is unafraid to take on a younger lover, and in fact a younger man may be able to keep up with her sexual drive and energy without attempting to put her in her place as older men are tempted to do. The Aries woman by nature knows her proper place, and she doesn't need to be told what it is. She quite easily makes that distinction for herself.

Aries stick to tradition, style, and convention as long as it serves their purposes and agrees with their lifestyles. Any inconveniences or obstacles are pushed to one side, as this formidable female sets about getting all she wants from life and lovers. The love of her life will always be held most dearest in her heart, however. And this career woman knows how to compartmentalize marriage, home, and family into manageable departments. She is a woman of her own making and much to be admired. She is forever the independent leader of new ideas, pioneering where other woman only dream of going.

Aries Health

Aries diligently adhere to a policy of hard work. You may abandon yourself freely to the pursuit of pleasure, but when the fun is over, you devote yourself to your labors and accomplishments. You have an intense interest in meal planning, loving to concoct gourmet delicacies for your friends and family. You seldom eat or drink excessively, however, due to your high regard for your body. It is a valuable instrument, a temple, to be as well cared for as an expensive piece of equipment, and to be ready to return to work. Illnesses for you are a major inconvenience, slowing your progress, restricting your freedom of motion, and preventing you from performing at your best in your endeavors. Your enterprising spirit leads you to cultivate a muscular, athletic physique ready for action.

Aries may require an abundance of sleep as compared to people of other signs. Plan large, well-ventilated sleeping areas that provide a constant supply of fresh air. A deep, natural sleep as opposed to a drug-induced sleep provides the most refreshing mental and physical rest. Attempt to plan a regular routine or sleep pattern, also scheduling the remainder of your day between work and recreation. Because of your active mind and body, you may have a propensity for headaches, eye problems, inflammations, and minor irritations or skin rashes. Make every effort to curb your appetites for luxurious surroundings and foods, social outings and an over active lifestyle. Plan to eat regular, well-planned meals providing nourishing foods. And curb your sweet tooth! Needless to say, you need to avoid alcohol and drugs as these will only acerbate your high energy level. You need to take care of your physical and emotional needs. A proper diet does much to forestall depressions or other general upsets. Be sure to avoid worry and anxiety and straining your brain which is sure to upset your general health.

Mars in Aries increases the vitality and energy level, but if afflicted can result in hasty temperamental displays and in a danger from fire and scalding, surgical operations, fevers, mental complaints, vertigo, and accidents. This can result in a mark or scar to the head or face. Becoming angry only deters from your general health. Be cautious of cuts and wounds or other accidents to the eyes, head, hands, and feet; of falls; and of danger from fire and explosions, firearms, and machines in general. Be careful of health disorders resulting from flatulence, digestive problems, and internal disorders of an inflammatory nature.

Aries rules over the head and is in sympathy with the stomach and kidneys. It is these parts of the body that are most susceptible to diseases. In particular, Aries are prone to colds, catarrh, high fevers, headaches, and problems with the eyes, ears, and teeth. You may frequently suffer from insomnia, convulsions, congestion, ruptures of blood vessels in the brain, dizziness and spasmodic pains in the head. There are possibly problems with trouble with eczema, ring-worms, neuralgia, sunstroke, stomach, kidney and liver troubles, nervous prostration, paralysis and other ailments resulting from nervous conditions. Discords in the domestic situation, such as frequent squabbles, may result in sick headaches. Troubles resulting from worry, anger, jealousy, impatience, and lack of physical exercise can easily develop. Calmness, self-analysis, exerting self-control, meditation and some form of regular, physical exercise can overcome these tendencies. Fresh air, daily walks, or even a break in your routine such as short trips in the country, can be beneficial. Provided that physical mishaps and accidents are avoided, Aries possess enough vitality and energy to insure a long and most interesting life. When the end does come, it is usually sudden, since Mars in Aries refuses to put up with illness, disability, or slow decline. Herbs beneficial to this sign are mustard, eye-bright, bay and others of a pungent nature.

HISTORY OF ARIES

Early Babylonian zodiacs did not include the Ram. It did exist, however, in Egypt where it was considered exceptionally important. And the Ram in early Egyptian times apparently did represent the constellation that later came to be called Aries. The Ram was the sacred animal of the god Amun, after whom many pharaohs were named: Tutankh-Amun, Amun-hotep, Amun-em-het. Amun was originally the Hidden One or the Unknown Force, an expression which might mean either the life-force or the ‚most high god’. The concept of a universal, all knowing god was known in Egypt and India prior to the time that monotheism evolved and eventually ripped religions into warring sects.

Before the rulerships of the twelve signs were allotted to the planets, they were ruled by gods or spiritual powers. In Plato’s time, Aries was ruled by Athena, the warlike goddess who sprang fully armed from the head of Zeus, so it follows that Aries rules the head. Athena was also goddess of wisdom and the inventor of weaving; she was not a single-minded entity such as Mars, the Roman god of war. The Greek name, Ares, has no connection with the Latin word, Aries which means ram. The Old Testament describes how, among the Jewish settlements, a lamb was sacrificed in every home at the time of the Passover. Its blood was sprinkled over the door in order that the Lord would "pass over" and not smite the house. The Bible describes the anger of Moses when he came down from the mountain top and discovered the people bowing before a golden calf. The shocking aspect of this sight was not the worship of the animal, but that the sacrifice of the he-lamb had been initiated among the children of Israel, and now they were regressing to the Egyptian cult of Apis, the bull, which, of course, was a belief that should have been abandoned after the Exodus from Egypt. However, even in Egypt, the worship of Apis was becoming the religion of Amen-Ra, the ram-headed god of the Hidden Sun. The bull and ram cults existed concurrently. It was the priests of Egypt, Chaldea and Greece who invested the signs, planets, houses, and aspects with their commonly accepted and applied significance and meaning.

ARIES

MARCH 21 - APRIL 20

THE THEBAIC CALENDAR

CHARACTER, PERSONALITY, AND DESTINY

The Thebaic Calendar represents the daily notes that the ancient astrologers wrote on burnt stones or papyrus. This is an easy and fast way to find information pertaining to your birth date. The native will often find his characteristics and destiny around his date of birth.

Whether Aries is a person's Sun sign, the Ascendant, on the cusp, or found in a House, the characteristics of Aries are evident. Each sign of the Zodiac represents certain characteristics, and Aries is the sign in which the Sun is exalted, indicating that the Sun bestows upon Aries the principle of new beginnings. Aries, the first sign, occurs in the Spring and therefore is indicative of the beginning of a new cycle.

DUALITY: Masculine   **ELEMENT:** Fire   **QUALITY:** Cardinal   **RULER:** Mars

The characteristics of Aries are manifested through a powerful psychological drive for the individual to prove himself or herself through action. Aries is a Cardinal Fire sign resulting in an enthusiasm by the individual which manifests itself with a strong desire to impulsively rush into physical, mental, or emotional action. The sign of Aries represents not only enthusiasm but raw energy as if solar powered and an impulsiveness bordering on the militant which can be either seen as rash or courageous. Aries is not a timid sign, and it becomes evident that this raw energy must be in some manner focused and channeled in order for the individual to be productive. There is within the Aries individual an innate feeling or desire to be in authority--to be the leader--almost as if this person were born to rule through a natural superiority. While Aries can be most charming and charismatic, there is found a tendency to use aggressiveness and even force, if necessary, to get one's own way. In other words, the patient use of diplomacy and tact may be attributes the Aries individual must strive to cultivate. When an Aries fails to learn the art of persuasion in their desire to be in charge, they can appear pompous and foolish to others. None the less, the Aries-born remains undaunted. His strong will power and inability to admit defeat, let alone a fault, sees him through any difficulties and any resulting failures. Having been hopelessly shot down into the depths of despair, Aries will turn around and simply apply his or her energy to a new plan, endeavor, or enterprise--especially if such an activity hints at adventure. He is inspiringly unquenchable in his ability to renew himself and his energies. The highly competitive nature of Aries compels him to be recognized as the best and the first, or he is not in the least interested in being involved. On top of that, he wants the recognition that comes with

76

being first--whatever is accomplished is due to Aries; whatever fails is the fault of the other person involved.

Being a Cardinal sign, Aries possesses a need for change and for new experiences both physical and mental which can either be seen as a positive trait or a negative one depending on how the individual focuses this desire. When this desire for new experiences or new plans is not focused, the individual may jump from one idea to another with a tendency not to see his or her plans through to completion. However, when this abundant energy and desire is focused and channeled into an orderly productivity, the individual's abilities to develop new plans and direct change are most beneficial. The pioneering and undaunting adventurous spirit of the Aries individual can be an invaluable personal trait and asset. Needless to say, the same thing can be said about the, at times, uncontrollable impulsiveness of Aries, which added to their apparent selfishness--they are of course the center of their own universe--deters them from the ability to fully appreciate one love at a time. It is almost as if Aries cannot slow down long enough to fully listen to or appreciate the needs or even the advice of another person. And when Aries finds him or herself in a situation that in any way limits or restricts him, he can become most restless, and that overpowering urge and need for change begin to stir within his very soul.

That is not to say that Aries cannot love. They love deeply and strongly, but their love is defined on their own terms. These are not individuals to be bound to a partnership in which they do not feel in charge of their personal situation. They must have a release for the immense energies, and they require a great deal of admiration from their romantic partners. Once that admiration so much as hints at fading, Aries loses interests, and before one relationship is ended will begin looking for another. This need to be admired and appreciated as well as loved both emotionally and physically underlies the most basic desires of an Aries individual. There may be that Aries that stays in an unhappy relationship, but they will no doubt be seeking not only pleasure but approbation somewhere else.

Aries seeks opportunities for action, and if one is not forthcoming, the Aries originates his or her own plans of activity. He loves to plan whether it is a new project, a day shopping, or a night out on the town. Dinner at home will find Aries planning the menu and adding the final flourishes to the festive entertainment. It is a rare Aries who needs or waits for someone else to come up with an idea. This person has no need for outside stimuli to prod him into action. Aries does, however, seek and desire knowledge and information to feed their restless minds. This is the self-starter whose only need in life is an entourage of happy and willing followers in order for them to feel fulfilled, energized, and ready to begin anew. As a positive masculine sign, Aries is by nature aggressive, active, and capable of initiating change--it is the completion of one project before beginning another that may be the biggest challenge for the Aries individual. The sign of Aries is manifested as the new cycle, the resourceful pioneer who can be fearless in taking on a new enterprise or reenergizing one that others have given up on.

Each of the twelve signs of the Zodiac are allotted thirty degrees, but it must be remembered that not all Aries, for example, share the same intensity of these characteristics. Each sign is further divided into Decans of ten degrees each, and each Decan has been shown to exhibit the characteristics of its sign in varying strengths.

THE FIRST DECAN

Within Aries, the first decan is designated as 0 degrees to 10 degrees of Aries and includes those individuals born between March 21 and March 30. The primary characteristic of these individuals is a need and desire to feed their ego and their self-esteem through recognition, praise, and admiration by either their partners, associates, friends, or lovers. When they receive this approbation, they strive through all their energies, actions, and efforts to live up to it. Born in the First Decan of Aries, this individual has a basic need to feel good about himself or herself, and this self-respect is gauged by the amount of appreciation they receive from others. They apply all of their energies into winning the approval of others. When this is done in a positive fashion, it produces admirable results. But reckless and impulsive Aries can also go the extra mile and ruin everything by over-doing. Their physical, mental, and emotional need for action and their impulsiveness, impatience, and fiery temper can just as well serve as a detriment to receiving the very praise and admiration they so desire--but no doubt they will obtain more than their share of attention with such actions and antics.

THE SECOND DECAN

The second decan is designated as from 10 degrees to 20 degrees of Aries and includes those individuals born between March 31 and April 9. The Second Decan bestows upon the individual an electrifying energy, a pronounced courage, and a strong self-confidence and self-reliance that impresses others. At the same time, this individual can be self-centered, self-serving, and an authoritative demigod who rules with a firm hand. They possess a strong will power which in many circumstances can be unbendable. The Second Decan Aries may be more recognizable as the person who possesses a tendency to see their plans through to completion. They also have the ability to round up their followers, inspire others to action, and oversee their plans, all the while remaining the central focus and the center of attention of any group. This Aries thrives on the thrill of excitement and adventure and new experiences--which includes and defines their romantic lives as well. They most desire prestige, position, recognition and, of course, admiration from others. Their ego drives them to compete and gain for themselves that which they most desire.

THE THIRD DECAN

The third decan is designated as being from 20 degrees to 30 degrees of Aries and includes those individuals born between April 10 and April 19. The Third Decan Aries may be perceived as being more refined and cultured than those of the first two Decans. There is a tendency for these individuals to pursue education, philosophy or perhaps theology. Less self-centered than other Aries, this individual may strive to better the community or to become recognized for public service. They remain natural leaders who are enterprising and creatively adept at organizing new plans. They retain all the natural energies of Aries as well and may be forever on the go seeking new outlets for their physical and mental energies. Being Aries, it goes without saying that they hold firmly to their personal beliefs and at their worst they must guard against being bigoted or narrow-minded. And of course, being Aries they thrive on recognition and the prestige it brings.

FIRST DECAN OF ARIES:

MARCH 21 - MARCH 30 - FIRST TEN DAYS

CHARACTER, PERSONALITY AND TEMPERAMENT:

The primary characteristic of these individuals is a need and desire to feed their ego and their self-esteem through recognition, praise, and admiration by either their partners, associates, friends, or lovers.

CARDINAL ELEMENT:

FIRE: Daring; aggressive; egotistical; pride; impulsive; brisk; passions rise to brutal force; risky actions; fiery, hot spirit and temperament.

DESTINY:

Gains and losses leads to violent dizzy heights and abrupt falling; resourceful attitude and everlasting energy.

STAR DATE OF BIRTH: MARCH 21

Fighting temperament, stubborn character. Serious difficulties to cope with all life. You are a resourceful and energetic individual who works hard but who is not overly successful at any one thing. You can be cunning, shrewd and even mysterious with a marked exotic approach and attitude toward your sexual relationships.

STAR DATE OF BIRTH: MARCH 22

Calm determination, self-esteem. Stubbornness. Dangerous adversaries. Your greatest difficulty is putting your creative ideas into action no matter how great your self-confidence. You are sexually self-assured and your sexual experiences feed your ego. Your lovers often remain loyal to you for lengthy periods, and you possess the ability to comfort those who have been emotionally hurt or rejected by others.

STAR DATE OF BIRTH: MARCH 23

Determination to lead and control without warnings and punishments. Delicate situations in life. You find the greatest satisfaction in creative endeavors. You possess a tendency toward unusual and unorthodox sexual practices. Those who are financially secure but emotionally insecure are drawn to you for comfort. You meet others who could enlighten you, but you have difficulty listening and attending to their messages.

STAR DATE OF BIRTH: MARCH 24

Brutal temperament; completely against contradiction. Tumultuous lifelong expeditions. But you are a natural at entertaining a crowd and tempting the temptress. Your romantic encounters add to your feelings of prestige and your aim to please is high even though you may strive to please yourself first. You are for sure the soldier and the poet enduring side by side.

STAR DATE OF BIRTH: MARCH 25

Patient character, working spirit. Career with a lot of activity and good material result. You are content with your position in life and your lifestyle and don't exhibit the ambition to change yourself for the sake of change. But sexually you can be demanding, and you tend to put on a commanding performance. Those persons involved in frequent travel or who are visiting your locality are attracted to you.

Star Date of Birth: March 26

The person is courageous and hesitant at the same time; reflections and decisions are late. Many failures because of the insecure character. Your creative and ambitious ideas often lead you to make money. You have an active sexual life, but you have a tendency to remain intellectually involved rather than emotionally. You are sexually stimulated by those who can match your intellect or by others who have been involved in the military or intelligence.

Star Date of Birth: March 27

Exuberance, tendency to tell everything to everybody; this represents a mistake; the life can be ruined because of too much devotion for other people. However, your cunning and shrewdness prove financially rewarding. You are an expert at attracting and seducing others who are drawn to your persuasive style and while you like to have a partner in your life you are not always faithful to the loved one.

Star Date of Birth: March 28

Excessive courage. Crazy decisions. Bitter experience all through the life, but never fatal. You particularly enjoy the time you spend out of doors where you can appreciate natural surroundings. But you are also drawn to formal occasions and love to dress the part. Sexually, you have an experimental and expanding nature that desires new experiences.

Star Date of Birth: March 29

Fine, tempered activity according to necessities. Self-control. Chance in difficult situations. Your possessive tendencies are at play whether with family, friends, or associates. And in love you are a possessive and jealous lover even though you stray and are drawn to that which is forbidden. You are attracted to attention-getting types.

Star Date of Birth: March 30

Excessive spontaneity, trust, imprudence. If the native is a woman, other people take advantage. You possess a desire for real property, land, or possessions. Sexually, you are attracted to other arrogant, self-indulgent persons who are just as jealous and possessive as you and who share your tendency to stray.

SECOND DECAN OF ARIES:
MARCH 31 - APRIL 9 - SECOND TEN DAYS

CHARACTER, PERSONALITY AND TEMPERAMENT:

An energy, a pronounced courage, and a strong self-confidence and self-reliance that impresses others. At the same time, this individual can be self-centered, self-serving, and an authoritative demigod who rules with a firm hand. They possess a strong will power which in many circumstances can be unbendable.

CARDINAL ELEMENT:

FIRE: Burning and blessed with enthusiasm; an energy and taste for creation and work; at times happy with a natural generosity; the native is a creator; innately creating a dominate enthusiasm around him; even after death the native influences his household; the native can unconsciously sacrifice slowly, slowly.

DESTINY:

Difficult life; travel abroad; cheerful old age; more stable and patient; also more industrious and persevering.

STAR DATE OF BIRTH: MARCH 31

Clean soul, filled with ideals; strength and feeling of balance. Happy existence, divided between home and social activity. Enterprising, active spirit, getting everybody's appreciation. These characteristics are valid also for the ones born on the 1st of April.

Star Date of Birth: April 1

You are a strong-willed, ambitious, and creative thinker. Sexually, you experience dramatic encounters and never forget former lovers who seem to reappear in your life over the years. Your true love may well be experienced the second time around.

Star Date of Birth: April 2

Courage, determination, isolation, sorrow; the individual is not appreciated enough; his good acts are not recognized. Your favorite companion may be yourself or someone willing to listen to you talk about yourself which may lead to loneliness in later life. Sexually, you find yourself attempting not to make the same mistakes again, but you often do just that despite yourself.

Star Date of Birth: April 3

Naive enthusiasm, boredom. Your curiosity and your impressionable mind lead you to develop an interest in the paranormal or occult subjects. Through the years, you find yourself becoming more open to sexual experiences and encounters which allows you to gain the knowledge shared by others.

Star Date of Birth: April 4

Taste for everything big; strong organizations, vast enterprises. General success. Married or not, your strongest bonds, friendships, or relationships are formed with those of the same sex. The highlight of your sexual experiences may occur during the summer months when you have a tendency to focus your attentions more fully on your sexuality.

Star Date of Birth: April 5

Skill for scientific research, especially astronomy. Calm and clean life. However, you have a tendency to be impulsive and even reckless in your younger years which can lead to speculative or risky adventures. Sexually, your impulsiveness can turn to an urgent compulsion as you experiment with finding the perfect partner who you can idolize.

STAR DATE OF BIRTH: APRIL 6

Strong character; calm during disputes and skilled to solve things with a smile. Successful life because of this skill. You are in love with the idea of love and romance and seek sexual fulfillment in an ego driven, intellectually curious manner. This interest may lead you to study, research, write about, or, in some other manner, more fully develop your knowledge about this subject.

STAR DATE OF BIRTH: APRIL 7

Ambition and aggressiveness. Any failures may be due to this aggressive aspect; malicious ambition. Your passions and sexuality may dominate a great deal of your thought processes and your life. And those you desire seem to come your way as your sexual encounters continue to expand your experiences in love life.

STAR DATE OF BIRTH: APRIL 8

Irrational optimism in all aspects of life. Long voyages, adventure. Your changeable nature may make you moody with a tendency to be stubborn and obstinate in getting your own way. You possess a natural sexual allure that has nothing to do with fashion, fads, or the latest styles or trends.

STAR DATE OF BIRTH: APRIL 9

Justified optimism; self-esteem and the skill to get the best from everybody. Positive success in difficult situations. You desire a peaceful life which leads to contentment, but you pass up what could have been worthwhile opportunities. Your congenial nature lends itself to a warm and lasting sexual relationship, and you are drawn to those who uphold standards and traditions.

THE THIRD DECAN OF ARIES:

APRIL 10 - APRIL 20 - THIRD TEN DAYS

CHARACTER, PERSONALITY AND TEMPERAMENT:

More refined and cultured than those of the first two Decans. There is a tendency for these individuals to pursue education, philosophy or perhaps theology. Less self-centered than other Aries.

CARDINAL ELEMENT:

FIRE: Daring, enthusiasm, wish and willingness to act and to be active; focus on art and love. Native has a great passion and his existence will be felt by this. Massive expenses.

DESTINY:

Creative with excellent, but expensive tastes; well brought up; learned and in charge of many things; native ends well.

STAR DATE OF BIRTH: APRIL 10

Laziness, sensuality, inactivity and a tendency toward a sentimental deception and complication. You are ingenious, flexible, and adaptable to new situations and new people. Your greatest challenge is in finding others who match your enthusiasm. Your secret loves may fan your flames more than other more conventional types.

STAR DATE OF BIRTH: APRIL 11

The individual loves partying; he has a lot of envious enemies; possible aggressions because of opposite sex. You see only your own ideas and opinions, many of which are developed at a young age, and you fail to recognize the importance of the ideas and insights.

Always others must adapt to your wants and wishes making you inflexible and dogmatic. In your sexuality, you are always looking forward to the next conquest.

STAR DATE OF BIRTH: APRIL 12

Sensual excesses; problems with opposite sex. You can be inflexible in that you resist change and are reluctant to accept the advice of others. You are hard working but not particularly ambitious. You are knowingly perceptive of the sexual desires of others while your own desires are often heightened by formal social occasions when you are dressed for success and can appear dignified or glamorous.

STAR DATE OF BIRTH: APRIL 13

Dull attitude; jealous feeling; controlling temperament. Suffers because of lover's infidelity. Your tendency to follow your own lead can make you appear at times non-traditional and unconventional. You seek challenges and this is especially true in your rather dramatic sexual encounters. You keep tabs on former and present lovers while forever looking for the next one.

STAR DATE OF BIRTH: APRIL 14

The native would be proud to have a famous lover. Good luck with opposite sex. Your basic fear of being inadequate leads you to prove yourself over and over and this is especially true in your sexuality. You can be overly possessive and jealous in regards to your lover while at the same time you seek the next encounter with which to soothe your vanity.

STAR DATE OF BIRTH: APRIL 15

Mocking, distant character. Lucky in business for men and women. You are drawn to challenges, secrets, mysteries, and solving the unknown through your diligent efforts. But your changeability and impulsiveness to follow new ideas effects your relationships and your ability to transcend to deeper, more meaningful sexual encounters.

STAR DATE OF BIRTH: APRIL 16

Tendency towards romantic love. Help from the opposite sex; materialistic character. You have a strong need to be accepted and well liked by others and this need for approbation leads you to respond to those who express love and desire for you, but you are continuously seeking that new relationship which you believe will prove fulfilling. The exotic or those of foreign birth appeal to your insatiable curiosity in life.

Star Date of Birth: April 17

Lack of determination and balance in everything they do. Hard life; achievements later in life. Your spirituality leads you to seek time to yourself for personal reflection. But you also seek a great deal of privacy for your more intimate, sexual encounters and abhor those who kiss and tell. You attract ambitious and successful people to you.

Star Date of Birth: April 18

The native needs to be sheltered and protected by their partner. Insecure life, unstable situations. Your shrewd and cunning mind combined with your impulsive and rash nature can lead you into questionable activities resulting in failures, loss, fraud, and scandal. Your sexual experiences fuel your ego driven nature and enhance your feelings of importance and self worth.

Star Date of Birth: April 19

Self-control, decision, ability. Rough life, filled with serious difficulties which will be overcome. Healthy old age. Your success is assured when you develop your innate intelligence and talents. If a man, your masculinity is important to you; if a woman, your femininity; and you are drawn to sexual encounters with others who share and understand this need.

Star Date of Birth: April 20

Ambitions without result; out of luck. You are ambitious and strive to prove yourself through your success. However, you prefer that your romantic relationships provide you with an outlet for fun, distractions, lightheartedness, and generally a good time enjoyed by both you and the other person.

Colors:

The most favorable colors for the natives of Aries are all shades of red, rose, and pink.

BIRTHSTONES:

The birthstones for Aries are rubies, garnets, and diamonds.

FLOWERS:

Favorable flowers for Aries individuals are the rose, the geranium, and the red tulips.

KEYWORD: "I AM"

POSITIVE   TRAITS:

Pioneering; adventurous; trustworthy; steady; endurance; persistent; creative; self-reliant; persevering; enterprising; practical; courageous; fearless; kind; careful; humorous; energetic; freedom-loving; magnetic; direct; constructive; enthusiastic; imaginative; kind; careful; humorous; energetic; freedom-loving; magnetic; proud; direct; constructive; leader; optimistic; defender of the weak; seeker of new experiences; an idea person with initiative; intellectual; strongly sexed.

NEGATIVE   TRAITS:

Selfish; self-centered; stubborn; unbending; blunt; domineering; hot temper; conceited; brisk; impatient; dogmatic; argumentative; covetous; amorous; lazy; lives in the present wanting everything now; jealous; possessive; impulsive; excitable; not domestic; hasty; sharp; overly competitive; resentful of restrictions; aggressive; irate; quarrelsome; rude; boisterous; foolhardy; brutal.

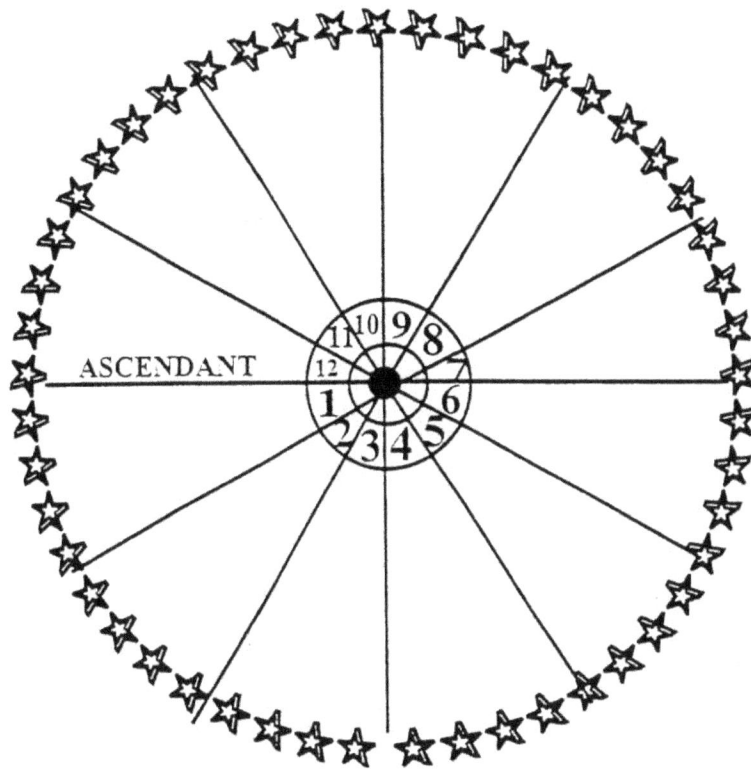

Aries

Personal Self-Expression and Mental Tendencies

1. Strong Wish, Demanding, Productive, Magnetism, Exploring, Gregarious
2. Proud, Hunter, Ideas to Create Change, Indomitable, Innovators, Pioneers,
3. Fighting, Courageous, Arrogant, Dexterous, Low self-sufficiency, Deceitful
4. Commander, Entrepreneur, Dangerous Situations, Energizing, Impusive, Positive
5. Good Will for Affirmation, Benevolence, Love and Travel, Selfish, Pugnacious
6. Spiritual-Force, Extremes, Attracted to Foreigners, Wanting Everything New
7. Efficiency, Follows, Instigates Power and Position, Rebellious, Being in control
8. Selfish, Prefers Not to be Questioned about Feelings, Self-effacing, Inconsiderate
9. Strong Stimulants, Holds Back in Intimacy, Selfish needs, Ruining Everything
10. Intellectually Guided, Restless Life, Balanced Soul, Short-Term Needs Important
11. World Constant Desire, Nice Soul Full of Ideals, Self-Focused Training, Satirist
12. Happy Life Divided between Home and Social Life, Noisy, Quick Tempered
13. Authoritative, Wishing to Impose Desire on Other People, Disrespect, Jealousy
14. Violent, Vicious, Unvanquished Will, Isolated, Disregard, Audacious, Vigorous
15. Belongs to Selfish Forces, Egotistic, Quarrelsome, Foolhardy, Self-Interest, Strong
16. Optimist, Enthusiastic, Drinking Vice, Violent Passion, Brutal, High-Minded
17. Instability, Activities Intense, Strong Personality, Imprudent, Insubordinate, Ardent
18. Impulsive, Fortunate, Harmonious, Industrious, Self-Assurance, Enthusiastic
19. Calm, Self-reliant, Feisty, Impetuous, Challenge, Inspiring, Forcefully, Impusive
20. Stubborn, Controlling, Blunt, Gambler, Talented, Mentally Alert, Violent, Bestial
21. Very Difficult, Defeatist, Impressionable, Have Many Roles in Life, Many Affairs
22. Adventuresome, Desires Affairs, Aries is Afire, Fighting, Impetuous, Easily Anger
23. Independent-Headstrong, Pioneering Leader, Big Ego, Easily Violent, Self-Value
24. Versatile, Demonstrative, Highly Motivated, Needs, Challenge, Arrogant, Outgoing
25. Manipulates Feelings, Half-moons Joined by Straight Line, Abrupt, Impulsive
26. Insensitive Toward Others, Inconsistent, Unrestricted, Blunt, Self-Secure, Religious
27. Self-satisfied, Everything Rotates Around Aries, Inconsistency, Defeated, Challenge
28. Multi-Faceted, Aries Looks Like the Horns of a Ram, Entrepreneur, Stimulated
29. Self-trusting, Dynamic, Impatient, Horny, Bitchy, Angry, Dynamo, Courage

30. Seldom Renouncing, Waiting to Fulfill Secret Sex in Public, Impressionable,
31. Impetuous, Self-conscious, Sexually Dominant, Impatient, Represssed, Unfaithful
32. Brisk, Susceptible, Sexuality in an Angry Relationship, Easily Angered, Controlling
33. Astronomic Studies, Poor Sexual Functioning, Stimulated, Social Climber,
34. Scientific Researcher, Orgasmic Impoverishment, Self-Centered, Adventurous
35. Extreme Jealousy by Partner in Home and Family, Impulsive, Dominating. Talented
36. Sexual and Emotional Exclusivity, Hesitations Agitate Life, High Self-Esteem
37. Ambitious Tough Pleasure, Boredom with Opposite Sex, Me First, Selfish
38. Creates New Things, Low Self-esteem with Repressed Anger, Easily Depressed
39. Manages Difficult Situations, Melodramatic Risky Affairs, Fights for Independence
40. Ascending and Descending, Sex Hunts, Multiple Affairs,Superior to Others
41. Combative Personal Relationship both Emotionally and Legally, Flamboyant
42. Self-impersonation, Independent Movement Controlled, Hypocritical Attitudes
43. Money-Making Schemes, Freedom Questioned, Free-Spirited, Foolish, Charming
44. Many Journeys, Sexually Dissatisfied, Never Stops Running, Wants Everything
45. Savage, Feels Unappreciated Without Control, Loves Sexual Experience, Powerful
46. Speculative, Risk-Taker, Mentally Stimulated, Challenged by Adversity, Expressive
47. Hasty Marriage, Divorce, Independent Direction, Falls in Love Easily, Obsessive
48. Powerful Personality, Self-Assertive, Emotional, Penetrating Mind, Magnetic
49. Nervous, Short-term Goals, Self-discovery, Falls in and out of Love Easily
50. Adaptable, Restless, Self-confident, Needs Experience, Easily Bored, Gregarious
51. Self-deceptive, Needs to Blow Off Steam, Penetrating , Convincing Liar
52. Separates from Family for Adventure to Find Love, Exaggerates, Idealistic
53. Follows Fashions, Involved in Business Enterprises, Opinionated, Exaggerates
54. Magnanimous, Vibrant Energy, Unfaithful, Audacious, Philosophical, Determined
55. Open-Hearted, Faces Change with Courage, Challenged by Fear, Impulsive, Clever,
56. Emotionally Stressed, Temporal, Ultra-Ambitious, Cultivates Soul and Mind
57. Lascivious, Penetrating, Speculates in Investments, Money Making Schemes
58. Indignant, Admirable, Intelligent, Responsible, Produces Success and Activity
59. Scientific, Philosophical in Male-Dominated World, Sinks to the Bottom, Elistist
60. Sharp, Progressive, Proud, Detached, Independent, Prone to Calamity, Charismatic
61. Determined, Expressive, Easily Angered, Vulnerable, Inspiring, Unhampered Spirit
62. Excitable Temperament, Fighting Spirit, Achieving, Leader, Outgoing, Fool-Hardy
63. Imposing, Interested, Self-righteous, Receptive, Passive, Low Self-Sufficiency
64. Vehement, Easily Shows Anger and Hurt, Enthusiastic, Foolhardy, Homocidal
65. Tribulations, Loss, scandals, High Spirits, Inexperienced, Likes Glamour, Foolhardy
66. Quick Recovery from Depressions, Judgements Made on First Impressions
67. High Self-esteem, Self-interest, Good Sense of Humor, Independent, Impatient

68. Susceptible to Accident, Emotionally Vulnerable, Cause Digestive Problems
69. Head Injuries, Face Inflammation, Optimistic, Watery Eyes Hands and Feet
70. Bold, Cunning, Fortune Hunting, Quite Self-confident, Extroverted, Melodramatic
71. Zealous, Critical, Cranky, Anxious, Suffers from Insecurity, Desires Knowledge
72. Pioneering, Commanding, Superior, Benevolent, Attempts What Others Fear to Try
73. Extravagant Love of Luxury Items, Resists Failure and Defeat, Problem Solver
74. Intellectually High-spirited, Manipulates Feelings-Love and People, Insomnia
75. Vain, Rash, Noisy, Pride is Double-edged, Reputable, Complex Personality
76. Reliable, Fearless, Noble, Generous, High Libido, Vulnerable to Rejection
77. Obstinate, Opinionated, Petulant, Quick-Spoken, Learns to Reject Others First
78. Resentful, Restless, Abrupt, Flattering Description, Dislikes Details, Risky Affairs
79. Vague, Tactless, Boisterous, Complex, Passionate, Cannot Keep Secretes
80. Sympathetic, Searching for Ideals, Surrounds Himself With Stimulating People
81. Self-controlled, Control-Dominate, Erotic, Survivor, Easily Wounded (Emotional)
82. Conquers Desires, Catalyst, Reluctant to Help Others, Demanding, Likes to Travel
83. Dislikes Details, Musically Inclined, Superficial, Hunters, High-Spirited, Inactivity
84. Intellect Relaxes Activity, Naturally Extroverted, Sensual, Sexually Romantic
85. Frustrates an Active Mind, Dislikes Secrets, Open Hearted to Himself Only
86. Always Planning Next Activity, Sweepingly Generous, Self-Centered, Worries,
87. Compartmentalizes Life and People for Own Needs, Fails Marriage, Fastidious
88. Possesses Leadership Powers, Responds to Compliments, Deceives Others
89. Seeks Satisfaction and Gratification, Demanding, Give of Gab, Irresistible
90. Gives a Lot to Win, Self-effacing, Inconsiderate, Falls Easily to Temptation
91. Win-Win Attitude, Highly Motivated, Prone to Gain Enemies, Unfaithful
92. Defies Social Convention, Luckey With Money, Appears to Be a Friend But Is Not
93. Flamboyant, Foolishly Charming, Hypocritical, Can Be Very Cunning, Impulsive
94. Multi-faceted, Powerful Aura, Demands Loyalty, Notorious, Very Fashionable
95. Sprightly, Mystical, Greatest Pleasure from Hunting, Brilliant Style, Antagonistic
96. Mysterious, Easily Bored, Convincing Liar, Gains Property and Money by Marriage
97. Obsessive, Wants Immediate Gratification, Feels Impelled, High-Spirited,
98. Desires Perfect Mate, Nosey, Enterprising, Kind, Sometimes Has Crazy Ideas
99. Easily Forgives and Forgets, Emotional Elitist, Susceptible to Headaches
100. Potent Chemistry, Attempts Things Others Fear to Try, Takes Chances, Vivacious

CELEBRITY BIRTHDAYS

MARCH   ARIES

21	Phyllis McGinley	Johann Sebastian Bach	Patrick Lucey
	Timothy Dalton	Cynthia Geary	Ed Begley
	James Coco	Shawnon Dunston	Rosie Stone
	John D. Rockefeller III	Rosie O'Donnell	Gary Oldman
22	Bob Costas	Werner Klemperer	Marcel Marceau
	William Shatner	Karl Malden	Chico Marx
	Stephen Sondheim	Lena Olin	Pat Robertson
	Stephanie Mills	Wernher von Braun	Orin Hatch
23	Lee May	Ric Ocasek	Marti Pellow
	Chaka Khan	Amanda Plummer	Marty Allen
	Joan Crawford	Princess Eugenie	Ron Jaworski
24	Robert Carradine	Steve McQueen	Norman Fell
	Thomas Dewey	Harry Houdini	Lee Oskar
	William Goetz	Dougie Thomson	David T. Suzuki
	Lara Flynn Boyle	Donna Pescow	Byron Janis
25	Bela Bartok	Frankie Carle	David Lean
	Howard Cosell	Sarah Jessica Parker	Elton John
	Simone Signoret	Arturo Toscanini	Bonnie Bedelia
	Gloria Steinem	Paul Michael Glaser	Aretha Franklin
26	Leonard Nimoy	Teddy Pendergrass	Diana Ross
	Tennessee Williams	James Caan	Erica Jong
	Sterling Hayden	Bob Woodward	Alan Arkin
	Al Jolson	Leeza Gibbons	Robert Frost
27	Maria Carey	Nathaniel Currier	Michael York
	Wilhelm Roentgen	Sarah Vaughan	Cyrus Vance
	Gloria Swanson	Quentin Tarantino	Judy Carne
	David Janssen	Talisa Soto	Tony Banks
28	Ralph Sanzio	Ken Howard	Diane Wiest
	Reba McEntire	Pandro Berman	Irving Lazar
	Carolyn Jones	Spyros Skouras	Salt
	August Busch	Nelson Algren	Dirk Bogarde

93

MARCH   ARIES

29	Jennifer Capriati	Ella McPherson	Eric Idle
	Pres. John Tyler	Warner Baxter	Pearl Bailey
	Walt Frazier	Eileen Heckart	Cy Young
	Denny McClain	Eugene McCarthy	Dirk Bogarde
30	Warren Beatty	Tracy Chapman	Turhan Bey
	Francisco Goya	Richard Helm	Eric Clapton
	Vincent Van Gogh	Frankie Laine	Celine Dion
	John Astin	Paul Reiser	
31	Rene Descartes	Rhea Perlman	Leo Buscaglia
	Cesar Chavez	Richard Chamberlain	Herb Alpert
	Liz Claiborne	Christopher Walken	Shirley Jones
	Arthur Godfrey	Franz Joseph Haydn	Red Norvo

APRIL

1	Rachmaninoff	Jane Powell	Lon Chaney
	Ali MacGraw	William Manchester	Alan Blakey
	Debbie Reynolds	Emil Mosbacher	Gordon Jump
	Otto Von Bismarck	ToshiroMifune	Wallace Beery
2	Emmylou Harris	Linda Hunt	Dana Carvey
	Alec Guinness	Charlemagne	Emile Zola
	Max Ernst	Leon Russell	Casanova
	Buddy Ebsen	Gary Steven	Jack Webb
3	Arthur Murray	Eddie Murphy	Doris Day
	Marlon Brando	Wayne Newton	Jane Goodall
	Tony Orlando	David Hyde Pierce	Alec Baldwin
	Marsha Mason	Washington Irving	George Jessel
4	Nancy McKeon	John Cameron Swayze	Kitty Kelley
	France Langford	Elmer Bernstein	Gil Hodges
	Arthur Murray	Robert Downey, Jr.	Howard Koch
	Anthony Perkin	Maya Angelou	Nick Mars
5	Michael Moriarity	Agnetha Faltskog	Bette Davis
	Melvyn Douglas	Roger Corman	Gregory Peck
	Spencer Tracy	Chester Bowles	Colin Powell
	Joseph Lister	Herbert Von Karajan	Gale Storm

APRIL   ARIES

6	Harry Houdini	Billy Dee Williams	Raphael
	Lowell Thoma	Michelle Phillips	Merle Haggard
	John Ratzenberger	Stan Cullimore	Ari Meyers
	Walter Huston	Marilu Henner	Jaso Hervey
7	David Frost	Irene Castle	Jerry Brown
	Walter Winchell	Ravi Shankar	Billie Holiday
	Percy Faith	Jackie Chan	James Garner
	Francis Ford Coppola	Mick Abrahams	John Oates
8	Sonja Henie	Barbara Kingsolver	John Gavin
	Mary Pickford	Clementine Churchill	Robin Wright
	Connie Stevens	Patricia Arquette	Betty Ford
	Julian Lennon	Catfish Hunter	Warren Avis
9	Jean-Paul Belmondo	Tommy Manville	Hugh Hefner
	Paulina Porizkova	Charles Baudelaire	Dennis Quaid
	Paul Robeson	Michael Learned	Ward Bond
	William J. Fullbright	Abraham Ribicoff	Carl Perkins
10	Don Meredith	Clare Boothe Luce	Brian Setzer
	William Booth	John Madden	Omar Sharif
	Steven Seagal	Commodore Perry	Bobbie Smith
	David Halberstam	Chuck Connors	George Arliss
11	Ethel Kennedy	Dean Acheson	Joel Grey
	Stuart Adamson	Lisa Stansfield	Oleg Cassini
	Quentin Reynolds	Neville Staples	Bill Irwin
	Gov. Hugh Carey	Richie Sambora	Delroy Pearson
12	Andy Garcia	David Letterman	Lily Pons
	Claire Danes	Shannen Doherty	Ann Miller
	Alex Briley	Herbie Hancock	Tiny Tim
	David Cassidy	Vince Gill	Jane Withers
13	Thomas Jefferson	Rick Schroder	Don Adams
	Saundra Santiago	Butch Cassidy	Tony Dow
	F.W.Woolworth	Howard Keel	Ron Perlman
	Garry Kasparov	Lyle Waggoner	Alex Briley
14	Julie Christie	John Gielgud	Pete Rose
	Loretta Lynn	Sir James Clark	Rod Steiger
	Brad Diliman	Dennis Bryon	Jay Robinson
	Ritchie Blackmore	Larry Ferguson	John Shea

APRIL   ARIES

15	Emma Thompson Alfred Bloomingdale Leonardo Da Vinci Algernon Swinburne	Elizabeth Montgomery Samantha Fox Claudia Cardinale	Roy Clark Bessie Smith Graeme Clark
16	Henry Mancini Charlie Chaplin Wilbur Wright Kareem Abdul-Jabbar	Jimmy Osmond Gerry Rafferty Dusty Springfield Nikita Khrushchev	Ellen Barkin Jon Cryer Peter Ustinov Bobby Vinton
17	Gregor Piatigorsky William Holden Harry Reasoner Billie Holiday	Thornton Wilder James Garner Boomer Esiason Stephen Singleton	J. P . Morgan Anne Shirley Pete Shelley Liz Phair
18	Huntington Hartford Leopold Stokowski Hayley Mills Melissa Joan Hart	Conan O'Brien Philippe Junot Barbara Hale Les Pattison	Jane Leeves Rick Moranis Eric Roberts James Woods
19	Dudley Moore Jayne Mansfield Hugh O'Brian Kenneth Battelle	Paloma Picasso Frank Viola Mark Volman Larry Ramos, Jr.	Don Adams Tim Curry Alan Price
20	Don Mattingly Ryan O'Neal Joan Miro Harold Lloyd	George Takei Luther Vandross Adolf Hitler Harvey Firestone, Jr.	Nina Foch Bob Braun Jessica Lange Craig Frost

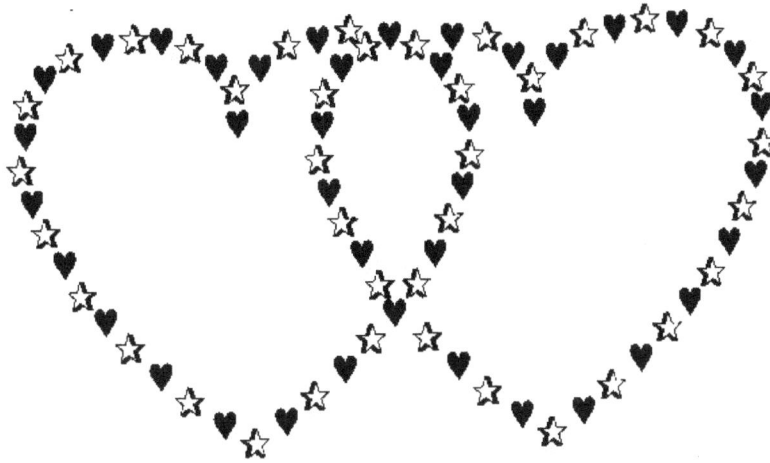

LOVE - SIGNS -INTRODUCTION TO RELATIONSHIPS AND COMPATIBILITIES

This segment of the book discusses that topic closest to the hearts of many people - ***Love, Romance, Relationships, and Compatibilities***. The descriptions that follow are based on generalizations pertaining to Sun signs. As has been discussed, individuals are strongly influenced by their Sun signs, but the natures of people are also a blend of the Moon sign, Ascendent and the planetary aspects. Thus, a truer indication of how a relationship may develop is discernible from the birth charts of the two individuals involved. But taking a look at the Sun signs is a beginning indicator of compatibility between two people. The better two people understand each other, the better are the chances of developing a lasting love and relationship.

Men and women are different, but within the influence of their Sun signs they also share many similar characteristics. Reading both the man and woman sections of the material which follows mav give the reader a broader scope of understanding of each sign in order to form a basis of comparison.

There is another aspect of astrology that needs to be mentioned in any introduction to a section on love and romance. Society and intellectuals may have a tendency to list romance as a less serious subject, but it this subject which most effects our daily lives, our futures, our fortunes, and our families. And discussing it openly, perhaps, will lead some to give it serious consideration rather than allowing their feelings or their logic to be the only guide to their decisions. Just because a romance is magical doesn't mean it will last, and the fact that a romance is logical and makes good sense doesn't mean it will be fulfilling.

The ancient astrologers devised within each Sun sign a list of characteristics for well-developed individuals and another list for individuals who were not well-developed. Many modern astrologers have disallowed these distinctions. Granted planetary aspects go a long way in influencing individuals to be one way or another. But this subject of whether an individual is well or poorly developed should also be mentioned when discussing a subject matter and decisions as important as love and romance.

A well-developed individual takes the gifts granted him or her and works on personal self-development throughout a life time. A poorly developed individual not only doesn't develop inherent gifts, but the gifts are often used to the person's advantage in a selfish manner. The point being that within each and every Sun sign are found individuals who lie, cheat, steal, misuse, and take advantage of others with only the most selfish of motives. Within each Sun sign are found individuals who are kind, caring, and sincere, and others who can't be trusted. The importance of taking the time to get to know one another can't be over emphasized.

Each individual is blessed with positive traits and gifts, and each person also possesses inherent negative traits. The challenge in life is to develop the positive traits while working to overcome the negative traits. Compatibility between two people is often an acceptance of both the wonderful positive traits as well as an understanding of the less desirable traits. All people can grow and develop and become better people. But, it seems, each person makes that determination and decision for himself or herself. Falling in love with the hopes of changing another person may work to some extent or it may be disastrous. The true challenge is to work to develop yourself and to be a role model for change in others.

Some people are willing to take a chance on love and others are more discerning. When you fall in love, however, to some degree you are casting your own destiny. Some people are bold and daring and willing to risk it all on love. Others are so cautious they never experience all there is to know. In between those two extremes are people who use good judgment and make wise decisions. Love is a blending and joining of emotions and intellect. The advice of the ancient astrologers was for the more impulsive Sun signs not to marry too young, and for the overly cautious individuals not to wait too long.

It is a serious subject. But much thanks are owed to its Inventor for also making love such an enjoyable and rewarding endeavor. Without love, our hopes and dreams are only that. Love brings reality, inspiration, and beauty into our lives. The reality of our strongest emotions transformed into inspiration and beauty.

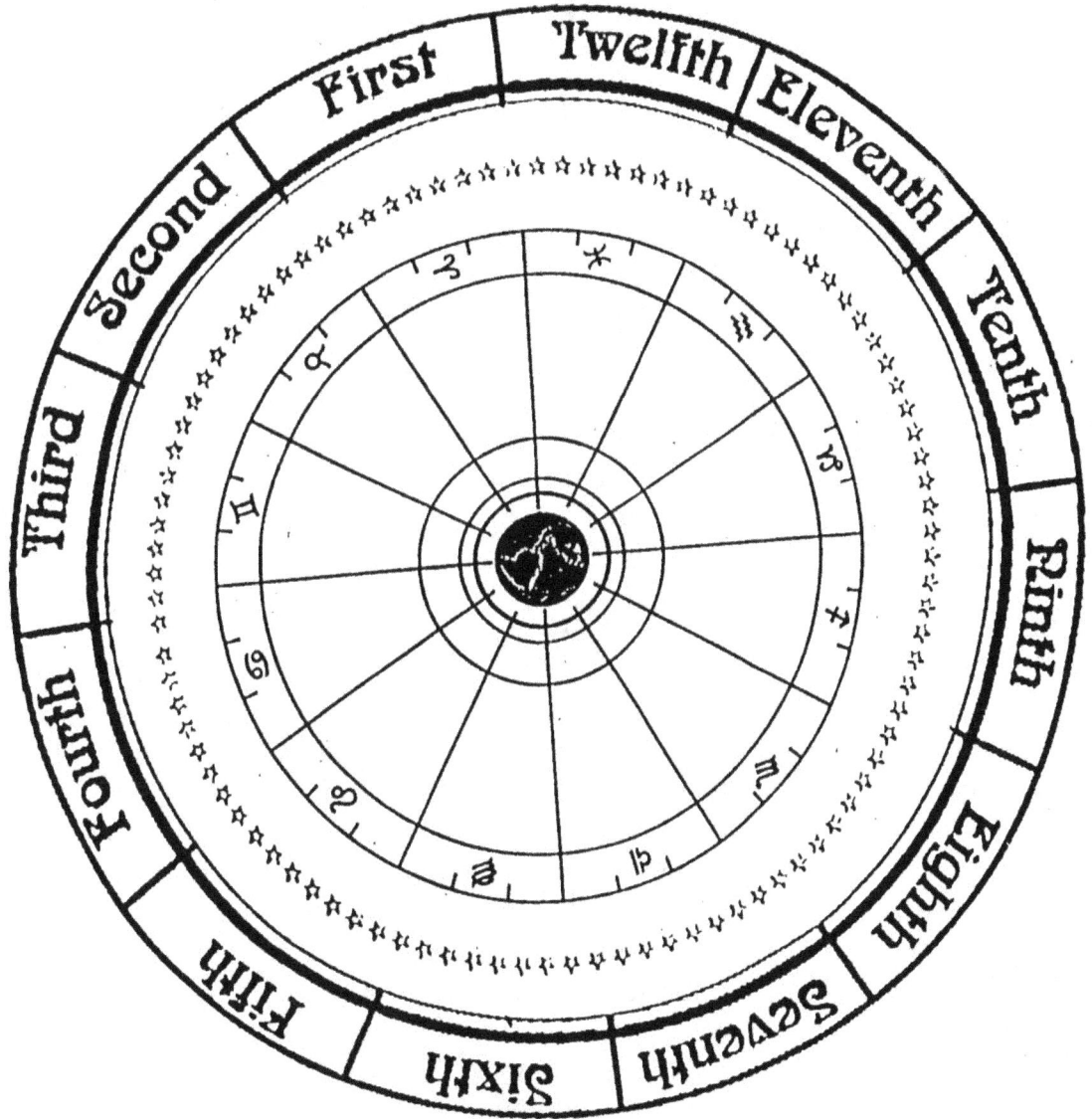

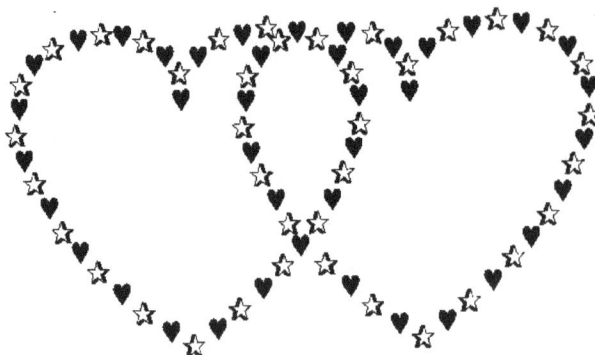

ARIES WOMAN - ARIES MAN
LOVE RELATIONSHIPS & COMPATIBILITIES

The combination of these two Fire signs may result in a combustible combination of energy, drive and enthusiasm with no one around to put on the brakes. There no doubt will be a shared empathy for each other's positive, open nature and extravagant, impulsive behavior. Their courage and drive will result in more plans and endeavors than either could envision alone.

He will strive to lead and maintain control over the relationship while being passionate, caring and generous. She will attempt to lead and maintain control while being loyal, supportive and appreciative of his efforts. He wants more than anything to be loved and appreciated, and she wants love, attention, and devotion. What they share in common is the ability to keep up with each other's outgoing, social, and fun loving ways. Both want to be on the go, experiencing life, meeting people, and leading an active life. Both appreciate the finer things in life and want their home to be well arranged, attractive, and suitable for entertaining. And both are passionate, explorative, uninhibited and ardent in the bedroom.

What problems could possibly exist? Combustible energy does just that. When these two Rams meet head on the result could be fireworks. Deciding who is going to lead, control, and dominate between two people who by nature are so inclined can easily lead to some interesting tugs of war. As much as they love each other, someone must decide how to reconcile the great question of who is winning the latest battle. It isn't a question of who is right and who is wrong. A Ram needs to win in any contest, and for many a Ram, life is an ongoing contest. Pacifying the Aries personality requires a gentle, kind and accepting hand. Neither can accept criticism which is a mighty blow to the Aries ego and pride. This combination requires two highly developed personalities who are capable of realizing that relationships are based on the give and take of compromise. If he realizes and appreciates that she is an independent, assertive woman quite capable of handling responsibilities, leadership, and decision making, this relationship stands a chance. She must realize, however, that he, with his fear of being rejected, has a strong need to control in order to feel secure. Both may have a strong preference for the seduction of making up after the battle which can result in bliss and a refreshed optimism and hopefulness that all will be well in the future. Between two highly developed individuals this could be a most productive combination. The endlessly, enthusiastic flair of ideas in their personal, business and social life

100

spells a constant rush of excitement. That neither gives much thought to the consequences of rash decisions on the long term could result in a roller coaster ride through life, but at least there will be no one around wishing it otherwise. These two possess the ability to accept in each other what someone else might see as fault.

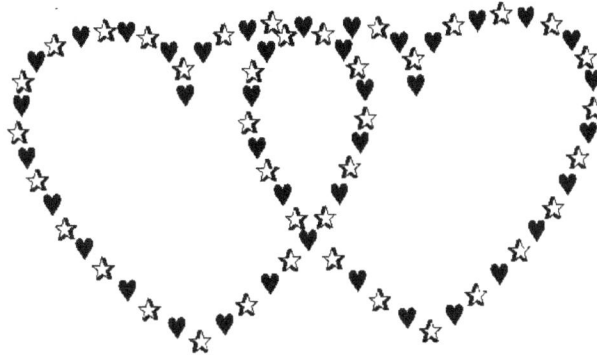

Aries Woman - Taurus Man
Love Relationships & Compatibilities

The Taurus man will appreciate an Aries woman who enthusiastically champions and supports his efforts. His is a Fixed, Earth sign, and he is patient, loving, kind, and tenaciously hard working. Hers is a Cardinal, Fire sign and she will follow him to the end of the world, devoted and loyal. They are both ardently passionate and she delights in creatively satisfying his earthy desires.

What this Taurus man must remember is that she is an idea person and driven to impulsively exploring the possibilities in life. What the Aries woman must remember is that he takes his time, deliberating and desiring all decisions to well thought out. She may push and pull and even demand the exciting alternatives in life while he remains firmly entrenched on a path that best produces results and security. She may jump to a decision immediately. He will want to think about it. And what Aries must remember about Taurus is that there is no amount of pushing or demanding that will persuade this individual to make up his mind before he's ready or to change his mind. He can be literally as fixed as the Earth. His patience, however, is unmatched by any other sign. He will endure her persistence, listen calmly to her arguments or persuasion, and refuse to budge against his decisions. If she's smart, at this point she'll rethink her demands, but there's every possibility that her fiery temper will lash out at the very thought of her demands not being met. And then this patient and understanding Bull may expose his own explosive temperament that has been simmering quietly below the surface. Fireworks doesn't accurately describe the results. Aries are known for fireworks. And when her fireworks fizzle out she'll be happy to forgive and forget. But whoever has experienced facing down an angry Bull will know she's in for a big surprise when this man loses his temper.

A smart Aries woman will recognize the strength of her Bull lover, and the positive qualities that he brings to the relationship. His may be a slower tempo compared to extroverted Aries, but he is dependable. And a smart Aries man will recognize that her driving desire for a little excitement in life adds a nice spark to the daily routine. Taurus is the sign of possessions, and she will probably find that her every material need is provided. All this couple really needs to decide is who is going to lead and make the decisions. Once that is settled, he can provide the steady hand needed by the idea a minute Aries intellect. She can provide the love and self-confidence that Taurus needs to feel secure.

This couple, as is the case with many pairs, will need to be well enough developed to be capable of working out their differences in a manner that builds a lasting relationship.

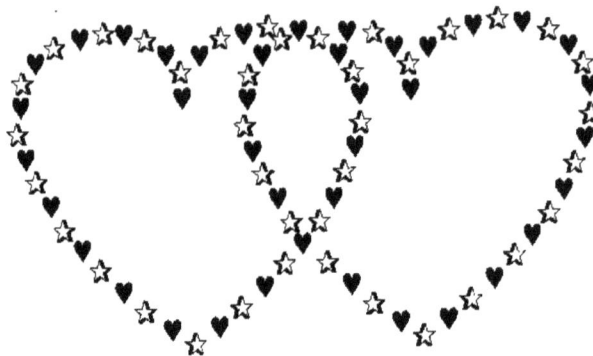

ARIES MAN - TAURUS WOMAN
LOVE RELATIONSHIPS & COMPATIBILITIES

As an Aries man, if you are looking for an attractive, romantic, passionate partner who can add steadfastness and stability to your relationship, the Taurus woman may suit your needs. And if you, the Taurus woman, are looking for a man who is intensely ardent and who can provide the initiative, direction, and plan for the future, then look no further. You share a desire for a pleasant, well-run and comfortable home and living arrangement.

She wants a home for security and comfort and may enjoy spending time there relaxing and pursuing her interests. He wants a place to come home to after he's exhausted his energies pursuing his other plans and activities, and he loves to entertain, especially guests who may have an interest in his future plans. The Taurus strength may endow her with enough energy to keep up with this adventurous spirit, but she may not share the desire to be always on the go and in the fast lane. He craves the bright lights and being where the action is while she may be just as happy contentedly sitting by the home fires. If she patiently waits for her man to return, he will. If she becomes disconcerted with his need for other people in his life, this couple will face strife and disharmony. Nothing is going to slow this man down. And nothing is going to speed up the deliberate pace of this lovely, feminine creature.

Finances are important to each person in this relationship. She seeks financial security, and he seeks finances for his latest plan. She wants money in the bank, and he wants money in his pocket. They both desire material possessions. For her, they are tangible proof of security. For him, possessions are a proof to others of his self-worth and manhood. After the necessary possessions, she may want an IRA, mutual fund, and retirement plan. He may need above all else an impressive car, boat, or plane.

He may demand control of their social, business, and personal affairs, but this woman will slowly build on what she decides is best for all concerned. And no matter how high tempers may flair, he's spouting fury uselessly against a will that cannot be forced. They share strong, energetic passions and if he can turn his well-planned fantasies toward sensual earthy desires, then she can match his erotic drive. They both may possess a fun loving sense of humor, but she must remember that he can't handle criticism not even in jest. She must also accept that he never lies because he sincerely and adamantly believes that whatever he says is true, correct, and right. And she will be able to keep count on one hand the number of times he admits to a fault. She will provide a patient and listening ear to his endless stories about himself, and he will provide all the excitement in life that she could ever desire. The longevity of this relationship may depend on these two people focusing their mutually strong will powers on maintaining the relationship.

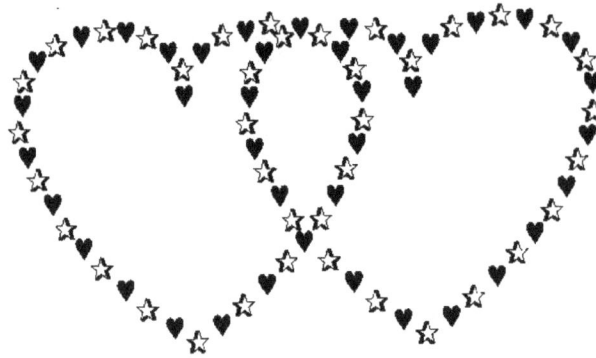

ARIES WOMAN - GEMINI MAN

LOVE RELATIONSHIPS & COMPATIBILITIES

Do not plan on tying this man down, and do not plan on dominating this woman. The two of you may share a love for fun, people, and exciting adventures. You both crave new and stimulating encounters with as many people, ideas and activities as possible. You are as active mentally as you are physically, and when this Aries female recognizes the Gemini man's need for mental stimulation there's no doubt she can match his desires and wishes. Neither of you waste time worrying over the long term outcome, fretting about what-ifs. You respond to a mutual attraction, trust your desires, and happily enjoy the moment while optimistically trusting that all will work out in the future.

She delights in his perpetually boyish grin, that bounce to his step and the magical twinkle in his eyes. They both share courage, initiative, energy and ambition. And a Gemini may be just the man who best appreciates and admires a strong-willed, assertive woman who challenges him mentally. In fact, he may encourage these traits seeing them as offering new opportunities rather than limitations. And besides, neither are overly impressed with convention. She may at times expect direct answers and actions, but this man will merely size up the situation and entertainingly dance around the Aries determination. Gemini, the communicator, is capable though of clearly expressing not only his desires and optimism but also his contempt and criticisms. But while his quick and sarcastic retorts may offend her pride and her willfulness may be too demanding, these two will not allow disagreements to slow them down for long. Both ate inclined to make-up, forgive and forget, and many of their disagreements may be fleeting as their attention and interest jumps to something new. She may be jealous and defensively possessive, but her Aries temperament may keep her too busy to observe all of his charming flirtations which he really can't avoid. He'll compensate by joining in and adding to her sexual delights and fantasies with both of them uninhibitedly exploring exciting heights of ecstasy. She and he alike will desire a large degree of freedom and personal space combined with love, admiration and acceptance. And if they choose to combine their abilities to communicate, persuade and sell their ideas, these two could face few boundaries to their potentials. They both love to be on the go and to entertain with a mutual desire for an attractive and comfortable ho-me setting. This is the couple who may with little fuss design separate financing which allows them both independence and mobility. The dynamic Aries woman will be enchanted by the ingenuity of personable Gemini. His Twin personality will more than add that spice to life that her explorative nature seeks. A strong mutual attraction and admiration between these two could quite well result in a lasting relationship.

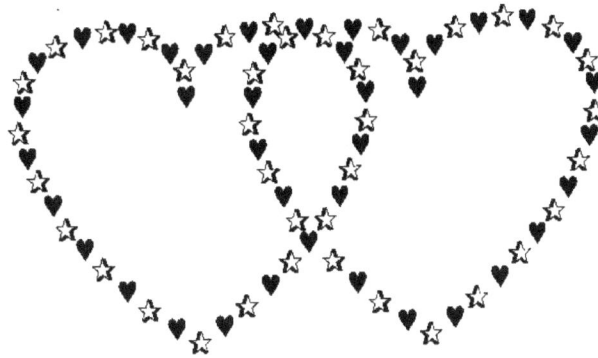

ARIES MAN - GEMINI WOMAN
LOVE RELATIONSHIPS & COMPATIBILITIES

The Gemini woman may be more than happy to allow the Aries man to think he is in total control. After all, she knows better. And the Aries man may delight in watching this woman bounce from one endeavor or activity to another. After all, that would be a woman after his own heart. Personable and sociable, neither of them would bore with talking about themselves and sharing the stories of their daily adventures. If she most desires a courageous protector who will relentlessly defend her against the challenges in life, this is the man for her. If he most wants a woman who can entertain his thoughts and passion while providing more of her own, this is she. In many ways, theirs may be a journey of exploring the possibilities and plausibilities in life. But attempting to figure out her elusive Twin personality will keep him spellbound. And attempting to follow his direct and straightforward direction, which is always changing with a bright new idea, will keep her anticipating tomorrow. Neither is afraid of change and both respond to the surge of energy derived from new undertakings. His Fire sign nature may thrive on the added energy of her Air sign. She thrives on congenial companionship, his and others. He can be jealous and possessive, wanting what is his firmly under his control. There's every possibility he's not the most faithful of men, but he demands just that from the woman in his life. If too demanding, he can drive her into a tizzy, but both will want to reconcile, makeup, and get on with life. Both can be charming and delightful when in public, and if this carries over at home, these two will share a mutual appreciation for each other. Happily impulsive, their whims will also fascinate the other person. That they may need a financial advisor is beside the point. She can be whoever he desires in the bedroom, and each will challenge the other in sensual antics. She will expertly counter his control-moves deciding for herself whether to allow him to make her over into a person of his own creation. He may find his mind too preoccupied with her dual nature to ever be disenchanted. The challenge for these two will be to accept each other as they are. He is aspiring, demanding, controlling, and self centered, and no amount of criticism will change him. She is as flexible and variable as the wind, and no amount of control will contain her, not happily anyway. The strength of this relationship is in what this couple share, and that is an adventuresome, exploring, seeking outlook on life. If they share common interests, objectives, values, and desires, then this couple has every chance of making a go of it. She expertly handles his egotistical Ram nature, and he rewards her with appreciating her changeability. That neither is tied to convention only adds spice to their love.

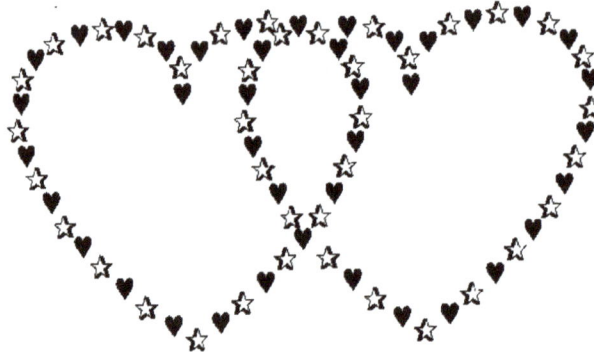

ARIES WOMAN - CANCER MAN
LOVE RELATIONSHIPS & COMPATIBILITIES

The heart of the Aries woman will be captivated by this enchantingly sensual and romantic Cancer man. He is imaginatively creative and shares her ability to be loyal and devoted. He possesses a subtly alluring magnetic charm that attracts her attention, and at the same time he is drawn to her electrically charged enthusiasm and strength. He admires her independent nature and wherever they go, he watches in admiration as she asserts herself toward the center of attention. Quieter and more cautious, he asserts himself less directly, in a round about fashion, but he gets where he's going with the same measure of success (if not more). If he's a well developed Cancer man, he'll know better than to attempt to harness the drive of her forceful nature. And if she's a well developed Aries woman, she'll know better than to attempt to invade this man's personal space. And they'll both have to be well developed in order to live together. The Aries woman may have her moods, but she springs back every morning with renewed hope and enthusiasm ready and eager to face the world. If she allows herself to be affected by his Cancer moods, or if she for a moment thinks that his moods are in any way related to her, she may find herself thrown off balance. His moodiness is beyond her influence or control, and there's nothing she can do but accept his periods of withdrawal as a part of his basic nature. He requires periods of isolation, to himself, to think and reflect and to allow his free-flowing mental processes and imagination to run its nature course. It would be impossible for him to allow another person into this private world of his own creation. If she's truly an independent woman, she'll go her own way and allow him his space. He is discerning and can be critical which may prick her Aries pride. And he is so sensitive that he can perceive any form of discussion on a personal level as some form of criticism. If she flashes her famous Aries temperament, he'll watch her in amazement then withdraw from the situation allowing time for the situation to change, but leaving her dissatisfied and frustrated with the outcome. She cannot win against his passivity, and an Aries needs to win. But being passive and cautious doesn't mean he can be controlled, and if she thinks differently she's only fooling herself. That is one possible outcome of this match, but if this couple is lucky enough to have positive Sun-MoonAscendant aspects, there is every possibility that this can develop into a lasting and rewarding relationship with Cancer creatively focusing the Aries drive into attaining home, financial security and success. Her extravagant "live for today" attitude will be balanced by his need to find security through planning for tomorrow.

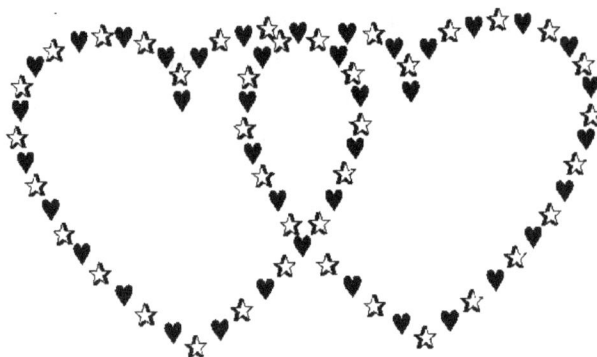

Aries Man - Cancer Woman
Love Relationships & Compatibilities

The Aries man may think he's found the perfect embodiment of femininity in this alluring, innocent, yielding and romantic woman. And the Cancer woman will feel like she's discovered a rock of strength to provide, care for, and to protect her. She is more than capable of giving him all the admiration he ever dreamed of, and she will come to depend on him, clinging to him for support. They may both be somewhat jealous and possessive wanting the total devotion of the other person. But Aries sooner or later will want his freedom to come and go as he pleases, and she'll want her personal space. When she withdraws into her moods, her periods of isolation, or her inward perspective, he feel at a loss to maintain control over her. And when he's too busy with his numerous activities to attend to her, she'll feel dejected. She can be charming, pleasant and sociable enough to please him, but not even she can control her moodiness. Sooner or later, the Aries man will spout forth his indignation, relying on his temperamental outbursts to settle all disagreements, and then he'll be faced with the Cancer's extreme sensitivity to anything the least bit unpleasant. Her moods may bring on his nervous tension headaches, and his temper may cause her nervous upset stomach. But with any luck at all, her tears will dampen the Aries temper, and if she doesn't withdraw from the situation altogether, she can allow him to soothe her wounded feelings in an amorous makeup session. Sex always improves the disposition of the Aries man, to him it will appear as a natural outcome to any disagreements between them. If she chooses to allow him to think he's in control, he'll be happy. But the truth be known, it's more than likely that no one ever really gets inside the shell of a Crab, let alone controls them. Her need for home and financial security can make her less gregarious than this Aries man, but then few people are as people-oriented as Aries. His tendency to be extravagant, believing there's always more where that came from, will leave her feeling insecure. To feel secure, this woman must have financial security and a home. The Aries man feels secure as long as he's got a plan in the works and he's actively engaged in an endeavor of his own making. Can these two work out their differences? That depends on how well developed each individual is and on the aspects of their Sun-Moon-Ascendant signs. No one can tell an Aries anything, he's always right. In this situation, if he figures out for himself that he is in control of everything but her, it may work. And if she can accept and admire him the way he is, this relationship may work. For true happiness, she may need to plan for her own financial security because their outlook on financial planning will always be different. She must want to stand by her man, support his every plan and effort, and make him feel secure and wanted on the home front. But most importantly, she'll have to come to terms with dealing with his temper. He must be capable of allowing this woman time to herself, admiring her for who she is, and appreciating her many creative talents. The Cancer woman desires kindness and admiration. The Aries man desires admiration and total devotion.

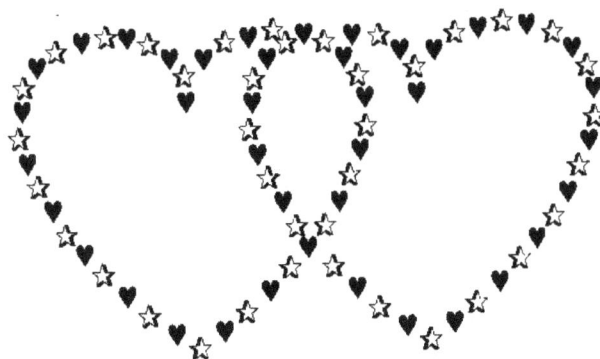

ARIES WOMAN - LEO MAN
LOVE RELATIONSHIPS & COMPATIBILITIES

This should be one for the movies. The lowly remainder of the Zodiac could sit back and watch these two representatives of the Fire signs arrogantly battle it out. A perceptive Aries female may realize that she has finally met her match, and an insightful Leo man will acknowledge that this is a woman whose passions equal his own. Both are gregarious, outgoing, fun loving, compassionate, caring and capable of kindness and generosity. And both share a love of elegant, even luxurious, and comfortable surroundings. Most importantly, both desire the spotlight. But while the Aries woman will utilize every ounce of her energy and strength to fulfill her aspirations, the Leo man will effortlessly claim what he perceives as being rightfully his, almost as a birthright. His dramatic flair and magnetism propels him to the center of attention, while Aries must strive to obtain just such a position. This may be what attracts her to him in the first place, and if this attraction turns into admiration, affection, devotion, appreciation, and love, he will respond in a most positive manner. He, on the other hand, needs an independent woman who can stand on her own, beside him, supporting and adding to his auspicious nature. If they can find a spotlight big enough for the both of them, this will be a happy couple. Actually, they have every chance of a happy relationship anyway once they determine who is the leader, who is going to dominate, and who is in control. No doubt, while this process is going on, there will be some exciting fireworks, tempers will flair, and the display of strong emotions will be endless. She will be dismayed to discover a man who effortlessly claims dominion over her, and in his condescending manner he will do just that. But while she possesses all the fiery energy of Mars, he possesses the might of the Lion endowed with the energy of the Sun. If and when he turns his kind-hearted warmth toward providing her the attention she desires, she will respond if full measure. These two people have every possibility of understanding the nature of the other person. And this understanding can easily develop into an intense and passionate affection. They may grow to understand, admire, and respect each other's nature because they may see themselves, to some degree, in the other person. The Lion's roar can easily be subdued by an Aries female who chooses to devote her efforts in that direction. And the Aries drive, however impulsive, can be directed and channeled by the more practical minded and organized Leo nature. Once these two decide on their goals in life, their biggest challenge may be finding the time to fulfill their aspirations and to participate in all of the activities which interest them.

ARIES MAN - LEO WOMAN
LOVE RELATIONSHIPS & COMPATIBILITIES

The vitality of these two will amaze onlookers, and their matching egos will delight each other. They share warm, personable natures with extroverted, sociable desires. Both are generous to a fault, but both may want to be recognized and appreciated for their generosity. However different their approaches, they both shine best in the limelight of admiration and attention. They also share strong wills, a fiery temper, an indomitable spirit, and the need to dominate and control the situation. It may be his plan, his contacts, and his pursuits, but she was born to authoritative leadership. She will have to accept that the Aries man doesn't even know that he's demanding, and he will have to be perceptive enough to realize that her regal manner is her most natural bearing. He may pour his energies into forceful demands or simply resort to a louder voice, but she will use her aloof condescending assertiveness to put him firmly in his place. His selfesteem may suffer until he acknowledges just how much this dynamic woman excites him. These two share other qualities including a self-centered selfishness that can't be helped, an overblown vanity, pride, and arrogance. He may become too overly involved in his plans and endeavors to give her adequate attention, and she may forget to listen attentively enough to his monologues. The positive side to all of this is once they recognize and accept the strengths and weakness in each other, they share the ability to be mutually appreciative. Here is a kindred spirit who understands an aggressive, willful, and aspiring nature. She will admire his determination and strength. He will admire her regal charm and personable nature. This is a good match as long as this couple can amiable share common interests, goals, and aspirations. Once they reconcile their differences and agree to who is going to lead on what day in what area of their lives, they'll discover the loyal devotion they 'most desire. There's a certain amount of magic and excitement between these two Fire signs which ignites in their love making. Both are sensual beings who love to explore with combustible energies. Both can be jealous and possessive, but he can pamper her beyond belief and she is more than capable of responding in like manner. one of them will have to take a firm grip on finances, probably practical Leo, because both are known for their extravagances. These two people optimistically love life and being surrounded by other people. They love to socialize and to entertain, delighting in being the perfect host and hostess. And both aspire to the good life lived in style and comfort.

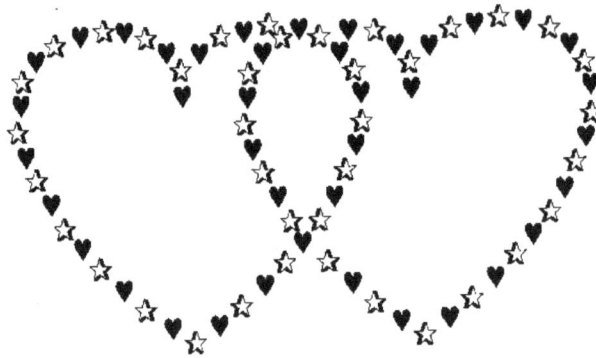

Aries Woman - Virgo Man

Love Relationships & Compatibilities

An Aries woman who decides on a Virgo man will have to curb her impulsive nature and at least appear to be sensible and cautious. The Virgo man can easily take caution to an extreme. He is detail-oriented, gathers facts, figures, and information and makes careful decisions. He doesn't have the slightest idea of how to be rash or to live for the excitement of the moment. He may even go so far as to tell her that if she doesn't learn how to make reasonable decisions, no man will ever want to marry her. She'll have to apply all of her energies to captivating this man because he's as cautious in love as in all other areas of life. He will admire her independent nature and her accomplishments. And before and after love makes them blind to each other's shortcomings, she will discover the best friend she could ever wish for. He may take control of her impetuous ways out of sheer determination and tenacity of which he has endless supplies. He has the energy to keep up with her social urges, but she may discover that he can be quite discerning about who to socialize with. They both share high aspirations, wanting a peaceful and lovely home and the means to provide it. He is more security conscious and willing to work hard to achieve what he wants in life. If she can appreciate his strengths, this relationship may work. But he can be critical and fault finding, and defensive Aries may not know how to accept this blow to her pride. He may see her temperamental flair ups as so much hot air and not be impressed in the least. She'll have to resort to persuasion or kindness or even learn to spout facts, figures and research data before he's swayed to her viewpoint. What these two share is a desire for appreciation and admiration, and if they can build on that they will also share a mutual and strong love. Virgo is more than passionate enough, but he may not fully understand the Aries need for thrill, excitement, and antics straight out of fantasy. Neither will he ever understand her extravagant spending sprees and her inability to save for tomorrow. Virgo isn't above shopping for fun, that is, after he has a healthy bank account, savings account, investment program, and a secure retirement plan. He can offer her security, but whether or not he can give her an adequate amount of attention, she'll have to discern for herself. She can add a magical spice to his life which, if he appreciates that quality, can make her indispensable. These two may find that they have to work on their relationship. To a large degree, the successful outcome of this relationship will depend upon the personal willingness of each person to devote their efforts to making it work, the development of each person, and on the other aspects in their birth charts. Both of them have much to offer the other person.

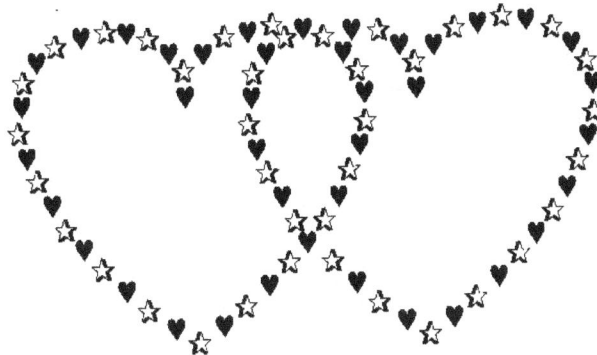

ARIES MAN - VIRGO WOMAN
LOVE RELATIONSHIPS & COMPATIBILITIES

The outcome of this pairing depends upon whether these two people bring out the best in each other or the worst. They both mean well, but they have different approaches to life. This Aries man can turn on so much charm and warmth that the Virgo female will think she as at last met the man of her dreams. And in her he'll find the devoted helpmate he's always desired. But while Aries is generous and helpful to others because it makes him feel good about himself, Virgo is a trusted and true friend who comes to the assistance of others out of a sense of responsibility. He impulsively initiates his ideas and plans, pouring every ounce of his energy and drive into forceful action. She looks at the plan and itemizes all the reasons why it won't work. Aries isn't preoccupied with whether or not his plans will work. of course they'll work, and if they don't it's someone else's fault anyway (probably hers for not believing in him). His optimism and warmth may soothe her pessimism and fears, and Virgo's practical approach to life may teach him a thing or two. Virgo will be quietly sentimental and somewhere in a back closet will be a stack of photo albums dating back to infancy. Aries too can tell you (endlessly) about his childhood experiences, but if he has mementos it's because someone else has collected and stored them for him. With this Aries man, she must be careful not to ever appear to be taking someone elsels side because this is exactly how he'll interpret any criticism of his decisions and actions. She is either for him or against him. He wants (demands) total commitment, and if he can get it, total submission and control. It's best for her to use gentle persuasion with this man, carefully molding her opinions, observations and criticisms into suggestions. If not, then she should be prepared to have him look at her like she's lost her mind. Then he'll either explode in a torrent of fury or decide to pout until she sees things his way, or he'll do both. Aries would have to be perceptive enough to see the sensitive, delightfully imaginative inner person of this Virgo female, and she would have to sense that this man can only be the way he is. They will have to accept each other and appreciate the good qualities inherent in both people. She derives pleasure from being of service to others, and

113

he expects to be served. If he's smart enough to appreciate all her efforts to please him, and if she truly admires him just the way he is, they'll make a lovely couple. That is, if he isn't too wrapped up in his business and social activities to pay her enough attention, and if she doesn't resort to nagging and carping. There is every possibility that the Aries enthusiasm for life will excite her in the bedroom, and he will find her devoted passion a sweet release. These two must make a mutual commitment to work on the relationship, but if their degree of loyalty is a match then so is the relationship.

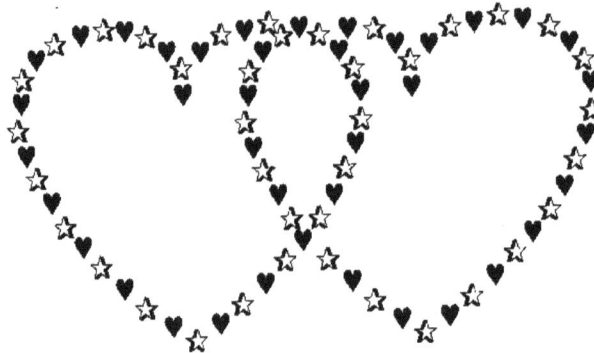

Aries Woman - Libra Man
Love Relationships & Compatibilities

Here we find two charming, intelligent, outgoing, and optimistic people who bring to the relationship what the other lacks. Aries offers excitement and challenge while Libra is endowed with balance, peace, and tranquility. Will these two opposites in the Zodiac find an equilibrium that balances out their relationship? The prospects are positive. This Aries woman will finally have met a man who can smoothly out talk her in the most pleasant of ways without ruffling her feathers at the same time. He knows intuitively to use gentle persuasion earmarked with the sincerest of praise and even flattery (Aries is susceptible to flattery). And she literally excites him beyond belief. He is magnetically drawn to her energy, drive, and impulsive actions which promise never a dull moment. Both are active, social creatures who love being surrounded by people. Both desire the finer things in life and pleasant, comfortable surroundings (although his taste may be more refined while hers are more ostentatious). She will have to accept his occasional indecisiveness, and he will have to expect the quickness with which she arrives at any decision. Libra isn't a control freak, but he will want decisions to make sense, and he can list pros and cons, endlessly attempting to find the perfect balance, selection, choice, or direction. He may be perfectly happy to have her make as many decisions as she likes, even to take the lead, but she will have to display the ability to make good judgments. She will have to develop just enough patience to explain her actions to him, then he'll be content to try anything once (Libras are easily persuaded once you know how, but it's best to entice them with fun rather than to attempt force or ultimatums). He is a good listener, wanting to learn all there is to know about this energy-driven woman, and he is capable of giving her all the attention she ever desired. She may have at last found that perfect person to whom she can truly and fully devote herself with no reservations. She will have to accept that as sociable as her Libra man is, there are times when he loses his energy and interest in being on the go. Then he'll want to take a break, find total relaxation, peace and quiet, and she'll be 'more than welcome to share these moments with him. He will have to accept that her need to be on the go is insatiable, and there will be times when its best to just wish her well and let her go to her heart's desire. Gentle kindness are the way to this woman's heart, and he possesses those qualities in abundance. She must remember that he prefers not to argue, but he does have a temper which is best left undisturbed (all that tranquility may cover a lot of repressed frustration and anger). He must remember that her stormy temperamental outbursts blow out as rapidly as they start, and underneath that fiery temper is a heart that burns just as warmly. There love making equates to total attention from both parties. As with all relationships, there are variables that can effect this one, but these two people may share a mutual attraction and a strong love for one another.

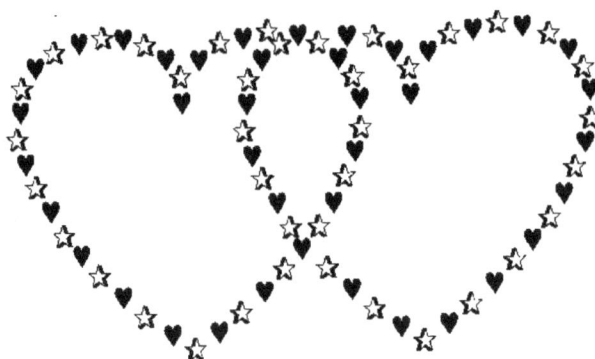

Aries Man - Libra Woman
Love Relationships & Compatibilities

This man will balance her scales for sure then take his time tilting them ever which way he can. But it was his hint at exciting adventure that captured her heart in the first place. While she won't ever understand his selfcentered and selfish ways, she is capable of appreciating his more positive traits and what she perceives as the goodness in his heart. The Libra woman won't submit to his controlling tendencies as much as she'll know intuitively how to manage his ego-driven and combustible nature. She'll oooh and aah, smothering his fiery temperamental outbursts with a charm reserved especially for him. He may talk louder, but she'll only wait him out, and then talk smarter, having aligned her facts and figures into a nice persuasive package. He'll think he's in control as she pampers him into submission. And Libra is more than capable of listening to her Aries man recite his endless monologues about himself, knowing full well that he's exposing just the information she needs to deal with him in the future. Her intentions are the best, and hopefully his are too. They can both turn on the charm and love entertaining, socializing, pleasurable and fun experiences, and the pleasant surroundings of home. She loves the way he wants to provide for and to protect her, but she may question always being named last on his list of possessions, somewhere after the house, boat, car, plane, and dog. But then once committed, he takes for granted that she is his for keeps. To achieve harmony, he may have to realize that his mischievous streak, little pranks, and instigating remarks can jar her out of her tranquility, resulting in even this mild mannered Libra woman losing her temper. She must accept that she has to abide his strong nature, and that from time to time she'll have to stand firm against his impetuous ways. He may feel that he can finally relax in the arms of a woman who strives for peace and harmony. Aries will have to recognize that this special package of femininity needs time off from the hustle and bustle of life to reaffirm her tranquil balance. And he shouldn't be overly dismayed if she responds to his long string of requests and demands with the quiet suggestion that they put it all off until tomorrow and simply enjoy today. They can both be impulsive, especially if there is fun and pleasure in the offering, but he will soon note her ability to postpone decisions for an indefinite period of time. Their escapades in the bedroom will leave each desiring the other all the more. And if their desire to live with each other is strong enough, these two will learn to balance their relationship successfully.

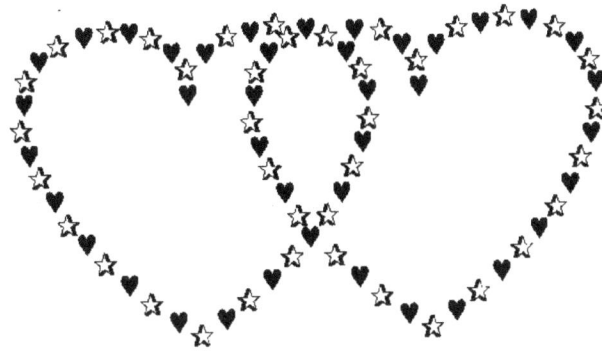

ARIES WOMAN - SCORPIO MAN
LOVE RELATIONSHIPS & COMPATIBILITIES

As an Aries female, have you ever stared into the blue depths of a body of water and wondered what mysteries were hidden beneath the surface? Did you for even a moment think you could control that body of water? Being Aries perhaps you are vain enough to think you can, and being that you aren't one to easily accept directions, you may not listen to this advice. However, be forewarned, you cannot control a Scorpio man. At first meeting, there may be an instant attraction between these two.. He knows intuitively that she's actively adventuresome in the bedroom, and she feels mystified by the mutual magnetism between them. He may think her superficial and less perceptive than himself, but he will admire her independent nature, assertiveness, energy and drive. She offers that element of excitement that all Scorpios are drawn to regardless of what mask they present to the public. He spends a life time coming to terms with secrets unfathomable by the other signs of the Zodiac. He's curious and drawn to mystery, investigations, and research. And he reads other people well. How does the Aries female capture his heart? She may want to let down her defenses, forget her fears of rejection, and display her warm, direct, honest, and loving ways. Being those are traits they share in common, he will respond in like manner. Aries is rash and impulsive, but if she can take two minutes to explain her actions and decisions, he'll probably allow her all the freedom she desires. Control might be an overstatement with Scorpio men. Perhaps it's more that he's glanced ahead, already considered the outcome of any given situation, and planned the best way to proceed. If he's truly perceptive, he'll realize she doesn't think that way, and he'll allow her the freedom to experience and discover life. He must remember she doesn't realize she speaks in that demanding voice, and she must remember that behind what appears as control, he means well and has her best interest at heart. He's as unpredictable as she is impulsive, but he's spent his life working on self-control and self development which allows him to deal with life intellectually rather than through his intensely emotional nature. He may shrug off her little impetuous flairs of fireworks, but she doesn't want to push him too far or make him lose his temper because then he loses his self-control, and in anger his mind works differently than hers. Long after she's forgotten what the argument was about, he'll remember. Whether Aries has met a quiet, reserved Scorpio or one as gregarious as herself, he'll want his space and freedom. He can be possessive and jealous, but this won't be a problem if he feels he can trust her completely. He may be happy with her controlling her own life, just don't try to control his. He is masculine, virile, and highly sexed. She wants to be sure he's a well-developed person because Scorpio can take her to the heights of spiritual enlightenment or the depths of emotional despair. Aries, on the other hand, is capable of offering true devotion or pure exasperation.

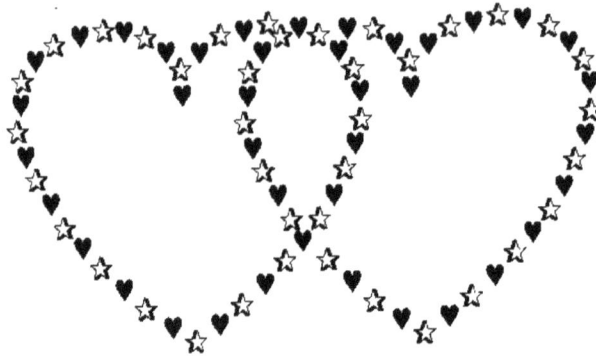

ARIES MAN - SCORPIO WOMAN
LOVE RELATIONSHIPS & COMPATIBILITIES

What is that enigmatic quality that draws an Aries man to a Scorpio woman? He must know he can never control her. He'll spend months telling her she's finally met a real man who can handle her. The truth be known, perhaps this fiery macho-ego driven man likes the relaxation of having someone else take control once in awhile, even dominate him a little. of course, he's not going to admit that. He won't believe the audacity she has to challenge his command, and then he'll keep coming back for more and more. She appears fearless and even laughs at his temperamental outbursts. Not even his tactless criticism rattles her into submission. Surely, he knows that Scorpio is silently working on selfimprovement, and she has already focused her analytical skills on herself. His tried and true control techniques won't work. What they share is a love of a dare, thrills, excitement, adventure, and exploring new territory. She is that mystery he can never quite comprehend nor predict. She is as compulsive as he is impulsive, and she will use all of her endurance to see a cause through to the end. And she will definitely see this self-centered, ego-driven man as a cause. Actually, Scorpio is drawn to strong egos and admires strength and courage, and she will overlook many a short coming if she is impressed with his power and might. She will expect, however, that he exhibit self improvement. Secretive? Perhaps protective is a better word. If he were open to listening, she might reveal what she's observed about this life and beyond. But being that he is caught up with the distractions of this life, chances are she can keep her secrets, and he'll never notice. She is jealous and possessive and doesn't want to hear him recite the names of the beautiful loves of his life, not repeatedly anyway. He is jealous and possessive, and if he's planning on adding her to his list of possessions, he should either forget it or at least list her first. Intrigue, mystery, fantasy, and excitement follow these two into the bedroom where she never fails to arouse his passion. He should not intentionally make her mad, especially for the fun of it. She remembers an injury and waits until the most opportune time to sting in retaliation. Revengeful? No, not at all. She only wants to teach a lesson, perhaps a string of lessons, and he should be prepared to learn. If he is at all perceptive, he'll take her along on social outings with business prospects, where she'll sit quietly in the background (Scorpio prefers to work on the side lines not in the center of attention). Afterwards, she can report who is friend, serious, sincere, or self-seeking. A well developed Scorpio woman, whether quiet and reserved or pleasantly outgoing, is a person of her own making. Does he want to make her over? He would be better off attempting to grow up and improve himself. This woman is capable of being a devoted, one man woman through thick and thin. To work, this relationship requires mutual honesty, devotion, kindness, caring, love, and these two should both forget about the control.

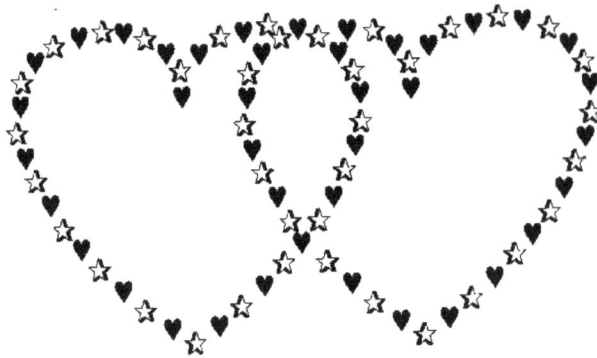

ARIES WOMAN - SAGITTARIUS MAN
LOVE RELATIONSHIPS & COMPATIBILITIES

The Aries woman and Sagittarius man share the natural affinity and friendship of two Fire signs. She will feel lucky with this Jupiter graced man who is as expansive as she is assertive. Her independent drive is just fine with him as he desires freedom even more than she does. He is cheerful, accepting, and optimistic, bringing out the best in her warm and caring nature. His mind takes a philosophical bend, and he seeks knowledge, experiences, and information. Both are energetically on the go, love new experiences, and are fond of pleasurable activities. If she shares his love of sports, music, or art, and outdoor activities,, they will have even more in common. Neither like restrictions, but this is especially important to him. He possesses a desire for the freedom to explore. Travel entices him, and these two can make the best of traveling companions. They are both fun loving individuals and people oriented. He is a true friend's friend, and will go to great lengths for a friend in need. She is also known for her generous qualities, and both will come to the aid of others. He enjoys the sights as much as she, but he may be less drawn to a crowd and may have little desire to be the center of attention. He says what's on his mind and can be well meaning but blunt and direct in speech, diplomacy not being his strong suit. She is also direct and open about her opinions, and both consider themselves right. She is right because she needs to be while he is right probably because he's well informed on the subject. Generally speaking, his honesty doesn't bother her unless his remarks are aimed at her. Then tempers may flair, but these two are both forgive and forget types who express their thoughts then keep on moving. He is more self-assured and selfconfident, perhaps from all that intuition and curiosity which has resulted in continual self-education. A well developed Sagittarius likes himself and may his own best friend. She possesses the Aries vulnerability and requires the approval and approbation of other people to feel secure. He is intuitive, prophetic and insightful and probably less distracted than she by the fondness for pleasure. He may be as happy in the urban setting as she, or the lure of wide open spaces may attract him. Both can be unconventional at times, but he is less tied to conventions, sentimentality, family, and roots. If he's bitten by wanderlust, he may travel far from his original beginnings. Bold and adventuresome Aries will travel along for the excitement, but she may not see quite as many colors in the elusive rainbow. This can be a most harmonious match with both partners allowing the other the freedom to explore life.

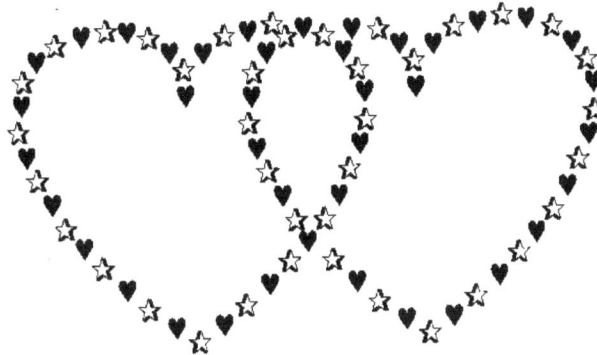

ARIES MAN - SAGITTARIUS WOMAN
LOVE RELATIONSHIPS & COMPATIBILITIES

With a Sagittarius woman, this Aries man has found a delightful companion who is thrilled with his initiative and drive.   Two Fire signs, both are enthusiastic and love fun, socializing, and the good things in life. In fact, he may be more serious than this Sagittarius lady who loves to explore the endless possibilities available to her. She may be happy enough to let him take the lead, allowing her more freedom of thought and expression with fewer obligations. Both are warm, friendly and caring, and any little spats are soon resolved in a kiss and makeup session. She can be as supporting, devoted and appreciative as he requires. Her whimsical nature, freedom-loving ways, and willful playfulness may make her not the easiest person to control as she avoids restrictions to her thoughts and movements. But then it was her carefree ways that first attracted him. Intuitive and perceptive she appears to know just the ways to keep her Aries man happy and satisfied. She can be quite companionable and may enjoy sports, the outdoors, and travel as much as he does. She is the romantic, and he will discover his own romanticism inspired by her loving nature. She requires a certain degree of freedom to expand her intellect and interests, and he requires the freedom to explore the possibilities of his ideas.   Both are highspirited, clever and amusing, and her humor and bright optimism adds spice to this relationship. Her best friends may be men, but he soon learns that she is loyal and faithful. They are both direct and outspoken and her blunt observations matches the Aries impulsive speech patterns. She may be less concerned with who is right than she is with her freedom to express herself. Both can be charming, warm and friendly individuals who are drawn to new experiences, meeting new people, and being exposed to the sights and sounds of interesting places. To win her heart, he will have to prove himself a true friend, caring companion, and sincere romantic. To her, life is an adventure, and bold Aries has all the qualities to prove her right. This couple can enjoy all that life has to offer, facing any obstacles and problems together. Her philosophical nature may open Aries mind, encouraging him to even greater achievements and aspirations.

They have much to share with each other, and there promises to be few dull moments between these two talkative and adventuresome individuals. She desires a certain portion of excitement to life, and that is just what Aries has to offer. To be truly happy, they only have to offer the other person the same liberty and freedom which they both desire.

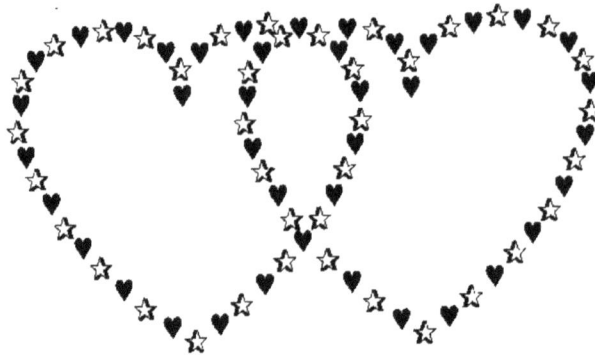

ARIES WOMAN - CAPRICORN MAN
LOVE RELATIONSHIPS & COMPATIBILITIES

In Capricorn, this Aries woman finds a man whose composure is reserved and dignified. A self-disciplined and often self-made man, he is cautious, stable and patient. He desires stability and ambitiously aspires to power and leadership. He steadfastly gets where he's going whether it be a mountain top or the top position in his company. He may find her vivacious, initiative, and lively, but he will view her impulsiveness as rashness. These two will not only act differently, they will think and perceive differently which can quite easily lead to communication problems. He most wants a help mate. Someone who will compliment his aspirations both professionally and socially. What they share in common are their aspirations. It is simply that they have different methods for achieving their goals. And he is methodical, well organized, and knows what he wants. Financial security is high on his list of priorities, and if she is extravagant and wasteful, he'll not understand her logic. If she truly wanted success and security in life, this independent, assertive, and ambitious woman would recognize this man's strengths and potentials. And it is more than likely his strong will power that first attracted her. She will have to accept that he may also have strong family ties and that he feels responsible for his relatives, a responsibility that he doesn't handle lightly. There is every indication that in love and marriage he is also responsible, loyal and faithful. But can he offer her that tinge of excitement she so much desires. Capricorn is an Earth sign, and his passion can be as intense and strong as the Earth. It may, however, be up to her to distract him from his responsibilities, duties, goals and aspirations. That should be enough of a challenge to excite any true Aries female. But can she be what he wants? If her desire is strong enough and if their mutual love and admiration creates a bond between these two very different people, they can develop a lasting relationship. She may want him to be more spontaneous, and he may want her to be more sensible and conventional. But she offers him that special spark of liveliness that comes with being energetically driven. And he offers her permanence and a sincere depth of affection. Her reward for her efforts will be a man who does lighten up and begins to enjoy life more fully, after he's acquired the security he desires. Capricorns are also known for reverse aging, and he will retain his youthful good looks as he ages. His reward will be loyal and devoted woman who retains her vitality, optimism and charm throughout life. Each provides the other with food for thought. The outcome of this relationship is totally up to the two individuals involved. It may require cooperation, a willingness to accept each other, and an ability to negotiate a compromise.

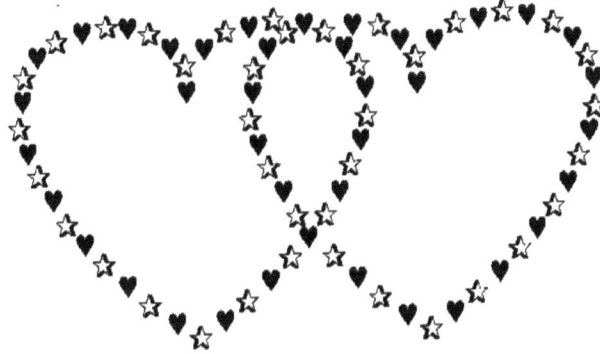

Aries Man - Capricorn Woman
Love Relatinships & Compatibilities

Aries have a tendency to either misjudge people or to make rash judgments regarding other people. This Aries man may see a quiet, demure and appealing female, but never realize her reserved, ambitious nature. While he's busy turning on the charm and that persuasive way he has with people, she is outlining her goals, objectives, portfolio, and plans for financial security and stability. He may be wearing the best of designer suits and driving an impressive car, but she is patiently studying the *Wall Street Journal.* Does he have an investment strategy? Give him time. He's working on it, but first there's one more impressive luxury item held like to acquire. She sees marriage (and she may prefer that idea to a string of fast romances) as having the potential to offer additional security not only for herself but for her future children. He sees marriage (though he may not admit it) as an experimentation in cohabitation. If it also happens to work, that's great. She is a capable and efficient female who uses self-control in order to make sensible and cautious decisions. His ambitious, energetic drive may appeal to her, but sooner or later he may also have to prove his logic. What excites her about him? He's Aries. His energy and magnetism intrigues everybody with whom he comes in contact. It would be helpful if these two had well-aspected Ascendants, Moons, and planets. There initial attraction to each other may soon grow into each person attempting to change the other. She wants him to grow up and be more responsible. He wants her to learn how to live for the moment and enjoy life. Neither is right nor wrong. They're simply different. If Cupid's arrow has brought about a compulsive and insatiable love between these two that cannot be denied or ignored by either, they must come to terms with communication, compromise, and promise. There is some promise in every relationship. If he came to appreciate her dependability, self-discipline, and conventional outlook, he stands a chance. If she can deal with his impulsive behavior, tendency to be constantly on the go, rash decisions, and his idea a minute intellect, she's in the game. Aries likes devotion, and he'll appreciate her concern for her family and relatives. If her family doesn't wonder where she met this character, then the chances are they didn't notice his faults, and they'll like him just fine. She possesses an earthy passion that appeals to Aries (everything appeals to Aries), and he'll be challenged by her cautious inhibitions. She will have to accept that his body may be covered with bumps, bruises, scars, and a couple of previously broken bones from rushing head first through life. She may also have to negotiate a way to handle the finances. What he promises her is never a dull moment, and if that's what she thinks she desires, it is a promise he's likely to keep.

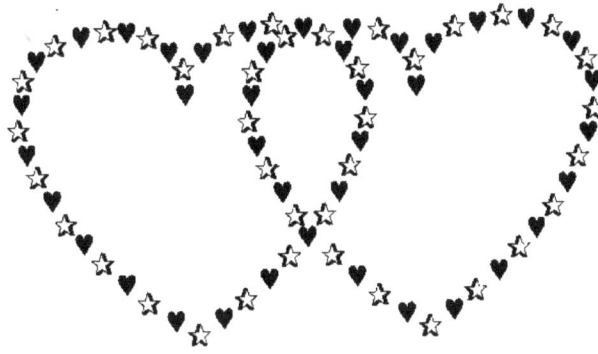

Aries Woman - Aquarius Man
Love Relationships & Compatibilities

Positive planetary positions can produce a mutual and dynamic attraction between these two amiable, charming and lively people. Both are sociable and like to entertain and be surrounded by people. Both collect people, but Aquarius will know and like more uniquely unusual people from different walks of life, and it makes little difference to him if they can help him socially or professionally. He has a genuine affinity for people in general. He is visionary in his humanitarian feelings and may express original perceptions and outlook on life. She is a person who initiates ideas while he, on the other hand, is inventive. They make think differently, but if they share common causes, interests, lifestyles, or likes and dislikes, then these two can communicate well enough to form an initial friendship. And friendship is the basis of all relationships with an Aquarius. If this relationship doesn't work, it will be important to him that they remain friends. While Aries is determined, Aquarius can be stubborn. He is intellectually open minded, develops lofty ideas, and broad minded concepts, but he has definite likes and dislikes, perhaps a personal routine, and firmly established opinions. She is independent and not the least bit clinging, and that is good because he will periodically withdraw from his throng of friends and want his privacy and space to be by himself or to pursue his interests. Both are capable of committing to relationship, but Aquarius, who is perfectly happy in an ongoing monogamous relationship, prefers to take his time and think about marriage. Her usual jealous tendencies will have to be controlled as she accepts that he has as many female friends as male friends. They are both fun loving, impulsive, and ambitious, but he may not share her intensity and drive. Neither is he as emotionally intense as this Aries woman. Aries can be passionately, even if it is only for the moment, driven in her pursuits. Aquarius is more detached, experiencing and enjoying his activities, but less emotionally attached. She lives for the moment and the present and to some degree immediate gratification, resenting any conventions that limit her. He is even more unconventional and envisions the future, skipping over what society may perceive as important, and seeing the larger picture in almost all aspects of life. He requires a great deal of freedom, and if he senses any limitations or restrictions to his way of life, he will either nicely get out of the situation or go so far as to rebel. Any attempts to change him or tie him down will only chase him away. But then neither does he place limitations on the freedoms of others. His curious nature draws him to this impulsive woman, and his at times erratic and changeable moods attract her curiosity as well. They promise each other an exciting adventure.

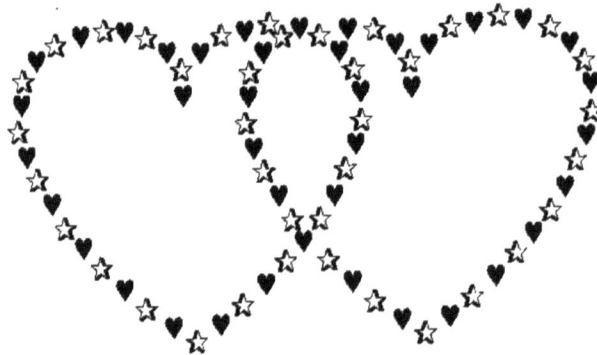

ARIES MAN - AQUARIUS WOMAN
LOVE RELATIONSHIPS & COMPATIBILITIES

Is it her unpredictable whims or her lively imagination that attracts this Aries man? He may at first attempt to redirect and reorder her life, but this is a woman who sets her own standards, holds her own values, and stubbornly holds to her unconventional thoughts and ideas. She is a creative romantic, but his intensity of emotions will never match her more detached intellectualized philosophy of life. He'll have to capture her heart through being a compatible friend who shares her love of people, socializing and interesting activities. Aries can manage that quite well enough, and while both can be impulsive, his boldness and adventurous nature may be just the unique attraction she seeks. She is neither intolerant, overly jealous, nor clinging, and likes the way he follows his latest dream. At the same time, she wants the freedom to enjoy her friends, many of whom are male. But then, in a relationship, she is as trustable as she is trusting, faithful, and devoted. He will need to respect her need to withdraw from the hurried activities of their fun-loving friends. She enjoys time to herself to pursue her own interests or simply to meditate on life in general. He initiates ideas while she dreams of world peace. With an innovative mind, she is a creative thinker who can be unconventional in her thoughts and ideas. Aries doesn't like societal conventions that impose on his life. Aquarius doesn't like conventions that impose on anyone's life. She is a bit of a free-spirit, deeply humanitarian, and desires the best for all. She wants a friend as well as a lover, and will do her best to insure that the friendship is secure above all else. Aries focuses his energies on his efforts to lead, but this female, who isn't domineering especially in her friendships, influences and at times inspires others. She has no desire to be the center of the crowd, but she wins friends effortlessly. Other people simply seek her out. Aries will either be proud of this lively companion or a little jealous of the amount of attention she receives with such ease. She is a genuine article. She is herself, even though her moods may change from one day to the next. She can be dizzy, erratic, or eccentric one day, and poetically quiet the next. Aries may be the explorer, but she is the social experimenter, wanting to observe the outcome of experiences, situations, and encounters. While he is forcefully direct, she is particularly fixed in her likes and dislikes and has her own special way of moving through her day. Aries would have to be secure enough to turn her loose to allow her to fly away, knowing that if their relationship is meant to be then she will return of her own free will. She can't stay where she isn't allowed to be herself, and Aries must abondon all hopes of ever containing this lovely female within a restrictive environment. If he can do that, then he will have discovered a most remarkable companion, trusted friend, and loyal mate.

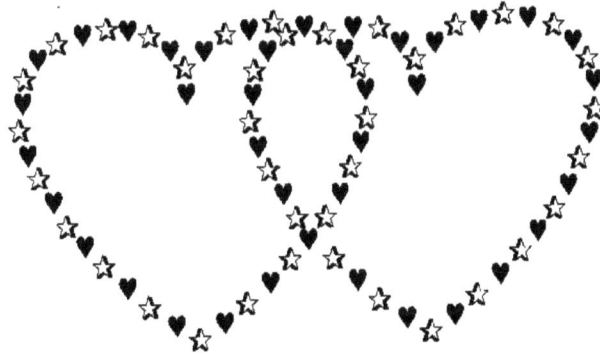

ARIES WOMAN - PISCES MAN
LOVE RELATIONSHIPS & COMPATIBILITIES

Aries flashes from thought to idea. Pisces flashes from one mental picture to another. If she is looking for a romantic, sensuous, attentive and dreamy escape from the world at large, she will discover it with this man. There are two types of Pisces. One who strives to achieve his goals by pulling against an inner nature drawn to the pleasantries of an easy life, and one who succumbs to flowing with the stream, enjoying life as it comes and seeking pleasurable outlets for his energies. Her particular Pisces man is intuitive, perceptive, and highly attentive to her needs. He either admires her courage and drive or is along for the ride. Aries can be easily mystified by this romantically charming man with his dreamy allure and preference for tender moments and enchanted, star-filled nights. He actually enjoys pleasing her and making her happy and fulfilled. He may attempt to soften her direct and forceful nature, displaying how much nicer it is to simply avoid conflict. He is sensitive and remembers past wrongs all the way back to childhood, and she must remember not to react too strongly to his list of complaints. Kindness and diplomacy will win his heart, and he will support her determination, but any direct criticism of him will wound him deeply. He may simply choose to withdraw from any form of aggressiveness or open conflict. If she wants to display her fiery temperament, she may find herself doing it to a mute or absent audience. Aries makes instant decisions while Pisces prefers to ask for advice. Not that he'll necessarily take it, he's just asking. She can direct and lead all she likes. He'll acquiesce pleasantly and then do whatever he chooses. She's wasting her time asking him to explain his actions. Pisces can easily be attuned and distracted to a higher consciousness, giving little thought to focusing too strongly on the innumerable procedures and conventions of daily life. He is compassionate, caring, and generous to others, especially to the love of his life. He either abstains from alcohol or enjoys his drink. He is either faithfully in love, or plays the field both before and after marriage. He admires beauty, natural settings, art and music, and wants to share this appreciation with a compatible mate. Both Aries and Pisces also appreciate beautiful surroundings and a pleasant home environment. They are both sociable, fun loving people who enjoy entertaining and an active social life. At the same time, he will seek his quiet moments to enjoy his creative imagination and fantasy-filled mental images. An Aries woman may find his romanticism a relaxing reprieve from the daily grind. And he may find her fiery forcefulness energetically stimulating.

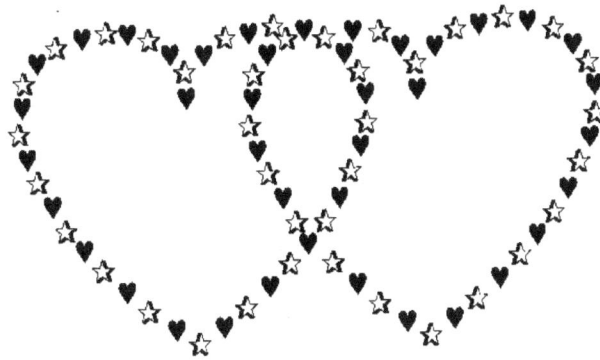

ARIES MAN - PISCES WOMAN
LOVE RELATIONSHIPS & COMPATIBILITIES

In a Pisces woman this Aries man will discover an attractive, sympathetic, and sentimental woman. She is a romantic at heart who is happiest when in love, and that should excite passionate Aries. A Pisces woman is either attracted to a strong and decisive men who can protect and support her, or to an emotionally or physically handicapped man who needs her care and concern. She may be drawn to a man who can offer her direction in life, or she may be passively aggressive, avoiding anyone who hints at wanting to control her. She absolutely glows when her attractiveness and allure is reaffirmed by an attentive, caring, and affectionate man. Pisces can be highly adaptable, and this woman will make every effort to change herself to be the woman he desires. But she retains her inner qualities, being creatively imaginative, magical and drawn to psychic awareness. Her mind perceives in vivid, graphic and colorful details and her mental pictures, dreams and visions can be more entertaining than the everyday world. While she may be physically active, she enjoys time to herself to lose herself in her dreams. Aries will delight in knowing that in exchange for his attentiveness, she can be erotically playful, loving every moment of their togetherness. He must remember that she is overly sensitive and even vulnerable to criticism, misunderstandings, or inattentiveness. She can be wounded deeply and suffer quietly to the point of sacrifice, preferring to avoid conflict at all cost (although there is that occasional Pisces female who will take just so much and then come out fighting). She much prefers compatible relationships based on mutual affection and caring as any disagreement can make her nervous and distraught. She can be as faithful, devoted, loyal and supporting as any Aries man would want, but he in turn must treat her with respectful kindness in order for the relationship to work. She may either like the direction he offers in life, or rebel against it totally. She likes to ask for advice, but may not always choose to follow it. She may decide to float along under the fiery umbrella of this man's strength simply jumping aside and dodging the fireworks he occasionally displays. And she won't lie to him in order to appease him, but she can create some highly imaginative fabrications just for the pure fun of it. And fun is something that both Aries and Pisces equally enjoy. The share a love of beautiful surroundings, a busy social life filled with people, and being actively on the go. They are an energetic couple with a love for a variety of interests and activities.

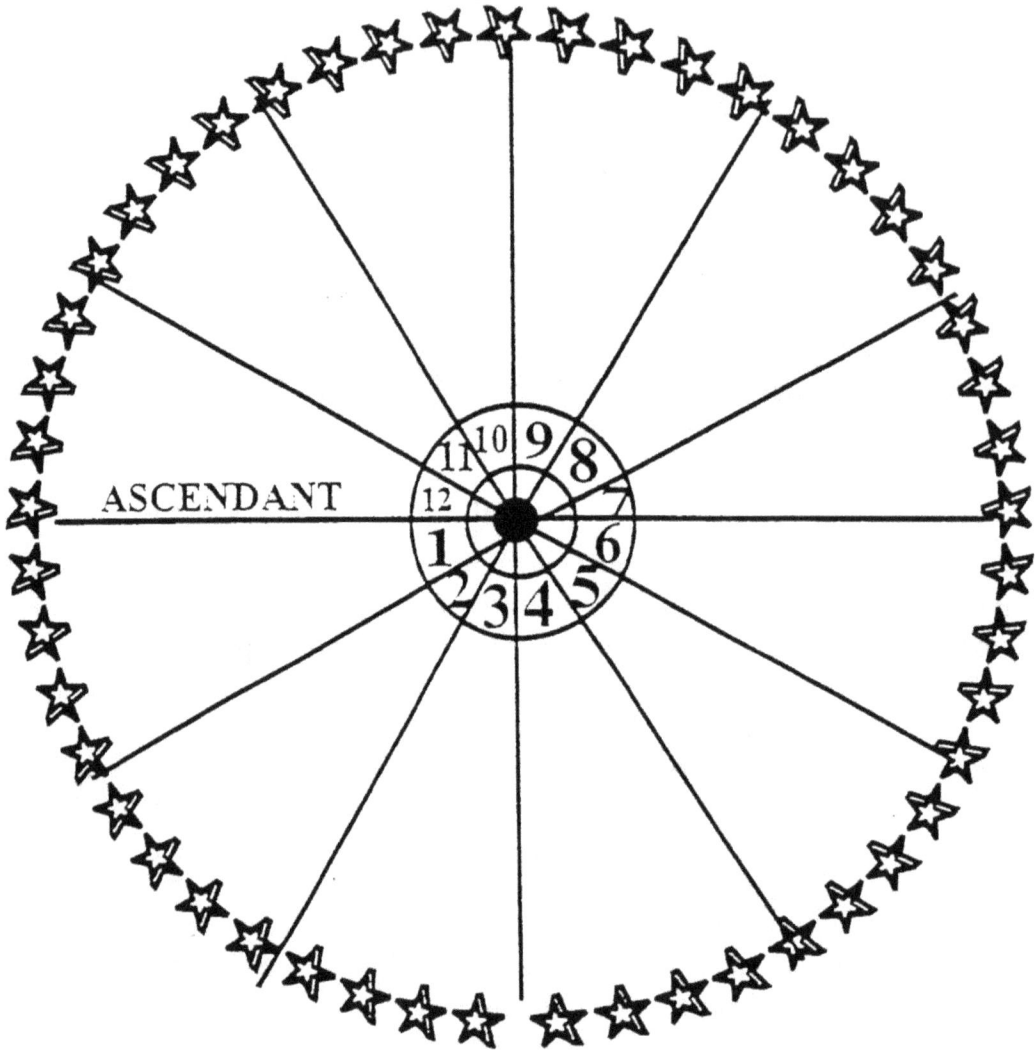

ASCENDANT

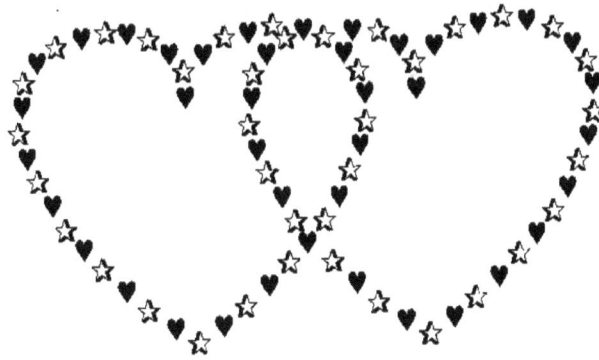

Taurus Woman - Taurus Man
Love Relationships & Compatibilities

Taurus individuals can be conventional people who are hard working and industrious, but who prefer to preserve their strength and energy. They are not impulsive, and when it comes to relationships, Taurus will carefully consider whether or not to become involved. Perhaps this is because once they have committed to a relationship, they have a tendency to tenaciously stick with it. Taurus, a Fixed sign, strives to build a lasting and permanent security, and once a decision has been made, they don't particularly care for making major changes, preferring to use their energies and to devote their efforts into making the relationship a lasting one. These two people are busy building and acquiring for the future and starting over isn't in the game plan. Unfortunately, many a Taurus will stay in a bad relationship far too long, believing that sheer endurance will win out eventually. Taurus are very likeable people, and this man and woman will discover in each other another warm, friendly, and fun loving person with a compassionate and caring nature. Their mutual love of the outdoors and nature may catch these two sunbathing nude in a favorite secluded spot or skinny dipping in the pool. They are both earthy and passionate lovers who don't care for being rushed in their love making. Both are devoted and loyal with reliable and responsible attitudes. They may have every thing in the world going for them, that is, as long as they don't oppose each other. Any form of opposition in the relationship would result in a clash of strong wills, an unwinnable tug of war with quite possibly little hope for a positive outcome. And each can be slow to apologize. It will be important for these two lovers to build on their strengths and to develop a manner of communication that doesn't in any way offend the other person. They both much prefer a well run home environment with an established routine. Chances are they are both busy people, and a routine that works makes their lives easier and less stressful. The spark that keeps this routine from becoming dull is their lively and quick sense of humor and their ability to see the parody in life. These two can develop numerous common interests whether it be a love of music, social events, entertaining, or shopping. Taurus is the sign of possessions, and they will both enjoy acquiring items for their home and lifestyles. There will also be some possessiveness and jealousy in this relationship, but these two Taurus individuals will most generally share a special compatibility. They will understand the needs and desires of the other person and appreciate the other's outlook on life. Learning to live with another person is a challenge in itself, but Taurus will face that challenge in the same manner as the rest of life. These two will pursue shared goals with determination knowing that their effort will bring them what they most seek. There is every indication for this to be a promising and fulfilling relationship based on love and appreciation for one another.

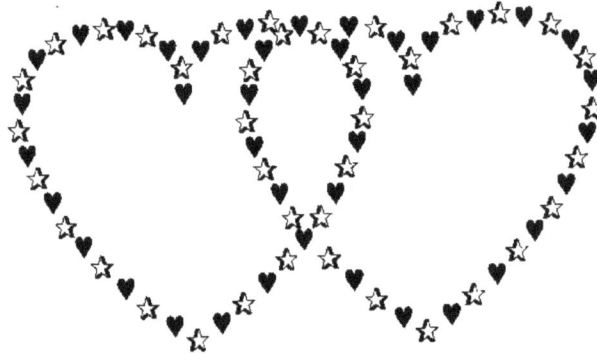

Taurus Woman - Gemini Man
Love Relationships & Compatibilities

The quiet practicality of this Taurus woman will surely be put to the test by the light-hearted, teasing manner of the Gemini man. While her energies and strengths are focused and goal-oriented, he divides his among diverse interests. It will more than likely be his amusing way with words that first catches her attention. They both can be sociable, warm and friendly, but Gemini may be more outgoing, needing more distractions and new experiences in his life. He is drawn to meeting new people, becoming involved in any number of exciting activities, and socializing with one and all. He is less down to earth, less emotional, and more able to rationalize his actions and feelings intellectually. He collects people, interacts with them, then moves on to another event or meeting. He is the communicator, quick with words, thoughts and ideas. He can also be impulsive and quick to act. Many of his decisions are made on the spur of the moment for the moment at hand. He may admire her personal strength, determination and will power, recognizing full well the stability she brings to any relationship. And she may admire his initiative and curiosity, finding his restless energy exciting and his unpredictable changeability intriguing. Both would like to achieve a good position in life, and he may see her need for possessions and acquisitions as ambition, not recognizing it as the basis of her sense of security. Their relationship may be bonded physically in a fun-loving, passionate affair that draws them closer together. She senses that life will never be dull with this exciting man, and he recognizes that her loyalty adds a special dimension to his life. He can be loyal and devoted as well, but depending on his planetary influences, he may have a susceptibility to outside stimulation. After all, he is a gifted flirt and well received by the ladies. This Taurus female will have to control her jealous and possessive nature, perhaps finding a way to express her concerns to him in a manner that doesn't threaten to restrict his personality. He can no more control his restless twin personality than she can control her resistance to change. As much as there is for him to like about this woman, he will sooner or later need to accept that arguing with her is useless. Her patience is overwhelming, but she is as slow to take decisive action as he is quick to act. And once she has formed an opinion, nothing changes it, whereas his opinions and even his direction are as changeable as the air. They are both as lovable as two people could be, but they are two very different people. Their shared interests, values, friends, and family as well as a strong love and appreciation for each other may well act to hold them together. To keep him interested, she will have to keep the fun alive, and to keep her interested, he will have to respond to her need for security and permanence. Interesting doesn't begin to describe this relationship.

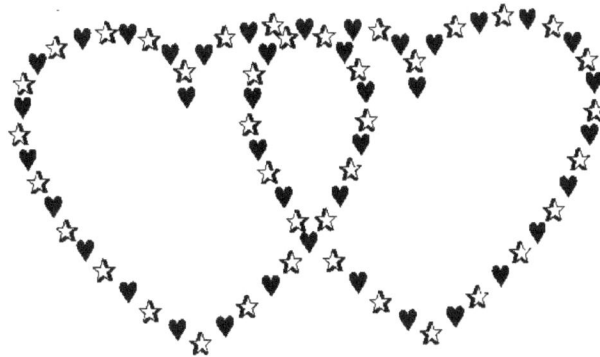

TAURUS MAN - GEMINI WOMAN
LOVE RELATIONSHIPS & COMPATIBILITIES

A Taurus man is sensible, hard working and down to earth, but the excitement of a Gemini woman can become a thrill as necessary as the air he breaths. And there is some quality about a Taurus man that is especially captivating. There is the allure of his warm, easy going ways, personable manner, and more than pleasant charm. Underlying that is his slow smile which reveals an interesting sense of humor and promise of fun. Then too, this perceptive Gemini woman may sense a prevailing strength beneath the surface demeanor of this man. He can be the easiest person to get along with, but he is definitely not a man to adamantly oppose. Attempt to push, pull or persuade him, and you can actually observe his facial expressions as he turns on his self-control and patience. She can not hope to get to know or understand this man by insinuating herself upon him. But if she displays an interest in him and allows him to be himself, he will show her in any number of ways just exactly who he is and what he's like. one thing she can be sure of, once he's made a commitment to a relationship he won't be quick to change his mind. He sets his mind and can become determined to stick with her through thick or thin or any obstacles life may set in their path. It may make life easier if she makes an effort to get along well with his friends and family, but she need not worry about even them swaying his opinions. Then too, he kind of likes the way this Gemini woman takes the initiative, and she may be especially fond of his fun-loving, athletic and nature loving ways. He also wants to provide her stability, security, and protection. Her friends will all love him, but he may also choose to show her how nice it is to stay at home enjoying just each other. Her restless nature and changeability may be just the spark he seeks to add interest and a sense of excitement to their lives. Taurus may be prone to establishing a routine but many a Bull is drawn to adding a little spice to life. His earthy passionate ways tantalize her need for a full and expressive sex life. He will have to understand her need for many diverse interests, activities, and social interactions. And she may be as intellectually curious as she is social. She can be quite happy as long as she doesn't feel tied down to someone elsels routine and conventions. She may or may not appear conventional, but either way, her dual nature will provide at least a part of her personality with a curious interest in what would be considered by more discerning individuals as unconventional pursuits. But then, that is probably what caught his interest in the first place. Once these two recognize and accept their differences and establish a harmonious lifestyle and pattern of communication, they are set for a lasting relationship.

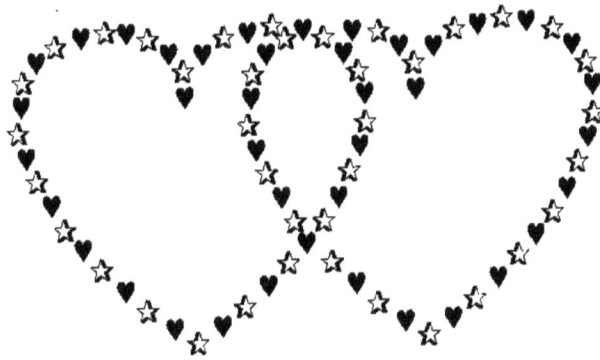

Taurus Woman - Cancer Man
Love Relationships & Compatibilities

This Taurus woman may take her time considering the advances of her Cancer man, but his congenial ways, com-mon sense, and sensitive nature may win her over. And he can be so creatively persistent and entertaining at the same time. Once the compatibility issue is out of the way, she'll discover a man who loves her pampering and responds to her affections. Cancer desires more than anything a companionable friend and lover with whom to share life, and Taurus's devotion, once the decision has been made, is everlasting. And they want the same things in life including home, family, and financial security. Both appreciate pleasant surroundings, a well furnished home, and a solid bank account. And both can be tenacious in acquiring the necessary possessions in order to feel secure within themselves. They share a love of good food, amiable friends, and pleasurable activities and past times, but both are drawn strongly to a well established routine focused on their home life. Both may love music, have a flair for acting, and an appreciation for art. Taurus's steady ways may provide the environment Cancer needs for his quiet moments of creative expression. He may also be moody, requiring time to himself to relax and recuperate from a busy life. The down side to the relationship may be his Cancer defensiveness. He does not appreciate criticism or an intrusion into his more private thoughts. Nor can he handle what she may see as discussions, but he will perceive as either reproach or a disruption to whatever he's doing. He can be considerate, thoughtful, and sincere, but when he wants his own time, he means just that and she must not feel abandoned or taken for granted. On the other hand, if he wants to go when she wants to stay, he will discover just how set in her ways this Taurus woman can be. She can be even more determined and set in her ways than he is. Her devotion and patience may draw him out, and his kindness and appreciation will win her over every time. The magic in this relationship comes from his sensual ardor which perfectly matches her passion, and together they can quite easily discover the meaning of desire and fulfillment. Taurus is also known for her reliable and responsible ways, and she'll appreciate his ties to his parents, relatives, and friends. Cancer needs to feel that he has someone in his life who he can depend on at all times, and that may be just what he finds in the strength and will of this Taurus woman. Their very natures appear to compliment each other, and all this relationship requires in order to work well is loving cooperation of the two people involved. Cancer's dreamy

135

creativity and active imagination will add a special spice to this relationship as will her ability to pamper him into contentment.

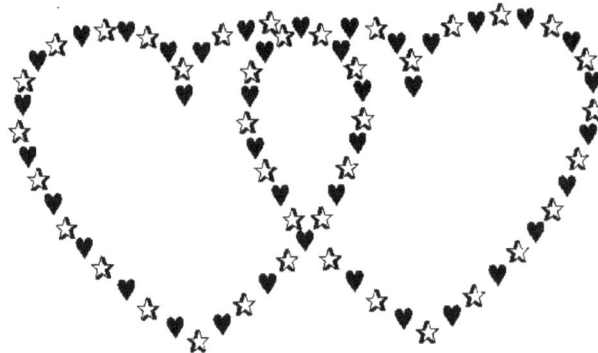

TAURUS MAN - CANCER WOMAN
LOVE RELATIONSHIPS & COMPATIBILITIES

These two share quite a bit in common. They both aspire to financial security, appreciate possessions, and desire a pleasant and satisfying home life. They may enjoy other people, entertaining, and an active social life, but they both center their attentions on establishing and maintaining a home. His personal strength, will power, and determination may provide her with a sense of protection and emotional security. She most desires a best friend, lover, and someone who she knows will be there when she needs a shoulder to lean on. And her imagination and creativity may inspire him to even greater devotion. Both are nature lovers, and if these two decide to romp in the woods, they may be play acting one of her fanciful dreams: she is a lost maiden, and he is a knight out on quest to save the troubled lady. She may appreciate his procrastinating nature, knowing that he takes his time, is never rash, and has their best interest at heart. She doesn't really like quick changes anyway because her own changeability is due to her moods rather than a restless nature. And her moodiness may have little relation to anything he has said or done. She escapes into her own space, becoming preoccupied and introspective from time to time. His own personality is somewhat more stable, reliable, and predictable which may serve to add a balance to her changeable nature. Add to this combination a shared interest in music, art, and the outdoors, and it equals out to the potential for a pleasant relationship. What each must remember is to curb a tendency to be critical or demanding of the other person. Taurus will become bull-headed against any obvious opposition, refusing to budge or give in any disagreement. Cancer, in comparison, is easily offended and hurt, and that will set off one her infamous pouty moods. He may as well accept that as agreeable and companionable as this lovely Cancer woman can be, she has her own mind and is prone to making many of her own decisions. Her overpowering need for security and personal possessions can also make her seem at times self-centered and selfish. Taurus can be possessive as well, but he has more of a tendency to be helpful, generous, and magnanimous, accepting what he may feel as responsibilities toward

136

relatives and friends. Both may have strong family ties. Sexually, they are responsive to their earthy passions which keeps them actively interested in one another. Her quick and creative wit compliments his need for humor and a sense of fun within the relationship. once he learns not to step on her toes, and she accepts that gentle persuasion works best with this man, they are on their way to a loving good time. Their warmth, enduring passion, and that fine sense of fun and humor, will only add to a most compatible relationship.

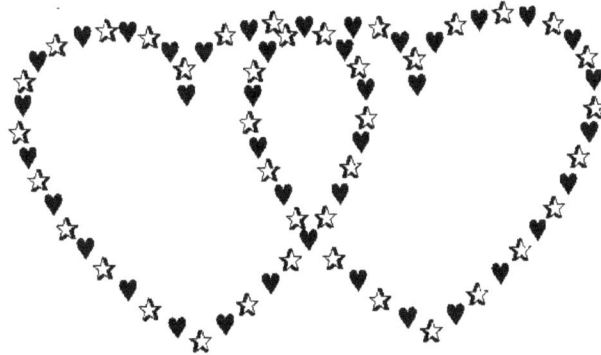

TAURUS WOMAN - LEO MAN
LOVE RELATIONSHIPS & COMPATIBILITIES

A Taurus woman may be greatly tempted to abandon her caution around a Leo man. He so easily impresses everyone, including her. Besides his outgoing personality and pleasing ways, his self-confidence shows in all he does. He aspires to leadership positions, is the center of attention wherever they go, and possesses a natural dramatic flair that he exhibits for one and all. He likes all the same things she does, including a nice home, nice things, and even a few luxury items. He can be as steadfast, loyal and faithful as she, however, she may want to compare who is the most hard working and diligent. Many a Leo has gotten through life primarily on personality and drive. Assuming this particular Leo man isn't in that category, then there remain a few things this Taurus woman will want to remember. While Taurus wants to be loved and appreciated, Leo wants to be loved, appreciated, and greatly admired for his many outstanding qualities. Not only does he have a commanding presence, but he wants to command, and he has a tendency to expect his admirers to follow his lead. She may find herself polishing the spotlight that Leo likes to stand in, and allowing him to accept the credit for any and all accomplishments in their lives. For the most part, though, Leo is a congenial person, both compassionate and generous, who enjoys social activities, a number of interests, and spending time with friends and associates. The same could be said about this Taurus woman who possesses a steady, self-sufficient nature, loads of patience, and who is slow to anger. What Leo will want to remember is that he can command all he likes as long as he doesn't attempt to pusb this kindly lady where she doesn't want to go. Her determination, tenacity, strong will, and finally aroused temper would prove a challenge for even fiery Leo. These same attributes (minus the temper) will be all the qualities she'll need to learn to deal with her arrogant Leo man. He may behave as if he feels his world should revolve around him and his needs, but that is what makes a Leo distinctly Leo. She will have to forget about changing him and learn to assert her own needs and wishes. He will probably respect her all the more, and these two can share the most intimate of companionship once the battle lines have been drawn, negotiated, and agreed to. Both are passionate lovers who attend to the needs and desires of the other person. Both like sex and this can develop into a special bonding between them that carries over into the other areas of their lives. He may from time to time be more extravagant than she is, feeling that boys must have their toys, and she may want to be sure that their financial strategy is well established so that she can feel secure within the relationship. Many a Taurus and Leo discover the happiness of a long lasting and fulfilling relationship based on mutual love and devotion.

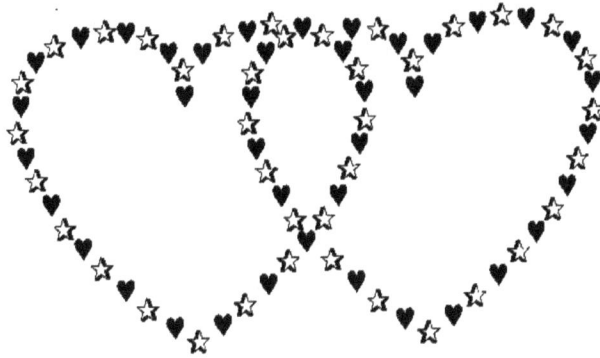

Taurus Man - Leo Woman
Love Relationships & Compatibilities

Leo are proud people, and this Leo woman will be more than proud of her handsome, congenial, and security-minded man. He actually wants to provide for her and use his masculine strength to protect her. He wants a home and all the things that go into building a permanent foundation for their future together. He will find that her outgoing personality and ingenuity adds a more than pleasant spark to his steadfast ways. Taurus doesn't really mind if Leo wants to be the center of attention as that's not one of his prerequisites anyway. But he will enjoy her vivaciousness and admire her independent and ambitious ways. He may soon discover, however, that since Taurus and Leo are both Fixed signs, they can both be determined to have their own way. She may use her natural magnetism, charm, and pleasing personality to gently persuade her strong-headed Taurus, but it would be a waste of time for these two to pit their wills against each other. She can be a tempestuous fireball, but he is as firm as the Earth in his opinions. He will find that she responds to kindness, admiration, and compliments, and that she positively radiates when flattery comes her way. She may be an incorrigible flirt and accustomed to receiving heaps of admiration and attention, but when in love she is quite capable of finding a great deal of selfexpression and fulfillment within the relationship. It goes without saying, however, that when in an one-on-one relationship, she will need what she feels is an adequate amount of attention. That should prove an easy enough task for a well-meaning Taurus man. Together they can develop their mutual appreciation for all the right things that make life both pleasurable and enjoyable. But he may have to keep an eye on her spending habits which are a bit more extravagant than his. She will be more than pleased with his fortitude in the bedroom, and they may well discover matching passions and desires. A Leo woman in love is intensely romantic, and she devotes all of her energy, drive, and devotion to the relationship expecting the same in return. A well developed Taurus man can accept her devotion and equal it in full measure. He has a tendency to stick with a relationship through any and all obstacles, and if she expresses her appreciation for all the good qualities he offers, then he is exactly the man she's been seeking. To make her feel admired, he may have to envision her on a throne, but more than likely she will respond whole heartedly. There is every possibility that together they can build an enduring and lasting relationship based on their strong love, shared interests, and common goals in life. Both are worth all the effort it takes to maintain a strong and healthy as well as romantic togetherness.

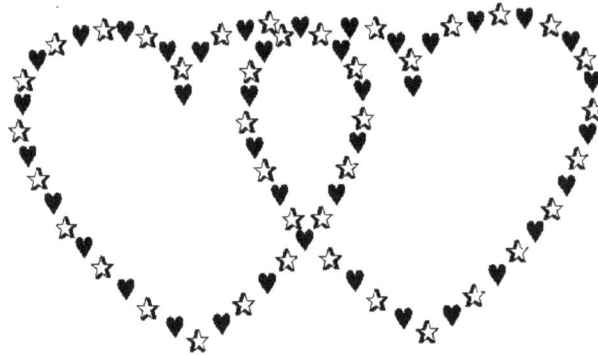

Taurus Woman - Virgo Man
Love Relationships & Compatibilities

Some relationships are just easier than others, and this may be the case between a Taurus woman and a Virgo man. Both share any number of similarities, interests, and perspectives. Both are seriously interested in establishing a home, building financial security, and planning for the future. Virgo can be just as hard working and diligent as Taurus, and these two may match their strides in all their efforts and endeavors. Both are cautious and not at all fond of making careless, rash, or spur of the moment decisions. Virgo is more detail oriented than Taurus, and will want to deduce all the facts to any given situation before proceeding. Virgo is a thinker with any number of intellectual interests, and Taurus may find that the best way to catch his attention is to be well informed on a variety of subjects or issues. These are two practical, down-to-earth, and sensible people who more than likely want basically the same things in life. He will learn quickly that she can be stubborn and set in her ways, but no doubt he will learn just as quickly that she responds to kindness and gentle persuasion not boldness. Taurus is determined to get where she's headed, and when this is combined with the analytical and rational inclinations of Virgo, the two find that their goals are most obtainable. Both share a distinct interest in financial security and possessions, and once their finances have been secured, this couple's favorite preoccupation may be shopping for their home and family. They relax best in a pleasant environment, filled with lovely things. And while they are both sociable and enjoy mingling and entertaining as well as social events, the week-end can just as well catch them working in their yard or on their home. Both Taurus and Virgo prefer to appear conventional, are discerning in their choice of friends, and tasteful in their selection of past times. one of his main interests may be health and diet, and this Taurus female will no doubt learn the meaning of low-fat. on the minus side of the relationship, both must watch a tendency to be critical. This only makes Taurus more obstinate and Virgo temperamental. But then to make up, both will respond to an attractive and practical gift and affection goes a long way with both these individuals. Taurus possesses all the qualities for awakening the Virgo passion, and these two share fulfilling, not to mention pleasurable, sexual experiences. Both Taurus and Virgo are compassionate, caring, and kind, and both cherish their families and friends. What these two have going for them is that they know what they want in life, and they apply themselves to obtaining just that. Other people can go their merry way, and these two would be fully satisfied living their life in their own way.

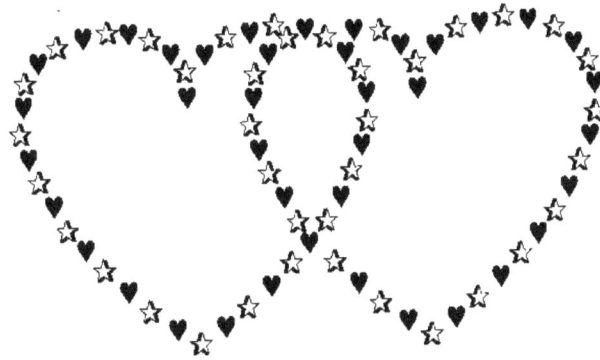

Taurus Man - Virgo Woman
Love Relationships & Compatibilities

All the same attributes and similarities hold true between this man and woman as mentioned in the previous section. What isn't mentioned is that both Taurus and Virgo are uncommonly cautious, at times even to the point of being distrustful. This especially holds true when it comes time to make that fateful decision on love and romance. The biggest obstacle the Taurus man and the Virgo woman may have to deal with is overcoming their respective caution, determining to at last make a decision, and then deciding to make a commitment. Neither wants to make a mistake by making the wrong decision, and neither wants in a relationship that won't last. And that is what is important to each of them. Each wants to make a commitment and stick to it, no matter what the future may bring. There is every possibility that these two will come together then back away from each other repeatedly while they attempt to navigate through their respective decision-making process. In the mean time, both can become frustrated and willful. He isn't swayed by friends, family, or her. He must make up his own mind. Neither is she easily won. If they finally discover mutual interests and establish that they have common goals and want the same things in life, these two will make a fine match. She must set aside her inhibitions and distrust and accept that he can't be bullied into revealing his inner nature. He must accept that what she really seeks is to know him fully. Now, once all that has been established, they may at last discover the warmth, compassion, and loving tenderness each is capable of giving and receiving. She will never tire of the strength of his passion, and her devotion will insure his arousal and interest. She can't fault that he is hard working and intensely interested in providing for the future while offering her the protection of his diligence and masculinity. If she is perceptive, she will notice that he is undeterred in forever returning to her side. They both have strong family ties, and it is probably important that both get along well with the other person's relatives because they will be a part of their lives. If Taurus and Virgo find that what binds them together is their capacity for team work, to get along well and to establish common interests, friends, and most importantly goals, then this relationship will work well for them. Both like to be of service to other people, and their friendships are important to them. And both can be easy going, companionable, kind and caring. Virgo has a tendency to worry too much, and Taurus must take care not to add to her worries. And with many of the signs of the Zodiac, both Taurus and Virgo will have to strive to accept each other as they are because neither is prone to changing their basic personalities. once all the decisions and obstacles have been dealt with, these two discover the power and durability of love.

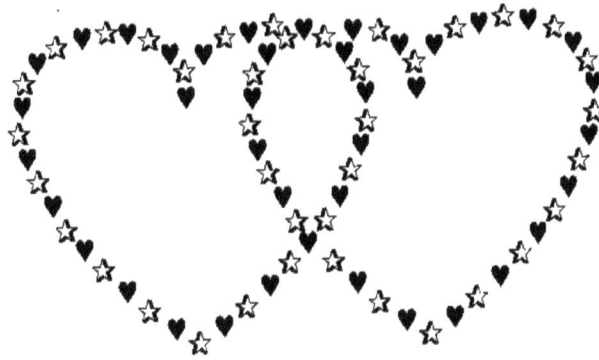

Taurus Woman - Libra Man
Love Relationships & Compatibilities

This Taurus woman has found herself marveling at the interests paid her by the most charming man in the Zodiac. She must be wondering if all that pleasant attention he pays her will continue as strongly after marriage as before. In answer to her question, the Libra man actually enjoys being attentive, charming and pleasant. He isn't acting that way just to please her. He strongly prefers that relationships are pleasant, all relationships. That's right, he's as pleasant with everyone as he is with this woman. The next obvious question would be can she control her jealousy and possessiveness and allow him to be the way he is. If she decides she wants to be a permanent item in his life, she'll probably have to exhibit the qualities of balance and harmony. He may possess a strong preference that all aspects of his life reflect a certain refinement and grace. He can be quite discerning, and if his attentions are focused on her, she can accept them as the purest compliment. One of the nice things about the Libra man is that he isn't difficult to get along with. He isn't obstinate, stubborn, or particularly difficult. He desires equity for all, however, and if his sense of justice is challenged, he can become argumentative. It would be a waste of time to attempt to out talk him in any disagreement because it can't be done. He doesn't use forcefulness. He uses diplomacy, tact, and persuasiveness. And while he does have a temper, it is as difficult to arouse as the Taurus's. Taurus may be cautious in making decisions, but Libra can be just down right indecisive. The fact is, he's judiciously weighing both sides of a decision, and in this case a steady, female Taurus would be a great help in arriving at an outcome. He won't think you're pushy if want to make a few decisions yourself, as long as they are the right ones. Financially, Libra may be as well set as Taurus, but Librals emotional security isn't based on possessions or his bank account. However, he does like nice things, pleasant surroundings, and a relaxing home atmosphere. All in all his thought processes, general outlook on life, and perceptions will be different from hers. In many relationships, it is just such differences which hold two people together. He will look at Taurus and see all of her good qualities despite any faults, but will expect her to be just as magnanimous. Taurus is intensely passionate, and Libra is intensely romantic. These two may be drawn together by a love and desire that is too strong for either of them to ignore, and if that is the case, all differences can be dealt with in time. Taurus will never suffer from lack of attention, caring and kindness, and Libra will discover a help mate in life who is devoted, and loyal.

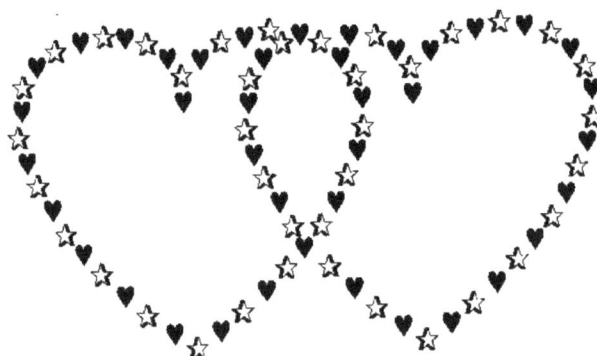

TAURUS MAN - LIBRA WOMAN
LOVE RELATIONSHIPS & COMPATIBILITIES

Libra perceives the good in the people she meets, and she'll be impressed with the any positive qualities of this Taurus man. These two Venus influenced signs are both genuinely sincere, kind and pleasant. That is the way he is, and that is the way she prefers to be. And he is determined enough to take her where she wants to go. Sensing that beneath his placid surface he is intense, she will use her sweet charm and graceful manners to keep him happily pacified. Libra works best when involved with a partner and preferable in an harmonious relationship. Now then, in order to balance her scales, Libra must deliberate both sides to any situation or decision and that can make her appear indecisive. She does appreciate input and opinions from others, but not rash, impulsive actions, nor does she like to be pushed or commanded to make up her mind. Taurus, on the other hand, is most patient, never rash or impulsive and is quite capable of giving her all the time she needs to arrive at a decision. He may come to realize that it takes a lot of pressure off her for someone else to make a decision, or to provide direction, as long as they are fair and sensible ones. If this Taurus man is really interested in this Libra lady, he'll also need to realize that she enjoys a spark of lively excitement in her life from time to time, not to mention a dash of lovely romance. Wanting the best for all involved and being open to suggestions, Libra can be gullible and even vulnerable to the influence of other people. Taurus will want to keep his cautious eye on her and help her to keep her scales wellbalanced. She isn't argumentative, but she can argue either side of a discussion and she enjoys a good debate. If he throws out a few facts or well phrased points, it will keep her mind contentedly preoccupied with weighing his opinions. After all, she isn't really arguing with him, she is discussing the issue at hand. And Taurus will want to keep his stubbornness in check. Libra isn't the least bit defensive, but she prefers compliments to criticism--they are so much more pleasant. Both Taurus and Libra enjoy comfortable living arrangements, good food and sociable outings. There's a good chance that they share a fondness for music or art. Libra adds refinement to his need to acquire possessions which

144

Taurus will like. His intense passion and ardor will hold Librals attention in the bedroom while her love of him and romance will keep him interested in returning to her sweet embraces. If Libra has dallied enough to satisfy her restless nature, then she may discover in this Taurus man what she has been searching for in her quest to find that perfect companionable partner. And a strong love can go a long way in feeling like perfection.

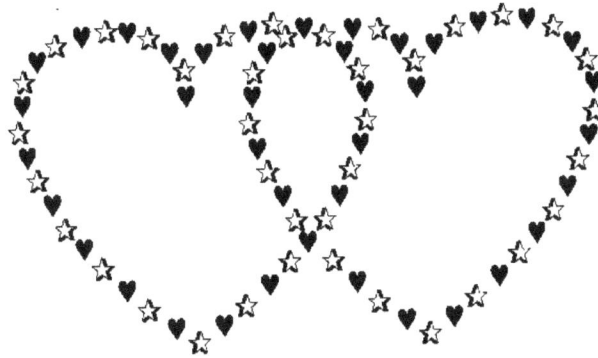

TAURUS WOMAN - SCORPIO MAN
LOVE RELATIONSHIPS & COMPATIBILITIES

Scorpio is drawn to a Taurus woman for all the right reasons. He likes her sensible, down-to-earth ways and her well-meaning intentions. Intuitive and quietly perceptive, he observes in her a sweet sincerity that soothes his inquisitive and seeking nature. At last he has found a woman who wants a home, security, possessions, and a future. Scorpio may not be completely comfortable knowing that her sense of security is based on those same acquisitions, but perhaps he will feel he can share with her a stronger belief system that brings a fuller measure of security, that is, if he is secure himself. Scorpio is either an enlightened individual who feels secure within himself, or he is terribly threatened, and unable to express, the workings of his mind. Whichever may be the case, there is a bit of mystery and allure about this man which will attract any sensitive female. He can be quiet and reserved at times, and then when the occasion arises, turn on a warmly pleasing personality that allows him to charm a crowd. He can choose to sociably work a room full of people or to stand off by himself and observe the interactions of others. He can be determined and decisive and just as ambitious as Taurus, but Scorpio isn't above a promising impulsive action. As opposite signs of the Zodiac, Taurus and Scorpio have something to offer each other--what the other is lacking. This can either draw them together or pit these two Fixed signs adamantly against each other. What they share is a strong will and determination, and once either makes a commitment, they both have a tendency to stick with it. Scorpio may find her jealousy and possessiveness flattering, and Taurus may find these same qualities in him rather admirable--almost like tangible proof of how much he cares. He may not be so controlling as he is impatient with her indecisiveness, and she has enough patience for both of them. Once they accept the other person's weaknesses and combine their positive strengths, there isn't much in life they can't accomplish. There is every possibility that they become a formidable team working toward mutual goals and aspirations. She will never complain about a lack of attention in the bedroom. Sex for these two is as natural and necessary as breathing. Scorpio reads other people, looks them directly in the eyes, observes their actions, and listens to their words, learning what it is that motivates that person. When he finds in this Taurus woman a reliable, trustworthy companion who is loyal and devoted, he will extend to her those same qualities. And while he may want to lead more than she cares for, he'll turn around and serve her breakfast in bed, admiring her for steadfast endurance of all his impossible traits. He also brings to her the promise that the mystery of love will always be there.

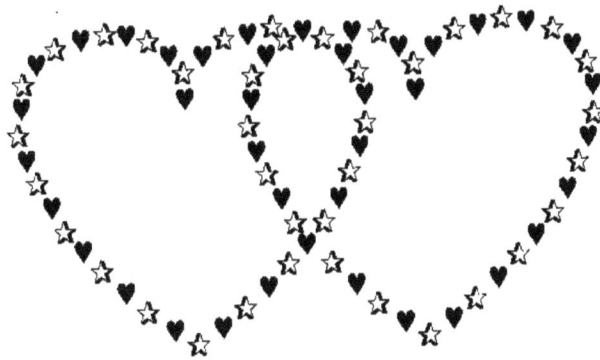

Taurus Man - Scorpio Woman
Love Relationships & Compatibilities

When these two individuals discover a mutual love and need for each other, it is bound to be one so intense and passionate that neither can ignore it. He is that fixed and steady rock in the turbulent storm--unlike the others who were more like passing ships on the open waters. Above all else, he wants to be possessed, and in return she compulsively wants him. After the first few years, when their passions have finally come down to Earth proportions, they'll find they both like establishing a routine and getting down to the business of planning a future together. She most admires him because he wants to plan for their security. He admires her because in all the tediousness of dealing with life, she never fails to add a touch of excitement. She senses in him the strength and ability to accomplish his goals. His tenacity actually arouses her. They are both ambitious and determined. She wants a person in her life who admires her the way she is, and he does. He wants to be appreciated for all his hard work, and this she does. She has all the endurance a person could ask for, but he is patient and persevering during the most difficult of times. She is accustomed to having people lean on her during difficulties, but in this Taurus man she discovers a person who she can lean on at all times. Granted, his caution slows her down, but that proves to be in her own best interest. She has a certain magic that seems to dispel his obstinacy quickly enough. It has something to do with her mischievous little smile and that appealing look in her eyes. The steadfast Bull may not admit it, but he loves a little mystery and excitement in his life. And Scorpio who is so good at searching out the secrets to a mystery, likes the fact that with Taurus you get what you see. He is open, honest and trustworthy. But more importantly, once he commits his love to her, she can finally accept that this is a person who means what he says. She reads him and likes what she sees, and he doesn't mind the intrusion. A Scorpio woman wants more than anything to be able to let down her wall of defenses and to be herself. She wants to devote herself full heartedly to the man in her life--one man who she can trust and depend on. Taurus, according to the traits of his sign, has the qualities that she is seeking. Now with all such matches, it's advisable to consider the Moon, Ascendant, and aspects of the planets as well. But if these two make the decision to commit their love as well as their lives to each other, they have every indication for establishing a fulfilling and lasting bond. It will require that they are determined for each other and not against each other. Once they accept that

147

the other person is there to stay, both may be happy to let go of their jealousies. But both Taurus and Scorpio will always want to possess the other person fully and completely.

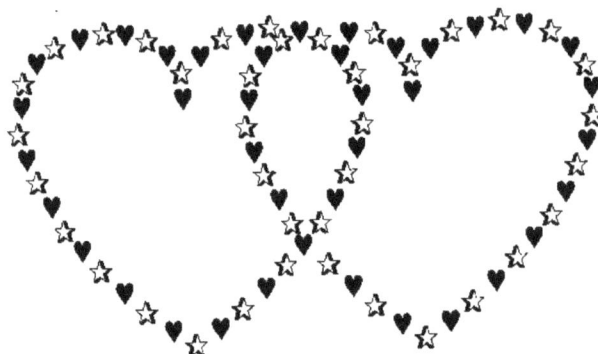

Taurus Woman - Sagittarius Man
Love Relationships & Compatibilities

A Taurus woman will be inspired by the optimism, cheerfulness, and imagination of a Sagittarius man, and he will like her warm-hearted ways. But Taurus is a wellgrounded individual, and Sagittarius has little or no interest in being grounded in any form or fashion. What Taurus perceives as a sensible routine, Sagittarius will consider a limitation. He seeks philosophical rainbows, and she desires tangible proof in the form of possessions. Both can be charming and pleasant people, but they are different. Taurus finds comfort in the acceptability of traditions and is more than happy with conventions. Sagittarius feels that conventions, and at times even laws, are a restriction to his personal freedoms. If he wants to try something different, he should be able to. After all, it is his life. Socially, whether he's quiet or outgoing, he's a witty, personable person who loves people and will go an extra mile for a friend, all of which Taurus may admire. on a more personal level, he has a tendency to say whatever pops into his head, not thinking that the truth sometimes hurt. Taurus isn't the best person for personal criticism, but she could criticize him all day without making a dent in his personal charisma. He may see her need for possessions and financial security as insecurities, feeling that things are nice to have as long as they don't become too burdensome an obligation. That's not to say that he doesn't like money. He does. How else could he do all the things he wants to do. It's just that she has more of a tendency to tuck it safely away than he does. There is a tendency for Sagittarius to love the outdoors and many are drawn to wide open spaces. If that takes him far from his family, he'll try to stay in touch. Taurus, on the hand, enjoys being caught up in the middle of family gatherings and is generally strongly tied to her family. He yearns to travel while she craves home sweet home. He's curious about life with a need-to-know attitude, forever seeking new knowledge and information. If he doesn't travel physically, then his mind is on a journey of its own. This relationship would require quite a depth of understanding on both of their parts and a great deal of acceptance. He is considerate, open minded, and tolerant and admires all her good qualities. She is compassionate, caring, and kind, but she may as well forget about being possessive with this man. If she decides to keep the home fires burning for this inspiring man, that's all well and fine. Or she may decide it's time to follow along and see just what it is that captures his imagination in the wide world of experiences. If their relationship is bonded on a strong friendship, then he will be true to his words. Just don't expect any promises that bind him to being grounded for life.

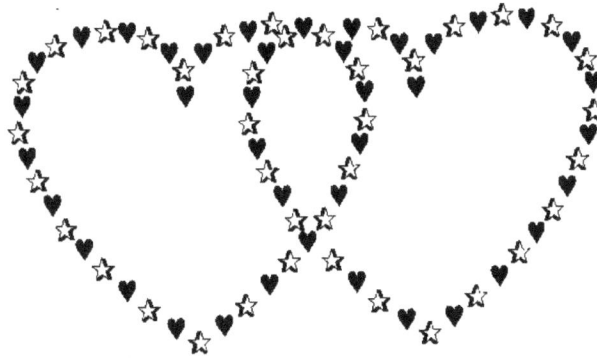

TAURUS MAN - SAGITTARIUS WOMAN
LOVE RELATIONSHIPS & COMPATIBILITIES

She may be a logical thinking idealist whose bright and sunny outlet on life leads her to do whatever he asks, in the name of friendship if nothing else, but this Taurus man shouldn't suppose that he can impose on her independent nature by demanding or ordering her around. A Sagittarius woman prefers a dependable man who is firmly assertive and ambitious, but she has no intention of becoming willingly submissive. She optimistically places a high value on friendship and expects her lover to be a good friend as well. She can be kind and considerate and when she turns her affections on this Taurus man she will also display her fiery, amorous nature. She is direct and unaffected, and speaks her mind openly if not at times bluntly. She can be temperamental and high spirited with an impulsive and changeable nature, and her emotions may vary with her moods from affection to indifference. But Taurus shouldn't make the mistake of thinking her cold or heartless because she is for the most part open-hearted, jovial and free of malice. She doesn't have a jealous or possessive nature and has a tendency to extend the same freedoms to others that she likes herself. A Sagittarius woman is unconventional in her relationships and greatly enjoys flirting, but the Taurus jealousy isn't necessary because she doesn't take flirtations seriously--they're just fun. Besides, her best friends may be men. She isn't especially timid and doesn't go to any lengths to hide her feelings. What she says and how she acts reflects how she feels and thinks. She'll appreciate the reliable, responsible nature of Taurus because she has a tendency to be too trusting and is at times vulnerable to unscrupulous people. It is her outgoing friendliness and imagination that perhaps caught the attention of this Taurus man who is capable of being sincerely friendly himself. Or was it his admiration for her many diverse interests? Together they share a love for nature, sports, athletics, music or any number of other interests. She expresses an interest in humanity and politics as it relates to social affairs, and she likes to discuss what she's learned. And while she likes travel and excitement, she's also open to new ideas and will follow an innovative idea right through to the end. Taurus shares that determination to build toward his future, but he may notice that at the same time Sagittarius can become distracted along the way. Her attention seems to wander to newer and more interesting ideas, and the Taurus steadfastness may greatly influence her to stay on track. This Taurus man and Sagittarius woman may find that a lasting relationship is built on accepting each other's differences for there will be many. Needless to say, that makes for few dull moments as they chart their future together.

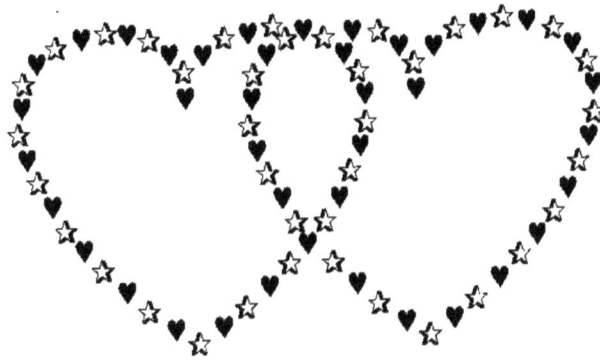

Taurus Woman - Capricorn Man
Love Relationships & Compatibilities

These two Earth signs share traditional values and a conventional lifestyle. In some instances, a Capricorn man in his early years may vacillate between chosen paths, but he is actually methodically gathering experience and organizing his thoughts for the road ahead. He applies a self-disciplined approach to his goal-oriented direction, ambitiously seeking position, preferably in a leadership role. Both Taurus and Capricorn are patient, Earth-bound types who diligently persevere in their efforts to achieve. He can be reserved and dignified or a bit shy, but underneath this calm demeanor is a man who knows what he wants and where he is going. He is a proud man who greatly wants to be appreciated for his efforts. He possesses the same caution as Taurus and will wait for the right lady who can share his goals in life and support his determination. He wants to be proud of her and will probably, without giving it much conscious thought, choose a woman who is an asset to his ambitions. And a Taurus female can be everything he desires in femininity, discernment, ambition, and common sense. They both want the same things including a secure home life with all the amenities and necessary possessions to make it comfortable and inviting. And they are both capable of working as hard as it takes to acquire what it is they want. Both prefer a well-organized and efficient routine that serves as a basis for their busy lives. Taurus at the same time is warm, friendly, and pleasantly humorous. Beneath his sometimes cool persona, Capricorn too is warm, sincere, and kind, and his humor is of the dry and witty variety. Capricorn likes to be well prepared for whatever obstacles may come his way, and his self-disciplined approach may make him more frugal than even security-conscious Taurus. She may exhibit more of an interest in acquiring possessions than he deems necessary. She may want to consider that in his drive to protect what is his and their future together, Capricorn can be controlling. He has their best interest at heart, and a smart Taurus woman may want to listen to his reasoning carefully. These two possess so many similar characteristics that there is every chance that their thinking processes are similar. While there may be differences of opinions, there is every possibility that they will choose to amiable settle their differences and refocus their attention to more important matters. Both take love and commitment seriously, and both are reliable, responsible, and trustworthy. Their intensity may be dispelled through their love making which is ardent and gratifying. She must never forget to

151

appreciate this man, and he must remember to express his love and affection to her. This is a good combination for success.

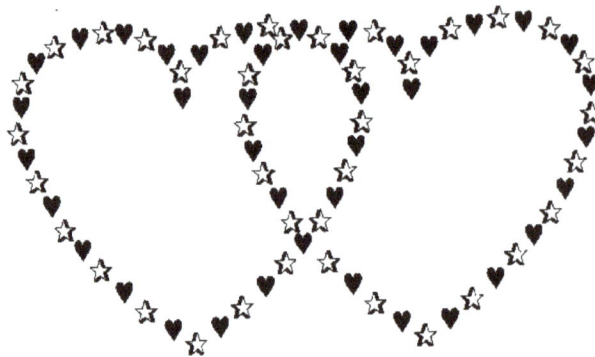

TAURUS MAN - CAPRICORN WOMAN
LOVE RELATIONSHIPS & COMPATIBILITIES

These two individuals do not take their relationship lightly. They share a need for security and permanence, and both prefer tangible proof of that security. That proof comes in the form of a well-run home, an organized life, a sensible routine, a satisfactory career or position, and the material possessions that reflect their position in life. It doesn't hurt that he is also warm, friendly, and personable with an entertaining sense of humor. There relationship is based on trust, and once that is established, she is the devoted help mate who makes life run all that smoother. She is proud of his convictions and strengths to say nothing about the way he wants to protect and provide for her. These two enjoy being conventional, adhere to the status quo, and find fulfillment in traditions. Her family obligations may match his own, and both will remain firmly tied and active in family affairs. His capacity for enjoying life with a little fun and frivolity will add that special ingredient of spice to her life. Her shy reserve may melt away under the attentions of this masculine and virile man. And he can't help but to have his passions aroused by this attractive and feminine creature who is so impressed and attentive with him. Music or art may attract either's interest, and they share a desire to be involved with each other. Once a mutual bond is established, these two may come to strongly depend upon one another. In her own career she may be independent and ambitious, but at home she sways between being a strong, self-willed person and a woman who is dependent on his attention, support and admiration. Both desire a relationship that will endure the test of time, surmount any and all problems and obstacles, and see them through their fears and worries to the best of life. And for these two serious minded individuals the best that life has to offer equals a secure life and an even more secure home life. She may be more prone to analytical and methodical thinking, but both are cautious in their decision making. And both are paranoid about engaging in risky or rash decisions or sudden changes of plans. These two are reliable, responsible, and conscientious. Will they have disagreements? That would only be natural for any two people, but these two aren't about to threaten their relationship over a disagreement. It might help if both he and she curb a tendency to be too inflexible and insistent on routine. Taurus can help Capricorn to be more physically active, but he will be happy to know that there is every indication that she will retain her good looks well into maturity. Capricorn can put her worries aside and trust that once this Taurus man makes up his mind that she's the woman for him, there is every indication that he won't change his opinion.

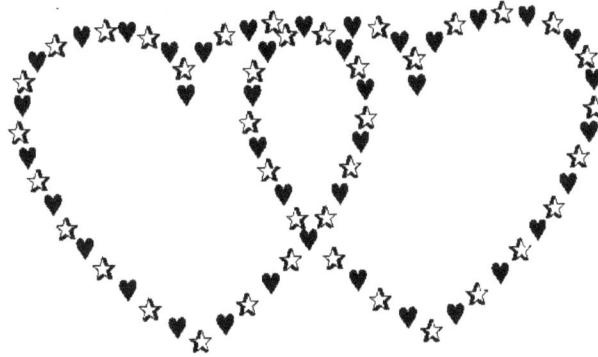

Taurus Woman - Aquarius Man
Love Relationships & Compatibilities

What does this Taurus woman see in this Aquarius man? It must be that he is everything she could never possible be. Unconventional Aquarius can throw caution to the wind then sit and watch it float curiously around his head (figuratively speaking of course). Traditions are fine for other people, but some how or another they simply don't apply to him. He'll be easy enough to love. After all, everyone loves Aquarius, but few people can explain why. That's because he is unexplainable. He's down the road, sitting in the future, dreaming of what could be. He can be eccentric or genius, the truth bearer or the biggest spinner of tall tales imaginable. It must be their differences that attracts this Taurus female to him. or perhaps her sensitive and protective nature has kicked in, and she wants to be there to offer him her support. She need not worry too much. Wherever Aquarius goes, people are drawn to him. He's a loner at heart, but he has an especially strong need for friends. And people for some unexplainable reason continue to seek him out for his companionship. People will put up with more faults from an Aquarius than any other sign, and just keep coming back. He's a very special person, and that's why this Taurus lady seeks him out. Whether the relationship works or not, they will always remain friends. If she wants to keep him in her life, she will need to forget about curbing his freedom or changing his ways. He goes where he pleases, when he pleases, and no one has as yet designed a strong enough law to bind his curious nature. He possesses a strong love of humanity and the ability to overlook the needs of the individual sitting next to him. She will never know exactly what's going on in his mind (no one does) which may intrigue this patient lady. She was certain that all the conventional, conservative rules and regulations made perfectly good sense until he came along and by his own life proved that any number of them are simply unnecessary. Aquarius is as unpredictable as Taurus is reliable. He can be sociable, likeable, and entertaining, however, he probably doesn't make much effort to be the center of attention, and he isn't much of a follower. He can be liberal, progressive, and intellectually independent, but in his home life he has particular likes and dislikes and is not easily swayed to change his mind. He likes to spend time at home, in his own personal routine, and perhaps will need some time to himself. But this Taurus female will have to accept that time at home also includes time with friends who will show up unexpectedly and Aquarius isn't the least bit discerning. He likes unusual people, and she may as well accept that she may wake up to discover a new friend sleeping on the sofa. To make this relationship work will require a very enlightened Taurus female who loves with all her heart and places her demands on herself and not on him.

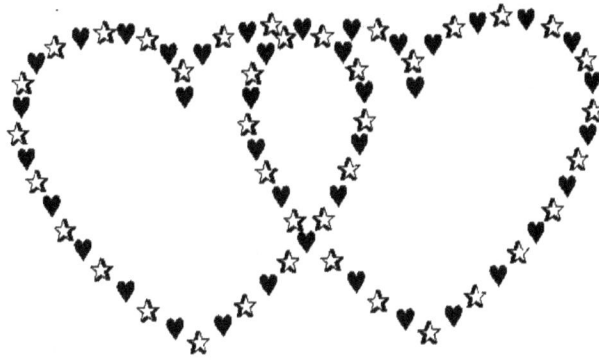

Taurus Man - Aquarius Woman
Love Relationships & Compatibilities

Whatever he thought life was meant to be, this lively Aquarius female will show him what life could be. Just when he thought he had it all figured out, a long comes a lady who effortlessly proves that all his conventional wisdom applies only to him. She lives life freely in her way meaning no harm to anyone and wanting no limitations on herself. She is an innovative and creative thinker who brings romance and imagination into his life. She is well liked, friendly, pleasantly attentive to one and all and finds Taurus a project worth investigating. She'll never rest until she has shaken him out of his conventional cocoon and exposed him to a glimmer of radiant light. The light of rainbows that is and of a future only she could imagine. Her smile will warm his heart, and he may find himself rushing home just to find out what she has planned for today. Possessions are fine with her, but hardly the necessity they are for Taurus. Her personal style is of her own making, and Taurus will forever wonder where she gets her ideas. She envisions a future while Taurus builds for the future. She admires him just as she admires all her friends. And this relationship will be based on friendship. Taurus will forever be amazed that she can throw caution and convention to the wind and yet people just like her anyway. He strives to do what is right, acceptable, and securely reliable. But she never fails to bring out his warm humor and to lighten his mental mood. If he really wants this charming lady in his life, he can forget about changing her in any form or fashion. She can't be possessed any more than the air. Once he decides to put her trust in her, despite their many differences, he'll discover that she's loyal and devoted. But he can't smother her freedoms or her liberty. She is a free thinker who delights in all the possibilities in life. That she doesn't cling to him possessively doesn't mean that she doesn't love him. If she's with him then she's where she wants to be. She likes his warm-hearted humor, the way he treats his mother, his strength and masculinity, and his patient, good-natured intentions. Although she may not share his outlook on life, with a few startlingly insightful remarks, she'll theorize why he's the way he is and leave it at that. There will be many a frustrating moment for this Taurus man, but she will never fail to amaze him while inspiring him to think. Whether or not they stay together, they will always be friends and both will always appreciate that each knew the other. If his determination keeps him by the side of this wonderful woman, then life will never be a dull adventure. She promises a luster that comes full of surprises, romance, and fun. And despite what anyone may say, Taurus does like to enjoy life and have fun.

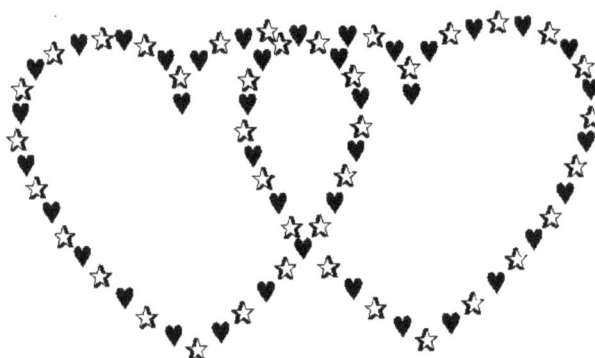

Taurus Woman - Pisces Man
Love Relationships & Compatibilities

In Pisces this Taurus woman may have found a man who needs her down-to-earth, practical approach to daily living. Forever romantic and sensual, he will appreciate her strength and emotional security. Taurus and Pisces both love the good things in life, and the possessions that make Taurus feel secure will make Pisces feel well grounded. For the most part, these are two easy going, friendly and congenial people who enjoy an active social life and entertaining as well as a pleasant home life. And both are sentimentally attached to home and family. He is a compassionate and caring individual who, if so inclined, can sacrifice his own needs for the benefit of others. He has two sides to his nature. One side is hard working and productive while the other side prefers to drift off into a dream world of fantasy and illusions. He brings his own special creativity to this relationship, and Taurus balances his moods with her capable direction and focus on goals. Many a Taurus possesses a creative bend as well, and if this is the case, these two can inspire each other with their talents and imagination. He adds a splash of color to her well organized life. Pisces doesn't respond well to criticism or being bossed around, and she may want to develop just the right incentives for curbing his tendency to dream away his days. And of course, he'll have to accept her ability to resist quick changes of plans. In truth, Pisces are people who function better if they think something was their idea to start with, and Taurus doesn't so much care whose plan it is as long as there is one being followed. Whatever their differences, these two passionate lovers can be found romping freely in the bedroom where his creatively romantic charms heighten her intense sensuality. And he responds to her possessiveness in a positive manner, feeling that it is more than adequate proof of her love for him. When Taurus and Pisces make a good match, then Pisces feels an overwhelming sense of security and peace, and Taurus likes nothing better than to feel secure. In love, a Taurus woman can be devoted and adoring which will only add to this man's feelinqs of well being. In return, she likes attention, praise and affection, all of which Pisces is more than capable of giving. He is one person who

156

genuinely enjoys giving, not just things, but also of himself. If the relationship is such that it brings out the good qualities in this Pisces man, then this particular Taurus woman will be more than delighted with her involvement with this man. And if he truly loves and appreciates the many good qualities she brings to the relationship, he will be able to watch their love grow and flourish. Together, they strive to seek happiness and fulfillment as much as anything else in life, and this relationship offers that probability.

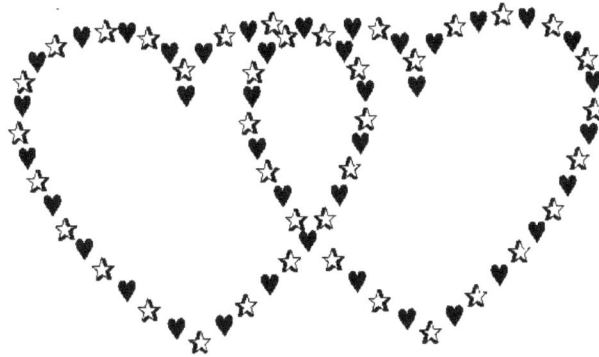

TAURUS MAN - PISCES WOMAN
LOVE RELATIONSHIPS & COMPATIBILITIES

Taurus sees in Pisces an attractive, imaginative female whose smile seems to add glitter to his life. And romantic Pisces see in Taurus the masculine embodiment of her dreams come true. His passion matches her romantic needs, and she never tires of dreaming up new excursions into sexual bliss. She needs a strong, steadfast person to lean on, and his ambitious nature suits her desires just perfectly. Much has been said about the Taurus need for possessions, but Pisces has a tendency to collect things as well, and she is most comfortable when surrounded by her things. They may be items that enhance in her creativity, or to which she places sentimental value, or which she simply enjoys. But in one way or another her many (always interesting) items reflect her distinctly personal taste and whims. There's every chance that each special item in her possession comes complete with a story of how it came into her life. She perceives pictures in her mind, and she needs those things in her life which enhances her imagination and creativity. And she most enjoys items that add a little glitter to life. The Taurus sense of direction will make her feel even more secure, knowing that she can work with him to build a future and still find time to dream purely imaginative escapes. She is intuitive and perceptive, and more than a few Pisces are psychically receptive. He is down to earth and practical, but this capability of hers will never fail to catch his attention and curiosity about matters he wouldn't otherwise think about. These two are both amiable, easy going people who like to take the time to laugh at life. Both enjoy pleasurable outings, sociable get togethers with friends, and activities that add fun to their daily life. They want their home to be comfortable, and both prefer a pleasant setting either for entertaining or for quiet evenings at home. Now then, he will have to understand that Pisces is

157

more emotional than he could ever be, and she is particularly sensitive to criticism. Neither does she unquestioningly accept orders. She will want to make him happy in every way she can, but Taurus will need to develop some tact and diplomacy to keep her truly happy. She will like his firmness, steady direction, and ability to work hard to acquire what he wants in life. And with her winning Pisces ways, she's probably just the person to persuade him to change his mind once in awhile just to suit her whim. She is a gentle and caring creature who just naturally adores the man she loves which is just what Taurus wants most in his life. He will discover that she is the most pleasant of people to come home to, and she will find that having him at home with her is a real dream. There is every indication that these two, together, can make their dreams come true while enjoying life at the same time.

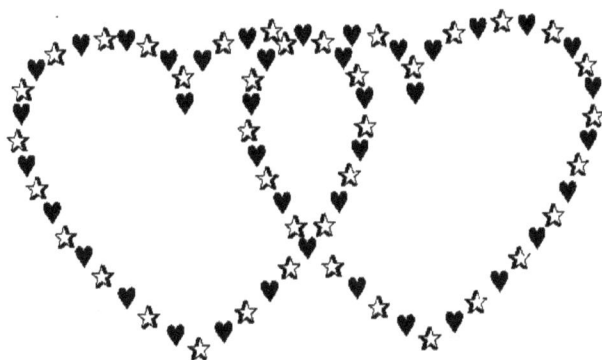

Gemini Woman - Gemini Man
Love Relationships & Compatibilities

These two may share a special compatibility based on mutual understanding. Finally he and she have discovered another person with a dual nature. Either may be that lively salesman who introduced you to the most innovative idea for your business or gave that unforgettable sales pitch for a new luxury item. Then again, Gemini could be that quiet, serious accountant with a phenomenal memory for facts and figures--but never doubt that there's another side to his/her nature that seeks travel, and new experiences, activities, and ideas (not to mention that Gemini has an appreciative eye for attractive members of the opposite sex). Gemini is forever the enigma of the Zodiac, not a mystery, but a puzzle. For these two, getting to know one another (and the dual nature of each) can be an ongoing life long affair. They are both curious, restless, highly persuasive and ready for change in one form or another. Their home life may be composed of an atmosphere that allows for freedom of thought, movement, and expression which is unhampered by jealousies, possessiveness and restrictions. These two bright and hopeful people love to toss around ideas and dreams. They are intellectual, logical thinkers, but don't forget that tendency to scatter creative forces in diverse directions. They both can be energetic, versatile, and adaptable to new situations and people. They bounce from one activity, mental pursuit, or interest to another, gathering experiences and lively companionship along the way. Gemini gathers information, and chances are, knows a lot a little about a number of different subjects. Either may express opinions on a wide range of topics or simply like to exchange gossip on the latest events. Both take an interest in some form of art, music or creative outlet. Each will need to expect the other to be one person one day and someone else the next. Both can alternately be warm and affectionate or cool and indifferent. They are sensitive people who don't respond to criticism or undue pressure well. And either can be quiet and reflective or turn right around and expose a cynical, sarcastic or irritable disposition. But these two can also be witty, amusingly charming, uplifting and fun, and in the case of any arguments, both are the forgive and forget type. Both abhor routine, and while many an astrologer will report that Gemini isn't highly sexed, it is more a matter that they are highly interested but don't overtly share that notion with many people. Sex is fun. Gemini most like fun. Therefore, Gemini most definitely does like sex. It isn't the intensely passionate and emotional sex of some of the other signs. No, Gemini perceives sex as a mentally stimulating and explorative search for new experience. And a Gemini person is on a mission of search and find for that perfect sexual partner, gathering new information and experiences along the way. These two people are quick in action and thought, and clever with words. When it comes to settling down into a lasting relationship, neither is cautious, but both want to be reassured that personal freedom is high on the list of priorities.

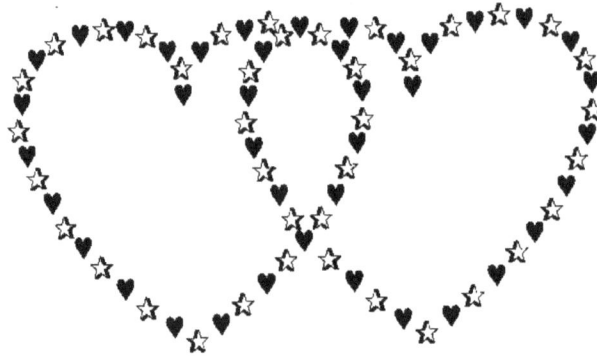

GEMINI WOMAN - CANCER MAN
LOVE RELATIONSHIPS & COMPATIBILITIES

A Cancer man can be tenderly sensual, attentive, and affectionate, and he finds this gregarious Gemini woman expressively romantic and charming. Both are highly imaginative and creative, each in a different manner, and both can be a bit self-possessed with their perspective day dreams. These two may have been attracted by a common interest in art, music, cultural events, or simply socializing with mutual friends. Cancer can be somewhat indirect in his approach, but she intuitively picked up on his attraction to her then approached him directly using her versatile charms and amusing wit to draw him out of the crowd. He likes attention, succumbs to flattery, is susceptible to any show of kindness directed at him, and glows when admired. How could he not be captivated by this perceptive female? Given a little encouragement, his mind turns to romance, and the thought of spontaneous sex sets his imagination in high gear. His receptiveness to spur of the moment erotic ideas excites Gemini as well. And there mutual compatibility in this arena is bound to spell excitement. However, he lives his life through his emotions, and intellectual Gemini may be more detached. Sentimental Cancer dwells on the past and probably has an interest in historical events, heritage, and his personal genealogy and family history. And he just as easily remembers past wrongs, slights, insults, and injuries, whether imagined or real. Gemini's wit can easily switch to sarcasm, and she will have to be careful of the Cancer defensive mode which might lead to one of his brooding withdrawn moods. Her own moods don't change, rather her entire nature changes from upbeat to coolly preoccupied. Cancer can be protective toward his usually lively Gemini, but she should be aware that this protectiveness can turn to possessiveness. As socially active as he is, he also likes to gear his life toward home, finances, and security. That's all well enough for Gemini, but this combination may produce that feeling of being hemmed in, of having her freedom limited. She has to watch her speech so she doesn't offend him, and now there's a feeling a restricting her movement as well. This might be too much for lovely Gemini to handle, unless of course we're talking about a love and romance which she can't possible do without. In that case, she must make some adjustments. Of course, it would be nice if Cancer adjusts also, giving her room to explore and experience life. Trust and understanding are important between these two, but they will also have to work on communicating because these two may well think, perceive, feel, and experience life differently. Gemini may find herself exploring ways to settle their differences, and Cancer may feel misunderstood. If they can match their dreams and similar interests, the rest is just a lesson in compatibility.

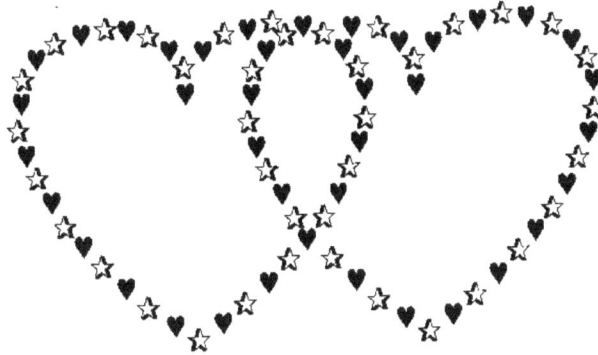

Gemini Man - Cancer Woman
Love Relationships & Compatibilities

She's entertaining, creative, imaginative, attractive, warmly affectionate and caring. This resourceful Gemini man is impulsively drawn to her good-natured ways. They share a creative but restless imagination that seeks new stimulation, experiences and change. But experiences for her may be centered around a home base where as Gemini is a little less prone to be bound by anything. They both love to travel, are socially active, and interested in art, music, or photography. She is so sensitive that she intuitively feels the emotions of others. He is so perceptive that he intuitively perceives the thoughts of others. She can become overwhelmed by her restless emotions, and he is at times submerged in his restless thoughts. She dreams fantasies while he dreams up new ideas, places to go, and people to meet. He can be attentive and affectionate one minute then gone to meet his friends the next. She most wants admiration and an abundance of attention. He most wants her understanding of his changing nature. They both want a relationship based on love, trust, mutual interests, and companionship, but those ingredients may mean different things to each of them. She'd like to be his central focus, but Gemini scatters his focus in numerous directions. She wants sex to be emotionally fulfilling, he just wants sex. He may be as impersonal as she is intense, but if the truth be known, when in love, he loves deeply and with all his heart. He'll make every attempt to be what she wants, but then his naturechanges again and he's off to follow his newest impulse.She wants thesecurity of home, sound finances, and personalpossessions. He wants those things too as soon as he's completed his latest endeavor. Both can be spiritually inclined, but again this is an emotional experience for her and an intellectually challenging one for him. He thinks while she feels. He'll learn to expect her moods which change with the sunrise and the phases of the moon. She'll learn that his entire nature changes subliminally and as are unexplainable to him as they are mystifying to her. If she clings, he'll only escape to where the air is freer and the atmosphere is less restrictive. Her possessiveness bothers him but no more than his periodic aloofness troubles her. Now quite fortunately, if these two are truly perceptive and intuitive, they know in their hearts that the other person means well, and both will accept their differences. After all, the world would be a dull place if everyone were predictably the same. Besides, these two know that neither of them is the easiest person to live with. Concessions will need to be made, but then it's time to kiss and make up and start all over again.

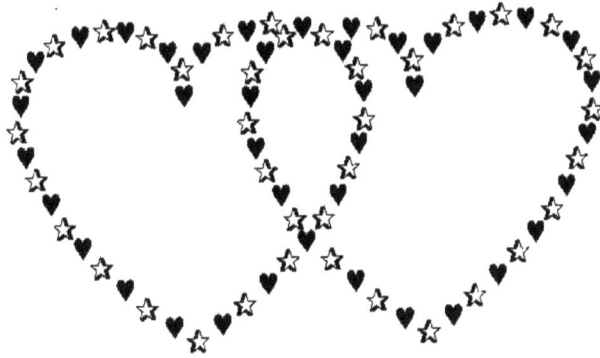

GEMINI WOMAN - LEO MAN
LOVE RELATIONSHIPS & COMPATIBILITIES

Leo the Lion at times needs a handler, and glib Gemini should be remarkably well versed for this position. He is proud and ambitious and all remarks made to him should be appropriately laced with praise and admiration. And flattery will get her everywhere. He is sunshine itself, beaming his warm, radiant magnificence and magnetic wit and charm for all to appreciate. His self-assurance and regal bearing work along with his dramatic flair to make him king of the show. He aspires to lead the attentions of others, focusing the spotlight on himself. At home, he may take it as his natural position to be catered to and served, and doesn't realize in the least that he can be demanding and overbearing. He's accustomed to receiving admiration and before this entertaining Gemini woman came along, he probably received more than has fair share of attention from his lady friends. A Leo man has a tendency to see the woman in his life has the perfect person who he is attracted to until the passions subside into everyday realities at which time he loses interest, falling in and out of love easily. But he will discover a basic compatibility with this special Gemini lady who shares so many of his interests with her unique zest for life. Leo can easily grow bored with routine, and there is nothing routine about Gemini. She shares his love for an active social life, a touch of excitement and adventure, and she thrills at his bold, courageous nature. She is perceptive enough to realize that beneath all that pomp and strong ego, he is sensitive and vulnerable and needs huge doses of reassurance and acclaim. And during one of his long lectures on her faults and shortcomings, his arrogance and overbearing, condescending manner can be cut short with her precisely to-the-point sarcastic observations. Luckily, they are both forgive and forget types who prefer to turn on their warm, friendly and happy dispositions and to enjoy the moment at hand. He'll want to protect her and lead her in the right direction, and Gemini most likely would benefit from a little leadership. But despite whatever faults she 'may have, he finds her uniquely entertaining and unpredictable. Her airy ways fan his fiery passions, and Leo may be too self-absorbed to notice she isn't overly emotionally intense. That he is generous, fun-loving, and kind only adds to his appeal. Both enjoy the good things in life that make it so much more comfortable and pleasing. He must accept her whims, changeability, and dual nature as part of the allure that holds his attraction. And she must accept his great need for appreciation, adoration, acclimation, and praise. But then the imaginative and versatile Gemini female is more than well equipped for this challenge in life. And truth be known she's probably as proud of her Leo man as he is of himself, and she expresses this thought freely.

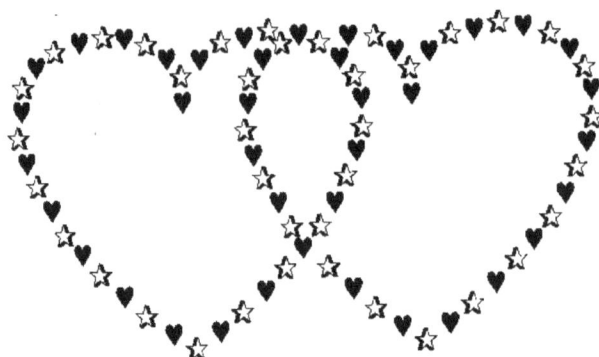

GEMINI MAN - LEO WOMAN
LOVE RELATIONSHIPS & COMPATIBILITIES

A charming and courteous Gemini man enjoys compatible companionship and once he's settled his mind on this enthusiastic Leo woman, he'll enjoy all the advantageous of a loving relationship. She admires his intellectual adaptability, and he is attracted to her independent and free-thinking ways. Her self-assurance makes him proud of her and makes him feel even more secure in this involvement. She beams sunshine and warmth, and he captures it in his words and returns it to her as a gift of appreciation. And every Leo woman is especially fond of not only appreciation but gift-bearing admirers. She is affectionate and cheerful and these two are both energetically driven to be outgoing, gregarious, and alive, making the most of the moment. They enjoy being surrounded by other people, either entertaining or being involved in a social whir of activities. In love, a Leo woman is loyal and devoted and although she can be controlling, no controls have yet been invented for the changeability of her dual natured Gemini lover. He'll recognize that she means well, and allow her as much control as he's capable of, but then he's off again on one of the tangents of his restless mind. What could possibly hamper these two is if they allow their daily lives to become routine which would result in both of them becoming discontent. When unhappy, he can be impatient, irritable, and cynical, and she can be temperamental. Both delight in a little excitement, something new to heighten the imagination and challenge the Gemini's intellect and the Leo courage. Gemini also likes to have someone listen to him, his ideas and thoughts, and if Leo perceives this as attention from her most admiring fan, she'll devote her full attention to him. That he is naturally gifted at meeting people, making contacts, and benefitting from influential people, will impress and inspire her ambitious nature. He is versatile and adaptable to new situations, and wherever they go her natural grace and bearing, to say nothing of her kind and generous nature, makes her readily acceptable and publicly admired. This Leo woman will have to learn to deal with any jealousy she feels when Gemini turns his charm and flirtations to any and all. His creative originality, selfexpression and ability to persuade others heightens her interest in his abilities. That they both appreciate art, music, or some form of creative endeavor may also inspire their interest in each other. Then too many a Gemini and Leo, liking the good life and pleasure, can be a bit too extravagant, and this is one area will mutual goals will need to be established. Leo has a basic need for an extra dose of excitement or challenge in life, and the duality of the Gemini nature may be just the added spice she seeks. When these two devote their lives to each other, their love is inspiring.

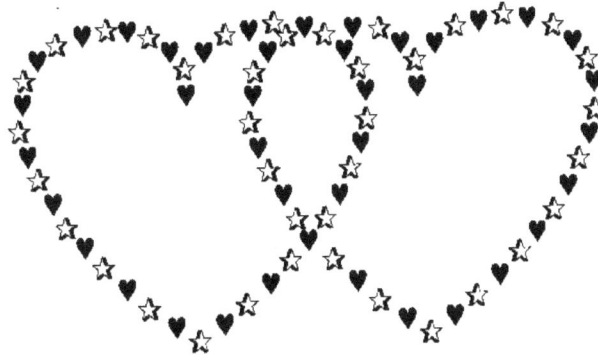

GEMINI WOMAN - VIRGO MAN
LOVE RELATIONSHIPS & COMPATIBILITIES

Gemini and Virgo can be the best of friends, partners or associates. Whether or not they make it as romantic partners will depend a great deal on the two individuals involved. Intellectually, they are well suited although Virgo is much more detail-oriented and his ideas may be more cautious, conservative, and limiting than the general nature of this Gemini woman. oh, she may be conservative as well, but she is more expansive and seeking in her outlook, exploring new possibilities and looking at the larger picture. Chances are she's gathered a little information about numerous topics, and will know just enough tidbits to keep Virgo fascinated with her far ranging opinions while he expounds on his own personal opinions and theories. He can be protective and a good provider, which she appreciates, and he most wants to be appreciated. But his overly cautious nature may dampen her usually restless nature. She wants freedom to explore new avenues of thought and activities, but in time he may feel she is superficial. He is most comfortable with dependability and routine and may feel uneasy when her amiability turns to cool aloofness. Both can kid and joke around, but he doesn't really understand her quiet and reflective moods when just yesterday she was planning a fun-filled excursion. She can be bright and hopeful one moment and act lost and lonely the next. She likes to create new ideas and then act upon them, but while he may play around with any number of ideas, his caution prevents him from action. He likes the tried and true. She likes anything new and innovative. He can be critical and analytical, intent on producing sound results, while she critically observes and perceives endless possibilities for expansion. Virgo is mentally restless, planning what needs to be done and aspiring to accomplishment and perfection. Gemini is mentally and physically restless, seeking change for the sake of change. He brings practicality to the relationship while she brings the ability to shake up his thinking processes and to persuasively goad him into action. If these two came to terms with their differences and accepted each other then they could combine their positive qualities and focus their goals on producing greater results. He must accept that she sees failure as a-stepping stone to success not a fall from grace. And she must learn to present her ideas in the most logical manner, which she is most capable of doing. She is also capable of distracting his logical thinking into more amorous pursuits, and then he reveals his more affectionate and tender nature and appreciates her appreciation all the more. These two are share the ability to keep each other happily preoccupied and busy with their endeavors and accomplishments. That there's a little give and take required may simply add to the development of a lasting and loving relationship.

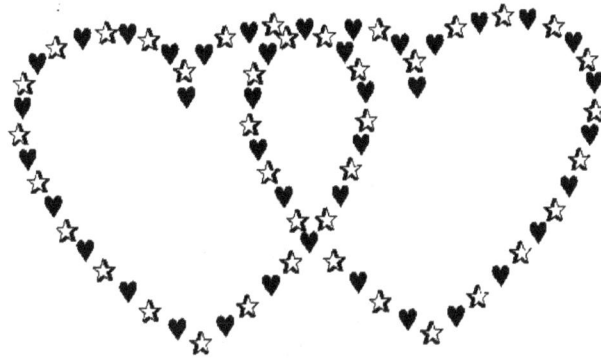

GEMINI MAN - VIRGO WOMAN
LOVE RELATIONSHIPS & COMPATIBILITIES

Gemini values freedom as much as Virgo values security, but he finds it is so restful and peaceful to go home to a warmly affectionate woman who is calm and dependable, especially after a day of competing with more assertive types. If he falls deeply in love with her it is because he recognizes their mutual similar qualities, but he also respects those qualities which she possesses and he lacks. In other words, she impresses him not only with her endearing love for him but with her predictable steadfast ways. Above all else she is a trusted and reliable friend, and while he has many friends, finding those qualities in another can be difficult. She is devoted and kind and added to all that is her enterprising intellect which matches his own. She can be amiable and humorous matching his quick wit and funny stories. Then too, in this Gemini man, the Virgo woman recognizes those qualities she'll never possess, and out of curiosity and pure attraction she will be drawn to see what new ideas and insights he produces in the future. He may rock her boat on occasion proving to her that her well-thought out and practical theories on life are just that, theories, while life can be so much more fun and exciting when you dare to take a chance. She may watch him in amazement and even vicariously live a more vibrant life through his antics. She can be precise and thorough in her deductions, but he never fails to amaze her with his simple little question of, "Yes, but what if... ". Both are affectionate and tender and even if his mind does tend to wander to far ranging topics, he forever returns for another embrace. They are a challenge to each other with her steadfast notions of how easy life could be if they just followed a few simple rules, and his insistence that she lighten up a little and explore the possibilities. Her sentimentality will make her all the more endearing to this impulsive man. That his nature changes from seeking and exploring to quiet introspection proves to her his need for her reassurances. Their intellectual natures don't prevent this couple from enjoying sociable activities and pleasurable outings both enjoying the companionship of other people. That he can't help his easy-going and mildly flirtatious manner may raise her eyebrow on occasion, but if she's smart she'll realize that it's her he continually returns home to and in that she must find her security. Being Virgo, she'll also want the security of home, position, and finances which is all fine and well with him because if this Gemini man is seeking life with this Virgo woman, then chances are he's realizing his own security through her. These two may spend a lifetime explaining their thought processes to each other, but in many instances that is what life and companionship are all about. And the friendship that develops is a strong base for a loving relationship.

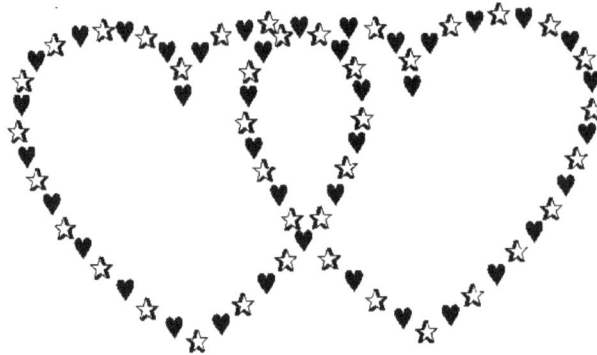

GEMINI WOMAN - LIBRA MAN
LOVE RELATIONSHIPS & COMPATIBILITIES

These two may well be a match. Both are easy going, friendly, sociable, and fun loving with an appreciation of pleasurable past times, elegance, grace and style. And not only are both charmingly gregarious and warmly affectionate, but he actually listens to her ideas and makes her feel important. With his judicious nature, he balances out any situation, deliberating with ease the many issues that face any couple in modern life. What he likes about her is her clever, inventive, and resourceful mind which never fails to give him something new to ponder and think about. The one aspect of their life that requires adjustments to each other is the decision making process. As mentioned, he deliberates, but she would rather apply her energies, make the decision, and get on with the next step. He may see through her dual nature, accepting it as being a basic part of her personality, and actually liking the unpredictability it adds to their life which promises to ward off boredom or too much routine. Libra likes a little excitement in life, and this is just what Gemini offers with her quick wit, willingness to attempt new things, explore new avenues, and most especially meet new people. Libra is inspired by meeting other people and listening to their ideas. Both are well informed people who intellectualize ideas, keeping each other filled with notions, perceptions, and information on a variety of subjects. Entertaining, travel, and their busy career lives may keep them too busy to argue much over the little things in life that seem to cause so much friction between other people. Both can be logical and analytical, but both are a bit restless for new stimulation. Gemini will most appreciate that Libra is dependable and desires a congenial partner with whom to share life. A Gemini woman can be a devoted and loving partner, and Libra will see this as the admiration and love he seeks. Their mutual attraction will draw them closer as they experiment with the possibilities available to them in life. They continue their exploring and the enjoyment of each other in their sexual relationship which is anything but dull. These two turn their charm on each other, both knowing the other is doing just that, and both enjoying every minute of the attention. And rather than be jealous, these two seem to take pride in the other's ability to charm others as well. These two may set out to prove that life can be a pleasant and enjoyable experience, shared with another, while experiencing whatever life brings their way. Any obstacles that happen their way will be dealt with in due time while this couple looks forward to what's ahead, knowing that bad times turn to good times. Life for them is a pleasant surprise just waiting to be lived.

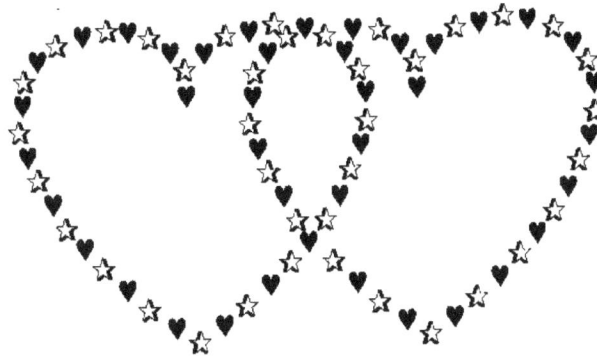

GEMINI MAN - LIBRA WOMAN
LOVE RELATIONSHIPS & COMPATIBILITIES

Libra has an affinity for comfortable living and pleasurable past times with her fair share of fun and frivolity thrown in. Along comes Gemini with his pleasing smile, charming manner, quick wit and way with words, and this Libra woman may feel sees found the perfect man. of course, none of us are perfect, Gemini included, but tolerant Libra looks past whatever faults he may have and sees his adaptable, versatile demeanor. She sees the basic goodness in his heart and that changeable, restless nature that seeks not only intellectual challenge but a spiritual enlightenment as well. He explores the possibilities in life influencing her to do the same. What he most likes about her is that she is open to new ideas and tolerant of other people. She retains a certain refinement in whatever crowd she finds herself, and uses her own special tact and diplomacy to win over the admiration of others. Both are logical thinkers, but she not only stimulates his imagination but listens to his new ideas. And Gemini, by the way, loves to have an attentive person listen to him. At the same time, they may both be a bit sensitive about preserving that feeling of freedom--the freedom to explore new ideas and meet new people. But she most desires a partner to share life's experiences, and he most wants a desirable companion. That his creativity is scattered in numerous directions doesn't especially bother Libra who sees this as the underlying nature of exploration and expansion in thinking. That he is creative delights Libra who possesses like Gemini a strong appreciation for music, art, or literature. Both are well informed, perceptive, and capable of observing the nuances in everyday interactions of other people. These two interact with others with ease, making contacts and benefitting from their many acquaintances. That they share a love of travel, a taste for adventure, and find exploration exciting, only enhances their relationship. Gemini can brood when things don't go his way, but

Libra offers him a fun reprieve when he's ready to go again. In the bedroom, fun and frivolity may rule the day, and in truth that's just what they seek. Now, that's not to say that these two aren't affectionate and loving as well, but both prefer a little excitement to perk up all that passion. And both understands that private little smile each reserves for the other which translates to "let the games begin". Either can be at times a bit superficial, but the more dreary aspects of life hardly appeal to these two energetic and lively people. Their impatience with life creates a yearning within them to get on with life, experiencing it while they may and holding off the doldrums for as long as possible. These are two loving and creative individuals who seek most in life what the other desires.

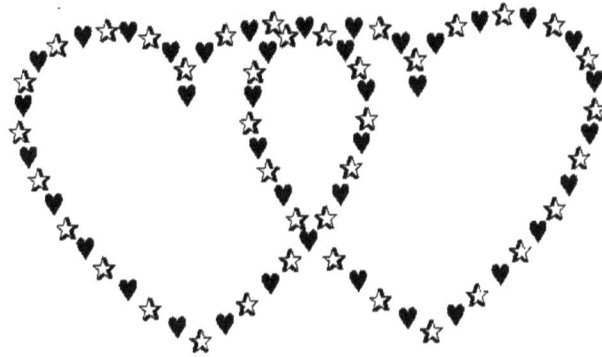

GEMINI WOMAN - SCORPIO MAN
LOVE RELATIONSHIPS & COMPATIBILITIES

The enigma of the Zodiac meets the mystery. She is not only attracted but curiously intrigued. And there's nothing Scorpio likes better than to solve a puzzle. Their initial attraction may have been instantaneous. His penetrating glance probed beyond her glib superficiality recognizing the duality of her nature that she charmingly holds at bay. Her intuitive perceptions noted his interest, however, that glance from this warm but reserved man revealed to her the strong will power he uses to control his intense nature. These two could spend a lifetime analyzing the psyche of the other. His emotional intensity adds a dimension to her life that she had previously only dreamed about. Her clever imagination captures his heart. Courageous Scorpio loves a bold adventure, and Gemini continually fulfills her promises to provide just that. Intellectually, they are both on a search and find mission however different their approaches. And if these two develop a lasting relationship, it will be their differences that bind them together. She offers endless ideas for Scorpio to consider, choosing and selecting which he wants to focus his strong powers of concentration on. He offers her determination and fortitude. He admires her capacity for devotion which a Scorpio can match full-heartedly. Needless to say, in her quest for experiences she never realized that sex could be such a thrilling and consuming part of life until she met him. Both like travel, change and novelty, and new experiences. In actuality, his moods and emotions can run the gambit of extremes, and her changing moods may bring on his own. Gemini focuses on freedom of expression, especially creativity, and Scorpio benefits from expressing not only his creativity but his emotions. She is to him the breeze that ripples over still water, stirring his mind and passions alike. Scorpio can be controlling, but with creative, imaginative people, he quite well understands the necessity of freedom. He will want affirmation that their finances are well-balanced because Scorpio always expects the inevitable obstacles that come his way. He can be single-mindedly focused on one tract or endeavor, but her ability to do more than one thing at a time fascinates him. In fact, there is a lot about her that delights him and vice versa. Whether or not they decide to stay together is a matter of personal choice, but they will always care deeply for one another. What these two share is a subtle empathy and understanding of the other that brings on an acceptance of their differences. What Scorpio knows about this Gemini woman is that when her passions collide with her intellect, she loves and cares

171

deeply, regardless of what mask she chooses to display to others. What Gemini knows about Scorpio is that when his passion is focused on her, her knees turn weak.

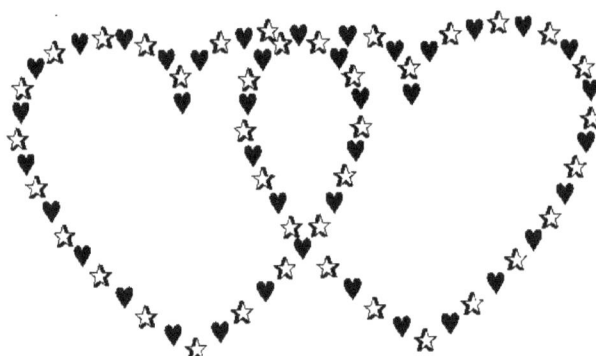

GEMINI MAN - SCORPIO WOMAN
LOVE RELATIONSHIPS & COMPATIBILITIES

This Scorpio woman may decide that the powers-that-be sent her to watch over this ingenious man. He actually needs someone in his life who is determined to stick with him and provide him the will power and determination to see his ideas through to completion or to stick with him when he changes his mind. And Scorpio thrives on being needed. It is the way that he pours his heart into all his many interests that catches her attention. It needs to be noted that every Scorpio woman should experience a relationship with a Gemini man at least once in her life. It is an experience which she will hold dear and remember fondly. Scorpio has no fear of a little excitement, and this versatile Gemini man's lack of caution and discretion has a tendency to draw him into difficult situations. Yes, he definitely needs a strong woman in his life. Sexually, he is drawn to her again and again, wanting to learn what it is she has to teach, and she will teach him what it is he needs to quiet his restless nature, at least temporarily. There's the chance that Scorpio may decide to hold her heart in check (using that infamous self-control) no matter how much she cares for him, waiting to see whether he stays or goes, so restless is his nature. once she devotes her heart to another, she has a tendency to want to possess that person mind, body and soul for herself, and Gemini is too captivating to ever want to subdue in any way. Can she have him and let him go too? That is her dilemma. She is perceptive enough to know he'll promise her the moon and mean every word, but the moon phases in and out. If a strong mutual love wins out between them then these two will spend a life time loving and growing, giving and taking. They will always love one another. Whether they decide to stay together, they must determine for themselves. What she learns from him is how to forgive and forget their differences. Not that she'll apply that to other people, but she'll surely be persuaded to forgive him his changing nature, knowing that he has no control over the matter. If they go their separate ways, then years later he'll send her a little note asking her to call. And when she does, they'll catch up on each other's lives and then he'll whisper his love for her and wherever she is or whatever she's doing, she'll return the sentiment. If they stay together, there's every possibility they'll learn to accept their differences and to harness their energetic drives into creating a pattern of successful accomplishment. Once devoted to him, she'll follow him to the ends of the world or to his next social engagement. He is adaptable and resourceful, and she is resilient. He brings her endless possibilities, and she smiles knowingly. Her intensity melts with his humor and charm, and together they laugh at all that could be.

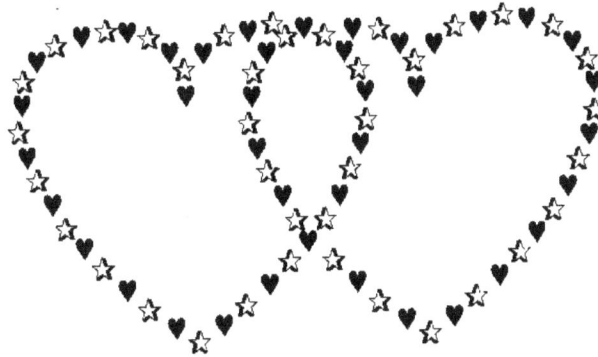

Gemini Woman - Sagittarius Man Love Relationships & Compatibilities

In a Sagittarius man a Gemini woman will have found a kindred spirit. He is optimistic, cheerful, and enthusiastic with a restlessly inquiring mind. Gemini gathers information on a vast diversity of topics, but Sagittarius becomes well informed and skillful in a number of different areas. These two individuals are unconventional thinkers prone to travel, exploration, new ideas and a change of scenery. Both Gemini and Sagittarius are friendly sorts who are well liked by other people. Gemini is freedom loving, and Sagittarius is independent minded, searching for philosophical wisdom and insight. Theses two prefer to be happy and to look for the bright side of any situation, and neither is overly emotional, clinging, or dependent on the other for personal success and happiness. They share an appreciation for each other's intellectual abilities and outlook on life. Neither is fearful of being exposed to a little change and both may need an element of excitement in order to experience life at its fullest. What these two must work at maintaining is that element of change found in meeting new people, being exposed to new ideas, or being involved in new activities. If trapped by their circumstances in a routine existence, either or both can become temperamental, high spirited, sarcastic and irritable. Saqittarius is by nature direct, blunt and outspoken, meaning no harm, but saying what is on his mind. Gemini's nature can vary from warm and caring to cool and aloof while the mood of Sagittarius can change from affectionate to indifferent. Luckily for both of them, these moods and swings in nature don't last long, and both cheerfully rebound. Luck is on the side of Sagittarius and that is the gift he brings to this fortunate Gemini female. These two may become more settled with maturity, but they will both retain numerous diverse interests. What is important for Sagittarius is that the relationship is based on mutual respect and friendship (not possession), and that suits Gemini well. These two impetuous people are charming and outgoing and just plain fun to be with. They are good conversationalist, imaginative and clever, versatile and always on the look for a new or innovative idea. Open hearted and jovial, Sagittarius is free of malice and makes every attempt not to interfere in the lives of others. Gemini isn't quite as straight forward, but she does admire all the good qualities in this man. Both are energetically mentally and physically active. Sagittarius brings a fiery, amorous nature to their love making, and Gemini fans his passions with her whimsical nature. She is more than happy to devote her good intentions to this man who grants her all the freedom to explore that she could ever possible want. Together they give to each other a friend, lively companion, and devoted partner in life.

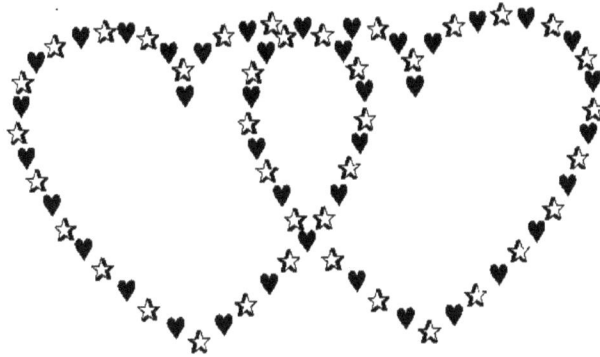

GEMINI MAN - SAGITTARIUS WOMAN
LOVE RELATIONSHIPS & COMPATIBILITIES

This Gemini man may sense the luck and optimism this Sagittarius woman brings to the relationship. Her outlook is expansive which promotes just the freedom he has been searching for in life. Neither of these two are eager to abandon their liberties and independent ways, and it may indeed feel like luck that pulled them together. Any relationship can automatically limit the opportunities for new experiences and impulsive travel, but Gemini and Sagittarius both seek the same possibilities in life. They are casual and flirtatious and love interacting with other people. Both lack jealousy and possessiveness which would be a waste of time for these two outgoing and personable individuals. She isn't timid, and she doesn't hide her feelings. She can be direct and outspoken, relating her opinions in an open manner. Neither Gemini nor Sagittarius is tied to convention, and they will seek whatever it is that satisfies their naturally inquisitive, restless and seeking natures. What she likes about him is his outgoing, congenial charm, and that he chose her to be his significant other. What he likes about her is that she is so captivated by him. Gemini loves to be admired, listened to, and praised for his innovative ideas and creative imagination. Sagittarius wants to be admired for her idealism, intellect, logical thinking, and lively romantic nature. These two are easily bored with an unchallenging routine, and to remain happy they will need to keep the excitement and sense of adventure alive in their relationship. When life limits their possibilities, both Gemini and Sagittarius can become irritable, sarcastic, and complaining. They most need to retain their respective abilities to improvise with new ideas and imaginative dreams. Sagittarius who is restless and changeable herself won't be offended by Gemini's dual nature. She is a true friend in time of need, and his duality will only call forth her compassionate and caring nature. These two can flirt, charm and tease each other from one room to another in their love making escapades. That he is so persuasive only adds to his charm as far as she is concerned. He may become impatient when she is expounding on her latest enlightening philosophy, but she only has to focus her light hearted humor on him to bring out his own quick wit and fun spirit. They may discover their solace in art, music or literature, but it won't be long before this gregarious couple is either entertaining or being entertained by friends, social activities, and congenial companions. That change is a part of their life is fine with them. They wouldn't have any other way. If Gemini was looking for an adventuress to share in his daring ways, then that is just what he discovers in this lively Sagittarius woman. Their own approach to life will determine their future dreams together.

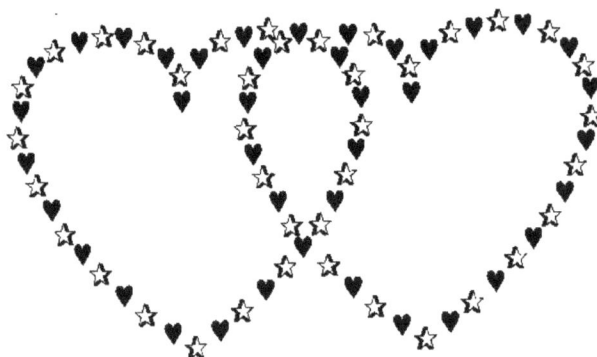

Gemini Woman - Capricorn Man
Love Relationships & Compatibilities

In the Capricorn man this Gemini woman discovers a conventional and traditional individual who in his own reserved and dignified manner patiently and steadfastly pursues success and security. He is responsible, practical, self-disciplined and ambitious, and in the Gemini woman he finds a loving and kind companion who is supportive, warm and affectionate. She may be just the diversion he needs from his serious minded endeavors. Capricorn can be sensitive, sympathetic, warm and reliable, and it is those qualities that assure this Gemini woman of being loved, protected, and provided for. She may not handle pressure well, but he takes it in stride as if it is just one more obstacle to deal with. Her ideas provide him with insights and entertain his intellectual curiosity. Her way with words and social skills, in fact, impress the Capricorn man who sees social interaction as a way to improve one's status in life. What she admires about him is his dedication not only to his goals in life but also to his family and to her. He is strong, supportive, and reliable. And Gemini chases the melancholy away from Capricorn allowing him the opportunity to relax and thoroughly enjoy his home life and the activities they share together. Then too, he catches her mind with his dry humor, sizing up people and events in a few precise words. She rebounds quite easily with her own quick remarks never failing to add a twist to his thoughts. But where Gemini works with ideas and prefers an outlet for her creativity, Capricorn prefers tangible and constructive efforts. All and all, they are different. They look at life differently and they approach life in a different manner. But that is what draws some people together, and it is their differences which they must come to appreciate in order to have a loving and lasting relationship. Once Gemini accepts that Capricorn is not the wandering type, she can relax and fully enjoy his companionship. His steadfast manner may give direction to her life, prompting her to focus her boundless energies on creatively producing results. This relationship is further enhanced by common interests, shared values, and common goals. Life is made even easier if there are well-aspected planets in the charts of these two lovers. Capricorns are noted for retaining their youthfulness well into maturity, and Gemini will note that once this dedicated man has fulfilled his ambitions, he will be more prone to relax and to enjoy more of life and more of her. Neither Gemini nor Capricorn is intensely emotional, but that's not to say that they don't love deeply. Capricorn is an Earth sign, and that special look he reserves for her speaks of earthy passions that never fail to excite Gemini. Together they seek to find fulfillment and happiness.

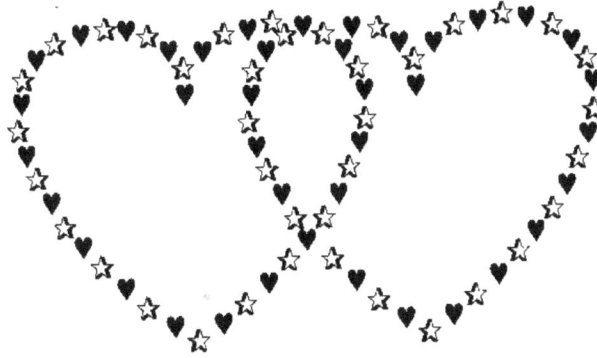

Gemini Man - Capricorn Woman
Love Relationships & Compatibilities

It goes without saying that Gemini sees in Capricorn many of the traits he lacks himself. When truly in love, a Gemini man will try his hardest to please this woman. And in actuality she doesn't ask a lot. She'd prefer that he settled down to a permanent career, that he promises to be faithful, and there's always the chance she'll ask him to give up playing in that funny little band on the week-end with those less than desirable friends of his. He will promise her everything, and he really will try, knowing that his sweet reward will be the admiration of this wonderful woman. Then that funny little urge, that restless nature of his, calls to him. He feels his best intentions slipping away, and there he is off with the guys again doing what guys do best. But then why does she stay with this impractical, unpredictable man? There's something about the roller coaster ride that he offers to her that draws her out of her more practical world. This is a competent, diligent, ambitious woman who knows that the sensible thing to do is to seek an advantageous relationship that promises to produce security for the future. What Gemini offers, however, is that magical dash of excitement and romance wrapped up in a charming and persuasive man. More than likely he first spotted her, perhaps working in her office, and then went to the trouble of finding out more about her before arranging for an introduction. She asked about and found out from those who know him that he's a very likeable guy so she accepted that first date. And it was on that first date that this ingenious, clever Gemini gave his award winning presentation--of himself. He knows that he's attracted a very special person who is one of a kind. She knows that she's never felt like this about anyone. The mutual entrancement is set, and once settled into a loving relationship, these two now discover their alarming differences. To her it's only a matter of establishing priorities and outlining the rest of their lives. To him it's a balancing act of making her happy and preserving his precious freedom. His mind goes into freefall, and he battles with all those ideas that are brainstorming in his head. The end result is the product of their own determinations. He can't change the duality of his basic nature or that part of him that yearns for new experiences, new people, and innovative ideas. She yearns for the sensible approach to attaining their mutual objectives. These two will meet at an impasse where each must decide the best route to follow. Surely, true love can win out if they're both willing to accept each other and live with their differences. Gemini is more than willing to accept her--that's how strong his love is. Now she must accept him, and love him just the way he is.

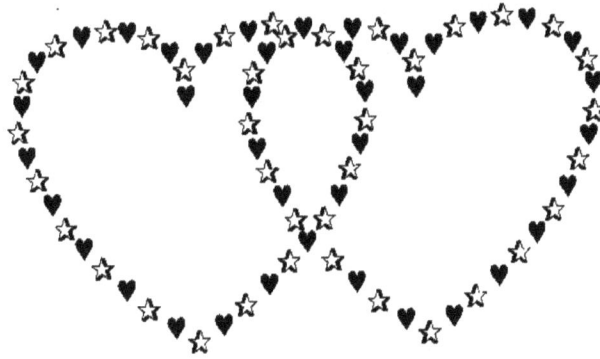

Gemini Woman - Aquarius Man
Love Relationships & Compatibilities

While some combinations of the signs must learn to accept their differences, Gemini and Aquarius must learn to live with their similarities. They share many of the sa-me positive qualities and good traits, but they also share similar faults. Gemini and Aquarius are fun loving, sociable types with outgoing natures who love to be involved in any number of activities. Both are experimenters, unconventional thinkers, and are seeking what is new and innovative. They are creative people whose minds play with original ideas and concepts. The Aquarius mind, however, is even more broad in its scope and produces loftier thoughts with an humanitarian interest that resents current limitations and seeks a future that offers freedom for one and all. These two people love their freedom and independence and neither are overly possessive or jealous. Each accepts the moods of the other person as a natural course of life. Arguing may be another form of discussion for this lively Gemini-Aquarius combination, and they will dispute everything from the proper method of hanging the toilet paper to the significance and influence of spiritualism. Aquarius develops extremely particular likes and dislikes relating to every aspect of life, and Gemini can be discerning in her preferences. This will create a need for adjustments to living with each other. Gemini can switch from funny and entertaining to preoccupation compared to the Aquarius shift from congenial and pleasant to erratic and withdrawn. But these two just naturally like each other, and that can turn into a fond friendship which develops into enduring love. Their diverse intellectual and social interests keep them actively involved and on the go. But both like to know that when they return home, there is a special person there, and home is where they are loved and accepted just as they are. Learning how to extricate themselves from their many friends and activities in order to spend time with each other is part of the fun as far as these two are concerned. They are more interested in romance and sex then they like others to know, and when together they intuitively recognize that in each other. Their light hearted ways carry over to the bedroom where they entertain each other at every opportunity. Gemini likes her friends and makes contacts easily, but while Aquarius shares this trait he is also sought out by more unique and eccentric individuals who he readily accepts into his life. Her imagination inspires his own to even greater heights, and these two find each other stimulating and fun. organizing their lives is not a top priority, but everything just seems to fall naturally into place which is acceptable to them. Their freedom and love of life and each other allows them to design their own personal and perfectly suitable lifestyle.

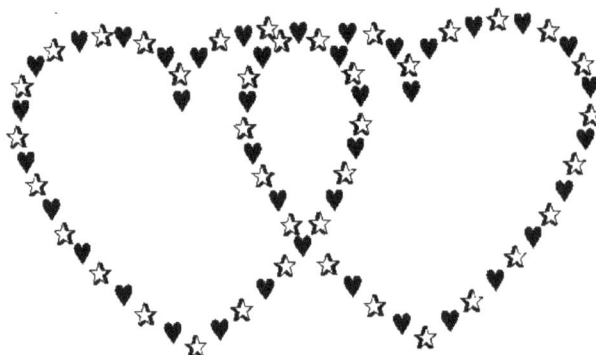

GEMINI MAN - AQUARIUS WOMAN
LOVE RELATIONSHIPS & COMPATIBILITIES

With their active minds and original ideas, Gemini and Aquarius are drawn to people of similar interests and interesting personalities. And that is just what this happy couple see in each other. Warm, friendly, outgoing, romantic, and imaginative, Gemini and Aquarius are good natured and kind and particularly fond of each other. She is tolerant and accepting and greatly admires his creative intellect, persuasive communication skills, and his overall outlook on life. Together they are fond of an active social life, like to entertain, and enjoy being surrounded by other people. That's not to say that she won't make an effort to find time for herself away from her many friends and activities, but Gemini can understand that need which he on occasion shares. His restlessness and his abundance of nervous energy that seems to propel him through life is accepted by Aquarius as what makes him unique. And the list of traits that make Aquarius unique are seemingly endless. In fact, it may be her individuality that most attracts this charming Gemini man. It's a great feeling to be loved, admired, and accepted just as you are, and that may be the basis for this relationship which more than likely began as a friendship and developed into compelling love. Gemini and Aquarius know that nothing in life is carved in stone, but today they are together so why not enjoy their time to the fullest. And if they are drawn together for a life time, it will just as likely be this same attitude that unites them. The nice thing about this relationship is that when they are together they can be themselves. They are free to be generous and giving of themselves. Gemini and Aquarius both like to be friends, as well as lovers, and to share common interests and ideas. They bask in their compatibility. She encourages his restless nature thinking that what other purpose could there be to life but to live it to the fullest. These two may well have their little arguments, disagreements and discussions, but deep-seated emotional arguments are not, generally speaking, their style. And both Gemini and Aquarius quickly forgive the other, forgetting the matter at hand, and moving on to something more entertaining. Both much prefer to remain friends then to allow disharmony to develop, and either will defer to persuasive and disarming charm to settle the matter at hand. Sexual compatibility also ranks high on their list of accomplishments, and Gemini and Aquarius, two Air signs, delight in delighting each other. Neither clings to the other, but curiously watches to see where all that freedom and independence will lead. Through in a little good natured stubbornness that adds to the interest level, and Gemini and Aquarius are set for an entertaining life. All they need to hold them together is a mutual commitment and an endearing love for each other.

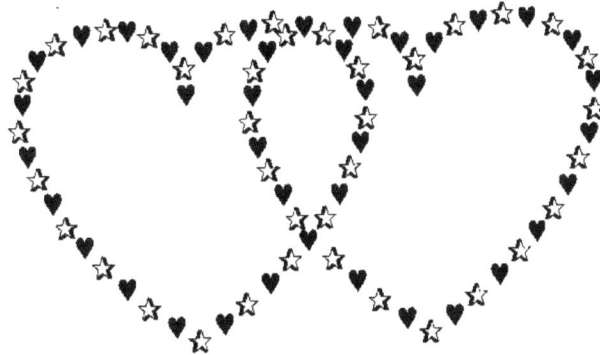

GEMINI WOMAN - PISCES MAN
LOVE RELATIONSHIPS & COMPATIBILITIES

Gemini and Pisces may be great friends and admirers, but they may have to disentangle themselves from their current romantic involvements before they discover themselves in each other's arms. They are two enchantingly charming individuals who are prolifically creative, social whirlwinds bent on discovering life each in his or her own fashion. After they have developed their friendship and flirtatiously dangled romantic overtures to each other, they will begin to notice certain disadvantageous to furthering a relationship. Either or both may lack the ability to give what the other most desires. Pisces can be selfsacrificing, highly romantic, emotional and sentimental, but most of all he wants to be admired through lots of devotion and attention. He wants to find emotional fulfillment through love, togetherness, affection and sex. That paints a pretty picture for this Gemini woman, but she may not fully understand just where she fits in. Gemini, on the other hand, may cleverly mold her words to fit the situation, is more than happy to say whatever it is he wants to hear to make him happy, and she does delight in making him happy. But Gemini is somewhat unsure about his sentimentality and emotional needs. She will gladly discuss it at length, but it doesn't quite sink in. It may appear to her, that logically one's emotional happiness is derived from one's self, so how can she further his well being? Perhaps they should discuss it again. But Pisces isn't as interested in all these discussions. He perceives through his intuitions and draws graphic images in his mind, and he wants her to know what he's feeling and perhaps to share in that emotion. By this time, the restless mind of Gemini has moved on to other ideas, and could they change the subject anyway because she would really like to discuss an innovative new concept. And so it goes, on and on, with never a real meeting of the minds. Now, nothing is impossible, and these two may be so in love and attracted by the imagination and creativity of the other that it holds them together. Witty Gemini will have to learn that what she considers funny, sensitive Pisces may take as personal criticism. And whether he admits it or not, he is easily offended. Pisces can also take Gemini's changeability personally. Seeing her once affectionate nature turning to indifference can leave Pisces feeling abandoned and unloved. It goes without saying that the outcome of this relationship depends a great deal on Pisces' ability to accept Gemini's less emotional nature. And which ever way the wind blows, there is little doubt that Gemini will forever be entranced by the magical spell of Pisces--a spell that cannot be logically explained away. Will they stay, or will they go? With these two it would be difficult to predict.

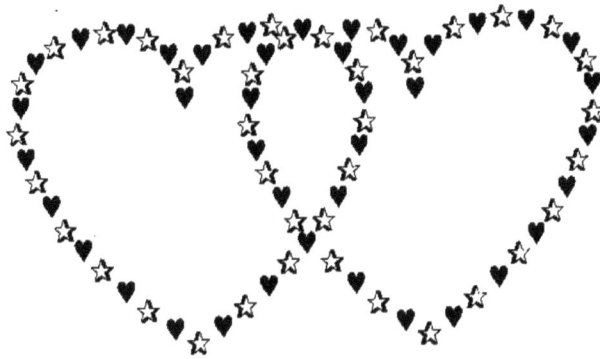

GEMINI MAN - PISCES WOMAN
LOVE RELATIONSHIPS & COMPATIBILITIES

What a magical creature this Gemini man has discovered in this Pisces woman. She appears to know intuitively just how to weave a spell that keeps him returning to her for more enchantment. Neither are the down-to-earth type. Gemini and Pisces can be industrious and hard working, but both insist on wearing a smile and making life and work as pleasant as possible. And after busy days that lead to busy weeks, both want time to allow their minds to free float through endless creative possibilities. Gemini brings lively conversation and wit to any social gathering, and Pisces brings a lovely enchanting smile and an amiable nature. Boredom and routine aren't for these two, but then nothing is ever boring when they're around. A Pisces woman will follow her man to the end of the world, sacrificing all that is necessary to make the relationship work. To logical Gemini this smacks a little of martyrdom, and if Pisces complains that he is somewhat self-serving, he may just remind her that she is at fault for giving so much. Pisces wants romantic love--to love and give with all her heart. But wouldn't it be nice to receive the same in return? And here the proble-m begins. Gemini's life is lived to a larger degree through his intellect. That's not to say that he doesn't feel deeply, but displaying his emotions and living them the way Pisces does is another matter. He can tell you what motivates people, and he knows all about persuasion, but pure emotion leaves him a bit baffled. In fact, it sometimes helps if a Gemini man has someone around to explain emotional responses to him. He certainly doesn't mean not to give her all the attention she needs, but it's just that his mind wanders to other things. That brings us to Pisces sensitive nature. Not only does she actually need attention, but it must be positive attention. She internalizes criticism in any form and takes it right to heart. This Gemini man may decide, as many do, that life without the magic of a Pisces woman would be unbearable in which case he must learn what it takes to please this woman. And that's not an entirely bad thing because there's a lot that Pisces can teach Gemini. She on the other hand, must accept that his moods have nothing to do with her--held be shifting in the wind with or without her around. But she will delight in his many ideas, and there's something about this man that captures her heart. Once she accepts Gemini as he is, he is a most lovable man. Yes, he is a flirt which wounds her jealous nature, but Pisces isn't above captivating a few hearts herself. These two entertain each other in the bedroom. This relationship requires two well developed individuals and well-aspected planets in their charts would help as well. But then, love endures all.

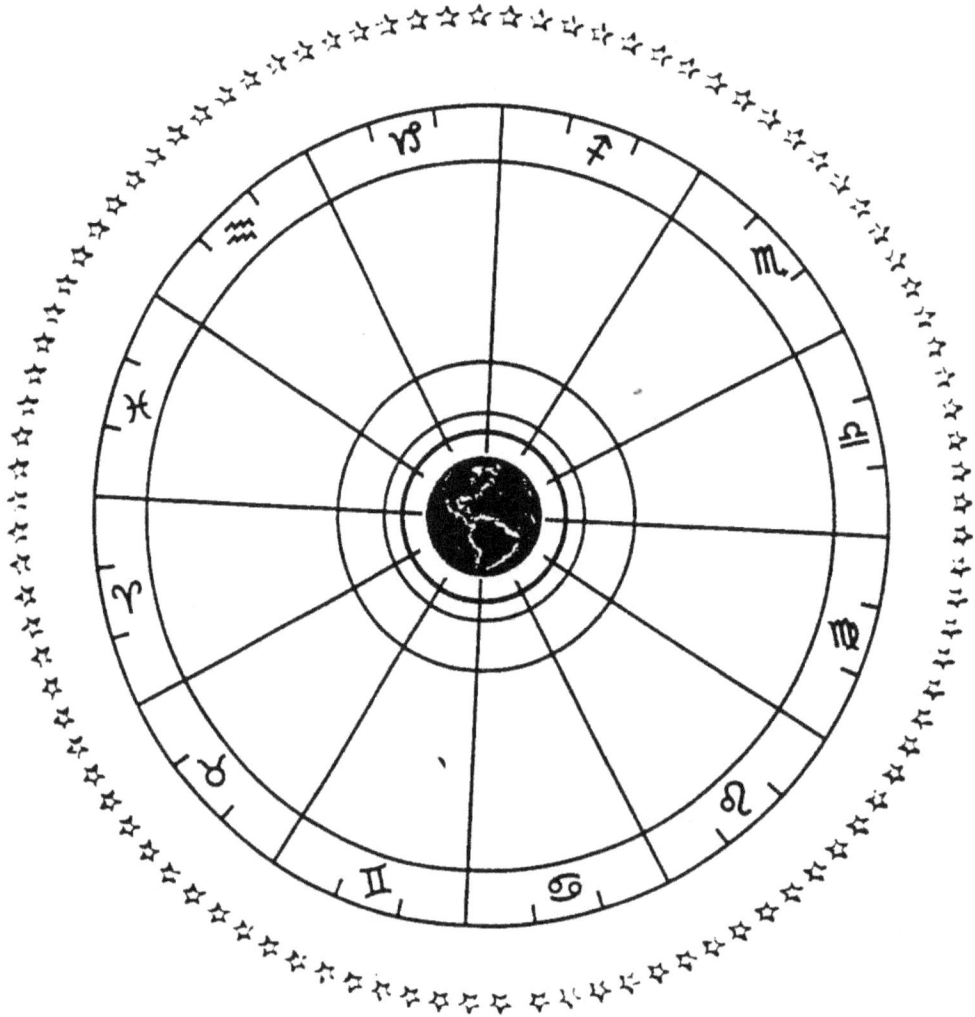

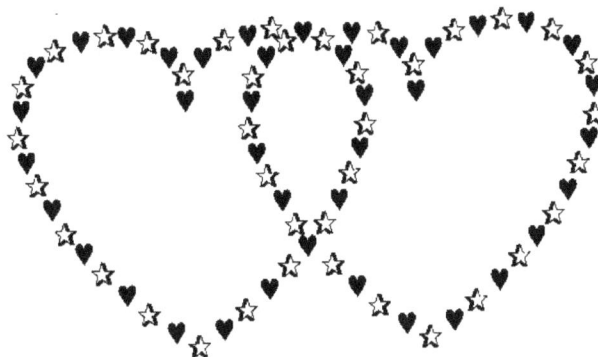

Cancer Woman - Cancer Man
Love Relationships & Compatibilities

An imaginative couple capable of great insights and perceptions if not fights of pure fantasy. These two abound in creative energy. They will have much to talk about-their common interests, historical perspectives, politics, religion, art, music, and their favorite movies, not to mention their feelings. Cancers perceive the world through their emotions. But while talkative, charming and personable, they keep many of their most private and personal feelings and perceptions to themselves, perhaps fearing rejection or ridicule. or, in many cases, Cancer protects his/her feelings and privacy just as determinedly as they protect their possessions, security, and finances. Cancers are big on collecting both items of worth and less valuable items of some sentimental significance, all of which are highly valued and protected, even secreted away. There is a close bond between a Cancer individual and his or her mother, or in some cases a father. If this bond was strained during adolescence, the Cancer native may have spent time with a relative or second family until that special bond was reestablished--they demand a large degree of maternal attention. Their defenses are highly tuned to protect an extremely sensitive nature, and they are so creative and defensive that they imagine slights and criticisms in the most casual of remarks. Their selfacclimation is realized through friendship which, needless to say, is of major importance to the Cancer self-esteem. They must feel accepted, loved, admired and appreciated to feel fulfilled. This is not an independent person, but rather a person who in the wrong circumstances is easily influenced. A discerning cancer learns to pick and choose friends and relationships carefully perhaps for this very reason. And upon developing a close relationship, Cancer will cling to it tenaciously. Crab-like, Cancer doesn't approach love and romance directly, but makes overtures, withdraws to think or to fantasize, approaches, then out of caution for his/her personal feelings, withdraws again. This withdrawing can require an adequate amount of privacy and time to oneself to consider the situation. Is it a beneficial relationship for me? Cancer perceives all the world through a personal perspective. Finally, the decision is made and this lively couple devotes all their attention to each other, gauging and qualifying the amount of attention that is returned. What saves these two selfpossessed people is that they are very likable and endearing, and, yes, lovable. Their lives are centered around home and security, but they desire travel, sights and sounds, and congenial companionship. She will discover that once she captures this Cancer man's romantic imagination, he can become direct, driven and pleasure seeking, desiring both a physical and emotional release. He is sensitive to her feelings, caring and considerate, and she will be more than pleased and excited. And a Cancer man possesses a special charm that makes a woman feel feminine and desirable. Personal adjustments are required in this relationship to keep his and her emotions and feelings balanced, but once they learn to give what the other desires, they are set.

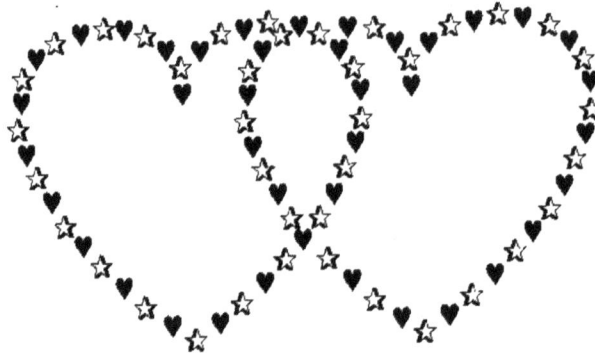

Cancer Woman - Leo Man
Love Relationships & Compatibilities

The imagination of the Cancer woman will no doubt be caught by the enthusiasm, energy, and cheerfulness of this Leo man. His self-assurance radiates enough magnetism for her to feel secure also. She is charmed by his humor and impressed with his regal bearing. She is proud of her man. This is a strong, determined, ambitious man who she can lean depend on. Busy, productive, and on the go, he may give her plenty of time for her privacy and flights of fantasy dreaming. However, when he focuses his attention on her she will feel like the center of his universe, and his generally sunny disposition drives her Moon-influenced moodiness away. The question that may make or break this relationship is whether or not he has the time to give her the amount of attention she desires. And whether or not she can admire him enough to soothe and fortify his ego. Also, Cancer likes being the center of attention once in awhile, but Leo may not like giving up that position. Leo can fume his indignation when things aren't to his liking, and Cancer's sensitivities are sure to be offended. This is a passionate man who knows what he wants, and his energies carry into the bedroom where he'll make her feel like a wanton woman. He is an intense man, but he doesn't always make contact with his emotions, and a Cancer woman practically wears her emotions, however aloof she'd like to appear. Cancer may decide she's happy on the side lines, and even happier to run a comfortable home where they can entertain their many friends (Leo likes to be surrounded by people), and that their times alone are all the splendor she needs. If that be the case then this is indeed a lucky woman who will make her man proud to have her in his life. Leo can be more than a little forthright and domineering at times, but he'll soon learn that as much as she means to please, a Cancer woman knows her own mind.

186

All the obstacles bring this Cancer woman and Leo man full circle back to their most inner needs. Cancer needs more than anything someone in her life who is strong and reliable and able to provide well for a family and home. Someone who she can lean on when she's feeling less than secure. Leo needs and desires a woman in his life who admires him for his many positive qualities, and who needs someone to lean on. That her creative imagination brings insights into his life is only added inducement for him. That his creative expressions put a smile on her face adds joy to her life. This energetic couple are bound to enjoy life, pleasure, and home and family life together. There are lessons to learn in life, and one of them is giving. These two will benefit and grow from the experience.

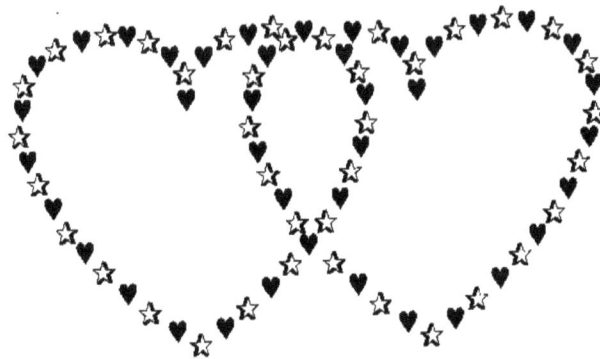

CANCER MAN - LEO WOMAN
LOVE RELATIONSHIPS & COMPATIBILITIES

There is every chance that a Leo woman who loves, admires, respects and encourages a Cancer man will find that he reflects those qualities back to her. She will find his romantic sentiments charmingly disarming and reassuring not to mention flattering, and remember Leo loves to be flattered. He finds her effervescent exuberance for life and her extroverted nature compelling. In fact, her outgoing congeniality may inspire him to do more, see more, and to strive for more out of life. He wants to please her because she can be so pleasing herself. Their differences run the gambit. Both can be creative, but his imagination carries him into intuitive, expressive modes of imagery while hers is more verbal and cognitive. She is at her best when displaying her flair for the dramatic, drawing the attention of others. But then Cancer's own flair for not only imagery but mimicry, humor, and fantasy can hardly be outdone. This is a courageous woman of strength and determination who fears only her self-doubts which she seldom displays. Cancer is less inhibited about expressing his emotions, doubts, and even fears, but he too keeps secret many of his inner conflicts. Leo can be at times arrogant, condescending, and picky, which Cancer resents. But then Cancer can be fault finding, critical and resentful of impositions, which Leo finds undignified. That they love a good time, social outings and gatherings, and an active life, may keep them too busy for fussing, but Leo must remember the importance of a more than adequate home life for Cancer to feel comfortable and at ease. While their basic natures are very different, they will share many of the same goals including a comfortable and pleasant home, and the importance of financial security to him will make her feel better about life in general. That the warmth of her Sun sign carries over to her passions in the bedroom will make him feel even more appreciated and loved. He needs a dependable friend who is there for him, and generous Leo can fill that order. She needs to be catered to and cared for, and this may make Cancer feel all the more needed. A Leo woman in love literally radiates her joy, and her pride in her loved one places him on a pedestal which is an attitude that will make this Cancer man feel like he is on top of the world. To sustain that loving feeling for the duration will require a degree of mutual consideration and adjustment to each other, but these two may determine to do just that. The Cancer nature is not necessarily weaker than hers, but these two possess definitely different approaches. She can be direct and forceful while Cancer arrives at his destination using a less direct but just as effective manner. Recognizing and admiring each other's differences bring this couple to the realization of what can be required of love.

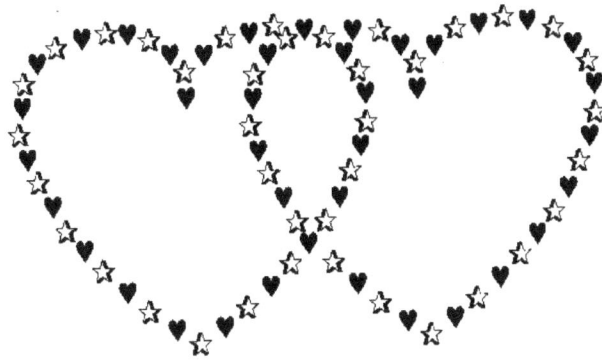

Cancer Woman - Virgo Man
Love Relationships & Compatibilities

This is one of those relationships that makes the world go round. While different, these two have much in common. In Virgo, Cancer will meet a man who is practical, reliable, responsible, and trustworthy. People seek him out for his trusted advice knowing that he will not only consider the facts but also be sincerely concerned for the other person's welfare. In that regard, he is not self-serving. But in his private life, he is cautious, reserved, and a steady hard worker. He does not take his romantic interests lightly or make impulsive decisions which he might later regret. He takes his career, family, and responsibilities seriously. He will be impressed with the Cancer woman's desire for home and security because that matches his ambitions in life as well. He likes a well planned home and pleasing surroundings which reflects his good taste, planning and care. These two appreciate the beauty and serenity of nature, and they share an affinity for pets with Virgo showing a preference for the smaller variety. Virgo, like Cancer, takes an interest in history, antiquities, memorabilia, genealogy, and heritage, but Virgo is a walking reference book of facts and data. Like Cancer, he is sentimental and sensitive, but his emotions are held in check. He is steady, lacking the moodiness of Cancer, but he will be drawn to protect her which can make her feel secure and loved. He takes pride in her creative imagination which broadens his analytical thinking. Like her, he has deep feelings, but he doesn't always express them well, however, his glance carries a thousand words. once this Virgo man truly trusts another person, he becomes more open to discussing his private thoughts and the reasoning that goes on behind his actions. once that trust and a reciprocal attraction are established, never doubt that he is all man because he can be assertive, virile, sensual and direct-- all that she dreamed of. Cancer will need to remember that Virgo's concentrated effort to be practical and to have his life well planned can make him at times demanding and fault finding. Virgo must recognize the sensitivities of Cancer and that her mood swings can produce crabbiness and criticism. But no doubt what drew these two normally pleasant people together was shared interests and activities. At home they may be hobbyists, but they also enjoy an active social life. Good food is another of their central interests, and she will learn that he is even more health conscious and diet regimented than she, but together they can plan a cookbook of favorite family recipes. Besides her charming nature and lovable manner, he most appreciates her security-

189

minded interests, and she appreciates that he takes her interest seriously. These are two people who bask in mutual appreciation for one another.

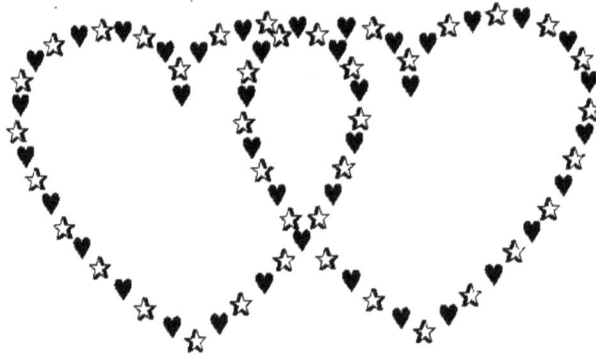

CANCER MAN - VIRGO WOMAN
LOVE RELATIONSHIPS & COMPATIBILITIES

The Virgo woman will like the subtle but sensual approach of the Cancer man as compared to the more aggressive and forceful types. His imagination, however, dances in his eyes and plays on his smile which he focuses on her. She is just as cautious, perhaps even shy, in romance as Cancer. To be clear, Cancer has more than his fair share of romantic involvements, but we're talking the serious, lasting variety here. He will want this Virgo lady to be not only infatuated by his charm, but impressed with him, admiring him for his many positive qualities. She is a serious minded person who also wants admiration and appreciation. These are two hard working individuals who strive for a secure future and a home to call their own. That he is gentle, sympathetic, caring and kind only adds to his allure. Cancer is intuitive and may sense that beneath her calm serenity her strong emotions and passions are held in check. Trust is important to these two people and may serve as the basis for building a companionable not to mention reliable relationship which provides them both with a feeling of security. Whether he's a self-directed man out to build a financial empire or a Cancer involved with artistic creative endeavors, she will feel drawn to support his efforts. They may both be somewhat conservative and traditional in their taste, but Cancer leads Virgo to exposure to sights and sounds that heighten the awareness and imagination. Entertaining and social activities may keep them active, but both enjoy time spent at home where they have more than enough hobbies and interests to keep them preoccupied and busy. A Virgo woman is not one to be won over with loving romance and then take for granted, and a sincere Cancer man shares these needs for continuing attention, time and affection. Both feel fulfilled when in a loving relationship that provides a supportive friendship, admiration and acceptance. Why else would Cancer have so many moody spells if not for a little loving attention? And in fact, romantic sensuality is one of Cancer's strong suits which Virgo will soon crave with anticipation. That his crabbiness may upset her usually gentle nature might be expected, but then exacting Virgo can at times be a handful also. That her mind is as active as his imagination will keep this attraction lively, but these are two are prone to worry whether it's necessary or not. Cancer is responsive to the emotions of others, and once she learns to express her emotions he will ingeniously find a way to either heighten them or soothe them whichever the case may be. That she likes his friends, shares his interests, feels responsible toward his family, and adores him, may be all this Cancer man could possible want. That he enjoys the time spent with her, adores her, and wants to provide and protect her from life's calamities, pleases her too.

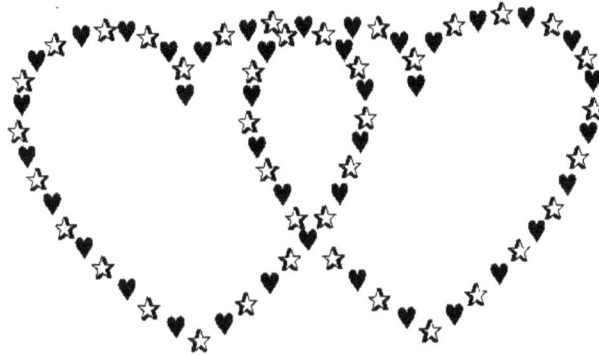

CANCER WOMAN - LIBRA MAN
LOVE RELATIONSHIPS & COMPATIBILITIES

Diplomatic, tactful, charming, and sensually romantic-what more do they need in common? Who will charm the other the most will have playful Libra smiling while this Cancer woman delights and shines in the center of his attentions. Librals refined mind and seeking nature is captivated by the imagination and creativity of Cancer. They share a fondness for beauty, nature, art, music, and literature. Librals desire for a companionable partner can make Cancer feel needed and appreciated. Establishing a lasting relationship, however, may require devoting their energies to learning to communicate. In his efforts to promote harmony, Libra dislikes hurting others or being unfair, and he may have a difficult time saying no or taking a firm position. But he strives to maintain a proper balance and may attempt to achieve this by either stating the positive side of any given topic or discussion or by deliberating the alternatives to any suggestion. Cancer can defensively see this as argument rather than discussion and can be offended that he would disagree with her. Libra applies his logic and analytical skills while Cancer responds from her emotions. Libra needs to talk things out, but Cancer has difficulty being open and direct and may not understand why all this talk is necessary or what benefit it is to her. She wants to be reassured of how any decision will directly affect her. Libra is simply caught in indecision, balancing and weighing, judging the possibility of success against the fear of failure. She may grow impatient with his indecisiveness, and Libra can become obstinate when faced with impatience. His generally well balanced scales can dip precariously making him annoyed, stubborn and quarrelsome, and with his adroit persuasive skills there's no winning an argument even if she did want to talk about it. She's cast into one of her gloomy moods feeling that no one

191

truly understands her. Sweet and gentle Libra will give her time to brood, turn on soft lights and relaxing music, and having regained his own balance, charm her into blissful submission. or was that her plan all along? Cancer can be shrewd, wanting to add to her growing bounty of treasures, but Libra may rate experiences as highly as treasure or monetary gain. She wants a variety of experiences for her imaginative mind to reflect on. Libra desires to know first hand the thrills of new experiences. Cancer can emulate others, adapting to any setting. Libra adapts to people and places, bringing along his own individualism while diplomatically striving to be accepted as he is and generally succeeding. Cancer who yearns to be accepted may grow a little jealous of the ease with which he interacts with others. To succeed in this relationship, the positives may have to balance out the negatives. Then Libra will be happy making Cancer as pleased as she can be.

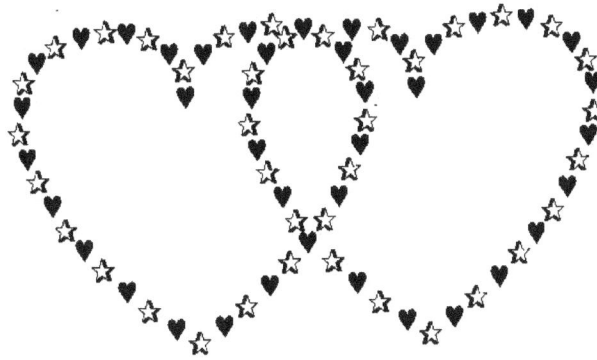

Cancer Man - Libra Woman
Love Relationships & Compatibilities

A Cancer man and a Libra woman may like each other immensely, establishing a friendship for life. But whether or not the twosome can develop a lasting romantic relationship may leave Libra in the qualms of indecision long enough for it to become a moot point. He is sensitive and sensual and in many ways the perfect companion. He is impressed with the way she can immerge from weeding her garden, change her clothes, look elegant, and be the perfect lady at the theater that evening explaining the nuances of the human interaction set before them on the stage. She is impressed with the way his imagination can transform a casual lunch date into a spur of the moment romantic interlude. She is accustomed to direct, assertive, forceful men who know what they want and go after it. But Cancer isn't like that--he's charmingly indirect. Does that mean he's interested or not? As far as Libra is concerned they can lay their cards on the table and in all fairness to each other discuss their feelings and intentions. But she accepts that Cancer can't do that and any attempts to help him discuss himself are met with that wary, defensive look which makes her feel like he thinks of her as a woman pursuing him which offends Libra. Libra is the listener, known for keeping confidentialities--everyone talks to Libra, that is, except this puzzling Cancer man. Libra simply does not like confusion--this is not the road to perfect peace, harmony and balance. What saves their relationship is that Cancer in his indirect manner finally gets where he's going, cautiously perceiving the benefits of doing so, catches her in her own indecisive, weak moment when she wants so much for someone to come along and make a decision for her, and captures her heart. Libra actually prefers that someone else take the burden of making the decision, that is, if it's the right decision. Once Cancer and Libra make a mutual decision both are capable of sticking with it (as long as it continues to be the right decision for Libra and beneficial to Cancer). That they share mutual interests, like people, have lively intellects, enjoy traveling, entertaining, music and the arts provides a basis for pleasant companionship. That they truly care for one another, faults and all, adds the perfect ingredient to a lasting relationship. They are different which they both knew from the start, but they are both dependable, good natured and kind hearted which brings them mutual admiration. Adaptable Libra learns how to mold her dialogue into non-threatening, uncritical praise and admiration, pleasing Cancer greatly. Cancer learns that she respects him most when he respects her. The plus side of a CancerLibra relationship is that these two bring out the humor and fun-side of each other. When these two decide to devote their energies to each other, little else matters.

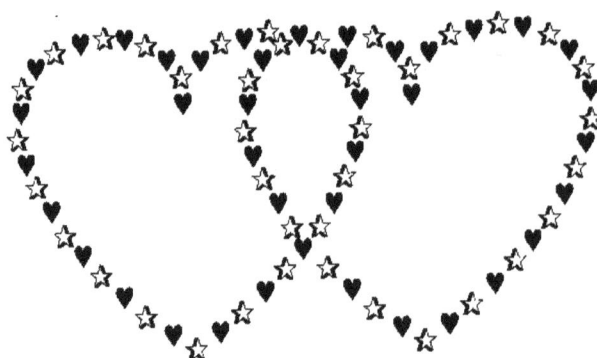

CANCER WOMAN - SCORPIO MAN
LOVE RELATIONSHIPS & COMPATIBILITIES

If this Cancer woman needs most of all a true friend as well as a lover, she will discover in Scorpio a dependable and loyal friend who will strive to protect and care for her. She should be forewarned not to attempt to apply her shrewdness to any dealings with this man because he will intuitively search out her true intentions and be greatly offended if they are self-serving. Scorpio is intense, direct but subtle, forceful when necessary, strong when in control and weak when all hopes of self-control are lost. Sex releases his passions allowing him to relax and regain his emotional balance. Cancer will be captivated not only by his intensity but by his great need for her. He can provide the relationship strength, determination, and will power all of which Cancer needs and admires. If she can devote her energies to creatively and lovingly taming his complexities, she will be greatly rewarded by his attentions. Loyalty will reduce the jealousies inherent in both of their natures. That both are greatly intuitive, perceptive, and like to please the other will enhance their togetherness. Scorpio admires the tranquil, domestic nature of Cancer who places such importance on home and security which in return allows Scorpio to feel secure. Scorpio can abide with Cancer's need for private moments, personal space, and time for moody reflection. But if she becomes overly critical, demanding or judgmental, she risks challenging his temper which Cancer is no match for. She can either withdraw or turn on her sweet charm, knowing that when he calms down he'll call forth his own special appeasing charm and beg her forgiveness. That his demeanor is naturally ruled by his intellect making him cool, reserved, and steady, doesn't quite rule out that he's emotionally intense as well. He needs someone in his life adept at diffusing situations not creating them, and it may well be that this special Cancer woman fits that description. She finds that when she applies her amiable nature and creative humor, he rewards her with his own. This is an active, creative and energetically ambitious couple who may set their goals and strive to attain them. They enjoy an active social life, but are just as entertained when together in their pleasant and comfortable home. She may spend a life time

194

attempting to probe his secrets while he has perceived and uncovered hers long ago through mere observation. His own secrets may be tied up in a history of daring little adventures that held prefer not to talk about. Cancer can relax and feel secure with Scorpio knowing that once he sets his mind and his heart on her, he'll never want to drift away. Scorpio can appreciate that he's found the woman of his dreams who appears to truly understand his complex nature and what he needs. These two make an entertaining couple intent on each other.

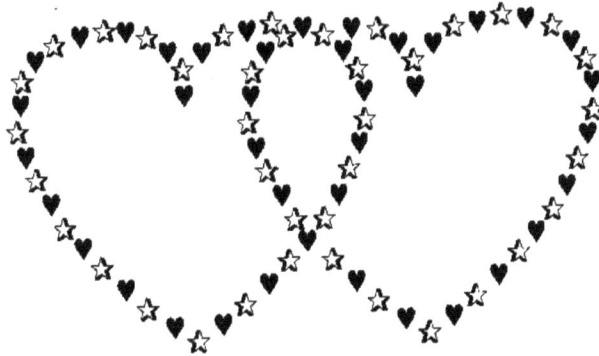

CANCER MAN - SCORPIO WOMAN
LOVE RELATIONSHIPS & COMPATIBILITIES

After the initial attraction, these two may develop a relationship based on a mutual bond of understanding. They may not always agree with the other's persons decisions or actions, but each accepts the other's faults, strengths, and weaknesses. They may not be able to explain or describe this understanding, but each intuitively knows the why behind the actions of the other person as well as his or her feelinqs and emotions. They both are capable of great kindness toward the other person. Cancer appreciates the approbation that he perceives in her kindness, and Scorpio may equate kindness as a part of her own perception of spirituality. And while Cancer and Scorpio never forqet a kindness, neither do they ever forqet an insult or wronq doing. criticism or any form of harm will cause Cancer to withdraw into his shell, nursing his wound in self-pity. Scorpio may withdraw in patience, havinq judged the weakness and vulnerability of the person causinq the harm and waiting to see justice served either with a little help from her or with the firm, intuitive belief that the person who wrongs others will in time do themselves in. Scorpiols challenge in life is to learn to forgive and this may be easiest to accomplish with a Cancer who she accepts and understands and who offers the same forgiveness in return. Cancer's challenge in life is to learn to share his emotions, thoughts, and feelings with another, and this might best be accomplished with this Scorpio woman. They possess the ability to bring out the gentleness, loyalty, intensity and imagination of each other--all the good qualities--to develop a compatible and harmonious relationship. A Scorpio woman knows little fear, and Cancer may question her boldness. But she in turn wonders about his caution and at times shyness which she may see as a lack of courage or direct action. In time, however, Scorpio will perceive the cleverness that Cancer applies to his actions and be impressed. Cancer may even come to emulate the Scorpio stronq will while at the same time giving her lessons in humor and how to laugh at herself a little--a lesson that will open her eyes to her own vulnerability. Once a Scorpio woman gives her heart it is only through trust that she learns to overcome her naturally jealous nature. A well developed Cancer man will know to instill that trust into the relationship. That their very togetherness brinqs out their mutual passions will continue to delight if not inspire these romantic lovers. That a Cancer man is receptive to the notion of adventure inherent in the female Scorpio will further entice his imagination. And what really binds the relationship is the ability of Cancer and Scorpio to allow their imaginations to run wild, finding joy, pleasure, and enlightenment through their shared experiences, thoughts and dreams.

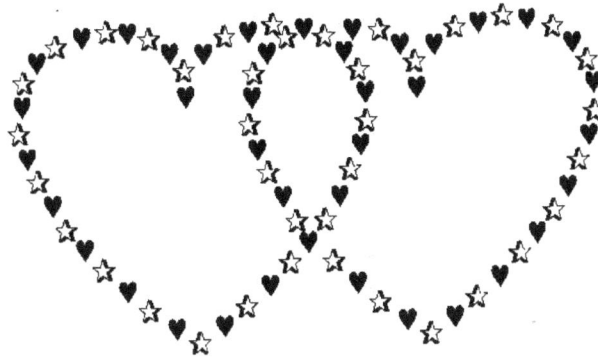

CANCER WOMAN - SAGITTARIUS MAN
LOVE RELATIONSHIPS & COMPATIBILITIES

The Cancer woman finds in Sagittarius a man who is open-hearted, jovial, and free of bad intentions. He willingly does favors for others not asking what is in it for him. He isn't interfering, possessive or jealous of others, and his sense of humor competes with Cancer's own play on words. He's a good conversationalist, imaginative and clever, versatile, and always moving on to some new interest. Cancer finds him fun to be with, impetuous and optimistic. Ever the philosopher, he may as a question a minute wanting to perceive the truths behind any given situation. And at that little trait, secretive Cancer may bristle, not wanting to be too open or to share her most private thoughts. He's not overly emotional which is another difference between these two, but he will make every effort to understand her moodiness. This man says what's on his mind, bluntly speaking the truth but meaning no offense to anyone. of course, this trait rattles sensitive Cancer, and there she goes again seeking the security of her shell. This relationship will make her question every conviction she's ever held, and it may be that in the self questioning she learns to grow and develop. That she prefers the safety of conservative conventions won't deter freedom loving Sagittarius from his unconventional approach to life. His independent nature is the backbone of his manhood, and he wants nothing to threaten that aspect of his life. He may be as ambitious as her, but money and possessions will never be the focus of his life--although he does respect money for what it can provide. It's best to never underestimate the tenacity of the Cancer female nor her changeability or even her adaptability. If this Cancer lady makes up her mind that this is the man for her then she undoubtedly has the ability to fit into his lifestyle. There may be a little friction from time to time as these two learn to adjust to each other, but that is one of the ingredients of any lasting relationship. Once Sagittarius decides he loves this woman he may return again and again until he finally decides to simply stay, devoting his attentions on her in his own free-spirited way. His lucky ways capture her imagination, and her creativity serves to expand his mind. And it may well be his expansive, seeking nature that is so bent on exploring the wisdoms and philosophies of life that compel Cancer to forget the differences in their natures. Their home will reflect their diverse interests providing an environment for learning and exploring. They bring a loving and sensual combination to their sexual explorations finding fulfillment in each other. These two are both fun loving, enjoying life as well as each other. That they are both good conversationalists, imaginative and clever only adds to the time they share together.

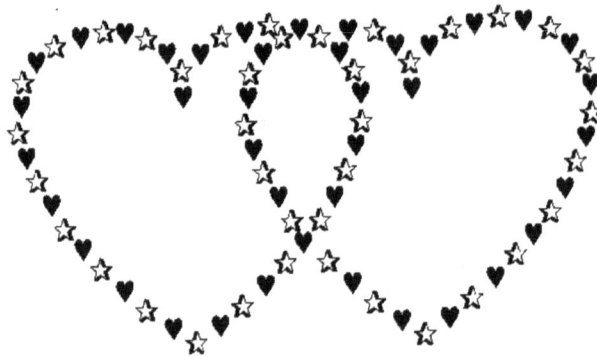

CANCER MAN - SAGITTARIUS WOMAN LOVE RELATIONSHIPS & COMPATIBILITIES

The Cancer man may profess and appear to be conventional and conservative, but there is something about the capricious humor of this self-confident and cheerful Sagittarius woman that attracts his attention. In fact, humor may set the stage for the initial attraction because she finds herself laughing with him at his impromptu caricatures and parodies on one and all. He may even find her direct, blunt remarks rather comical especially when they never fail to draw disapproving or shocked looks from others. That she is a knowledgeable and intellectual only adds to her appeal. That he is intuitive and perceptive serves to fuel her seeking and expansive nature. If he is that type of Cancer man who yearns to travel a bit and be exposed to new places and people, she is the perfect match for him. That home and security are important to him are fine with her as long as the home environment fosters freedom of expression and the freedom to explore new ideas. He is a amiable and good conversationalist as long as the topic of discussion doesn't focus too strongly on his personal perspectives. But then Sagittarius is open minded enough not to probe too deeply into the affairs of another, preferring to maintain a strong friendships and neither does she want to be pinned down to a list of what's acceptable and what isn't. If the attraction is strong enough and love is in full bloom, these two may find themselves easing into a compatible relationship once they learn how to live with the other person's personal traits. Cancer may bask in the optimism and good luck that seem to ride with this special lady. And she'll have enough interests of her own not to be offended when he wants time to himself for contemplation and to let his imagination soar to new heights. Her own moodiness is easily dispelled much to his delight. They carry a special magic to the bedroom--a combination of her excitability and exploring nature and his sensual, imaginative approach. What pleases her intensifies his passions making his own all the more erotic. His jealousy may be centered more on her intellectual accomplishments and self-assurance than on her male friendships which he accepts as simply a part of her unique character. And although not possessive, Sagittarius may be a little envious of the talents displayed by Cancer. But those are small matters compared with the pleasure these two find in their companionship. He will learn that she can be loyal, trusting and pleasingly affectionate which is what Cancer desires most. There are enough inherent differences in traits and characteristics between these two that common interests and goals serve to balance out what could otherwise cause problems. It is that curious little way she has of applying a philosophical twist to life that continues to capture his heart.

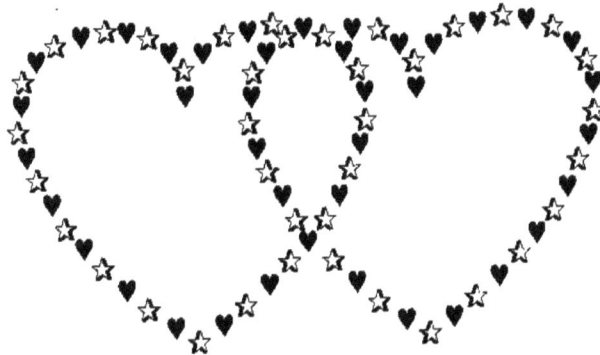

CANCER WOMAN - CAPRICORN MAN
LOVE RELATIONSHIPS & COMPATIBILITIES

A Cancer woman with a Capricorn man walks with her head held a little higher, proud of his many strong traits, his ambitions, and his respect for home and security. Adaptable Cancer finds in Capricorn traits that she feels are well worth emulating and she eases into the role of being his special partner in life. She is intuitive enough to know when to charm him and when to reassure him of how much she appreciates not only what he does for them but who he is. It may have been their ambitions that attracted them to each other and their desire to seek not only career success but social position as well. They are active in their community, interested in politics and social affairs, and responsible in their civic roles. Their home reflects their good taste and many interests. They like comfortable surroundings but are not prone to overspend for luxury items. They save and invest wisely while teaching each other the meaning of a dollar earned and how to be frugal when necessary. Her caution suits his reliable and dependable nature making him even more pleased with all her efforts. Capricorn is patient with her mood swings seeing them as a reflection of her more intuitive nature. For this relationship to work well, Cancer will need to be an active person who has developed enough of her own interests to keep her busy because Capricorn can become preoccupied with his ambitions. Cancer may prefer more attention, but she is perceptive enough to realize that obtaining what they want in life depends upon hard work. She wants a strong man and that is just what a Capricorn man offers. He handles well all the obstacles he faces in life through determination and self-discipline. Capricorn accepts his family obligations and responsibilities which is what Cancer needs to feel secure. And her gentle nature and creative humor makes home a place where he wants to relax and enjoy her companionship.

199

She likes his dignified manner and is especially pleased that he retains his youthful appearance through the years. Beneath his caution and stable composure, Cancer discovers a warmth spiced with a dry humor and sensible reserve. This is a man who can truly appreciate all the special qualities of Cancer, and being appreciated and sincerely loved balances her moodiness making her a loyal, devoted and trustworthy person. That they have their differences of opinions goes without saying, but these two appear to learn from life how to bend and adapt to each other. Their romantic overtures only add to their pleasures in life. Once Capricorn makes a commitment, he prefers to stay with the relationship wanting most a stable, steady home life that augments his busy professional life. Cancer's own stability is reflected in setting goals with Capricorn that bind them together in this relationship.

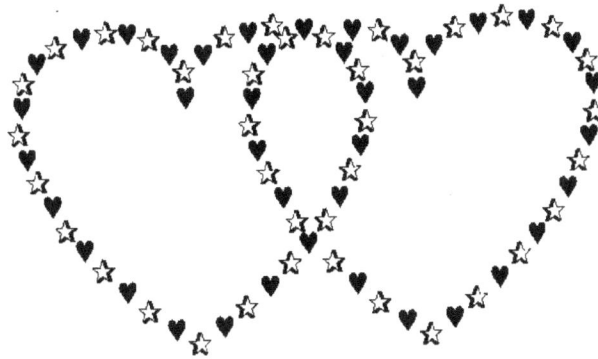

Cancer Man - Capricorn Woman
Love Relationships & Compatibilities

A Cancer man recognizes in a Capricorn woman a person who is sensitive, kind, warm and sympathetic. But she is also reliable and responsible, and she takes his ambitions in life seriously. Both are conventional people who feel secure with traditions and accepted practices. Her focus on financial security and perhaps even her efforts to succeed in a career impress Cancer who wants the same things. They have a strong interest in establishing a secure home that provides them a pleasant, safe, and relaxing haven from their busy daily lives. That she is practical and determined only reassures him that he has found the perfect companion. Both Cancer and Capricorn are loyal, trustworthy and protective and want to be appreciated for their good qualities as well as their efforts. Generally speaking, they are not risk takers, and to some degree they find comfort in a well organized routine that allows them to lead busy, productive lives. Both appreciate a little quiet time to themselves to either relax, think, plan or create. Her devotion brings out his sensual nature which in turn fuels her own earthy passions. While both are the nicest of people, either can be at times shy or reserved. But this is a persevering woman who adds determination and strength to the relationship for which Cancer is grateful and pleased. She also instills her own form of persistent control wanting to be reassured that they are headed in the right directions and not making unnecessary mistakes. That they share a way with words, a mutual interest in social affairs, and are involved in numerous activities brings out the best in each person. She affords him the opportunity to be responsible and caring for his home and family. He offers her the opportunity to dream a little, travel, and reflect on all their shared memories. Add to that is special blend of humor and Capricorn relaxes, smiles and laughs along with this endearing man. That their signs are opposites in the Zodiac either works for them or against them, but there is every indication that it can be a positive influence between two industrious individuals who continue on a path of self development and accomplishment. Cancer and Capricorn are two people who benefit from the added balance of the positive traits of the other. That differences will emerge and that they will need to not only accept each other but learn the best way to communicate and share their thoughts and opinions presents those obstacles that Capricorn is so well known for overcoming and dealing with effectively. She is analytical and methodical where he relies to some extent on his emotions, but that is only another example of the balance they bring to the relationship. Cancer and Capricorn are two people who do well in life when they decide to that is their goal. Their love for one another only grows in warmth and congeniality.

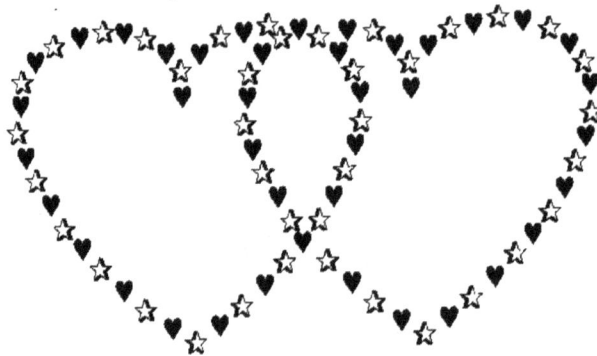

CANCER WOMAN - AQUARIUS MAN
LOVE RELATIONSHIPS & COMPATIBILITIES

At some time in her childhood this Cancer woman fell in love with her dreams and decided when she grew up she would fly with the wind. She tucked that dream away and got on with her life, but then along came an Aquarius man who showed her that dreams can come true when you throw the rules of convention to one side and live life on your own terms. She is back in dream land (that is where she would most love to be if only life permitted it, and that is the well guarded secret that Cancer protectively hides from the world while she play acts being the perfect lovable, well adjusted person). His unpredictability entrances her mind leading her from one fantasy land of her own making to another. Unfortunately, reality comes along all too often and dispels the dreams, but it would be wonderful if life could be that way and she yearns to dream some more. If her life is centered on creative endeavors in art, music, or literature, Aquarius may well be the catalyst she needs for her lively imagination. What she may like best is that he affords her the opportunity to play any number of roles as people float in and out their lives. That she meets everyone from the banker to the most eccentric, unique characters may compel her to stick around to see who shows up next. He is an original thinker who invents futuristic social theories on everything from the packaging of cereal to the redistribution of the world's population. Fortunately, Cancer is security minded, but Aquarius is sure to criticize her for her limited thinking. Will she be offended? Sooner or later, Aquarius manages to offend most everyone he knows, but he is such a friend to one and all that everyone forgives and returns, seeking him out. Whether or not he's successful in life depends upon too many variables to safely predict, but there is that definite possibility. For Cancer and Aquarius to live together would definitely be a learning experience for both of them. He doesn't mind her possessions, but he finds suspect her motive. Her possessiveness of him may prove her love, but it will hardly slow down freedom loving Aquarius. At the same time, he forms firm opinions and strong likes and dislikes, and it is a waste of time to argue with this man. He does respond to kindness, caring, and empathy and a respect for his ideas. Cancer will need to be totally smitten and truly in love for the sake of love. She can feel secure in knowing that he will be a friend for life, and that once he finally decides upon a relationship, he has a tendency to prefer monogamy. He is active and exploratory in sexual relations if not somewhat eccentric, but that only mystifies the fantasies of Cancer. Either their differences will drive them apart on friendly terms, or draw them together in a complimentary blend of contrasting characteristics.

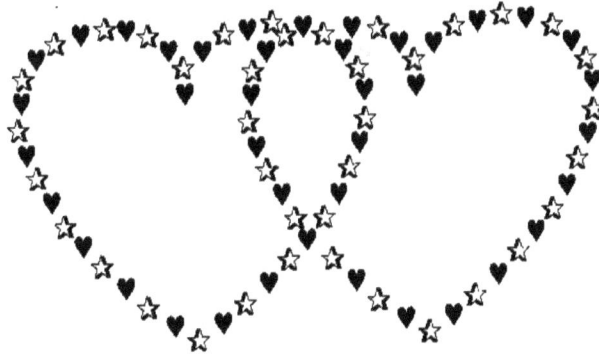

CANCER MAN - AQUARIUS WOMAN LOVE RELATIONSHIPS & COMPATIBILITIES

Aquarius is drawn to interesting people with similar interests, and this Cancer man is a most interesting person. He is captivated by the way people just seem to seek her out. He makes every effort to be pleasing and charming and to put his best foot forward, but she is uniquely herself. They are very much different, but then alike in wanting to be surrounded by people and then, at other times, to be alone. He can be introspective, thinking about his life and dreams, designing his creative endeavors in his mind. She can be introspective, thinking about the world at large, what it means, and how she fits into it. He will ponder how best to carry out his goals and to secure a home and possessions. She will add to his thoughts by explaining that the blue collar worker is the backbone of society. Both are fun loving, congenial, and happy when in love, but Aquarius can be much less emotionally attached. This detachment has nothing to do with how she feels about him, but it may take even perceptive Cancer some time to figure that out. Cancer wants to be loved and cherished and to find the kind of devotion that equates with how his mother did or should have felt about him as a child. He wants approbation, attention, fulfillment, and loyalty. When he finds the right woman, his heart opens to let her in then closes to keep her there. This Aquarius woman will gladly explain that there's an entire world out there and she can't sit happily in his heart and let the world go by. She is independent and wants her freedom to live her life. That's not to say that she doesn't appreciate all that Cancer has to offer. A secure home, lovely possessions, a sensual, and caring man is just what she wants, but she also wants the freedom to be herself. It is after all her independent nature that holds his attraction. These two ease into the bedroom and it is there that each finds the reassurance needed to fulfill all their dreams. Dreamy Cancer is at his best when held in her warm embrace. That her unpredictable rationale leaves him guessing is an understatement, but then she must contend with his mood spells as well. She is tolerant and willing to accept Cancer the way he is and ready to listen to his problems. That she is compassionate and caring eases his temporary periods of self-pity and doubt and places him back on top ready to face whatever may come. They are both romantics at heart and when their imaginations get carried away there's nothing these two lovers can't dream and envision. The down side to the relationship is that if they allow their moods to turn into criticism and complaints, neither responds well. Cancer becomes defensive, and Aquarius loses interest. Cancer and Aquarius function best with each other when the positive qualities of each sign are in full force. Then it is their imaginations and strengths that lead the relationship.

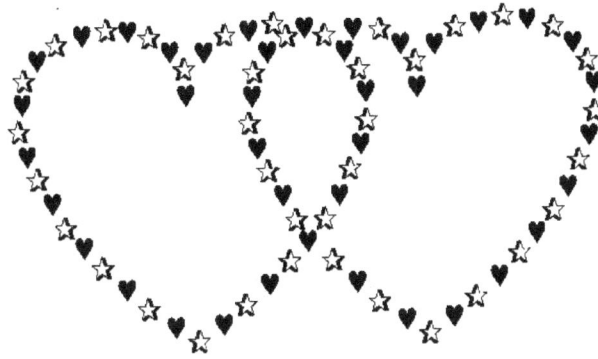

Cancer Woman - Pisces Man
Love Relationships & Compatibilities

This is an interesting couple, drawn to each other out of love, imagination, dreams, magic and fantasies. They capture each other's minds, create soft music together, and paint a series of rainbows that only the other person can see and feel. No one could be more sensitive than a Cancer woman except a Pisces man, and no one could understand her sensitivities as well. He is attentive, caring and genuinely concerned with her happiness and well being. Not only that, but he listens to her express her mind and emotions, not resenting it in the least and wanting to understand her completely. Pisces likes the gentle, unassertive ways and shy, indirect approach of this Cancer woman after having been offended by so many strong, independent and forceful women in his past. Both Cancer and Pisces like a warm, caring and sincere person, and both share a love for home. They may like to travel for the experience and to see the sights, but each will want a comfortable home to return to. Cancer may be more concerned with home, security and her possessions, constantly counting and reevaluating her financial security and checking to see if there's any way she can make it grow faster. Pisces may hate to be bothered with the details of money and finance, but many a Pisces has a tendency to keep a reserve safely tucked away which makes him feel secure knowing there's money in the bank. That erases his fears and allows him to enjoy life more fully. Pisces is a fun loving, happy person with the best of dispositions. Worries and even a hint of depression may slow him down, but his general optimism and cheerfulness returns bestowing on him that special smile that entrances this Cancer woman. Cancer and Pisces are forever ruled by their emotions making them secretive, sensitive, moody and changeable, but never dull. Cancer can be a bit more conventional than Pisces, but that only makes him like her more. Both can dwell on the past and remember hurts and fears from long ago, but both can change and laugh about the good times as well. They possess a special magic between them that is only found in a purely imaginative response to life, joy and pleasures. Either of these two is capable of letting the pleasures of life get out of hand, but when well developed, they learn how to balance temptation with temperance, harmonize joy with hard work, and how to set their sights on fulfilling not only their dreams but their goals and ambitions. No one works harder than Pisces once he sets his mind to completing his aspirations. That he is smart enough to enjoy life at the same time is a positive trait that is shared by many a Cancer as well. Both Cancer and Pisces also need to be needed in order to feel complete and fulfilled. This is a magical relationship enhanced by love and affection.

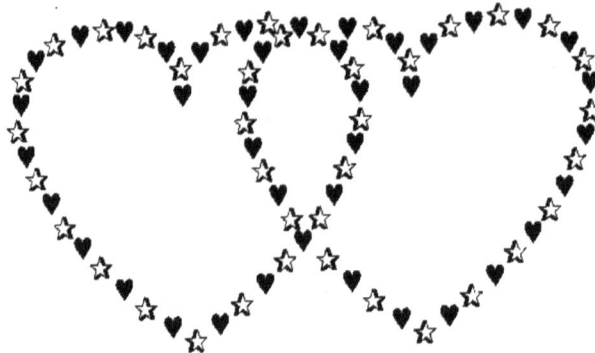

Cancer Man - Pisces Woman
Love Relationships & Compatibilities

The magic of a Pisces man runs second only to that of the Pisces woman. She is a tender and gentle soul filled with unselfish humility, sympathy and genuine concern for others. This Cancer man can pour his heart out, and she will listen to every word. Not only does she need to be needed but she has a desire for others to be happy. Whatever her circumstance in life she will seek to make it pleasant and enjoyable, and she fills her home with items that reflect her creativity and add to the overall comfort and pleasant feelings of being there. She likes to be pleasing, accommodating, and attractive, and she generally succeeds. Her personal style will always represent the uniqueness of her nature whether it be by adding glitter, native beads, or a feather. She never tells a harmful lie but she will create her own reality by fabricating to her heart's desire. She keeps her personal secrets just as the Cancer man does and relishes in the mystery she creates. She is well liked wherever she goes and floats through numerous friendships retaining the best in all of her experiences. She and Cancer are moody and at times unpredictable, but both know how to regain their charm and allure. She can be so well meaning and sincere that her feelings are easily hurt, and she is deeply wounded. Cancer can be sensitive and easily hurt but in a self serving way. Pisces is hurt because confrontations mean that things aren't working out the best for everyone concerned. She can be vulnerable and may need a strong arm to lean on, but Pisces isn't a person to be bossed around. She has her own methods, her own ideas, and her way of accomplishing her goals. She is generous and wants to help others but may come to resent her better nature being taken advantage of. Perceptive and insightful, she can be influenced by the bad moods of others, and when this happens she worries, frets, and may even become either despondent or irritable. With Cancer, Pisces may want to let him be by himself when his moods become dismal just to protect her own susceptible nature. But if this woman can't dispel the Cancer moodiness then no one can. She brings to any relationship an especially magical quality that she invented herself. Once smitten by this Pisces woman, Cancer will want to cling to her as

206

tenaciously as possible, but he'll have to learn her ways and whims to keep her happy and content. There is no one as joyful as a happy Pisces nor anyone as discontented as an unhappy Pisces. What makes her happy? Sincerity, caring, kindness, pleasant days and evenings, a home built on shared experiences and togetherness, and lots and lots of loving warmth and affection. Cancer will want to come out of his shell and prove this is the destiny for him.

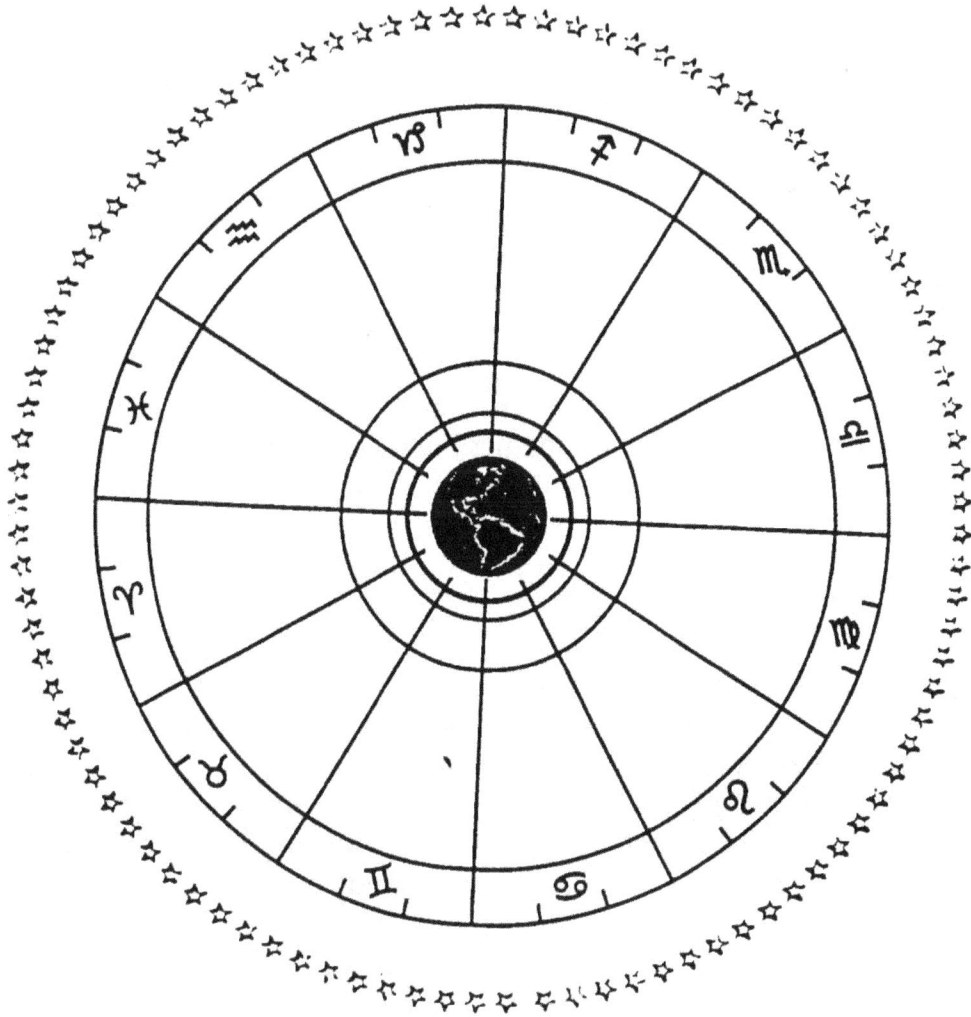

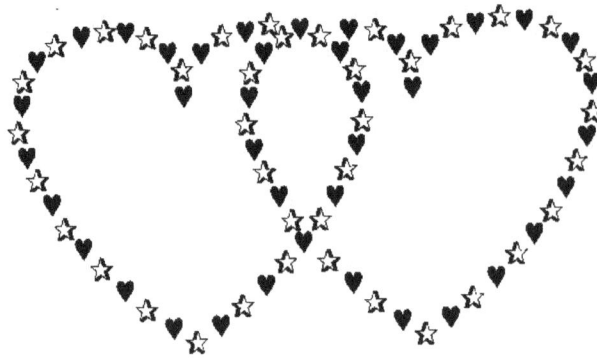

LEO WOMAN - LEO MAN
LOVE RELATIONSHIPS & COMPATIBILITIES

When royalty meets royalty, they know instinctively how to defer to the other with the greatest protocol and diplomacy. These two may get along well because there is something so rewarding about the companionship of another regal person. They know how to treat each other and how to react to the vanity of the other person. They understand how to appease and admire the other and how not to offend. And there is every chance they will be more respectful with each other than with a mere commoner. These two share immense egos. cheerfully enthusiastic, extroverted, and powerfully intense, Leo wears his self-assurance in his/her regal bearing. They literally radiate a magnetic, sunny, energetic aura that draws attention to them. Naturally entertaining and compelling, the words to hold the attention of others appear to role off their tongues with little effort. These two just naturally create an image and that image is important to them. They may spend money on entertainment or on creating an ambience of comfort in their surroundings. Even the shyer Leos create a kingdom over which they rule and dominate the position of center of attention. A Leo isn't a loner. They must have other people in their life in order to shine at their best. They are dignified, loyal, noble and convinced of their own abilities to succeed. In fact, they are so convinced of their own self-worth that they actually need the admiration, adoration, and praise of others, making Leo just a little vulnerable to flattery and compliments. Leo doesn't like deceptions, though, nor criticism, and arguments can quickly result from offending this powerful ego. These are two people blessed with common sense, organization skills, capabilities, creativity, and tho ability to lead. Two Fire signs can expect to ignite their passions in the bedroom, pleasing each other with their intense natures. A Leo woman is happiest and most radiant when in love and she will devote herself to making this Leo man the center of her universe, expecting his appreciation in return. These two possess a strong, at times, inflated pride and must receive praise, kindness, and acknowledgment of how wonderful they are. If they are as proud of each other as they are of themselves, this should come easily for them. They may have to delineate the areas of their lives where each will rule or come to some agreement on rulership of their daily lives. No doubt, both will have busy careers at which they expend a great deal of energy wanting to achieve success and make it to the top. A Leo man may need his pride and ego bolstered if the Leo woman in his life outshines him in her career. He doesn't take easily to being upstaged whether it be in their personal lives or professionally. These two both like to be catered to and without realizing it can be demanding. And in their effort to lead, Leo can be vain and overly critical of others. Remember that tact and diplomacy work best when dealing with the wounded pride of Leo. What highlights a Leo-Leo relationship is that if life isn't exciting, they will create their own. These are two dynamic people who devote their energies and love to each other.

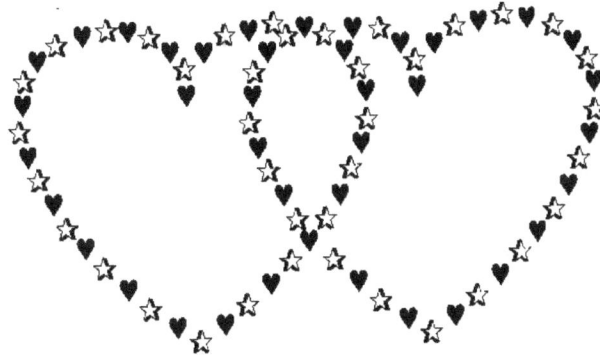

LEO WOMAN - VIRGO MAN
LOVE RELATIONSHIPS & COMPATIBILITIES

To captivate this Virgo man, this Leo woman had to overcome his cautious nature proving beyond a doubt that she was the woman for him. Virgo seeks someone who lives up to his expectations and deserves his admiration. Her list of positive traits are practically endless, and Virgo is most certainly impressed with this practical, capable and reliable woman who is as ambitious as she is warm, affectionate, and loving. She may pull him out of his well established routine showing him how expansive life can be when they take advantage of the many opportunities to expose themselves to cultural events, social activities, entertaining and being entertained. He may be ambitious but being the focal point of attention isn't necessary for him. He may, however, be proud of the way she draws attention to herself and glows in a crowd. Her cheerfulness and optimism may balance out his worries and that nagging pessimism that upsets his disposition. This is not a man, however, to be forcefully dominated. Decisions must be arrived at logically after prodigious thought, and to this he applies his critical and analytical nature. Virgo can be selfeffacing applying his critical nature to himself as well as to the others in his life. He will have to accept that Leo is not a person to be criticized. She is literally above criticism which distracts from her positive picture of herself. Together, they can create a lovely home and pleasant environment, but Leo will have to understand that Virgo is thrifty and wise when it comes to expenditures. The thought of wasting money or being extravagant literally makes him cringe in fear that his savings and future security are being depleted. Her investments may include a closet full of stylish clothes and a bounty of tangible possessions that proves her worth, makes life interesting,' and brings her acclimation. His nagging concern with the details of health and diet may make her feel all the more loved, protected and cared for, proving that he is concerned with her well being as well as his own. Her fiery passions in the bedroom excite his earthy desires, and his total attention to this lovely empress appeases her vanity. That he is loving, gentle, kind, and sincere add to the pleasant qualities of this man who at times can be a bit shy and reserved. She will know that when he gives her the praise and adoration she needs and desires, he is being honest, sincere and genuine. And when she generously radiates all that exuberant, open-hearted admiration on him, he will -indeed know what it feels like to the king of the jungle. It helps to have well aspected planets between this alliance of a Fire and Earth sign, but these two may well prove what determination, courage, and devotion can produce. They have both found a person worthy of love and admiration.

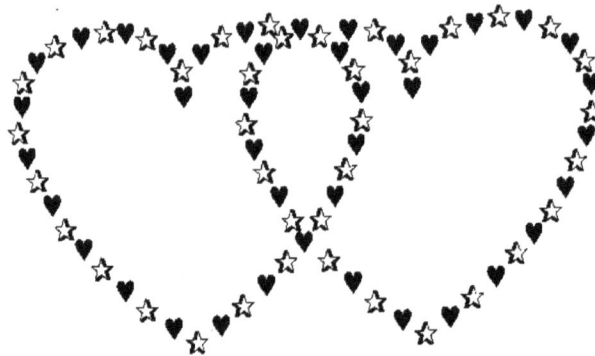

Leo Man - Virgo Woman
Love Relationships & Compatibilities

Her intense pride in her man fuels, fires, and sustains this relationship. She has applied all the rationale of her analytical processes and arrived at the conclusion that he is the perfect man for her. He is a strong, authoritative leader who provides direction and purpose to their lives. He deserves her total trust, loyalty and devotion, and that is what Virgo is capable of giving along with all the admiration and adoration that Leo needs. That his sunny disposition never fails to put a loving smile on her face is added gratification. He is witty and entertaining, and that he loves her makes her feel complete and fulfilled. Leo is capable of enjoying the moment and has his own way of making any occasion memorable and exciting. That he can be overbearing and is at his best when catered to may not overly distract this Virgo woman from his more positive charms. Being overly analytical, a she may be able to outline her own faults--something Leo is incapable of doing. If he admits to a shortcoming it may be presented as a complaint that his family or someone else feels that he is too vain, flamboyant, self-centered, conceited, bossy, or arrogant. After such an admission, he will expect the sympathy of his Virgo lady to ease the pain that anyone would criticize him. She will have to reassure him that he is perfect and others must be mistaken. He is after all a caring and generous person to all his friends even if he does want to be recognized for his efforts. Virgo is sensitive and sentiraental and by quieting his fears she may dispel her own as well. She is a reliable, trusted and true friend, and that she derives the greatest degree of fulfillment and pleasure by being of service to others can make her just the person Leo most desires in his life. In return, Leo will have to come down off his self-made pedestal and proclaim her the true love of his life. She has a need to protect her loved ones, and Leo may need his pride protected from time to time. She is steady and reserved and has deep feelings that she doesn't always express. Leo isn't the best at getting in touch with his own feelings, but he will be gratified by her loving attention. There is always the possibility that both Leo and Virgo can be demanding and fault finding, and in such instances it helps that both are forgive and forget types who don't carry a grudge or nurse a wound for long. His optimism returns and her faith in him rekindles. Their romance is inflamed by the combination of his fiery passions and her earthy needs. She may be wise enough to realize that it is his very nature that propels him into action leading him to achieve and succeed. He may be wise enough to realize when he has found a woman worthy of keeping company with a king.

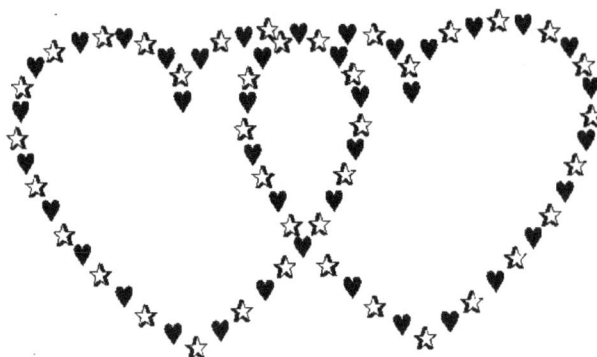

Leo Woman - Libra Man
Love Relationships & Compatibilities

She is charmed off her throne and compelled to find out more about this romantic, easygoing, personable man. He is fun and so is she. He likes a little excitement in his life, and Leo thrives on excitement. She can entertain an audience with her lively conversation, and Libra can talk circles around her. Libra likes to make other people happy, and if it makes her happy to be the center of attention wherever they go, that's fine with him--it saves his energy for more important endeavors. In some instances, her energy may drain him of his own, and he will need some quiet time to regain his balance. But in his efforts to make her happy he will intuitively recognize her need for adoration and praise and will be more than willing to supply it, making her feel like the queen she believes herself to be. Libra much prefers harmonious, pleasant times and an ambience of comfort and ease. Soft lights, pleasing music and the companionship of his favorite person make him feel content and happy. Both Leo and Libra enjoy the pleasures of life liking good food and drink and a home that reflects their refined taste and need for comfort. Both enjoy entertaining and being entertained as well as involvement in social activities, cultural events, and interests that attract their intellects and enhance their need for stimulating experiences. She may be more forceful, intense, impulsive, and strong willed, but Libra is the diplomat of the Zodiac knowing exactly how to persuade and appease the nature of Leo. Leo should be aware, however, that Librals easygoing nature covers nicely an adamant temper once it is aroused. He'll take his time making a decision but then become fixed in his opinions. Libra has been told so many times that he is wonderful that he no longer needs the same degree of constant approbation and praise that Leo desires, but she will learn that compliments and niceties will go much further with Libra than complaints and fault finding. The' real saving grace of this relationship is that Libra admires a person with strong ego. He will recognize it, call it what it is, but still admire Leo for possessing such an intense and ego driven nature. It adds that unique spice to life and touch of electricity that Libra is so fond of despite his own balancing act. If she precariously tips his scale in just the right degree, she may glimpse his own strong ego, but then the scales regain their balance and he smiles knowingly content to maintain his harmonious bearing. .She has dignity. He has refinement. They combine their natures to produce a comfort-loving environment providing each other a touch of grace that sublimates their needs. He adds balance to her fiery

212

nature, but inspires her to roam free in their love making. Their life together can either evolve into a balancing act or perfect harmony.

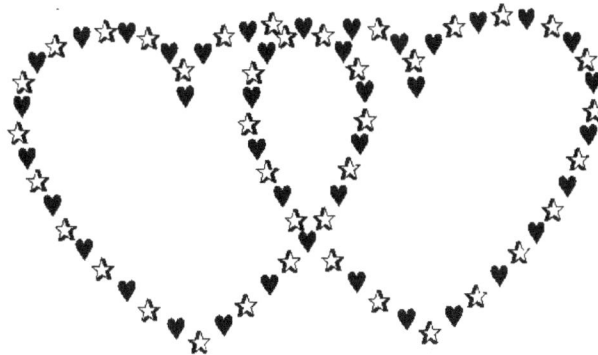

LEO MAN - LIBRA WOMAN
LOVE RELATIONSHIPS & COMPATIBILITIES

Leo needs to act on his impulses and Libra needs to think. But in the midst of her indecision she is easily persuaded and swayed by a strong willed man who knows what he wants. They are easily impressed with each other. He is magnetically electrifying and she is alluring and charming. He can be flamboyant, witty, talkative and entertaining while Libra wins his heart with her most pleasing and enticing smile. He seeks her out as the grand prize that proves his superior prowess, courage and masculinity. He is the champion full of pride, a natural flair for excitement and drama, and self proclamation. He needs another person in his life to fulfill his picture of himself. Once he has captured the heart of this lovely lady and is convinced that she is his, they will settle into a busy life of careers and social activities. It may be at that time that Libra is allowed to see the behind-the scenes vulnerabilities of strong-hearted Leo. It is best that she doesn't outshine or achieve more than Leo in any aspect of their lives and that life always provides a bit of excitement and no hint of routine or boredom. Because he possesses no faults, he projects to the other person any feelings of insecurity or inadequacy. When displeased, he can be arrogant, smug, aloof, and full of false pride. He can lecture endlessly pinpointing the other person's shortcomings, and if he runs out of complaints he can condescending describe her physical imperfections. For example, her upper lip may not be long enough to please his royal preferences. That physically she finds him quite handsome even if his nose isn't perfectly symmetrical, leaves her confused. All of this can come as quite a shock to easygoing Libra especially after he was so nice and complimentary during the initial stages of their romance. Leo has her attention, and now he wants her to know beyond a doubt who is the best, most admirable, and most desirable. Libra's scales may become permanently off balance leaving her distraught, miserable, irritable, discontent, and even depressed. Passing insults aren't enough to upset Libra, but his arrogance, pomp and selfimposed circumstance may be enough to prompt Libra's anger to flair. Then she'll deflate his ego swiftly and surely. The last section on Leo-Libra described the best case scenario, and this section describes the worst. Historically, this woman would have been advised to give up her career and to make every effort to become a loving, devoted, and submissive woman. That statistically that advice no longer works well for the modern woman is real-life. If the relationship continues on an abusive course, she must face facts and leave. This in no way implies that Leo and Libra can't find happiness. There are different people of different levels of development, different stars, planets and aspects, and any number of probable outcomes.

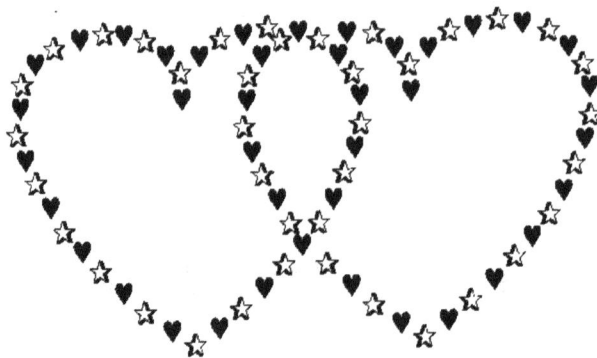

LEO WOMAN - SCORPIO MAN
LOVE RELATIONSHIPS & COMPATIBILITIES

The strong-willed, powerful and intense natures of Leo and Scorpio may make them think they feel the same about much of life. His calm, steady, compassionate and kind nature enhances the vibrancy of Leo making her feel secure and protected. Socially, the more reserved Scorpio may possess perfect timing, knowing when to compliment and when to charm, but he has little interest in copying Leols flamboyant and dramatic entrances. Generally, Scorpio is not as ostentatious or conspicuous as showy Leo. Either Scorpio is accepted for who he is or others may as well leave him alone. Leo is talkative and congenial with a quick, witty way with words. Scorpiols conversation and humor reflect his intellect and thoughts. There is much about Leo that Scorpio admires and respects including her strong ego and energetic drive. Scorpio can lavish praise and admiration the same ae any other person, but he isn't one to over inflate the pride of Leo. Leo must recognize that his compliments are sincere as are his affections, but constant adulation isn't part of his repartee. They share a certain blend of courage and boldness, a taste for .excitement, and a yearning desire for adventure. Their sexual passions may be a perfect blend of intensity, and Scorpio's robust desires will make Leo feel wanted and ndeded not to mention fulfilled. She can dominate all she wants as long as she acknowledges that he is in perfect control. And it may well be the self-control of Scorpio that makes Leo feel tamed and appeased. She wants to create occasions that are memorable and happy, and when in love a Leo woman achieves her happiest moments by knowing that the man in her life is comfortable, satisfied and pampered with pleasure. And in order to make those wishes come true she desires a warm, elegant, and cheerful environment and home. All may be well and good between them if she can contain her regal pride and if he can control his jealous and possessive nature. Leo won't take to being possessed easily, but will want her freedom to be herself--outgoing and admired. Both Scorpio and Leo need to be respected and treated with tact, diplomacy and kindness. Scorpio is a Fixed, Water sign, and Leo is a Fixed, Fire Sign making them strong in opinions and not people to be forcefully pushed or dominated. Both Leo and Scorpio give themselves full-heartedly to love. These two can be devoted, loving and determined to make the relationship work. Between two well developed individuals of Leo and Scorpio, a relationship can be blissful and enlightening, each giving their best. In different circumstances this can also be a disastrous relationship bent on competition. These two individuals will want to know themselves well and to allow themselves time to know the other person before committing their hearts and love.

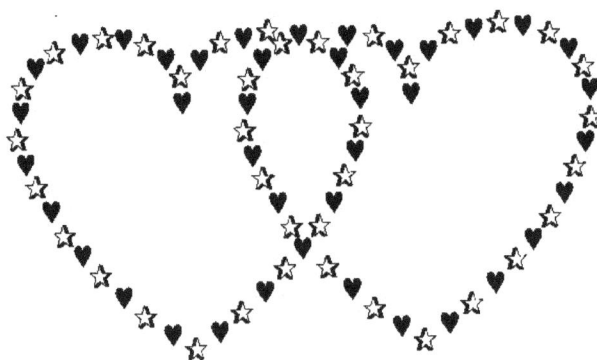

Leo Man - Scorpio Woman

Love Relationships & Compatibilities

When Leo and Scorpio wish upon a star, they both wish for happiness. And if they keep that wish foremost in their minds, they can discover it with each other while developing a loving and lasting relationship. Mutual interests, common goals, and learning to treat each other with respect and kindness may be the key ingredients. Another is mutual admiration for the other person's positive traits and acceptance of any weaknesses or faults. Dramatic and showy Leo has a tendency to place the woman in his life on a pedestal believing that she is the perfect woman for him until she proves otherwise by exposing her human frailties. With Scorpio, however, he would be wise to continue treating her well, making every effort to keep her happy and satisfied. When she is happy, she will in turn work tirelessly to make his life pleasantly fulfilled. Leo is drawn to the camera, and -if his hobby is photography, she'll help him take lots of pictures of himself, but evasive Scorpio may be more camera shy than photogenic Leo. Outside interests are also a necessity for Leo to find amply opportunity to expend his competitive energies. She will be happy to let him lead to his heart's desire on the home front as long as he proves himself worthy and as long as he uses kindness, tact, and diplomacy. Scorpio doesn't take readily to demands. These two strong willed people no doubt will make their best efforts to be appeasing, but tease the Lion or antagonize the Scorpion and watch the real show begin. He may destroy her calm faith in herself, and she may smash his precious camera. Leo may as well forget the competition because he is no contest for Scorpio (who has been so loving and kind up to this point). In a disastrous relationship, Scorpio can put insecure Leo in permanent counseling. There's nothing sadder than to see proud Leo whimpering that he feels like she's trying to crawl inside his head which any Scorpio can do with ease. Inside the head of a well developed Leo she will discover many wondrous and impressive attributes including his energetic drive to succeed in his endeavors and with her, wanting only her admiration in return. Inside the head of a poorly developed Leo she will discover very little except a person who has gotten through life on the merits of his winning personality and who still wants personal acclaim and admiration. A well developed Scorpio, on the other hand, brings to a relationship the wondrous ability to devote her heart and soul to her endeavors. A poorly developed Scorpio will manipulate and destroy anything in her path. And neither of these two types adapts well to being used. Expansive Leo and determined Scorpio will want to know for sure that this is the right person for him and her. A well-matched pair of Leo and Scorpio can call forth the heavens for their delight. Their robust energies satisfies the other.

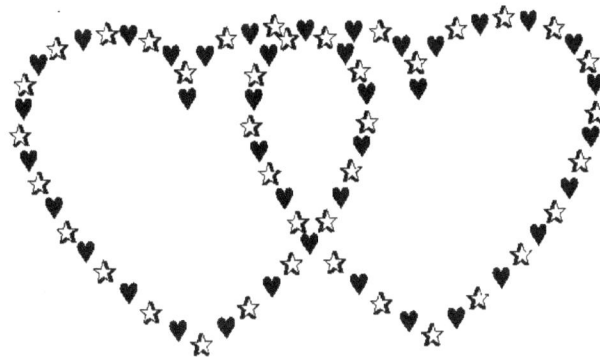

Leo Woman - Sagittarius Man
Love Relationships & Compatibilities

What a delightful pair these two Fire signs must make. Leo is drawn to the optimism and cheerfulness of Sagittarius whose witty and insightful humor inspires her own. Both possess an easy going manner and bring out the positive qualities of the other. These two possess an urge to live life to the fullest with a yearning for change, new experiences and novel situations. He is adaptable, versatile, expansive, and seeking, wanting nothing to slow down his exploring nature. Attempting to dominate a Sagittarius man would rapidly drain Leo of her energies, and she's much better off allowing him his freedoms, free of any limitations. He, in turn, has no interest in dominating or controlling independent Leo which allows for her personal growth and the opportunity to express herself. A Sagittarius man seems to delight in discovering the nature and characteristics of other people, and he will find an outgoing Leo woman a delight to watch. He can admire her to her heart's content, but he is also blunt and outspoken by nature not really meaning any harm in his candid comments. It is his good intentions that win the day, however, if Leo recognizes that he's only being himself. Their fiery passions keep these two enjoying each other, craving more intimate moments together. They also enjoy travel, the good things in life, and a comfortable home. Sagittarius may have spent a life wandering from here to there and back again, but Leo's sunny magnetism may be what it takes to attract him to a permanent and lasting relationship and the home she adorns so well. So proud of her is he that he may brag endlessly to his friends about her many wonderful qualities which makes Leo shine all the more brighter. A Sagittarius man gets his way by intuitively knowing how to win over the other person, and Leo will be impressed with all his winning efforts. Like any couple these two will have their obstacles to overcome. The emotions of the Sagittarius may vary with his moods from affectionate to indifferent, and he can be temperamental, high spirited, impulsive, and changeable. But his bad moods don't last long, and he generally looks for the bright side of any situation. Leo can turn from being sunny and warm to being self-righteous, arrogant, overbearing, and giving in to a tendency to lecture and to be bossy. Luckily, they are the forgive and forget types who are usually too busy to hang on to an argument for long. Neither likes a boring routine, and both will want to be actively engaged in numerous pursuits and interests. This is an advantageous match for -both parties concerned made especially fortunate by well aspected planets in both of their charts. Sagittarius will feel like his good luck has come through again when he finds himself in love with this lively Leo woman.

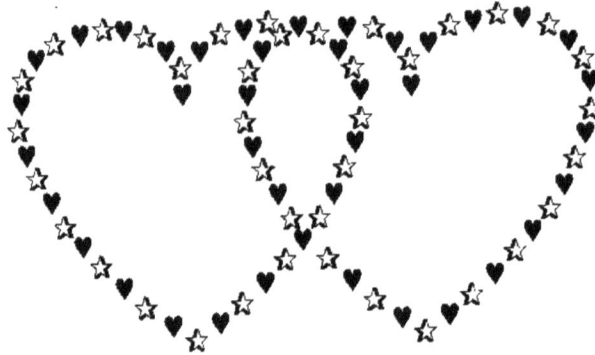

LEO MAN - SAGITTARIUS WOMAN
LOVE RELATIONSHIPS & COMPATIBILITIES

When Leo and Sagittarius turn their energetic enthusiasm toward entertaining each other, they stand the chance of falling hopelessly in love with the enchantment of the other. There seems to be no boundaries to what these two can accomplish when they join forces and pursue common goals in life. Her restless nature may be caught by the fiery magnetism of this Leo man whose noble bearing catches the attention of so many. Both love comfort, ease, and gracious living combined with a busy and active social life of entertaining and pleasurable outings. They share many of the same interests in life which balances out their differences. Dignified Leo may be caught off guard by the unconventional methods of Sagittarius, but both can be practical and sensible or at times just a bit reckless and irresponsible. Leo can be bold and daring which fascinates impetuous Sagittarius. They are both capable of being kind, considerate, charming and just plain fun to be with. They like good conversation spiced with the right amount of humor and congeniality. A good-natured Sagittarius woman will have the best of intentions even when she's dropping a few straight-forward remarks. And her candid observations may help Leo see himself in a new light, providing him the opportunity to grow and expand. She is somewhat more open to new and innovative ideas, but, as impulsive as Leo can be, he may show her how to apply a practical approach to her actions. she is versatile and adaptable compared to Leo who can be more fixed in his outlook on life. Given the opportunity, either can be generous, extravagant, and even wasteful, but common sense generally rules the decisions of this couple. These two are also enthusiastic about their sensual passions finding excitement and pleasure with each other. She likes that he is dependable, strong and assertive, but she may not particularly care for being bossed around. Rather than demanding, Leo must apply his natural congeniality and ask rather than command. Direct and unaffected, Sagittarius loves her freedom, liberty, and friends. She yearns to travel, see the sights, meet new people, and gather experiences. Leo loves his independence as well, but both would also like an companionable person with whom to share their lives and experiences. An unhappy Leo can be a beast in the jungle while an unhappy Sagittarius is reduced to becoming cynical and sarcastic. Keeping the magic alive requires new experiences, common interests, and mutual admiration, kindness, and respect. But a daring Leo will capture her heart while her own -optimism suits him just as well. His intensity and pride are softened by her open-hearted and caring ways. And she is just as impressed with his own open-hearted and giving approach to life. Together they share life to its fullest.

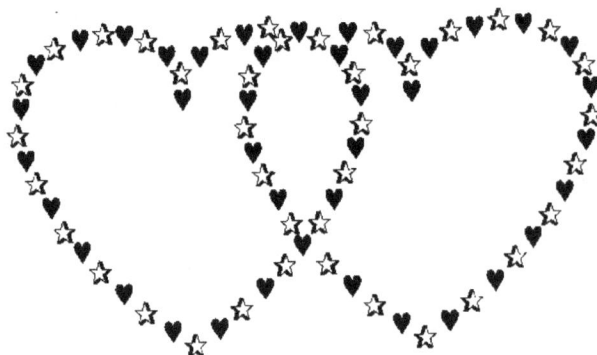

Leo Woman - Capricorn Man
Love Relationships & Compatibilities

Leo is blessed by the Sun with a courageous selfassurance and a powerful, expansive nature leading her to feel inherently that she was born to prominence, a feeling which is displayed in her bearing and dramatic flair. In contrast, the planet Saturn bestows on Capricorn the inherent feeling of obstacles to face and surmount. Capricorn succeeds based on the merits of his hard work and diligent efforts to overcome obstacles, restrictions, and limitations to his driving ambition for prominence and position. His is a calm, steady, dependable, conservative and cautious approach to achieving. He may appear reserved and even shy, but his restrictive nature is quietly calculating how to acquire not only position, but prestige, money and possessions. And he prefers to control his life and his home, not wanting anything to deter him in his efforts. He may be impressed with Leols congeniality, warmth, energy and ambiti6n, but if she is the least bit extravagant he'll teach her the meaning of frugal. This is a reliable man who takes his responsibilities and duties seriously including his duties to his family. Leo will have to share his good intentions with the rest of his family. Love can conquer all, but this relationship may also need large doses of cooperation from both of these individuals. Leo will want her freedom not only to express herself but to acquire new experiences and to pursue her many interests. If she is in the least domineering, she will have to acquiesce. What may soothe her heart is that this man makes every effort to provide well and to protect his loved ones. He is not extravagant, but he does appreciate a comfortable, well planned home and a pleasant atmosphere. He is well organized, conventional and at home with traditional values. That Leo can be devoted and loyal meets with his approval. That she is proud of his accomplishments and his sincerity. also makes Capricorn content. She brings to Capricorn a touch of dashing excitement, and in the bedroom these two find the kind of passion derived from two strong and intense natures. Leo is even more pleased and proud if she marries well, and Capricorn who calculates all of his cautious decisions, prefers to marry for prestige or position. He will like the way she carries herself so well in social outings and her interest in social activities. What seals their commitment to each other may be their shared interests and common goals in life. Both want a good home, to be actively involved socially, and prominence or good standing in the community. He works hard, achieves his .accomplishments, then relaxes to enjoy life. That she enjoys all of life benefits him as well, helping him to laugh and to see life through a different perspective. That his many positive qualities include a warm and loving heart guarantees Leo that she is loved and admired.

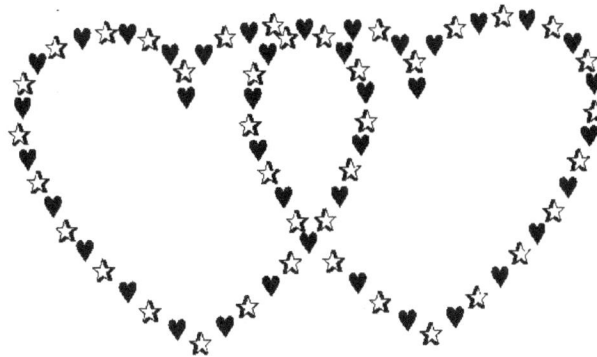

Leo Man - Capricorn Woman
Love Relationships & Compatibilities

Leo ego may well expand tremendously if he captivates the heart of a Capricorn woman. she is industrious and willing to work as hard as it takes to achieve her ambitions. She applies herself to her education, her career, her family, and her home. She is responsible and diligent, but loving and kind as well. She has her own special charm--not the outgoing, personable gregariousness of Leo--that exudes a pleasant warmth, understanding, and kindness. She is well liked and appreciated by her family and friends. This woman in her own quiet, sweet way takes charge of her family and organizes their daily affairs. While other people are flitting about trying one thing then another, selling themselves short, and explaining why they can't apply for that top position, this Capricorn woman merely applies for the position, gets it, works hard and keeps it, never batting an eye. However quiet, reserved and even shy she may be, she isn't intimidated by the aura of position. What she may see in Leo is that touch of excitement that his flamboyant nature offers. She is drawn to his ideas, his energy, his forcefulness, and his .ambitions. Capricorn may vicariously discover excitement and adventure with Leo, but sooner or later he will need to prove himself as well. Industrious Capricorn may want to be sure she hasn't found a lazy Leo who offers a flair for enjoying life but who at the same time lives off her hard work. She likes comfort and security and a well balanced check book. It should be mentioned that either Leo or Capricorn can also be selfish, driven to acquire what they want from life. Given the opportunity, either will consider marrying for position, prestige, or financial security, or the prospect that it will be achieved. That's not to say that love can't turn their heads, and once infatuation develops into full-fledged, can't have enough, love and affection, these two will be drained of their energies and passions. Through cooperation, give and take, negotiating, and finding shared interests as well as developing common goals, they learn to live with another. A smart Capricorn woman will know how to soothe Leols ego and let him think he's in charge at the same time. She has a way of getting what she wants, and she knows that, so she doesn't fear losing her freedom. Leo can be generous, but Capricorn sizes up a situation and gives what is necessary. If she deduces it is necessary to feed Leols pride with admiration and praise, she will do just that. Whether or not the relationship works, of course, depends upon the two people 'involved. They will love and work and love some more. Leols great strength and congenial ways will add to her comfort and good feeling about life. This relationship requires mutual understanding, love and lots of affection from both parties involved.

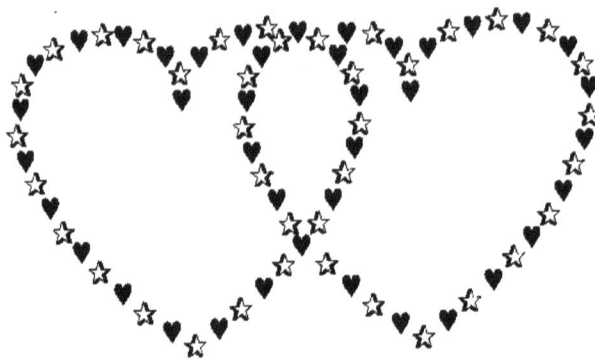

Leo Woman - Aquarius Man
Love Relationships & Compatibilities

Everyone loves Aquarius, but can Leo find happiness with him? Aquarius is pretty busy expanding the universe, and Leo is preoccupied with expanding her audience. That he is unique goes without saying. Creativity may draw them together, and Aquarius likes everyone so Leo does stand a chance of winning his heart. If they make better friends than lovers won't be surprising. But there's always the chance that his inventive streak amazes her to say nothing of that quiet genius-at-work attitude. She is congenial, easy going, very likeable, amiable, friendly and a witty conversationalist. But can she understand that routinely there will be a stranger sleeping on the couch who was passing through town and didn't have a place to stay? If she has any inhibitions due to convention and traditions, she may now forget them because they are no longer necessary. She is at last free to be whoever she would like to be. She may be ambitious and driven or lazy and indolent--it matters not to Aquarius. No one as of yet has discovered a means for controlling unpredictable Aquarius. She may try, but he'll either firmly and fixedly change her m-ind once and for all, or he'll simply leave. If she wants him, it will be on his own terms. In return, he is faithful, loyal, kind and considerate--when he isn't preoccupied with other people and other interests. His mind wanders from social activities to pursuits too various to describe. He is the greatest of humanitarians, and Leo will need to make every effort to follow his thinking. He thinks in the future, what the world could have been could still be once the restrictions are forgotten. Lovely Leo may want to know more or perhaps she's fallen deeply in love with this man who influences others not by dominating but by the strength of his ideas. He may be as fun-loving as she, enjoying being surrounded by friends, but his quiet moments will take up a certain amount of his time as well. He likes money for the freedom it buys, but money and possessions take on an entirely different meaning to Aquarius. Prestige and impressive luxury items are fine for Leo, and he will enjoy them as well. Just don't expect him to base his selfesteem on what he acquires. He is good natured and kind, most of the time, and can be a charming and lively companion. He is imaginative, romantic and slightly eccentric leaving bold and courageous Leo sensing adventure. He'll happily stay around as long as the relationship isn't confining, but he can wait what seems like an eternity before he hears the call of wedding bells. Love endures -all, and if this relationship doesn't work out, the two of them will have a friend for life. Life's glamour loses it glimmer in comparison to the innovations of Aquarius.

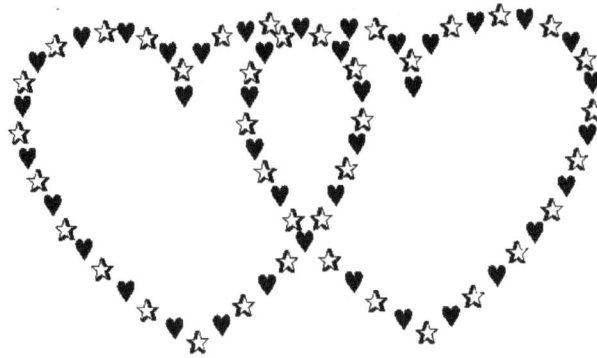

Leo Man - Aquarius Woman
Love Relationships & Compatibilities

This could be the story of the man who feel in love with his best friend after he realized he would never find another so compelling nor quite so entertaining. Most of her friends are male making that scenario quite reasonable. She knows exactly how to keep the surprises coming without giving it much thought at all. Her list of friends may leave Leo envious, but since he's included on that list he can't complain too much. That she's fun and loving at the same time attracts his interest, and she can be a social butterfly or entertain herself alone if she chooses. She may understand his nature better than he does, and if receiving all that praise and all those compliments makes him feel so good, then she'll be glad to offer them. That he beams that sunny smile when he sees her and never fails to make her laugh adds to her amusement. He has enough enthusiasm, strength, self-assurance, and courage for the two of them, and all he seems to lack is her ingenious way with life itself. She has her own distinct lifestyle with no plans of changing it in the near future, but being that they are friends, he won't begrudge her that. That she wants her freedom to come and go and do as she pleases makes her who she is. All Leo knows for sure is that when she is pleasing herself she's often pleasing him as well. He wants a trusted companion in his life who adds a whimsical twist to the excitement he creates. These two may dance through life with hardly a care. That's not to say that reality doesn't set in sooner or later, but there's something about the Aquarius nature that withstands limitations and obstacles. And of course, Leo is undaunted in his efforts to achieve the course he sets for himself. They capture the mind of the other and nothing else seems to matter. She soothes and bolsters his pride making him feel like he is truly king of the wild. Leo is convinced of his own abilities, and with her encouragement, his ego feels almost like a tangible possession he can feel beating within his , breast. No, that's her beeper that she put in his pocket so she wouldn't lose it and when her friends called he could take the call and relay the message that she would be back soon. Leo doesn't like routine, and while Aquarius has particular likes and dislikes, her routine may include getting up in the morning with the rest of the day open to new possibilities. He loves her because he knows her so well, and yet he realizes he will never know all there is to know about what goes in inside her head. If he gives her her freedom to do as she pleases, she won't wander far. Leo finds he has been mastered by someone who never tried nor competed for his attention. She won his heart on the merits of being who she is, and if he stays his happiness will depend upon himself. That's a mighty order for Leo, but one he is equal to in full measure.

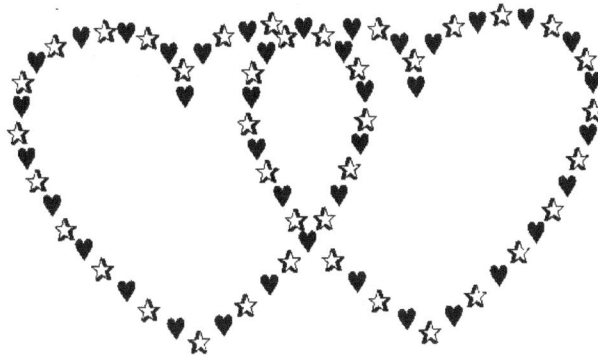

Leo Woman - Pisces Man
Love Relationships & Compatibilities

Fire and Water combine in this relationship through a natural respect and admiration for each other. Pisces is a highly emotional, changeable and sensitive sign, and this man admires Leols confidence and self-assurance. That she is radiantly sunny, warm and affectionate also draws the attention of Pisces. Leo admires the many positive traits of Pisces who responds so well to affection and devotion. They are a fun-filled couple who enjoy pleasant outings, social gatherings, travel, meeting and greeting new people and an occasional adventurous experience. They like the good things in life, pleasant surroundings and an inviting and comfortable home that reflects their good taste. Pisces can be as showy as Leo but she may prefer traditional styles to his more eclectic preferences. Conventional, thoughtful, and practical Leo is expansive, wanting to express herself in the best light possible, but in Pisces she finds a man who is particularly individualistic and who finds his own ways to express himself, his creativity and his passions. Pisces is especially drawn to strong people, and Leo finds herself drawn to his individualism. These are two very different types of people who may feel compelled to explore their differences while building a relationship based on love and compassion. And compassion is the strong suit of Pisces who can sacrifice all for another. It is this very humility that he offers to teach Leo, providing her the opportunity for growth and progressive expansion of her own nature. of course, she has much to teach Pisces as well, such as a firm belief in himself. Both like their approbation, each glowing in the attention of others, and both Leo and Pisces can flirt just for the fun of it. His flirting will upset Leo who can turn jealous and temperamental, and whether he shows it or not, Pisces silently simmers in his own jealousy and possessiveness over this wonderful woman who he's placed first in his life. He may never express those feelings, keeping them as one of those secrets that Pisces holds dear to his heart. But Pisces is sensitive and vulnerable to hurt feelings no matter how well he attempts to hide that from others. All that aside, these are two loving and kind individuals who can do well together if they truly like the differences in their natures, want to learn how to live with each other, and want the best for the other person. Pisces intuitively knows how to make Leo feel like the grandest of people which makes her feel loved, contented, and at peace with herself. That Leo is at her best when in love brings out her most caring, tender and affectionate nature which is what Pisces most desires. Both are ardent lovers who delight in keeping the adventure alive in the bedroom. Both like the unique dazzle that the other brings to the relationship. Making it a lasting relationship is left up to these two different people.

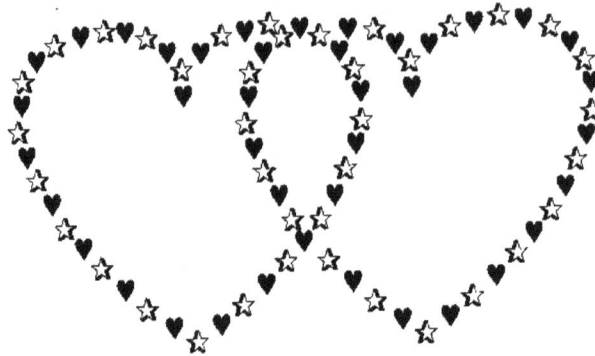

Leo Man - Pisces Woman
Love Relationships & Compatibilities

A strong, powerful Leo man wants to take his natural place in any relationship, that being the leadership position. This Pisces woman admires that about him, and Leo radiates and glows when admired. This brings the discussion to another well kept Pisces secret. Allowing him to make the decisions may make life easier for her in many ways. However, it is just as likely that she knowingly gives the impression of not being controlling when in her own passiveassertive manner she is effortlessly the one in charge. And never think that behind all that winning charm there isn't a thinking mind that knows that admiration and pleasantries can rule over most people, especially a Leo. Pisces can make the Lion purr in ecstasy feeling that he's finally found someone who understands his needs. These two will coo at each other until Leo is smiling his gratification and Pisces is affectionately loving every minute of her accomplishment. Pisces soaks up the Sun-sign warmth of Leo, needing the affection, caring, and protection which this confident man provides. Leo doesn't in any way feel less superior when around Pisces, just more protective. There is a vulnerability and sensitivity about Pisces that makes all the strong signs feel protective of her. What else is strength for? Pisces teaches the Lion humility and caring for someone other than himself. It's when he falters in his caring that he runs the chance of actually damaging Pisces. She wants to give and give of herself but when taken advantage of or taken for granted, she is deeply wounded. She'll swim mightily upstream attempting to prove her strength, but knowing that with the right person in her life the burden would be lightened. Obstacles in love threaten the very existence of this romantic and highly emotional woman. Leo must come to an understanding that she needs him, but he also has to accept that she determines how much she needs. She'll ask for advice, but she doesn't always follow it, pulled in different directions as she is, and this can perturb Fixed and practical Leo. Leo functions best in a well organized home which leaves him free to think about his busy life and many activities. Pisces finds dealing with the details of organization frustrating because it takes up too much of her time. She can usually find whatever it is she wants and doesn't understand the fuss and bother. She may not understand why it is so important to him that the cabinet doors are kept shut and that order prevails in the pantry. Her casual attitude can unbend the Lion who isn't rigid by any means, but he finds these little distractions annoying. They will learn that those are the small things that make or break a relationship right along with balancing the checkbook and finances.

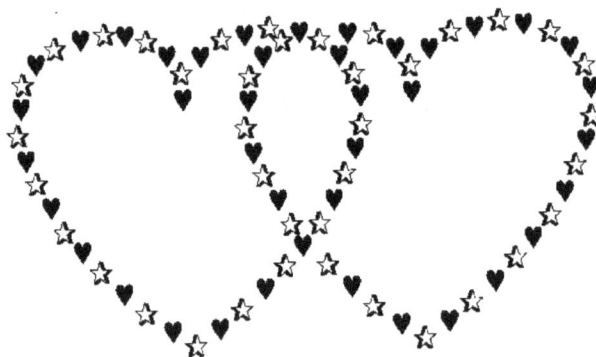

VIRGO WOMAN - VIRGO MAN
LOVE RELATIONSHIPS & COMPATIBILITIES

Virgo individuals derive pleasure from work, family commitments, and the responsibilities of a home. The rewards can be tangible, but it is just as self-rewarding to Virgo to be of service to others. They can enjoy the fun and pleasures of life as well as the next person, but these pursuits are second place to the satisfaction of being responsible, dutiful, and hard working. These two are cautious about love, relationships, and most especially marriage. A discerning Virgo is a detail-oriented, analytical, and critical thinker. They are capable of excelling in any field which requires the assimilation of details and facts. A Virgo who is a history buff will spout forth information, in great detail, leaving the listener astounded at their memories. And no matter how shy or reserved, they do love to talk. These are not impulse driven people full of new, rash, or innovative ideas. They are conventional, traditional, patriotic, and civic minded people who want the best for themselves, their families, their communities, and their country. Their interests are centered on activities, hobbies, diet, health, food, and personal security. Many of the obstacles that Virgo faces in life are self-imposed. The apply their critical natures to themselves, worrying excessively about their own faults and shortcomings. Many a Virgo brings about his or her own anxiety-related health problems. They are always available when a friend seeks advice, but Virgo will also turn their critical nature toward their friends analyzing the other person's rationale in life. In romance, they can think about the possibility until the opportunity no longer exists. There is a Virgo tendency to over-analyze the relationship rather than enjoying the companionship of the other person. These two Virgo individuals may understand each other well, and they may also understand that the best way to a Virgo heart is to establish a trusting and true friendship first and then allow romance to develop in its own sweet time. If neither is in a hurry, then patience pays rewarding returns. Two Virgo people will have much to talk about and may well share similar interests. They relax best in natural settings away from their busy lives, perhaps hiking, fishing, or just seeing the sights. They enjoy social activities, but Virgo may not be overly interested in crowded or noisy places. Whether at home, work, or play, Virgo is actively busy, running off nervous energy. Even sitting still, he/she exhibits some sign of nervous energy, whether it's a tapping foot or drumming fingers. Relaxed, Virgo has a tendency to be leaning forward as if thinking on the verge of dashing into another room. When it comes to the subject of marriage, or even involvement, the Virgo caution puts on the brakes, and many a Virgo waits until later in life to marry. When these two decide on a relationship, they pour their devotion and loving attention into pleasing each other. Beneath that exterior reserve is the warmth, caring, and love of the Virgo heart.

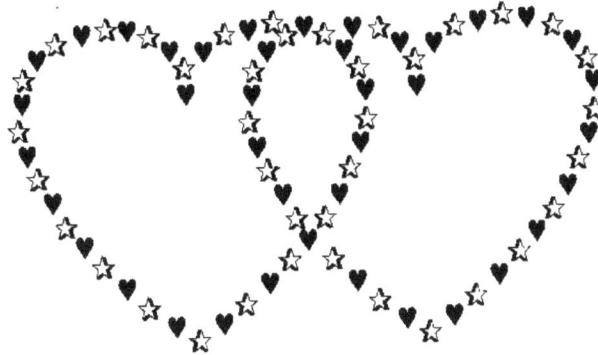

VIRGO WOMAN - LIBRA MAN
LOVE RELATIONSHIPS & COMPATIBILITIES

The Virgo caution is no defense against the charms of a Libra man. This may be her first love or the love of her life, but it will create memories for a lifetime. Libra is all harmony and balance which brings peace and relaxation into Virgo's life, and one thing a Libra man knows is the importance of enjoying the pleasures of life. Libra finds practical sensibilities with this Virgo woman and in return teaches her the value of experiencing life now. Virgo is impressed with the ease with which Libra moves through life, diplomatically and tactfully presenting himself to others. He is at heart a romantic who knows that beneath the Virgo caution is a warm, compassionate and caring person. She must have the most giving of hearts to want to protect it so determinedly. Life is never boring for Virgo and Libra because these two love to talk, to discuss, and to communicate at length. Virgo wants to cover all the details in any discussion which is just fine with Libra who is balancing and weighing the merits of each fact, perhaps baiting her a little with an abstract thought or two or catching her making over generalizations. Libra finds he can relax with Virgo who isn't pushing him to make a spur of the moment decision. And Virgo likes the way Libra judiciously encourages her to make decisions for herself. Libra has a tendency to like things perfect which pleases Virgo, but they must sooner or later define perfection. These two could quite happily spend a lifetime defining and qualifying perfection. Libra will not procrastinate about taking the lead in their sexual life, proving to tentative Virgo that their experiences together can be more rewarding than any other facet of life. What Virgo wants most is to let down her guard with a man in whom she can place all her trust and love. onc6 that trust is established, she may well take the lead and teach him a thing or two. Libra actually needs more rest and relaxation than Virgo is accustomed to allowing herself. But here again, Libra may perceive that Virgo really needs to slow down and discover the pure joy of being perfectly at ease.

And that Virgo is steady and reliable is just what Libra needs--those qualities add not only a dimension but a direction in life toward which Libra can apply his purposes. If their good natures win out over life's trials then Libra and Virgo enjoy the best of life and of each other. On the flip side of that coin, their relationship deteriorates into nagging, carping and fault finding. The development of this relationship depends a great deal on the two individuals involved, but the stars seem to shining on a happy and fulfilled life that adds a touch of joy and grace to both Libra and Virgo. Mutual devotion, commitment, and a need for each other is all these two need once love is declared.

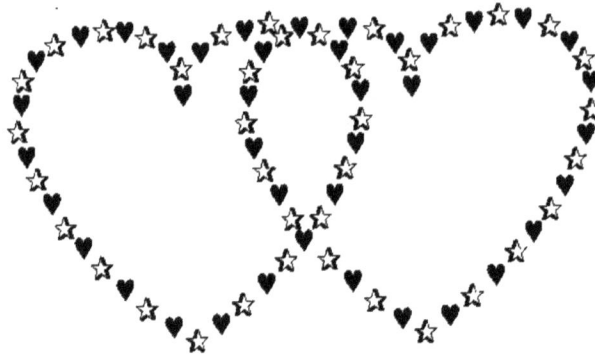

Virgo Man - Libra Woman
Love Relationships & Compatibilities

Many a Libra woman takes her career life seriously as well as her home and family life. What she admires about this Virgo man is his responsible, reliable nature. His capabilities allow her the freedom to follow her own pursuits without worrying that he will be offended or wandering off in a different direction. It is her way with people and the tendency she has to enjoy life that catches Virgo's attentions. Not only is she a gracious hostess but she handles business meetings with a diplomatic if not entertaining manner that puts others at ease. Virgo does well with people, but it is more of an effort for him to relax and truly enjoy the experience. He discovers that Libra effortlessly takes the pressure off him, insuring that he enjoys himself. If they have common interests, whether it be politics, national affairs, or the economy, then their discussions can be endless. Both are talkers while Libra is a dedicated listener as well. It won't take Libra long to deduce that Virgo is impressively detail-oriented, and she'll know enough about the subject matter to catch him in any unbalanced conclusions, gently pointing out the bigger picture and the alternatives he's failed to analyzed. Openminded, tolerant and accepting, Libra also enlightens Virgo when he's too conventional in his thinking. She is further impressed that no matter what abstraction she introduces, he immediately grasps the concept, considers it, and doesn't mind complimenting her on her thinking. she is somewhat bothered that he is so critical of himself, and that he wants to analyze her decision-making rational. But she is pleased that at last someone actually wants to help her in her deliberations and decision making. When all this talking stops she is especially delighted to learn that she excites him physically as well, and Virgo beams with pleasure that she is just as interested in him. Romantic Libra discovers a man who is warmly sensuous, and sincerely caring, tender and kind. She needs to remember that this is a man who takes life seriously, protecting a sensitive nature that few people actually see. He needs to remember that she responds to kindness, diplomacy, and fairness, and a strong arm to lean on as well as a ready ear to listen to her when she's trying to make a decision. They both appreciate a comfortable home, pleasant surroundings, nature trips, and enough social outings to keep life interesting. He offers her a well thought out security. Easy going Libra offers him the know-how to relax, experience life, and enjoy their time together. All couples disagree sooner or later, but their disagreements can be just that with the opportunity to learn, explore, and love with the security of knowing the other's good intentions. If these two know that what they want in life is each other, then this relationship can work. Love blends differences, and it is differences that many times makes living so very interesting.

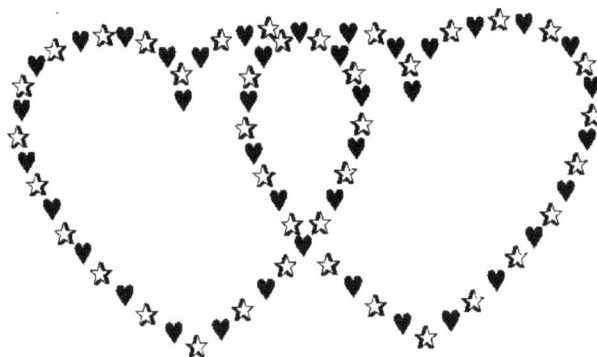

VIRGO WOMAN - SCORPIO MAN
LOVE RELATIONSHIPS & COMPATIBILITIES

These two are a challenge to each other. virgo's caution amazes Scorpio, and Virgo is in turn challenged to analyze Scorpiols intensity. Scorpio and Virgo both have strengths that are manifested in different ways. Scorpio has a tendency to be used by others for his strength, courage and abilities and progressively becomes suspicious of the intentions of others. But Virgo receives intrinsic rewards for being of service to others and doesn't use the talents of others, succeeding on the merits of her own hard work. Scorpio finds in Virgo a self-sufficient person who doesn't attempt to take advantage of the his strengths or his abilities, who doesn't play control games nor compete, negating the necessity for Scorpio to control or compete. Thus, he is more at ease and feels he is able to relax in the warm assurances of this practical and sensible person. Scorpio realizes that her self-criticism and analyzing of others is her method of seeking understanding, knowledge, and self-improvement, and that she means no harm to the other person. Besides, Scorpio is known to have strong analytical and critical abilities himself. She exposes Scorpio to details he has overlooked, and he exposes her to more broad-minded concepts. And Scorpiols courage and apparent lack of fear calms Virgo's worries and anxieties. He doesn't quite understand her preoccupation with health and diet, but that, in his mind, is a minor issue. Virgo, in her caution, doesn't take risks. Scorpio takes risks, has experienced the agony of failure, dealt with it, and has a pragmatic attitude about it. (Less daring people see Scorpio pragmatism as a ruthless and cold demeanor.) Virgo knows that Scorpio is warm, kind, compassionate, and loyal, and having delicately over time through questions and answers drawn out Scorpiols rationale, she vividly sees a lack of fear of failure. As long as the sun rises in the morning, Scorpio sees nothing to fear. If he does become distraught or anxious, chances are it is out of concern for friends or family or someone else has drained his energy. Scorpio treasures a trusted friend and in this relationship may apply sexual self-control, knowing that sex is his arena and wanting to protect Virgo who stands a chance of losing her caution with him. If she gets up her courage, she should have no fear of rejection from him. Scorpio is always ready to assist a woman in need. Having made that decision, this woman should be prepared for a daring adventure. This is a good combination between two well developed people. A less well developed Virgo would provoke Scorpio with her incessant fault finding, and a poorly developed Scorpio would take advantage of

232

Virgo's virtues. That they take the time to get to know one another before proceeding in a relationship provides the proof in the making.

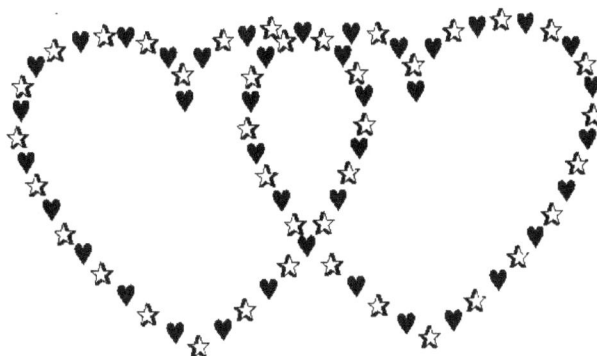

VIRGO MAN - SCORPIO WOMAN
LOVE RELATIONSHIPS & COMPATIBILITIES

It would be impossible for a Virgo man to go through life collecting all those details and analyzing each and every aspect of life and not realize that the strength inherent in this Scorpio woman was wrought from experience. She has gone boldly into life, been trampled on, picked herself up, and continued on still looking for one more adventure. When she meets this Virgo man, she is pleasantly surprised. Remember, Scorpio loves a good mystery and his caution is just that to her. She doesn't have to secondguess his intentions because he wants to be friends first and to get to know one another. out of a compelling curiosity she takes a break from the impulsive risk-takers in order to explore Virgo. She didn't realize it would take so long--it's been months now and he hasn't made his first romantic move. This is new territory for Scorpio who with any other man would know what to do. Now, Virgo has her thinking. If she approaches him, will she scare him off? And if that doesn't happen, wouldn't it feel like taking advantage of him to initiate a romantic involvement? After all, he's bound to be susceptible and vulnerable to her sexual prowess. She's feeling protective and once a person arouses this instinct in Scorpio, he has made a loyal friend. (Granted, another Scorpio would rope him in and play with his affections, but this particular section is discussing well-developed individuals.) Neither Scorpio nor Virgo are casual people--they both possess inherent strengths in differing capacities. Scorpio now discovers that he is also protective of her, an altogether new experience because few strong-willed Scorpio women are in need of much protection. But Virgo's good intentions delight her, and with him she finds herself relaxing, becoming tranquil and at ease. She explains tactfully that he is wrong to be so critical of himself because he has many good attributes. They discover that they can talk to each other, openly and freely. She calms his worries, explaining that nothing could be as important as all that--why not relax and enjoy a little of life? Which is exactly what Virgo does when he's with her. With only one area of life left to explore, Virgo discovers Scorpiols henceforth unveiled romantic passions, and, as she predicted, he is enchanted. If one were to predict, it may take a couple of years, but their passions will finally subside enough for them to begin looking for new interests to explore as well. As with all relationships, this one is enhanced by shared interests and common goals, but this is a good combination between two loving and compassionate people. Both are capable of great devotion and loyalty to the other, and as they discover, they want the same things in life.

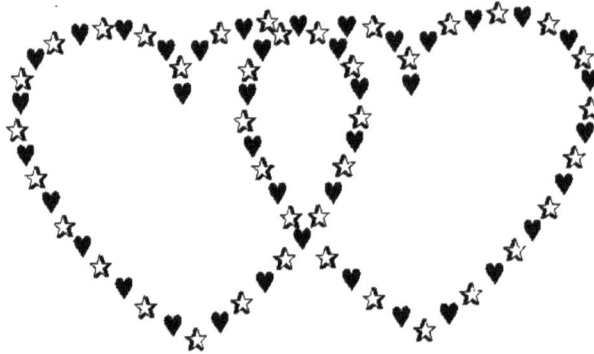

VIRGO WOMAN - SAGITTARIUS MAN
LOVE RELATIONSHIPS & COMPATIBILITIES

There are some relationships that develop with seemingly little effort and there are those which require so-me work and determination. Virgo and Sagittarius may have to expend some effort and work on understanding and accepting each other's similarities and differences. These two communicate well in practically all areas of life, but they go about life differently. First of all, Virgo is practical, sensible, and precise wanting to get the facts right down to the last detail. Sagittarius is more easy going, naturally persuasive, and will present the facts in the best manner for the occasion. And if exaggeration helps to get a point across, well then why not exaggerate a bit? Practical and methodical Virgo is preparing a tidy nest egg for the future. But while Sagittarius may not necessarily be a spendthrift, he is inclined to spend on what he wants or feels he needs. Sagittarius is incredible skeptical of the Virgo caution which seems to him to be pure inhibition. He is unafraid of change and likes to try new things. If they don't work out, he can always go back to the old ways of doing things. Virgo diligently decides upon a path and follows it with fortitude and determination. If Sagittarius is unhappy in a situation, he looks for another whether it be in career, location, or relationships. Virgo cautiously decides to patiently wait and see how this relationship works. Sagittarius is extremely hesitant about getting tied down in a relationship that limits his freedom of thinking or movement. There may be a Virgo female who decides to find out what all the Sagittarius excitement is about. And there may be a Sagittarius who decides that maybe she knows something he doesn't, and he'll give it a try. These two must be careful not to go against their natures and in the long run make each other extremely miserable over the years. Either it is a good match or it isn't. He doesn't really appreciate her critical fault finding remarks, and his blunt, direct opinions can sear her tender heart. Virgo can be attached to home and family, but Sagittarius, if born to roam, can lose contact and doesn't hold much to sentimental or binding ties. What holds them together? It could be that he somehow philosophically inspires Virgo to take a dare and risk an experience for the pure adventure of it. Or that he teaches her what pure fun life can be when you forget all your worries. It could be that she provides him with just enough ties to the Earth to allow him to focus on his pursuits and to develop his abilities, potentials, and dreams. She represents home and the warm assurances that go with being accepted when you return there. He represents those dreams she was afraid to allow into her life until she met him. They learn from each other, develop and grow, and produce a relationship filled with the wonders of love.

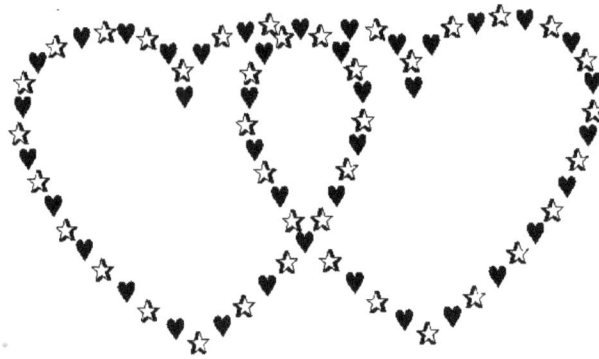

Virgo Man - Sagittarius Woman
Love Relationships & Compatibilities

Well, okay, according to his calculations Sagittarius isn't the most perfect woman for him, but she makes him laugh and for some reason he can never quite have enough of her companionship. Detail-man has collected his own repartee of jokes he has been saving for someone who really appreciates good humor. And Sagittarius is so witty, she plays with words just for fun. More often then not, she shrouds her blunt and direct observations in funny little phrases that don't make Virgo feel quite so vulnerable but which gets her point across just as well. Virgo may even laugh at himself a little which surely will help him relax and put all those worries to one side for awhile.

Intellectually, these two communicate with an ease that astounds them, parlaying facts and interesting subject matter back and forth between them. Virgo may take pride in the way this woman chats up a storm with other people too, but he may question that she knows full well that there is no law against flirting and she takes full advantage of every opportunity to do just that. She will make it clear that she doesn't like to be tied down to a lot of unnecessary rules and regulations from him or anyone else. Life is to be lived--now. If in a career which she loves, she will stick to it, but if she's unhappy, there is every chance that she will change her occupation using her natural luck to find something more suitable. Unnecessary changes alarm Virgo who doesn't understand not applying yourself diligently to whatever it is you happen to be doing-happiness is found in the self-rewarding fact that you are working. And just for her information, he has every intention of enjoying life fully as soon as he has enough money to do just that. That logic doesn't suit philosophical Sagittarius who must have her freedom to enjoy life now, and there she goes again, making the most of every opportunity. About the only thing in life that destroys the Sagittarius luck is restrictions or being trapped in a longterm, unhappy relationship. Perhaps she intuitively knows this and is a little skeptical of being bound by a permanent partnership. But Sagittarius, like many a female, is susceptible to the romantic overtures of a promising male, and her dreams may turn from sand castles to the casa that Virgo envisions. She respects much about the steady permanence that he wishes to bring to her life, recognizes his good intentions, and admires his reliable nature. Then too he can be so sincere and considerate. It is difficult to imagine attempting to find another quite like him. Pure attraction draws them together, he offering her the ties that bind to people together in shared love and passions. She brings a joy to the relationship that she desires to share with another in a loving embrace.

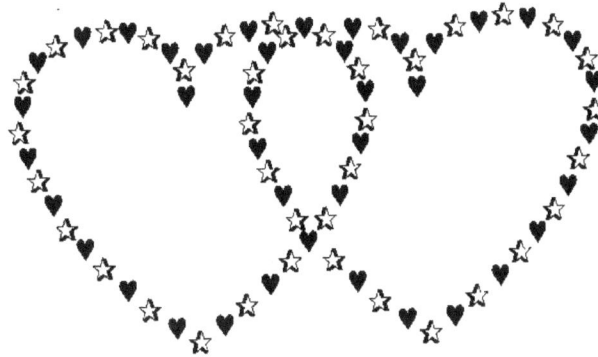

Virgo Woman - Capricorn Man
Love Relationships & Compatibilities

The Virgo woman and the Capricorn man, both serious in nature, may take their time and allow the relationship to develop slowly, giving both ample time to consider the consequences and the long term benefits. Neither one is rash nor impulsive, and each gives careful consideration to any decisions. Once each decides the other has passed the final inspection, they may form a mutual admiration society, join hands, and not let anything under the Sun come between them. Finally, two serious, well meaning individuals who want nothing else but to achieve their ambitions and goals in life, establish a secure home, and build for the future. Virgo and Capricorn succeed on the merits of their own efforts, and these two apply all their strengths and efforts in realizing their plans. He is methodical, well organized, practical, and strives against all odds and all obstacles to reach his destination. He aspires to top positions in his field or to owning his own business. And if it is required that he spends more hours at work then at home, this Virgo woman understands that necessity. If he needs a partner at home or at work, he has found the right woman. A practical perfectionist, she attempts to match his efforts. Together, they plan a sensible home, count pennies whether they need to or not, and save for the future. Capricorn can be even more frugal than Virgo if necessary. These two both take an intense interest in their families, accepting any and all responsibilities for relatives. If at some time Capricorn must take care of an aging relative, Virgo understands completely offering to help in any way possible. If not immediately set upon a path as a young man, Capricorn naturally matures to desire and aspire to succeeding in life. He can be reserved and dignified with an air of silent knowing that others respect and admire. He and Virgo pursue activities and interests related to their careers, the community, social functions, and their civic duties. These two are comfortable with conventional, traditional lifestyles finding security in well set rules and regulations that benefit one and all. Unlike other people who must spend a life time learning how to communicate and live with each other, Virgo and Capricorn are capable of falling into a set routine rather easily. In some instances, however, that is where the problem begins. Their life can become too routine, too methodical, and too organized. Virgo worries incessantly with no one to relieve her anxieties, and Capricorn grows even more reticent. These two, remember can overcome any obstacles, and with thought will realize they need to reinstall that special spark into their relationship that first attracted them to each other. Capricorn grows younger with age making this an attainable goal for himself with the help of this lovely Virgo lady. And Virgo can be restlessly receptive to wanting to fulfill his wishes.

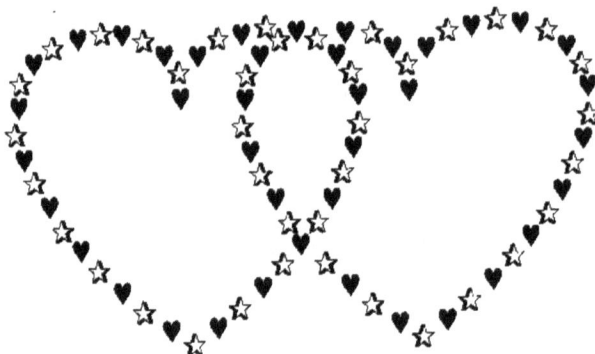

Virgo Man - Capricorn Woman
Love Relationships & Compatibilities

No matter how reserved, a Capricorn woman can be a charmingly pleasant companion. She is not adverse to working for what she wants, and will pursue her goals steadfastly. A serious-minded Virgo man can't help but be impressed with this soft-spoken, well meaning, and attractive woman. They form a friendship based on trust and loyalty which develops into a full blown romance. She is tender and loving, and he is compassionate and caring. This is a well-thought out relationship designed to produce effective results, and that smile on her face and twinkle in his eye prove their efforts weren't in vain. Without much fuss or bother, she can easily manage a household, handle the finances, and pursue a career. With like-minded goals, control probably doesn't become much of an issue as long as these two are making steady progress. Capricorn is more assertive than aggressive, and she possesses a softness to her nature that eases away some of virgo's anxieties. She'll soothe his self-critical nature, knowing that to perform at his best in the world, he must have a strong self-concept and feel good about himself. These two are ruled by their minds not their emotions, but that's not to say they don't understand the importance of a strong emotional well being. Analytical Virgo may throw out a criticism or two, but Capricorn catches them, applies logic to them and displays them for him to re-analyze--all the while smiling with that special charm and enchanting tilt to her chin. She wrote the book on competence and yet she is feminine, fragile, and pleasantly disarming with an elegant grace that captures his Virgo heart. Virgo is strong, reliable and self-sufficient which are all admirable traits that combine well with the self-discipline of this Saturn influenced female. She aspires to accomplishment of her goals and knows she will face numerous obstacles in obtaining what she wants in life. Virgo feels a sense of accomplishment when he can be of service to someone else and offers Capricorn all the help she may need. Each are responsible people who remember the help they receive from others. These two have strong family ties and accept their responsibilities, duties and obligations as a matter of course. Both are self-sufficient and manage themselves and others well. If they remember to throw in a little fun and frivolity and a few laughs, they'll also manage their relationship well. What love brings together with these two endures through a lifetime of fond memories and the rewards of working together. If they part, it will be amiably and against their better wishes. These two don't accept changes in their lives easily and both much prefer to make love work and last. Virgo tempts Capricorn to be true to her nature.

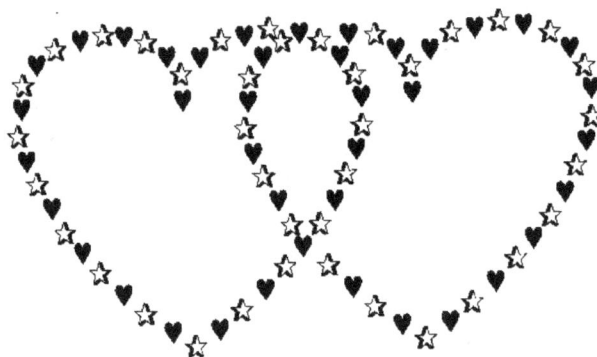

Virgo Woman - Aquarius Man
Love Relationships & Compatibilities

Why one might ask would this soft-spoken, reliable and sensible woman be drawn to the rebel of the Zodiac? Perhaps in her dutiful manner, she wants to take care of him, protect him and be sure no harm comes to him. His reactions to any situation are unpredictable as are his changeable moods and inclinations. True he has a penetrating and analytical intellect that produces profound, far-seeing, and at times genius insight, but does he work hard like Virgo? That depends a great deal on the personal philosophy which he has developed for himself. Aquarius is as unconventional as Virgo is traditional. His preference is to write his own rules, and he may perceive the rules and laws of society as not applying to him because he had no part in making them. He can be a cool mixture of practicality and eccentric instability. He's congenial, friendly, funny when he chooses, and a pleasantly charming flirt. Soft spoken and courteous, he likes to loose himself in the companionship of his many friends. At other times, he is intense, fascinating and intriguing then changes to being diplomatically sympathetic and caring. Perhaps because he feels others will never understand him, he remains rather impersonal even with his closest friends, and from time to time will withdraw from the crowd seeking solitude. Like Virgo, he seeks friendship first in any romantic relationship and won't be in a hurry to make it permanent. Like Virgo, many an Aquarius marry later in life. In romance, it is his experience that his lady friends eventually attempt to change him in some way, and he determines for himself what changes he is willing to make. Aquarius is a person who will borrow from one person to give to another, and perhaps more than any other person, his friends willingly support and care for him and back his ideas or inventions no matter how outlandish. He impulsively lives for the future and dreams of the perfect society. He can easily loose himself in his thoughts and not consider the consequences of his actions, at times hurting the other people in his life. If this Virgo woman is determined to keep him in her life, she will need to apply all of her patience, allow him to come and go as he pleases, and keep the refrigerator well stocked with his favorite foods and beverages. He adamantly wants his home well managed to suit his preferences and is not open to discussing this issue. Analytical Virgo can attempt to rationalize his thinking, but few people can follow the Aquarius mind that wanders on another wavelength unconnected to the precepts of logic and conventional thought. Does she love him against all odds and want to stay? If not, they'll be friends for life. His romantic charm may inspire her to do just that.

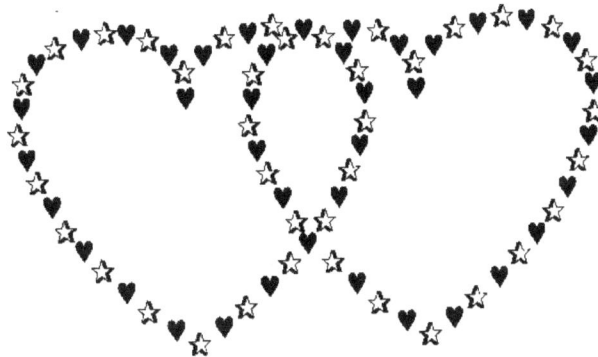

VIRGO MAN - AQUARIUS WOMAN
LOVE RELATIONSHIPS & COMPATIBILITIES

Virgo may have thought he had his life all figured out, but then he happened upon this ingenious, sparkling female and began questioning himself all over again. She may keep him waiting for that dinner date, but she was vague about the time. Maybe she had to stop off and see a friend on the way, or there was an unexpected emergency. His anxiety level starts to rise, and he considers the benefits of getting her a beeper or a cellular phone so he can stay in contact with her. It can't be a flat--he just bought her new tires which, being Virgo, he wouldn't usually do, but he was afraid hers wouldn't get her to where she was going and then he would have to rearrange his schedule to help her out anyway. There she is now, but who are the other two people with her? He thought this was to be a special occasion just for the two of them. Better not complain. She's always pleasant, but if he complains she doesn't return his calls for a few days, and once it was a couple of weeks before he heard from her. He knows she cares for him. She has made that clear in any number of ways. Now, if only he understood her thinking, he would be able to also understand how to deal with her. But it is difficult to ask her questions. The last time he asked her why she was late she said something to the effect that time is a man made construct primarily devised to restrict the freedoms of other people and without time man would probably have already figured out how to make contact with the future ... then there was something about a dimensional feasibility that left him secretly researching the subject for weeks. She loves his home, adores his parents, and has a special communication with his poodle. Now, if he could only communicate with her as well. He knows she needs him, and he wants to protect her, but he needs to think about this relationship some more. Fortunately, she is in no hurry and she certainly isn't pushing him to make a commitment like so many other woman would be doing. The nice thing about her is she can be funny, charming, and so socially presentable and gregarious all in her own way. She presents the truth to him molded to suit her own perception, and while she does everything she says she's going to do, she's not overly willing to accept obligations that might tie

241

her down. But despite all that, their romance bloomed, and she has certainly sexually inspired him to a new variation or two. She is open-minded and tolerant of all his faults which he felt compelled to tell her about, and she remained impersonal, not getting overly emotional or concerned that he wasn't perfect. Why does she stay with him when she knows so many others? Because to many a Virgo and an Aquarius, friendship comes first, and neither of these two willingly wants to lose that special relationship that they have developed. This combination depends entirely upon the two people involved.

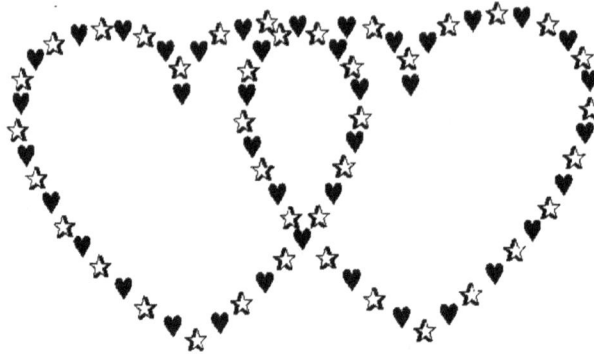

VIRGO WOMAN - PISCES MAN
LOVE RELATIONSHIPS & COMPATIBILITIES

The combination of Virgo and Pisces produces a relationship between opposite signs in the Zodiac, and as is often the case, opposites do attract. Pisces is a sign which brings unbelievable abilities to dream and an inclination toward mysticism to any relationship with the individual many times relying on intuition and perceiving people and situations through their emotions. Virgo is the sign representing work and service to others, and this individual most often reflects on facts, practicalities, and sensible decisions while seeking reality. As with all opposites, they bring to each other what the other person lacks. And their opposite characteristics can either blend together to produce a harmonious blend, or these two could find themselves at odds while attempting to understand and to change each other. Virgo offers Pisces order to life, and the Pisces creative imagination offers Virgo a most certain break from the routine. There is a natural flow of conversation between these two very different people which may help to relieve their worries. Each are prone to worry and fret and to imagination situations and problems being worse than they actually are. The busy activities of Pisces may distract this Virgo woman from her worries allowing her to relax and to enjoy life more. And her compassion and caring will certainly ease the mind of tentative Pisces who relaxes best when he feels loved and accepted. She brings a gentle direction to his life encouraging him to follow his dreams and to develop his talents and abilities. If romance develops into love and marriage, Virgo effortlessly organizes the home and manages their daily lives allowing Pisces more freedom to pursue his efforts in life. And a loving and caring Pisces will teach Virgo the warmth and depth of emotions involved in lovemaking. That's not to overlook the fact that Pisces also loves to laugh, and his gaiety adds a new dimension to Virgo, easing her serious outlook on life. These two share a fondness for comfortable living, a pleasant home, and a variety of interests. They love the outdoors and nature as well as social outings with friends. All goes well, but this couple will have to address the issue of finance. Virgo doesn't comprehend the Pisces decision making process when it comes to the dollar. Pisces likes to save, that goes without saying, but what he does choose to spend money on at times seems to Virgo like unnecessary extravagance. And it is difficult to argue with the practicalities of sensible and logical Virgo. There is also something about the Pisces secretiveness which may upset orderly and well meaning Virgo. Each may want to discover the planetary locations of the other before making long term plans, but overall, there are indications for great possibilities for this couple once they learn to blend their differences into positives.

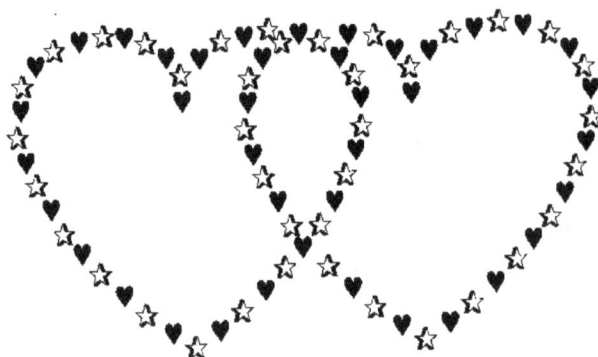

VIRGO MAN - PISCES WOMAN
LOVE RELATIONSHIPS & COMPATIBILITIES

The Virgo man and the Pisces woman love to talk and to laugh, exchanging pleasantries and enjoying life almost as easily as picking up the phone. Virgo is one of best at analyzing and critiquing another, and he will have no problem understanding the emotions that propel this woman through life. Next, he must decide if he can live with that level of high-intensity emotion on a full time basis. But he may be a pushover for the enchantment that this lovely Pisces woman brings into his life. He offers the protection provided in his strength and good intentions, reliability, sensibilities, and a practical approach to life. Virgo will take a quiet pride in the creative expressions of Pisces which fascinate him. Her laughter distracts him from his many worries, and he finds himself relaxing with her as a companion. She finds it difficult to believe that Virgo has as many faults as he claims to have and disagrees with him on this point. And feeling protective of sensitive Pisces, Virgo may keep his criticisms of her to himself. She is lovingly warm and affection and always greets him with the most cheerful of smiles. That is pie in the sky for Virgo who wants more than anything to be appreciated for himself. Virgo must learn, however, that Pisces has needs as well, including lots of attention, admiration, and expressions of love. Whether it is a bouquet from the florist or a flower from the garden, Pisces will be pleased as long as he remembers to think about her often. And when Pisces is happy she is at her best, charming and glowing with an energy of her own making. She brings to Virgo glimpses of insights and visions that enlighten his mind pulling him out of reality into the consideration of what dreams are made of when one is free to dream. Do they find everlasting happiness together? That depends a great deal upon the two individuals involved in this Virgo-Pisces relationship. They think differently. Pisces must truly admire Virgo for his practical, logical mind and respect his decision making abilities and the way he manages their lives. He means well, and he does well. Virgo, on the other hand, must accept Pisces as she is because there is no changing her. She likes financial security as much as Virgo, but it is a necessity for her to have interesting things in her life. She needs his strength and direction, and he needs her sparkle, fun, and magic. Opposites in the Zodiac, they either accept and blend their differences or the relationship deteriorates into quarrels and disagreements. Their conversation is good, and their sex is great. Now, these two must decide upon the rest of their lives. Astrologically, there are strong indications for good possibilities between the combination of Virgo and Pisces. When these two love, it is magic in the making.

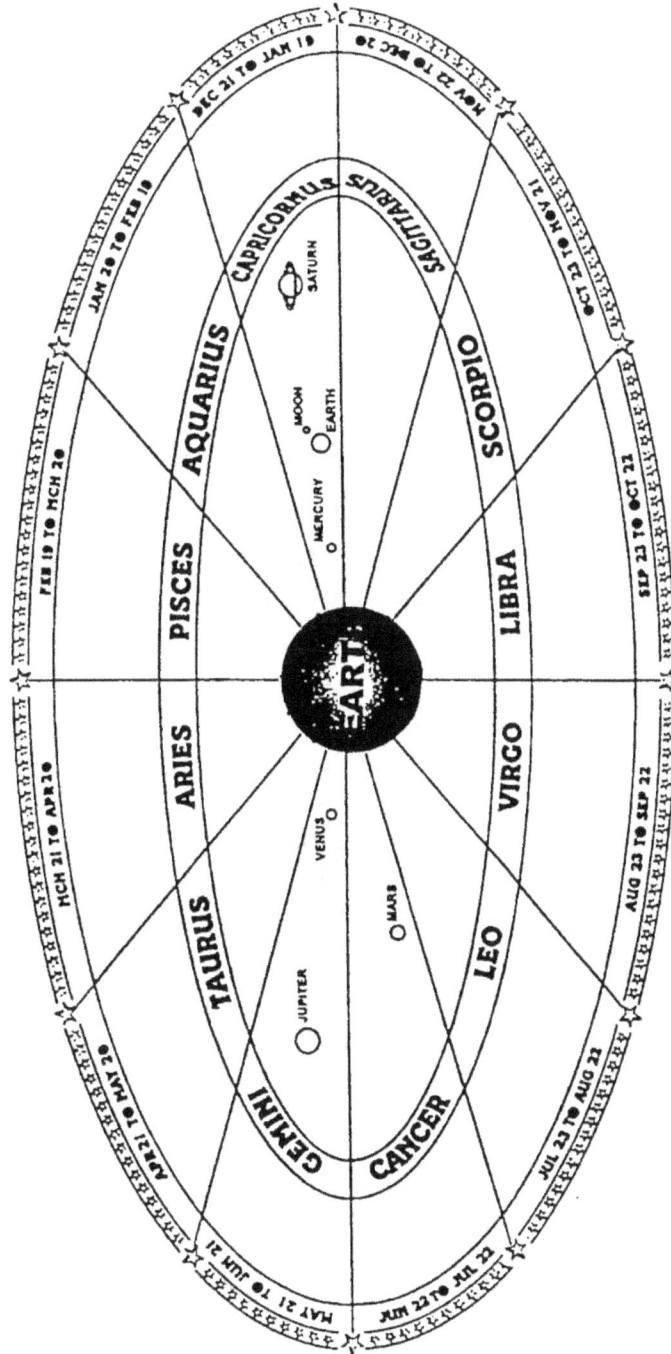

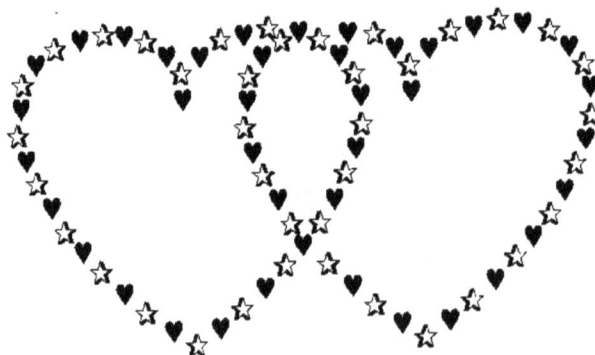

LIBRA WOMAN - LIBRA MAN
LOVE RELATIONSHIPS & COMPATIBILITIES

These two make every effort to be fair and just in a relationship seeking harmonious togetherness, pleasantly beautiful surroundings, fulfilling careers, and an active social life. They are drawn to their lively conversations, discussions, debates, deliberations, and, yes, even to their occasional arguments. They match each other well in charm, graciousness, diplomacy, tact, and persuasion. But Libra has an unconscious tendency to like to have the last word in any discussion, and these two will have to make a conscious decision on how to end the talk. Their logical intellect precludes an interest in varied and diverse subjects, seeking ideas and forming opinions on either side of an issue. They may feel extremely comfortable with one another recognizing each other's Air sign need for verbal expression. Libra is not the silent, sulking type who withdraws from a situation or a conflict. These two want to talk out whatever is on their minds. She discovers a man who is as considerate and kind as herself. Each is compatible, generous, and compassionate. They much prefer being nice to each other and are just as amiable to other people as well. They may share an interest in art, music, or literature, and not only does each want to express his or her opinions, observations and criticisms, but each wants to listen to the remarks of the other person as well. Libra likes to work hard, and they like their pleasures. They make diligent efforts to produce good results in their endeavors, but Libra also needs time off from busy schedules to rest and relax and regain their equilibrium. Libra and Libra combine and blend their positive traits well, but they also bring to the relationship the same negative traits. Libra loves fun, pleasure, and socializing, and these two must strive to maintain a balance between their pleasures and work. Overindulgence in pleasures whether it be food, drink, or sex results in problems. Then too, there is that little tendency to argue and if arguments turn into ongoing conflicts, it unbalances Libral scales emotionally. Most often, the optimism of Libra results in the scales regaining their balance, the conflict being resolved, and other matters attended to. Libra would prefer to compromise than to prolong an argument. These two are romantically well suited with each other, both liking soft lights and music, expressions of love, and lots of affection and attention. Bright lights make them squint and loud music is distracting and who else would possibly understand that but another Libra. These two don't like to be rushed into making a decision, but once they decide on each other, they begin to hear bells. Libra prefers marriage to ongoing affairs which is only fair it seems. The stars predict every indication of good things for Libra and Libra when they decide upon each other. These two who are so much in love with the idea of love may well discover perfect harmony and balance with each other--all things being equal that is.

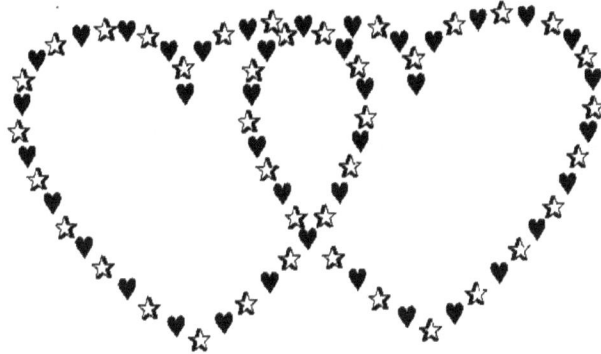

LIBRA WOMAN - SCORPIO MAN
LOVE RELATIONSHIPS & COMPATIBILITIES

Libra is not at all opposed to a strong, forceful man who is passionately ardent as well as equally hard working, ambitious and enthusiastic about life. Hers is a masculine sign ruled by the feminine planet, Venus, making her wonderfully female but not easily intimidated by the strong, silent types. Both Libra and Scorpio are kind and considerate people, and she'll be intrigued with his compassion and caring. She will, of course, want to know more about him and to discuss his opinions, their relationship, and his feelings. This brings her to one little problem in this relationship. Scorpio enjoys the easy going rapport of Libra, but he isn't as open to discussing everything there is to know about his life let alone his feelings. Scorpio is cautious and just a bit distrustful of all this talk even though he truly cares about her. Besides, no matter how adaptable he is, his opinions and likes and dislikes are firmly set. And opposition to his opinions can frustrate him. What Scorpio may fail to realize is that Libra is only talking or perhaps discussing, maybe even debating a bit. She doesn't necessarily mean to challenge his opinions--this isn't an argument, it's a discussion. This is one issue that Scorpio can be somewhat thick-headed about-- he never quite grasps her logic on this matter. He can also be rather sensitive in this regard. At the same time, he is patient with Libra and encourages her in all her endeavors. At other times, his perceptive nature leads him to be suspicious of her optimistic outlook on life and the way she sees the bright side of all situations. He may even think Libra naive and unsuspecting of what troubles may lay ahead. The reasons for his own actions are well thought out, but he may not be able to express them as well as Libra would like. That he is self-confident and self-assured is what Libra likes about this Scorpio man, and she may have to forego finding out what secrets he keeps in his mind. Libra needs companionship, a partner in life, and expressions of love, affection and lots of romance. Scorpio needs to be accepted as he is and for her to realize that not all communication is verbal. His silent glances and small gestures hold plenty of meaning. These two are equally curious about each other, and Scorpio is every bit as interested in romance as is this lovely Libra, and in that department he will give her plenty of attention and expressions of his true meaning. Scorpio brings his own special warmth and understanding to Libra, learning not to tip her scales out of meanness. Libra does her balancing act, smoothing and soothing his intensity and learning not to step on his Scorpion tail just for the fun. These two both learn through their give and take how to love and live with another.

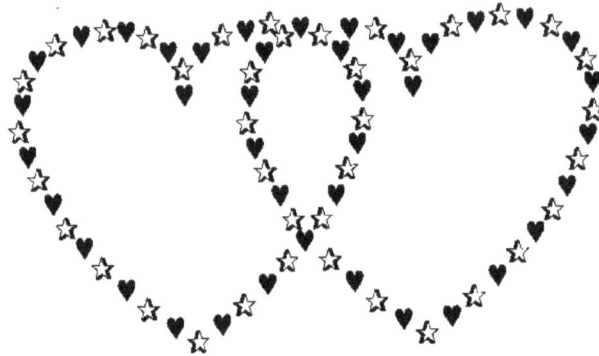

Libra Man - Scorpio Woman
Love Relationships & Compatibilities

The Libra man may most admire the intensity exhibited in everything that Scorpio does. He likes her strength, her self-confidence, and her enthusiasm. And she is surely charmed by this man who so easily expresses all that he wants to say and do. His speech is eloquent and romantic, and she finds herself curiously looking forward to just listening to him talk. Both possess logical, analytical intellects, and respect the thoughts of others. Scorpio may not agree with everything he says, but he says it so well that it's a pleasure to hear him speak. Perceptive as Scorpio is, it won't take her long to realize that he easily takes an advocate position for either side of a discussion and that he recognizes the pros and cons to both sides of any argument. His general optimism has a way of making her feel better about life as well. This man is fun to be around, and Scorpio likes to have fun as much as the next person. She accepts that every once in a while he talks himself in circles without really making a point, and she does wish that she could have the last word just once. But how she loves it when he turns all that charming persuasion toward making her happy. This soothes her sensitive nature, and she empathizes all the more with Libral's need for fairness and all his endless efforts to keep his scales well balanced. She makes every effort, herself, to keep him happy, but Scorpio from time to time likes a good argument-not a discussion--in order to balance out her own nature. It rids her of her restlessness, and she is calm again and ready to appease her Libra man by enticing him with her warm embraces. She does so love his romantic nature, and as far as she is concerned, he's free to be as romantic as he likes. In fact, a couple of more hours of practice and undoubtedly they will have it perfectly refined. Libra learns that a silent glance from this enticingly sexual female is a romantic stimulus all by itself. There is a weakness this couple must be careful of. An off-balanced Libra can easily become distracted by pleasure, and a weak Scorpio may find escape in alcohol or drugs. That warning aside, both Libra and Scorpio possess strong inclinations to pursue serious careers and serious interests in life. Libra seeks a peaceful, relaxing setting, and Scorpio desires tranquility. They both like pleasant surroundings and a comfortable home that is accommodating for either entertaining or for those quiet times they spend alone together. Common interests and shared values add to this relationship as does intellectual stimulation and a touch of excitement and adventure in life. In fact, Scorpio just may bring to Libra that daring dash of excitement which seems to thrill and spice-up her imagination. Differences, curiosity, and an unexplainable attraction called love holds them together while they learn all there is to learn about each other.

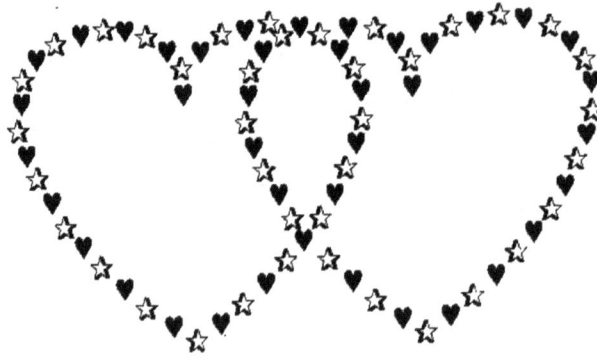

LIBRA WOMAN - SAGITTARIUS MAN
LOVE RELATIONSHIPS & COMPATIBILITIES

This is an interesting combination between two interesting people. These two thrive in a relationship with another intellectual person who likes to share ideas and thoughts. Both Libra and Sagittarius like to talk, ask questions, read and think. Even a quieter Sagittarius can ask endless questions and surprise Libra with his quick wit, funny little practical jokes, perceptive insights, and imaginative dreams. They have their differences, but Libra likes this man and is comfortable with the way he thinks. They are best suited if they share similar interests, ideals, and values. Sagittarius values friendships but even more so if the friend expresses similar ideals and philosophies. Libra, the romantic, needs and wants a companionable partner in life, and there are any number of Libra women who either marry too early or too impulsively. Sagittarius, on the other hand, takes his time exploring and expanding his freedom-loving ways and experimenting in romance. Sagittarius isn't usually anxious to get tied down early in life, and if he's still roaming about, it is advisable for Libra to allow him to get it out of his system before they consider a serious relationship. If these two have arrived at that point in life where a lasting relationship is what they both want, they'll discover that their own special combination produces opportunities for a harmonious romance. These are two people who are optimistic, always seeing the good in whatever life brings their way. Each can turn obstacles and negatives into positive situations. Sagittarius isn't a submissive person. He resents limitations and restrictions on his freedom and thoughts and movements, but at the same time he doesn't always like the responsibility of leading and making all the decisions--obligations can limit his need for freedom. Libra is more than willing to manage and lead, but she does like input in the decision-making process. Libra will have to polish her balancing act because while she's managing, she has to remember not to be bossy or controlling. She may find that adaptable Sagittarius likes spur of the moment decisions and activities, and he's energetically ready to be on the go. That's fine with Libra if she's in one of energetic spells, but Sagittarius also needs to recognize that she isn't being lazy or withdrawn when she decides she wants to rest for a few days--she needs her rest to regain and maintain her balance, peace and harmony. The Fire sign Sagittarius also energetically pleases the Libra need for frequent affection and romance, and he'll find her receptive to his advances and just as

250

pleasing as he dreamed she would be. There is every possibility that these two blend their dreams quite well into a loving and lasting relationship.

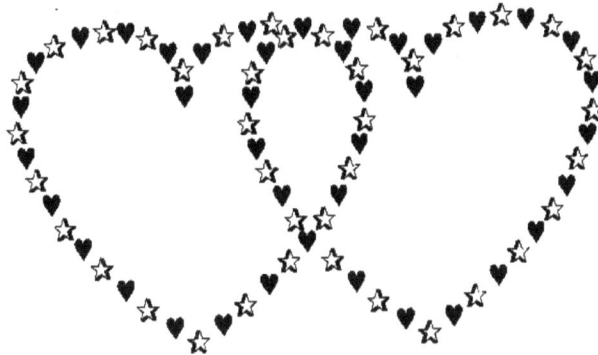

LIBRA MAN - SAGITTARIUS WOMAN
LOVE RELATIONSHIPS & COMPATIBILITIES

The romantic charmer of the Zodiac has so many lady friends that he may postpone making a decision about a firm commitment, dangling prospective partners along until he makes up his mind. That suits this Sagittarius woman as well because she has any number of male friends who enjoy her company as well, and she isn't in a particular hurry to be confined by a commitment. But the more they talk, the more they look forward to talking some more, and these two form a friendship based on shared values and ideals. He seeks fairness and justice, and Sagittarius is philosophically idealistic. Libra likes that Sagittarius is generous, witty, and gregarious, but he is also drawn to her intellect. He may lead the discussions, but she is adept at insightful and perceptive remarks that add to any conversation. Sagittarius effortlessly expands the Libra mind and thought process, adding to his ideas and helping him to balance his arguments and to arrive at his conclusions. That she often does that through humor is what amazes Libra. But Sagittarius can also be blunt and direct in her remarks, not meaning any harm, and Libra has to learn not to take offence. Libra also likes that Sagittarius is even more optimistic than he is and always finds the silver lining in any cloud. A Libra man may naturally want to take the lead, which is fine with Sagittarius, but she doesn't want to be controlled. She likes his diplomacy and tact and his persuasiveness, but she is rather fixed in her opinions. At the same time, she is adaptable to new ideas, loves to meet people, and to travel and explore new horizons. If Libra shares those interests, these two have many a fun time together. Libra may want to note that a Sagittarius trapped in a dull and boring routine can become sarcastic and discontent with life. Libra likes a little excitement in his life, and Sagittarius thrives on an ingredient of change and new experiences. Both do better with plenty of mental stimulation to keep their minds occupied or either can become restless. She is a lively, independent woman who is self-assured and self-confident. If her intuitions led her to this romantic, sentimental Libra, she will be pleased with their shared interests and outlooks on life. She has to remember that he is only discussing, not

251

arguing, and he has to remember that she isn't shooting arrows at him, those are only perceptive observations that she is making. They may discover that luck and opportunity enhances their relationship, or perhaps they feel so lucky because they found each other. She is curious, experimental, and energetic about love and romance, and their sexual encounters are pleasantly entertaining and satisfying. That Libra and Sagittarius both share a fascination with a challenge will lead them smooth over any differences to produce a loving, kind and affectionate relationship.

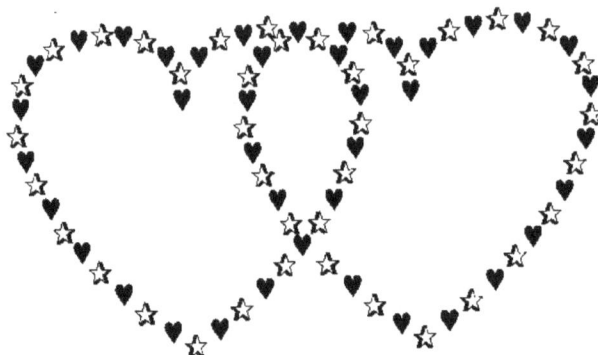

LIBRA WOMAN - CAPRICORN MAN
LOVE RELATIONSHIPS & COMPATIBILITIES

Libra and Capricorn may share determined and ambitious natures, wanting to succeed in their endeavors and to attain leadership positions, but they use different methods to achieve what they want in life. He is practical, methodical, dependable, and reliable, readily applying self discipline in order to achieve self-control. He is comfortable in a conservative setting and with a conservative outlook on life and is quite fixed in his opinions. Both Libra and Capricorn can be kind, considerate, and warmly affectionate, with a gentle nature that expresses compassion and caring. But Capricorn in his effort to be decisive, dutiful, and responsible, pushes himself to accomplish. He doesn't postpone decisions or actions and has little interest in procrastination which he may view as laziness. He isn't rash or impulsive, giving careful thought to his decisions, but he is comfortable with making a decision. Librals need for deliberation and discussion are seen by Capricorn as a waste of time. Libra may find Capricorn too stubborn and too conservative if not somewhat overbearing and controlling. He doesn't even succumb readily to her charm or powers of persuasion. There is much that Libra does like, however. For one thing, Capricorn isn't inclined toward loud and angry outbursts. He remains calm and purposeful in all situations, and Libra much prefers peaceful and calm settings. But Libra is capable of working hard and playing hard finding the pleasures in life a reward for all that diligent effort. Many a Capricorn, while they aren't adverse to enjoying life, views pleasures and play as an extravagance which can wait until after they make their fortune and own a comfortable home. Libra is all for making a home and building a fortune, but postponing pleasure indefinitely can appear more than a bit dreary to this fun-loving woman. But Capricorn does appreciate the Libra optimism which brightens his day and soothes his own rather pessimistic outlook. And Capricorn likes the ease with which she handles social functions. Libra is also more flexible and adaptable than Capricorn, attributes which add possibilities to life. Libra senses Capricorn's deeper earthy passions, desires and emotions and proves that romance can put a smile on his face any day of the week. They both must develop a strong desire to make love last by developing a true understanding of each other as well as tolerance and acceptance of their differences. Capricorn is an excellent manager and leader, but he may have to accept that Libra has excellent ideas and wants to express them. The best way for these two to overcome their differences is to focus on their similar positive traits and to down play their negatives. Capricorn what really binds them together is a lasting love they can not ignore nor live without.

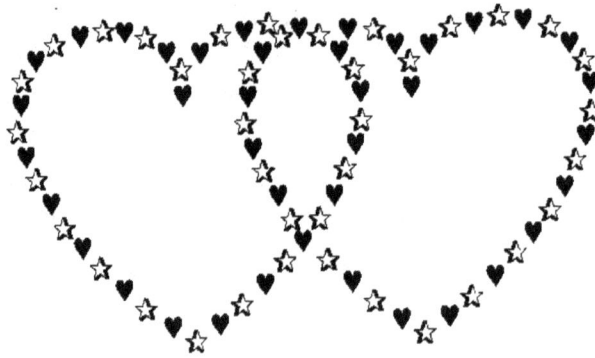

LIBRA MAN - CAPRICORN WOMAN
LOVE RELATIONSHIPS & COMPATIBILITIES

It may be impossible to convince this romantic Libra man that the quiet, gentle, sweet woman he has fallen in love with is also determined and ambitious for success. She is warm, sensual, affectionate and appreciative of his charms. She is reserved and calm and effortlessly manages a career and home. She may manage him as well, but it is always with the best of intentions--she wants him to be successful--and her decisions are always sound and reliable. He really didn't mind giving up his second car--the sports car--so that they could invest in a profitable retirement program. In truth, financially, he's never been so sound. And they did splurge on that trip last vacation to go home and visit her family. Libra is thoughtful, logical, and tries to be reasonable and fair, and that appeals to this Capricorn woman. Each prefers harmony and peaceful settings, and they share similar taste in music and art. Libra brings to Capricorn the ability to not only see the advantages of material gain but the wonders of enjoying life and appreciating beauty in all its forms. What he likes most about her is that endearing smile that lights her face when he walks in the room. What she likes most about him is that his romantic smile warms her heart and stirs her earthy passions. These two most appreciate the positive qualities they find in each other. The Libra optimism lightens what would otherwise be a more pessimistic outlook on the part of Capricorn. She comes to understand that he expends his energies working and playing hard and then needs to time at home to rest and relax. She learns that rest and relaxation benefit her as well and eases her tendency of striving for achievement. Capricorn can be a home body, artistically creative, or socially active, and whichever the case may be, she finds her life more balanced by the dreams and imagination of this Libra man. He seems to know that if she appears aloof and preoccupied, for him she will become as passionate as any Earth sign can be. Libra, on the other hand, is more mentally romantic, but he never fails to be drawn to her emotional nature. Capricorn teaches Libra the advantages of self-discipline, and Libra teaches her the joy of enticing pleasures. That she is never rash or impulsive, but listens to his deliberations and gently helps him arrive at decisions and directions, eases Libral tendency to lose his precarious mental balance. These two bring differences and the ability to blend them into a meaningful and lasting relationship. The decision of whether or not to do so is completely up to them, of course. They will discover that bossy, but together they form a special admiration and love that makes their differences seem unimportant.

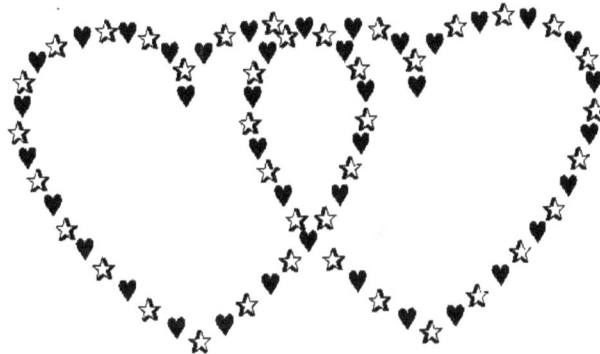

Libra Woman - Aquarius Man
Love Relationships & Compatibilities

Libra and Aquarius have a tendency to make good friends and to share interests and ideals. She admires his humanitarism, and he admires her intellect. Both seek understanding and knowledge and both enjoy social outings, travel and meeting people. Aquarius recognizes that Libra makes every attempt to be fair, and these two strive to give each other space and freedom. However, Librals tendency to see both sides of any issue and to want to discuss issues comes up against the Fixed Aquarius nature. There are times when he sees only his viewpoint and doesn't understand the need to discuss it further. In fact, continuing the discussion after he's emphatically stated that it's concluded, can make Aquarius frustrated and angry. Then too, he may resent Librals habit of always having one more last word to say about anything and everything. Librals curiosity may lead her to want to explore the Aquarius mind, but this isn't a particularly good idea. He doesn't like for his thinking processes to be questioned or discussed. He sees Librals alternatives and list of pros and cons to his thinking as disagreement and arguing. Librals best approach is to humbly tell him that his opinion is interesting and could he tell her why he feels that way. Then he'll feel good about himself and admire her for respecting his thoughts, think about it a minute and give her a brief reply about the logic of his likes and dislikes. Whether or not his thinking appears logical to Libra, she must learn to simply accept it. After all, it is his thinking and he is free to think however he wants, and his mental processes and logic are quite different than Librals. It's best to diffuse any Aquarius anger by not opposing it. Pleasantness and kindness are the way to the Aquarius heart. His eccentric behavior may unbalance Libra, and he can become emotional in an argument which tips her scales even further. After all, Libra requires harmony, or she may become nervous, anxious or ill. Their arguments, however, will probably flair up and blow over because they possess a great deal of admiration for each other. After his fuming and fanning, he may even apologize for his outbursts, but Libra must accept that Aquarius can't be pushed into doing anything. That they are both Air signs gives them an understanding of their needs, and this carries over into the bedroom where they make each other romantically happy. Librals optimism leads her to see fairness and justice, but Aquarius is more inclined to see injustices and unfairness with the only hope being for a better future after the present is remade. Libra admires in Aquarius what she is not--a rebel who is capable of throwing caution and decisions to the wind. He can be stubborn, and she can be stays where he is appreciated, loved and accepted, growing younger and more youthful with age until he catches up with gregarious and fun-loving Libra. Together, they plan a loving and happy future.

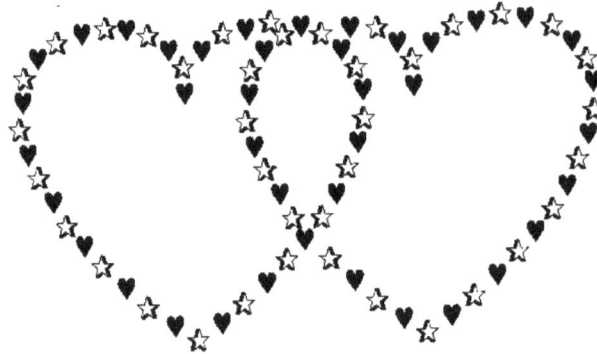

Libra Man - Aquarius Woman
Love Relationships & Compatibilities

Libra desires peace and harmony but he also possesses an appreciation for a little excitement in his life and that is precisely what the unpredictability of Aquarius offers. He is as sociable and entertaining as a person can be, but Aquarius often changes plans or entertains on the spur of the moment. Aquarius is the sign of friendship, and her home is always open to her friends. But both Libra and Aquarius are changeable and at times moody, and just when Libra thought there would never be another quiet moment around the house, Aquarius may decide she would like a spell of peace of quiet. Libra, on the other hand can work hard and then turn his energies to socializing and pleasures until he's exhausted his resources and needs a nice, long rest to recuperate and re-balance his equilibrium. Their friendship is easy and uncomplicated, and their love life demands only that they accept their individual needs and differences. Libra is adaptable, flexible, and open to new ideas, but Aquarius seems to have written the book on unique, if not eccentric, ideas and thoughts. of course, that makes her all the more lovable. In his efforts to be accommodating and to please her, Libra can take a middle-ofthe road attitude, and Aquarius will notice that he doesn't really like extremes. When Aquarius truly admires and loves a person, though, she has a tendency to be considerate of their preferences as long as those preferences don't become confining or limit her own lifestyle, wants and needs. Libra much prefers a partner and doesn't really like to be alone, and if these two truly love each other he will find a way to make her happy and to make her his. All that stuff about romance actually fascinates Aquarius who may never publicly admit it. She likes to keep her deepest feelings to herself, and Libra may be just the person to discover how much she truly yearns to hear all those sweet things he has to say. Two Air signs are well matched emotionally--neither is particularly clinging or overly emotional. But these two do enjoy a good romance and either one is capable of a tear or two over a sad ending to a favorite movie. Both Libra and Aquarius have good intellects. His is logical and analytical while hers is of her own making. That is what he likes about her--her thoughts never fail to amaze, entertain, or inspire him. She is an innovative and unconventional thinker who needs another person in her life just as much as Libra needs a partner. She won't settle for just any partner, though, and Libra will need to display his ability to understand and accept her the way she is because she may have no plans of changing any time soon. Libra will discover that when he falls in love with Aquarius he wants to protect her and support her in all her endeavors, and that is the kind of attention Aquarius most needs.

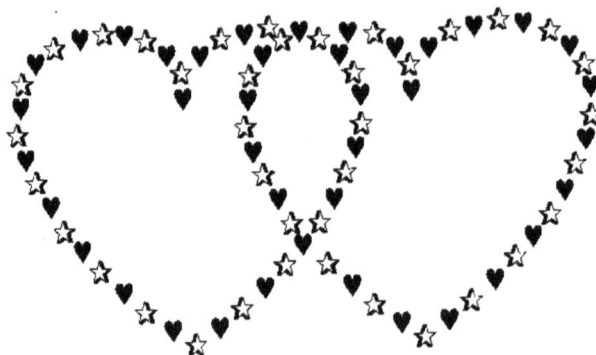

LIBRA WOMAN - PISCES MAN
LOVE RELATIONSHIPS & COMPATIBILITIES

Libra finds in Pisces a man who is as romantically charming as she herself can be. Intuitive and perceptive, he understands her need for romance and that she is in love with love. The sign of Pisces loves to serve and if this is what Libra wants then he'll do his best to satisfy her in every regard. She loves the attention and the magical enchantment that be creates by his very presence. On an intellectual level, it may be their curiosities about each other's nature that attracts them. She likes to be mentally stimulated, and, again, the creative imagination of Pisces can possess the attention of any thinking person. Libra has a strong appreciation for art and music, and the Pisces creativity only adds to this appreciation. The Pisces ability to dream and fantasize also inspires Librals own dreams. But no matter how curious they are about each other, they may discover that they don't really understand the other person's thought processes. Libra is logical, analytical, and even critical while Pisces is intuitive and emotional. Pisces perceives through his emotions and relates to the world from his perceptions. Wanting to be helpful, Pisces will listen intently as Libra talks--Libra loves to think aloud--and he will offer her advice or consoling, which ever she needs. And both prefer peace and harmony--Libra to find balance and Pisces to find the peace needed to lose himself in his dreamscapes. The Libra logic may not always apply to the Pisces thinking. He wants to feel good about all decisions while Libra simply wants all decisions to be fair and just. Pisces has a tendency to be moody and at times emotional while Libra has her own tendency to be moody. Discussions can easily turn to arguments with these two with Libra attempting to make a point and Pisces being offended that Libra doesn't readily accept what he feels to be the correct decision or opinion. Pisces isn't open to discussing his logic or the pros and cons. If a person loves him, then they agree with him, and that should be simple enough logic. There goes Libra scales tipping to one side as she yearns to talk things through and to explain her logic. When unbalanced, Libra can become frustrated, irritable, and even bossy. And one thing Pisces doesn't like is a bossy person. Ask Pisces nicely and he'll deliver the moon, but boss him around and he becomes a fish out of water. The extremes of Pisces emotions can keep Libra on edge wanting a clarification of matters. Libra does best to give up and give in and just sit back and watch as Pisces dispels bad moods, switches to a good mood and enlightens his audience through the creative magic that he understands so well. These two delight each other

258

with warm embraces and soon their shared magic of enlightened romance claims their hearts again.

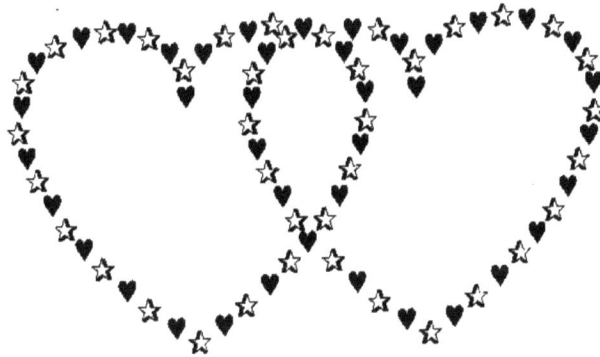

LIBRA MAN - PISCES WOMAN
LOVE RELATIONSHIPS & COMPATIBILITIES

The Libra man, forever the romantic, can't help but to be attracted to the fascination of Pisces charm. They are both congenial and pleasantly outgoing, both happy when mixing and socializing with other people. Each likes relaxing surroundings and a comfortable home. Librals taste are refined while Pisces prefers her home to make a statement that reflects her individuality and unique likes and dislikes. Librals sensitivities can be thrown off balance when things are out of place, and Pisces has difficulty understanding the need for a semblance of order much preferring a less demanding structure. Pisces sees Librals ability to take either side of a discussion as manipulative, but Libra wants to review the alternatives. Pisces likes affirmation of her decisions and actions in order to feel admired, but Libra may not realize this in his effort to discuss other possibilities. Both are sentimental and sensitive, but Pisces is inore so. She deals with life through her emotions and wants to understand how daily events and the actions of others relate to her own life. This makes it difficult for Libra to carry on his intellectual discussions with Pisces who personalizes and internalizes all discussions. Sensing her sensitive nature, Libra attempts to be diplomatic but the natural ability of Libra to communicate is thrown off balance as he slows his thinking and attempts to choose his words carefully in order not to offend her. Now, Pisces intuitively detects that Libra has changed his tactics, and she thinks he is trying to take advantage of her by agreeing with her. By this time, Libra is frustrated. He wants to talk, to have an open-minded discussion in which both are free to speak their minds. Pisces is further offended thinking that he is frustrated because he can't have his way. Pisces withdraws into a sulk, proving she's wiser because she refuses to argue. Libra is suddenly mentally, physically and emotionally exhausted. He could recuperate immediately if only they could talk, but he knows if he approaches her now she will either look at him like he's mean and wrong, or she may lose her Pisces control and start throwing things. Libra contemplates how a person who can choreograph her own dreams can have so much difficulty dealing with a simple logical discussion. Pisces wants to know how a man who is so charming, romantic and kind can be so insensitive to her feelings. Time may take care of their differences as they learn to live with one another because each is very much impressed with the many positive traits of the other. Her imagination never fails to brighten his day, and his sincere regard for her makes her feel loved and appreciated. Both Pisces and Libra desire another person with whom to share life, love and happiness. And it is a strong love for one another that draws this couple together.

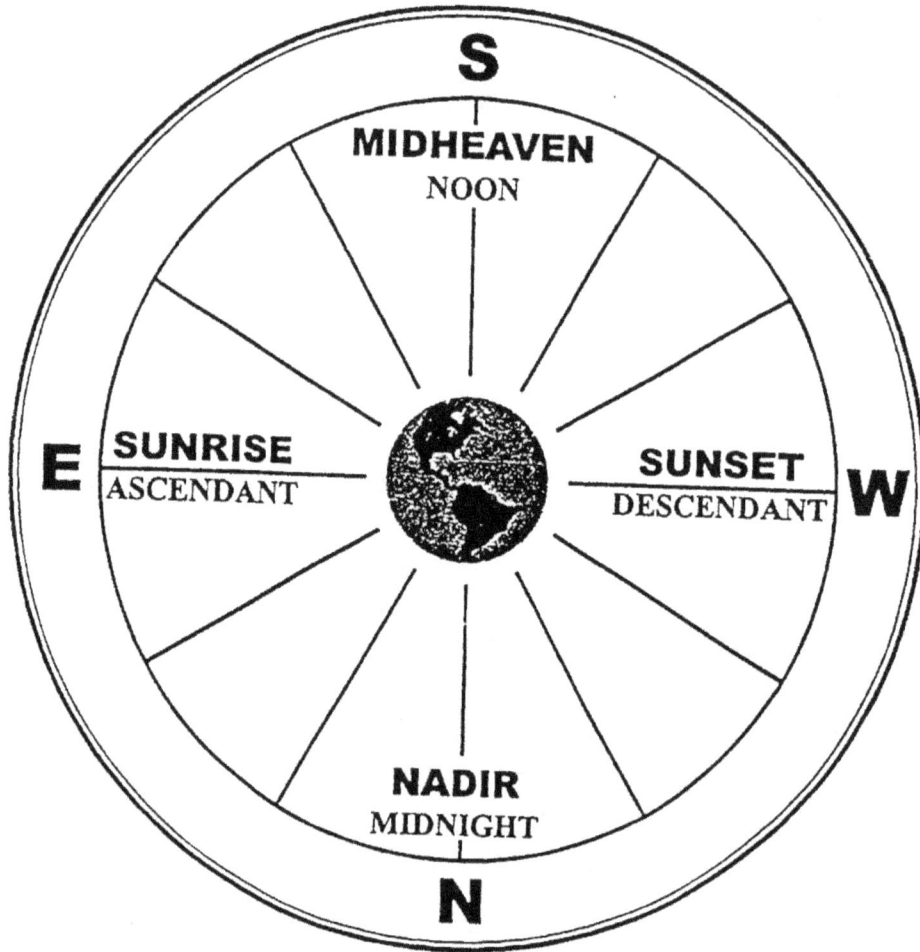

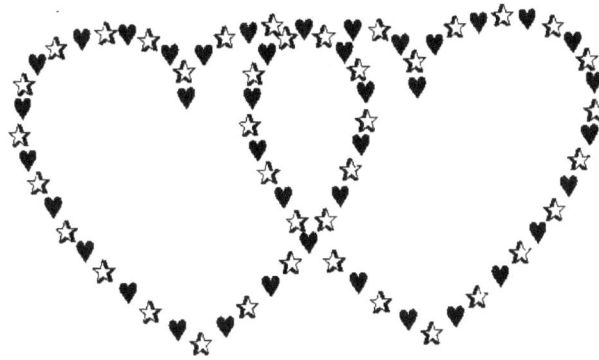

SCORPIO WOMAN - SCORPIO MAN

LOVE RELATIONSHIPS & COMPATIBILITIES

This can be an intense, even emotional, couple who want to possess each other mind, body and soul. What aids their relationship, is that they may intuitively understand the needs and desires of the other person. To have a fulfilling relationship, they need to have common interests, values, and goals. Scorpio are warm, compassionate and caring people, who, when in love, give their all, hoping to receive the same in return. Scorpio has by nature a jealous and possessive streak which subsides only through establishing mutual trust and respect for the other person. These two are happiest when they share a strong commitment with another person. They can be tranquil, loving people who also possess a yearning for a little excitement if not just a bit of the daring escapade from time to time. But these are strong-willed people who also like to think through their actions and decisions with a certain amount of caution. Then that daring impulsiveness comes along, and they are off to seek a new experience. When these two share a sense of purpose, they focus on it with all their combined intensity wanting to see it through to a final accomplishment. They are resilient to failure and will start over from scratch if need be, and if well developed individuals they don't succumb to defeat. A less well developed Scorpio, however, is susceptible to not only failure but to drowning his or her emotions in alcohol or drugs. A combination of Scorpio and Scorpio finds two people who are capable of experiencing their inner storms, then riding them out and providing shelter to each other from the storms of life. They may experience every emotion known to man from the joy of enlightenment to the depths of a bottomless pit. They can take each other to great heights or slowly destroy the other person with their passions. A Scorpio man can be loyal, faithful and devoted, or he can feel challenged when he meets a new woman--he wants to make all the women happy. To know and understand a Scorpio takes time, and these two will want to know each other well before they make that final, lasting commitment. There is that Scorpio secretiveness to be accepted, but perhaps these two learn to share a secret or two while developing their trust and their love and caring. They relax best in the calming surroundings of their own home either entertaining or delighting in the companionship of each other. This relationship has every possibility of working out well for the two people involved, or of not working out at all. Scorpio has a tendency to want to stay and make it work. But if all indications are that long-lasting problems exist, it is better not to prolong it because of their ability to destroy one another and in so doing learn the meaning of hate. When love overrules, and these two discover that special compatibility that draws them together, it is a rewarding and fulfilling relationship. Their mutual passions and energies fuel their desires for each other.

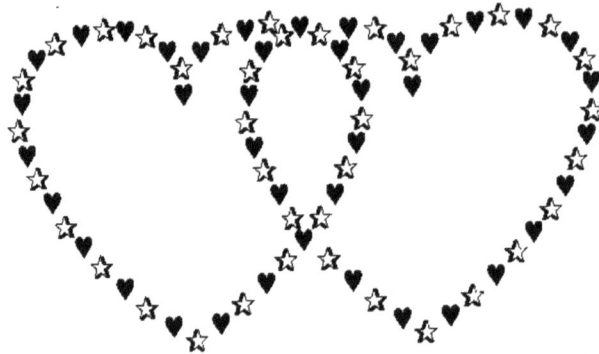

Scorpio Woman - Sagittarius Man
Love Relationships & Compatibilities

A Scorpio woman and a Sagittarius man like each other and make the best of friends, communicating and talking about their common interests and expanding their intellects in the process. In a romantic relationship, they may discover problems in their basic philosophies. Sagittarius is Mutable Fire sign with plenty of energy and passion, but he is adaptable and versatile and seeks new experiences, new people and new places. He may, after a time, commit his heart, but his intellect and his soul will also be his. If he perceives the Scorpio possessiveness, he may prefer to view it from a distance, immediately feeling the desire to be somewhere else doing something else. But Sagittarius intuitively perceives the passionate adventures which Scorpio hints at with her provocative, mysterious glances, and can't resist the temptation to learn more about this interesting woman. Scorpio likes the response she senses in Sagittarius and his restless nature that seeks a good adventure. She also likes his idealistic nature and his tendency to turn any conversation into a philosophical dialogue. If these two were to combine their natures, Sagittarius would discover the intensity he needed to follow through on his endeavors. And that Sagittarius can further enlighten Scorpio adds to her interest in him. He offers her a new perspective for viewing life and the world, giving her food for thought but also lightening her mood. Then too, there is that infamous Sagittarius way with words and spur of the moment humor. The humor Scorpio loves because it reflects his thoughts, his optimism and his quick mind. That he can be blunt and direct in many of his remarks catches Scorpio off guard, but she may learn to laugh at herself more. It goes without saying that these two need common interests and goals to share and to draw them together. In so doing, they discover the positive traits of each other. Both are compassionate and caring and concerned about social issues. She must learn not to be overly controlling, however, and he must learn not to attempt salesmanship-like persuasion.

Both are intuitive and can add up the strengths and weaknesses of the other, but neither should spend too much time complaining about weaknesses. Sagittarius will be driven away, and Scorpio will be offended. These differences aside, they may share a love of nature, outdoor activities, social gatherings, and intellectual pursuits. Once their fondness for one another grows into love, it may be that they can't get enough of each other. And when their heads clear, they discover their hearts and their lives intertwined with each other in a lasting embrace. They learn from each other what differences can add to a relationship, and accepting that, they decide to stir up a new adventure together.

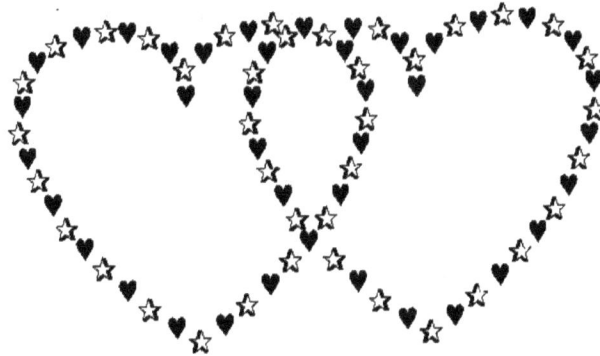

Scorpio Man - Sagittarius Woman
Love Relationships & Compatibilities

A Scorpio man is as susceptible to optimism and cheerfulness as the next person, and the warm, Fire-sign nature of Sagittarius attracts his attention from the very beginning. Scorpio makes the most loyal and devoted of friends and can be just as warm, pleasant, and congenial as Sagittarius. But the chances are the Sagittarius woman is more open and free and expresses who she is in her words and Actions. Scorpio, more intense and emotional, is more subtle and less open and it takes longer to get to know him well. These two people both possess a highly curious nature. Sagittarius explores and questions, wanting to know as much as possible while Scorpio is more compulsively drawn to seek out knowledge and the answers to mysteries and secrets. The more serious inclinations of Scorpio are distracted by the light-hearted ways of Sagittarius, and he finds himself enjoying her humor, quick wit and even quicker way with words. For the most part, Sagittarius looks for the bright side of any situation, possesses the best of intentions, and doesn't consciously mean to offend anyone with her open, direct and often blunt remarks and observations. She is simply out-spoken and is often quite shocked to discover that few others share her ability to hear and see the most obvious of observations. Inherent in her nature is the desire to experience and see as much of life as possible. Her restless desires require change, stimulation, meeting new people and being active and involved. When life or relationships limits her with confining or restrictive circumstances, she can become temperamental and high spirited and her optimism is deflated leaving her moody and depressed. Her direct remarks can turn sarcastic and cynical, and now she stands the chance of offending her loving and compassionate Scorpio man. Sensitive Scorpio doesn't respond well to criticism, and while changeable Sagittarius may alter her moods and forget her words, Scorpio remembers the injuries. Either they learn to appease one another or these little episodes can build into prolonged tension placing a strain on the relationship. Sagittarius is capable of leaving and forgetting, and Scorpio is capable of never forgetting but ignoring the other person for life. on a more positive note, when these two develop their positive traits, one of which is seeking wisdom and knowledge, they grow closer together. Scorpio is highly protective of loved ones, but he is also drawn to new experiences and challenges the same as Sagittarius. When their lives provide for the necessary change of pace, the stimulation of new people, travel, and new experiences, they both benefit. Impetuous and charming Sagittarius is drawn again and again to the sexual fulfillment found with her loving Scorpio man. And Scorpio is drawn to her clever imagination and offer of lasting friendship and love.

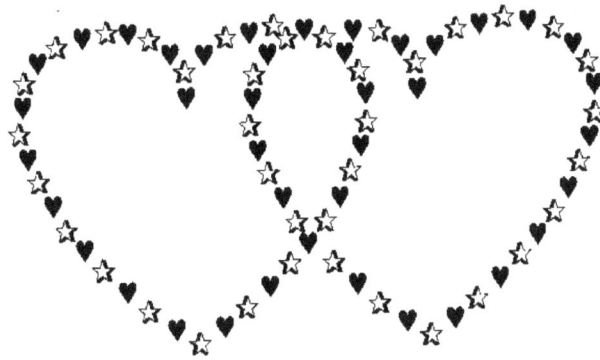

Scorpio Woman - Capricorn Man
Love Relationships & Compatibilities

A Scorpio woman may greatly admire a Capricorn man for his focus, direction, ambition and drive. And she may be the only distraction he allows in his well-organized life. That suits Scorpio fine and she may work to protect him from any other possible distractions interfering with their lives or his goal-oriented drive to succeed. Capricorn is even more analytical, methodical and logical than Scorpio who learns from his practical, determined and persevering ways. Capricorn highly values his time and is a good planner and organizer, and he won't want to waste time on intense emotions that slow down progressive accomplishments. This benefits Scorpio who may need a distraction from her emotional, inward thoughts as much as Capricorn needs an occasional distraction from his ambitions. That these two are also warm and kind and the most sincere and loyal of people also benefits their relationship. Scorpio knows how to arouse the earthy passions of Capricorn, taking his mind off business and his busy activities, and proving that sex can be as beneficial to one's well being as all else in life--a natural way to relax, exercise, improve circulation, and feel good. Both Capricorn and Scorpio are highly protective, loyal, trustworthy, and devoted, and want to appreciated, admired, and loved. They can be jealous and possessive, but each translates this as love and admiration which makes them feel secure. Capricorn likes to lead and is firm in his opinions and decisions, but generally speaking he isn't prone to angry outbursts or harsh words-which he may also see as a waste of time. This works well with Scorpio who is easily offended by angry remarks. That isn't to say that they won't have their disagreements because Scorpio also likes to be in control of the situation. If they learn to negotiate and mediate any different opinions which occur, they have every possibility of both being winners. Both Capricorn and Scorpio can seem at times aloof or withdrawn, but each can also be affectionate and sentimental in their own way. And both can be subtle in their own way, which they learn to appreciate in each other. These two save the demonstrative expressions of their affections for the privacy of their own home. And each prefers a home which is comfortable, relaxing and wellsuited to their lifestyle. Capricorn is patient with that little streak of impulsiveness that Scorpio exhibits. And Scorpio teaches Capricorn that a little impulsiveness adds a certain amount of spice to life. Together, they develop not only their self-discipline and self-control, but also their sensitive, sympathetic and warm and reliable natures. There is every indication that their love can develop into a deeply fulfilling and lasting relationship.

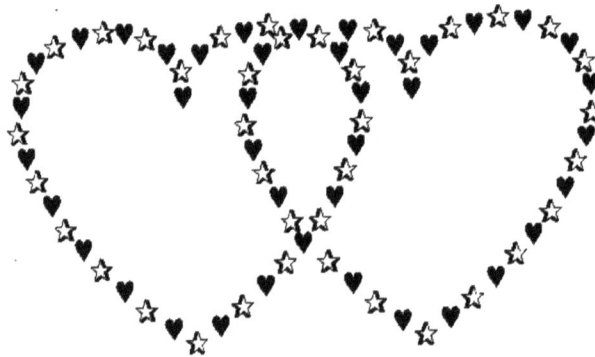

SCORPIO MAN - CAPRICORN WOMAN
LOVE RELATIONSHIPS & COMPATIBILITIES

Scorpio is first caught by her attractive feminine ways and then finds his mind captivated as well by her calm, logical and well meaning intentions. She is capable, reliable, and quietly goal-oriented with a subtle approach that he can appreciate. They can be congenial, warm and amiable, but both also like their quieter moments which they share with a natural affinity for the other person. When well-matched, these two make a good team, each benefitting from the positive traits of the other. She is highly organized and efficient and Scorpio adds his own shrewdness and insights to their endeavors. Both like to control and to lead, but if they communicate well this doesn't develop into a deterrent to their accomplishments or to their relationship. Capricorn likes a forceful and protective partner, and the Scorpio possessiveness makes her feel secure and loved. That she can be at times stubborn and fixed in her opinions may arouse an occasional temperamental outbursts from Scorpio, but generally he will be too considerate of her gentle nature to be overly forceful with her. She wins with kindness, gentleness, and those charmingly subtle ways that he can't resist. He wins by shrewdly evoking her loyalty and devotion, and these two kiss and makeup. Their love life is another area that continues to develop and become fuller and more meaningful with time, and in their passions they never seem to tire of one another. He respects her need for security and tangible possessions and her conventional outlook on life. She learns to respect that his curiosity leads him to explore various interests, but that he continues to return home to her. Their home is a well-planned, tranquil and comfortable haven away from the busy lives they lead, and it is there that they seek each other and their mutual companionship. Capricorn is cautious and doesn't much appreciate any risk taking, and Scorpio makes every attempt to comply. He is cautious as well and likes to think through his actions, but every so often he finds himself compelled to act on an impulse. But she likes the way his curious nature leads him to seek knowledge and even enlightenment. This relationship, of course, works best with shared interests, values, and common goals which act to draw these two closer together and allows them the opportunity to get to know one another well. Capricorn shouldn't be concerned with the secretiveness of Scorpio, which harbors no ill well, because over time he will come to be more trusting and will share more and more of his thoughts with her. These two both do well in a relationship based on trust and love with plenty of affection and admiration added to the combination. They protect and harbor each other providing the security the other desires. Their love adds the magic.

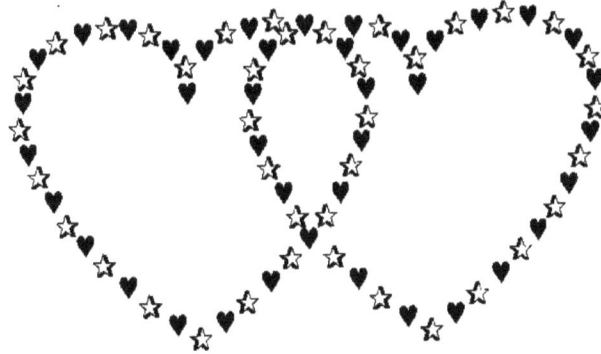

SCORPIO WOMAN - AQUARIUS MAN
LOVE RELATIONSHIPS & COMPATIBILITIES

This could be an exciting relationship and if it lasts it would be a learning experience for the two people involved. Aquarius generally begins a relationship through a friendship and even with this introductory alliance, they will notice immediate and apparent differences in their approaches to life. She may think her way, and he may think his way, but the intensity of Scorpio holds little sway with Aquarius. He is simply not a person to be possessed by another let alone influenced to change his lifestyle. He is happiest with the freedom to come and go as he pleases and expends much of his time and effort on a diversity of interests. If Scorpio loves Aquarius with the intensity she is known for, she may decide to stick with him in an attempt to understand him and to learn to live with him. That Aquarius doesn't respond well to temperamental outbursts will be her first lesson. And that he explains his actions and thoughts in philosophical dialogues may be her second. Scorpio deals with realities in what she feels is a logical and sensible manner. All her truisms are now put to the questioning proof of the Aquarius visionary rationale. She may prefer the straight path forward, but Aquarius is routinely off on a side road experimenting with what he thinks may be an easier way to do things. Both can be impulsive, but Aquarius at times seems driven to explore the road less taken or to invent his own path to suit his preferences. Sexually, he is imaginative, inventive and exploring which does interest and intrigue the passions of Scorpio. Aquarius is a challenge to Scorpio in almost all aspects of life, and she finds herself wanting to know and experience more. She can be strong-willed, forceful and independent, but after all is said and done, it is the Scorpio patience that sees her through this relationship. Aquarius is unpredictable, changeable, and restless, but he likes the determination of Scorpio and her streak of bold daring that entices her to experience a new adventure. Aquarius can talk himself into predicaments, and from Scorpio he learns how to face them unflinchingly and to talk his way out. He learns that her strength is enduring and that she goes to great lengths for the person she loves. She is a person who instinctively protects her loved ones and this makes Aquarius feel secure in the relationship. But again, it is a growing experience for both of them with the outcome greatly depending upon the two individuals involved. They will either develop a loving and lasting relationship or grow apart. The Scorpio intensity can serve to focus the creative endeavors of Aquarius, securing him in productive relationship that brings beneficial results. His humanitarian ideals heighten the insights of Scorpio who seeks wisdom and understanding. They love and experience and then love some more.

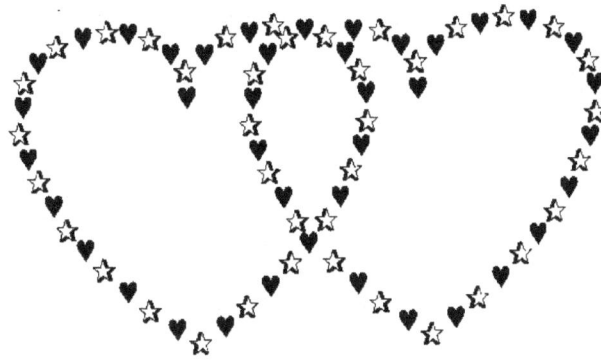

SCORPIO MAN - AQUARIUS WOMAN
LOVE RELATIONSHIPS & COMPATIBILITIES

The Scorpio man would have to be seeking an enlightening experience that opens his mind to new possibilities and experiences in order to develop a lasting relationship with this Aquarius woman. She wants to be the best of friends, on her own terms, and isn't open to being possessed, confined or otherwise restricted by a limiting lifestyle. She creates her own lifestyle and welcomes her friends to join her in any number of experiences. She and the Scorpio man may be intrigued by the differences in each other, and both being curious, they may decide to pursue a relationship in order to discover what the other has to offer. Being friends, they relax easily with each other and enjoy exciting and fun times when together. Each can be pleasantly outgoing and personable, but they are both prone to a mood change that compels them to spend time alone with his or her own interests. Each is drawn to a challenge, but for different reasons. Scorpiols curiosity leads him to uncover hidden meanings, secrets and to delve into the mysterious. Aquarius seeks the eventual outcome of any given situation wondering what would happen if she did this or that. Aquarius is adaptable, tolerating and open to other people, but in her own lifestyle she can be set in her ways and opinionated with strong preferences and likes and dislikes. Scorpio can develop definite preferences of his own with distinct opinions and little wish to change or to be persuaded by others. If their lifestyles are compatible, then there is always the chance that they can develop a companionable and loving relationship. She wants to admire the man in her life, and Scorpio strongly desires to be admired and appreciated. Aquarius is not as intensely emotional as Scorpio which may be just as well because actually he possesses enough intensity for the two of them. He is strong-willed, determined, courageous and, at times, boldly daring and brave. This is a man who will risk his life for his loved ones if necessary, and in everyday life, he wants to protect and cherish. Aquarius admires all that in Scorpio, but on a day-to-day basis, she may also want an ample supply of freedom to run her life her way. If Scorpio can learn to control his possessiveness, then he stands a chance of keeping Aquarius satisfied and happy. Aquarius only needs to prove herself trustworthy, devoted and loyal, and she will win the Scorpio heart. She is after all the independent, unique individualistic person that he fell in love with--now he must accept her the way she is. Sexually, Scorpio reads her needs and desires and intuitively knows how to make her happy and fulfilled. She responds with her own thrilling

269

initiatives and together they explore each other and the possibilities life has to offer. These two find love the greatest adventure of all.

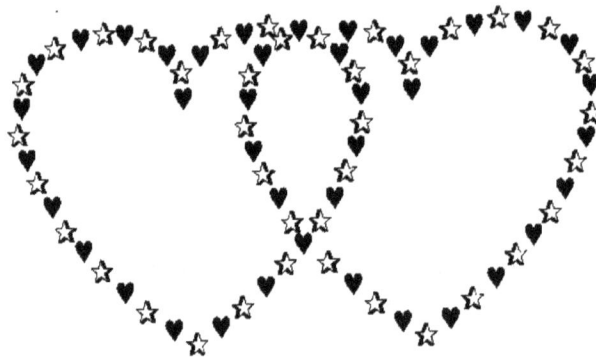

SCORPIO WOMAN - PISCES MAN
LOVE RELATIONSHIPS & COMPATIBILITIES

Scorpio can serve as an excellent sounding board for the creative imagination of Pisces. Listening intently to all he has to say while he expresses his dreams and fantasies, she is forever intrigued by the workings of his mind. she intuitively senses his deep emotions and admires his sympathetic and sentimental nature. She sees through his laughter and light-hearted ways to the warmth his heart holds. Pisces can easily be a man who is capable of great sacrifices for his loved ones and this trait endears him to Scorpio who.is just as willing to use her strength and fortitude for the protection of those she loves. They are different but alike in many ways, and intuitive Pisces perceives in Scorpio her own strong emotions, intensities, sympathies and sentiments. They are trusting, loyal and devoted, and Pisces responds to Scorpio by selflessly listening to her describe her emotions, thoughts, plans and ideas. Pisces likes her strength and determination and isn't offended in the least by her possessiveness and jealousy which proves all the more how intensely she loves and needs him. Scorpio is proud that he is an unique individual who adds his own special·magic to her life. Each can be moody, but both Scorpio and Pisces seem to know how to entice the other out of a bad mood just as each knows when the other person needs time alone to think, meditate, or just to relax. There are even times when these two can sense the emotions and thoughts of the other person and their silent communications become just as important as their conversations. Each keeps more than a few secrets which adds to their mystique, but don't be surprised if sooner or later they begin bartering away one or two just for the fun it brings them. And don't doubt that Scorpio and Pisces enjoy their fun, games, and laughs. They can be kind, pleasant, charming and congenial liking social activities and lots of interests. But each likes the comfort of home and the special companionship of the other. Sex is a romantic adventure for these two--an emotionally charged togetherness of passions and desires. In fact, their greatest challenge in life may be not allowing their pleasures to distract them from their more serious goals and endeavors. Their curiosities lead them to explore the intrigue of unexplainable phenomena, and they may be drawn to the mystical. Scorpiols urge to control melts under the charms of Pisces, and Pisces feels tempted not to be quite so stubborn for no apparent reason. Each adds insights, enlightenment, intuitive perceptions and a compelling depth of emotions to the relationship. As with all relationships, the final outcome depends greatly on the two individuals involved, but there is every indication for a strong and lasting relationship based on love, desire, and a mutual commitment to one another.

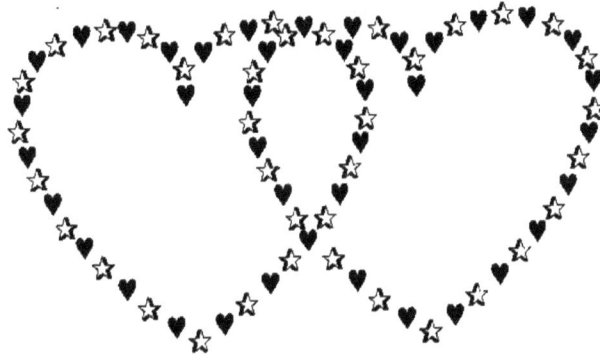

Scorpio Man - Pisces Woman
Love Relationships & Compatibilities

There is every possibility that he will appreciate her sensitive and intricately creative mind while she will like his quiet, reserved manner and strong will. There may well be a mutually mystical appeal between these two highly intuitive and sensitive people. She is passionately emotional, and he is intensely emotional. He willingly provides her a strong arm to lean on and the protection she desires, and at the same time she senses the warmth behind his cool demeanor. Her imagination and talents will inspire Scorpio, and she brings to him all the glitter and shine that reflect her magical heart. These two both desire a trusting relationship to which they can fully devote themselves. They are both givers, and they want to give of themselves totally and completely, to submerqe themselves within each other and become one. They are possessive and jealous knowing what they want, and that they share the same desire may make them feel secure with each other. Scorpio can easily provide the strength and determination to help Pisces journey upstream. They discover that one of their deterrents is that each is also susceptible to the pleasures of life and together they must guard against not being distracted from their goals. Two less developed individuals will resent the possessiveness of the other, and these two will find that resentment growing and festering and their arguments binding them together. It is when Scorpio and Pisces learn to blend their positive traits, commit their trust, and accept each other that this relationship results in a beneficial and fulfilling combination. Their emotions and passions serve to satisfy their sexual desires as well bringing their love into full bloom. Compassionate, kind and caring, these two sense the needs of the other and are caught up in the mysterious, mystical and maqical moments of their togetherness. Each is capable of listening to the other with genuine concern, and they develop a rapport that is a special communication between them. Each is sensitive to criticism, misunderstanding or inattentiveness and needs the affirmation and admiration of the other. Disagreements upset them leaving Pisces moody and nervous and making Scorpio irritable and distraught. When in tune with one another, she, of course, brings the possibility of lighthearted laughter into his life, and he responds with his own warmth and congeniality. They are amiable and sociable, liking to entertain and be entertained, but they reserve their most special moments for each other. There is every possibility for mutual compatibility between Scorpio and Pisces and this is what each is seeking. Their love grows and flourishes and Scorpio knows he will never find another as magical as Pisces to fill his days and nights. Together, they find the fulfillment they seek.

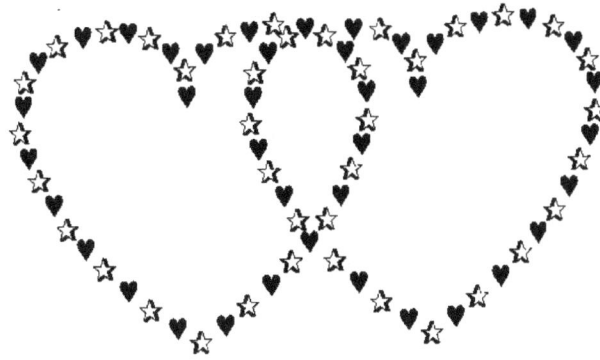

SAGITTARIUS WOMAN -
SAGITTARIUS MAN
LOVE RELATIONSHIPS & COMPATIBILITIES

Together they share laughter and playfulness and where it will take them no one knows. The masculine Fire sign of Sagittarius is ruled by Jupiter, planet of good luck, which influences these two to be outwardly optimistic, generally cheerful, fun-loving, independent and freedom prone. They seek new challenges, explore new ideas, are energetic and ambitious and known for an abundance of thoughts and an expansive nature. There are different types of Sagittarius natives from the quiet, reserved and apparently conservative ones who turn around and make quick, perceptive jokes and surprise others with their dreams to the outgoing types who like to play and party and drive their sports cars too fast. Others read and think and pursue serious-minded careers in research, writing, science or religion. But all appear insatiably curious and ask innumerable, direct questions or seek answers to their probing thoughts. They like a taste of excitement and are drawn to travel. While adaptable and versatile, Sagittarius is also restless and impulsive and does not take well to boring, routine activities or paper shuffling jobs. They prefer open spaces to small, cramped rooms or offices, needing room for their expansive natures. These two are curious and experimental about romance, liking the romance part but backing away from commitments which can feel restrictive, limiting, or more like an obligation. In a relationship, they most seek friendship and compatibility. Romance is fine, but there must also be a meeting of the minds and plenty of intellectual stimulation. The philosophers of the Zodiac, their Mutable sign makes them communicators. These two understand each other well and communicate easily with one another developing along with their easy going rapport a form of silent communication as well. If they make good traveling partners and are headed in the same direction, half of their problems are solved. Sagittarius are known for cheerfulness, a quick wit, and an ability to bluntly say what is on their minds. However well meaning, tact and diplomacy are not character traits, and they have a tendency to put their foot in their mouth. When these two Archers turn their arrows, lack of tact and brutal honesty toward each other, the result can be a fiery demonstration of escalating offence and anger. And in their efforts to apologize, they may inadvertently add insult to injury, making matters worse not better. of course, bad moods don't last long and when their optimism returns, these two forgive and forget and kiss and makeup. They play jokes and pranks on each other, and their playfulness carries over into their lovemaking where they develop an intimacy that only gets better with time. They must remember they are both restless people who require excitement or outside interests in their lives. If their lives become routine, each can become irritable. The best way to get Sagittarius out of a bad mood is to give him or her attention, but don't interrupt their introspective moods when they are dreaming and traveling in their minds. Lots of love, caring and attention draws them together and the freedom to be themselves keeps them loving and embracing.

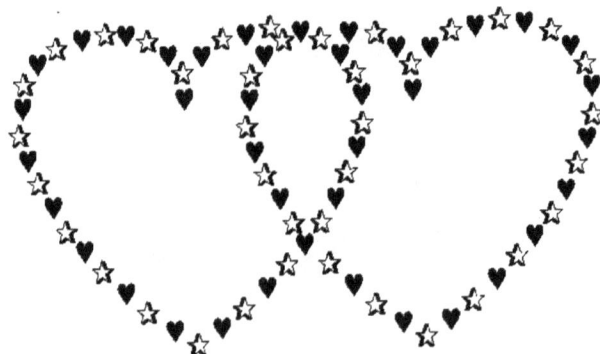

SAGITTARIUS WOMAN -
CAPRICORN MAN
LOVE RELATIONSHIPS & COMPATIBILITIES

Sagittarius may see opportunities where Capricorn sees obstacles. These two approach life quite differently. As congenial and pleasant as he may be, he is conservative and cautious preferring the tried and true to any unmarked paths. Sagittarius, on the other hand, is impulsive and restless with a daring nature and a willingness to take chances or to make compulsive risky decisions. Capricorn in his efforts to succeed can stick with a job, overcoming obstacles and steadily climbing the successful career ladder. If Sagittarius is unhappy with her job or career, she will switch to another in an effort to find personal happiness and fulfillment. Capricorn likes the laughter she brings into his life, but he may question her unpredictability and the manner in which she makes decisions. She is independent, which he likes, but he doesn't quite understand her wish for freedom--freedom to do what? We are all free, aren't we? Now, that's settled, let's get back to work. We'll have plenty of time for freedom when we are successfully retired. Neither are overly emotional types, which is good, but Sagittarius has basic needs. Among them are activity including both mental and physical. She is physically energetic and active, but mentally she wants stimulation as well. She searches for wisdom by exploring new ideas and thoughts. All that aside, Capricorn realizes she is a fine person who doesn't interfere with his lives or the lives of his family. She's an excellent conversationalist at social gatherings, and one day soon she may even learn to cook. She is straight forward, honest, and direct in her comments so that Capricorn always knows what she's thinking which makes dealing with her a little easier. And she can be so imaginative and clever. But Capricorn definitely must do something about the way she spends money. Financially, she can be somewhat reckless and irresponsible, but that's only a matter of teaching her to be more economical, something he probably thinks he can easily teach her. She, of course, admires his ambitions and knows he only wants what is best. Industrious and hard working Capricorn may learn to relax and laugh more, but he will -more than likely insist that she control her restless nature and apply herself to the tasks at hand. Their attractions prove compelling and she is capable of bringing out the warmth of his Earth sign passions while playing tenderly with his heart. He uses his great patience and self-control to teach her the meaning of love and happiness, home and family. Well-aspected planets help this combination tremendously as does a fulfilling and trusting love.

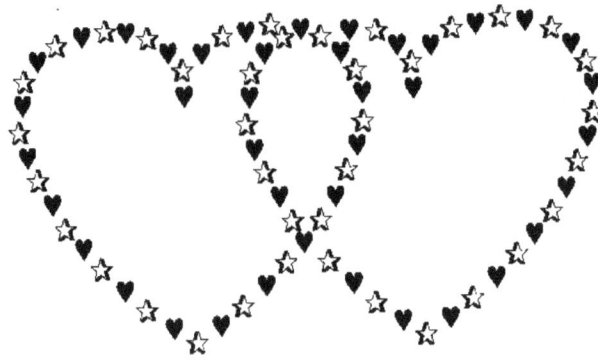

Sagittarius Man - Capricorn Woman

Love Relationships & Compatibilities

asual and easy going Sagittarius may wonder what is the secret to the compelling attractiveness of this Capricorn woman. She is soft and feminine, beguiling and bewitching and all without really trying. She possesses a quiet, demure charm that intrigues and fascinates him. Capricorn has the ability to be in charge without really letting the other person know they've taken charge. And that being the case, she may unobtrusively set Sagittarius in a direction and focus his energies, imagination and optimistic spirit on achieving and accomplishing his goals. Capricorn is kind and compassionate, congenial and friendly with a dry sense of humor which Sagittarius will appreciate. She likes his quick wit as well and his outspoken way with words hardly phases her. If he is blunt and direct, then she knows exactly what he's thinking. She quiets his restless spirit by keeping him mentally stimulated and feeding him additional food for thought. If he likes sports, either as a participant or a spectator, she may realize that it's another interest that keeps his mind off moving to Alaska to pan for gold. She is more than capable of handling the household finances, investing and saving for the future, budgeting his expenses, and acting as his personal secretary which allows him all the time he needs for his many and diverse interests (and she likes the managing responsibilities). All she has to do now is convince him to visit her family over the holidays, and all will be perfect. If he isn't a stubborn and obstinate Sagittarius, he will recognize immediately the benefits this determined woman brings to his life. If he doesn't appreciate her, and becomes irritable and discontent and manages to turn his flaming arrows of criticism her way, he may encounter the firm determination and strong will of her Earth sign ways--she is firmly set on her path. An unhappy Sagittarius eventually loses his luck and his charm withdrawing into a dismal existence. These two will need a reality check to be sure they are well suited for each other and that they share the same goals and values in life. That being the case, his romantic attentions bring her to the realization that she truly appreciates this inspiring man. Sagittarius is capable of pursuing different interests at the same time whether it be two sources of incomes, a job and studies, or two romances at the same time. Capricorn will want to be more than sure that he has roamed the earth to his heart's content before they settle down to establishing a home. And to make Capricorn truly happy, he will want to be just as sure that home and security are upper most in his mind as well. Once all that is established, they spend a life time learning all there is to know about the other, sharing and growing in love and togetherness.

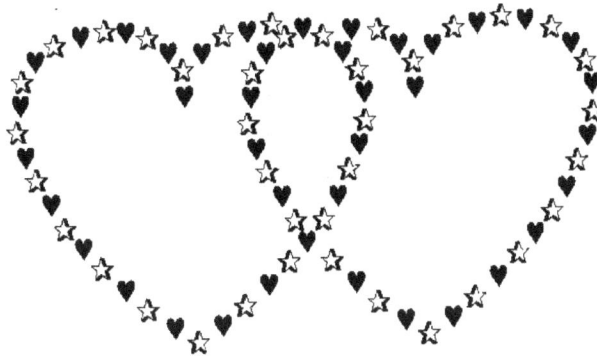

SAGITTARIUS WOMAN -
AQUARIUS MAN
LOVE RELATIONSHIPS & COMPATIBILITIES

To start with, they like each other tremendously and make the best of friends. She is idealistic, independent, fun-loving, inquisitive, and philosophical. He is idealistic, independent, fun-loving, inventive, questioning, and a humanitarian visionary. They admire each other and like the other's lifestyle and sense of freedom. Each is unique and individualistic in his or her approach to life. They both like meeting new people, exchanging ideas and exploring innovative thoughts and concepts. Both place a high value on friendship, and either will go to great lengths for friend. Each can be sociable, outgoing, congenial and the life of the party, or more reserved and introspective. And both delight in practical little jokes and pranks and displays of humor. Each can be unconventional, if not in lifestyle then in some other aspect of their lives. But Aquarius is not only unconventional in his own way--he is also eccentric in some manner. Sagittarius is a Mutable Fire sign which can turn her cheerfulness and adaptability into short lived but fiery temperamental outbursts. Aquarius is a Fixed Air sign meaning that no matter how much he would like to change the world, he is very fixed in his opinions and preferences. When this man makes up his mind nothing short of full fledged negotiations changes it and then it is reluctantly. Talkative Sagittarius is guilty of an exaggeration or two, and Aquarius is capable of inventing tall tales just to hear how they sound. Her blunt and outspoken remarks don't offend Aquarius, but any direct criticism can easily put him in one of his moods. He will answer her many questions with questions of his own or turn mute on any subject or respond with a reply that takes days to decipher. He is predictably unpredictable, but then the actions of impulsive Sagittarius can be difficult to predict as well. He likes her exploring nature and that she is always ready to travel or to seek a new experience. She likes all that is unique about him especially his original thinking process. Both may like nice things but neither is pretentious. Their traits blend well in the bedroom where they are exploring, inventive and playfully delighted with each other. These are two very lovable people and that they love each other is hardly surprising. Their challenge will be deciding upon a direction and then sticking to it or not sticking to it which ever they decide. A little change in direction is not a matter that greatly upsets these two. In fact, it is change and everything new, exciting and challenging that compels them along the road of life. Whether or not they stay together is left completely up to them--considering that there is no predicting an outcome. That they love and laugh and make the best of friends and turn romance upside down just to see how it works is what makes them so very charming.

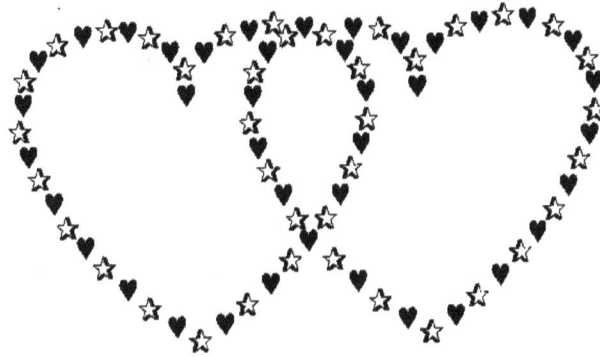

Sagittarius Man - Aquarius Woman

Love Relationships & Compatibilities

He sent a message through their grapevine of friends saying that he would like to ask her out, and she sent a message back telling him that sounded like fun. Or, if not already friends, they met on a hikinq trail, bike path, science lab, computer class, math workshop, observatory, at a party or a night out on the town, or on a plane, train, or ship. Their attraction is a natural, easy goinq affair based on pleasant conversations, plenty of humor and good jokes, and an affinity for discussing any variety of topics. Sagittarius can become easily bored and restless seeking some activity either mental or physical and much preferring to be on the go meeting friends or planning an outing. There are times when Aquarius can grow bored if she discovers herself standing still for two minutes, and she will seek an instant distraction, activity or a friend to help her fill the time. Both are unpredictable and their moods can change, leaving Aquarius wanting to be alone to pursue some thought and Sagittarius resting for the next qo around. It would be difficult to imagine a relationship between these two ever being dull. In all probability this is a casual couple with unique preferences based on their individuality. if their values, interests, individualism and uniqueness blend well, then their relationship soars with their love and friendship for one another. There will be a mutual stimulation and appreciation of the ideas, opinions, attitudes, and philosophy of the other. If on the other hand, there are too many differences and their preferences are too diverse, they will find themselves wonderful friends but seeking romance in other directions. In either case, sooner or later, Sagittarius learns that while Aquarius responds beautifully to his outspoken and direct remarks, she doesn't respond well at all to criticism or anger which can make her resentful and belligerent. Aquarius learns that he is cheerful and optimistic but on occasion little things are irritating or he snaps out a sharp retort. Neither have the time to stay angry for long, and they forget their spats, kiss, and start afresh. Their lovemaking is spontaneous, responsive and fun and grows even more satisfying with time. Neither are the overly emotional, possessive type--these two prefer for romance to be lighthearted and enjoyable. Sagittarius and Aquarius grant each other all the freedom necessary to be independent individuals. These two want to explore as much of life as possible, perhaps inventing it as they go along. There is every indication that if they choose to stay together, it is a very good choice. Together they throw convention and caution to the wind, and take a risk on life being the greatest adventure of all.

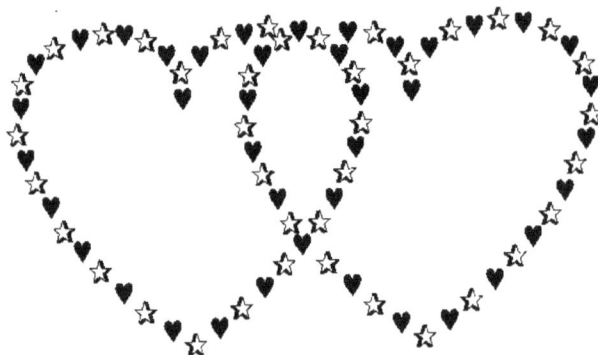

SAGITTARIUS WOMAN - PISCES MAN
LOVE RELATIONSHIPS & COMPATIBILITIES

Sagittarius finds in Pisces another person who is funloving, congenial and sociable. He loves pleasant activities, people, stimulating conversation, and being on the go. Pisces, with his creative imagination, offers Sagittarius a taste of the exotic. And her innovative nature adds a new dimension to his already provocative thoughts. There is also the possibility that he adds depth to her free flowing ideas. He especially likes her optimism, good luck, and cheerfulness, being a most naturally cheerful and easy going person himself. That they excite each other mentally as well as physically may draw them together and keep them together. And, of course, common interests, friends, similar values, and shared lifestyles add to their special compatibility. Add to all that the romance and love that only a Pisces man can conjure up, and Sagittarius may find that she has discovered all she wants in life. Being a Mutable sign, Sagittarius is adaptable and versatile and adjusts well to new situations, places, and people. But then too, she possesses the strength of a Fire sign and restlessly yearns to be free and independent to explore life. Pisces, when he sets his heart on a loved one, can be possessive and jealous, and this is one area where they will need to make some adjustments. He is also sentimental, compassionate, kind and caring, but extremely sensitive. It may take Sagittarius some effort to realize how deeply wounded he can be by her direct and blunt remarks. But, if she is the least bit perceptive, she will recognize (as the other Fire signs do) that his sensitivities, as tiring as they can be at times, are what add that special magic he brings to the relationship, and she will become more protective making every effort not to intentionally upset his sensitivities. This is the very demonstration of caring that Pisces responds well to, and he in return will make every effort to please her in all the ways he knows how. This is not in any way to imply that Pisces is weak--his own strength is based on a deep emotional base that is capable of great service and great self-sacrifice. These two learn from each other and grow from the experience, or they choose to go their separate ways. If they decide to stay, it is a learning experience in which each grows and expands. And Sagittarius desires expansion in wisdom and truth. That they both love to travel rounds out the relationship as they seek new experiences in faraway places. Well-aspected planets help them to set their sights in a positive direction, but they will have to decide who is the captain and who is the navigator. These two learn to let their humor and good will ease any tensions that spring up between them. They also learn to trust in love.

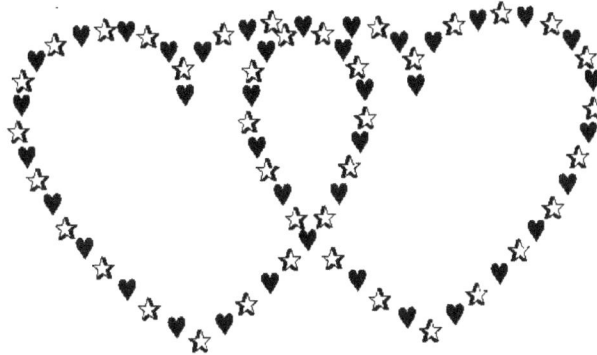

SAGITTARIUS MAN - PISCES WOMAN
LOVE RELATIONSHIPS & COMPATIBILITIES

Any healthy, well-developed Sagittarius man will find himself helplessly wanting to explore this enchantingly magical Pisces woman. She is the physical embodiment of emotions, spiritualism and light-hearted laughter. She seems to know intuitively how to temper his fire or fuel his passions. She laughs at his jokes and bubbles over with mirth at his senseless little pranks. His restlessness and seeking nature compel her to explore for herself what it is he seeks beyond the garden gates. But, being Pisces, what attracts her the most is his forever optimistic spirit and the way he turns a bad day into a better one by always pointing out the bright side of any dilemma. And no one could appreciate a lucky streak more than Pisces who actually believes in magic itself. There is probably no other sign in the Zodiac who could expand the Sagittarius mind as much as Pisces. Her sensitivities are based on intuitions, perceptions and insightful dreams. She is an enchantress and effortlessly more entertaining than most other people he knows. And all bodes well in the land of enchantment until her mood changes, or he grows restless and becomes distracted. Pisces is overly emotional and seeks confirmation of love with lots of attention and devotion. She can be jealous and possessive of the man she loves, and this can make freedom-loving Sagittarius more than a little anxious--he does not want to be possessed. That he trips over his words and isn't always aware that his blunt comments are hurting her feelings only adds to their problems. Pisces should be aware that Sagittarius, as a group, are not known for fidelity until they've sampled more than their fair share of opportunities. If he is ready to settle down to one woman and a lasting relationship, he can be the best of companions. otherwise, it is simplest to grant him his freedom. These two can also be tempted by pleasures and the good times in life. Pisces will want to know that Sagittarius plans to swim with her upstream and distract her into floating aimlessly downstream. These two can develop fine ambitions, pursuing their goals and developing their talents, or they can forever swim around in circles trying to make up their minds in which direction to go. In a good situation, they learn from one another and establish a special rapport and communication based on love and compatibility. But no matter how many questions Sagittarius asks, Pisces will keep her a secret or two to herself if for no other reason than to surprise him when he least expects it. That they are both full of surprises adds to their passionate embraces and these two love one another with enough gusto to keep the spice alive in their relationship. They travel together on new roads, adding love and meaningful expressions to the experience.

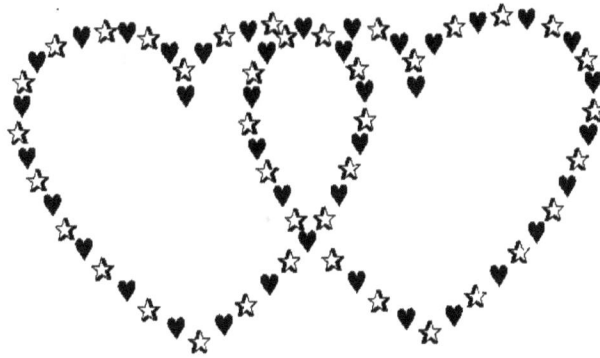

CAPRICORN WOMAN -
CAPRICORN MAN
LOVE RELATIONSHIPS & COMPATIBILITIES

Capricorn may start off life by getting their bearings and direction and experimenting with one idea or another, but once that direct is set, they are capable of applying great self-discipline and self-denial combined with a formidable will power and determination to achieving their ambitions. These two are conventional thinkers who are quite comfortable with tradition and tried and tested methods. They work hard toward their goals, are not rash or impulsive, and apply themselves diligently to all of their efforts. They approach decisions cautiously always considering the future outcome of whatever they do. An Earth sign, they are warm, kind and caring with great deal of passion which may be held in check in a reserved and again self-restrictive approach to romance. And in love and romance, they are as cool and decisive as in all other areas of life. They want to make the best possible decision in choosing a mate, desiring a permanent relationship. And once a commitment is made, Capricorn is a loyal, faithful and devoted partner intent on building a lasting togetherness for the future. They are responsible and dutiful to home, family and relatives and willing to take on family obligations. These are discerning individuals who seek another person who lives up to their own standards. If it is a wise decision to marry for financial security, position or social status, then that is what Capricorn does with the best of intentions. For all their reserve, they are known for a rich sense of humor and a warm congeniality. They are also known for a reverse aging process. As they age and become more financially secure, they retain their youthful looks and remain physically and sexually active. Two Capricorns center their attentions on a comfortable home, financial security, community activities and involvement, and family responsibilities. They possess earthy passions, but these two must guard against allowing work and obligations interfere with love and romance. These two save and save, and if need be, are frugal in order to achieve their goals. They may find that adding a trip or two or some other excursion or activity that changes their routine, keeps the relationship on an even and peaceful keel. They aren't people prone to angry outbursts, preferring quiet and peaceful settings and settling disagreements in a sensible fashion. Capricorn is a Cardinal sign, and they both have a tendency to lead, but this shouldn't be a problem as long as each feels they are headed in the right direction. Either can become gloomy or pessimistic and a little change or a warm embrace and a loving smile may help to keep the gloom away. They face obstacles together, love one another, and plan for a future of lasting togetherness. These two approve of each other and don't waste time on criticizing what they only see as strengths. Capricorn are known for accomplishing their goals and once they settle in with the perfect partner, they succeed as well with love.

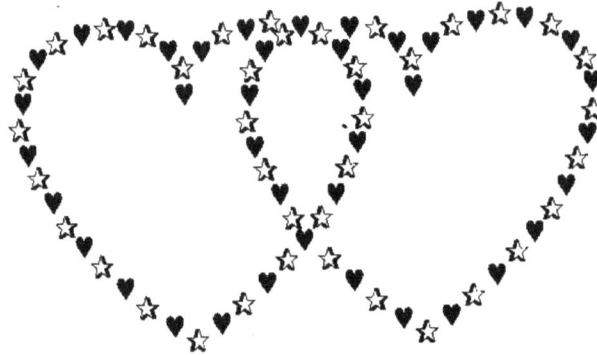

CAPRICORN WOMAN - AQUARIUS MAN
LOVE RELATIONSHIPS & COMPATIBILITIES

There is the possibility that well-aspected planets allow these two to blend their positive traits. And there is the possibility that love blinds them to their differences. Like Capricorn, Aquarius may choose to wait to marry until later in life, but for different reasons. Funloving and freedom-minded Aquarius isn't anxious to give up his independence while serious minded Capricorn may patiently wait for the right person who fits into her lifestyle and plans. or perhaps they met when they were very young, and Aquarius impulsively fell for her captivating smile, and Capricorn mistakenly thought his uniqueness was an attempt to be charming. They live and learn that Capricorn applies sensible, conventional wisdom to all aspects of life and that Aquarius simply does not comprehend the ideology of the wisdom of convention. He makes his own rules to life and those made by others in many instances just don't seem to apply to him. With a little effort, each could benefit from the other. He could learn to live within the boundaries of convention--to some degree anyway--and she could learn the scope of visionary inventiveness. on the other hand, they may fuss and feud from dawn to dusk. No, Capricorn doesn't like to argue and any disagreements will make her distraught and nervous, but she is, after all, a Cardinal sign which means she doesn't give in all that easily once she's made up her mind in a sensible manner. The outcome of this relationship is as unpredictable as any Aquarius situation, but one thing Capricorn can be guaranteed of--life will never be routine again. Of course, Aquarius does benefit with her in his life. After all, she never complains about managing his affairs which can be a rather dreary job as far as he is concerned. And it doesn't bother him if she saves for a rainy day. Aquarius is not particularly materialistic and is happy as long as he is comfortable today and even happier if someone is backing his latest invention. Capricorn, while imposing limitations and restrictions on herself, will learn that attempting to impose any on Aquarius will only create a distance between them. There is always that occasional Capricorn who lives vicariously off the dreams of others, but when reality sets in, she may begin to wonder what they actually have in common. All things being equal, they are distinctly different. But there are those individuals who make the most of differences and teach each other their strengths and lead each other happily along the road of life. He may find her materialism selfish and she may interpret his tall tales as lying, but for some reason they spark an interest an interest in each other. She wants a man she can love with all her heart and trust and devote her life to. Aquarius wants to be accepted, loved and understood by someone he counts as a friend and lover. These two love and live and learn together.

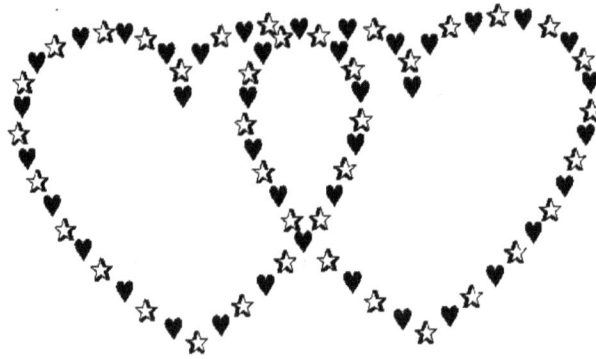

Capricorn Man - Aquarius Woman
Love Relationships & Compatibilities

The Capricorn man finds her attractive. She comes from a good, respectable family, is well educated, socially entertaining, personable, witty and an excellent conversationalist. And his family likes her. Aquarius thinks there's something charming about his interests in tradition and his conventional tastes. He is also so kind and caring and with a surprisingly good sense of humor. And he is so responsible and dependable which must mean he cares a lot about her. Not only that, but he was very patient when she explained that she couldn't make it to Sunday dinner with his great-aunt because she had just been given free round-trip tickets to Seattle in exchange for house sitting and dog-watching for her friend who just got offered a job in Miami and can't use the tickets which aren't refundable. After all, Capricorn is so economical, Aquarius figures he will certainly understand the logic of using the tickets and she is only going to gone a week and since he's so dependable maybe he could watch her dog, water her plants, and check her mail. Now, that does prove that he loves her. And when she told him she had always wanted to be in business for herself, he sat down and outlined and organized a plan right down to how to get a small business loan. Then he explained something that had been bothering her for some time-- how to balance her checkbook, but it is so inconvenient to write down all those figures instead of keeping a running tally in her head. Granted, he isn't all that tolerant of all of her friends, but those two artists had been sleeping on the couch for over a week which was okay except when she felt like a little much needed privacy. He is so pleasant to be with when she wants to get away from the crowd and spend time alone with just the two of them. And he respects her opinion on a lot of different issues, like her refusal to wear fur coats. It is also reassuring that he is close to his family when so -many people don't seem to stay in touch with relatives all that much. She is fascinated and absorbed by the way he thinks. And he is more than a little surprised by her thought processes especially when she gets that faraway look in her eyes and starts talking about subjects that never occurred to him. In fact, it is her original thinking that intrigues him the most. She is unlike anyone else he has ever met. And she seems to need him which makes him feel very protective toward her. She's wonderfully independent and doesn't demand all of his time, and she understands when he must work late or spend time with his family. Each may decide to give it time to see how it develops. This relationship depends entirely on the two individuals involved. If love brings them together, it may keep them together as well.

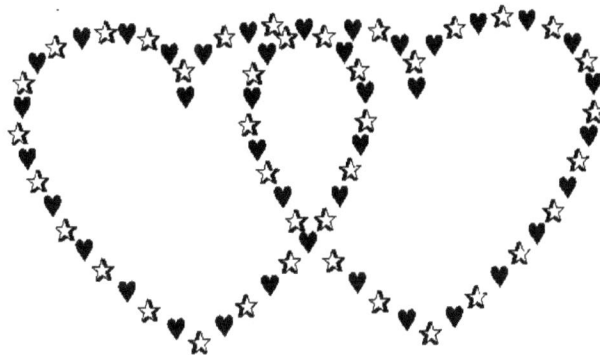

CAPRICORN WOMAN - PISCES MAN
LOVE RELATIONSHIPS & COMPATIBILITIES

It was his charm and charismatic flair that first attracted this Capricorn woman to this attentive Pisces man. Without even asking, he guessed her favorite flower and sent a lovely bouquet along with the sweetest poem. Her heart wanted to rush out to him, but she took her time and gave it some thought. What may win her over is that the Pisces man wants a permanent and lasting relationship. He is drawn to her sensible approach to life, and she is drawn not only to his creative thinking process but to his sincerity which matches her own. He is sociable and likes to be on the go, but he likes for her to be with him. And at other times he wants to be alone, just the two of them to talk and share their thoughts. His affectionate nature continues to catch her pleasantly by surprise. She has never known a more tender or loving man, and with him she feels she is learning to trustingly be the same. Granted, they think differently on a number of issues, but he doesn't like temperamental displays or arguments any more than she does. In fact, he says one of the things he likes best about her is her tranquility. She is learning that he is very sentimental and sensitive about a number of things and his emotions are much more intense than hers. But her calmness seems to reassure him. He listens to her intently and comforts her when she becomes the least bit depressed. She had to use a little finesse to reorganize his schedule and personal affairs, but once he recognized how much more efficient her system was, he seemed genuinely pleased although he continues to revert to his old system or lack of system. But with her help, his career is running smoothly which makes both of them extremely happy. He likes it that she is planning and saving so carefully for the future, but he gently insisted that they enjoy life now as well. They compromised on that one, and she discovered that life is more fulfilling when she relaxes with him. Romantically, he is thrilling filling her with anticipation. He may play around and make her laugh, but he is never fully content until her passions match his own. That they share many of the same interests made it seem easier for these two to establish common goals. other wise, the relationship may not have developed so smoothly. Pisces light-hearted ways may dispel Capricorn's pessimistic moods, and reliable Capricorn may ease Pisces, own moodiness. Pisces is inspired by the determination and ambitions of Capricorn to develop his own positive traits and abilities. Capricorn is rewarded for her diligent efforts and hard work by the gentleness and caring that Pisces offers. Pisces finds that obstacles seem less daunting when viewed through the Capricorn perspective. Capricorn learns that without Pisces all her efforts would be much less satisfying and she would feel less complete. Love allowed to flower and bloom becomes what these two most desire.

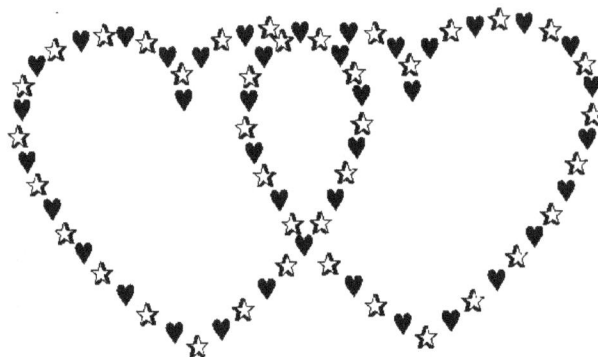

CAPRICORN MAN - PISCES WOMAN
LOVE RELATIONSHIPS & COMPATIBILITIES

He silently dreamed for years of meeting the perfect woman who would fill his heart with tender love and romance and who would want to be his for now and ever more. Nothing in life is all that easy and Capricorn anticipates obstacles to whatever he wants. But this special Pisces woman does appear to be all he ever dreamed of finding. She is attractive and charming and moves easily within his social circle. She listens to him in all sincerity and caring, and she is genuinely concerned with the welfare of his family, respecting his obligations and the time he spends with them. She is active in the community and volunteers her time to help others when she can. She can be so kind and sympathetic and at times appears to need his strong reserves to lean on for support. Her feelings are easily hurt, and he must guard against appearing insensitive to her feelings, but she makes being nice to her the easiest thing in the world to do. She appreciates his ambition, his career, and his efforts to succeed, but she enticingly persuaded him that a little more relaxation--with her--would make life all the much better. And he was pleasantly surprised to discover that in this regard she was right. Her taste in clothing, furnishings, and activities are somewhat more offbeat than his, but he has to admit that it does add a pleasing and distracting element to their lives. She enchantingly allows him to make all the decisions and to lead, but she intuitively knows how to get her way whenever she wants. She can work hard and then turn around and have magical dreams that hold him spellbound. The obstacles he expected were there, and he had to learn that he loved her the way she was and he had to guard against attempting to change her in any way. Pisces, as well, learned that the

Capricorn nature can be firm and unbending and responds to caring and kindness rather than criticism. That both much prefer finding pleasant alternatives rather than allowing their differences to turn disruptive, helped them tremendously or the relationship wouldn't work as well. She learns to coax him to spend more time with her loving and learning each other better. Her romantic nature entices his earthy passions and he can't help but want to experience more of this delightfully magic creature. Her laughter can fill a room, her smile catch him unawares, and her embraces totally entrance him. She learns from him that direction in life can take one far, and he learns from her that the journey can be enjoyable. The relationship needs a firm foundation based on love, caring and devotion for each of these two to feel truly content. He surprises her by never growing old but becoming even better and younger with age. He feels as if he's been enchanted, and he loves every minute of it.

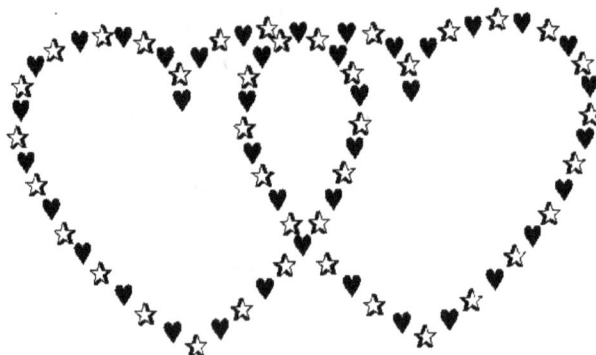

Aquarius Woman - Aquarius Man
Love Relationships & Compatibilities

The Aquarius man and woman possess a unique glamour that results in a magnetic appeal. These two are either distinctly alike and understanding of one another or they are just as easily distinctly and individualistically different--although they may be more tolerant and accepting of their differences than other people. Aquarius function in a world of ideas, many of which are most original and reflect an inventive nature. They are warm and friendly with their own brand of caring, kindness and social skills. They are concerned about others on an humanitarian level, love to be surrounded by friends, and will go to great lengths for a friend. But their friendships remain somehow on a loose, impersonal standing rather than becoming overly personal and attached. Their personal relationships are less emotionally intense that those of the other signs and this applies to romance as well. They are detached and logical thinkers however erratic and original their thoughts. Their minds are functioning somewhere in the future, and perhaps they doubt anyone else could possibly understand their thoughts let their alone their personal feelings. In their own efforts to understand others or even each other, they are quite analytical, wanting to know the why behind the actions and statements of friends or loved ones. For these two people, romance is fantastic as long as it is fun, exciting, and filled with the joys of sharing in true friendship manner. Aquarius prefers a lover who is intellectually stimulating, accepting an tolerant, and who is receptive to new ideas. They also much prefer an element of intrigue in romance, and are not excited by people who are an open book and too easy to read. Sex is an affectionate and tender adventure for these two complete with experimentation and exploring. And however strongly their rebel natures seek change for the world, each remains firmly fixed in opinions, preferences and lifestyle, and likes and dislikes. There is a tendency among Aquarius natives to view all people as being of equal importance whether they be friend, family members or strangers. And not being materialistic, their is always the chance that Aquarius will view all property as belonging to everyone. It is difficult for Aquarius to come to terms with the feelings of others toward possessions, rules and regulations. Aquarius may even develop a Robin Hood outlook on life. But being notoriously unpredictable, it would be difficult to over generalize about the natives of this sign. They are neither jealous nor possessive and once they make a commitment of love and togetherness they have a tendency not to wander far. They can be nonchalant until opposed, easy going until the situation calls for determination, and undecided until some one else attempts to make a decision for them. But it is an Aquarius in love who displays the best of his positive traits. Always a friend, and devoted, they love with a loyalty equal to none other, but which they invented on their own terms.

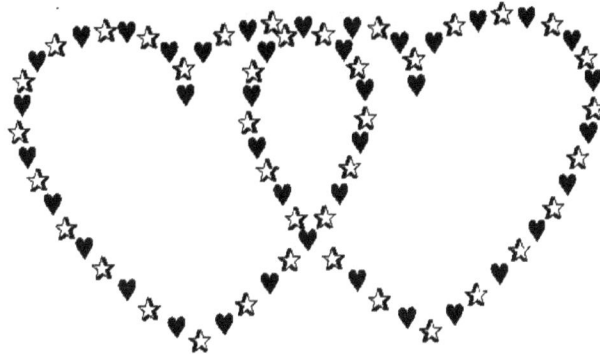

Aquarius Woman - Pisces Man
Love Relationships & Compatibilities

This Aquarius woman finds her curiosity instantly intrigued by the sensual imagination of the Pisces man. He finds that her attractiveness is highlighted by her visionary ideals. Pisces is a person who can take service to others to the extent of self-sacrifice, and he can't help but be enticed by the humanitarian outlook and caring of his lovely Aquarius companion. He is intuitive and perceptive and sensitive to his surroundings, but she uses logic, observation and an analytical approach to size up people and situations and come up with the most far thinking conclusions. She, with little effort, adds scope to his imagination and creativity, but he provides her with a perspective entirely different than her own. It is a most interesting and unique relationship with no predicting who is the most entertaining. They both love friends, socializing, and a constant variety of activities. And each requires a certain amount of quiet time to themselves. Each is unpredictable in their own way. Pisces is emotional and sensitive, and his moods may vary with his feelings. Aquarius deals impersonally with realities, but her own moods vary from time to time with her thoughts. Pisces may make every effort to follow his ambitions and swim determinedly upstream, or he may prefer a more easy going lifestyle that allows the current to carry him downstream. And Aquarius may float in the air above his head waiting to see which way the wind blows. Two well developed people will, of course, find a balance between diligent effort and the pleasures in life, but again this is unpredictable with changing natures. Aquarius has a tendency to shy away from a relationship which places limitations on her freedoms and independent ways, and Pisces will have to accept that too much possessiveness can drive her away. He, on the other hand, likes lots of time and attention and to develop a relationship on an emotional level. Here again Aquarius may not be able to match his level of emotional intensity. All of that may take time and effort in order to develop a truly loving relationship, and if their love was based on friendship and common interests to begin with, these two may find a foundation on which to build lasting and permanent togetherness. It comes down to that magical word love which Pisces envisions as the most wonderful of experiences, and Aquarius associates with true friendship. These two dare to love and love to invent their own mysteries and intrigue blended together for pure magic and adventure. There is every possibility and indication that this relationship works well for the people involved, and then again there is that possibility that it doesn't work at all. The final outcome depends greatly on the two individuals and what they decide they want most in life.

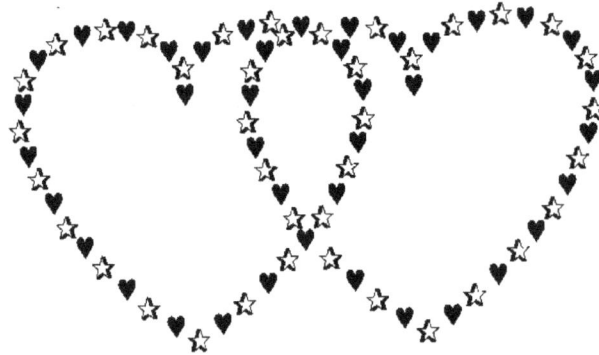

Aquarius Man - Pisces Woman
Love Relationships & Compatibilities

At heart, he is always the rebel looking for a worthy cause and true ideals, and in her heart she is always the dreaming child looking for the purest vision. Pisces not only wants to possess her love but wants to be possessed as well. Aquarius takes a less subjective approach to romance, being the realist, and doesn't respond that well to all this possessiveness. In a romantic relationship, as far as he is concerned, the other person should also be a friend as well as lover, and friends should know the boundaries and limitations of friendship. Aquarius doesn't care for interference with his independent ways and has a preconceived notion about how things should be done. He will listen to the opinions of others, but once he fixes upon a personal opinion, preference or like or dislike, he is not easily persuaded to change his mind or his behavior. Pisces may be more sensitive to the opinions of others, but Aquarius is not bothered in the least if any aspect of his life is unconventional. For the relationship to work well, these two learn to accept each other and their differences. Aquarius, on some logical plane that only he understands, grasps that Pisces is truly very sensitive and emotional, and most generally he makes every attempt not to offend her sensitivities. Pisces realizes that he is truly a very a very unique individual and intuitively perceives that he must be free to live his life his way however insensible it is to her. If he is very trustable, she allows him to enter her dream world of imaginary and vivid flights of fantasy. And if she is very trustable, he allows her to share in his visions of how wonderful the world would be if man opened his mind to the greatest of possibilities. They love to laugh and frolic and play and then dream some more. And Pisces enchantingly distracts him from his many interests to remind him that sexual fun and games are equally as enlightening. Pisces can present enough of an intellectual and intriguing challenge to Aquarius to keep him wanting to know more. He can analyze and study to his heart's intent and never discover all her secrets or charms. Pisces discovers that he is full of surprises and unpredictable and is every bit as challenging as she is herself. They may take a chance on love or decide that their friendship is complete enough. In love, their are any number of adjustments to be made, but they can be certain that their relationship will never be dull or routine. He is protective, kind and caring, and she is all those things and plus generous and giving. Together they devise a lifestyle that accommodates their many interests, friends, and activities, and they find time to share those special moments with each other. She learns that love is not a exciting and fulfilling as one makes it to be.

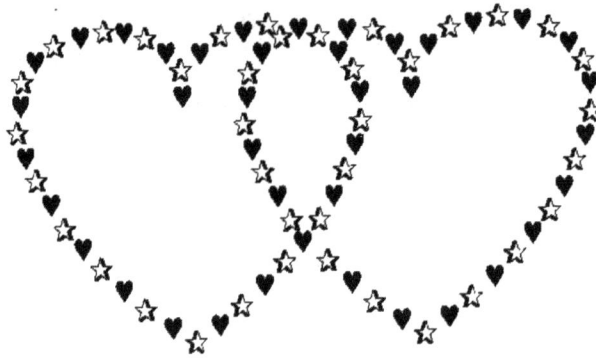

Pisces Woman - Pisces Man
Love Relationships & Compatibilities

Pisces is the physical embodiment of emotions, spiritualism, and an endearing charm unlike any other in the Zodiac. These two are generous and kind and want to give of themselves completely when in love. Love and romance for them elevates emotions to a spriritual oneness. These are not casual lovers. They seek love and togetherness in order to feel complete. Being susceptible to their emotions, it is quite possible they have been taken advantage of and hurt by others in the past. But having so much to give, and wanting to care for another, Pisces never quits looking for that special someone. They are sympathetic and willing to suffer any sacrifice, giving up everything and anything, for their loved ones. That's not to rule out those Pisces who follow their pleasures allowing their lives to be led by the temptation of good times and an easy life. Pisces are funloving and sociable and like people and pleasant activities. Pisces can also be moody, allowing their emotions to run rampant and resulting in discontent and confusion, but like all the signs, the moodiness passes and Pisces is back in charge of their lives. Pisces likes to be surrounded by nice things with a preference for all that glitters and shines, and some are extravagant spenders. But many a Pisces feels most secure with a comfortable and growing savings that guarantees a comfortable future. Pisces is creatively imaginative, and they may paint a picture of what they want in their minds and then work and struggle to obtain it. But often when they attain their goals, the effort has been so overwhelming, and the cost to their personal lives so great, that they no longer want it. Pisces is gifted with sensitivities, perceptions, and intuition, and is challenged in life not to ignore their intuition of fear. They are not weak, but knowing their own sensitivity, Pisces learns to be cautious. Being a Mutable sign, Pisces is adaptable and changeable. But the Pisces intellect again is ruled by emotions and intuition, and the thinking process is different making them not easily led by pure logic and reason once they make up their minds to follow a particular direction. These two learn that in romance there is love and there is loss. Love gives and loss takes. If these two discover that they strongly want the same things in life, each other, then they are free to trust in love and pour their hearts and emotions and many positive traits into making it last. They are a loving and fun couple, capable of both laughter and working hard to develop their dreams into reality. These two have the ability to turn the most routine events into a special occasion. And their sexual relationship is anything but routine as they play and frolic and instill a mystical quality into their love. Their direction is set by wanting the best for each other. Their home is filled with the lovely objects that reflect their inner most personality and charm. And when they take each other by the hand, their imaginations take them on the purest flights of fantasy.

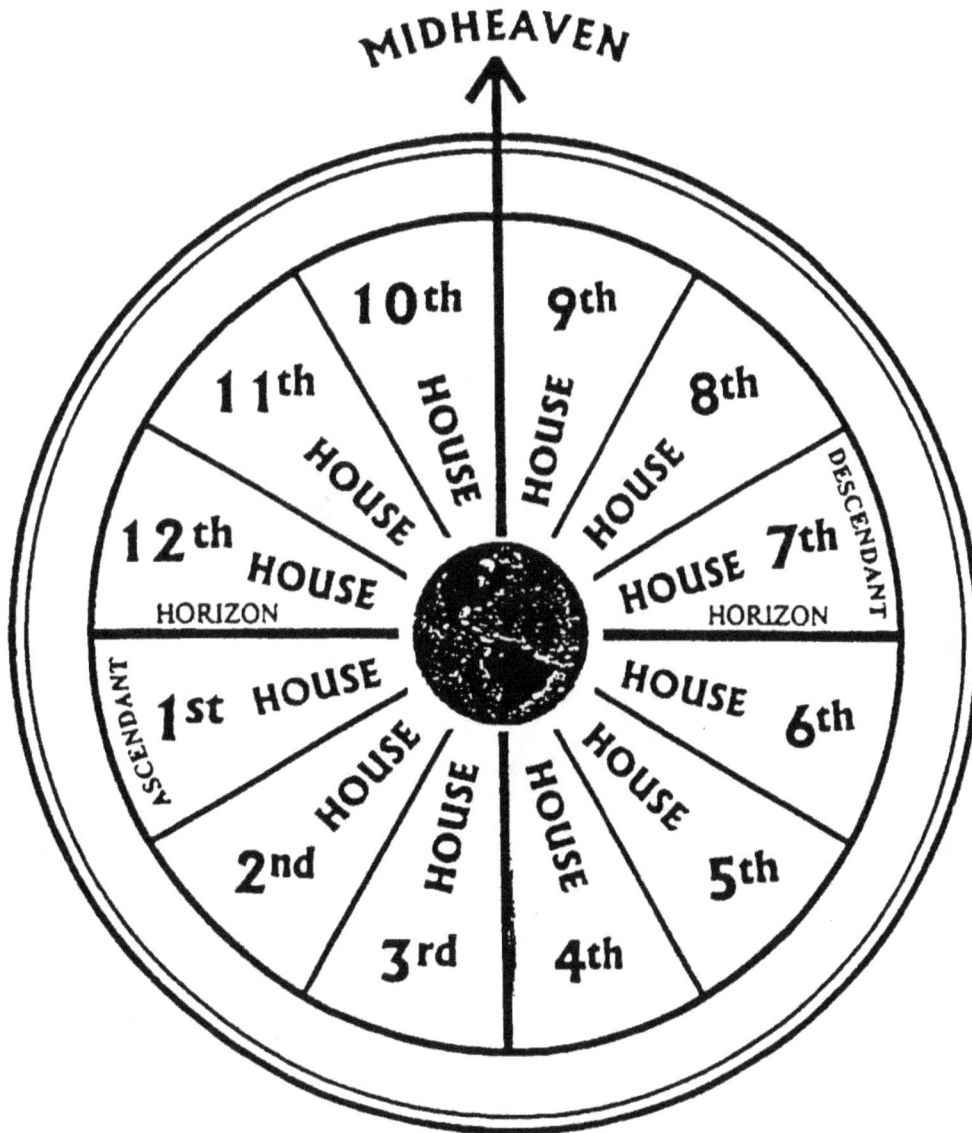

HOUSE RULERSHIPS

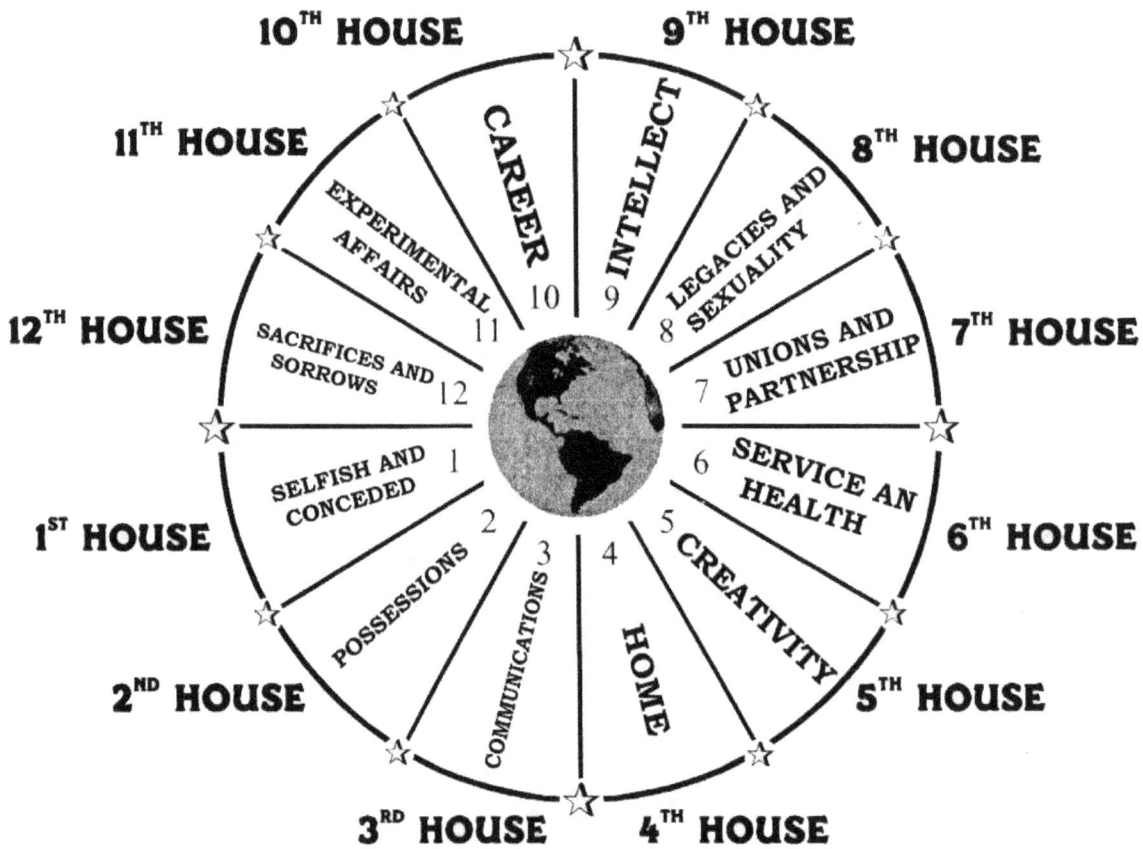

10TH HOUSE

9TH HOUSE

11TH HOUSE

8TH HOUSE

12TH HOUSE

7TH HOUSE

1ST HOUSE

6TH HOUSE

2ND HOUSE

5TH HOUSE

3RD HOUSE

4TH HOUSE

CAREER

INTELLECT

EXPERIMENTAL AFFAIRS

LEGACIES AND SEXUALITY

SACRIFICES AND SORROWS

UNIONS AND PARTNERSHIP

SELFISH AND CONCEDED

SERVICE AN HEALTH

POSSESSIONS

CREATIVITY

COMMUNICATIONS

HOME

10 9 8 7 6 5 4 3 2 1 11 12

THE TWELVE HOUSES OF
THE SOULS

In astrology, the signs are considered the fixed divisions of the celestial sphere of influence. The inner circle of the Birth Chart, however, is divided into twelve sections which are referred to as the Houses. These twelve Houses relate to the everyday activities of life. These twelve divisions of the Birth Chart or celestial sphere intersect at the ecliptic at points referred to as cusps. The Houses begin at the Ascendant, or rising sign, continuing counterclockwise down along the circle and to the right in the direction of the Earth's rotation. The planets orbit clockwise passing through these divisions every twenty-four hours.

The cusps of the First House, known as the Ascendant, begins at the nine o'clock position or division of this pie-shaped Birth Chart. The Descendant is located at the three o'clock position, or the Seventh House which is exactly opposite on the chart. The line running between the First House and the Seventh House is referred to as the horizon. The Houses remain in these locations, never changing positions. The Ascendant is always the eastern point of the horizon, and the Descendant is always the western point of the horizon, corresponding to the rising and setting of the Sun. The line or meridian intersecting the horizon indicates the Midheaven (Medium Coeli), or cusps of the Tenth House, in the twelve o'clock position, and the six o'clock position indicates the lowest heaven (Imun Coeli) at the cusp of the Fourth House. The Houses can be divided into categories of the first six houses found below the horizon, and the second group of six houses located above the horizon. The first six Houses are related to the second group of Houses in the areas of life that they represent. For example, the First House represents the personality, and the corresponding Seventh House represents relationships.

On the Birth Chart, the Midheaven marks the location of the Sun at noon on the day of an individual's birth. The sign located in the Midheaven influences the outward expression of an individual, the ego, and that person's career choices. Those planets located below the horizon are called the day planets and represent extroversion and objectivity. Those planets located below the horizon are called the night planets and represent urges, instinctual feelings, and subjectivity. The rising planets are located in the eastern half of the chart and numerous rising planets indicate a strong will power and take charge attitude. Numerous setting planets located in the western half of the chart indicate flexibility and a willingness to become involved with others.

The Houses can also be grouped in divisions which correspond to the Cardinal, Fixed, and Mutable signs. The first of these divisions is called Angular Houses which refer to the First, Fourth, Seventh, and Tenth Houses that mark the four angles of the Birth Chart. The planets influences are intensified when located in Angular Houses and are said to be indicative of potential and achievement in life. These planets are said to be accidentally dignified.

297

The Succedent Houses, or those which succeed the Angular Houses, are the Second, Fifth, Eighth, and Eleventh Houses. Planets located in these positions are not as powerful but they are indicative of stability and purpose and are referred to as the financial Houses.

The Cadent Houses are those which fall away from the Angular and Succedent Houses including the Third, Sixth, Ninth, and Twelfth Houses. Planets in the Cadent Houses do not have the same potential for opportunity as the Angular Houses nor do they possess the same stability as those located in the Succedent Houses. Rather, they are indicative of flexibility, adaptability, a strong intellect, and an ability to communication and to develop interpersonal skills. The Angular Houses are the most powerful, with the Succedent Houses being next in line followed by the Cadent Houses.

Houses can also be classified in groups of four, corresponding to the four elements of Fire, Earth, Air and Water. Group one relates to the Fire triplicity and as it is personal it corresponds to the Houses of Life including the First, Fifth, and Ninth Houses. These are Houses of energy, enthusiasm, motivation and spiritualism.

Group two, the Houses of Wealth, relates to the Earth triplicity and regards possessions. It includes the Second, Sixth, and Tenth Houses, and respectively cover money and movable possessions, career, and aspirations. Groups three, the connectives, is of the Air triplicity and includes the Houses of Relationships of the Third, Seventh and Eleventh Houses. Groups four, Water triplicity, is subjective and relates to the Houses of Endings which includes the Fourth, Eighth, and Twelfth Houses which include not only endings but death and regeneration and in the Twelfth House, the subconscious.

Other astrologers consider the Twelve Houses to be the periodical influences of the stars upon people. The influence of the astrological Houses, it is believed, starts with the beginning of an individual's life. The First House starts its influence from birth lasting until the first birthday, at which time the influence of the Second House begins, and so on until a cycle of twelve years is completed. At the age of thirteen, the First House would begin its influence once again, with this process continuing throughout life. Using this process, an individual determines which House is presently influencing his or her life, by counting from one to twelve until the actual number or years or age is reached.

Each of The Twelve Houses is Ruled by One of The Signs of The Zodiac and Influences Certain Areas of a Person's Life.

First House of Self & Personality   Aries

Personality, character, disposition, outlook on life, mannerisms, inclinations, style, physical appearance, early childhood, destiny, ego, personal actions, likes and dislikes, self-interest.

Second House of Possessions &   Taurus Accumulations

Possessions, sense of values, earned income, security, money, finances, worldy good and one's attitude toward these, use of material resources, gains and losses, physical substances which support the body, acquisitions.

Third House of Communication &   Gemini Daily Travel

Personal environment, brothers, sisters, relatives, neighbors, family relationships, school life, intellectual pursuits, education, communications, speech, books, publications, letters and writings, short trips, self-expression.

Fourth House of Home,   Cancer

HEREDITY & ACCOMPLISHMENTS

Heredity, mother's influence), beginnings and endings of life, the home base from which one operates, the residence, the psychological aspects of self, childhood conditioning,

FIFTH HOUSE OF CREATIVITY   LEO

Personal self-expression, personal will, children, love affairs, artistic creations, games, sports, amusements, recreations, hobbies, talents, pleasures, holidays, enterprises, speculation, affections.

SIXTH HOUSE OF WORK,   VIRGO
SERVICE & HEALTH

Health, employees, career, skills, duties, responsibilities, dependents, diet, hygiene, nurturing, attitudes toward subordinates, care of pets, aunts, uncles, and the subconscious mind.

SEVENTH HOUSE OF PARTNERSHIPS   LIBRA

Close relationships of a personal or business nature, partnerships, social consciousness, cooperation or lack of, peace or discord, marriage or divorce, adversaries, legal contracts, court, formalities.

EIGHTH HOUSE OF LEGACIES   SCORPIO

Legacies, expenditures, elimination, sharing feelings with others, big business, the stock exchange, insurance, research, crime, and attitudes toward sex, death, and regeneration.

NINTH HOUSE OF INTELLECT,   SAGITTARIUS
IDEALS & DISTANT TRAVEL

Long journeys, goals, planning, purpose, direction, philosophy, mental interests, religion, foreign residence, search for new ideas, prophecy, higher education, and moral ideals.

TENTH HOUSE OF CAREER &   CAPRICORN

POSITION IN LIFE

Aspirations, ambitions, positions, authority, honor, prestige, fame, professional position, father, politics, diplomats, social status, self-discipline, the personal image, corporations.

ELEVENTH HOUSE OF FRIENDS & AQUARIUS PROTECTION

Friends, acquaintances, clubs, groups, associates, business associates, altruism, the rewards from ambitions, hopes and wishes, humanitarian efforts, and others who share your outlook on life.

TWELFTH HOUSE OF SACRIFICE, PISCES SECLUSION, SECRETS, ENEMIES & SORROW

Service to others, self-sacrifice, escapism, the unconscious, karmic influences, secrets, repressions, neuroses, deceptions, hidden enemies, hidden resources, self-undoing, prisons, hospitals, and institutions, self imposed limitations.

THE FIRST HOUSE

The First House is Angular, ruled by Aries, and represents identity or the self. This is the House that is indicative of the personality, the tendencies of the individual and the natural disposition. The First House is an individual's rising sign or Ascendant, and it is the most important, most personal and most powerful House in the Birth Chart. The Ascendant is the beginning point of the Birth Chart and determines where the other Houses which follow will be placed. This First House represents you, your character and outlook on life, your mannerisms, inclinations, style and appearance, disposition and temperament. It is indicative of your personal perspective on life, and it is the First House which influences the outcome of the remainder of the Birth Chart and the destiny of the individual.

This is the House which indicates your preferences, your likes and dislikes, and how you see others and the world around you. It also represents how you present yourself to the world, and therefore how others not only see you, but how they accept you and your ideas. It is the first impression that you make on others. Even your subconscious attitudes are represented here as well as your entire approach to life. The First House is indicative not only of your physical appearance but also your health and your early childhood. It is how you approach and look at life, your philosophy of life, and the beginnings of each activity as well as the improvements of your character that you strive to make in life.

The First House rules the self-interest of the individual and the worldly outlook on life. It rules the early childhood as well as destiny in the making. The parts of the body that this house represents are the face and head.

THE SECOND HOUSE

The Second House, a Succedent, is ruled by Taurus. It represents your worldly possessions (but not real estate) and financial affairs as well as those resources available to you including money, talents and values. It is indicative of your sense of values and your basic security but also of your physical senses. The Second House relates to your personal feelings of self-worth, your striving for achievements, your goals and objectives.

This House is indicative of the physical aspect of life, the physical substance of the body, and an individual's desire to accumulate personal possessions and an earned income. It reflects on your outlook regarding money, possessions, and what you want to gain, materially, from life. It is the desire to accumulate personal possessions and material objects in life. Not only gains, profits, and investments are influenced but also losses. It effects personal liberty and personal debt. To some extent, the placement of the planets in relation to the Second House gives some indication of how financially successful an individual will be and which endeavors might be most successful.

The Second House rules your financial affairs and prospects, including money, personal freedom, movable possessions, and acquisitions. The parts of the body it represents are the neck, throat, base of skull, and ears.

THE THIRD HOUSE

The Third House, ruled by Gemini, is Cadent and considering the influence of Gemini it is most naturally indicative of communications and your personal environment. This includes your relationship with your brothers and sisters, your relatives, and your neighbors. It represents your intellectual interests pertaining to your studies, writings, letters, speaking, interests, inclinations and abilities. That aspect of your life that relates to your daily transportation, travel, commuting, and getting from one place to another is also covered. This Houserepresents how you accept and deal with new ideas and concepts as well as how you function within your personal environment or home setting. The early environment is highlighted and all learning experiences including motor skills, education, and the psychological adjustment of the individual as well as the ability to study and to learn. The acquisition of new concepts, knowledge, and perceptions are also included in this area. This is your cognitive ability and inclinations which pertain to those areas of interest to you which you decide to pursue or study. The parts of the body ruled by this House include the shoulders, arms, hands, lungs, collar bone and the nervous system.

THE FOURTH HOUSE

The Fourth House which is ruled by Cancer is an Angular House. It is indicative of your home, the parent who supported you, family environment, and domestic situation including the home you will establish on your own as an adult. It represents your early home life and your present and future home. It also represents endings or the condition of life you will encounter at the end of life. In addition, it oversees real estate, mines, properties, and the conclusion of endeavors. The Fourth House could be considered your home base or your base of operation and those influences in life which determined your behavior conditioning, your biases and prejudices, and your psychological perspective on life. It most generally represents your place of residence, the home that you make for yourself and your family, and the influences which you find there. Your domestic situation is covered here. This is your personal life, your most personal feelings, and what you plan for your home life for the future. It is your beginning environment, your immediate domestic situation, and what you strive to establish for your later years. It is indicative of what you hold most dear to yourself, what you protect most in life, and what you consider the most personal aspects of your life, both physically and emotionally. The parts of the body ruled by Fourth House includes the breast, stomach and the digestive tract.

THE FIFTH HOUSE

The Fifth House, a Succedent, is ruled by the sign of Leo and represents creativity and personal self-expression. This covers how you project yourself into the world including children, affairs of the heart, pleasures, and new endeavors as well as your artistic creations. Not only romance and amusements are covered in this House, but also holidays, vacations, sports, games, speculation and gambling, hobbies and other past times. It is indicative of your emotional attitude and of the affections you hold in your life time rather they be for friends, favorite people in your life or for your favorite pets. It also represents your enterprising nature and that spark of originality inherent in your personal make up. The Fifth House shows your dramatic flair, literary aptitude, artistic talent, or that creative urge you feel in other areas of your life, particularly that urge to leave something of yourself behind when you die. It is indicative of your ability to enjoy yourself, of parties and gifts on the lighter side of life and more seriously of publications, politics, the finer arts, and social gatherings as well as pregnancies and the education of your children. If a planet is afflicted, this House rules the over-indulgence of pleasures. The parts of the body the Fifth House represents are the heart, sides and upper half of the back.

THE SIXTH HOUSE

The Sixth House of health and service is Cadent and is ruled by Virgo. This House represents your daily work, your health, and your personal habits. It rules your relationships with your colleagues and fellow workers, your employment and any employees, and the conditions under which you work as well as the tools or equipment you use. It oversees not only duties, responsibilities, and all those daily tasks which must be accomplished, but also your attitudes toward your work. Your daily expenses are covered here too as well as any overhead, maintenance expenses, utilities or landlords. This House is also indicative of your general health, your susceptibility to diseases and illness, personal hygiene and your diet, and all conditions directly effecting your health. In addition, it covers the services you provide for others, your daily wardrobe and clothing, and your care of pets and small animals. It is indicative of aunts, uncles, personal adjustment and your subconscious mind. The parts of the body ruled by the Sixth House are the solar plexus and the bowels.

THE SEVENTH HOUSE

The Seventh House ruled by Libra is Angular and rules partnerships including your spouse, business partners, the public and any enemies. As the First House represents you and yourself, this House represents how you deal with others in close relationships and includes marriage, separations, divorces, and remarriage. It is indicative of your attitude toward your marriage, your spouse, and also points to what kind of relationship you establish with your spouse. In business affairs, it relates to contracts, lawsuits, agreements, litigation, any court proceedings, formalities or any involvement in the public or in politics. This House is indicative of your social consciousness, your cooperation or your lack of it, and your success or failure at relationships. Not only your social awareness but your awareness and concern for others is shown. Your enemies, competitors, adversaries, or anybody holding a grudge are covered here. The First House represented your strengths, and conversely the Seventh House represents your weakest personality traits. The part of the body ruled by this House are the veins, kidneys, ovaries, and the lower half of the back.

THE EIGHTH HOUSE

The Eighth House, a Succedent, is ruled by Scorpio and represents legacies and the support you receive from others including financial, moral, physical or spiritual. It rules over the possessions of others and the financial affairs of partners, but also death and all matters connected with death and regeneration. It includes trusts, wills, taxes, insurance, inheritances, and investigations, secrets, sex, spiritual and physical regeneration and rebirth, degeneration and the end of life. The life-force elements of sex and birth, and the personal attitudes toward death and the after life are indicated. It shows elimination, the extraction of essences, expenditures, and rules over businesses, corporations, the stock market taxes, research, restoration, as well as psychoanalysis. This House reflects occult inclinations, sleep, and secret affairs and hidden assets. Surgery and types of illnesses are shown here. This House has also been referred to as the House of Crime. The parts of the body ruled by the Eighth House are muscular system, the bladder and the sexual organs.

THE NINTH HOUSE

The Ninth House is Cadent and ruled by Sagittarius. It reflects the intellectual exploration of the higher mind which provides a sense of purpose and direction. Your more profound thinking is indicated here as well as your aspirations and search for new meanings and

305

understandings of life. This House is indicative of distant travel, residence in foreign countries, and journeying to remote places far from where you were born. It reflects your dealings with others from foreign countries, your exposure to different lifestyles, cultures and ways of thinking. It shows connections with other countries in commerce, big business, imports and exports. Here too is shown your dreams, visions, insights, psychic experiences, education, and intuitions. It covers higher learning, philosophy, religion, psychology, science, the law, your intellectual interests, and the lessons you learn in life as well as your view of the Universe. It represents your search for the meaning to life, wisdom, and spirituality as well as your moral ideals, conscience, dreams and expanding consciousness. This House rules advertising, publicity, organized sports, and domestic and wild large animals. The parts of the body ruled by the Ninth House are the liver and thighs.

THE TENTH HOUSE

The Tenth House which is ruled by Capricorn is Angular and represents your career, reputation, public standing, the parent who nurtured you, and your employer. It shows your aspirations, ambitions, and hopes. This House rules over fame, honors, recognition, prestige, promotions, and positions of authority and leadership. It represents your status and influence, attainments, successes, your business and social involvement, your employers, the government, or others in authority over you. It relates to self-discipline and those areas of life regarding outward appearances and your business and social image. It is how others regard you and your standing in the business world or in your community or neighborhood. The Tenth House rules your public image, social position, fame and success reflecting those qualities or positions that you aspire to achieve. The parts of the body ruled by the Tenth House are the knees, joints, skeletal system, and teeth.

THE ELEVENTH HOUSE

The Eleventh House ruled by Aquarius is a Succedent and is representative of your capacity for friendships, associations, and your hopes and wishes for the future. It rules over your social contacts, others who share your ideals, and professional contacts, and includes your involvement in clubs, organizations, political parties, professional associations or unions, communes, and how you interact with masses of people. It is indicative of the financial condition of your employer. These could be considered your more detached or impersonal relationships of day-to-day life, but these relationships to a large degree reflect your ideals and outlook on life. How you feel toward humanitarian and philanthropic concerns is shown here. This House reflects the harmonious cooperation of groups of people, but on a personal level shows individual expressions of personality. The Eleventh House also indicates your preferences of intellectual pleasure, and your dreams, objectives and goals in life. Your ability to overcome obstacles may be influenced by this sign as well. The parts of the body ruled by the Eleventh House include the ankles and calves.

THE TWELFTH HOUSE

The Twelfth House, ruled by Pisces, is Cadent. It represents the limitations placed on an individual's life many of which are self-imposed. Perhaps the most mystical of all the Houses, it has been referred to as the house of self-undoing, the hell of the Zodiac, the house of the evil demon, and the house of Karma. On a less dismal note, it includes bad habits and vices. This House reflects unseen or unexpected troubles, secret enemies, hidden dangers, clandestine affairs, restraints on personal freedoms, and limitations on aspirations. It shows seclusion, isolation, disappointments, and silent sufferings. Self-sacrifice, devotion, and service to others is also indicated in this House, and it is indicative of hospitals, prisons, and other institutions as well as confinement. Self-imposed escapism is shown and in some individuals neuroses and psychological disorders. The Twelfth House, at the same time, is associated with psychic abilities. This House reflects what meaning one discovered in life, and from a karma perspective reflects the rewards and punishments each person receives in life. The parts of the body ruled by the Twelfth House include the feet, toes, phlegm and mucus.

THE HEAVENLY HOUSES

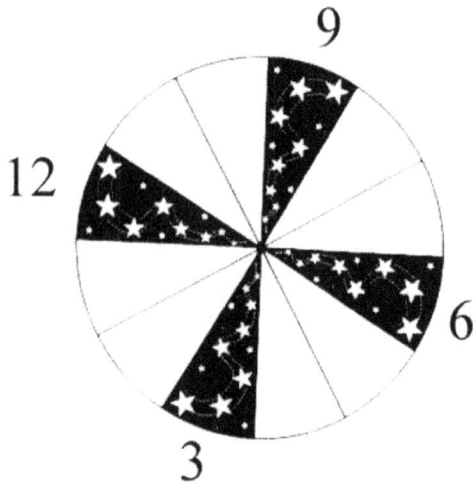

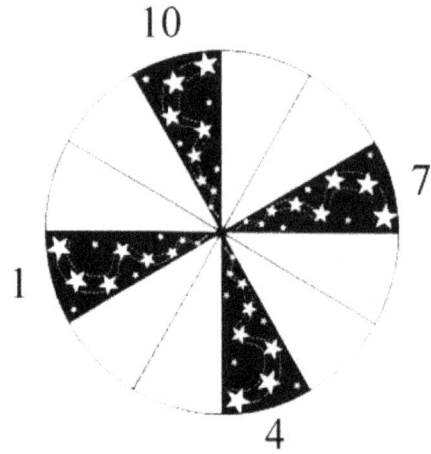

CADENT HOUSES

ANGULAR HOUSES

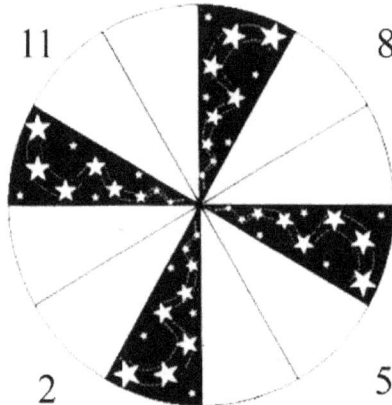

SUCCEDENT HOUSES

Planets in The First House Ruled by Aries

The House of Self and Personality
A Planet in The First House Possesses a Very Powerful Influence.

This placement intensifies the Sun sign making you confident, radiant, optimistic, and outspoken. Ambitious and proud, you are more than ready to take on the world in order to achieve your successes in life. You are considered firm, forceful when necessary with a strength of conviction and of morality. You possess a quick perception and decision-making ability with leadership qualities and a constructive nature that impresses others. You strive through your own enthusiastic efforts to attain the forefront, leadership or coordinating position in all that you do. Your vitality and energy are focused on pursuing your goals, and you are not easily swayed by others. You strive to be recognized not only for your abilities, but for your ideas, plans, actions, and the results you achieved. You enjoy being the center of attention and feeling important, and you work extra hard to gain that position and to keep it.

Frankly outspoken, you speak your mind openly unafraid of allowing your forceful and driving nature to show. You are self-reliant and believe in your own abilities, ideas, plans, and talents. You are impressed with yourself and with your dignified manner, you have the strong ability to impress others. At the same time, you are generous, kind and humane. Your love of power and prestige is naturally derived from your independent, sometimes combative and defensive ambition, but it is combined with a loving, hopeful, and caring disposition. You simply radiate confidence, and your ability to persuade others is undaunted. You, therefore, easily pull others together, influence decisions, and accomplish tasks, all of which results in you achievements, attainments, and bettering yourself in life. You seek and find positions of trust, influence and responsibility. If well-aspected, this position tends to a happy childhood and a good health.

If afflicted, the native is arrogant, over reactive, too defensive and sensitive, prideful, argumentative, and is ruled by his or her libido and pleasure seeking nature. This person becomes dictatorial, dominating, egotistical and pompous preferring to rule rather than to lead.

Your lofty motives and drive lead you to honor, general success and advancement with the good will of others.

THE MOON IN THE FIRST HOUSE

You are emotional, sensitive and changeable. Every aspect of life is experienced through your feelings which set the tone for your decisions, responses, visions, and your interpretation of events in your life. You can be inherently shy and at times moody, but when these inclinations are dealt with, you approach other people in a positive and successful manner. Change is highlighted in your life, and this may be in finances, residence, occupation, or relationships. Your mind is receptive, ingenious, and intuitive granting you a creative imagination and a nature that has a flair for fantasy.

You may find yourself building walls of self-defense to protect your sensitive nature from the world, but you are at the same time ambitious to attain security, support and recognition, and self satisfaction. You have an interest in public life and with your refined taste and sympathetic nature, you find yourself responding to the concerns of others. You can be receptive of new people and places, and your flexibility and desire for change may lead you to roam about looking far and wide before you decide to settle. Located in a Fixed sign, the nature of the individual is less changeable and more content.

You can be romantic, impressionable, dreamy and fanciful, you are receptive to psychic experiences. You want most to be appreciated and admired, and your ambitious nature leads you to aspire to fame or fortune. Family, home, and loved ones are also important to you.

Needless to say, the negative traits of this location of the Moon indicate a person who is oversensitive, moody, self-centered, unaware of the needs of others, resentful, sentimental, susceptible to suggestions, fanciful, and changeable with a tendency to scatter efforts and thoughts in different directions.

The Moon in the First House possesses a tendency to elevate and benefit the individual with indications for advantages in public, social life, and domestic life.

MERCURY IN THE FIRST HOUSE

You are active and volatile, adaptable, and changeable with a tendency to be restlessly nervous. Quick-witted, curious and inquiring, you enjoying discovering new information and may know a little about a lot of different topics. You are resourceful and observant with a comprehensive intellect that seeks knowledge. At the same time your nervous energy and active mind leads you to seek new experiences, to meet new people, and to adapt to new situations easily. You have the ability to fit in, to gather the information you need, and to put it to good use. Always aware of others and your surroundings, your logical but quick mind has a tendency to think and then to act accordingly. Perceptive and studious, you possess an appreciation for literature, informative books and material, and other sources of information. Your opinions are distinctly personal, and being persuasive as well as expressive you may speak or write well. Your need to express your opinions may lead you to speak out impulsively on occasion.

Analytical and rationalizing, you are quick to see an opportunity for advancement or for self-improvement. You have a tendency to feel that any situation can be improved for the better, and you arrive at this rationalization from the use of logic not from smugness. This logic along with your intellectual energy and quick wit impresses others. One of your greatest challenges may be understanding others who are more emotional than you for you tend to see the world from your personal perspective of logic and self. This same rationalization and logic leads you to see the varying alternatives to situations and decisions, and at times you may find yourself adding up pros and cons while you make plans based on contingencies.

If afflicted by other planets, the individual is overly restless, indecisive, and self-centered with the ability to take advantage of other people. This person may gather much information, study in a number of different areas, or travel restlessly, but never finds a specific focus in life.

Mercury in the First House grants numerous changes in life as well as the opportunity to travel, but there may well be a tendency toward restlessness and nervous anxiety. This person is quick in thoughts, speech, and actions with an inclination to approach his or her personal affairs logically and rationally. You are intelligent and excel at being able to express yourself effectively.

Venus in The First House

With Venus in the First House you are charming with a beauty all your own. Harmonious, well-balanced, graceful, and kind, you enjoy good luck and a sociable, happy disposition. You most want to be loved and appreciated by the other people in your life, and this desire appears to come easily to a person who is easy going, pleasant and refined. One of your chief talents appears to be getting what you want, and with your personality, others are only too happy to help you along the way. You prefer to charm others rather than to be assertive or forceful. Not one to cause problems or rock the boat in any way, you use your intuition, peaceful nature, and the art of compromise to either to accomplish what you want or to find balance in a situation. You have a tendency to either put up with the harshness of others or to ignore it. More than likely it was a person with Venus in the First House who developed the art of diffusing a situation, calming tempers, and making everyone feel better.

You are amiable and trustable with a cheerful and sympathetic nature along with an affectionate disposition. Unafraid of emotions, you are both responsive and receptive to love and romance, and members of the opposite sex find you appealing. You prefer to enjoy life and seek pleasurable activities and the companionship of others. You love to socialize, and when surrounded by others, you are cheerful and entertaining preferring that others are happy too. You love to spoil yourself and to be spoiled by others. You have a taste for fashionable clothing, attractive styles, pleasant surroundings, and a cultured lifestyle. In addition to all that, you possess an appreciation for art, music, and the theater.

You have a tendency to develop your own perceptions of what is socially acceptable or attractive, and you may find that you are easily offended by what you consider the harsher, more unpleasant realities of life. You have a strong preference for beauty, pleasure, harmony and peacefulness in life. This may make you a bit judgmental with a tendency to avoid what you perceive as the unnecessary unpleasantries of life.

If afflicted, this native is self-centered, self-indulgent, and develops a love for leisure and pleasure, preferring the easier, softer life to hard work or diligent effort in any form. There is a tendency toward denial of any personal problems and avoidance of obstacles, struggles, or difficulties.

Venus in the First House bestows a tendency toward good fortune in life and affairs.

Mars in The First House

Mars in the First House and you are a rugged and boisterous individual who possesses a dynamic energy that propels you into life. You are assertive, ambitious and enterprising, and you are an active participant in your surroundings and not an idle bystander. Self-confident and aspiring, you find yourself carving out your own place in life and creating your own destiny. You are practical but uninhibited about acting on your impulses and desires. Courageous and combative, your warrior outlook on life leads you to seek to win at all competitions and endeavors, and you believe you can. You possess a positive outlook on life that adheres to personal liberty, independence and freedom. Along with that you have practical and strong executive abilities and in many instances are a natural leader.

You are a forceful individual whose vigorous self-assertion leads you to plunge, sometimes impulsively, into new projects, ideas, and physical exertions. Your strong will power forces you to attempt to overcome any handicaps or obstacles. And with your great energy and stamina you find yourself not only working hard but accomplishing more than others find possible. You are that audacious contender who scorns defeat and is daringly reckless of danger. Your fiery, passionate nature holds true in romance also for you possess a strong sex drive.

Your drawbacks are that you don't like to take directions or orders from others, and you can be a bit too rash and headstrong. At other times, there is a tendency to be too forceful in getting your own way which happens when you lose your patience with a situation or with other people. With Mars in the First House, you should guard against being accident-prone. There is an inclination for scars to the head or face or to the body part associated with the sign occupied.

If afflicted, this native is overly ambitious acting out of rashness and impetuousness, or is too headstrong, obstinate, forceful, impatient, and volatile with violent tendencies.

A self-starter, you prefer to initiate your own projects, and then are not afraid of the hard work required to see your projects through to completion. You find yourself caught up in the present moment, and you focus your energies and drive on what you are attempting to accomplish. You may find that it is necessary to work hard during your early years which helps you to develop beneficial habits and skills.

313

Jupiter in The First House

Jovial and optimistic, you are a high spirited person who prefers to be cheerful, pleasant and amiable. You face all aspects of life and especially new experiences with enthusiasm, confidence and hope. Good natured and benevolent, you are kind, generous, and faithful. You have a tendency to inspire others and often find yourself in leadership positions with your natural good luck carrying you through any difficult situations. You most aspire to be noble and just and with your humane nature, you find yourself always helping others. Prudent and sincere, others appreciate your courteous and pleasant manners and good intentions. Jupiter in the First House grants you honesty, truthfulness, and trustworthiness which makes you well-liked and popular among your friends, associates and colleagues.

Your natural poise and dignity along with your determination and executive ability enable you to attain positions of authority, leadership and power in society, business, education and religious matters. At times, your mind takes a philosophical bend, but generally you are open-minded, logical and possess a good reasoning ability. Energetic and vital, chances are you also excel at sports and love to travel. A bit restless, you also have an exploring nature that grants you a love for the wide open spaces, fresh air, and boundless skies which you find inspiring. At times it appears that your interest know no limits, and you find yourself pursuing any number of either intellectual, social, physical, or pleasurable activities.

Jupiter offers protection and luck and this at times appears just in time to save your present situation. If you aren't careful, you find yourself depending too much on this natural luck which can make you complacent, taking your advantages for granted.

If well aspected, there are indications for attaining positions of power, responsibility and leadership. If afflicted, success is moderate, and the native is too pleasure seeking, self-indulgent, unfaithful, lazy, rash, loud, gullible, extravagant, impatient and conceited with a tendency for weight gain which can cause health problems. This person is prone to over exaggeration in order to gain the confidence of others.

You possess a buoyant, cheerful disposition and the ability to inspire confidence in others. Jupiter endows you with luck and good fortune and you find that things work out for the best in your life. Others seek you out for your friendship and good will.

314

Saturn in The First House

With Saturn in the First House you are influenced to be reserved, serious, conscientious, and patient. When well-aspected, Saturn grants a thoughtfulness and consideration for others. More emotional types, however, may find you cool and aristocratic, but chances are you prefer to contemplate life from a viewpoint of discretion and prudence. Diligent and economical, you prefer to work from a systematic approach that reflects careful attention to details.

You most desire to achieve in life through your own efforts, hard work, and diligent efforts. You persevere facing obstacles and hardships with a tenacity that grants you the ability to handle responsibilities and difficult situations. Although reserved and somewhat grave at times, your calm and serious nature sees you through life's trials. You aspire to better yourself and to attain prominence and the power to control your own life. Limitations in early life provide you with the self-discipline to achieve your aspirations. You apply industriousness and a steady, and a methodical, well-planned approach to your endeavors. Your persistence, practical and learned ability, continued effort, patience, and wise decisions earn you a good reputation, honor and credit.

You consider life to be a challenge, and to this you apply order and self-development in order to bring about the desired results. Whether shy or simply cautious, you choose your own time to act or to make decisions, preferring to test the waters and to seek practical, sound solutions to problems and situations. Others consider you reliable, thoughtful and responsible. You may be a bit mistrustful of the intentions of others preferring to be patient in making judgments about friends and associates. You can be subtle, preferring to think through decisions and to move cautiously through life. This can give you a tendency to be stand-offish with the opposite sex, but when in love, you are faithful and considerate and willing to endure any hardship for your family or loved ones.

If afflicted, this native is gloomy and discontent, secretive, stubborn, obstinate, overly mistrustful, negligent of personal affairs, with poor habits and a lack of opportunity. Sorrows and disappointments are indicated.

You possess the inclination to overcome limitations and aspire to achievement, power, responsible positions, and success. Your diligent efforts and ability to endure hardships grant you the wisdom to excel in life.

315

URANUS IN THE FIRST HOUSE

With Uranus in the First House chances are you are the adversary in any discussion, capable of taking the opposing viewpoint and arguing it effectively. You are an advocate of freedom, equality, innovation and progress and firmly believe that even the most popularly accepted ideas, opinions and practices can be improved. The chances are good that you have unconventional ideas that at times question tradition and existing rules and regulations. You much prefer the expansion of ideas and thoughts and see formalities as limitations. You are capable of accepting revolutionary ideas whether in theory or related to societal changes, academics, sciences, or religious dogma. It is not that you are aggressively forceful, quarrelsome, or overly antagonistic, but you do tend to take the side of the underdog because oppression in any form is an open attack on what you perceive as personal freedoms and liberties in the society at large. You are a person who either makes or breaks accepted practices and the law.

You are a friendly, easy-going person who most enjoys staying active, detached and intensely independent. You avoid any limitations or restrictions to your activities, thoughts, studies, interests, communications, or personal style. This may make forming lasting relationships difficult unless you find a person who fully understands your nature. At times, you prefer your solitude in order to pursue your interests. And you most resent anyone who attempts to control you or who is domineering. You would prefer to listen to your own intuitive perceptions and ideas. Whether it is your nonconformist approach, your at times eccentric ideas, or your magnetic appeal, you stand out in a crowd, and your ideas draw attention because you can be direct and outspoken in your views.

Uranus rules originality and creativity, and this endows you with the creative spirit of innovation and invention. You are curious about unusual and unordinary subjects. Information is important to you too, and you seek material which relates to all areas of science, technology, space, electronics, or communications. If Uranus is well aspected, you possess a strong intellect, a superior intelligence and you may be a genius. Whatever the case, you have a strong inclination to experiment. You can be changeable and restless with a nervous energy the compels you to seek adventure or at least new experiences in different places. This may lead you to relocate or to travel also seeking new knowledge. Guard against electrical accidents.

If poorly aspected, this individual is unorthodox, eccentric, stubborn, inconsiderate, sarcastic, critical, easily offended, erratic, overly restless and too changeable. An unpredictable nature leads to many changes in life.

Well aspected, Uranus in the First House grants a strong intelligence, originality, an independent nature, and, if Mercury is also well aspected, the ability to express ideas well.

NEPTUNE IN THE FIRST HOUSE

Neptune in the First House produces a person who is gentle and refined, but who may prefer dreams and fantasy to reality. You can appear vague to others, but the chances are you prefer to keep your more private thoughts and visions to yourself. You are curious about the world around you with a tendency to delight in the beauty of nature and natural surroundings including the oceans or other bodies of water. Your sense perceptions make profound impressions upon you, and being highly imaginative, you may be either musically or artistically talented. To others you appear glamorous and mysterious with a magnetic charm and charisma all your own.

You are highly impressionable, and Neptune in the First House represents inspirations, romance and emotional involvement. Your dreams and visions are vivid and powerful, and you possess a strong inclination for unusual occurrences, thoughts, perceptions and experiences. You may be either visionary or idealistic, but your thoughts are highly original if not mysterious. You have a quick mind and your perceptions are often accurate and correct. You meet unusual people with out-of-the ordinary interests.

You can be enthusiastic about life, but must guard against being easily swayed or impressed by others. You are most capable of changing your mind to suit your mood, and this may lead you to jump from one endeavor to another. To enhance your creative mind and willed power, you must stay away from alcohol and drugs. Your dreamy mind makes you appear absent-minded and at times lazy, and if left to your own desires, you might prefer to dream away your days.

However, if afflicted, this native is lazy and filled with self-delusion with a strong preference for luxury, passion, and pleasure. This person is often confused, uncertain, procrastinating, sensitive and overly emotional, excitable, changeable, unstable, indolent, and any enthusiasm and energy is dispersed into random efforts. There is a tendency to drift through life, for imagination to become morbid, and there is indicated danger through schemes and deception, many moves, and changes.

If well aspected this person is sensitive, original, creative and intuitive, and may be receptive to psychic experiences. You are gentle, loving, kind, and compassionate with a generous and caring nature.

Pluto in The First House

Pluto in the First House represents a person who is strong-willed, individualistic, creative, and intense. Strong and resilient with a magnetic personality and a determined ego, you may crave power. You can appear moody and restless or energetic, enthusiastic and passionate. Chances are you even choose what impression you want to make on others and do so effectively. You can be unconventional with a will of your own and a tendency to write your own rules as you go along. You perceive everything from a personal viewpoint, and are determined to follow through in your efforts, to finish what you start.

You are a self-reliant person who may prefer your private life to remain just that. You may seek seclusion or private places to protect your personal and private life. At times, you can even be secretive if not a bit mysterious. On your own, you are the competent individual, perhaps a loner, who can survive anything life sends your way. In love, you prefer a total commitment based on acceptance and trust. There is a part of your personality that craves adventure, and this leads you to experiment with life learning new skills and developing your talents, and forever seeking the new experience whether it be mountain climbing, flying, scuba diving, skydiving, or fishing off that remote reef in the South Pacific.

If afflicted, this individual feels unaccepted and incapable and can be argumentative, uncooperative, moody, changeable and restless, vindictive, ruthless, or violent. There is indicated the possibility of exile or seclusion or in the least a lack of direction.

Pluto in the First House grants the power of transformation, and this makes you capable of becoming who and what you want to be. You use your enthusiasm, energy, and intellect for self-development, your determination for achievement of your goals, and your strong will power to acquire what you most desire in life.

Planets in The Second House Ruled by Taurus

The House of Possessions and Accumulation

The Sun in the Second House makes you a person who has either developed your own value system and perspective on life or is seeking to develop values you can trust and abide by. In some regards, your personal outlook on life leads you to be a person who also places value on accumulating money and possession. And you do appear to attract money, but it seems to go as easily as it comes. You appreciate the luxuries in life and the things that money can buy, and you tend to spend lavishly sometimes on items that are more status symbols than necessities. You expend time and effort on creating a fashion statement and style that is individualistically of your own making. Your personal style may well reflect refinement, good taste, and a sense of appreciation for beauty, color, and form.

You possess a strong desire to be appreciated, accepted and admired. Friendly, sociable, and fun-loving, you can be generous and well meaning, but it is important to you that your good qualities and deeds are recognized by others. It is quite likely that you know influential people and make friends with all the right people. It is also just as likely that you come from an affluent home or have successful parents. And financial success appears just as likely to be in the stars for you too. Depending upon your personal values, you are either a person who gives lavishly of yourself to others, or who spends extravagantly on yourself. In any event, your interest in life center on making money, social interactions, pleasurable activities, luxury, and sports. You are also a romantic who is drawn naturally to love.

If afflicted, this individual is ostentatious, greedy, possessive, prideful, self-centered, snobbish and overbearing. There is a desire for social position, fame and recognition, or superiority.

If well aspected, you are cheerful, open and accepting of others, and you appreciate pleasurable activities, family, social events, and self-enrichment. You find success in life based on industrious effort and positions of responsibility.

319

THE MOON IN THE SECOND HOUSE

The Moon is forever changing, and placed in the Second House of possessions it represents fluctuation and financial ups and downs. All the same, you possess a good business ability and an appreciation for possessions and financial success. Your creativity and imagination enhance your talents and abilities, and in addition, you are highly persuasive. You develop values based on knowledge, education, information and communication.

Tenacity and determination are your strong points, and knowing that you face obstacles and limitations, you strive to obtain security and a sense of well being based on long-term plans and goals. The Moon favors a female influence or the mother, and your financial endeavors may be enhanced by either with special emphasis placed on business contacts with women. You are a natural at sales or you may discover gains through public employment, real estate, politics, the food industry, businesses associated with water or liquids, domestic products, commodities, or an ability to predict or forecast supply and demand.

A romantic at heart, your possessions hold sentimental value to you, and you feel more secure when surrounded by items you have collected through the years. Sensitive and reflective, you prefer a home environment that enhances your need for balance and security in your life. You desire to be appreciated and accepted especially by your loved ones. While money and possessions are important to you, you also value your personal security and the security of your family and home just.

If afflicted, this native is moody, changeable, wasteful, careless, stingy, over sensitive and sentimental. There is a tendency to shift from one plan to another and to feel like a failure.

You are considerate, generous and kind with an inclination for financial success, however, you may experience numerous gains and losses before you achieve the security you desire. You place a high value on your home life and the welfare of your family.

MERCURY IN THE SECOND HOUSE

Mercury in the Second House grants you a skill in commerce and a shrewd manipulative ability in finances. You are capable, practical, rational, and oriented toward business and finance. You possess an alert mind and are able to make quick decisions and to produce results. Ingenious and versatile you rely on your ability to retain information and details. Intellectually, you develop an appreciation for the written word, and you collect the writings of your favorite authors.

Your inclinations draw you to the fields of education, economics, philosophy or theology, writing, lecturing, communications, advertising, publishing, travel, business or commerce, sales, distribution, or any endeavor requiring a proficient middle man to handle transactions. You may have more than one source of income. Depending on the positions of the other planets, you may either hold tightly to money or be a free spender. You absorb information and use it to the best advantage. While you prefer that your ideas and plans progress quickly, you are capable of being patient and of waiting for the opportune time to initiate new plans.

To a degree, you focus on money and possessions, but developing your ideas and your intellect are just as important to you. You seek knowledge for knowledge sake recognizing the importance of being well-informed and current on affairs of the world. You know that possessions come and go and can be replaced, but your intellect must continually be developed.

Your curiosity leads you to be a collector of books, mementos, gadgets, crafts, and eye-catching items of interest. You possess an insatiable desire to find that unusual item or just the right gift for a friend. Congenial, you seek out friends who share similar interests. And in romance, you prefer companions who challenge you intellectually.

Adaptable, your nature can lead you at times to desire change or new experiences, and mobility doesn't frighten you. In fact, you find exciting the idea of travel, meeting new people, or being exposed to new ideas, people and places. Your varied interests lead you to explore new possibilities wherever you are.

If afflicted, this individual is uncertain, stubborn, careless, spendthrift, impractical, changeable, restless, and vulnerable. This persons uses trickery and manipulations in order to profit materially.

You are best known for being a person with varied interests and activities who possesses an alert, active mind. You may find that you have two groups of friends, associates, and sources of finance.

VENUS IN THE SECOND HOUSE

Venus in the Second House grants you the magnetism to attract those things you appreciate and find pleasurable in life. You possess a natural talent for financial affairs, and being lucky and quite fortunate, you are generally able to obtain money and prosperity. You are refined and pleasure-loving, and use your resources on fashionable clothing, jewelry, accessories, entertainment, and attractive items for your home. You most desire harmonious surroundings and find contentment when surrounded by luxury and comfort. You have an eye for beauty and a taste for physical comfort. You may find success through the fields of art, music, entertainment, the hotel industry, flowers, decorating, fashion or apparel, jewelry, the food industry, recreational activities, real estate, or any position dealing with the public. You find that your social contacts, friendships, associates, marriage, and contacts with women benefit you. Partnerships and any endeavor related to the female consumer are enhanced. Status and social standing in the community are important to you, and your strongest traits are your winning charm and sociably attitude.

You are particularly kind and generous, finding enjoyment and pleasure in making other people happy. Men with Venus in the Second House are known for spending money on female friends. Women with this placement can be extravagant in their spending habits. Your peaceful, fun-loving nature draws you to music or singing, dancing, adornment, and fine food and beverages. But whatever your spending habits, you find that when you need assistance, you are more than likely to find the help you need.

New experiences delight and thrill you, and you are considered open and accepting of others. You like meeting new people, but also have a fondness for friends, appreciating your relationships with others. You are quite capable of both giving and receiving, and your relationships are plentiful, rewarding, and satisfying.

If afflicted, this individual possesses a weak will power, is extravagant and self-indulgent, pleasure and sensation seeking, greedy, possessive, insatiably materialistic, and rejecting of new experiences and other people.

This is considered a fortuitous placement for Venus. If this planet is found in your Second House, you are fortunate to the point of being lucky and financial gains are yours when you focus your efforts on success and the results it can produce.

Mars in The Second House

Mars in the Second House and you are a highly competitive person who gains through your own energetic and resourceful efforts. Your inherent drive leads you to focus your strength and will on achieving financial success, and generally speaking, you possess a profitable earning ability based on your own merit and tendency to work hard. You may be a wheeler-dealer or simply a person who is unafraid of taking risks. You find yourself curiously attracted to speculation or get-rich-quick schemes, and in this regard there are times when you impulsively make rash decisions. At the same time, you may find it difficult to hold on to money which at times runs through your fingers. You possess a sense of pleasure in your ability to be an extravagant free spender who is generous with friends and associates.

You may have a strong preference for owning a business and being self-employed, allowing you to run the show under your own steam. Your inclinations may lead you to endeavors involved in the fields of mining, steel, chemicals, the timber industry, ranching or farming, engineering, machinery and mechanics, the military, or government positions. Then again, you may prefer sales or to manage other people as an agent or promoter. Whatever your endeavors, your physical energies and aggressiveness propel you to action. You have an inherent driving force within you to succeed and to accumulate what you want from life. You are direct, forceful and uninhibited about exploring new possibilities. At times both daring and adventuresome, physical exertion doesn't deter you and you will fight to protect your possessions. Left to your own desires, you would prefer to be a self-made person. And your initiative and directness augment that desire. You prefer efficiency and expediency, becoming quickly impatient and frustrated with sentimentality, indecisiveness, confusion or anything distracting from productivity. Obstacles, problems, financial ups and downs, and competition are nothing new to you, but your enterprising nature and drive is sufficient to see you through any crisis. You may relocate or change directions several times before you settle.

Planetary afflictions result in an individual who is careless with money, rash, impulsive, argumentative, and dishonest, and who suffers through losses, problems, and financial misunderstandings.

You realize financial gain through the efforts of your own enterprising nature and hard work.

322

JUPITER IN THE SECOND HOUSE

Jupiter in the Second House endows you with an optimistic spirit of well being, increasing your chances for prosperity and success. Your self-confidence and enthusiasm enhances your driving ambition producing a talent for finances. In fact, the chances are you possess an exceptional ability for handling your business affairs realizing a productive growth and development, and no matter how little you start with, you turn it into gains and profits. You are cheerful and likable, and others are attracted to your appealing nature. On occasion you benefit from social contacts.

Your positive and open-minded attitude often leads you to seek new experiences or new information. You enjoy traveling, meeting people and seeing new sights. And your expansive nature and philosophical inclination combined with an easy-going attitude makes you accessible to others. You are known for your generosity and sincere efforts to be supportive. Others know that you are honest, trustable and responsible.

With Jupiter in the Second House, you may find yourself drawn to the fields of banking, finance, the stock market, securities, sales, government positions, law, insurance, education, sales, import-export, medicine, domestic goods, food, real estate, psychology, literature and publishing, or the travel industry. You also possess an interest in science, theology or philosophy. Then too you can be somewhat of a visionary who is always initiating and speculating on new ideas and innovative approaches for the most productive uses of available resources. You accurately appraise your current affairs and make plans for the future.

The negative traits brought about by planetary afflictions make this individual a careless spendthrift who is greedy, self-indulgent, showy, changeable, restless and dissatisfied with acquisitions; financial judgment is questionable and money slips away.

Overall, Jupiter in the Second House enhances your opportunities for attaining financial success, security, and good fortune. Your ability to inspire trust in others gains you positions of responsibility, and through careful planning you benefit from your endeavors. Your nature leads you to seek out the most beneficial decisions not only for yourself but for the other people in your life.

Saturn in The Second House

Saturn in the Second House produces firm inclinations toward caution and conservatism. You much prefer traditional, well-tested methods and procedures. And you aren't hesitant to work hard for what you want to achieve. You strongly prefer sound investments with guaranteed profits and abhor any thought of speculation, preferring slow but steady increases as opposed to any chance of risk. You also guard and protect your possessions in order to minimize any risk to your security.

At times, life appears to be an uphill struggle and you face numerous obstacles, realizing slow but steady and profitable gains after much hard work. Opportunities present themselves but you are either not in a position to take advantage of them, or your cautious nature prevents you from taking decisive action. You face either real or self-imposed limitations in your efforts to succeed, but at the same time, experience has taught you to expect intermittent, inevitable, and frustrating delays. Persevering, your tenacity sees you through any and all difficult situations. You prefer your possessions to be tangible items or real property. You can be economical, thrifty, or even frugal in some matters, knowing full well the value of a dollar earned. With this position of Saturn, you may have inclinations toward the fields of real estate, mining, produce, storage and warehousing, construction, salvaging, heavy equipment, machinery, or labor. Then too, you can be shrewd in business matters with the ability to drive a hard bargain, evaluating and assessing your decisions while you seek your money's worth. Pennies add up to dollars, and you carefully watch where your pennies are being spent. When adding up your expenses on a project, you never forget to add in the postage stamp.

If afflicted, this individual suffers from nervous anxieties, is miserly, stingy, clingy, selfish, greedy, self-serving; chances of loss or poverty; may have unnecessary fears related to possessions; faces numerous obstacles; problems with land, property, or inheritance.

When well aspected, Saturn in the Second House favors a sound financial ability, and a person who is economically thrifty, conservative and solid. Gains are earned through cautious investments, diligence, hard work and effort. This position indicates benefits for the individual through inheritance or support from the father or employer.

You are known for being an ambitious person who is unafraid of working for what you want in life. You seek financial gain and success for the security it can offer you.

URANUS IN THE SECOND HOUSE

Uranus in the Second House endows you with a streak of individualism that propels you along a path of freedom and independence. Your interests are prone toward the unusual, and you satiate your curious nature by forever seeking unorthodox or stimulating experiences, knowledge, and people. An established routine fails to hold your attention. You have a tendency to establish your personal values based on your own observations and evaluations rather than accepting conventional and popular beliefs. You may develop a fondness for material things or you may decide that you have little interest in accumulating possessions. And the chances are that what you do acquire will have either an intrinsic or utilitarian value to you.

You possess a unique ingenuity that attracts you to unusual and original occupations and sources of income. You are inclined to having any number of fluctuations in your income, experiencing ups and downs and moving from sudden lucky financial opportunities and windfalls to losing money. Your finances may appear to be unsettled, but you most likely don't allow yourself to be overwhelmed by your financial situation. You consider money as a means to gaining freedom from restrictions and limitations. It may be that you are continually pulled between striving to make money and the desire to be unencumbered by responsibilities, possessions, and the other aspects of life that require a steady income to support. In fact, your individualistic nature may lead you to minimalize your lifestyle rather than to buy into a consumer mentality.

With your sudden insights and intuitions combined with your strong will power, you may decide you prefer going into business for yourself. Those fields which you may excel at include science, inventions, electricity, machinery and mechanics, writing, music, antiques, gadgets, curios or advertising specialties, railroads, technology, or electronics. Your interests may also include astrology or astronomy. You may receive money through inheritance, partners, friends, or the government. Your detached attitude toward money allows you to speculate without being overly fearful of loss, however, if you have difficult aspects in your chart, this is not a good position for speculation. If well aspected, you can expect to receive overall gains in the long term.

If afflicted, this individual can be a stubborn, domineering, rebellious, unresponsible type person who isn't above lying, cheating or not repaying loans or bills. This person is materialistic, wanting money and possessions, usually the fastest way possible.

You are a unique individual with a special interest in the rare and unusual. You mind is inventive and resourceful, and when the right opportunity comes along, you will no doubt realize it.

NEPTUNE IN THE SECOND HOUSE

Neptune in the Second House grants you a strong creative outlook on life and a desire to support philanthropic concerns. Sensitive and aware, you have a tendency to donate to charities and humanitarian causes. You are idealistic with a refined perception of beauty, quality, and the finer things in life. You possess an appreciation for luxury as well as music, art, cultural events, nature, and well prepared food. You delight in the senses and want to sample what life has to offer. At the same time, you are for the most part nonmaterialistic, regarding possessions as either necessities or developing an appreciation for their esthetic value and beauty.

Intuitive and imaginative, you make money, but your financial situation is at times questionable mainly due to money problems caused by debts, liabilities, or over-spending. It may be that your financial judgment isn't good, or that, being creative, you prefer not to adhere to logical, business-like approaches to finances. It is most important that you guard against being susceptible to fraud and schemes. The chances are that you will experience extremes in gains and losses. If well aspected, you may excel in a creative field such as music or art, or in careers related to water, institutions, investigations or the secret service, or in a public position.

If afflicted, this native is impractical, lazy, extravagant, careless regarding finances, confused, vague, and is prone to over eating, alcohol or drugs; realizes losses through impositions, fraud, and trickery. This person may even come to be dependent on others for support.

You possess the potential for displaying compassion and love for others and for achieving through your creative efforts. Your natural intuition will lead you to opportunities.

PLUTO IN THE SECOND HOUSE

Pluto in the Second House inclines you to stubbornly and decisively pursue what you want in life. Intense, you face life's obstacles with a single-minded determination and drive. In just such a manner, you have the ability to turn failures into success and liabilities into assets. You can be at times an adventurous risk taker, and then too you are capable of waiting out bad times which you know will invariably turn into better, more prosperous situations. Your financial situation is prone to change, but your powerful drive and ambition, and your strong desire to succeed, makes you resourceful. You are not adverse to having more than one source of income. Success comes your way, perhaps even in a sensational manner, and you prove yourself competent to handle it and you finances well. You are comfortable with your assets and develop an appreciation for material possessions.

This is also a good position for handling other people's money, and you may find success in the fields of banking, investments, securities, research, financial counseling, taxes or corporate law, corporate financing, mining, the oil industry, or the entertainment or movie industry. Industrious, you develop a preference for efficiency and utilization of time, effort, and resources.

You are unafraid of hard work, diligent effort, or going the extra mile to achieve completion of your plans and realization of your objectives and goals in life.

If well aspected, this individual is astutely goal-oriented with the strong ability to achieve and to accumulate financial security and possessions. If afflicted, the native is selfish, grasping, greedy, unscrupulous, wasteful, possessive of things and people, with a tendency to develop neurotic cravings for possessions and pleasures, including sexual addictions. This person will stop at nothing to obtain financial, public, or political gain. Loss of friends and law suits are indicated.

You possess uniquely diverse abilities which you put to good use, quite often to your advantage. While you most likely will experience changes in your financial situation, you realize success in your endeavors through determination and a strong will power. Your intensity in all that you do leads you to the top.

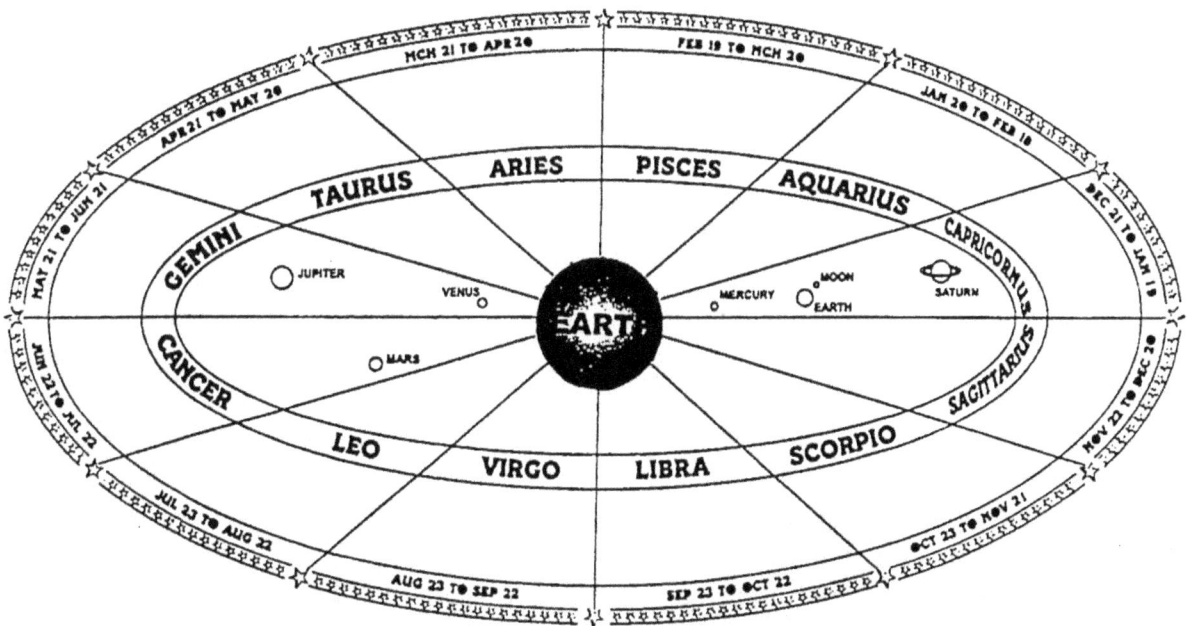

Planets in The Third House Ruled by Gemini

The House of Communication and Daily Travel

With the Sun in the Third House you possess an intellectual self-expression. You are optimistically observant of life and communicate your feelings to others. You have a tendency to be in the right place at the right time and to make good decisions. Your strongest inclinations lead you to be flexible and this is seen in the manner in which you accept and adapt to other people and different situations. Your curious nature compels you to develop your intellect through education, travel, and by exploring new subjects and different fields of interest. Then too your strong intellect, cheerful personality and your unique creativity adds to your fluent ability to express your ideas, thoughts and opinions about a diverse range of topics. You perceive the world around you and new information in a clear and logical manner.

Your lively and alert mind grants you a creative slant on life. And at the same time, you are highly energetic and enthusiastic about your daily life and endeavors. Your achievements in life may well be associated with intellectual accomplishments, and you may find you have an affinity for teaching, writing, publishing, or any field pertaining to collecting and disseminating information. Then too your family, especially any brothers or sisters, are important to you, and you more than likely will benefit from associations with relatives or with neighbors.

Impartial and self-reliant, you have a tendency to transform abstract concepts into concrete accomplishments. You are resourceful and ambitious of success in your field and recognition for accomplishments. Your inner nature leads you to desire to communicate with others on an intellectual level while at the same inspiring, uplifting, enlightening, or benefiting them in some manner. And this desire you accomplish with your magnanimous, charming and winning personality.

If afflicted, this individual is often snobbish, arrogant, disorganized, overbearing, domineering, prideful and indecisive with a strong inclination for numerous misunderstandings with relatives or neighbors and problems connected with letters, publications, agreements, or false statements.

328

The Sun in the Third House grants you the ability to express yourself well, and this position inclines you for achieving success and leadership in your chosen field. Your capabilities lead you to intellectual pursuits.

THE MOON IN THE THIRD HOUSE

The Moon in the Third House leads you to experience numerous changes in your interests, pursuits and career. You are both reflective and introspective while at the same time retaining information based on data you have gathered and on the experiences you've encountered in life. Your strong imagination and flights of fantasy grant you a dramatic and intriguing personality. Your studious nature is compellingly curious and inquisitive, but at the same time restless and changeable. You are inclined to desire not only change but travel, meeting new people, and seeing new places. Your intellect pulls you to investigate new sources of information and an endless number of diverse interests. Adaptable, you have to be on guard not to be too easily influenced or swayed by other people or your present situation. You are prone to mirror those around you in order to fit into your environment.

You are prone to changing your opinions either to suit your fancy or as you gather more information about a particular subject. And your immediate environment greatly influences not only your opinions but your decisions. You may adopt one fad, lifestyle, or fashion after another until you find the one that suits you best. You are striving to find yourself and a mode of self-identification and self-expression, but you may try on a variety of different hats, exploring and experimenting, until you feel at home within yourself. Fanciful, you are expressive, and this is reflected in your writings and creative endeavors either in art or music.

You may discover that the past intrigues you leading you to a career in the field of history, anthropology, archaeology, theology, ancient languages, astrology, science, or antiquities. This is also a good location for advertising, public relations, research, writing, or social science. At the same time, you possess a strong affinity for your community, public affairs, politics, and world events. More than likely you also have an interest in the lives of celebrities, famous people, artists or writers. You develop strong connections and associations with family, friends and neighbors, and your home is an integral and important aspect of your life.

If afflicted, this native is moody, temperamental, unstable, interfering, gossipy, and easily bored and dissatisfied with personal situation. There is a tendency to daydream, to live in a make believe world of fantasy, and to dwell on unimportant issues. There is an indication that accomplishments and educational pursuits may not be completed.

When well aspected, the Moon in the Third House is an excellent position for studious and intellectual pursuits. Your intelligence, creativity, and likable fanciful nature grant you the ability to express yourself in public and to realize your desire to achieve public recognition.

MERCURY IN THE THIRD HOUSE

Mercury in the Third House influences you to be alert, versatile, lively and changeable. You are mentally energetic and stimulating and physically active as well. Mentally astute, you are aware of everything going on around you, and miss out on very little. You pick up cues from your environment and use sound judgment and logical thinking to analyze your situation. Intelligent, talkative and well informed, you enjoy expounding on numerous subjects and engaging in discussions on a variety of topics. And you express yourself well in a meaningful and productive manner. Then too, your curiosity leads you to seek new information and to ask questions in your drive to obtain all the necessary data. You are more than likely decisive with the ability to make accurate, exacting and quick decisions.

You possess strong inclinations toward an active life that among other things includes writing and numerous short trips. Practical, keen and efficient you are capable of compiling details or of shrewdly applying your knowledge to a broader objective. With your inquisitive nature, you may develop an interest in investigation or research. You most desire to broaden your mind and to expand your intellect and understanding with the latest information. Your varied interests lead you to develop strong study habits and you enjoy reading, speaking, writing, teaching, lecturing, science, and current events. Or you may discover that you are inclined toward careers involving dealing with the public in either sales, presentations, public or government positions or in public relations. This compelling curiosity about the world around you may lead you to change directions in life as you pursue your interests and thoughts. Combined with this strong intellectual nature is a tactful, sociable, witty and fun-loving, clever personality which others appreciate. You maintain strong bonds with family, friends and associates.

If afflicted, this individual is anxious about family, prone to worries, indecisiveness, arguments, exaggerations, deceits, cheating, and stealing; indication of problems with contracts.

When well-aspected, this native enjoys traveling for business or pleasure, intellectual accomplishments, and successful endeavors and pursuits. There is indication of success through pursuits related to communication and the ability to express yourself well.

VENUS IN THE THIRD HOUSE

With Venus in the Third House you are refined with a charming personality and adaptable intellect. You most desire to please others and are proficient at the art of give and take. Perceptive and agreeable, you are capable of seeing both sides of an issue, and generally you prefer to find a harmonious course that is acceptable to you and to the other people in your life. Your interests include an appreciation for the arts, music, poetry, literature, and cultural events. Cheerful, sociable, and brightly optimistic, you find that others both appreciate and enjoy your company. Your natural charm spills over into your communications and whether speaking or writing, your thoughts are perceptive, descriptive, and often others find your expressions delightful and endearing. You tend to be refined, creative and artistic and this flair is exhibited in all that you do. You love to see and be seen and are caught up in a flurry of activity, gracefully moving with ease from one pastime or engagement to another. Short trips and excursions excite you and add variety to your life.

You can be discriminating in your judgments, but you prefer to be both fair and logical, applying discretion to your life and rationalizing your thoughts, perceptions, and actions. You share a mutual respect and love for your family and friends, and enjoy meeting new and interesting people. You are quite fond of pleasurable activities including travel. In fact, you may meet a new love or discover a favorable financial gain through one of your trips. You are also fortunate in artistic endeavors.

Unfortunately, if afflicted, this individual possesses too strong a love of pleasure, tends to be lazy, self-indulgent, superficial, emotional, or decadent, and has numerous problems associated with being changeable and indecisive.

Venus in the Third House leads you to be a charming communicator who enjoys entertaining, guesting, or hosting special occasions. Your special charm adds a flavor to life which others find delightful. And you are more than capable of expressing your feelings and perceptions in speech and writing.

MARS IN THE THIRD HOUSE

Mars in the Third House and you are mentally alert and physically energetic. Direct and forceful, you communicate by speaking your mind and can be most adamant about making your point. You are adroit at using either your wit or your sarcasm depending on the situation at hand. You are cleverly skillful, resourceful, and ingenious, preferring to come straight to the point in what you perceive as being a just and correct decision or direction. If at all possible, you prefer to win, to come out first, and if you feel you can't win, you may decide not to compete. Vigorous and decisive, you are unafraid of being argumentative or aggressive, and you excel at debate often winning by sheer will power. You know quite well how to use words to your best advantage, and at times do so almost impulsively and instinctively. And once gaining the advantage, you aren't inclined to give up. Then too, your mind is actively curious, and you find yourself exploring and investigating all avenues of new information and sources of news. You find yourself striving to display strong, persuasive, and responsible leadership abilities, and may discover an astuteness for education, literature, journalism, or executive positions in communications or transportation.

You are a do-it-yourself type person, and develop skills requiring manual dexterity and a mechanical mind. Machinery fascinates you, and you may find yourself collecting the latest gadgets or tools to be used at home, in a shop, or at work. You also have a strong interest in the latest technology and electronics, preferring to be up-to-date, well informed, and aware of the newest developments. If well aspected, you may possess an imaginative, inventive ingenuity. As far as travel is concerned, you more than likely should take precautions against accidents.

If afflicted, this native is tactless, impatient, inconsiderate, overly critical, nervous, restless, and inattentive to details, while being argumentative with family and friends. Problems may occur in regards to relatives, friends, associates, neighbors, travel including driving, communications and law suits. This person is combative or even violent and loses control easily.

While being mentally alert, and under some aspects even of genius proportions, you are a person of ideas, creativity, and persuasive verbal and written communications.

JUPITER IN THE THIRD HOUSE

With Jupiter in the Third House your optismism and cheerfulness brighten the days of your family and friends. Your expansive mind gathers knowledge, pertinent facts, and relevent information in order for you to formulate your ideas, thoughts, communications, and even philosophy of life. This pursuit results in a refined intellect, but you are, at the same time, known for being kind, thoughtful and sympathetic to others. Witty and easy going, you enjoy pleasant relationships not only with family members but with friends, neighbors and associates as well. Practical, with high ideals, you possess an intuitive nature and an abundance of common sense which allows you to be capable of giving and receiving in relationships.

Then too, your intellect is energetically restless, and you are compelled to get your ideas across in a straightforward and direct manner. You are candid, honest, and outspoken, and you express yourself fluently in any conversation. This carries over into your written work too where you can apply yourself as an insightful critic or express your thoughts in a concise and meaningful style. Quite possibly you develop an interest in the welfare of society and form a somewhat liberal, tolerant consciousness. Your mind drifts toward expansiveness not limiting, restricting or narrowminded ideas. Then too, travel, rather short distances or long trips, allows you experiences in life that broaden your mind and concepts.

Jupiter in the Third House grants you luck in communication, and you may find yourself entering the field of writing, journalism, broadcasting or commentator, lecturing, advertising, public relations, education, publishing, or sales. You discover that you are capable of adapting to new situations or new ideas, and at the same time you are sincere in your effort to be conventional, appropriate and accepted. Your associates appreciate your reasonableness and your sociable, earnest and outgoing personality. In addition, your philosophical inclinations may lead you to develop an interest in theology or subjects related to religion or spiritualism.

If afflicted, this individual can be too talkative, imprudent, restless, impractical, superficial, prone to exaggerations, overly tactless, reckless and often outspokenly inconsiderate of the feelings of others. Affliction brings problems with relatives, neighbors, and friends.

If well-aspected, this native experiences benefits from travel, relatives, education, literature or publishing, and friends and associates. You are able to share your ideas and feelings.

Saturn in The Third House

Saturn in the Third House makes you patient, kind, tactful, and serious with a matter-of-fact outlook on life. You have an orderly, methodical mind and you generally prefer to approach situations in a practical manner. You systematically gather information and formulate plans, thoughts, and ideas. Your communications are well thought out and delineated, and you have a tendency to develop not only your thoughts but your approaches to the subject at hand. You view information from a utilitarian perspective, wanting to put to good use your knowledge. With Saturn in this position there is a strong likelihood that you had to overcome obstacles in order to obtain an education or the necessary training to attain job skills.

Your natural inclinations lead you to be cautious in your pursuits, but you are also somewhat restless. Faced with obstacles, you have a tendency to fret, worry and become anxious. But your powers of concentration are strong, and as you learned to overcome any limitations in life, you developed a contemplative, diplomatic nature which allows you strong self-control, reasoning powers, and cognitive abilities. You find that as you mature, your intellect continues to grow and expand, seeking facts, information and knowledge from numerous sources. Part of the limitations and restrictions you faced in early life were due to struggles within the family unit, and discord among siblings or other relatives. There is a good chance that the opportunity for travel hasn't been available, or you are too busy to indulge in travel for anything but business or family obligations.

Your methodical and orderly reasoning ability may lead you to pursue a career in the field of science, math, computer programming or analyst, research, technology, physics, medicine or in a field requiring mechanical ability. You may find that with your strong powers of concentration, you prefer dealing with empirical data rather than abstract theories. Your natural curiosity leads you to develop many interests, many of which are time consuming, but you must guard against your cautious nature making you a procrastinator or indecisive.

If afflicted, this native suffers from numerous problems, loss and sorrows, despondency, pessimism, moodiness, and is narrow-minded, rigid, skeptical, and overly conservative, defensive, and sensitive with feelings of inadequacy. Delays in education, communications including writings, and development of family problems.

Saturn in the Third House grants you a responsible nature that adheres to a thoughtful, persevering, and conscientious pattern of life. If well developed, your intellectual nature inclines you to philosophy, and your written communications reflect a penetrating depth and profound reflections.

Uranus in The Third House

Uranus in the Third House influences your life to be one filled with new places, unusual people and rather out of the ordinary occurrences and experiences. You are highly intuitive, insightful and receptive to your perceptions, senses and feelings. Open to new ideas, your inventive intellect leads you to be unconventional in your thoughts and ideals. More than likely you follow your own lead, unheedful of the normal course of events or the everyday paths followed by others. You may view conformity or even convention as unnecessary crutches used by others seeking the easier, least resistant road to follow. It is as if information and ideas leap into your mind, and others simply don't have the same information available to them. Curiously ingenious, you seek out the extraordinary and profound whether it be ancient and forgotten or new and beyond the perceptions of ordinary man.

It may well be that your inventive nature is of genius proportions, but be that what it may, your mind has a strong scientific bend. Your intellect may lead you to excel in the field of electronics, computers, transportation, technology, astronomy, sociology, or theology. You are drawn to research, investigations, and sudden trips that add information, experiences, and insights into your life. Others find your communications, especially your writing, interesting, informative, original, perceptive, and avant-garde. You are one of those persons capable of pursuing more than one line of action at a time, and to others this may make you appear eccentric or scattered. Needless to say, you are too busy to pay much heed to what others are thinking or doing. But all the same you are friendly and easy going with a sociable, if somewhat detached, air about you. Adaptable and tolerant, you are accepting of others. Unfortunately, your mind set, unconventional thoughts, or at times rebellious nature causes occasional difficulties with family members.

If afflicted, this native is more than a little rebellious, eccentric, headstrong, indifferent, restless, impractical, fidgety, indecisive, and prone to separations from family and to accidents while traveling; public criticism regarding writing, ideas, or projects.

Versatile and creative, you remain forever your own person despite the disapproval of more conventional people. You may discover psychic abilities or healing powers.

Neptune in The Third House

Neptune in the Third House makes you imaginative, fond of travel, and prone to numerous and strange adventures. Then too your interests lead you to unusual studies, philosophies, perceptions and thoughts. You are intuitive and insightful on a psychic level which you may or may not decide to develop. You possess a strong interest in the psychological factors of life, perceiving experiences from an interrelated viewpoint of mind and matter. Your mind may drift from one thought to another as you attempt to envision the meaning of it all, or with your strong spiritual inclination, you may prefer to mediate in order to achieve a higher consciousness. Art and literature are of interest to you, and you love to communicate your ideas, perceptions and visionary insights to others as well. You have been known to either change your name, use nick-names, pseudonyms or an alias.

Depending upon other aspects, Neptune in the Third House influences a person to either be a charming salesperson or a slick con artist. Many journeys are indicated as are difficulties with family members. Unusual occurrences may include strange perceptions and feelings, and out of the ordinary experiences. The ability to plan is either elevated or given to outlining schemes, plots and deceits.

Under affliction, this native is prone to fantasizing and dreaming, can have a morbid or weak nature, suffers from hallucinations, or in some cases depravity, is confused, discontented, indifferent, and vague, and suffers from misunderstandings with relatives.

Your artistic and creative ability are inspiring and reflect your strong idealism and intuition. You are productive, thoughtful and prodigiously insightful.

PLUTO IN THE THIRD HOUSE

Pluto in the Third House endows you with a practical intellect. You desire pertinent information that you can use and lose interest rapidly in subject matter that you perceive to be unnecessary to your efforts. However, with relevant information, you make every attempt to absorb as much as possible. You possess strong opinions and are uninhibited about speaking your mind. Your communications are straight forward, direct and to the point. This directness may put off some people, most especially family members. But others appreciate your intensity, and your drive to express yourself through speaking or writing. You can also be opinionated and are rarely easily swayed or influenced. Chances are, you are the person, through your self-reliance, who is persuading or influencing others.

You are a resourceful person and may find that you have a strong interest in science or scientific research. Then too, you may find research, investigations or solving mysteries intriguing and find yourself drawn into secret affairs as an undercover agent, spy, private investigator, or law enforcement officer. Your excursions and travel may lead you on one adventure or another, often of a secretive, sensitive or highly private nature. Quick to the point, perceptive, and intuitive, you may be inclined to the fields of journalism, psychology, education, or legal affairs.

It is quite possible that you experience numerous changes in your life, some of which are sudden or drastic, and others brought about by family members or your writings. Other obstacles come your way as well, including danger in travel, and you use your practical and resourceful nature to overcome any difficulties. You draw on your strength and will power to make whatever adjustments are necessary in life.

If afflicted, this native is suspicious, obstinate, brooding, defensive, narrow-minded, intolerant, angry to the point of being violent, manipulative and dominating. There is an indication of sorrow through siblings and problems associated with friends, neighbors and associates. Under some aspects this native can become a creative criminal.

You are best known for your creativity and highly personal outlook on the future. Pluto in the Third House leads you to develop your own perspective on life, and you follow through on your ideas with an intensity of purpose. Independent and resourceful, you are your own best counsel, and your self-reliance sees you through any and all endeavors.

PLANETS IN THE FOURTH HOUSE RULED BY CANCER

THE HOUSE OF HOME, HEREDITY AND ACCOMPLISHMENTS

The Sun in the Fourth House grants you an intense pride in your home, heritage, and ethnicity, with strong parental ties. You possess a strong desire to be established and settled in life. Your ambitious and enterprising nature leads you to realize your greatest hopes and wishes. You are fortunate in inheritance and gains associated with your parents. You develop a strong identity and self-respect based on the security you derive from the close personal ties of your home life. You enjoy reflecting on your home life, talking about your family, telling family stories and jokes, and reliving the past through photo albums or home movies. At the same time, you are highly protective of your home and family, not appreciating it when others take advantage of your time or invade your privacy.

This is a good position for gains through property and real estate, and you may decide to pursue a career connected to these aspects of life. Or you may be the adventurous individual who decides to begin a business from your home. Then too, you may discover good fortune in careers connected to natural resources, female consumers, the food industry, decorating, design, or household products. At the same time, your entrepreneur spirit leads you to invest wisely in either real estate or securities in order to provide well for the future of your family. You most desire recognition and approval from the other people in your life, and you thrive on the attentions and affections of your loved ones.

Under affliction, this native develops an early desire to leave home, experiences misfortunes, obstacles, and limitations through the family, home, inheritance, or property, and is basically insecure, fretful, and worrisome.

Well aspected, the Sun in the Fourth House is a good position for honors and fortunate circumstances later in life. There is some indication for an interest in spiritual matters or psychic experiences at or near the home.

You are not only fortunate, but successful in your ambitions. You can expect to enjoy good health in your later years.

337

THE MOON IN THE FOURTH HOUSE

The Moon in the Fourth House makes you not only reflective but receptive of the attitudes of others. You may find that you change residences often during your lifetime, but, be that what it may, you remain protective of your home and family. You possess a strong desire for personal security and a sense of belonging to your home and community. You are charming, intuitive, and popular with friends and family, but others admire you most for your supportive and nurturing nature which leads you to become a caring and resourceful parent. While you may experience mood swings, you retain your perceptions and attitudes which enhance your overall outlook on life. You strive to build security and to provide it for your loved ones. Strongly patriotic, you stay well informed on national events, politics, and state and community affairs. You most desire peace and harmonious situations that provide contentment and balance to family life.

This position of the Moon grants you a sound business ability, and you may find that your prefer being in business for yourself. Your interests lead you to consider careers in the food industry, farming, real estate, household products, or education, history or fields related to heritage. You realize benefits through parents, the family, the home life, or properties. Chances are you are an accomplished collector and this hobby or side-business leads you to fill your home with antiques or other items of interest. Drawn to the water, you may find yourself either living near a body of water or engaged in a water-related business.

Under affliction from other planets, this position of the Moon influences an individual to be self-centered, restless, dissatisfied, unrealistic, moody, and overly protective of self and family. There is an indication of obstacles and problems associated with family; loss from theft or fraud; possibility of poverty and numerous disappointments in life.

If well aspected, this person can expect to lead an independent and successful life receiving honors, position, or inheritance. Assistance from a member of the opposite sex is indicated.

Your strong ability to handle personal finances, your property, and to manage your home life results in a productive, secure life surrounded by family, friends and neighbors.

Mercury in The Fourth House

Mercury in the Fourth House grants you a strong inclination to work out of your home, to change residences often perhaps in connection with your business, and for your life to be anything but routine. This could well be the planetary location of the wanderer, that person who chooses not to establish a permanent home, and whose security is not based on putting down roots. At the same time, you are proud of your family and heritage, and possess a strong love for family members. Chances are you are economical or simply don't need unnecessary possessions in your home life. You overcome any obstacles in life with sheer determination and will power, and base your sense of security on your intellect, abilities, or spirituality. Even so, home life can present cause for concern leading to worries and anxiety, and many of the problems you face in life relate directly to your home or family.

Your curious nature and strong intellect lead you to investigate or study any number of subjects and you may develop an interest in such diverse topics as the natural sciences, ecology, archeology, literature, mining, real estate, antiquity, or education. You may decide to teach, write, become a journalist or musician, or enter politics, your intellectual interests capable of carrying you in any number of directions. Most likely, you seek out others who share your interests in life, and you develop numerous friendships with people living in different localities. Also, you like to collect items of interest including gadgets, electronics, favorite books, stamps, shells or lucky stones.

Under planetary affliction, this individual is high-strung, irritable, restless, inconsistent, and experiences unexpected changes, difficulties, losses, limitations or a lack of opportunity. There is an indication for loss through theft, fraud, or fire.

If well aspected, the Moon in the Fourth House indicates an active, sociable lifestyle, and a person who is popular with family and friends. Unexpected profits from real estate or possessions are indicated as well as opportunities for experiencing success through intellectual pursuits or an inheritance. There is also some indication for unusual perceptions such as psychic experiences.

Mentally active and energetic, you deal rationally with family and with your home life. You home is filled with activity and reflects your interests and pursuits in life.

Venus in The Fourth House

Venus in the Fourth House and you are an optimistically charming person who prefers a harmonious home life and to be surrounded by love, warmth, and acceptance. You have fond memories of your parents and your childhood and strive to create a favorable domestic situation as an adult. Allowed your preferences, you favor filling your home with beautiful and comfortable furnishings for yourself and your family and for entertaining friends. In fact, you may feel so at ease in your home that it requires an effort on your part to go out and socialize. At the same time, your gracious demeanor draws others to you with ease. Then too, you are a bit protective of your personal security and home life, and you find yourself wanting to know people well before allowing them to enter your personal life to become acquainted with the real you and your family.

Your creative artistic flair may lead you to develop an interest in floral arrangements, home furnishings, interior decorating, gardening, design or art, catering, receptionist or hosting, or hotel management. In fact, your sociable nature is conducive to any situation requiring meeting the public or making others feel comfortable and relaxed. Your bearing reflects a quite natural refinement and others consider you knowledgeable and cultured.

When well aspected, Venus in the Fourth House is a fortunate and agreeable position for domestic situations. There is an indication for profits from pensions, investments, property or inheritance. Happiness in marriage may come later in life. Maturity finds you in a peaceful and comfortable situation having realized general success in life.

Under affliction from the placement of other planets, this position of Venus can result in an individual who is extravagant, demanding, dictatorial, jealous, too generous, careless, and who uses poor judgment. This person may experience sudden losses, disappointments or sorrows in life.

Gracious, diplomatic, warm and accepting, you promote harmony wherever you are. Your strong love for your home, community and country are reflected in your general attitudes. You are sensitive to your surroundings and prefer not only a well arranged but a well-organized home, and these tendencies carry over into your personal affairs and your relationships with other people. You are highly receptive and find yourself striving to learn not to be easily influenced by the opinions and desires of others. Your strongest goal in life may be to establish an independent, secure lifestyle while at the same time remaining supportive of your family.

Mars in The Fourth House

Mars in the Fourth House grants an energetic pursuit of owning one's own home and becoming prosperous. Your inherently aggressive nature strives for security, but your forcefulness may make you prone to a disruptive home environment. Because of misunderstandings with your family or relatives you may find yourself relocating away from your immediate family and striving to establish yourself and your home away from your beginnings. You may even decide to remain single, feeling that it is easier to maintain your independence when you are on your own and unencumbered by the responsibility of others. If you do marry, you may find that your strong need to establish control over your personal life may lead you to be dominating over your family and all that goes on in your home. This may result in many contentions, quarrels, unpleasantness and disappointments unless your spouse if very understanding and willing to be submissive to your strong nature.

There is a good chance that you are a self-made person, and you develop an interest in home repairs and hobbies. If it's broken, you are often successful at fixing it yourself, and your mind imagines various ways of improving your home. Changes persist in your home environment including relocations, but you may decide to work from your home. Then too, you may be a military person who expects order and for things to run properly both at home and at work. If you develop an interest in the environment, you want to see it protected, preserved and well maintained. You strive to develop self-control, but this may not deter your forceful nature or strong emotions. Your powerful constitution grants you mental and physical energy even as you mature in age.

Under planetary affliction, this position of Mars influences a person to be quarrelsome, argumentative, disorderly, contentious, belligerent, and who suffers from numerous obstacles, disappointments, strife, and losses through fires, accidents, or theft; health is affected by disposition causing digestion problems. There is an indication for loss through property or investments.

When well-aspected, Mars in the Fourth House influences a person to be energetic, active, forceful and enterprising. You strive to establish a secure home and endeavor to be successful in acquiring personal possessions. Your strong nature and dynamic, energetic attitude sees you through life's obstacles, and your forcefulness overcomes any limitations you face.

JUPITER IN THE FOURTH HOUSE

Jupiter in the Fourth House grants you luck in having a comfortable and peaceful domestic home life. Your security is tied to the harmony you establish in your domestic affairs, and you become devoted to your family and home. You either came from a large family, and enjoyed the influence of your parents, or find yourself surrounded by family members in your adult life. Your restless nature may lead you to relocate, even to a foreign country for awhile, or away from your original beginnings. You are also expansive and most enjoy space to think or dabble in your pastimes. The chances are that you prefer a home that is either roomy, spacious, or set in the country or on a hill with a view of the sky, trees or surrounding area. This tends to satisfy somewhat your need to roam and your expansive nature giving you a feeling of not having limitations placed on your mind or intellect. Your desire for open spaces does make you prone to traveling in order to experience other places or simply to enjoy the open road. You find yourself steering clear of obstacles, limitations and restrictions on your personal freedoms, thoughts or ideas preferring the companionship of others who are open and accepting. You desire the companionship of people who like peaceful and harmonious situations, and you really have no appreciation for what you see as unnecessary discord or antagonism. You have little patience with trouble makers who seem to like to stir up problems and bad feelings.

You may find that your luck carries over to good fortune in dealings with real estate, property or possessions. You either inherit property or possessions, or a strong sense of security from your family. Then too your spiritualism may be strongly connected to what you learned from family members in your early life.

If afflicted, this individual experiences problems with family members who cause limitations, is at times extravagant and greedy but overgenerous with immediate family members, and suffers from loss by fire, lawsuits, property, inheritance, or difficulties with the law.

Jupiter in the Fourth House, when well aspected, brings good fortune and an easy, comfortable life with success and position in the latter life, and luck in the city, state or country of your birth.

You enjoy success in your endeavors and pursuits, and your generous, outgoing personality promises acceptance and popularity with all those who meet and get to know you. You face obstacles optimistically, intuitively feeling that the chances are good your natural luck will pull you through.

SATURN IN THE FOURTH HOUSE

Saturn in the Fourth House leads you to be not only self-disciplined but the disciplinarian of your household. You prefer to set standards for your home life and conduct and to establish and adhere to a regularity of routine. Your ability to accept responsibilities perhaps lead to you being handed many of the household chores as a child, and this led to a tendency to be capable and efficient in household management. You may not be considered overly demonstrative with your feelings, but you are caring, concerned and devoted even to the extent of being self-sacrificing when necessary. While there are others who can't be inconvenienced, you are available for the care of a family member. Conservative, reserved and cautious, you place your trust in solid, tangible possessions, property and investments. Self-restraint may lead you to also be cautious of change, much of which you perceive as unnecessary. If the circumstances calls for it, you can be somewhat manipulative in your effort to maintain control over your situation.

You apply the same tenacity to facing obstacles and difficulties, and hard work and burdensome responsibilities don't deter you from you drive to acquire a secure home and possessions. There is the possibility of the early loss of a parent, difficulties with property, and dissatisfaction with the home life. Your anxieties about procuring a home and proper security for your latter years can lead to excessive worries which cause digestion problems or nervous disorders. You take your mind off your problems by developing hobbies and interests such as genealogy, antiques, restoring furniture, and collecting old letters and family photos.

Under planetary affliction this individual can be controlling, over sensitive, emotional but unable to express feelings, neurotic, dogmatic, overly fearful of the future or any change, and misfortune in the home town with separation from family. When well aspected, this native benefits from property, businesses related to property, farming, ranching, natural resources, oil or mining.

Life teaches you to be self-reliant and independent, and you develop your abilities through self-discipline, self-control and restraint placing self imposed limitations on yourself as you strive to acquire the necessary security to feel successful. You most desire to be recognized and admired by your family for your efforts. You discover a talent for dealing with property and real estate.

URANUS IN THE FOURTH HOUSE

With Uranus in the Fourth House the chances are good that you had an out-of-the ordinary childhood filled with extraordinary experiences. As an adult, you are free roaming and independent, but still you do have a strong preference for having others in your life. There is an indication for much change in your life, including partners, homes, and careers. While it would be nice to have a well-established home or home base, it isn't a necessity for you to feel secure. You are quite capable of taking care of yourself, and your inclinations lead you on a road of experiences and encounters with any number of people. Your immediate family members don't always understand your decisions, but while others attempt to tie you down to an ordinary, routine lifestyle, you persist in living your life your way. Limitations and restrictions may offend you, and while you appreciate the opinions of others, their intentions can feel like ropes binding you down.

You find yourself drawn to unusual, new or innovative things, people and ideas. Your interests include a fancy for gadgets, electronics, cars, motorcycles, bikes, or perhaps a jet ski, boat, or surfboard. Anything that excites and challenges the mind and that part of your personality which wants to go just one more step beyond. Or you could develop a preference for an alternative lifestyle experimenting with back-to-nature ideas, communes, or backpacking across America. That's not to say that you always land on your feet, but alternating circumstances, ups and downs, rags to riches, and moving from one uncertain predicament to another doesn't erase your curiosity about what could happen next.

Planetary afflictions would quite possibly cause misfortune through home, estrangement from family, loss of property or inheritance, a brush with poverty; there is danger of accidents, violence, or loss through theft, deceit, vandalism, floods, hurricanes, earthquakes or other natural disasters; you will have impulsive, rash behavior, poor judgment and problems with the law.

Your life is full of good times and bad times, and you become an adroit story teller, relating your many experiences in life to others. You are either a person who entertains other with ease, keeping them spellbound with your latest adventure, or you choose to be a loner in the crowd, keeping your desires and preferences to yourself. Either way, other people seek you out to explain the nature of life to them, for surely someone as interesting as you has plenty of answers.

Neptune in The Fourth House

Neptune in the Fourth House indicates relocations or changes in the domestic affairs. You may dream and fantasize about the perfect, ideal home and family situation with the best of intentions. Your romantic heart craves the stability of a happy family and home. Your more private nature, however, shields your real desires from others, and you may find yourself keeping secret many of the events or happenings that evolve through circumstances in your home. Due to the confidential nature of either your problems or the problems of your family, you are not prone to disclose family information to others. This may make it seem difficult to build close friendships as you are somewhat cautious or distrustful of becoming too close to people outside your family. Even with understanding and accepting people, you find it best to keep some aspects of your home life private. All the same, with family members you build strong and lasting emotional ties.

You may have a strong preference for living near the water, whether it be an ocean, lake or river. And your inclinations lead you to develop an interest in art, music or both, and an enjoyment of travel. Compassionate and caring, you are compelled to help others and this may lead you to work with the disabled or with others in an institutional setting. You may enjoy entertaining or prefer to keep your own company, but either way your flights of fancy and dreamy moods make you a delightful companion when you seek others out. Sensitive, you may develop psychic abilities.

Under planetary afflictions this individual may experience loss through theft, fraud, scams or misfortune and misunderstandings through the family; nervous disorders may effect the health; unusual living conditions; and loss through real estate. However, when well aspected, this person enjoys numerous benefits from family, personal property, and investments.

When well developed, this individual may find inner peace and security after extended traveling or seeing the world. In fact, you may decide to live far from your beginnings. In other circumstances, staying in one place produces the same benefits. Whichever the case may be, once you find your way in the world, you become determined to turn your dreams into reality. You may turn your deepest fears and anxieties into expectations for a secure and happy future. Your spirituality sees you successfully through life and you are quite capable of handling whatever life sends you way.

PLUTO IN THE FOURTH HOUSE

Pluto in the Fourth House and you most desire privacy from prying eyes. You may decide to tuck your home out of sight behind trees or shrubs or at the end of a winding driveway. That not being the case, you will insure privacy and security inside your home. Your home and family are extremely important to you, and you want to both provide well and to protect your loved ones and your possessions. You are especially intense and may have a strong tendency to oversee the affairs of the household, at times being overbearing or somewhat dominating. There is strong indications for you to experience changes in your home life. Your outlook on life may include a questioning of the accepted values of society, and you may strive to develop your own personal values based on your perceptions.

You possess an interest in subjects pertaining to nature and the Earth. This may lead you to study science or to develop hobbies associated with the outdoors. Your inclinations may lead you to a career in geology, mining, exploring, research, archeology, ecology, ranching or farming, real estate, minerals or gems. If not a profession, your interests will develop into time consuming hobbies, and you find yourself spending countless hours locating and researching information. You may collect rocks, artifacts, fossils, petrified wood, or other examples of the process of nature at work.

Under affliction, this native experiences profound changes in the home, sorrow from death of parent, an unusual childhood, family upsets, or strict, overbearing parents, and may become rebellious.

You are a responsible person with a strong interest in your family and your home life. Devoted, you can be self-sacrificing and supportive of others who may depend on you. You can expect a major transformation developing sometime between youth and the latter years which you may bring about yourself. There is an indication for success in your endeavors.

PLANETS IN THE FIFTH HOUSE RULED BY LEO

THE HOUSE OF CREATIVITY AND LOVE

The Sun in the Fifth House of creativity produces a person who effortlessly strives to magnetize, radiating a personal essence that draws attention. You are happiest when you are center stage, and having an abundance of energy and a great potential for creativity, you may just succeed at this endeavor in the arts, music, acting, or in sports. If life doesn't take you in that direction, you find yourself the center of the crowd, entertaining and projecting your best self to others. You strive to be a leader and to influence others. Highly self-aware and filled with self-confidence, you express yourself fluently, with a flair for just the right words or witty saying. You possess a natural appreciation for enjoying life, pleasures, fun, and good times in the company of others. You desire to be admired, appreciated, and recognized by others. All of this comes to you with little or no effort, and your greatest obstacle in life is overcoming self-pride. If not careful, you come to expect this adulation and lazily choose not to develop deeper cognitive abilities, thinking that all in life will come easily to you. There is a possibility that your perceptions are intensely personal, and if situations don't go your way, you simply imply that wasn't what you really wanted anyway.

Active, well liked, creative and self-indulgent, you have a natural appeal with the opposite sex and may enjoy any number of love affairs. You may find financial success in a business you developed from a hobby, through creative expressions in art or music, sports, executive positions, teaching, lecturing, consulting, investments, speculation, amusements, pleasures, or the entertainment industry. You are at ease with children and are fond of them, but chances are you will have a small family. Honest, with a strong sense of honor, at some time in life, you may decide to develop your spirituality. Your greatest obstacles are overcoming your self-illusions and developing the ability to share your feelings and emotions with your loved ones. Strong-willed and powerful, you have a tendency to dominate others in your life.

Under planetary afflictions, this individual is arrogant, prideful, self-centered, dominating, overbearing, jealous, egotistical, dishonest, pleasure-seeking and can exploit others or be an exhibitionist. Loss is indicated through speculation or dishonesty, pride brings troubles with love affairs, and problems with children. If well aspected, you are an honorable person who attains achievement of your endeavors and enjoys successful relationships.

346

THE MOON IN THE FIFTH HOUSE

The Moon in the Fifth House inclines you to be a romantic at heart with a tendency to create your own self-image and an image you project to the world. Your strong emotions may lead you through a number of romantic affairs, and at times you are rather impulsive in your pursuit of love, pleasure, and fun. Your creativity can grant you a dramatic flair and an exciting lifestyle which may make you the center of attention. A love affair or a successful endeavor may well bring you public recognition. Your romantic liaisons may also bring you criticism from your family who at times attempt to influence your choices.

You also possess a natural artistic flair, but the productivity of your artistic talents may depend to a large degree on your moods and temperament. And with your innately pleasure-seeking temperament, you may very well develop an interest in businesses dealing with amusements, resorts, the entertainment of adults or children, or other creative enterprises center around recreation, hobbies and pastimes. You may also find pleasure in speculative ventures and in gambling with changing luck.

You may find that you have to work at finding or creating a balance in life between emotions and your intellect. Your mind may tell you one thing, and your heart another. Disappointments in life may center around finding love with a person who is poorly suited for you. In this situation, you must guard against becoming disappointed to the point of despondency which would change you from being a loving person to one who shuts down the emotions and becomes cold and indifferent.

With planetary afflictions, this individual is prone to being overly protective, possessive, clinging, dependent, and suffers loss through gambling and speculation, or through love affairs and children. If well aspected, this position is indicative of public success as either a child or an adult.

You are fond of children and may decide to have several or even to adopt. You experience any number of changes in all aspects of your life.

Mercury in The Fifth House

Mercury in the Fifth House and you are a person who is intellectually inclined. You gather information and transform it into creative concepts which you express dramatically well either verbally, in print, or artistically. You enjoy stimulating change whether it be going to new places, meeting interesting people, or exchanging ideas with other well informed people. You are drawn to people who attract your intellectual interest, and even lovers must prove their mental merit. You possess a strong fondness for pleasurable activities, fun and games, and time spent with the opposite sex. Then too, your competitive nature may lead you to excel at games requiring mental acuity such as chess, word games, or competing against the computer. You are fond of children, but depending upon your lifestyle, you may or may not decide to have children of your own. You are a person who has experienced his or her full share of worries, anxieties, and perhaps sorrow through family.

You are at home in the world of ideas and may find success in fields such as teaching, lecturing, writing, acting, travel, entertainment, computer graphics, or as a critic or agent in the arts, literature, movies, or theater. As a journalist you show an active interest in the lives of public personalities. Then too, you communicate well with the public, and this ability could lead you in any number of directions. Your ideas are well thought out, but you are at times overly opinionated. If well aspected, there is an indication for luck in speculative ventures.

With planetary affliction, this individual is conceited, opinionated, overly critical, nervous, and experiences problems with love affairs through scandal, divorce, estrangement, and lawsuits. There is a strong indication for losses through speculative investments. When well aspected, Mercury in the Fifth House is strongly indicative of success in your personal and professional life, as well as gains realized through investments, entertainment or travel.

You are a leader in thoughts and concepts, and your intellect evolves with your many interests. You find enjoyment in stimulating the mental processes of others including children and young adults, and education is important to you. Your emotions are processed through your mind, but you also develop a strong affections for the loved ones in your life. It may be that your creativity brings you success through your prolific ideas and concepts and through your ability to express these ideas well.

Venus in The Fifth House

Venus in the Fifth House grants you a deep love for life and a romantic desire to fulfill yourself emotionally. Optimistic and sociable, you possess a positive personal charisma that charms, inspires and persuades others. Your social life would tire a less energetic person, and you move through love affairs with the grace of youth. Affable and refined, you develop a flair for a distinctive personal style that naturally draws attention and admiration. Then you expertly handle this approbation with a diplomatic nonchalance. You find success in your endeavors through social and productive relationships with others, whether friends, associates or lovers. You are fond of amusing pastimes and pleasures, finding delight in entertaining, the arts or the theater.

Creative with perhaps an artistic talent, you find good fortune in matters related to art, or, if well aspected, in investment, speculation, real estate or property ownership, business, acting, music, activities related to children such as education or amusements, parks or resorts. You are, of course, a natural at teaching bringing the gift of inspiring and delighting young minds by holding the attention of pupils with your sincere and fun-loving ways. In your personal life, you find that you are most happy when in love and have a strong desire for spouse, children, home and family. Chances are, your children become the highlight of your life bringing pleasure, joy, and pride through their merits and accomplishments. Venus is the Fifth House is indicative of good fortune and comfort through your children.

If the planets in the chart are under afflictions, this individual is careless, rash, impulsive, unconventional, indecisive, indiscriminate, suffers poor health through over indulgence of pleasure such as of food, drink or habit forming substances or other addictive activities. There is an indication for problems associated with the opposite sex, romantic affairs, children or investments. Then again, this person may possess all the natural inclinations and traits of this position, but must work harder to develop positive traits and to achieve through personal endeavors.

You possess the natural attributes necessary for being in the spot-light, and you excel at drawing attention to yourself through not only your charm but your creative talents as well. Your greatest goal in life should be to develop your talents and creativity in positive and beneficial ways. This position of Venus favors success in your endeavors and especially in love, romance, marriage and children.

MARS IN THE FIFTH HOUSE

With Mars in the Fifth House you have created yourself through your own energy, will power, and assertiveness. You pursue all aspects of life vigorously whether it be serious acquisitions or games, pleasure, love or sex. You find all of life challenging and you attack it with all out forcefulness. You excel at competitions in all aspects of life, but most especially are drawn to athletic or strenuous endeavors. For example, your nature draws you to participate in sports, racing, or any activity offering the opportunity to win, and you most definitely compete with winning in mind. In both your personal and professional life, you strive for victory and that includes socially and with love. Whatever aspect of life you are engaged in, you may find yourself turning it into a competition. All the same, you exhibit your own personal creative style which is more than likely that of the fearless, competent and well-prepared warrior than the aggressive caveman.

You strive to create your own empire, and once it is built, you protect it with all you might. In many instances, you are a natural leader, displaying all your abilities and inspiring others to follow your directions. Your internal, energetic fire propels you to quick, decisive action, but at times you are rash and impulsive. But in whatever you do, you remain uninhibited and with little fear of failure. You must guard against being carried away by your emotions, your ardent passions, or any over indulgence in pleasures which can quite easily result in financial or social problems and perhaps even physical injury.

With planetary afflictions, this position of Mars is indicative of an individual who is egotistical, quarrelsome, domineering, a bad loser, foolhardy, fickled, overly rash, impulsive, reckless and extravagant. This person may experience problems, even disgrace, due to a love affair. There is an indication for loss through speculation, gambling, and pleasures-seeking, and problems associated with the children. When well aspected, this native is an inspiring and magnetic leader in his or her community and enjoys success in professional endeavors and investments.

You are a sociable individual who enjoys others and who strives to be admired and appreciated. You are fond of children and naturally become the disciplinarian of your home. This is a favorable position for Mars, granting you the ability to face life with fortitude and the tenacity to overcome any and all obstacles. While you focus and direct your enormous energies into creative pursuits, you find yourself also developing within yourself the necessary self control for positive results.

JUPITER IN THE FIFTH HOUSE

Jupiter in the Fifth House grants you a strong appreciation of grandeur, a fondness for children, and an appreciation of all types of fun, recreation, pleasure and amusements. Your expansive nature draws you to various types of sports as well as social events, community affairs, and cultural attractions. Your self-assurance and happy-go-lucky attitude promotes your creative streak in both your social and professional life. You can be forcefully direct and outspoken when necessary, but chances are you are sensuous and caring in love. You explore life and all its opportunities, taking great satisfaction in meeting new people, making friends, and enjoying the companionship of others, especially new romantic liaisons.

You come to expect your natural good luck to hold true in all areas of life, and this quite possibly is the case in your personal life, business, investments, speculations and even with gambling. You more than likely are a productive person who turns opportunities into realities. You may find that you enjoy working with children and become a teacher or counselor, or your life may lead you to become involved in a business associated with schools, entertainment, finances, or organizing public or social functions. Then too, you may become the self-made entrepreneur, or it is quite possible that your interest in society or spiritualism leads you to enter politics or an area of religion. Your good luck carries over into your family life, and you may find that your children are also fortunate and dutiful bringing you additional happiness and comfort.

Under planetary affliction, the luck of this native holds, however there is an indication for it to be modified with additional obstacles and problems causing losses especially in speculative ventures. This person may strive to gain through love affairs, and is indiscreet about relationships with the opposite sex. If well aspected, success and good fortune can be expected through love affairs.

Acceptance and popularity appears to come to you with little effort on your part as you are a good natured and well meaning individual who expresses sincere concern for others. You like the adulation, but then who wouldn't? Once settled in life, you are happy with your spouse, and your family may be large with a number of children all of whom love and respect you. Jupiter in the Fifth House grants you good fortune and luck.

SATURN IN THE FIFTH HOUSE

Saturn in the Fifth House inclines this individual to experience any number of obstacles and problems especially with love affairs. Perhaps this is because of your strict sense of self-discipline and your serious nature. You desire most to find respect, understanding and appreciation for your sincere, and well meaning efforts. You respect others and you would like to receive that respect in return. The chances are that your cautious, earnest nature prevents you from taking a chance on love. You much prefer to patiently wait for that perfect lover of your hopes and desires, and preferably that person will measure up on your list of pros and cons. The love of your life may be an older person who you respect. You are somewhat reserved about pleasure and having fun, perhaps feeling that those pursuits are too extravagant or a waste of time. That's not to say that you don't enjoy life, because you do--it's simply that you take it a bit more seriously than many people. You may follow sports, for example, gathering information on players, games, wins and losses. The chances are you are a person who firmly believes children should be seen but not heard.

Your creativity is expressed in serious form as well with a preference for good investments in art and music. Responsible and dutiful, you make an adroit manager or agent in the entertainment industry, and excel at finances, investments, politics, law, science, or as an administrator of an institution, school, or business. Efficient and reliable, you are a decision maker with executive ability. In life you have come to expect obstacles and you strive to overcome them through your own merits and tenacity.

If afflicted, this individual came be shy, timid, or a reticent person with an inclination to worry or be anxious. There is an indication for loss through speculation, the danger of accidents, and poor health related to nervous disorders or complications with the heart, and disappointments in romance. If well aspected, Saturn in the Fifth House grants favor in investments in property, real estate, or mining ventures.

You have a tendency to view life as an opportunity, and in all areas of life you gauge what those opportunities are. Your romantic affairs may be seen from the viewpoint of whether they are socially or in some other way advantageous to you. Or, if you are spiritually inclined, you may be drawn to a religious study or to marriage with a minister. Whatever the case may be, you are conscious of your duties and responsibilities and are considered dependable and trustworthy.

URANUS IN THE FIFTH HOUSE

With Uranus in the Fifth House, you are prone to being uniquely individualistic, and this carries over into your relationships and romantic affairs as well. Highly self-aware, you realize that life is a process of change, development, modification and inevitable transformation. Your likes, dislikes and personal preferences change as well, and you have a subtle understanding that what you like now may not be what you desire in the future. Flexible and accepting of others, you are susceptible to sudden romantic liaisons and infatuations which may end as abruptly as they began. You are wonderfully romantic, but find yourself drawn to others who excite your creativity and imagination. This heightens your attraction to people who are distinctly unusual and strong characters either in personality, lifestyle, fashion, or ideology. The run of the mill person fails to catch or hold your attention. Unconventional and impulsive, you experience any number of bizarre, secret, strange or out of the ordinary love affairs. The idea of marriage fascinates you, and you become engaged more than once with the situation changing. Even so, you make every attempt to remain on friendly terms or in touch with former lovers. Marriage must promise to provide space, equality, freedom and friendship before you become totally accepting of the idea.

The greatest love in your life may be your liberty and personal freedom of expression. You flaunt and display your creativity, boldly challenging the world to take notice. Your interests and pastimes take you in any number of directions, and you are prone to original diversions, unusual distractions, and daring pleasures. Highly inventive, you are prone to experimentation and novelty. Chances are you are not a stranger to scandal, which you don't necessarily enjoy, but which you assume can't be avoided. You may be attracted to gambling, speculation, or risks or chances, but this is not a good position for such activities. Your children may be unaccepting of you or you may not understand them. For whatever reason, problems, estrangement, or separation may result with your children along with difficulties in your domestic situation.

Under planetary afflictions, this individual exhibits anti-social behavior, is rebellious, reckless, irritable, impatient, abrupt, detached, and aloof who has disdain for convention or the ordinary; children are different in some manner. When well aspected, the children are creative and gifted.

Your individualism may lead you to have little patience with the niceties of social conventions in that you prefer to be accepted based on your own merit, just as you are.

Neptune in The Fifth House

Neptune in the Fifth House and you are an illusory personality in that you may prefer fantasy to reality. Romantic with insightful creativity, you are drawn to all expressions of drama. The movies, theaters, dinner clubs, comedy clubs, casinos acts, or any other form of entertainment offering the projection of illusions, fantasy, or a surreal non-reality compels your attention. Besides show business, your own creativity may be expressed in art, music, photography, or even in financial affairs. This is considered a fortunate position for actors, entertainers, musicians, or painters, or any endeavor in which images are used to portray life. You have a tendency to instill fantasy and dreams into your love life as well, transforming lovemaking into a drama of sensuality. Idealistic about love, you find yourself moving through a number of disappointments, and unusual or chaotic experiences. You have a wonderfully open, receptive and innocent nature that accepts others with high expectations of sharing, receiving and giving. Therefore, you give and give and give only to find that it seems that others are always on the receiving or taking end of the relationship. No matter the disappointments in life, you have a tendency to stick to your romantic notions and dreams that an individual will come along who is honest, caring, generous, sincere, creative enlightening, and out of the ordinary. You may regret your mistakes in love, or you may consider your experiences a growth and learning process. If life becomes too harsh or realistic, it may be that you have to guard against isolating yourself, or shutting yourself away from the world, even becoming celibate, in your efforts to avoid any additional mishaps or disappointments. You are idealistic about your children as well, and chances are they will be highly sensitive, intuitive and creative individuals. You find that you are as giving in your relationship with your children as you are in all areas of your life, and you must guard against spoiling them by being overly generous.

Planetary afflictions indicate a person who is pleasure seeking and vulnerable to losses through gambling, speculation, deceits, or disloyalty as well as experiencing trouble with unfaithfulness and confusion in love affairs; illicit love affairs or with a married person; and children who are in some way unusual. If well aspected, the individual is assisted in life by a benefactor or influential person perhaps of the opposite sex. Success in investments is indicated either in the petroleum industry, shipping, or through businesses associated with water.

You are sensitive to the influences of life and are highly tolerant and compassionate of others. Ideally, you feel the world would be a better place if others were more concerned with the welfare of others. You may discover that chance meetings with other people bring you opportunities.

Pluto in The Fifth House

Pluto in the Fifth House promises a person who transforms creativity into passions whether in art or in love. You are the born risk taker whether it be in emotions or in business. You have realized profits through taking that daring chance that others would back away from. Romance for you centers on eroticism which excites your innate desires for heightened, intense sensuality. You have a strong tendency to follow your impulses and flashes of intuition which adds a flavor of excitement to your endeavors. You may for the most part be uninhibited about spending money on unnecessary expenditures or for pure pleasure and delight. Perhaps you feel that money can be replaced, but the chance for new experiences must be acted on before the opportunity is lost. At the same time, you have a powerful and intense pride that is projected into your life in displays of competence, capability, and a practical acceptance of responsibilities. This doesn't preclude you from following your desires, and you may be overly tempted to gamble, speculate or invest in get rich quick schemes. You find balance and harmony in life through your creative expressions, but you also have a strong tendency to maintain control of your life by doing things your way, following your plans and under your direction.

Under planetary affliction, this individual is overly self-aware, severe, resentful, dominating, possessive, obsessed with pleasure and addicted to sex; indications for associations with organized crime, illegal forms of recreation, and loss through gambling and speculation. When well aspected, this native pursues creative outlets through art or dancing, or strives to become well developed through spirituality. This placement of Pluto grants a strong indication for your children to be creative and talented.

Intensely creative, you strive to be a person of your own making. Your sense of independence of thought and movement is important to you. Numerous changes may influence your life.

PLANETS ARE THE DAUGHTERS OF THE SUN BY SCIENCE, PAIN, LOVE, OR BY DEATH

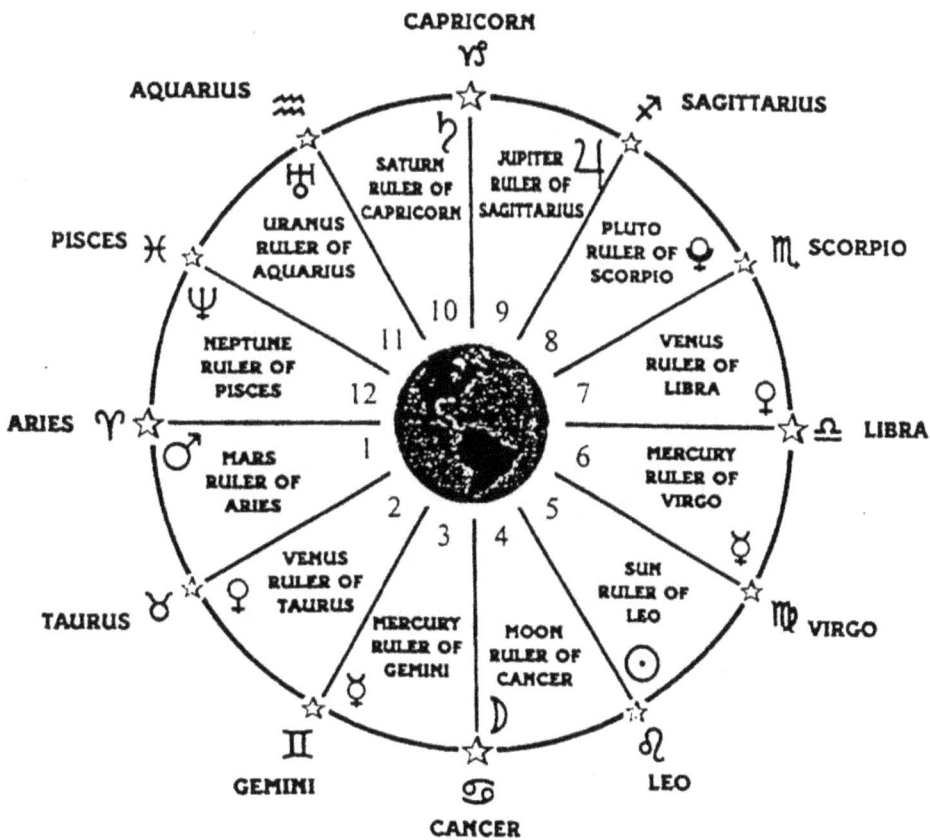

CAPRICORN
♑

AQUARIUS ♒   SAGITTARIUS ♐

SATURN RULER OF CAPRICORN

JUPITER RULER OF SAGITTARIUS

URANUS RULER OF AQUARIUS

PLUTO RULER OF SCORPIO

♏ SCORPIO

PISCES ♓

NEPTUNE RULER OF PISCES

VENUS RULER OF LIBRA

10 9
11   8
12   7
1   6
2   5
3   4

ARIES ♈

MARS RULER OF ARIES

♎ LIBRA

MERCURY RULER OF VIRGO

VENUS RULER OF TAURUS

SUN RULER OF LEO

♍ VIRGO

TAURUS ♉

MERCURY RULER OF GEMINI

MOON RULER OF CANCER

♊   ♌
GEMINI   LEO

♋
CANCER

355

Planets in The Sixth House Ruled by Virgo

The House of Work, Service and Health

With the Sun in the Sixth House your self esteem is strongly tied to your career. You are a faithful, conscientious, capable and productive worker who applies your vitality and talents to the tasks at hand. Detail oriented, you strive to perfect your work skills whether you are the executive in charge or the employee performing the actual work. You take a great deal of pride in a job well done and this is exhibited in your orderly, well organized and meticulous methods and procedures. You possess a strong determination to succeed at your efforts and to be recognized for your zealous efforts. You also apply this same determination to problem solving and to making decisive judgments which produces effective results.

This placement of the Sun in the Sixth House is indicative of health related problems. It is important for person with this placement to develop a health regime including diet and exercise. Finding time for mental relaxation is also important because it takes the mind off daily worries and anxieties related to work. Reducing stress and striving to create balance, harmony and a positive outlook on life promotes good health as well as a healthy attitude. Remember to make every attempt to be aware of and to bring your overly perfectionist compulsions under control. Physical fitness also augments mental relaxation as does pleasurable experiences.

Under affliction, this individual is overly critical, defensive, nervous and anxious suffering from emotional disorders and from a weakened health system that produces susceptibility to contagious diseases and poor recuperative abilities. If well aspected, the individual protects the health through nutrition, exercise, rest and relaxation, self-awareness and education which promotes good health and the general welfare.

You are especially successful at endeavors related to service to others, worthwhile humanitarian causes, or in work that benefits others such as medicine, counseling, or promoting employee benefits. You strive to achieve recognition and distinction in your work and service to others.

THE MOON IN THE SIXTH HOUSE

The Moon in the Sixth House is reflective of changes in occupations, goals and direction. You are a considerate, hard working individual with the ability to turn personal effort into practical results. You seek to find that area of life offering an occupation that is not only of service to others but which is also of interest to you in order to feel fulfilled and worthwhile. You want to enjoy you career. This results in you trying on a number of hats, obtaining different training or skills, and experimenting in life until you find a niche which you instinctively feel was made for you. You have a natural inclination to protect, nourish and take care of others in some way. This may lead you to seek a career in the food or beverage industry or catering, health or medicine, sanitation, social work, counseling, or civil service. You are also fond of animals and nature and may prefer to work in some area related to pets or the out of doors. You possess a strong domestic nature and enjoy the preparation of food, home improvements, and beautifying your surroundings.

You are observant and analytical and spend time reflecting on your experiences. You can be a bit self-critical which can cause anxieties and nervousness. In fact, your self-analysis can result in psychosomatic health related problems. You may find that work-related stress results in stomach problems or indigestion. Mental relaxation, a well-balanced diet, an exercise program, and stress reducing activities promotes good health for you. Peaceful and harmonious settings and pleasant interactions with others also takes your mind off your personal problems.

Under planetary affliction, this individual is highly nervous, defensive, overly critical, grasping, indecisive, changeable, clinging and dependent on others; there is an indication for poor health related to nervous disorders, stomach, lungs, headaches, and poor circulation; trouble through dishonesty and disloyalty from employees, colleagues, associates. If well aspected, this person enjoys good health as well a gains through the career.

Your personal habits, lifestyle, and career undergo several changes that are at times reflective of your moods. You remain, however, intuitive, imaginative and creative with a dramatic flair for life.

MERCURY IN THE SIXTH HOUSE

Mercury in the Sixth House of work, service and health, finds a person with a practical mind who is an analytical and critical thinker. You apply yourself to all you do in a methodical, well organized manner, wanting to produce the best results possible in any situation. It may well be that you are never quite satisfied with your own results and that you continually attempt to maintain what you perceive as perfection. You strongly prefer that your work and your personal life run on a well programmed routine that best allows for efficiency and productivity. Somewhat reserved, you observe all that goes on around you, detecting the necessary details and mentally processing them. You are drawn to mental work as you actually find an intrinsic reward in putting to use your intellectual and cognitive abilities. The areas of health, diet, hygiene, education, communications, medicine, literature, writing, chemistry, engineering, science, technology, electronics or any field requiring detailed work, expertise, or advanced training is of interest to you. An excellent planner, you are very suitable for any number of positions in the world of business or higher finance.

A diligent and hard worker, you are the person who is periodically guilty of overworking thus taxing your mental and nervous energies. You are prone to stress brought on by either working or worrying too much. If you are obsessed with details and perfection, wanting everything to fall into place in a systematic and orderly manner, it may be that you are never quite satisfied with your performance. You forever strive to do even better, to produce even more efficient and productive results. This can very easily eventually wear on you resulting in health problems connected to anxiety, headaches, stomach problems, or despondency and depression. You benefit from stress reducing activities, a healthy diet, and an exercise program that provides not only enjoyment but which serves to add balance to your life.

Under planetary afflictions, this individual is nonproductive, lazy, worries too much, irritable, and is mentally unstimulated. Poor health related to the nervous system, excitability, headaches, and stomach disorders are indicated. Well aspect, Mercury in the Sixth House indicates profits through mental work, but concern about either your health problems or the health of someone else in your life.

A prodigious and productive worker, your analytical mind combined with your many other favorable characteristics can produce favorable results in any and all aspects of your life.

VENUS IN THE SIXTH HOUSE

Venus in the Sixth House and you are a delightfully refined person with exquisite taste and a creatively artistic flair. This is a favorable position for Venus for work and health. You like to feel of service to others with a strong preference for harmonious relationships with colleagues, associates, the boss, or with employees. You are drawn to your work, finding enjoyment, pleasure and fulfillment out of any job that offers you the opportunity to do what you love and find pleasant. Diplomatic and congenial, most generally, you prefer work that allows you to come in direct contact with other people or the public. You do well in a position in the fields of art, appraising, or any business related to the female consumer such as cosmetics, fashions, or decorating. Then too, with your pleasant, tactful and charming personality combined with your compassionate nature, you feel fulfilled when helping others, and you may gain a personal feeling of satisfaction by working in the areas of counseling, teaching, mediating, arbitrating, personnel, public relations, social work or in the health profession. You have a strong inclination to augment beauty, excellence, and high standards in all areas of your life and are constructively discriminating and critical of foods, beverages, and other products. You can discern those products with the best ingredients, quality, workmanship, or style. Almost as if subconsciously you are instantly repelled by physical labor or work requiring you to get your hands or clothing dirty. You are most likely genuinely enchanted by beautiful surroundings, attractive fashions and styles, and nature with a love for small animals and pets.

With planetary afflictions, this position of Venus can produce a tendency for the individual to be overly indulgent in food, beverages or pleasures with a lazy attitude toward work or responsibilities. There may be health problems resulting from weight problems, rashes or irritations of the skin, or alcohol or drug use. When well aspected, there is an indication for gains through work associated with women.

Venus in the Sixth House is a strong indication of discovering romance through your work situation. Good health is indicated when the individual takes care of his or her health and uses discretion in regards to proper nutrition, refraining from excesses in food, drinks, and other indulgences. You do well in circumstances where beauty, comfort, refined taste, and value are expected and encouraged.

359

Mars in The Sixth House

With Mars in the Sixth House you are boldly unafraid of hard work, demanding positions, physical labor or manual jobs requiring using tools, equipment, or instruments. Energetic and assertive, you strive to accomplish your tasks. You are a productive, diligent worker with an interest in both increasing and improving your knowledge and skills. You are active and enthusiastic in your endeavors with an independent nature that perhaps leads you to prefer to work alone on projects of your own design or undertaking, to direct the work at hand, or to look for ways to initiate new methods. You drive yourself to succeed and excel, and others may find it difficult to keep up with the pace you set. It may be that you are the natural athlete who enters professional sports. You can be sociable and congenial, but at work you can also be demanding that others perform at their best. Then too, somewhat temperamental, you may feel that you know how best to do the job at hand, disliking criticism or directions from others. This may result in arguments, quarrels and disputes with co-workers or employees. This position of Mars is also indicative of losses and thefts associated with the job or of colleagues or employees taking advantage of you in some way. This is a good location of Mars for the military, civil service, workers unions, or for positions in the fields of welding, engineering, machinery or mechanics, heavy equipment, teaching, or surgery. You either want to be your own boss and self-employed, or you prefer to leave the administrative duties to someone else while you devote your energies to completing the job. Healthy and vigorous, you may find that your health problems are related to injuries, burns, and accidents caused by overwork, impulsiveness, or carelessness on the job. Some form of surgery is indicated.

Under planetary afflictions, this native is argumentative, intolerant, and abrupt, indiscreet, and extravagant with an inclination for work related problems caused by disputes and quarrels. There is an indication for inflammatory illnesses, accidents, injuries, surgeries, and danger through physical activity, large animals, theft, poisoning, foul play, or surgeries.

Your abundant energy and enthusiasm lead you to enjoy an active life filled with work, play and leisure activities. Your biggest problem may be your tendency to do too much and too work too hard. You must strive to control your impulsive nature and your physical body and to exercise caution in your daily life in order to prevent unnecessary accidents or injuries.

JUPITER IN THE SIXTH HOUSE

Jupiter in the Sixth House and you are congenial, cheerful, easy-going, and enjoy good luck in work related matters. Although you may not be drawn to overly detailed work, you are well organized and capable of establishing a systematic approach to your duties. Your leadership abilities allow you to organize workers to complete the project at hand. Your strong points are your generous, compassionate, and caring nature that instills in others a wish to settle disputes and to get along in a harmonious manner. You are well liked and respected for your loyal service and devotion on the job, and you intuitively know how to diffuse a situation, restore harmony, and revive order and good will. You are particularly well suited to administrative, supervisory, personnel, mediation, or arbitration type positions. Then too, your expansive nature may lead you to pursue a career that allows for freedom of movement or even travel. The chances are you enjoy your work and through diligent effort you move up the corporate ladder, advance in your own business, or find success in your career field. There is also a strong indication that you succeed through your career or in religious, philanthropic or social welfare efforts. You enjoy your work and may do well in the areas of natural resources, forestry, wildlife and nature, or in the travel industry, construction, import export businesses, medicine, journalism, education, advertising, sales, law, publishing, writing, or any area allowing you to deal with the successful completion of projects.

Your good luck holds in the area of health, and if you do need medical treatment the chances are you will receive beneficial and good diagnosis and treatment. There is a strong indication that your presence augments the health and welfare of others as well.

Under planetary afflictions this individual is arrogant, lazy, snobbish, self-indulgent, and has feelings of being better than other people. There is an indication for this person to suffer from health problems related to over indulgence and weight gain, liver problems, tumors, respiratory, blood or digestive disorders.

You are a well liked and respected person who is generally admired and accepted by colleagues, associates, your boss or your employees. Your strength lies in your ability to get along well with others, to work hard, and to bring endeavors to completion. You are more than likely lucky in all that you strive to accomplish and this carries over into other aspects of your life.

361

SATURN IN THE SIXTH HOUSE

Saturn in the Sixth House makes you an efficient and reliable worker with the ability to be exacting, careful, and detail-oriented. Conscientious and dutiful, you take on any necessary tasks required for the completion of the job at hand. You prefer a well ordered organization that allows for the smooth running of the operation. You are serious about your responsibilities and have taken the time to develop and improve your work skills. Your critically analytical mind may lead you to a position in the fields of medicine, science, engineering, mechanics, civil service, municipal or government positions, writing, editing, accounting, mining, mathematics, or construction. You would be excellent at writing procedural manuals, instructional manuals, or in any other position requiring retaining and analyzing facts and details. You are not always assertive, but you are exacting, and this may cause you problems with fellow workers who don't possess your natural abilities. However, for the most part you are well liked and respected for your hard work and diligent efforts. Your cautious nature leads you to think through decisions rather than to jump impulsively to conclusions, but there are times when this same caution produces undue stress, anxieties and worries. Having been exposed to your full share of problems, obstacles, and situations beyond your control, the chances are you developed your cautious, serious nature in response to these circumstances. It is quite possible for your health to be affected by stress related illnesses or depression, nervous disorders, colds, viruses, the flu, headaches or stomach upsets. Before this occurs, it would be wise to adopt stress reducing activities, a healthy lifestyle, an interest in diet and nutrition, and an exercise program that builds your body while taking your mind off your problems. Taking care of your health must become just as important to you as your career in order not to miss out on opportunities because of problems related to illness.

Under planetary affliction, this individual can be skeptical, critical, discriminating, dogmatic, narrow minded, and controlling. There is an indication for this person to be unsuccessful with any number of obstacles holding him or her back including chronic illnesses, accidents, or operations. If well aspected, this person is successful at career efforts.

You are best known for being reliable and responsible, for following through and completing your endeavors with sincere efforts. Learning to relax, accepting those things in life that can't be changed, and finding enjoyment through your work experience will benefit you greatly.

Uranus in The Sixth House

Uranus in the Sixth House grants you intuition and imagination with the ability to produce innovative methods and original ideas. You may specialize in a field requiring a productively inventive nature and creative abilities. Rather than patience, diligence and discipline, you apply yourself to the tasks at hand in a manner that allows for a great deal of latitude, expression, and freedom of ideas, thoughts, and movement. At the same time, your mind has a technical bend, and you may be drawn to the fields of science, electricity, computers (hardware or software), electronics, engineering, or aeronautics. Machines and all the latest electronic gadgets fascinate you, and you find yourself preoccupied with how these things work and how can they be improved. Your mind has the ability to flow effortlessly through this mental process, and you dislike being interrupted by others or by the daily occurrences in life. You develop your own way of doing things, managing your life and daily affairs in a such a way that it allows for your independent nature. And if others leave you to your natural inclinations, you are fine. Problems develop with other people insist on directing your activities or thoughts or on having tasks completed their way. If you don't get along with colleagues or if you find yourself working with a controlling person, you have a tendency to simply change jobs or make a career move. Then too, there are times when your restlessness or curiosity leads you to do the same thing. You can be extremely sensitive to your surroundings, that is, the immediate physical environment, and this may to some extent explain the occurrences of unexplained illnesses or discomforts. Or it could be that a low tolerance to stress or nervous anxiety causes these persistent or nagging complaints. There is an indication that sudden changes or events may produce illnesses or bring about health problems.

If afflicted, this individual is irritable, impatient, disorganized, highly obstinate, resentful or rebellious, changeable, and restless with an indication for poor success in the career and strange or incurable diseases. If well aspected, Uranus in the Sixth House grants unique opportunities and the ability to successfully produce effective results. This person may also have an inclination for psychic abilities.

You are a highly original and inventive person who strives to maintain your independent focus and freedom of thought. Your innovative ability to improve accepted methods and procedures brings you personal satisfaction.

NEPTUNE IN THE SIXTH HOUSE

Neptune in the Sixth House allows for a nature that is enamored of illusions whether it be fantasy, glamour, or dealing with images. You are highly idealistic, inspirational and sensitive preferring to search out the best environment and situation in order to satisfy your restless search for the best place to be to produce the best results possible. This searching may also lead you on a spiritual journey of enlightenment which is reflected in a need to be of service to others. You may be inclined to pursue a career in art, photography, acting, entertainment, production, advertising, or the fashion industry. Or you may be drawn to working in large institutions such as hospitals, or the hotel and restaurant industry, art galleries, clubs. The planetary influences of Neptune could possible lead you to working in the oil or chemical industry or in a position related to water. This is also a good position for the medical field, psychiatry or humanitarian endeavors in that you are more than willing to make personal sacrifices for the benefit of others. Then too, you may be drawn to unusual careers which excite your imagination. The chances are good that you are not drawn to positions requiring overly tedious, mundane or routine task performance. You must guard against theft, deceit, or scams as well as problems associated with employees. Your health is at times somewhat unpredictable as you may be susceptible to unexplained or peculiar illnesses. You may find that you are sensitive to medications or that medications don't have the desired results.

Under planetary afflictions, this individual is lazy, prone to drifting, a loner, indulgent in pleasures, and suffers from severe illnesses. This person must develop an awareness of medications and the resultant effects on the body as well as an awareness to any reactions to chemicals in surroundings, clothing, or food. Care should be taken to associate with others with good intentions and healthy habits. When well aspected, this native is highly perceptive to his or her environment and intuitive about other people.

You are highly receptive and must guard against exposure to not only illnesses but the thoughts of other people. It is advisable for you to develop healthy habits, a sound diet, an exercise program, and to relax your mind through meditation. If well developed, your sensitivity leads you to develop psychic abilities.

Pluto in The Sixth House

Pluto in the Sixth House promotes individualism as well as intense powers of concentration. You are capable of not only searching out and seeking answers, but to analyzing problems and efficiently producing results. Your open mind looks for the most suitable approach to difficult situations or seemingly unsolvable problems. You apply yourself to discovering the most efficient and practical use of, for example, natural resources. You do well in all areas of research, science, or higher education, or in jobs which deal with the preservation of the environment, or with air and water pollution and contaminants. On the other hand, you may well be an individual who enjoys a personal sense of fulfillment from helping others which may lead you to the fields of medicine, nutrition, counseling, social work, or psychology. You are hard working and not afraid of applying yourself, and you strive to be competent, effective, and productive. In fact, there are times when you overwork which can cause job related stress and undue anxieties. But if you allow yourself to worry exceedingly or to become anxious, you are prone to nervous related disorders, stomach and indigestion problems, headaches, or may suffer from lack of energy due to nervous exhaustion. Reducing stress and adding activities into your life which promote health are beneficial to you. You must guard against poor nutrition brought on by not taking the time to eat properly. A healthy diet, proper exercise, and a good frame of mind will augment how well you perform your duties at work. By applying the same efficiency to your health as you do to your career, you find that you only gain in benefits becoming even more productive in your career.

With planetary afflictions, this native is intolerant, critical, shrewd, harsh, obsessive and has a tendency to be difficult to work with. When well aspected, this individual can be an inspiration and very helpful to others.

You are a person who can transform problems into results. You are most likely to find yourself collecting and processing data, then turning that information into workable systems which produce effective results.

PLANETS IN THE SEVENTH HOUSE RULED BY LIBRA

THE HOUSE OF PARTNERSHIPS

The Sun in the Seventh House and you are a person who prefers working closely with others and developing strong personal relationships. You have come to depend on the people in your life and what happens to you is influenced by them. Your relationships can buoy you up, adding balance and a sense of well being and optimism to your life, or they can drag you down making you distrustful and questioning of the intentions of others. Your reactions to daily occurrences are tied to how well you feel your relationships are going. When all is going well, you feel ready to take on the world and are confident and self-assured. Difficulties with your partners bring on a preoccupation with relationships which distract you from your more immediate goals or desires. But then many of your goals in life are tied to not only other people but more especially to those with whom you feel a particularly close connection. In other words, your entire life seems to be interrelated to your relationship with other people.

When the planets are well aspected, the Sun in the Seventh House indicates a most favorable, happy marriage which augments or adds to your success in life. This is also a good position for other personal relationships as well as business partnerships which promise popularity and acceptance. If afflicted, this individual experiences numerous conflicts, obstacles, problems, and disappointments brought on by personal relationships as well as loss and misfortune through choosing the wrong mate. This position may also bring on negative public attention or notoriety.

You are a person who much prefers using tact, diplomacy, and good will in your easy-going efforts to promote agreeable relationships. You often diffuse difficult situations, divert problems, and prevent delays by your ability to work well with others. These naturally likable qualities make you a person who is inclined to profit and prosper through your partnerships, associations, and business relationships. Being a person to whom marriage is important, this prosperity carries over into your personal life as well.

THE MOON IN THE SEVENTH HOUSE

With the Moon in the Seventh House, you are both sensitive and responsive to others. You strongly desire security in your life, relationships and domestic situation which makes you somewhat cautious and guarded in entering into friendships and especially in choosing a mate. While your relationships are very important to you, you are not always open to becoming deeply involved with others. You hold back, waiting, allowing yourself to get to know the other person. Then too, you are highly reflective. When around others you have a tendency to emulate and copy their attitudes, likes and dislikes, patterns, actions, and lifestyles. It is almost as if you are uncertain of who you want to be so you try on the personalities of other people. At the same time, you closely guard the real you, building walls of defensiveness and protection, and not allowing anyone to become too close. Your need for security leads you to see all relationships in regards to how they will benefit or provide for you. If you don't see an advantage, chances are you won't pursue the contact. But you want above all else to find that special person, friend or associate to whom you can feel close. When you do find someone, you can become dependent to the point of being clinging. This is after all, your security, and you are going to hold on to it. And you may hold on to the point of being personable, likable, and submissive, but then swinging into moodiness and withdrawing into your own secluded environment that offers peace, quietness, and the opportunity to enjoy your private idealistic fantasy world. In marriage you may choose a mate who is protective, supportive, and mature with strong, responsible characteristics, or someone who attracts your attention and fantasy-prone mind by exciting you with an unsettled nature and a likeness for change and travel.

Under planetary afflictions, there is an indication for discontent, strong likes and dislikes, and unpopularity which bring on discord, disappointments, lawsuits, sorrows, separations, and unexpected and unusual experiences in relationships as well as numerous changes. If well aspect, this individual can expect a fortuitous marriage and success in business partnerships. Under some aspects, these individuals marry hastily then give their affections to another; numerous changes or relocations are indicated.

You possess a strong desire for acceptance and admiration, and you have the ability to fit in with other people. Your domestic nature leads you to seek security through marriage, home, and family.

MERCURY IN THE SEVENTH HOUSE

Mercury in the Seventh House and your strong point is your ability to communicate, especially in one-to-one relationships. Your nature is more intellectual than emotional, and you may spend a great deal of time thinking about your relationships, rationalizing which one is going well and which one is not. Charming, flexible and adaptable, you enjoy meeting new people and getting to know them. The chances are you are an active person who enjoys his or her freedom to move about enjoying old and new friendships alike as you prefer. Your likes and dislikes change with your moods, and your relationships may undergo changes just as rapidly. You can just as easily develop an honest, close relationship with one person, then move along to another. Or just as easily your versatile nature allows you to be involved in two or more romantic relationships at once. You may eventually meet your marriage partner through travel or perhaps writing. This person may be younger than you, an employee, or distantly related to you, and marriage tends to be based more on an intellectual affiliation than on an emotions. There is an indication for more than one marriage in your life. In the other areas of your life, your personal and business relationships are numerous, and you constantly add to them, meeting people through other contacts and travel. You may keep in touch with some of these people for a life time or choose to contact some as you feel it is necessary. People also fall by the wayside as you move on to new situations. In other words, people come and go in your life, most often as a result of your own choosing.

With planetary afflictions, this individual can be sarcastic, deceitful, bickering and temperamental and experiences an unsettled and inharmonious marriage. Problems, strife and difficulties are experienced through business, associates or partnerships, and in regards to contracts, communications and writings. If well aspected, the individual is active, quick thinking, and open minded experiencing good fortune in marriage and partnerships.

You can be verbally creative and entertaining, attracting others to you easily. Other people are important to you and to your life, and you are adept at communicating effectively with other people in personal relationships, partnerships, and in business. You possess a strong preference for meeting and developing relationships with people who are articulate, clever, intelligent and talented in some way.

Venus in The Seventh House

Venus in the Seventh House directs you to strive for harmonious, pleasant, and fulfilling relationships based on congenial good will and sincere intentions. You find that you are most content when surrounded by beauty, and you creatively apply your skills to creating a harmonious environment where relationships will flourish and grow. You may dedicate yourself to promoting your relationships and friendships, taking especially good care of your relationship with your spouse. You much prefer for all things in life to run smoothly, and you feel that can best happen if you direct your energy, charm, and diplomatic skills to insuring success in your relationships. You feel that all aspects of life could run easily if only others would allow it to by working together for common and decent goals. When others oppose you or cause discord in your life, you may develop deep resentments that life or people can be so unjust and unfair when it isn't necessary for it to be so. You perceive that experiences and life can be enjoyable, fun and pleasurable, and it is disappointing to you when problems arise to disrupt what would otherwise be a pleasant time. Venus in the Seventh House grants strong indications for a happy and successful marriage which includes social gatherings, pleasurable experiences, and financial success. There is also an inclination for conflicts to be resolved peacefully, and for success in all dealings with associates, partners and in public relations. With your sociable, charming personality, your suitors may be many and whether or not you marry, or who you marry, is left to your own discerning judgment. You are well liked, popular, and possess refined and artistic taste. Your personal as well as your business relationships are numerous as other people are attracted to your sincere personality and likable manners. This is a good position for legal matters, a career in law, or luck with legal contracts.

Under planetary afflictions, this native experiences difficulties, delays, or sorrows in marriage and problems with partnerships or associates. Loss is indicated through lawsuits or court actions. When well aspected, this position of Venus is fortunate for the native.

You possess a great love for your personal friendships, relationships with other people, and most especially for spouse. Your perceptions of the world are focused through your interpersonal relationships. For you, life is most enjoyable when you are surrounded by caring, well-intentioned people.

Mars in The Seventh House

Mars in the Seventh House inclines you to be fiery, passionate and impetuous in life and love. You have a strong, forceful personality with a tendency to be aggressive and at times controversial. You strive to prove your self worth and value. It seems that you attract competition, opposition and even verbal disputes by your very nature. You are strongly drawn to vigorous and active people who stimulate your mental and physical energies. At the same time, you possess a strong sense of direction and often initiate meeting new people or other social contacts, and your independent nature attracts others to you. With your confident and self-assured nature, you take the lead in relationships, selecting the time, place, and person to suit your wishes. In marriage and partnerships you also take the lead, driving through any obstacles to meet your personal objectives. There is an indication that you will marry young, perhaps impulsively or rashly, and that you may be married more than once in your life. The chances are that you will experience strife and difficulties in your marriage relationship. You will also have any number of obstacles and problems in personal and business relationships.

If planetary afflictions exist, this individual is excessively aggressive and forceful, or becomes just the opposite and is lazy, dependent, and indecisive. There is indication for separations in love affairs and marriage, numerous obstacles which develop through relationships, the death of a spouse or partner, loss through law suits, and violence. If well aspected, these aspects are modified and the individual is more fortunate in personal and business relationships.

Much of what happens in your life depends upon the extent to which you strive to become well developed and mature. An impulsive nature can lead to rash decisions which may bring changes and obstacles into your life of your own making. Then again, you may find that as you mature and gain life experiences, you think through your decisions more fully, making wiser and fortuitous decisions. Your strong aggressive nature and self-confidence brings you admiration from many, but at the same time it is important to develop wisdom in the decision making process. Your personal decisions affect not only your life and relationships, but the lives of other people. Although you like to have your own way and to have other people agree with your opinions, you also possess a strong need for others to accept and appreciate you. As you mature, you learn much through your relationships and personal contacts with other people.

JUPITER IN THE SEVENTH HOUSE

With Jupiter in the Seventh House you are most fortunate and lucky in marriage and other partnerships and find success and gain through both. You are known for being kind and friendly with an open and generous nature. There is a tendency for you to prefer honesty and integrity in your personal relationships meaning that you have little interest in the, intrigues or surprises that some people find exciting. You are accepting and tolerant of other people which not only attracts people to you but insures their loyalty, faith, and support to you. Other people consider their relationship with you important, significant and inspiring. Then too, you are naturally outgoing, enjoying any number of activities with a preference for nature, sports and recreation. You apply your enthusiasm, charm and general optimism to meeting new people and forming lasting relationships which benefit both you and the other person. In marriage, you and your partner enjoy a faithful and lasting relationship based on an intensely emotional love, care, friendship and passion. There is some indication for more than one marriage. Your strongest characteristic may well be your ability to promote cooperation among people, leading others to form beneficial and successful relationships in the community, socially, and in business affairs. At the same time, you have the natural ability to impress the right people, seemingly with little exertion gaining approval and support for your ideas or projects. Then too, you effortlessly receive popularity, prestige, power and social standing.

Under planetary afflictions, this individual can be over-generous, arrogant, irresponsible, or overbearing with inclinations for gambling, scams, deceits, unfortunate speculation, and trusting the wrong people. Delays and difficulties in marriage are experienced and losses through lawsuits. When well aspected, the individual enjoys success and good luck in marriage, partnerships, business dealings, and in regard to social standing as well as realizing gains in legal affairs.

You possess strong tendencies to seek self-improvement by expanding your intellect, education, skills, or philosophies, and you have a tendency to want to share your knowledge and good will with others. If well developed, you are a spiritual person who develops his or her intellect as well as intuitive abilities. Enthusiastic about life in general, you want to share what you have learned in life with others. This both augments and enhances your personal relationships and partnerships.

SATURN IN THE SEVENTH HOUSE

Saturn in the Seventh House grants you a powerful inclination toward responsible and sensible personal relationships based on sincerity and justice. You possess a strong tendency to be particularly cautious in choosing your friendships, relationships, and partnerships. You prefer to patiently take your time, guardedly waiting to see how a relationship will develop before continuing it for any length of time. The chances are you are somewhat emotionally reserved when it comes to forming friendships or more serious relationships. You quite deliberately think through your decisions and actions carefully choosing the correct response for the situation. You much prefer that everything adds up and makes good common sense promising results that are advantageous. There are indications that when it comes to marriage, you select a partner who is older or well established and who will benefit you socially, in business, or financially. While you may not be overly demonstrative, you are well meaning, faithful, and stable. As with your other partnerships, you take your commitment to your marriage quite seriously wanting only what will benefit both you and your partner in the long run. In an unhappy marriage situation, you would choose to continue the relationship rather than to upset your carefully formulated plans and methodical routine. At the same time, you are independent and often strive to be the leader in your personal situation as well as in your business partnerships. With a mature, responsible attitude, your friends and colleagues turn to you for advice and direction. Your reserved nature may reflect either a certain amount of shyness or inhibition or on some occasions a well chosen restraint on your part which allows you to control your situations and plans.

Under planetary afflictions, this individual is arrogant, egotistical, and indifferent and may well face non-responsiveness, incompatibility, and lack of passion through the marriage. There is an indication for suffering through sorrows, obstacles, with numerous difficulties experienced in partnerships and other relationships which bring on financial downfall through contracts, enemies, competitors, lawsuits, legal actions, or deceit. When well aspected, there is indication the individual prospers through enduring relationships, partnerships, and marriage.

Your self-control and self-confidence influences other people to trust in your good judgment and common sense. You are generally well meaning and make a sincere effort to do the best you can in your personal relationships and in your partnerships.

URANUS IN THE SEVENTH HOUSE

With Uranus in the Seventh House you find that your partnerships and relationships are greatly influenced by changing situations and the unexpected actions of other people. You possess a tendency to follow your impulses, starting new relationships easily. Your spontaneity uplifts other people who are more than willing to see where these quick flashes of insight will lead you. You follow your heart, protecting your freedom and independence in being able to do what you want and go where you desire. You are tolerant, open and accepting of other people wanting to know as many people as possible. This leads you to form many new relationships, partnerships and friendships. Some of these are long lasting and others last as long as the mutual interest endures. Your relationships and partnerships are prone to be either compatible and serious or extremely superficial, and you are drawn to unusual people from various walks of life. You may decide on impulse to marry whether from infatuation or a desire to have a meaningful relationship. There is an indication for your marriage to be sudden and romantic or even secret, but the results may not be long lasting. This position of Uranus may lead to more than one marriage or serious romantic relationship. Generally speaking, your relationships and partnerships are best described as unpredictable. It may be that as far as you are concerned, all of that can't be helped. It is almost as if you are addicted to that rush of excitement brought on by meeting and becoming involved with new people. Your interactions with others are intensely stimulate your imagination, giving you a driving desire to experience more of life.

When well aspected, this individual marries a person with unusual, genius, talent or perhaps a person from another culture or country who is out of the ordinary in some regard. Under planetary afflictions, this individual is willful, obstinate, nervous, distrustful, jealous, rebellious, suffering through sudden marriage resulting in unhappiness, disputes, a lack of understanding, divorce or separation, scandal, or sorrow from the death of the partner. There is an indication for obstacles, problems, conflict and loss from relationships with strangers, partners, enemies, and the law. Numerous changes as well as unexpected opposition and actions of others are experienced.

Other people respond to your inventive creativity and flair for ideas. Your independent nature brings you much in the way of new experiences through relationships and partnerships.

Neptune in The Seventh House

With Neptune in the Seventh House you are a remarkably creative and imaginative person. Highly intuitive, you read other people well, and this awareness of others leads your own moods and decisions to be influenced and affected by the feelings and opinions of others. The chances are that you are a person who paints pictures in your mind and just such a picture you paint of your ideal lover and soul mate. And it may be that your entire life is lived with you looking, however subliminally, for this ideal person who will fulfill and complete you and make life even more worthwhile. In marriage, you either place your partner on a pedestal, believing that you have found that special person, or you are forever somewhat disappointed, believing that the other person will never be able to live up to your expectations. This attitude of yours makes you more than a little vulnerable to that type of person who will play out the role you have designed for them until you eventually wake up one day and realize what that person is really like. You may also find that you are vulnerable to deceptions on the part of others. In that you are a sensitive person this could lead to disappoints in your romantic relationships and it other areas of your life. On the other hand, it could be that your highly developed intuition leads you to see beyond superficial appearances to the person within, and if that is the case there is some indication that you will discover true love and computability with a person who is mentally well developed but physically impaired. There is also an indication that you develop strong psychic links with other people, and this may underlie your partnerships and relationships. To you, your goals may seem simple, that is, to find others who want a peaceful, gentle and stress free relationship based on compatibility, wants and desires, and perhaps a shared vision of life. Your artistic flair forever paints the idealistic vision which you most desire.

Under planetary affliction, this individual experiences domestic upsets, scandal, mystery, confusion, deceits, jealousies, death of a partner, problems with partnerships, contracts, and with involvement with the public. When well aspected, the prospects improve for partnerships and marriage.

Above all else, your sensitivity leads you to be responsive and caring of your partners wishes and needs. There is an indication for more than one marriage or serious relationships.

Pluto in The Seventh House

With Pluto in the Seventh House you appear ceaselessly energetic and dynamic, appealingly magnetic, more than a little temperamental, and forever changeable. You are intensely involved in your relationships and seek other people who are strong willed and forceful. You find yourself in partnerships in which you are either the dominating person or the other person dominates you. Or perhaps there is an on going push and pull competitiveness in your relationships in an effort to determine who will win out and dominate the other person. You can be judgmental, sizing up other people to evaluate and rate them as compared to yourself. People may become things to you, and are either important objects that you want and need or unimportant objects to be discarded at your will. Romantic partners may become objects with which to fulfill your sexual drives, and they are possessions to keep around for as long as you feel the urge. You have been hurt in the past and carry your grudge around with you like a wound constantly needing attention. In fact, you may develop relationships for no other purpose in mind than to fulfill a revengeful need to get back at someone who has done you wrong. Some type of mystery or secrets form a part of your life, and being distrustful, you look for the hidden motives or secrets in other peoples lives as well. You can be demanding, insisting that other people prove themselves to you which has the effect of draining the other person's energies and emotions. There are strong indications that you will marry in secret, elope, marry for gain, or marry a person from a foreign country or different culture.

Under planetary afflictions, this individual experiences problems with unstable partnerships, jealousies, strife, the disappearance of a partner, divorce, enemies, and difficulties with legal affairs, laws and lawsuits. When well aspected, the individual gains through a public position with the fame being shared with a partner.

You see your partnerships as a reflection on yourself, and in your marriage you strive to provide and take care of your partner to augment your own prestige and public appearance.

Planets in The Eighth House Ruled by Scorpio

The House of Legacies

The Sun in the Eighth House is a good position for an energetic and long life. There is an indication for inheritance or gain through marriage or partnerships. And your financial well being continues to improve after marriage. Whatever honors you expected or deserved in life, it may be that posthumous fame and honorable recognition is most indicated, and this recognition may be due to some heroic, or outstanding act, or through sacrifice on your part. On a personal level, you possess an interest and curiosity in the secrets of life which leads you to explore and to investigate any number of sources of information, always looking for plausible answers to the great mysteries surrounding us. One of the mysteries which attracts your interest is the afterlife, spirit world, or the possibility of other dimensions. Your intuitive perceptions lead you to also be intrigued and forever fascinated by other people and what motivates them to respond to life and situations the way they do. The Sun in the Eighth House is a good position for handling finances well, whether yours or other people's, and this may lead to a career in banking, economics, finances, or investments. This is a particularly good position for the insurance business or businesses dealing with legacies, inheritances or death benefits. Also, with this position there is an indication for your parents to proceed you in death as well as your spouse. Your father may have some form of strong influence in your life either through legacies or spiritual leadership and influence. There is a likelihood that you receive gains through the death of a family member or a generous partner. At the same time, it is important that you protect your health and guard against difficulties with your heart, circulation, or blood pressure.

Under planetary affliction, this individual suffers problems associated with legal problems regarding inheritances, mismanagement, or deceit on the part of a partner; violence, danger, and fighting for survival; sudden or violent death; spouse proceeds you in death; illnesses during travel. When well aspected, this individual can expect steady gains throughout life although the early life may be difficult.

Your pride leads you to be responsible in your personal and business affairs. You make efforts to be efficient in the uses of your resources and have a tendency to eliminate the inessentials in your life.

THE MOON IN THE EIGHTH HOUSE

With the Moon in the Eighth House you most desire security, and you may hide your true or inner feelings from others in an effort to avoid being rejected or criticized by them. This sense of security is so important to you that you can become intensely possessive and self-protective which in personal relationships can produce dependencies, resentments and jealousies if you don't feel you're receiving adequate attention and compensation. You strive through your creativity to devise a perfect persona attempting to build your self-esteem by being of service or helpful to others, but wanting in return to be appreciated and admired for your efforts. You can be overly defensive taking offense at the slightest remark. The influence of the Moon leads you to take an interest in the more sensual aspects of life, studying your reflection in the mirror to create the most sensual expressions, developing a wardrobe you feel augments your features, and appreciating the admiration of others for your physical appearance. Romance, love and sex are important to you as well. Then too, you are highly sensitive, intuitive, and, if so inclined, you may develop an interest in psychic matters, the afterlife, and some form of spiritualism. There is an indication that you will receive financial gains through a public position, inheritance, partner, from some connection to your mother's personal or business affairs, or through matters related to women.

Under planetary affliction, this individual may suffer from the early loss of the mother or in a man's chart the wife, an unstable financial situation after marriage, an intense interest in sensationalism or sensuality, a public death through either accident, notoriety, treachery, drowning, drugs, infection or degenerative disease or disability, or sudden violence. If well aspected, a natural death after a fortunate life.

You are intense and quietly passionate about all you do in life, using your creativity to enhance your perceptions of life and drawing upon your intuitive perceptions to become aware of the possibilities in life. When well developed, you strive to become spiritually aware and lead and inspire others in spiritual growth.

Mercury in The Eighth House

Mercury in the Eighth House leads you to be insightful, penetrating, and intuitive. You are somewhat secretive about your personal thoughts, feelings, interests, and intuitions, preferring to share your insights only after you have established a trusting relationship with another person. Your awareness that there is more to life than simple answers may well lead you to develop an interest in psychic matters and astrology. In fact, the idea of intrigue in any form fascinates your curious intellect, and with an innate slyness only you can understand, you delve into ferreting out the unknown answers to questions preoccupying your mind. You can slice away at details, discarding and eliminating the unnecessary and inessential from your mental list until you feel you have reached some form of viable conclusion or at least a feasible analogy. This tendency can lead you to be a skillful researcher studying profound subjects or the neighborhood gossip gathering information on one and all. Your interests in other people is usually based on your attempt to understand the motives and incentives that lead to their actions, emotions, and reactions to situations. And your analysis of other people can be delivered in cutting and sarcastic repartee whenever the occasion presents itself for you to gain an advantage, repay a grudge, or seek revenge.

This position of Mercury is advantageous for handling the financial affairs or inheritances of others such as in banking, finance, taxes, or insurance. Then too, this is a good location for a public office or political position, or your natural inclinations may lead you into some field connected with investigations. In your personal or business life, you may experience more than your share of obstacles, quarrels, strife, and difficulties, and you experience problems with partners or others pertaining to their finances. There is an indication for sorrow because of the death of a relative, colleague, neighbor, or close friend. Your sexual inclinations lead you to experiment with sex at an early age.

With planetary afflictions, there are indications for this individual to be susceptible to poor health brought on by complications or accidents injuring the brain, respiratory illnesses, or serious nervous disorders which in some cases result in death. When well aspected, this individual is alert and mentally aware up to and preceding death.

In whatever manner you decide to use your cognitive abilities, you are quite capable of obtaining and learning the facts, arriving at an analysis of the situation, and formulating conclusions.

Venus in The Eighth House

Venus in the Eighth House and you are charming and sociable with extremely intense emotions. This intensity is reflected in your attitude toward sex which you consider pleasantly pleasurable, fulfilling and exciting, and there is every indication that your relationships are harmonious and enjoyable. In other areas of your life, you are fortunate in that you receive financial benefits either through marriage, partnerships, inheritance, or insurance. Then too, your fondness for refinement, beautiful surroundings, and the better things in life may entice you to develop an interest in financial affairs which can easily lead to a career in banking, investments, business, or perhaps financial writing or journalism. Your perceptions and good taste combined with your natural awareness of the likes and dislikes of others grants you the ability to foresee trends, fads, and consumer buying patterns making you a natural at not only forecasting but exploiting this ability in your own business. Then too, you are that person who can walk into any store and immediately point out the best and most expensive item for sale. This natural ability to assess goods and property makes you a skillful buyer, and you love to do just that, enhancing your personal surroundings with tasteful or artistic objects, decorations, and accessories. Your personality and optimistic outlook on life is also reflected in your personal style, adornments, and fashion statement.

With planetary afflictions, this individual is overly indulgent, pleasure seeking, too interested in sex, self-absorbed, jealous of others, and possessive of things and people. There is an indication for sorrows, difficulties, strife and disappointments with love affairs, the death of the spouse, and the death of the individual in connection with ill health caused by pleasure or over indulgence in food, alcohol, drugs, or sex. When the planets are well aspected, Venus in the Eighth House is most indicative of a long life and a peaceful, natural death.

Diplomatic, tolerant and accepting of others, you form partnerships and friendships easily. Other people are instantly drawn to your gracious charm and appealing manners. If you are a well developed individual, you possess an inherent desire to fulfill your spiritual nature, and you want to share your feelings about these matters with others. Your intensity inspires and delights other people many of whom consider you a remarkable and generous person.

379

Mars in The Eighth House

With Mars in the Eighth House, you are a person who is emotionally intense and somewhat mysterious or secretive about your personal affairs. The mysterious of life may intrigue you as well, and you investigate the subjects of sex, death, finances and money, and the actions of other people. In addition, you are curious about psychic phenomena, astrology, the occult, the afterlife, and perhaps healing, medicine, or health in general. Realistic and pragmatic, the subject of death doesn't frighten you as it does some people as you consider it simply the natural outcome of living. You are also adept at deciding how to extract and eliminate that which is no longer necessary or relevant. You may find that with your natural inclinations and skills this is a good position for a career in research, investigations, politics, medicine, dentistry, or psychiatry.

In your personal life, when you are in the mood, you are passionate, earthy, sensual and lusty, and you are drawn to an active sex life. It should be noted that this particular position of Mars is indicative of marriage to an extravagant person who exhibits a remarkable talent for spending your money which results in difficulties and problems associated with finances. You also may well experience conflicts and difficulties with other family members regarding either legacies, wills, inheritance, insurance, or property. Strong willed, you face your problems in life making every attempt to overcome obstacles, strife, and disagreements.

When planetary afflictions exist with Mars in the Eighth House, it is indicative of either a drowning, a fatal accident while flying, a sudden illness resulting in death, or a sudden and violent death. The financial affairs are unfortunate with losses suffered through conflicts, partners or spouse. When well aspected, death is the quick and sudden result of illness or an accident. When this position of Mars is aspected by Neptune, psychic involvement can result in upsets to the individual.

With your intense and energetic drives you learn to survive all the obstacles, trials and tribulations life has thrown your way. You apply at all times your natural ability to persevere with patience and will power. Your strength is drawn from this strong will power, your natural energy, and your ability to think and act independently. Your intellect leads you to perceive all problems objectively and in relationship to solutions. Thus, you become proficient at research, investigation, analysis, and then turning your findings into viable answers.

JUPITER IN THE EIGHTH HOUSE

With Jupiter in the Eighth House, you are subtly resourceful, and this is especially true in regards to financial matters. The remarkably good fortune and optimism of Jupiter influences you to be skillful, clever, and ingenious with the intricacies of handling your partner's and other people's resources such as in the areas of accounting, banking, taxes, business management, finances, or businesses related to death benefits or pertaining to death in some fashion. You have the ability to shrewdly salvage operations and to produce profits from what others would overlook, dispose of, mismanage, or waste. In your personal affairs, you also are just as capable of good management, handling decisions with little effort. It may well be that your good luck carries over into your marriage which results in prosperity and financial gain. In addition, there is every indication that you will realize additional financial gains through inheritance, legacies, insurance, or a partner. You are that lucky person who has wonderfully happy dreams and generally good thoughts about your life and the lives of other people with whom you are associated. You possess a rather healthy sexual attitude and appetite, both enjoying and bringing joy to your relationships. Then too, your personal attitude toward life and death is pragmatic and realistic, an aspect of life which you take in stride with little anxiety. Perhaps you feel that way for good reason because there is a strong indication that you will live a long life and that your death will be peaceful and due to natural causes. At some point in life, though, it may well be that you develop a curiosity about matters dealing with the investigation of psychic abilities, other entities, or the life awaiting after this one.

Under planetary affliction, this individual is cunning, wily, and crafty with a tendency to mismanage other people's financial affairs and to face problems related to lawsuits, loss of partners or friends through disputes, and poor health through heart problems, diseases of the blood, degenerative diseases, or tumors.

You may develop a personal philosophy of life which perceives the goodness inherent in man, and this carries over into your relationships, partnerships, friendships and with your family. Realizing that all people have faults and shortcomings, you are more than capable of accepting and over looking those faults in order to appreciate the goodness in the hearts of others. In fact, it could be that you develop a personal philosophy which others find enlightening and inspiring.

Saturn in The Eighth House

With Saturn in the Eighth House, you are a person who is cautious and controlled and who takes financial responsibilities seriously. Other people, including your spouse, can rely on you to be dependable in regard to their financial affairs as well. At the same time, you must work diligently and hard to produce profits, and when you do, you exhibit a facility for saving and investing wisely, holding on to your money in order to provide for a secure future. Aware that money doesn't come easily to you and that you must strive for gains, you don't look on marriage as a way to increase your profits. If and when you marry, the chances are that it will be for other reasons rather than to improve your financial standing. You have faced obstacles before and probably realize that after marriage you will continue to struggle, building on your own abilities to produce, provide, and save for the future. In a protective way, you may develop a cautious nature toward expressing your emotions as well. It has become necessary for you to maintain a control over your life, emotions, and the other people in your life in order to insure that the future will be secure. You have learned that frivolous mistakes can easily lead to ruin and disappointments. It isn't that you aren't optimistic about the future, but you remain reserved, even somewhat secretive, about your real feelings, waiting to see what others are going to do or how any particular situation will develop. Life has taught you to wait for others to prove that they can be trusted, but somewhere within you may be this fear that eventually others will either turn on you or in some way cause you more troubles and problems. In the same way, you develop a deeply ingrained distrust of authority including perhaps the government. You may even feel that others are plotting against you. You feel this way because of past experiences, but you struggle with the reasons why other people blatantly choose to cause problems in life. Your approach to sex, love and marriage is just as serious, and not a subject you regard lightly. It could be that you may develop an interest in psychic affairs and unnatural phenomena.

Under planetary afflictions, this native is highly possessive, jealous, controlling, manipulative, resentful with bizarre sexual attitudes. With Saturn in this position, there are no indications for financial gains through business partners, legacies, inheritance or insurance; lawsuits; legal battles resulting in prison confinement; and difficulties with money problems after marriage. Death is the result of a slow and lingering illness, drowning or other accident. When well aspected, a long and dignified life and death from natural causes is to be expected.

A self-imposed form of self-discipline compels and leads you to work diligently to provide for a secure future. And you place this dedication above all else in life including your social life or personal life.

URANUS IN THE EIGHTH HOUSE

With Uranus in the Eighth House, you may possess somewhat of an experimental outlook toward financial affairs which could easily result in unexpected gains or losses through a partner. Friendly, open and freedom loving, you adhere to a desire to create change just to observe the results. And the results can be fortuitous, beneficial, inventive, creative, and just as likely sudden and unexpected. There are strong indications for you to experience benefits and gains through marriage, partners, inventions, or unexpected sources, or for you to experience sudden difficulties and losses in financial affairs after marriage, with partners, or associated with the losses of others. You may also experience unexpected gains or then again difficulties and problems associated with inheritances or legacies. Then too, yours may be the story of the self-made person who progressed from a poor beginning to a prosperous adulthood. Preferring to avoid restrictions on your freedom of thought and movement, you can develop either unconventional or somewhat detached feelings toward sex. Whichever the case may be, you aren't traditional or accepting of the more repressed and inhibited societal attitudes toward sex. You may have a tendency to develop sexual relationships with a person who you know isn't available or who can't completely fulfill your needs. Your curious nature, unusual Technicolor dreams, and premonitions compel you to investigate paranormal phenomena, or you may decide to develop your psychic abilities or interest in astrology. The chances are that your death will be as sudden and extraordinary as the other events in your life, and will perhaps be the result of an accident.

Under planetary afflictions, this individual suffers from worries, anxieties, and financial problems associated with inheritances, legacies, or insurance, with unusual or unexpected events occurring in connection with deaths. When well aspected, unexpected financial benefits and gains are to be expected for this individual.

You are more than likely a well-intentioned person who takes your responsibility toward others seriously, preferring to stay on good terms with other people.

NEPTUNE IN THE EIGHTH HOUSE

With Neptune in the Eighth House, you are highly intuitive, receptive and aware. Your awareness may well lead you to develop a soul searching approach to spiritualism, mysticism or psychic affairs. It may be that your strange dreams, nightmares, or visions cause you to view life somewhat differently and more perceptively than others do. The chances are that you have developed the ability to attain alternate planes of consciousness through meditation, ESP abilities, or the ability to channel or act as a medium. Your dreams and visions can be most unusual and insightful, compelling you to seek meaning and wisdom in life as well as an understanding of the afterlife experience. There is a strong indication that you will experience unusual or peculiar financial gains through a partner or other person, or just the reverse. This position of Neptune can be fortunate for public office or politics because it grants the native a natural charisma that inspires others. Idealistic and visionary, you are capable of believing in grand illusions which can make you susceptible to disappointments and deceits in sexual relationships. More than likely you have experienced disappointments and problems as well with deceptions, secrets and scams in financial matters which have caused reverses and financial losses resulting in you being cautious of all finances affairs handled by a partner. These experiences and obstacles combined with your well developed spiritual nature have led you to the conclusion that there is more to life than material possessions and financial gain. There is some indication that, unless you are cautious, you are easily influenced or swayed by others, and you are highly receptive to hypnosis.

Under planetary affliction, this individual can become involved with secretive and deceptive financial practices with partner or partner's money; experiences numerous financial difficulties after marriage; loss through complications with partner or others; fraud through legacy, insurance or inheritance; and problems associated with disreputable practices of partner. Death is the result of a peculiar or unusual occurrence. When well aspected, the native gains through unusual sources. Death is related to water, poison, drugs, or occurs during an operation while under anesthetics.

You develop highly idealistic values and standards and are always aware and helpful to other people. Your insightfulness can quite easily lead you to be inspiring to others.

PLUTO IN THE EIGHTH HOUSE

With Pluto in the Eighth House you are powerfully emotional with an intense desire to achieve. You are analytical and use this process to perceive the ways and means to attain the achievement you seek. Spiritualism and the meaning of life and what follows is important to you as well. And your spiritualism augments and enhances your life allowing you to subtly perceive those changes which will naturally occur in your life. You may not know what these changes are, but you know that they are coming. The chances are you will experiences reverses and losses in life, and with your forcefulness, will power, and determination, you act to overcome them, rebuilding your life and even starting over with a fresh beginning if necessary. In fact, these incidents of rebuilding and starting over may occur more than once in your life. Rather than being destroyed, the obstacles in your life lead you to develop an inner strength and determination to hold on to your faith and beliefs and to endure all that life may bring. You have learned to hold your emotions and beliefs close to you, protecting yourself from others who would use any information they could get to disrupt your life. Your secretiveness is for good cause. You have a strong curiosity and a natural inclination to investigate, learn, and to obtain knowledge. You also possess good financial abilities and learn to use money to its best advantage. If necessary, you are capable of eliminating all of the nonessentials from life (at times out of necessity), but you have the capacity to enjoy life at the same time. Your sexual drive is strong, healthy and uninhibited based on an outlook that sex is but a natural and enjoyable part of life. You may develop an interest in research, investigations, science, medicine, psychic phenomena, or affairs related to death. It may be that your understanding of death and the afterlife is more perceptive than most, but not something that causes you any fear.

Under planetary afflictions to Neptune, this individual can be prone to obsessive and at times behaviors of either a philosophical or unhealthy sexual nature. When well aspected, this individual develops a strong sense of good character and responsibility.

You are a strong person who is self-willed, self-reliant, and creatively resourceful. You are capable of displaying heroic efforts.

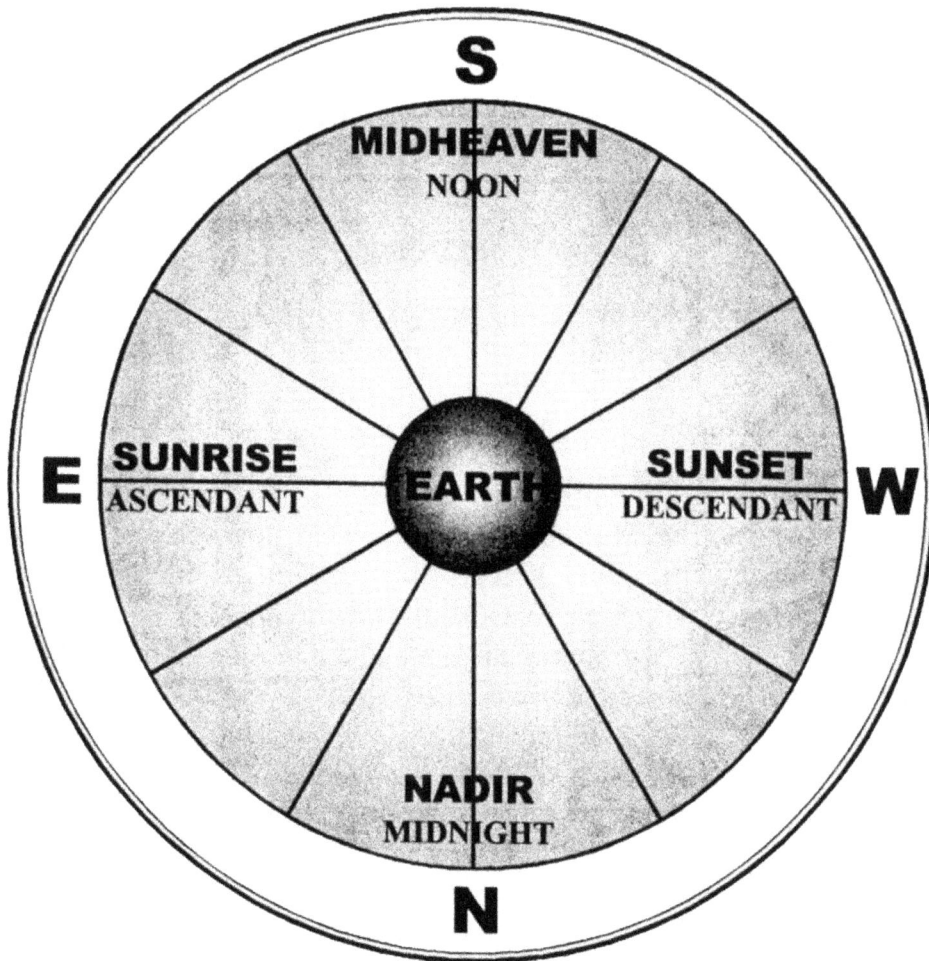

Planets in The Ninth House Ruled by Sagittarius

The House of Intellect

The Sun in the Ninth House and you are a person who possesses noble aspirations and ambitions. You strive to gain knowledge and to improve your intellect developing an interest in philosophy, theology, law, literature, cultures, science, art or music, and higher education. Your intellect is restlessly exploratory, seeking to expand and promote all avenues of thought and perceptions. You may find yourself striving to understand the broader, deeper and more profound implications of the subject matter you pursue. Then too, your curious nature may lead you to explore the world of thought, ideas and concepts through distant travel which allows you to experience differing cultures and lifestyles. And nature and the outdoors may well enhance your spiritual inclinations offering you the visions which produce spiritual and uplifting benefits. You approach the intellectual side of your life with a fiery intensity which allows you to communicate your thoughts and concepts to others. There is a strong indication for success and recognition related to religious affiliations, higher education, the law, or from a public position, writing or communications, or as a result of travel, research, or exploration. This person may live and work in a foreign country during some period of his or her life.

With planetary afflictions, this individual is condescending, narrow minded, prejudice, opinionated, outspoken, and bigoted with extreme religious beliefs; problems and accidents through foreign travel; difficulties with legal affairs, writings or publications, church, partners. When well aspected, this individual is responsible, judicious, patriotic, and courageous, and receives recognition for accomplishments. There is indication for happiness and financial gains with good aspects of this position of the Sun.

You possess a firm and ambitious nature and are self-reliant and confident in your intellectual pursuits and ideology. Your sincere faithfulness gains you the acceptance and appreciation of others.

THE MOON IN THE NINTH HOUSE

With the Moon in the Ninth House there is a tendency for you to be easy going, friendly and gregarious. Your perceptions of life are formed through your intensely emotional and sensitive nature. You possess good moral values and a strong spirituality with a desire to provide for and to protect your family and home. With your receptive and imaginative intellect, you pursue a variety of subject matter in order to further your abilities, satisfy your curiosity, and benefit your mind. You have an innate feeling that your creative fantasies and flair for the dramatic will be enhanced with additional information gathered from as many sources as possible. You prefer to use your mind to fill your time, enhance your thoughts, and entertain your moods. You find travel an excellent way to gather insightful information, experience different sounds and sights, and add to the repertory of your impressions. It may well be that your ingenious mind leads you to research and investigate any number of subjects adding to your ability to invent new and innovative ideas and concepts. While your intellect is penetrative, you are also a person who is reflective, taking the time to ponder and think out what it is you have learned and how that knowledge can best be applied to broader, more significant issues. This position of the Moon is indicative of benefits and gains through change, and you are drawn to new concepts, ideas, and places. You strive to maintain your freedom of thought and movement as well as your ability to entertain a variety of new concepts and theories or simple novel ideas and notions. But your thought processes and rational, however many facts you collect, are based on your emotions and feelings rather than on logic. Your dreams, visions and psychic experiences are illusory and remarkably graphic.

With particular planet afflictions, this individual is eccentric, impractical, overly romantic and dreamy, vague, restless with a tendency to roam, and can become fanatically religious or unorthodox perhaps joining a cult. With this position of the Moon, there is an indication for difficulties, problems and sorrows experienced in relationship to religious matters, travel, writing, or with a family member of a partner. When well aspected, this individual gains through in-laws or relatives of the spouse, and enjoys the experiences gathered through travel.

You are a person who wishes to inspire, guide and instruct, and you may be a naturally gifted teacher or communicator who desires to enlighten others with your intellectual knowledge.

Mercury in The Ninth House

Mercury in the Ninth House and you possess an ever alert and active intellectual ability with a love of knowledge. It may be that your bank of knowledge is vast while you are at the same time an intellectually stimulating person with a profusion of ideas, thoughts, concepts, beliefs, and opinions which you strive to express and share with others. You place a high value on your personal freedom, your exploratory nature, and your ability to satisfy your somewhat restless and changeable curiosity as to what may be over the next hill, either figuratively or literally. Your hunger for knowledge may lead you to explore such fields as science, art, literature, philosophy, theology, law, cultures or some area of higher education. With your innate desire to explore different cultures, you yearn to travel, gathering information and broadening your experiences as you do so. With your ability to learn new languages, you may even yearn to live in a foreign country in order to immerse yourself completely in a new culture. Your mind is so adaptable and open to new thoughts that at times you find yourself pulled in different directions as you seek to satisfy your current curiosities. There are even times when you find yourself pursuing one direction, then perhaps losing interest and going in a different direction altogether. You must also guard against your tendency to doubt yourself and your decisions which also leads you to change course in midstream or before you complete whatever it was you set out to do. Mercury in the Ninth House is considered a good position for teachers, professors, attorneys, historians, anthropologists, or for the fields of advertising, communications, radio and television, journalism, or writing.

Under planetary afflictions, this individual is overly restless, indecisive, doubting, procrastinating, opinionated, dogmatic and intellectually snobbish, interfering, worrisome, with efforts that are scattered in too many directions. There is an indication for problems associated with religious matters, the law, lawsuits, writing, travel, or in-laws. When well aspected, this individual is studious, intuitive, even visionary and intellectually advanced and experiences success in matters related to travel.

Ingenious, earnest and clever, you desire to express what you have learned to others and have the ability to influence and persuade the opinions of others by putting your own personal slant on your communications.

3Venus in The Ninth House

Venus in the Ninth House and you are delighted with new concepts and ideas that would benefit and better relationships among people. Kind and sympathetic, your desire to be understanding and helpful to others leads you to seek knowledge and to broaden your intellect through various forms of information. Along with your gentle nature, you possess an optimistically philosophical outlook on life, perhaps based on your religious background, and you appreciate the opportunity to share your optimism with others through lively discussions with well-informed people. Your inherent and natural appreciation for developing your intellect leads to an interest in all types of artistic expressions, music, and entertainment, as well as the ideas of contemporary writers and speakers. Generally nonjudgmental, you possess a strong preference for truth, justice, fairness, and equity for all of society which may lead you to take an active interest in social welfare and sociological concerns. The chances are you get along well with many people and that you enjoy a pleasant relationship as well as benefits from your in-laws and relatives of your spouse. With Venus in the Ninth House there is a strong indication for a marriage to someone from a foreign country, marriage aboard, or marriage to a person involved in theology, science, art, or literature. This is also a good position for Venus to enhance your intellectual capacity and to aid you in avoiding problems and difficulties in your life. It may be that the majority of your travels are for pleasure and the purely enjoyable sights, sounds and experiences you share with other people. Your intuitions and perceptions of your experiences and the diplomatic affect you have on other people enhance your creativity and artistic expressions. At the same time, you more than likely express your ideas and feelings well verbally, adding emotion and impact to your conversations.

Under planetary affliction, this individual can be indifferent and lazy with a tendency to desire and wish for the unattainable. There is every indication for disappointments and difficulties through unrealized hopes and dreams. When well aspected, this individual receives honors and recognition, general success and good fortune, and is happy in marriage.

This is an excellent position for Venus on your chart and promises that your charming and pleasant disposition will be appreciated and recognized by others.

Mars in The Ninth House

With Mars in the Ninth House, you are intellectually energetic and enthusiastic, forming opinions and beliefs which you adhere to adamantly. You are capable of assertively upholding your convictions and will try with all the powers of your persuasive abilities to influence others to your way of thinking. Independent and strong willed, you achieve an education, even if it is through self-education, and continue to broaden your intellect through additional knowledge and experiences. If you are a self-made person, that doesn't deter your determination or efforts in anyway. You possess an adventurous nature, and once committed to an effort will crusade its cause undauntingly. You may become involved in social reform, evangelism, left wing causes,

389

right wing causes, politically correct reforms, or the tenants of conservatism. Whatever your intellectual persuasion, you stick to your beliefs and attempt with all your energies to persuade others to your point of view. Your tenacity leads you to experience any number of obstacles, strife, and problems, but you face any and all adversaries with the forcefulness of your convictions. And the chances are that you back up your words with decisive (and at times bold) actions. For you, travel offers the opportunity for broadening your focus and for expanding the breadth of your knowledge and base of information. The fundamental principles of concepts attract your curiosity, and you find yourself exploring the depths and hidden meaning of contrasting theologies and philosophies. It may be that your liberal ideas and love for freedom of expressing well devised concepts leads you to study and explore as much as possible, often in direct opposition to narrow-minded principles. There is some indication for problems associated with travel, legal affairs, violence, in-laws or relatives of your spouse, and with distressing ideas or dreams.

Under planetary afflictions, this individual is often overly headstrong, fanatical, skeptical, narrow-minded, aggressive, and condemning of anyone with opposing viewpoints. There is an indication for many problems and disputes with lawsuits, relatives, in-laws, travel, and religious beliefs. When well aspected, this individual is enterprising and independent, realizing success in legal matters and self-development.

Whether your interest is in law, politics, philosophy or religion, you explore and seek out new ideas and concepts, forever developing your intellect to better perceive and process new information.

JUPITER IN THE NINTH HOUSE

Jupiter in the Ninth House and your expansive, open-minded, and optimistic nature leads you to explore extraordinary philosophies, thoughts and concepts. Jupiter, the planet of good fortune, when in the House that it rules, confers an especially benevolent and tolerant attitude toward the ideas and viewpoints of other people. You possess the understanding faculty for clear and intuitive forethought and anticipation of the underlying feelings and emotions which lead others to adopt particular beliefs and concepts. This understanding also leads to an appreciation of the good or common points of various philosophies, theologies, and precepts. Then too, your perceptive abilities may compel you to an interest in the occult, metaphysics, or physic phenomena. Whatever your interest, you seek as much knowledge and information as you can possibly absorb while you develop and add to your own principles and beliefs. Your faithfulness and devotion to your beliefs or values develops within you the aspiration for higher and more profound education, intellectual freedom of thought and expressions, and in addition, every available opportunity for expansion of these thoughts and insights. The idea of travel excites your adventurous nature, and you yearn to experience new places, meet interesting people, and exchange ideas on a variety of levels. It may well be that you have a flair for languages and, with your congenial manners, get along well and easily with people who you meet through foreign travel. You may find that both education and travel provides you also with new opportunities for advancement and success. You express your ideas well and may discover this success through writing, education, or publishing your ideas.

Under planetary afflictions, this individual is arrogant, overbearing, ostentatious, proud, self-righteous, boastful, and extreme in beliefs, religion, or philosophies. There is indication for danger and accidents through travel, and problems with religious affiliations, legal affairs, philosophy, and relatives. When well aspected, this individual is serene, open-minded, rational, and successful enjoying honors and recognition through education, religion, law, philosophy, or humanitarian efforts. This position is indicative of good luck and fortunate circumstances through travel, visionary insights, international concerns, science, higher education, occult interests, inventions, communications, or transportation.

Your optimism and bright outlook on life serves as an inspiration to others while your higher aspirations compel you to seek new knowledge and information while broadening your mind and intellect.

Saturn in The Ninth House

With Saturn in the Ninth House, you are serious and conscientious with a methodical and well organized approach to improving your intellectual abilities in order to pursue your goals. Your interests may lead you to develop a somewhat orthodox philosophical outlook with a cautious tendency toward new approaches, methods or ideas. This caution may even develop into a distrust of new procedures, theories, or philosophies. At the same time, you develop an interest in science, law, geology, politics, travel, writing, teaching, lecturing, archeology, economics, theology, or metaphysics. Your sincere and earnest desire to studiously search out all the facts results in you being well informed and thorough in your knowledge of any particular subject matter. Then too, once you have gathered information pertaining to a subject of interest, you become contemplative and meditative, reflecting seriously on the impact or outcome of your research. Your well trained mind sets high standards for yourself and you are inclined to apply those same standards to others. And those standards are no doubt based on conventional and traditional ideas and values. You may have a tendency to put pleasure and good times on the back burner, especially early in your career, while you remain preoccupied with the more serious aspects of pursuing success and security in your professional life. Travel, for example, may be undertaken for business rather than for relaxation or exposure to new places. It may well be that once you have achieved your goals in life, you relax more and your ideologies become more tolerant. You may face obstacles and problems associated with receiving an education, but generally you face all limitations with determination to succeed.

Under planetary afflictions, this individual is overly dogmatic, austere, intolerant, bigoted, and judgmental and at the worst is mentally unstable or even perverted. There is an indication for obstacles and problems brought about by travel, affairs in foreign countries, legal difficulties, and with in-laws and relatives of the spouse. When well aspected, this individual possesses idealistic principles and philosophies.

You take life seriously and are capable of handling responsibilities and duties diligently. You develop a faithful devotion to your religious or spiritual principles.

Uranus in The Ninth House

With Uranus in the Ninth House, you may have more than the average share of an adventuresome spirit. The chances are you have come to expect unusual and unexpected occurrences in your life. But then your viewpoint is unorthodox with a tendency to explore the unknown and unexplainable. You have a tendency to be interested in philosophy, occult, metaphysical, or unnatural phenomena. Your inventive intellect is resourceful, and with your independent nature you love to roam and travel, exploring new avenues of thought and experience. Intuitive and open to new ideas, you are tolerant of the viewpoints of others, perhaps feeling that you can gain understanding and insight by exploring different perspectives. Your travels expose you to out of the ordinary experiences, including some danger, and exotic people and places. Your spiritualism or personal philosophy may lead you to develop an humanitarian interest in the welfare of the common person. At the same time, your studies, observations, and exposures to diverse cultures and peoples has lead you to be open-minded and accepting of nontraditional or unconventional thought patterns. You don't hesitate to question the cultural dictates of Western culture perceiving them as provincial, restrictive, and limiting. You are the intellectual free spirit who values your personal ability to think for yourself and to make your own decisions in life. And those decisions can be very original and novel. The run of the mill, conventional person may see you as peculiar and eccentric, but then that is probably the least of your concerns. Your interests and inclinations may lead you to teach, lecture, research, preach, enter politics, or become a social reformer.

There is an indication for sudden, or unexpected trips, problems and unusual experiences while traveling, exposure to some danger, and difficulties with in-laws and relatives of your spouse. Reversals with legal affairs or contracts and unexpected problems with them. With planetary afflictions, this is individuals is impractical, rebellious, or fanatical, and may join cults or anti-social movements. When well aspected, this individual is insightful and highly intuitive with prophetic visions.

Your philosophies and ideas are progressive and many times original, inventive, and advanced. Your adventuresome nature leads you to be open to not only to new ideas but to new experiences and people. You seek out the unorthodox, willing to explore and sample the unconventional.

NEPTUNE IN THE NINTH HOUSE

Neptune in the Ninth House leads you to develop a spiritual nature with an interest in philosophical and inspiring subjects. Your intellect questions the orthodox and investigates the unorthodox, leading you to explore mysticism, astrology, or other concepts. You are intuitive and quite possibly receptive to clairvoyance, visions, premonitions, or at times what appears to be prophetic visions. The idea of long trips and travel to faraway places entrances your imagination as well, and you yearn to experience and to be exposed to as much as possible in life. You have a love for languages, cultures, forgotten philosophies, and emerging insights and theories regarding ancient times. Your often unusual dreams, perceptions, feelings, senses, and experiences leads you to believe that there is more to this life than man has come to understand, and you seek to use your intellect to gain some understanding of the possibilities of the unknown and unexplainable. At the same time, you have a tendency to be impressionable which exposes you to others who attempt to lead and influence your thoughts and decisions. Learning to trust your personal intuition rather than to follow the opinions of others becomes a lesson for you in the realities of life. When you do follow your own nature, the chances are you develop a highly profound standard of spiritualism, religion, or personal philosophy. Insightful in this regard, you can also be inspiring to others who also seek knowledge and enlightenment. You may become interested in teaching, counseling, consulting, social work, or helping others in some way.

Under planetary afflictions, this individual is highly impressionable, imitative, indecisive, exaggerating, discontented with life, impractical, or even extravagant. There is an indication for this native to experience troublesome dreams, feelings, and psychic occurrences; problems through trips and travel; difficulties with legal affairs; and troubles with relatives of the spouse. When well aspected, this individual develops highly inspirational philosophies.

You are visionary, insightful and highly imaginative with a tolerant and good heart. Your inclinations lead you to develop an interest in helping others especially those less fortunate than yourself. From your efforts, you gain an appreciation for the self-rewarding, intrinsic value of developing your inner nature and higher aspirations.

Pluto in The Ninth House

With Pluto in the Ninth House, you possess a compelling desire to investigate and to get to the bottom line of whatever subject matter your intellectual curiosity has lead you to. And, based on your investigations, you may have an ever more inherently compelling feeling that the right amount of change would transform life for the better for one and all. But then restless and eager for change, your nature seeks the more adventuresome path in life. You are the chance taker, willing to try most anything once including walking on the edge and daring the powers that be to send you even more thrilling experiences. Travel, meeting new people and unusual characters, and being exposed to a variety of personal philosophies has a huge impact on your personal reflections. The broad scope of your experiences exposes you to thought patterns, perceptions, beliefs, lifestyles, and life choices that are eye opening and inspiring. And this inspiration may lead you to develop your own personal philosophy concerning the nature of man and man's propensity for good and bad. Hypocrisy, inconsistencies, bureaucratic incongruities, and the unnecessary rules, regulations, and traditions that place limitations and restrictions on the freedom and liberties of individuals upset you. In fact, you may even feel that law makers are producing unnecessary laws that no one bothers to follow simply to keep their jobs in tact. Your own spiritual nature may be well developed, and you find that you easily influence and sway the opinions of others while inspiring them to lead fuller lives. Your personal philosophy, however, may grow, evolve, develop, and change as you progress through life. As you mature, you gain an appreciation for what you have learned through your experiences and for the wisdom and insight you have gained. Your ability to follow your aspirations, regardless of the obstacles you face, leads you to an acceptance of success and failure, and you learn to appreciate both. Your spouse may be from a foreign country or another culture.

Under planetary afflictions, this individual is overly changeable, rash, impulsive, either indifferent or opinionated, and can become fanatical in religious, social, or radical political movements. There is an indication for danger in travel, difficulties with the relatives of the spouse, legal problems, and lawsuits. When well aspected, the individual gains insights and understanding from travel, people, and experiences.

You possess an insatiable desire for knowledge, information, travel and experiences. Your understanding, sympathetic, and accepting nature draws other people to you.

PLANETS IN THE TENTH HOUSE RULED BY CAPRICORN

THE HOUSE OF CAREER

The Sun in the Tenth House influences you to strive for achievement and success in your chosen field. Your ambitious nature leads you to aspire to positions of authority, responsibility, power and prestige. This position of the Sun is favorable for success and gain through your profession with indications for recognition, honor, and even fame. This is a particularly good location for politicians, persons in public offices, or other careers dealing with the public and public recognition. If not a public figure, then you are more than likely active in your community or well known in your profession. You are more than willing to work hard and to apply your efforts to achieving your career goals even if it means putting your personal life, family, personal relationships and pleasures on hold. The Sun in this location acts much as it does in the sign of Capricorn, and Capricorn is recognized for diligence, application, and tenacity. The natural strength and vitality of the Sun allows this type of perseverance, but at the same time you accept responsibilities and duties based on a strong sense of values and morals. In other words, you set high standards for yourself and then follow through accordingly. You are independent thinking with a resourceful nature and a dignified bearing that automatically impresses others. There is indication that influential people are impressed with your abilities, ambitions, decisiveness, and leadership.

Under planetary afflictions, this individual is overbearing, arrogant, self-serving, rebellious, and even dictatorial and power hungry. While the Sun in the Tenth House brings benefits, there is the possibility for reversals. When well aspected, this individual receives honor, fame, recognition, and success in life.

You have the ability to achieve success while influencing and inspiring others with your leadership abilities. Honest and trustworthy, other people look to you for responsible decisions and actions.

THE MOON IN THE TENTH HOUSE

With the Moon in the Tenth House, you are inclined toward a public life striving for recognition, prominence and success in your career. And this natural inclination leads you to dream and visualize about being before the public or crowds. Whether this is actualized in your career or social life, you feel compelled to act upon your desires for recognition and appreciation. For one reason or another, however, you may experience any number of changes in your professional life, realizing successes, gains and then again reversals in positions and popularity. There is a strong indication that your career moves and your profession are in some way influenced by a woman. This may be your mother, another female member of your family, or someone else who is concerned with your success and achievements. The Moon in the Tenth House is a good position for prominence, success and public recognition, and this location is advantageous for careers in marketing, advertising, design, consumer products for women, decorating, designing, photography, acting, music, art, fashions, food or catering, commodities, shipping, or traveling. Or you could just as easily choose to be an entrepreneur in a field indicated by your Sun sign. You may find the most success in a career that allows for change. Wherever you desires lead you, more than anything you strive for advancement, recognition and appreciation from others. This may lead you to be so involved with others that your private life is put on hold or even ignored. But while you may be somewhat careless with your personal finances, there is every indication for gain through property or possessions.

Under planetary afflictions, this individual is too changeable, restless, driven, and dissatisfied if not appreciated. There is an indication for public scandal, problems associated with notoriety, public discredit and disapproval, success followed by failure, and numerous business difficulties. When well aspect, this individual enjoys appreciation, success, popularity and financial security; benefits through association with a woman.

When well developed, this native possesses the ability to be concerned for the social welfare of the public, and to use personal charisma to influence public opinion.

MERCURY IN THE TENTH HOUSE

With Mercury in the Tenth House you are better at planning and organizing than dealing with minute details. Friendly and outgoing, you know how to communicate your ideas and concepts well. In fact, this may be a perfect position for the Moon for a career in communications such as writing, publishing, or a position which allows you to put ideas before the public. If the job calls for a person who is energetic, quick, decisive, and responsible, you are more than well qualified. Then too, you work well with other people and exhibit natural leadership abilities. You may be called upon by others to share your ideas and abilities and to utilize your charisma and natural charm by entering politics. Or, it may well be that you possess a strong interest in literature, teaching, public speaking, consulting, traveling, psychology, or astrological research. If you decide to develop the skills associated with your natural manual dexterity, this could lead to a career in computer hardware, electronics, electricity, or transportation. And your versatility and creativity doesn't preclude turning your ideas into inventions. You are drawn to facts rather than opinions and abstractions, and your mind gathers and processes the needed information in a rather rapid manner. Your personal preferences lead you to new situations and people who are intellectually stimulating and exciting. New ideas, concepts, and the opportunity for utilizing information compels you to imagine new and innovative approaches to problems and methods. The idea of change doesn't bother you, and, in fact, you may have a tendency to change positions or careers if such a move offers the opportunity to be exposed to new ideas, people, or methods. And chances are you prefer positions that allow for freedom of movement, thoughts, and flexibility. Then too, it may be that you change positions if you find yourself stuck in a situation with uninspiring, limiting or restrictive-thinking people. Adaptable, penetrating, and resourceful, you prefer that your intellectual outlook not be restrained by procedures, rules, regulations, or the personal incompatibilities of other people.

Under planetary afflictions, this individual is overly changeable, too restless, unstable, deceptive, impulsive, and experiences problems and obstacles in business. When well aspected by other planets, there is an indication for success and honors in the career.

Your strong memory, ability to process information, and fluent speech and writing capabilities provide you with the skills necessary to realize success in any number of careers. You may have more than one job or career at a time, or change professions sometime during your life.

VENUS IN THE TENTH HOUSE

Venus in the Tenth House influences you to aspire to social success, and you apply your diplomacy, tact, and caring nature toward this aspiration. This is a good position for Venus for awards, honors, recognition, popularity, and friendships which are based on your personal charms, abilities and personal merit. Perceptive as well as receptive to the feelings and inclinations of others, you read a crowd and are capable of using your powers of speech and voice modulation to inspire and influence others. Your natural abilities may lead you to an interest in art, music, literature, or cultural affairs. Then too, with your appreciation of beauty and elegance, you may find yourself drawn to a career dealing with women, fashions, beauty, cosmetics, jewelry, accessories, entertainment or amusements, luxury items, or a position which requires you to interact with the public. Congenial, affable, and likable, you much prefer harmonious and pleasant situations, and you are talented at making other people feel at ease. This ability to relate well to others carries over into your career, and you handle business meetings and gatherings with ease. You are particularly skillful in dealing with women and their concerns. There is indication that this is a favorable position for Venus for partnerships and/or a successful marriage which augments the career in the some manner. It is also a good position for a favorable and fortunate home life which enhances successful parenthood. It may be that a parent influences and aides your career in some manner, but along the way other people who are impressed with you offer their support, advice and help as well.

With planetary afflictions, this individual is a social climber who faces limitations, obstacles, lack of opportunities, or subordinate positions. There is some indication for scandal, notoriety, or disappointments associated with the public or with women. When well aspected, the individual receives honors and social recognition, success in career, and the support and favor of influential persons.

Your grace and poise lead you to be well accepted by the public as well as by your professional colleagues. Your genuine concern for others and your efforts to promote harmony, peace, and beauty draws the appreciation and social acclaim that you seek in life.

Mars in The Tenth House

Mars in the Tenth House influences your bold and energetically daring drive and ambition to achieve success in your career. Self-reliant, you depend upon your initiative, self-development, and the acquisition of skills to carry you to the top in your chosen field. You know that your achievements in life will be based on your own merit and effort and not on the support or assistance of others. Decisive, competitive and independent, you acquire the necessary organizational abilities to responsibly handle executive positions or to manage your own business. Your nature is aggressive and, if necessary, forceful in your efforts to push through your ideas and concepts. Quick in perceiving important facts pertaining to any situation, sizing up people, and making decisions, you rely and often act on your immediate impulse and inner feelings in order to accomplish your objectives. You are not preoccupied with the 'what ifs' or the list of possible consequences. Rather, you are prone to vigorously rearranging the situation to best suit your decisions, then seeing them through to completion. Your passionate nature and the strength of your will power enable you to face the numerous obstacles, problems, strife, and difficulties that continuously crop up to deter you from your objectives. You may also experience either benefit or a problematic situation related to your father. Independent and freedom loving, your courage and enterprise draws you to competition with the desire to win. There is an indication that you achieve either fame or recognition, or notoriety and scandal. You may pursue a career that uses your mechanical ability or seek success in the areas of engineering, drafting, architecture, construction, design, sales, dentistry, sports, medical surgery, the military, politics or acting. Some area of your life will involve physical endurance and strength, and you are unafraid of risky enterprises.

With planetary afflictions, this individual is overly forceful, dominating, forceful, and overbearing with little regard for the opinions or concerns of others. The aggressive nature results in difficulties and problems with other people; physical labor is involved on the job; business troubles, reversals and failure due to dishonesty or poor ethics are indicated. When well aspected, there is indication for success, financial gains, and prominence in the career based on personal merit, skills, and abilities.

You are a person whose aspirations, drive, and ambitions lead you to success in your business enterprise and career. Undaunted by the obstacles thrown in your path, you pursue your goals relentlessly.

JUPITER IN THE TENTH HOUSE

With Jupiter in the Tenth House, fate opens windows of opportunity to you which you view with optimism and enthusiasm. Self-reliant, confident, and trustworthy, you possess strong leadership abilities, an authoritative demeanor, and the capacity to interact well with others. Proud and ambitious, you aspire to managerial or executive positions of leadership and authority. The chances are you also have high moral standards and you seek fairness and justice in your dealings with other people. You recognize the importance of being socially active as well, and in this area of your life you find as much success as in your career. It may well be that you are drawn to the fields of banking, corporate finance, politics, law, the justice system, sports, politics, government, diplomatic positions, religion, economics, or investments. Then too, you may prefer the opportunities for freedom and expansion offered by owning your own business. Jupiter in the Tenth House offers success from opportunities, social contacts, knowing the right people, and being in the right place at the right time. There is indication not only for career success but for financial gains through marriage, sports, or public office as well as honor and recognition, assistance from influential friends, and benefits from superiors. It seems that your good luck holds in social, political or public positions with appointments, offices, or gains realized.

Under planetary afflictions, this individual can be arrogant, indifferent, overbearing, and snobbish. There is indication for difficulties, obstacles, losses, and reversals in business, social life, and travel; some losses due to dishonesty; minor position in career dealing with the public. When well aspected, this individual enjoys the personal acclaim and public recognition of honors, social success, and distinctions as well as responsible and successful career positions.

Your expansive nature seeks broad horizons and opportunities for freedom of thought and expression even though you are most likely a conventional person in your outlook and perspectives. You most enjoy surroundings and career positions which allow for your mind to explore and for your energy to find focus.

Saturn in The Tenth House

With Saturn in the Tenth House, you are drawn to responsible positions with your ambitious nature compelling you to aspire to power, positions, and advancement. Your accomplishments in life are based on your tenacity, hard work, diligence, perseverance, industry, persistence, and personal merit and effort. The chances are your achievements in life stay with you only if you possess the ability to endure the hardships and to overcome any and all obstacles. This prospect leads you to be serious and conscientious, accepting your responsibilities and devoting yourself to being worthy of any position you acquire. You much prefer to apply common sense, good methods, and a cautious approach to decision making in your business endeavors. Then too, your dignity, demeanor, and self-reliance brings you the respect of others who look to you for accountability and good reasoning. You are management material and may aspire to an executive position of authority and leadership. You may perceive life as being one long climb requiring all your efforts to achieve a top position or success in your career. You are capable of studying and examining the system in order to ascertain the best methods to use to realize your goals. You do well in any position requiring a methodical, well organized approach, and you may decide to enter the field of banking, government, law, science, business management, construction, mining, or research, or politics.

Under planetary affliction or when the individual is not well developed, Saturn in the Tenth House is considered a position which is known for those who find success through their own efforts and then experience reversals, losses, and business failure. Little or no opportunities are indicated in this position, and all accomplishments are gained on the basis of personal effort. There is also an indication for problems, obstacles, delays, and prolonged, dull periods showing little accomplishment; financial failure with undeserved dishonor and discredit; defeats and losses through politics and public affairs. When well aspected, this individual accomplishes goals and objectives and achieves success through hard work, personal merit and effort.

There is an indication that once a person with this placement of Saturn achieves a satisfactory position in his or her career, it is best to hold on to it. Your diligent nature leads you work hard for achievements in life, and you more than anyone else know that whatever you acquire is well deserved. You earn the respect and recognition of colleagues, associates and partners.

Uranus in The Tenth House

With Uranus in the Tenth House, you seek a career that allows for your independent nature. You dislike limitations, restrictions or strict authority over your freedom of movement, exploration, and expressions. The chances are your career will be unusual or eventful in some manner. You are creative and imaginative with a definite inventive bend to your thinking processes. You much prefer developing new methods, procedures, or thought patterns and abhor following conventional methods just for the sake of tradition or because that's the way it's always been done. Unafraid of following your own inclinations, you pursue your personal concepts and ideologies preferring to investigate and invent procedures as you go. You are totally uninhibited about trying unconventional approaches, at times astounding or shocking your colleagues, partners, family and friends. You possess broad minded theories of what is acceptable behavior and what is not, looking at the general effect and outcome of actions in relation to the benefit of the whole. You see many laws and regulations as being unnecessary restrictions which are offensive primarily because you weren't involved in creating them, therefore you don't understand why they apply to your life. Your career and professional life brings you changes, sometimes unexpected, in status and position. It may be that you undertake two different careers or jobs at the same time. There may be times that you feel that others don't understand you, and indeed that may well be the case. While you are friendly and generally easy going, you experience problems with superiors, employers, and persons in authority. When you discover a cause that catches your attention, you can become doggedly determined, persistent, and forceful. While there is indication for Uranus in the Tenth House to bring extraordinary experiences in business activities, socially, or through public affairs, there is also seen obstacles, discredit and reversals which you must overcome in order to be successful. Your inclinations lead you to the fields of electronics, science, humanitarian concerns, social work, psychology, teaching, research, investigations, flying, journalism, electricity, writing, acting, music, explorations, metaphysics, or perhaps a career requiring mechanical ability. Then too, you may much prefer to be your own boss by owning and running a business.

Under planetary afflictions, this individual is eccentric, rebellious, restless, and experiences numerous difficulties dealing with authority figures whether it be with parents, the law, superiors, or in public affairs. There is an indication for separation from family, friends, partners or loved ones; and hazardous, daring, or dangerous employment. When well aspected, this is an especially inventive person who experiences unusual or unexpected changes.

Your creativity and imagination combined with your inventive skills brings you much inspiration in life. Once you set your goals and objective and follow through with personal effort, you realize success and recognition in your endeavors.

Neptune in The Tenth House

Neptune in the Ninth House and you are quite possibly a person of vision and idealistic approaches to humanitarian concerns. Neptune influence brings an illusionary quality which leads you to pursue either careers or past times which allow you to cast yourself in a role of your own making. This is an excellent position for actors, comedians, musicians, entertainers, writers, social scientists, social reformers, scientist, psychologists, astrology, religion, philosophy, or careers associated with water. Then too, there is a mysterious quality endowed by this position of Neptune, and you may feel inclined to a career involving secrecy, confidentiality, or in which you use an assumed name. In fact, mysteries intrigue your imagination and curiosity which may lead you to explore or investigate phenomena seeking solutions to so far unanswered questions. Intuitive and perceptive, many people find your ideas and concepts inspirational and insightful while the more conventional person may see you as unusual or different. With Neptune in this position, there is indication for success, gains, honors, recognition, and public acclaim through a unique approach to your career. You may receive assistance from your parents, but if not, you aspire to achievement and accomplishments based on your own merit. This location is often associated with the film industry where success can be glamorous but also transitory.

Under planetary afflictions, this individual can scatter his or her efforts in too many directions. There is indication for an unusual or out of the ordinary career filled with obstacles and complications as well as scandal or notoriety which is not always the fault of the native. When well aspected, this idealistic individual is creatively talented and possesses the ability to inspire others with either his or her concepts or performances.

Your mind may be filled with dreams, visions, illusions, and ideals for the perfect world or the perfect picture, but you pull your ideas together in a manner which translates ideals into realism.

PLUTO IN THE TENTH HOUSE

With Pluto in the Tenth House, you are driven by an intense desire to succeed at your endeavors. Self-assertive, strong willed, and determined, you use your persuasive abilities to pull the support of other people to you. Once you have an idea in your head, you can become compelled to successfully follow it through to completion. At times impulsive or rash, you must guard against not following the wrong ideas, pursuits or goals for too long before you finally accept failure. But then you have the tendency to accept failure as a lesson in life and to move on to new or even more challenging endeavors. You can apply your talents and skills perceptively and effectively, and when necessary you face down obstacles, authorities, or limitations and restrictions. Your business acumen and flair for success leads you to aspire to leadership positions of responsibility and authority. However, you may most desire independence and the power that comes from making your own decisions and deciding your own direction in life. Courageous, tenacious and willing to work as hard and diligently as necessary, you can lead, direct, innovate or invent, depending on what the situation calls for. You possess a dynamic energy, but your drive is more than likely based on your strong will power and determination. Not wanting to be distracted by unnecessary problems, you prefer to exert control over your personal and business affairs, sensing intuitively the best direction to pursue and the most efficient method to follow. You can, at times, lose patience with others who are procrastinating and indecisive when the situation calls for what you perceive as rather simple undertakings or procedures. Quick thinking and decisive, more cautious people can have difficulty following your thinking or keeping up with your logic. You also strive for the a job well done, preferring or striving for perfection whenever possible, and you don't appreciate nonproductive practices, sloppiness, or lack of industriousness.

If afflicted, this individual is dictatorial, manipulative, resentful, neurotic, antisocial, and intimidating. There is indication for obstacles, strife, and problems through enemies, secret affairs, associations with organized crime, psychic dealings, and faulty business practices. If well aspected, this native experiences success in endeavors as well as recognition and honor through the career.

You are quite capable of succeeding at your endeavors once you decide on a career field and your chosen direction in life.

403

Planets in The Eleventh House Ruled by Aquarius

The House of Friends

The Sun in the Eleventh House acts much like the Sun in Aquarius, influencing you to possess a high regard for friendships. At the same time, you are an independent person with a freedom loving nature. This leads you to desire to know as many people as possible, to be sociable, and to socialize through entertainment or social events. At the same time, you hesitate to allow others to infringe on your personal life by placing limitations on your freedom. This leads you to withdraw at times to your own sanctuary seeking privacy and the opportunity to allow your thoughts or interests to roam at random. You follow your own whims and have the ability to influence others to join in your escapades and adventures. You also possess a distinctly and uniquely humanitarian outlook on life, perceiving the good in people and mankind in general. You are open, tolerant and accepting of other people, cultures, and groups, believing that everyone has something to offer toward the betterment of society. You enjoy planning and organizing gatherings either for pleasure, entertainment, or just to pass the time of day. Your mind focuses on ideologies, and often you find yourself discussing serious subject matters with your acquaintances. And this is a fortunate location for lofty desires and ambitions. This is also a good position of the Sun for you to receive benefits, assistance, or support from influential friends.

There is indication that you acquire friendships and associations with powerful and influential people who are impressed with your loyalty, dignity, honesty, and self worth. You achieve prominence, honors, and recognition through social success. With planetary afflictions, this individual is often domineering and self serving. When well aspected, the native is genuinely concerned with the well being of other people.

You are quite capable of accepting responsible positions of leadership in humanitarian causes, politics, recreation, amusements, or cultural events.

THE MOON IN
THE ELEVENTH HOUSE

With the Moon in the Eleventh House you possess a compelling need for friends, especially one very special friend who you feel will be there for you and will remain a friend for life. You become very attached to your friends, dependent on their influence and input into your life. But while you may know a large number of people, a good number of your friends may surprise you by being unreliable, disloyal or unfaithful. There is an indication that you enjoy much success in dealing with women, children, and young adults, but you may not develop many lasting friendships. You love to be surrounded by people, involved in group activities, and included in social events, but many of these types of encounters are somewhat superficial. Sociable, pleasant, and charming, you have a tendency to reflect the social climate in which you find yourself, aspiring to please others and to fit in with the situation. Other people are attracted to you, and this makes for a pleasant outings, but others don't get to see who you really are. And that may be what you had in mind because in actuality you are a very private person who allows only the most trusted person to ever get to know you well. Perhaps you fear others wouldn't accept the real you, or perhaps you don't really trust just anybody. Whatever the case may be, you remain a social butterfly, happy with your numerous activities, clubs, associations, or get togethers.

Under planetary afflictions, this individual is self-serving, narcissistic, self-absorbed, and easily influenced. There is an indication for sorrows, losses, disappointments, sudden changes, delays, limitations, separations, and scandals through friends, acquaintances, and social encounters. When well aspected, this individual is favored by friends and acquaintances. There is an indication for hopes and desires to be realized.

This is a good position for the Moon for success in social desires and wishes. You do well in volunteer work or activities requiring organizational abilities and a creative flair. Your imagination grants you the ability to be dramatically entertaining with a natural intuition for reading the group or the crowd and knowing how to respond. You are quite capable of being either entertaining or inspiring, or then again you may choose to turn on your famous charm or charisma. With this particular position of the Moon, you may need to be careful of people who influence you in a negative way or who take advantage of your giving nature. You meet and enjoy a wide assortment of acquaintances some of whom are influential or well known personalities.

Mercury in Eleventh House

With Mercury in the Eleventh House you prefer the intellectual companionship of well informed and well spoken friends and acquaintances. You are intuitive, but you perceive the world through your mind rather than reacting to situations through your emotions. You are capable of rationalizing and deducing the pertinent aspects of a situation, and you use this approach in your interpersonal relationships. Perhaps somewhat reserved, your active and original mind grants you a witty sense of humor and a way with words that others find insightful. You enjoy a large circle of acquaintances and may join a number of clubs, groups, associations, or societies. Then too, you may find yourself pulling groups of people together to exchange ideas, dialogue, and viewpoints on a range of topics. You appreciate being exposed to differing ideas and are capable of listening to opposing perspectives without being offended when the opinions of others differ from your own. Tolerant and accepting, you can understand opposing viewpoints even if you don't agree with them. Logical and practical, you add these experiences to your bank of knowledge while pursuing additional new ideas and facts. Good literature, science, astrology, research, investigations, or humanitarian issues intrigue your imagination. Not a loner, the number of people you know steadily grows, but you may find that you develop few close and lasting friendships. This may be due to your preference for group interactions, activities, and communications. Somewhat idealistic and original in thought, you desire ideas and most appreciate being exposed to new people who can interject a fresh slant or perspective on a subject matter. You especially appreciate the novel or differing perspectives of younger people.

With planetary afflictions, this individual can be at times impractical, cynical, critical, or eccentric. There are indications for problems, obstacles, worries and anxieties caused by unreliable friends; undependable advice from friends; and distrustful or dishonest friends. When well aspected, this native can be inspirational to others and often receives benefits from friends.

While your resourceful intellect is adept at developing creative concepts, solutions and new ideas, there is an indication that you should choose your friends carefully in order to prevent unnecessary problems, scandals, or public embarrassment. Your versatility and adaptability makes you at home in many situations, meeting new people and acquaintances with ease. Your intellectual outlook on life can add insight and inspiration to your conversations and interpersonal relationships.

VENUS IN THE ELEVENTH HOUSE

With Venus in the Eleventh House, your friends are an important aspect of your life. Many of your friendships may be formed with creative, talented or artistic individuals who add beauty, insight and inspiration to your life. Your openness and outgoing nature also attracts many acquaintances of the opposite sex with whom you form congenial relationships. You can be an idealist, preferring to be surrounded by pleasant, happy people in harmonious situations. And in fact, your friends do provide much happiness while at the same time supporting you in your projects and ideas. In fact, it may be that this support group of friends and acquaintances provide the leverage and networking that you need to achieve your hopes, aspirations and dreams. Socially active and popular, you find that you gain through the large number of people, contacts, and friends who you associate with. Gregarious and at ease in the companionship of others, you delight in making other people feel comfortable and relaxed. You can be caring, giving, and entertaining, much preferring that your friends enjoy the best you have to offer. Life for you should be enjoyable for one and all and to that end you have a strong desire for the best of food, drink and pleasurable times. Then too, you possess a strong appreciation for the arts, theater, cultural affairs and relaxing activities where people gather in an amiable and refined atmosphere. With this location of Venus, it is quite possible that you will meet your spouse through your social contacts and activities, and that your marriage will be beneficial and happy. There is also an indication for benefits, gains, and favors from female acquaintances.

With planetary afflictions, this individual can be too interested in fun and pleasure, choosing the wrong friends who lead the person astray. Under adverse planetary influence, unreliable friends cause problems, loss, scandal, or delays through faulty advice. There is an indication that the hopes, desires, and goals are frustrated by others. When well aspected, this position of Venus influences an individual to enjoy pleasant and happy associations and benefits from friends.

Your diplomatic, tactful, and gracious nature leads you to enjoy being surrounded by friends and acquaintances who appreciate your ability to interact well with others. Your pleasant charm brings you much happiness and the fulfillment of your dreams and desires.

407

Mars in The Eleventh House

With Mars in the Eleventh House, popularity is less important to you than being surrounded by others who appreciate and share your ideas and opinions. You can be aggressively active in group activities often taking a leadership role. You may have a preference for the companionship of other people who are forceful and outspoken or unafraid of voicing their personal opinions. Independent and enthusiastic, you may champion particular causes or voice strong opinions about community, national, or international affairs. With your strong opinions, you have the ability to stir interest and action through group involvement's for worthy causes and concerns. It may be also that you possess a strong and patriotic appreciation for veterans and military personnel who served their country. The chances are your forthright and independent nature leads you to quarrels and disagreements with friends and associates. But then controversy doesn't necessarily dispel your energies. In fact, just the opposite may be true, and you find your adrenaline level fueled and your energy level set on high when in the midst of a conflict. When it comes to associates, you may be rather choosy, preferring to have only a few close friends who you trust and know you can count on. At times, somewhat impulsive or rash, you are not afraid of taking a risk or being involved in daring adventures, strenuous sports, or unusual activities. At some time in your life, this adventuresome nature of yours combined with the influence of your friends may have lead you into questionable or dangerous activities. You are familiar with obstacles, problems and sorrow, quite possibly having had to face the death of good friend in the past. If you were to find yourself placed in the right circumstances, you could easily become a revolutionary, seeking change and benefits for society.

With planetary afflictions, this individual is argumentative, impulsive, disruptive, offensive, quarrelsome, sensitive, easily frustrated, or indulgent of pleasures and inclined to risky, troublesome, or treacherous friends who cause problems and loss through poor influence and faulty, bad advice; problems with the law; financial difficulties; and death through risky ventures or death of friend. When well aspected, this individual is responsible and helpful to friends and acquaintances and gains success through friends.

You are strongly individualistic with a preference for friends with strong wills and natures. You are energetically enterprising in meeting people and leading others in worthwhile causes and work hard to promote your goals and ideas. You may well be a social reformer, leader, or promoter.

JUPITER IN THE ELEVENTH HOUSE

With Jupiter in the Eleventh House, your expansive nature leads you to fortunate circumstances surrounded by loyal and trustworthy friends. Your optimism and enthusiasm shows in your relationship with influential people of high standing in your community such as business people, legislators, bankers, judges or other professional people. Your social success enhances your professional growth and development and you find yourself benefiting from your many associations, acquaintances and long time friends. Your ambitious and self-reliant nature as well as your own trustworthiness and honesty brings you recognition and credit from others. Your acquaintances also appreciate your generous nature and your interest in the welfare of other people. You appear to others to be the genuine article, true to your word, industrious, and possessing the best of intentions. You can be a natural leader who others trust to follow, and your aspirations may lead you to executive positions of authority and leadership either in your profession or through your involvement with social groups, clubs, or associations. Your acceptance and popularity brings you much happiness in life, and your stroke of luck at just the right moment only adds to your optimism and enthusiasm in initiating activities, projects, or social gatherings. It would appear that this same luck holds when you meet your spouse through your social contacts or friends because marriage turns out to be a happy affair for you as well. While you may be independent and freedom loving, you are also generous, well meaning, responsible, and caring. You take the time to develop numerous and diverse interests, meeting others who introduce you to new topics of conversation or stimulating and entertaining activities. Ever open to new and different ideas and thoughts, you are a good listener with a sensitive ear to the feelings and opinions of others.

Under planetary afflictions, this individual is pleasure seeking, lazy, indifferent, deceitful, unresponsible, and either uses friends and associates for personal gain or is taken advantage of by friends; problems and difficulties brought on by jealous friends. When well aspected, Jupiter in the Eleventh House is a lucky and fortunate position for friendships.

Your magnetic charm and personal outlook on life draws other people to you. When well developed, this individual is insightful and inspiring serving as a role model in responsible, caring, and giving behavior.

Saturn in The Eleventh House

Saturn is the planet of self-discipline and self-imposed limitations. With Saturn in the Eleventh House, you are somewhat reserved and cautious in your choice of friends and acquaintances. Industrious and hard working, you may prefer to select friends carefully based on your preconceived notions of whether or not it is a wise decision. In other words, you don't want to take a chance on risky associations with the wrong people. It may appear at times that you cultivate friendships with influential people or with those who will benefit you in some way. However, this may just be a reflection of your discriminating nature because among your friends you are known for your caring, responsible and attentive nature. In fact, you may have friends who are older or else in some way needy of your support and assistance. You are a loyal and faithful person who can become devoted to the welfare of others. This at times leads you to be self-sacrificing to the point of inconveniencing yourself. Accustomed to facing obstacles and problems in life, you take this inconvenience in stride, feeling a strong desire to patiently complete what you set out to accomplish whether it be the care of someone else or the attainment of your goals. Rather than socializing on a grand scale with a large number of people, you may prefer the companionship of a few close and personal friends who share your interests in life. Superficial relationships hold little attraction for you perhaps because you view them as a waste of time. You probably prefer mentally stimulating and informative conversations with knowledgeable people. Professionals, well educated or well informed people with an interest in science, politics, public affairs, economics, or business may attract your notice. Your involvement in groups, clubs or associations is primarily to gain knowledge, and you take a serious interest in whatever new information you can gather. It is important to you to feel respected by your friends and associates, and you strive to be a person who deserves that respect.

With planetary afflictions, this individual is either lonely or an extravagant show-off. There is indication for this individual to be used by deceitful friends who take advantage of the him or her; responsibility for the care of another person; many obstacles, difficulties, sorrow, strife and failure through delays of friends and acquaintances; friendships with unfortunate and needy people; faces numerous frustrations in accomplishments. When well aspected, this individual is a responsible person with high aspirations who must face and overcome any number of obstacles and problems in life. Your responsible and serious nature earns you the respect of others. You are drawn to other conventional and traditional people who appreciate and share your interests.

410

Uranus in The Eleventh House

With Uranus in the Eleventh House, your visions, hopes, dreams and aspirations are focused on a better world for all humanity. You are open and receptive to most anybody, developing an appreciation for the differences in people as well as for the unusual or unique viewpoints, concepts and lifestyles of other people. You are also open to that chance encounter or the sudden opportunity to meet new people, no matter their background. You fit in and easily make friends with people from all walks of life, no matter their social standing. In fact, the chances are you have personal friends who are influential, prominent and prestigious as well as friends who are homeless and others who fall somewhere in between these two extremes. In one way or another, your friends and associates consider you uniquely individualistic. At the same time, you strive to preserve your freedom, privacy and opportunity to be by yourself when you feel like it. Pleasantly well-mannered and quietly friendly, your shyness may keep you subdued in a large group, but others soon notice you and are attracted to some mysterious quality about you. The chances are you are a nonconformist with a liberal, innovative viewpoint, but you don't tolerate limitations placed on your freedom of movement, thought, or expressions. And when others attempt to impose limitations on you, you are capable of becoming quite rebellious. You also have a bit of a daring streak in you that leads you and your friends on one adventure or another.

Under planetary afflictions, this individual experiences difficulties, sudden separations, unexpected estrangements, impulsive and chance encounters which lead to developing unusual aspirations and strange romantic relationships; eccentric and unreliable friends. When well aspected, this individual benefits from the most unusual and remarkable friendships with insightful and brilliant people.

You receive the benefit of insight, inspiration, hopes, desires, and wishes through your associations and friendships which lead you to develop innovative and inventive new approaches to dealing with humanitarian causes and concerns. If you are not eccentric then you are a most unusual person who is greatly admired and appreciated by others for your caring and concerned attitude and unique outlook on life.

411

NEPTUNE IN THE ELEVENTH HOUSE

With Neptune in the Eleventh House, you meet the most unusual and unique people. You may be associated with a group with strong artistic abilities or others who are gifted, talented or highly skilled. Then too, the chances are you know more than one unusual character who is remarkable for being strong willed or outrageously different. You are generous, tolerant, helpful, and accepting of your friends and associates, and they in turn open their hearts to you. Your closest friends share a spiritual awareness with you that offers insights and different perspectives on questions that arise through your life, thoughts, and meditations. You appreciate people not for what they have to offer materially, but for what they offer in the way of insight and inspiration. And you know quite well that the panhandler on the corner may have more insight than the most successful business leader in the community. Intuitive, you perceive rather correctly what is in the heart of the other person, whether good intentions or bad. But chances are you see the good even in the worst of characters. You join clubs, associations or social groups out of a desire to share a common interest or ideals with other people. Your ideology may be as unusual and different as your friends, but you are well liked and appreciated for those particular qualities. And your highest ideals and aspirations are focused on humanitarian causes and concerns. You paint visions in your head of the perfect utopia in the best of all possible worlds.

When well aspected, this individual forms beneficial friendships with unique individuals such as artists, poets, entertainers, writers, musicians, mystics, psychics, clairvoyants, and crystal ball readers as well as others with unusual past times and interests. There is an indication for success or benefits through spiritual associations.

Under planetary affliction, this individual is eccentric, erratic, impulse driven, antisocial, scheming, and suffers disappointments, problems and obstacles through the treachery of friends; losses through poor advice; and complications associated with undesirable people.

Caring, giving and generous of your resources, time and effort, you earn the appreciation, love and acceptance of the people who get to know you well. Even those who deceive you or take advantage of your kindness may call you later on to tell you how much they appreciate your loving nature. Your spiritualism inspires others to share their inner feelings with you.

PLUTO IN THE ELEVENTH HOUSE

With Pluto in the Eleventh House, your strong and independent nature leads you to form close and personal relationships and friendships. Your friends may see you often, or they may live on the other side of the world and contact is intermittent. But then your friends remain close no matter how long the separation. You are open and tolerant of other people and accepting of differing viewpoints whether those ideas agree with yours or not. But you develop your own perspectives and may be the person who pushes through or leads social reforms. Life teaches you that there are times when it is best to keep your ideas to yourself, and you learn to be secretive, or at least closed mouthed, if necessary in order not to offend others or to make unnecessary enemies. At the same time, you seek to transform problems, obstacles, and limitations into benefits for yourself and others. Your friends appreciate your caring nature and your interests in political, social, and community welfare. The chances are you are the person who is always available to help someone in need, and you become actively involved in the lives of your friends. Your intensity is focused into this caring about the lives of other people, and your friends recognize and appreciate that aspect of your personality. There are times when you prefer to be the loner, spending time to yourself to think through ideas or to enjoy your solitude.

Under planetary afflictions, this individual can be self-serving, pleasure seeking, extravagant, easily lead astray, and susceptible to changes caused by friends and associates. There are indications for problems, difficulties, delays, separations through friends; sorrow from death of friend. When well aspected, this individual is a successful leader among groups, social organizations and associations.

You are recognized for your intensely loyal nature, your abilities, and your desire to transform and reform. Given the opportunity, you form plans and initiate innovative ideas. You offer your help and assistance to others when they are in need, but you are just as capable of being on your own and by yourself. Your friends and associates come to depend on your strength, tenacity, and ability to work hard. You must guard against other people using your strength for their personal benefit to the point that you are emotionally drained. Take care to provide for yourself as well as for others.

Planets in The Twelfth House Ruled by Pisces

The House of Sacrifice, Seclusion, Secrets, Enemies and Sorrows

The Sun in the Twelfth House influences your nature to be sensitive and imaginative with a strong tendency to seek solitude to allow for privacy and contemplation. Your need for privacy is so great that you may seek to create a persona for the outside world, but you defensively guard against others ever really knowing your true self. You are reticent, preferring not to share or discuss your personal feelings openly with many people. This may be due to a deeply seated shyness or a strong preference for a personal and private life away from the curiosity, interference, and criticism of others. This privacy allows you the time and personal space to meditate or to develop your interests without having to explain yourself to anyone. After all, it is really not anyone else's business what you do in the privacy of your own home, and your interests can be unusual, unique, or highly creative. You may develop a successful interest in occult or psychic affairs, science, medicine or the healing arts, gardening and herbs, chemistry, art, research, or writing. You may be drawn to helping others by working in an institution such as a hospital, prison, or school, or you may be so talented at role playing that you become an actor. There is an indication that you will encounter obstacles and people who cause you problems, but you can successful overcome these limitations by using your creativity and ability to work hard. Other people are willing to assist you when you need it most. You may feel that you are happier in an obscure position, allowing others to seek the lime light and to receive the recognition. Then too, it is more than likely that you feel most self-fulfilled when helping others.

With planetary afflictions, this individual can be extremely shy, lonely, retiring, and reticent, or can be withdrawn and neurotic. There are indications for obstacles, problems, sorrows and misfortune. When well aspected, this individual becomes self-sacrificing and persevering, overcoming obstacles, seclusion, or obscurity through his or her personal efforts and merits.

You use your compassionate, caring and charitable nature to benefit, heal, or help other people. You have a refined sense of beauty and appreciate nature, art, and peaceful settings.

414

THE MOON IN THE TWELFTH HOUSE

With the Moon the Twelfth House, you view reality through your feelings, instincts, and intuitions. You are sensitive and receptive, responding to the changing feelings of those around you. You seek privacy to withdraw from exposure to the influences of others, preferring to create your own illusions and secret world of visions and dreams. You respond to beauty in art, nature, music and literature, but may most prefer outlets which provide an insight into a fantasy world where all problems are resolved through a happy ending. Your sensitivities leave you at times vulnerable to losing your self identity as you emulate, adapt to, and adopt the tendencies of others. Only by withdrawing and building protective walls around yourself are you able to protect your grand illusions of what you would prefer the world and reality to be. You develop a strong curiosity for the mysterious, secret or unexplained, seeking knowledge about the occult, astrology, or mysticism, or else you use your own creativity to invent the solutions to the mysteries of the human conditions. Highly defensive and seeking perfection in yourself and your world, you don't appreciate the remarks or criticism of others no matter how constructive, and you have a tendency not to admit to a fault, a mistake, or an error in judgment. In fact, you are greatly offended by even imaginary slights, taking to heart the slightest nuance of what you perceive as an insult. And to protect yourself from the opinions of others, you can become secretive or in extreme cases, sneaky. Secret love affairs may excite your imagination as well, but any indiscretions can bring problems, loss and sorrow into your life. There are indications for obstacles and limitations in your life, but you gain from behind-the-scenes activities. Your caring and compassionate nature may lead you to work in hospitals or institutions, or your need for privacy may lead you to seek a position in a quiet, peaceful or remote location. Your curiosity and love of the unknown leads you to enjoy traveling and visiting places which expose your imagination to new sights, sounds, and sensations.

Under planetary affliction, this individual is shy, overly sensitive, defensive, neurotic, and can be unstable and easily influenced and lead by others. There is an indication for problems, obstacles, worries, and sorrow through friends, females, family or mother, secrets, or imaginary fears; and limitations, restraints, imposed early retirement, or an extended illness or hospital stay. When well aspected, this individual becomes a well developed and caring person who is compassionate and concerned with the welfare and needs of others.

Your sensitivities, intuition, and receptiveness can lead you to develop a psychic or other profound ability. By developing your creativity, insights, and intuition, you become truly inspiring to others.

415

MERCURY IN THE TWELFTH HOUSE

Mercury in the Twelfth House and you are insightful, contemplative, and romantically imaginative and receptive. You possess a tendency to make decisions based on feelings, intuitions, and emotions rather than on logic and facts. You can be shy and self-absorbed, rarely allowing others to know what you're really thinking, but you prefer to exhibit a pleasant and personable personality. Your secrecy extends to your feelings about other people which you also keep to yourself because you are capable of reading meaning into the subtle nuances of conversations, voices, gestures and actions. And it may be that through meditations, precognitions, insights, and psychic abilities, you absorb and observe more than you can possibly express or explain verbally to others. You can be capable, however, of analyzing other people's problems clearly. Your inclinations and personal moods can change from being charitable and giving to the point of self-sacrifice to becoming disillusioned with your efforts, deciding to pamper yourself instead. Your curious nature is attracted to investigating the mysteries of life, and you seek knowledge through occult or mystical affairs, secret societies, science, medicine, art, music, or literature. Then too, risky or secretive adventures compel you even when there is a hint of danger involved. You are sometimes preoccupied with small inconveniences and petty complaints and may prefer to work by yourself, in seclusion, or in quiet places.

Regardless of abilities, skills, and talents, under planetary afflictions, this individual faces obstacles, concerns, problems, and animosity through family, lack of opportunities, writings, and slander. When well aspected, this individual is successful in his or her endeavors after overcoming obstacles and limitations.

Your self-confidence and self-esteem is often bolstered by time spent in meditation and through rest, peaceful settings, and seclusion. When well developed, your mind may function well on the psychic level.

VENUS IN THE TWELFTH HOUSE

Venus in the Twelfth House and you are inclined to be romantically adventuresome, emotional, and sensitive. You are capable of being giving, loving, kind, selfless and self-sacrificing. Caught up in the energies you receive through love, you may find yourself involved in secret romantic attachments and affairs. Creative, imaginative, compassionate, caring, and sensitive, you have a tendency to seek comfort and relaxation in seclusion. Then too, you possess a refined and highly developed appreciation for beauty in nature, art, music, and most importantly in your surroundings. You have a strong preference for peaceful and harmonious settings. And in your personal relationships you most enjoy the perfection of harmony, peace and beauty as well. You may be drawn to perfectionists who turn their critical natures to perfecting you in which case you remember them fondly as you move on seeking that perfect harmonious relationship. You may marry early, but give your heart to another, and there is indication that life brings you intrigue through your relationships, and animosity through the resentment of women. Or, on the other hand, you may decide to repress this inner nature and become self-sacrificing to the point of entering a convent or finding some other method of serving others. On your own, you discover that your inner resources are abundant and you can be quite content relying on yourself for companionship. If you develop your spiritualism your curiosity leads you to investigate mysticism, psychic affairs, or the occult. Then too you are drawn to healing, medicine, chemistry, nature and animals, and discover rewarding experiences through becoming involved with charitable organizations.

Under planetary afflictions, this individual is overly sensitive and too interested in excessive physical and emotional pleasures. There is indication for separation, divorce, estrangement, disappointments, or sorrow through love affairs. When well aspected, this individual focuses energies on artistic, creative, and caring, charitable endeavors.

You enjoy peaceful, quiet, refined, and harmonious settings, at times preferring to relax in seclusion away from the harsher realities and problems of life. You are capable of creating just such an environment where your mind is free to meditate on your creative urges. When well developed, you become spiritually inspiring not only to yourself but to others who know you well. You are capable of serving others through giving and caring whether through charitable organizations and institutions or through your relationships.

Mars in The Twelfth House

With Mars in the Twelfth House you sense limitations to your energies and freedoms. You either find yourself fighting adamantly for the underdog against opposing authoritative forces or you sublimate these tendencies by losing yourself in work perhaps in large institutions where you blend into the crowd. You may protect your private life and personal views by becoming reserved or secretive about your inner feelings thus avoiding the criticism or animosity of other people. You possess a tendency to be secretive about your real desires, motives, objectives, and intentions. And while you strive to control your inner nature, there are times when you act out of impulse or compulsion which in some instances results in unfortunate misadventures and misunderstandings with other people. The chances are you are not being paranoid if you think your enemies are plotting against you in secret. There is an indication that you suffer from false accusations, physical injuries, danger from burglars, violent enemies, accidents while working with animals, the poor health of a partner, and problems in love. You may feel like you are dodging obstacles in all aspects of your life, and that it is up to you to overcome these problems in your own way using your strengths, energies, and courage to do so. If well developed, you set goals and visualize yourself going through the actions necessary to attain them, knowing that allowing self-doubt to enter into your mind will result in failure. Your imagination is active, creative and ever alert, resulting in you focusing your energies on goal-oriented results.

Under planetary afflictions, this individual is rash, restless, impulsive, and disceitful with a tendency to experience problems, strife, obstacles, treachery, and distressful situations through poverty, lack of opportunities, enemies, injuries, imprisonment, hospitalization, reversals in finances, bankruptcy, scandal, notoriety, and social disgrace, with a worst case scenario being death while in confinement. When well aspected, this individual strives to overcome any and all obstacles through endurance, perseverance, strength, energy, and a strong will power.

Your personal inspiration evolves through self development, resulting in you relying on your personal reserves of strength and character to successfully accomplish your goals in life. Your active imagination, energy, and assertive attitude propel you through life on your own terms.

JUPITER IN THE TWELFTH HOUSE

Jupiter in the Twelfth House grants you luck when you most need it or provides a great protection in times of difficulty. You find yourself most resourceful during difficult periods of your life. And faced with obstacles brought on by competitors, opponents, or even enemies, you overcome such difficulties perhaps becoming friends, or at least on friendly terms, with the very people who were set against you. Your difficulties and obstacles in life are usually followed by more successful experiences, and at times you find that you even gain from the bad times. You are a compassionate, caring, giving, empathic, and charitable person who most likely shares and helps others either anonymously or in some quiet or secret manner. You enjoy the time spent with others, but you also seek out time to yourself to either pursue your thoughts, meditate, or simply to allow your mind the opportunity to expand, pray, study, and reflect. These periods of seclusion can lead your active imagination to create entertaining mental fantasies, or at other times you develop especially inspiring thoughts and concepts. Your expansive nature leads you to explore spiritualism, mysticism, astrology, or psychic experiences as well as the fields of medicine, chemistry, research, poetry, dancing, acting, or social work. You feel most successful when helping others perhaps in work associated with institutions or hospitals. There are times when you are filled with self-doubt, and you wonder if you are doing the right things with your life. Then too, it is important for you to feel needed by other people, and there are times when your self-esteem is dependent on how others react to you. It is very likely that your friends, associates, and family assist you when needed in a confidential or secretive manner. There is an indication for you to experience unusual occurrences in relation to romance, religion, higher education, public offices, politics, or international affairs and business.

Under planetary afflictions, this individual is too self-doubting, rash, hasty, self-indulgent, impractical, extravagant, unrealistic, dependent on the opinions of others, and preoccupied with fantasies. There is some indication for reversals in life which result in the individual either being a charity case, institutionalized, or imprisoned. When well aspected, there is an indication that this individual gains through difficulties, enemies, unusual occurrences; reversals followed by gain with success being realized in mid-life; and assistance coming in a quiet or secretive manner from an unexpected source.

You can be compassionate, charitable, and inspirational to others. Learn to listen to your intuition which often serves you well in times of need or difficulty.

SATURN IN THE TWELFTH HOUSE

With Saturn in the Twelfth House, you are reserved with a tendency toward isolation, seclusion, or reclusion. It may be that you are at your most productive and creative during these periods of isolation. However, it may well be that you are cautious and sensitive with an inner fear or self-doubt that quite often results in a lack of confidence and self-imposed limitations. You have difficulty sharing your feelings with others perhaps because you don't fully understand

419

them yourself other than to sense an unexplainable sorrow and despondency that you carry with you. You may feel that fate itself is against you, setting yourself up for whatever may come. There is some indication for secret enemies who cause you difficulties and for false accusations, and this may be what you sense. However, too much time in isolation, brooding over your problems, can cause you to lose mental and physical energy to despondency and depression leaving you nervous, filled with anxieties, and panic-prone. In other words, your mental imaging and fears may act to draw to you what you most fear. At the same time, you are known for being a hard worker who strives to acquire security, position, and possessions. To this end, you may find that you are at your best and are most inspired when you either work in seclusion, behind the scenes, or in situations such as large institutions where you are for the most part unnoticed. As far as you are concerned, fame, glory and recognition can go to others, you are most content with doing a good job, receiving your just rewards and benefits, and living a quiet, peaceful life.

Under planetary afflictions, this individual is fearful of fate, harbors anxieties, secrets, sorrows, with feelings of disappointment, despondency, and depression leading to physical and mental illness. There is an indication for secret plans by adversaries, false accusations, confinement, imprisonment, unexpected or unusual problems, scandal, public embarrassment or discredit, and danger through violence, burglaries, or theft. When well aspect, the native faces obstacles and problems in life but experiences success through a working in isolation or seclusion.

Use your active and powerful imagination to see yourself happy and successful in life, thus producing positive results. Plan and enjoy life one step at a time rather than focusing too seriously on what could go wrong in the distant and far-off future. Look forward to the good things in life, and enjoy today to the fullest.

Uranus in The Twelfth House

Uranus in the Twelfth House grants you an original perspective on life which leads you to strive for personal independence and the ability to think for yourself. You are more than likely liberal in your viewpoints and accepting of the thoughts, philosophies, and lifestyles of other people. At the same time, you resist any limitations, conventions, or restraints placed on your own thoughts and actions. You may find the demands and conditions of society as well as the consumer mentality restrictive and confining. You most prefer to set your own standards and to decide for yourself your values and what is important in life. Your open-minded tendencies may also lead you to unexpected and secret love affairs, experiences and adventures. At the same time, you are highly intuitive and perceptive, and you may be a gifted psychic with a compassionate, caring, and humanitarian nature. It may be that during some period of your life your curious nature either leads you to travel extensively or to live in another state, country, or locality away from your family. Then too, your work habits are as individualistic as the rest of your nature, and you exhibit a preference for intellectual, behind the scenes, secretive, unusual, or creative practices and procedures. Introspective and prone to deep thought and meditation, this is a good position for research and investigations, and you may find yourself curiously interested in occult subjects, mystical experiences, astrology and unsolved phenomena. With your unconventional attitude, you may unwittingly be the cause of many of the problems and obstacles you face in life.

Under planetary afflictions, this individual is eccentric, secretive, rebellious, and in extreme cases even violent. There is an indication for sudden reversals of fortune, sudden and unexpected occurrences caused by adversaries, problems of a mysterious nature, scandal and public disgrace, institutional confinement, and problems associated with psychic experiences. When well aspected, this individual experiences success through psychic abilities, occult investigations, institutions, unusual or secretive ventures, or behind-the-scenes activities.

Your detached, compassionate idealism leads you to associate with other people who are independent thinkers and doers. There are times when you must guard against being overly fearful and vulnerable about losing your individuality. Finding balance in life leads you to maintain your personal well being which allows you the independence and freedom you desire.

Neptune in The Twelfth House

With Neptune in the Twelfth House, you are intuitive with a strong cosmic consciousness. Sensitive and aware, the chances are you possess an artistic ability or musical talent or at least an interest in art, music, drama, the theater, or perhaps a preference for refined amusement and entertainment, fine dining and dancing, and gracious living. You have a preference for a peaceful, quiet life that allows for a more than sufficient amount of personal privacy and an atmosphere conducive to meditating, thinking, or creative activities. Your highly developed awareness may lead you to utilize your conscious awareness of the mysterious, subtle forces at work in life. Your curious and intuitive nature may lead you to investigate psychic affairs, or the occult, or to develop an interest in mediums or other mystical phenomena. At the same time, you are a compassionate and caring person with a great need to help and to be of assistance to humanitarian causes as well as directly beneficial to other people. And your insights may lead you to develop an interest in science, medicine, the healing arts, laboratory work or other types of research, or perhaps detective work catches your imagination. There are times when you must guard against any obstacles or difficulties in life leading you to become paranoid, fearful, anxious, or overly apprehensive, suspicious and critical of the actions, motives, thoughts, and expressions of other people. Highly imaginative and creative, you must strive to maintain balance between reality and self-delusions which can lead to self-doubts and insecurities. You function best when your daily affairs are private, and you may even prefer a certain amount of secrecies in your personal affairs. This is a good placement for Neptune for doctors, nurses and medical staff or for other types of work in large institutions.

With planetary afflictions, this individual can develop fears, anxieties, and inhibitions regarding the harsher realities of life as well as the future; loneliness; overly critical of others; delusions leading to emotional or physical illnesses. There is indication for danger from psychic experiences, deceits, fraud, and secret adversaries, and for scandal, public disgrace, and problems from secret sorrows, grief, and disappointments. When well aspected, the native gains from success in psychic and occult research, large institutions, or secret research and investigations.

You are kind, compassionate and helpful toward others with a sincere and caring nature. You possess a great love for the mysterious.

Pluto in The Twelfth House

With Pluto in the Twelfth House, changes and transformation can be expected during periods of your life involving restrictions and limitations. This is a strong position for Pluto for psychic experiences and occult activities which inspire you to investigate and research. You may find that you work best in private, keeping your personal thoughts and interests to yourself until you know others well enough to share your more personal insights. Or perhaps you prefer to maintain your privacy until you meet other people who share your interests and inclinations. Then too, you may find that you work best in private or in behind the scenes activities. It may be that secrecy serves your purposes also, preventing the world at large in following your activities and judging your personal preferences. Strongly independent with a desire for personal freedom as well as freedom of thought and expression, you prefer not to be tied down to convention, social values, or to a restrictive system. With your strong desire to understand and comprehend not only other people, but the way of the world as well as the unknown forces at work, you feel you understand other people's needs for conventions and tradition, but you find it difficult to accept any system without a lot of personal thought and exploration. Then too, wanting to live your own life in your own way, you may not want others aware of your active sex life, and you develop an intense desire for discretion, even secrecy, in this area of your life as well. You may not be overly demonstrative in affections, but you are deeply emotional, caring, and concerned with the welfare of others. At times, you feel the need for periods of isolation or seclusion in your life primarily because you have the capacity for sensing and absorbing the feelings and emotions of others. The problems of other people can cause you much distress, and when you feel overwhelmed, you have a tendency to withdraw in order to renew your inner strength.

Under planetary afflictions, this individual can suffer from psychic or mediumistic experiences which become too graphic and threatening. There is an indication for restrictions, limitations, even confinement. But when well aspected, this native possesses strong intuitive insights and psychic abilities.

HOUSES OF THE SKY

The Earth is divided into two sections called hemispheres. It is shaped like an oval. It rotates around its axis which is not vertical but slanted. The Earth follows along a path called the Zodiac, moving around and orbiting the Sun. This path is referred to as the Zodiac belt or band. This band around the Earth is divided into 12 sections, each 30 degrees wide, corresponding to the 12 signs of the Zodiac and totaling 360 degrees. The Sun and its Planets are walking along this band. In reality, the sections are not equal in width.

In order to determine the position of the Zodiac at sunrise when the person is born and also the position of the Sun, Moon, and Planets, one has to imagine that the Sky is divided into these 12 sections which are referred to as the Houses of the Sky. Each House has a special meaning for the individual life.

HOUSE 1 -- Represents the body and the individual's life, personality, character, appearance, head and face. Hunter, selfish, high self-esteem, dominant, proud, arrogant, impulsive, leader, dynamic, insensitive, risk-taker, charismatic, multi-affairs, adventuresome, self-centered.

HOUSE 2 -- Money earned by own activity; benefits; salary; wealth; metal; factories; commerce; trade; rates; budget; neck and the back of the head. Artistic, dogmatic, lazy, stubborn, tenacious, greedy, persistent, affectionate, tolerant, builder, game player

HOUSE 3 -- Short journeys; mechanical transportation; mail; letters; manuscripts; sisters; brothers; neighbors; shoulders, arms, and hands. Capricious, unpredictable, dramatic, changeable, multifaceted, neurotic, high sex drive, stimulating, broad minded.

HOUSE 4 -- The end of life; tombs; graves; cemeteries; adverse situations; inheritance; foundations; property; father; lungs and stomach. Manipulative, high sex drive, crabby, magnetic, imaginative, moody, intuitive, materialistic, dramatic, self-centered, selfish.

HOUSE 5 -- Children; education; pedagogy; theater; clubs; races; love; ambassadors; diplomacy; favors; speculations; heart and spine. Demanding, magnanimous, lax, amorous, fiery, romantic, authoritative, strong, vain, proud, creative, warm.

423

HOUSE 6 -- Illnesses; moral crisis; doctors; employees; subordinates; crowds; farms; kitchens; small animals; intestines and bowels. Undemonstrative, variable sex drive, critical, nervous, compulsive, organized, hyper-energetic, dedicated, tidy.

HOUSE 7 -- Marriage; associates; unions; law suits; divorces; separations; civil suits; contracts; enemies; war; treaties; adversaries; failures; animosity; material crisis; thief; assassins; kidneys. Self-protective, diplomatic, controlled, seductive, sensual, manipulative, cool.

HOUSE 8 -- Death; infinity; destruction; decomposition; corpse; disappearance; forgetfulness; oblivion; suicide; inheritance; wills; dowery; rents; tradition; antiquity; rectum and genitals. Vindictive, power user, stubborn, arrogant, secretive, asexual, adventurous, lusty, passionate, compulsive, leader.

HOUSE 9 -- Long journeys; marina; religion; morality; dreams; science; higher education; philosophy; occult science; justice; wisdom; magistrate; referee; ribs. Intuitive, independent, philosophic, versatile, blunt, eager, optimistic, impulsive, lucky, jovial, loves travel.

HOUSE 10 -- Profession; documents; situations; enterprises; businesses; patrons; managers; directors; kings; honors; titles; power; politics; authority; credits; celebrity; mother; stolen articles; knees, joints. Critical, moralistic, self-sufficient, vulnerable, purposeful, loyal, very hard worker, family orientated.

HOUSE 11 -- Friends; acquaintances; reunions; desires; projects; faith; trust; fidelity; hope; popularity; ministers; parliaments; calves and leg joints. Proud, quirky, offbeat, shy, quixotic, sensual, erotic, pornographic, uninhibited, aloof, self-centered.

HOUSE 12 -- Hidden enemies; envy, sorrows; melancholy and depression; conspirators; jealousy; hospitals; sanitariums; prisons; labs; correctional institutions; maternity; chronic illness; exile; vice; labors; difficulties and obstacles; doubts; financial deficits; losses; social problems; sabotage; parasites; sadism; large animals; wild animals; stable; toes and soles. Escapist, artistic, self-sacrificing, isolationist, easily hurt, indirect, low-self-esteem, introverted, self-denigration, self-deprivation, sentimental, humanistic, often orphaned.

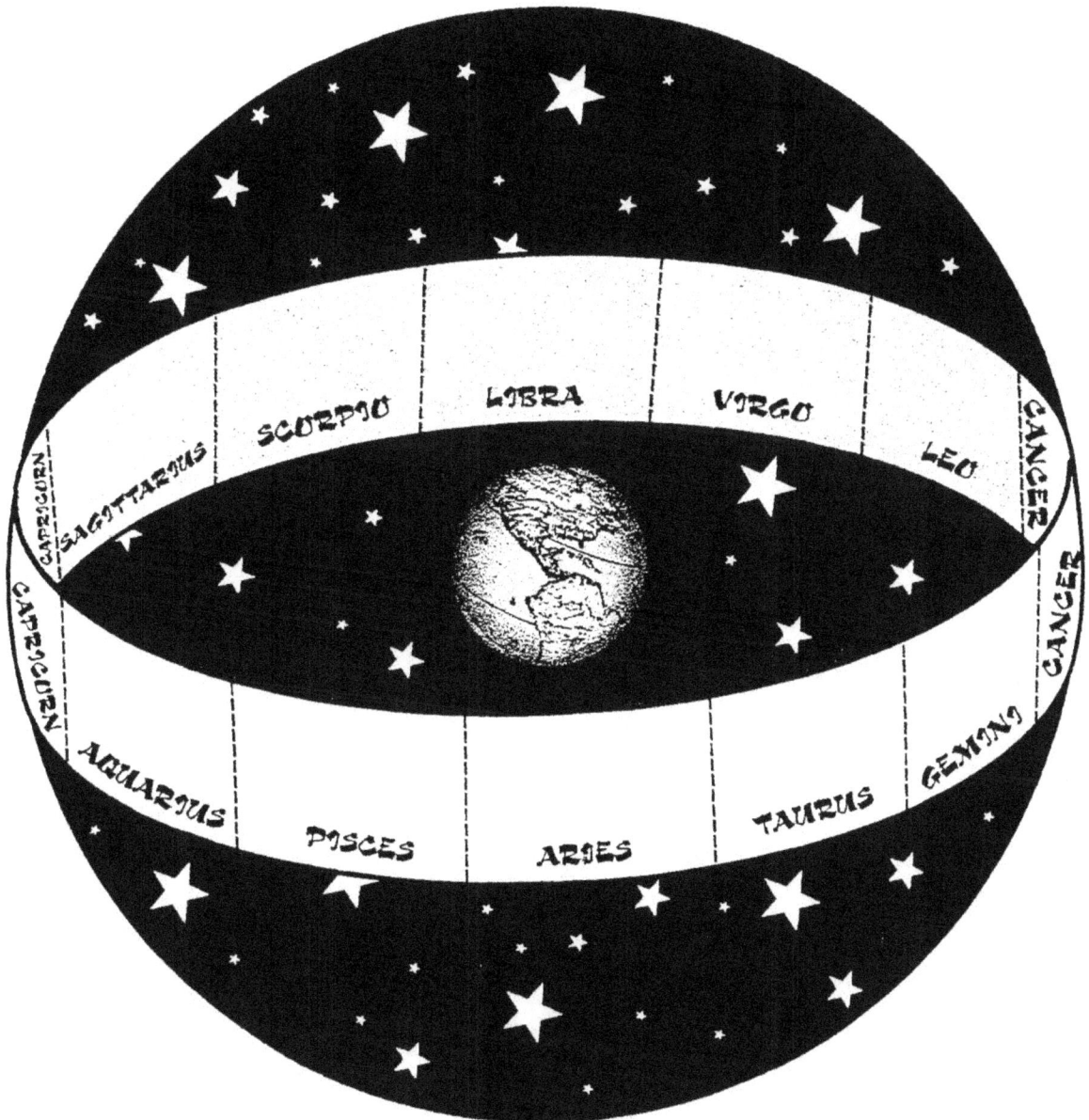

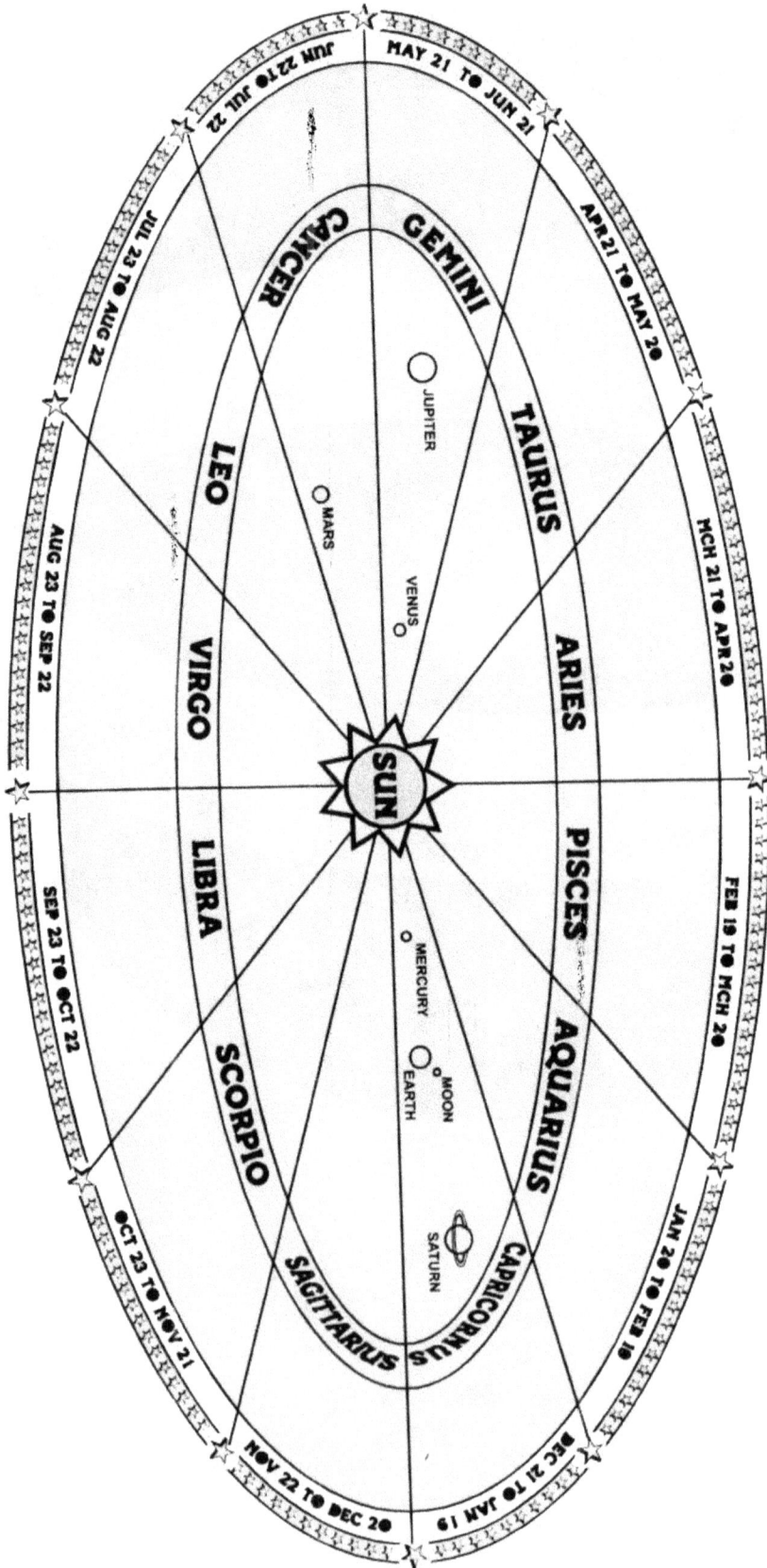

426

THE INFLUENCE OF THE PLANETS

The study of Astrology dates back to a time when the Earth was considered the center of the Universe, and it was believed that the celestial bodies orbited it. Thus it was described by Ptolemy, and it wasn't until 1543, that Nikolaus Copernicus initiated a new idea that had been floating around for centuries. That is, that the Sun is the center of the Universe and all the planets, including Earth, orbit it. Scholars and theologians alike opposed this new idea presented by Copernicus, and it was considered heresy. The fact of the matter is that Astrology along with astronomy and the other sciences has evolved over time to encompass new information. Today, it is accepted that new information will continue to influence our lives, and astrologers continue to study the planets and the influence of the celestial bodies on horoscopes. And by ascertaining the positions of the planets at the time of birth of an individual, a person's birth chart is formed.

The word planet in Greek means wanderer (stars), and it was these wandering stars that attracted the attention of astrologers from the earliest of times to the present. Is it that the planets possess inherent qualities that effect our lives, or is it the motion of the planets as they make their transit through the signs of the Zodiac which influences lives? It is accepted that the Moon has an effect on the Earth's tides as well as other aspects of nature. Do these other planets effect our daily lives as well? The study of these questions is the basis for the study of astrology.

In astrology, those planets orbiting the Sun inside the Earth's orbit are referred to as inferior. The inferior planets, therefore, are Mercury and Venus. The planets outside the Earth's orbit are the superior planets, Mars, Jupiter, Saturn, Uranus, Neptune, and Pluto. When compared to the Moon which takes 28 days to complete one cycle, Mercury requires 88 days to complete one orbit of the Sun, Venus requires 224.5, Mars takes 22 months, Jupiter spends 12 year in each orbit, Saturn's orbit is between 28 and 30 years, Uranus requires 84 years, Neptune takes 165 years, and Pluto's orbit is 248 years. Thus, the time each planet spends in each sign of the Zodiac varies.

Each planet rules one, sometimes two, signs of the Zodiac. When the planet is located in the sign it rules, it is said to at home, or in Domicile. When the planet is placed in the opposite sign to the one it rules, it is in Detriment. Each planet is also most harmonious or most powerful when it is located in another sign, referred to as its Exaltation. When located in the sign opposite where it is exalted, the planet is in its Fall. A planet has the most influence when located in its Domicile, and next its Exaltation. Its influence is weaker in its Detriment and the weakest in the location of its Fall.

Ancient astrologers classified the Sun, Mars, Jupiter and Saturn as masculine. The Moon and Venus were referred to as feminine, and Mercury was androgynous. Jupiter (the Greater Fortune) and Venus (the Lesser Fortune) were considered benefic while Saturn (the Greater Infortune) and Mars (the Lesser Infortune) were malefic. The Sun, Moon, and Mercury, being

427

neither benefic nor malefic, were referred to as common. Modern astrologers in many instances ignore many of these ancient classifications, preferring to think of the influence of the planets as being either positive or negative.

The ancients also assumed that these wandering stars moved in a fairly circular pattern, but it was later determined that planetary orbits could better be described as ellipses. Then too the retrograde movement of planets was observed, that is, what appears to be the backward movement of a planet in its orbit. Retrograde occurs when an inferior (faster) planet overtakes Earth, or when a superior (slower) planet is overtaken by the faster moving Earth.

Each planet is felt to influence a particular aspect of the lives of individuals, whether emotions, love, temperament, intellect, subconscious, or luck. Neptune and Pluto are also believed to have a generational affect because of the length of their orbits and their length of stay in each sign. By planning a birth chart based on the time and date of birth, the influences of the planets on an individual life can be determined.

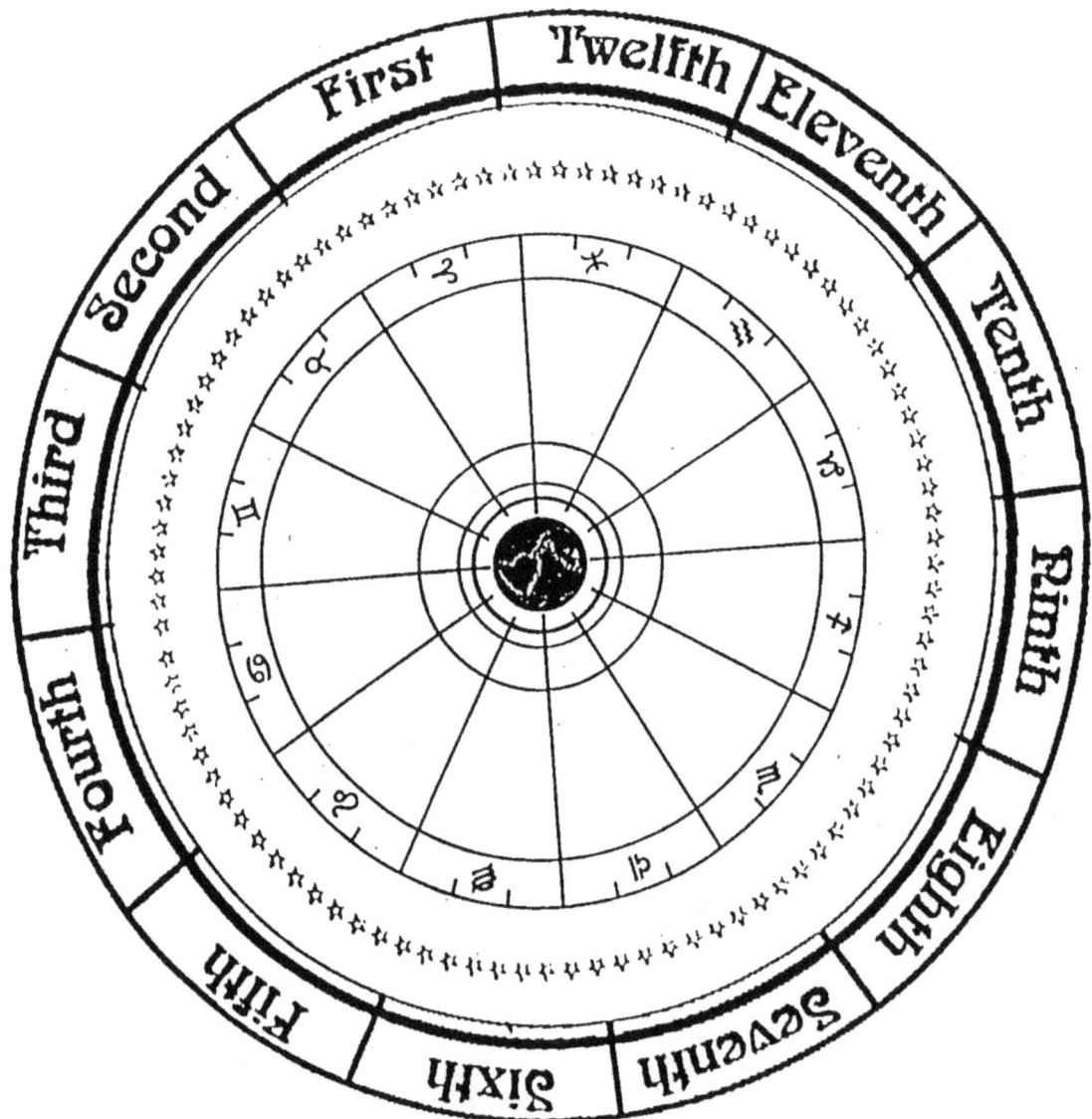

MERCURY

Rules: GEMINI and VIRGO

KEYWORDS: Ideas, the intellect, communication, conversations, mental activity, facts, statistics, sensory perception, mental processing, mental interpretation, logic, short trips, siblings, neighbors, colleagues, health, diet, medicine, employment, skills, transportation, surroundings, critical thinking, inquisitiveness, documents, writing, teaching, worry, anxiety, nervousness. Mercury rules Gemini and Virgo; is exalted in Virgo; is in detriment in Sagittarius; is in fall in Pisces.

The task of Mercury, the wing-footed messenger of the gods, is to serve as an emissary for the Sun. Mercury's orbit is closest to the Sun, and since there is always a twenty-eight degree distance between them, Mercury is either in your Sun sign or in the sign preceding or following your Sun sign. Orbiting back and forth with wave-like motion in its short orbit, it collects and weaves the sense impressions into practical and meaningful connections.

Mercury is variable, convertible, neutral and dualistic. It represents the practical mind with its intelligence enhanced by matter and is influenced by whatever the Moon is reflecting, thus it suggests the quality of changeability. Mercury collects the sensory perceptions and indicates a person's reactions to sights, sounds, odors, tastes and touch reflecting the person's response to the material or physical world. In other words, it is the messenger through which your physical body and your spirit reacts to the world. The benefit of Mercury is the ability to analyze, and it signifies not only how a person perceives the world but how the mind works. Therefore, it communicates and channels the will of the person allowing man to connect the perceptions with the intellect. In modern terms it is the central processor which collects and deals with the sensory input, channeling it into thoughts and actions. Mercury is the planet of mental activities, communication and intellectual energy which rules over intelligence, perception and reason, memory, speaking and writing. It has influence over the nervous system, bowels, hands, arms, shoulders, collar bone, and tongue as well as vision, perception, comprehension, interpretation and expression. Mercury enhances both the Sun's ability to act and the Moon's ability to react. Mercury also has some influence over daily travel, short trips, and it rules over transportation.

The rulership of Mercury influences natives to be clever and shrewd, quick in speech with an alert mind, fast to discern, eager for knowledge, likes to investigate, inquire, research, and explore. They are good speakers, singers and actors.

If afflicted, Mercury inclines its native to be overly nervous and worrying, hasty, irritable, forgetful, controversial, critical, sarcastic, argumentative, and to possess a tendency to be sly, to lie and commit fraud, forgery, or scams. It is associated with mischievous, childlike and amoral behavior.

Ancient scholars referred to Mercury as Thoth or Hermes, the messenger of the gods and was depicted as a youthful person flying with wings on his heels. Mercury represents duality, speed and wisdom. Mercury's nature is neutral and dualistic. Its colors are blue and gray and its metal is silver.

The influence of the planet Mercury is neutral, dualistic, cold, moist, sexless and convertible. Mercury is associated with the mind and the intellect. It expresses according to its position, aspect and location in the Zodiac. It can either be good when in favorable aspect to other planets or malefic when adversely aspected. When well-aspected Mercury influences persons to acquire knowledge and to communicate it to others. It bestows good reasoning and intellectual powers and the ability to be perceptive, clever, versatile, superior in debate or argument, and with good attention to detail. If poorly-aspected this planet produces a person who is inconsistent, critical, cynical, sarcastic, questioning, argumentative and lacking in purpose or direction. Nervous energy results in stress.

MERCURY IN ARIES

Mercury in Aries produces a person who is aggressive and brilliant but also impulsive and fiery. You possess a quickness in thought and speech which produces a faculty for public speaking, debating, or argument, but at times you consider only your own opinion. If afflicted, there can also be a tendency to be contentious, antagonistic and disputing. You can be expressive, earnest, demonstrative, liberal, inventive, unique, interesting and clever, but with a tendency to exaggerate. And whether funny or sarcastic, you are clever, outspoken, enthusiastic and most often original and quick in thought. Changeability is seen in opinions and projects. There may be a restless nature that at times lacks stability of purpose or a sense of order. However, there is an inclination for your first decision to be the correct one. You possess sharp and alert reactions to sense impressions. Often, music harmonizes and balances your nature.

MERCURY IN TAURUS

Mercury in Taurus makes for a happy and pleasant person who may prefer to ponder and think before making a decision. Then this person sticks obstinately to that decision. You have a practical, stable, and constructive mind which is determined. Good judgment and reasoning ability is seen and this person is persevering, discreet and diplomatic, however, with strong likes and dislikes. There is a strong desire to for financial success and material possessions, and a talent for handling money. Sociable and refined, there is seen a fondness for the opposite sex, pleasure, recreation, music, art and cultural amusements. This person is a strong visual learner who perceives the world best through the sense of sight. There will be a strong preference for harmonious and pleasant surroundings. Likewise, the sense of touch is well developed, and this person can see how a material will feel or feel how something will look. While taste and smell are adequate, hearing may not be as strong. This person can tune out sounds and may not correctly hear the sound of his or her voice, sounding at times a bit flat or unfeeling. Learns through practical experience.

MERCURY IN GEMINI

Mercury in Gemini grants a quick and ingenious mind that is logical, clever, inventive, resourceful, and well informed. There is a preference for travel, change, novel experiences and speculation. This person longs to be free and while lucid and expressive in speech and thought with a rational, curious and seeking mind, at times there is seen no need to be overly practical. This person is sympathetic and generous but not given to sentimental and emotional inclinations. Being perceptive, observing, and shrewd, there is a tendency to categorize and organize ideas. The outlook is unbiased with a lack of prejudice. This is the phrase maker, whose quick wit, humor and charm is noted in his or her clever remarks. This person has strong senses and reacts to variations and shades of light, color, texture, and sound. Failing to tune out all of the sensory perceptions in the environment can leave a person at times tired, and there is a need to seek solitude in a relaxing and quiet setting.

MERCURY IN CANCER

An individual with Mercury in Cancer is diplomatic, tactful, and sociable with a strong desire to please others. Readily adaptable to their surroundings and other people, they can change their opinions easily. There is a tendency to be influenced and swayed and at times this person tries too hard to please others by saying what he or she thinks others want to hear. This person is sympathetic and tolerant of others and appreciates the kindness and admiration of others. There is seen a keen imagination, but at times this person is sensitive, melancholy or moody. The mind is at times restless and reflective, requiring knowledge or informative material. The intellect is clear, sensible and reasonable, and the mind is retentive with an interest in historical times or family histories. This person enjoys social occasions, pleasures, picnics and family reunions. There is a spiritual inclination for this person. Being sensitive, this person personalizes the sense impressions seeing and hearing either beauty or at other times noise and distractions. There is a found a fondness for music and a creatively artistic streak.

MERCURY IN LEO

With Mercury in Leo, a person is ambitious, confident, and articulate and possesses a warm and magnanimous personality that can sway the opinions of others. Persistent and determined, the mind is lofty if not fiery and quick tempered. Able to concentrate and to communicate ideas and concepts well, this assured speaker and thinker may become a bit conceited and dogmatic lacking an appreciation for anyone who doesn't readily agree or accept his or her ideas. Distinctive, aspiring and persuasive, this person seeks to be understood, admired and accepted. This person is kind and sympathetic with an intuitive intellect and noble ideals of honesty and justice. There is seen a positive mind which tends to govern, control and organize. This person is known for a strong will power, an expansive personality, and a progressive mind. Outgoing and fun-loving, this person shows a preference for children, animals, music, arts and culture, sports and pleasures, and may be prone to self-indulgence. This person is more attuned to his or her own image, voice or projected self-impression than to the sights and sounds of the environment. Having fixed opinions, this person most perceives those images which agree with these opinions producing a person who is unobservant. Because of a lack of interest, this person may be slow to react.

MERCURY IN VIRGO

Mercury both rules and is exalted in Virgo. This is a pragmatic person with a mind that is comprehensive and practical. There is a tendency for this person to be cautious, prudent and discriminating while at the same time being versatile and inventive, but less innovative than adaptive. Studious with a good memory, this individual is perceptive as well as intuitive. This person is precise in observing, organizing and categorizing details and information. There may be a compulsion to be correct. This person can be persuasive in speech but may lack confidence, and being self-critical, this person may be unwilling to take a firm position. The nature is quiet and serious and can at times be critical and skeptical. This is not an easy person to convince without facts, as he or she will want to see, know and understand before making a decision. There is an inclination toward math or literature. This individual has a tendency to intellectual the senses preferring to name, describe and put in a slot every sight and sound thus diminishing the pleasure of simply feeling. With effort, learning to appreciate feelings can be developed.

MERCURY IN LIBRA

Mercury in Libra grants a flair for being expressive in both speech and thoughts. This person is refined and graceful of mind and spirit with a preference for being easy going. In an effort to balance, this person's mind is less concerned with details than it is with how the details relate to the overall pattern of the situation. The intellect and the emotions combine to assess the value of perceptions. This is likely to be a quiet, impartial, caring and judicial person who prefers to compare and contrast before arriving at a reasonable decision. Wanting to weigh and consider differing viewpoints, there may be a tendency to be indecisive and vacillating. This is a favorable location for intellectual pursuits, and the person may possess natural abilities for music, math, or inventions. This person prefers to apply discerning balance and judgment to all of the sensory perceptions preferably from the standard of art or of good taste. This person is sensitive to the environment preferring sights to be neat and attractive rather than offensively messy, odors to be appealing, and sounds to be pleasant rather than loud or offensive. This sensitivity may be appeased by the natural beauty of the wilderness setting, and offended by the man-made clutter.

MERCURY IN SCORPIO

Mercury in Scorpio influences the individual to be bold but obstinate with an inclination toward research and solving mysteries. This person is ingenious and shrewd possessing the ability to size up people, situations and deceptions. This perceptive mind is curious and seeks knowledge, but is at the same time critical, suspicious and adept at discovering secrets and solving puzzles. This person can be the persistent investigator or may prefer to delve into the mysteries of life. This person can be sarcastic and reckless and if involved will be vindictive, holding a grudge for a life time. The nature is fond of the opposite sex, friends, and pleasures. There is indicated a mental resourcefulness, a practical ability, but problems with disappointments and troublesome friends and relatives. This person's sensory perceptions are filtered through a critical filament of discernment. The observations are astute, comparable to the eye of an eagle. This person is constantly aware of what is going on as if there were an eye in the back of the head. These critical observations, while not always kind, are more often than not accurate. This person may well develop an interest in the occult, mysticism, or other unsolved mysteries of mankind or the universe.

MERCURY IN SAGITTARIUS

The person who has Mercury in Sagittarius will find that the nature is purposeful and ambitious, the mind is quick and bright, and the spirit is expansive and loves freedoms of expressions and movement. This is a sincere and generous person who is independent and, if freedom is restricted, can become rebellious. Changeable, restless and impulsive, the progressive mind is constantly seeking stimulation, new information and knowledge. This person is both physically and mentally active and can become prophetic, wise and philosophical. At times, this person is outspoken and blunt. There is a fondness for nature, travel, home, family, sports and animals. In regards to sensory perceptions, this person has a tendency to scatter the attentions in many directions rather than paying close attention to any one stimulation. There may be a tendency to overlook things, to not hear all of a conversation, as if the person is thinking about something else.

MERCURY IN CAPRICORN

Mercury in Capricorn precludes patience, prudence and practicality focused through a sharply acute and penetrating mind. You are tactful but curious, diplomatic but critical. You are thoroughly careful, economical, and will systematically finish what is started. There is a sensible and dignified demeanor about you with an ability to speak clearly. There is a tendency to be rational, calculating and methodical in decision making. You have a dry humor which at times is pessimistic. If afflicted, this Capricorn native can become narrow-minded and rather stiff and opinionated. You appear to see and hear all with sense perceptions that cut to the basics presenting a realistic and accurate portrayal of your surroundings. Your mind is seldom in the clouds, and you don't linger on abstractions when you could be focusing on details and facts. You solve difficult problems with practical solutions. At times you can be disapproving of less serious-minded folks.

MERCURY IN AQUARIUS

Mercury in Aquarius produces a person who is refined and original, comprehensive and inventive, with a penetrating intuition. You possess a good reasoning ability and powers of concentrations. You are observant and perceptive of human nature, and being sociable and kind, you make friends easily. You are forward looking and futuristic in your approach to life. You most like to circulate freely, with no restrictions on your thinking and freedom, and you enjoy new and stimulating ideas and experiences. Innovative and progressive approaches appeal to you, but you may find that many of your ideas, especially about humanity, are too progressive to be accepted. Your senses are strong, alert and sensitive, and you may find beauty where others don't see anything. Your values lead you to possess a realistic approach to experience that results in you appraising all things based on their utilitarian or artistic merits.

MERCURY IN PISCES

Mercury is in detriment in Pisces, and this individual resists using a purely logical approach to life. After all, what fun are hard facts? You much prefer to be kind, charitable, flexible, imaginative and then again at times impressionable. Much of your knowledge is based on perception and intuition, and you appear to be able to memorize and absorb your environment. You can choose to be emotional and secretive or bubbly, fun-loving and talkative. You have a fondness for pleasure, travel, and socializing with friends. While not materialistic, you may love beautiful things, and you know how to save for your future wants. There are times when you choose to isolate yourself in order to retreat into your private world. Chances are you possess psychic tendencies. You can be analytical but diplomatic, cautious but versatile, ingenious and above all else you most probably possess numerous creative talents. You are selective and personal in your senses and prefer to pick and choose what you want to see, hear, taste, or smell, and perhaps you simply have a strong desire not to see the world as it is.

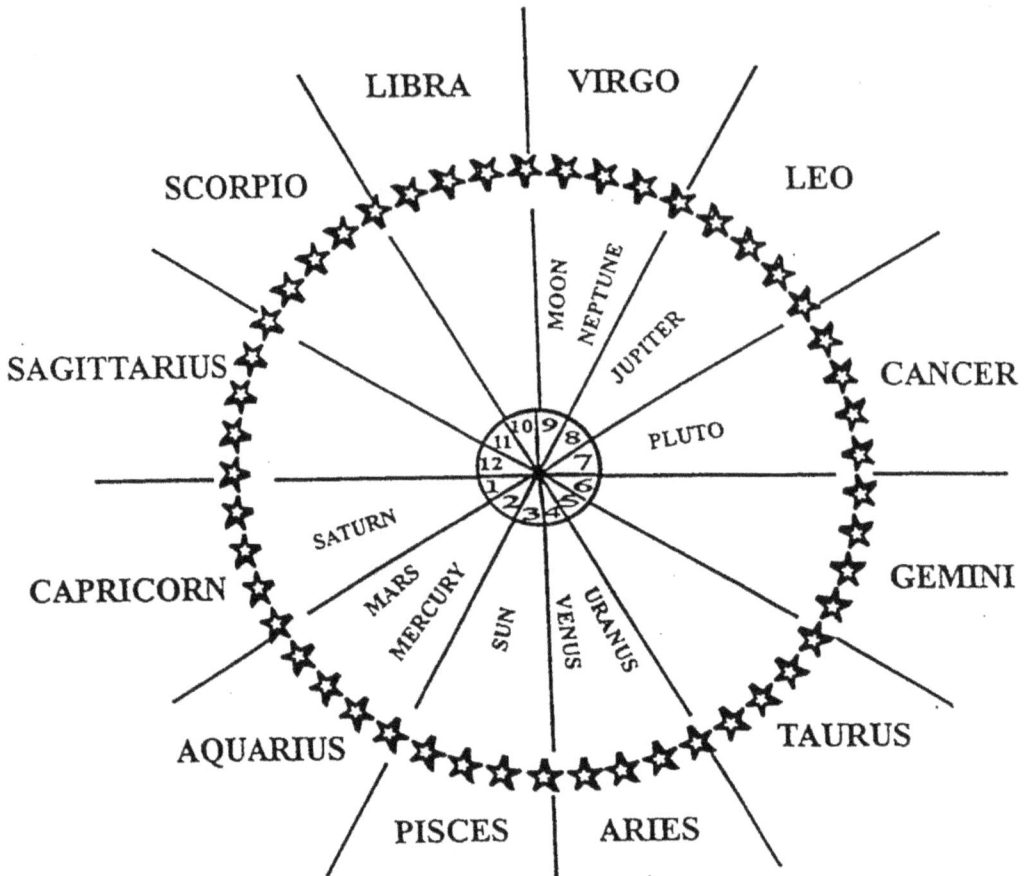

VENUS

Rules: TAURUS and LIBRA

KEYWORDS: Love, beauty, desire, attraction, partnerships, personal relationships, relationships with the opposite sex, romance, art, music, adornment, luxury items, valuables, power to attract, acquisitiveness, values, harmony, vanity, refinement, appreciation for beauty, indulgence, laziness, ostentatiousness, retention. Venus rules Taurus and Libra; is exalted in Pisces; is in detriment in Aries; is in fall in Virgo.

Venus, named for the goddess of love and beauty, governs emotional responses. In the influence of Venus, the Sun is found to energize the emotions and relationships. The principle of attraction is emphasized which brings feelings into an artistic pattern, and procreation is channeled into artistic creation. The Venus influence tends to bring balance or harmony to the basic sexual desires, helping to create cooperation and acceptable forms of behavior. The Venus influence is generous, kind, humorous and loving.

In mythology, the goddess Venus, known for her beauty, instructed mortals in the ways of love and seduction and possessed legendary skills in this regard. This alluring goddess who taught the pleasures of life was also known to be temperamental and sensitive, and at times vindictive.

The orbit of the planet Venus falls between the Earth and the Sun, and is never more than forty-eight degrees from the Sun. In your horoscope, Venus is either in your Sun sign or falls in one of the two signs before or after your sign.

Venus influences our emotional reactions to other people, ruling over our personal relationships and our love affairs as well as art, beauty, manners, decor, affections and friendships. Venus is a feminine planet which rules the sense of touch and influences our disposition. This influence inclines toward the higher attributes of the mind such as music, poetry, art, and literature. In its elevated aspect, it is the higher quality of love reflecting devotion, happiness, and grace. In the body, it rules circulation, nerves and impulses, the throat, kidneys, veins and ovaries.

Venus in relation to your birth sign indicates your attitude toward emotional experiences. If Venus is found in the same sign as your Sun sign, emotions are important to you and effects your actions, making you graceful and congenial. If Venus occurs in your Moon sign, again emotions are important and they influence your inner nature making you more self-confident but sensitive with a loving heart. With Venus in the same sign as Mercury, your mind and emotions work together so that you idealize the world through your senses and interpret emotionally what you perceive.

Venus in Aries

Venus in Aries influences this native to be ardent, affectionate and to attract. You are demonstrative and fall in love easily with a powerful erotic compulsion. More intense than sympathetic and tender, you are sensual, idealistic and imaginative. You are inclined toward love and admiration while being warm-hearted, passionate and attracted to the opposite sex. You are persuasive with a tendency to be controlling, but you are a natural at making friends. Often, this person will have an impulsive attitude toward money and will dream up money making schemes. You are known for being generous and charitable. Venus, a feminine sign, is in detriment in Aries which may give you a tendency to seek pleasures and gratification. Fiery, intense Aries becomes impulsive in emotions under this influence. If Venus is afflicted, there are arguments, restlessness and emotional upsets in relationships. Your sensory perceptions are personal and you see the world as how it relates to you and your pleasures. You are warm and sociable, but sensitive and you show more concern for those who admire you than you do for the world at large.

Venus in Taurus

Venus in Taurus produces an affinity between the planet of love and the sign of material possessions which more than likely will prove fortunate to affairs of the heart and to security. This person may be inclined to marry for money finding it easier to love in comfort. However, in your emotional relationships you are passionate and affectionate but also possessive. You desire to enjoy the best of life and all it has to offer. Both Venus and Taurus are closely associated with money and art, and while you work toward financial security, you also cultivate an appreciation for the arts. At the same time, you have a desire for pleasures and the best that money can buy. In love, you have deep, lasting feelings, are loving and faithful if not tenacious. Sociable, friendly, and generous, you possess fixed and stable feelings and opinions. Earthy and sensual, you believe in love, both physical and spiritual and look for both.

Venus in Gemini

Venus in Gemini may refine the intellect making it imaginative and poetic, but it leaves Gemini flirtatious, lively and lighthearted. Your emotions are elusive while you remain discerning of beauty and virtue. You are naturally friendly, intuitive, inventive, and original with a good sense of humor and an appreciation for light, airy and mental recreations. You may be rather cool and indifferent to the idea of marriage and obligations until you find that partner who shares your intellectual outlook. You most enjoy the fun and excitement of romance and a social life that is filled with other fun-loving companions. A thinker, you prefer ideas to being overly emotional. Your duality and amorous, easily aroused nature gives you an inclination toward more than one affair at a time. You are emotionally aware, but you are not particularly sensitive or touchy. In fact, you may be able to tell or write about emotions better than you actually feel them, and you seldom care to argue about them. This is a positive position for speculation in trade.

Venus in Cancer

Venus in Cancer grants an affectionate, charming and sympathetic nature, and feminine Venus bides well in Moon-ruled Cancer with both being concerned with reproduction and growth. You are sentimental, sympathetic and affectionate, cherishing those you love especially your family, and you may have a strong relationship with your mother. You are loyal and devoted, and strive to provide a good and secure home for your family and children. If well-aspected, Venus influences this person to be charitable and kind and to desire to be cherished and admired. Your emotions can run high and at times you are sensitive. If afflicted, you may be possessive, susceptible to flattery, shy, and excessively emotionally. Receptive, imaginative and responsive to emotions, you may indulge in several love affairs of a secretive nature and perhaps a relationship with an older person. While not selfish, your need for home and security gives you a deep sense of self-preservation and there is a tendency to maintain a protective shell. You may find that your are more emotional than physical in your perspective of life.

Venus in Leo

Venus in Leo leaves this powerful nature wanting to adore and exalt a lover while dominating at the same time. Venus grants Leo a graceful and artistic desire for self-expression. Leo, the sign of personal creativity, becomes endowed by Venus with an affinity for beauty, good taste, and fashion. You are sympathetic, charitable, kind, and often generous with a tendency to be sincere and ardent in love. Strongly attracted to the opposite sex, you can be demonstrative, pleasing, entertaining and amusing. You enjoy friends and pleasures. You lean toward the dramatic with a flair for excitement and romance, wanting life to be significant and meaningful. You love to be loved, appreciated and admired. You have a tendency to idealize love, and can become disappointed when reality sets in. Not spontaneous or hypocritical, your emotional responses can be honest but somewhat calculating. You are capable of turning your emotions on or off at will. You are not easily swayed, and in your affairs you have a tendency to listen to your own words and to do most of the talking.

Venus in Virgo

Venus in Virgo produces a discriminating and restrained influence that applies rational analysis to emotions and love. You have a quiet nature and seldom expressed deep sympathy. However, while you are sensitive, at times you can be overly critical of others in your life, avoiding involvement by finding faults and imperfections. Virgo works hard to produce tangible results, but may overlook sentiment and emotions. Venus and Virgo, both Earth signs, possess a love of nature which in this position is practical and realistic rather than awe-inspiring. You are generous, but hold your emotions in check perhaps with a concern for your reputation or standing in the community. You often shine in the business world, and may enjoy gains through business or investments, but emotions may be experienced through a well-organized code of conduct. Cautiously, you hold your emotions in check perhaps fearing someone will take advantage of them. You most desire someone who will appreciate you and consider you unique and deserving.

VENUS IN LIBRA

Venus rules Libra endowing this native with kindness and sympathy, affection and a love for nature. You are graceful with refined manners and taste and an alluring magnetism that appeals to others. Friendly and sociable, you are popular and well liked and know how to captivate an audience. You love music, poetry, the arts and cultural entertainment. You are a romantic, in love with love, but you may turn love into an ideal complete with rules of conduct, ethics and good manners. Being tolerant but versatile, you may breeze through a number of relationships before finding the love you desire. There is luck in finances and business for this position. Emotionally, you are direct, to the point, and crystal clear with a youthful but sometimes sensitive outlook on life. The struggles of life don't dampen your regard for beauty, emotions, and love, and you usually bounce back happy as ever. You prefer to think the best of others and attempt not to hold a grudge. And you seek emotional experiences of life with no limitations, clarifying your responses to suit your whims.

VENUS IN SCORPIO

Venus in Scorpio is at its sexiest increasing the passions and emotions. You are ardent in love and demonstrative in affection, loving sensations, luxury and pleasure. Venus is in detriment in Scorpio, meaning that you who are already preoccupied with sex become even more seductive and sensual and your emotions are susceptible to temptations. You may have a sultry charm but find that you make every effort to channel this emotional energy into more productive pursuits. Even so, the emotionally indulged judgment of this person knows infatuations, love affairs, and endless flirtations. Relationships are highly emotional, and you are at times jealous and possessive in love. You may experience trouble and disappointments and numerous problems with your love life, even attacks on your reputation. You make every attempt to hold yourself to high standards in love, and your vivid emotional personality elevates love to a glorious plane. Your sincerity and willingness to sacrifice earn you respect and admiration.

VENUS IN SAGITTARIUS

Venus in Sagittarius makes this person eager to experience emotions, but with a desire to remain free as long as possible. You idealize love, turning it into an experience of the mind, and you are unafraid of loving and being loved. You are impulsive but sincere and loyal in your affections. You possess a refined nature, loving beauty, but are fun-loving and impressionable while remaining intuitive and imaginative. Charitable and generous, you may enjoy travel, art, romance, sports and amusement all with the same degree of enthusiasm. You also equally pursue knowledge and intellectual and spiritual enlightenment. Sociable, you have many friends and acquaintances and enjoy a busy and active life. Loving to travel, you may find yourself developing attractions and affections for members of the opposite sex in far away countries. You possess a reverence for life, freedom, philanthropy and may express love as goodwill towards others. You may choose freedom, or a long leash, over long-term affairs or marriage. In marriage, your partner must understand your need to explore and experience life. You are sensitive, but no matter how many times your heart is hurt, you will continue to seek that new experience.

VENUS IN CAPRICORN

Venus in Capricorn influences this native to be wise, trusting, responsible, and seldom found in compromising situations. Your affections are serious but restrained. Emotionally, you are ambitious, diplomatic and honorable, and you may choose to marry for convenience or social position. If you have emotions, you hold them in check and refrain from displays preferring to use tact and instinctively saying or doing the right thing at the right time. When well-aspected, this person is loyal, trustworthy and dependable. Your first love may be your career. Venus turns your personal affections into emotional discipline, and for you true love may need time to grow and blossom. If afflicted, this is a person driven by physical pleasures with a self-serving ego. This can be a productive position for Venus granting a sense of order, discipline and proportion and success in endeavors. You seldom struggle between emotions, love, desire and ambition and duty. They all blend together quite naturally for you.

Venus in Aquarius

Venus remains unemotional in Aquarius finding an individual who is kind, charitable and an humanitarian. Your emotional responses have a tendency to be frank and open serving your aesthetic outlook on life. You have a love for ideals and may idealize love as well. You are intuitive, philosophical, and generous. You possess a flair for the exotic and may find yourself experimenting with love and emotions but settling in life. Your lover must be a friend as you hold friends and friendships in high regard. Your tendency is to love humanity as much as any individual and you may not devote your attentions exclusively to one person. You may be unconventional in love and attracted to stronger, more independent types who aren't as demanding on your time and affections. You have a strong fondness for pleasure and social life, easily make friends and acquaintances from all walks of life. While you are faithful as long as the affair lasts, you may find that you encounter sudden or unexpected experiences, secret affairs, and a love for a person either older or younger. You are sensuous but not necessarily sensual, and are perpetually pure of heart seeking freedom of expression and personal independence.

Venus in Pisces

Venus brings out the best in Pisces compelling a person to respond deeply to emotions, perhaps more so than you can express. Venus elevates and refines your sentiments bestowing you with a nature that is charitable, sympathetic, and inclined toward relieving suffering and pain in others. You are found to be compassionate and sensitive, emotional, psychic, idealistic and inspirational. You are ruled by the emotions, and in a relationship can be overly sentimental but genuine. You are willing to sacrifice for your love and for your family. You receive genuine joy from giving. You love all things that are beautiful including poetry, music and art. You are cheerful and congenial and prefer peaceful settings and comfort and luxury. If you aren't careful, you can become a bit lazy and indolent, and must strive to overcome this tendency in your nature. You are faithful and devoted with a tendency to idealize your partner, and you most desire to share the pleasure you find in life with another person.

443

MARS

Rules: ARIES

KEYWORDS: Energy, initiative, desires, new beginnings and ideas, motivation, physical exertion, forcefulness, ambitions, effort, competition, combativity, courage, bold, daring, impulsiveness, direct action, adventure, aggressive, fearless, sexual drive, temper, violence, destructiveness, passion, fires, quarrels, pain, war, weapons, accidents, cuts, bruises, fevers. Mars rules Aries; is exalted in Capricorn; is in detriment in Libra; and is in fall in Cancer.

Mars, named for the Roman god of war, is indicative of physical energy, the natural flow of energies into channels, and the most effective uses of energy. Mars manifests as hot, dry, masculine, and pertains to ambitions, initiatives, desires and the animal nature. The planet of Mars, because of its red color, is considered fiery.

Mars is referred to as a superior planet, orbiting outside of Earth from the Sun, and is not as closely associated with the Sun as the inferior planets, Mercury and Venus. Mars remains in each of the twelve Zodiac signs for a little over two months, taking about two and a half years to travel through all of the signs. It represents the energy or actions which express the reactions of the mind (Mercury) and the emotions (Venus).

If Mars is in your Sun sign it endows you with abundant energy which is at times directed into a fiery temper. In the same sign as your Moon sign, Mars grants the ability to use and realize your most inner nature and desires. In the same sign as Mercury, Mars sharpens your senses and makes you quick in speech, thought and actions. In the same sign as Venus, it makes your emotional responses quicker and causes you to act on them, making you ardent and passionate with an earthy awareness.

Mars rules over energy, ambition, actions, boldness, tenacity, and courage. Mars, the warrior of the Zodiac, was known in Greek mythology as Ares, the god of battle. This planet represents the union between matter and spirit, and it is the energetic influence of the planet Mars that sets out to conquer the limitations of the human experience, refusing to submit to the necessity for struggle and pain. Positive traits of Mars include ambition, strength, decisiveness, independent, direct and forceful, leadership, and the defender of others. It is strongly sexed, passionate, and forceful. The negative traits include aggressive, irritable, rash, impulsive, brutal, selfish, argumentative, rude and boisterous. Mars rules over fire, earthquakes, violence and war, and the negative influence can cause accidents, injuries or illnesses. Mars is associated with the muscular and sexual system, adrenal glands, red blood cells, the kidneys, bruises and burns, the male hormones in both sexes, heat, action, weapons and sharp tools.

MARS IN ARIES

Mars rules Aries and when it is positioned in this sign, it grants the native initiative, abundant energies, and powerful force. It influences you to be positive, self-assured and active but combative. You are originally enterprising and probably have mechanical ability as well. You can be fiery and electrically inspiring. You are frank and outspoken, know what you want, and love your independence and freedom. Your nature is at times impulsive and if you choose you can act rashly, but always on your own initiative. You possess a love of enjoyment, pleasure, sports, adventure and excitement. You are intellectual and love knowledge of all kinds, but at the same time you are sexually active. If Mars is afflicted, you have a fiery temper. Courageous, you are at your best when not limited or restricted by others. Your self-interest is strong, and you will push your ideas forward with or without encouragement from others. You are abrupt and aggressive in speech, and a formidable adversary reacting with strength and vigor to any challenges.

MARS IN TAURUS

Mars in Taurus can turn an otherwise stubborn person into an obstinate one who sees 'red' on occasion. But usually, your energy is more tempered and is used in practical and persevering ways. The impact of Mars compels you to force your way through obstacles and any resistance to attain your achievements. You have a quiet ambition, quick wit and plenty of plans for the future. You possess good executive ability and excel at organizing and directing. You work tenaciously and with determination to turn plans into practical applications. Mars in Taurus can alternate from being peaceful and aggressive, stoic or indulgent, generous or self-seeking. You are ardent and stable in love, and focus your energies on your security. You have a strong preference for doing things your way. You have the strength to achieve your basic objectives in life and love. Your passions are earthy, passionate, but possessive. You gain financially, materially and in pleasure, and you spend freely. If afflicted, there is a tendency toward loss, and the temper is hasty and at times violent. This position of Mars indicates opponents and difficulties, but you persevere.

Mars in Gemini

Mars in Gemini and you project your ideas forcefully with sharpened insight and perceptions. You are intellectually quick and energetic, but mentally combative and forceful. You are direct and plain spoken. You can be restless and changeable with a tendency to expend your energy in many pursuits. You are a nimble talker who prefers to change words into action as quickly as possible. Your sudden inspirations and impetuous ideas propel others to actions as well. You have a way with words and can talk yourself out of most difficulties being convincing or at other times sarcastic and cutting. You love the adventures in life and have a need to circulate, your mind requiring action both mentally and physically. Rarely bored or boring, you can wear others out with your energetic outlook on life. If Mars is well-aspected you like information, travel, and science, and you are inventive, ingenious, and practical. If afflicted, you can be disagreeable and critical with a restless and indecisive mind. Your energy flows naturally to your speech, and in love you are a sensualist who likes the physical expressions of love.

Mars in Cancer

Mars in Cancer focuses energy on the emotions, and this person must constantly strive to rule the emotions rather than having the emotions rule. You want security, and you strive to acquire and to protect what you have. You may find that you hold your emotions in check and then periodically, you suddenly blow up. The well developed native will strive to direct this energy into productive causes and accomplishments. You are tenacious, ambitious and boldly industrious, but those temperamental outbursts cause you problems. Sensuous and fond of luxury, you are prone to nursing bad feelings for those who have offended you. You have a rebellious streak, but can be originally creative and strongly independent. If Mars is afflicted there is an indication of an early death of mother or separation from; trouble in home life and marriage; many worries and sorrows; changes in residence; trouble through inheritance of property; accidents to home through fire, storm, earthquake, theft; danger through water; stomach disorders and problems related to sight.

MARS IN LEO

Mars in Leo grants enthusiasm and a strong sense of purpose. You are candid, fearlessly independent, free and enterprising and strive to be honest and conscientious. Your energy flows through positive, self-centered channels insuring that you always make a good impression. You are ambitious, active, trustworthy, industrious and capable of responsibilities and positions of authority. You are sociable, friendly, warm and kind, and ardent in love and pleasure. You have a tendency to be hasty and impulsive in love, emotions, and passions. There are times when you are aggressive and defiant, even forcefully so. You have a preference for projecting ideas in a dramatic manner, and will take an action regardless of consequences. There is a tendency for you to be impatient with less courageous types. A fiery planet in a Fire sign makes you doubly assertive. Mars makes this individual motivated enough to push forward purposefully with style and presence. Mars endows you with strength, courage and generosity. Your ego is in control of your energy. If Mars is afflicted, there are disappointments in love and fortune.

MARS IN VIRGO

Mars in Virgo makes you original, bold, hard working and enterprising. While you are usually successful, Mars places difficulties and struggles in your path. Your energies are directed into systematic and orderly ways in. Logical and precise, you may do well in scientific endeavors. Mars and Virgo are a vigorous combination, and you are shrewd and adroit with mental and physical finesse. Through specialization and skill, you rise in your profession, at times spending more time on your career than you do on your love life. But whether you are ardent in love or at work, you strive for perfection and results. The problem with this position of Mars is a tendency to focus on details rather than the bigger picture, losing your energy for more important things. If Mars is afflicted, there is a tendency to be irritable, rash, proud, stubborn, reserved, secretive, revengeful, and you suffer from loss of friends. Otherwise, Mars in Leo grants financial gain in later life.

447

Mars in Libra

Mars in Libra leads you to float between being languid and passionate. Either way, you are perceptive and observant with a clear vision and refined taste. You are intuitive and idealistic, but enterprising. You may have a love for science or fondness for law or business. In love you possess a strong attraction for the opposite sex, and can be ardent but rash, passionate but impulsive. You believe in moderation, however, and your energies are controlled by judgment. By nature peaceful, you are exposed to opposition and adversity which requires your strength, wit and skill to overcome. In spite of yourself, you become involved in arguments and can be belligerent. You are sociable and magnetic, but emotionally impressionable, and you strive against being overcome by stronger personalities. You are sensitive to love, and your energies flow effortlessly in that direction. If Mars is afflicted there are many separations and difficulties between. Your energies and your emotions are always working either with each other or not, and you express your energies both emotionally and physically.

Mars in Scorpio

Mars in Scorpio makes you deeply emotional. This position of Mars can either be the best or the worst location. If positive, these energies make for personal security both financially and in love. You are magnetic with a forceful ego which attracts others. You are passionate, determined, practical and relentlessly striving toward accomplishment. You possess executive skill and mechanical and inventive ability. You may appear cold to more emotional types, and can be rash and impulsive, selfish and even revengeful. But at the same time, you are diplomatic with a sharp mind and acute awareness that produces results. At its worst, Mars indicates a fear of not attaining security, producing a person who seeks escapes and can be timid or quarrelsome, self-indulgent and weak, dangerously cruel, jealous and revengeful. This position of Mars requires a great degree of strength of character and self-control. If afflicted, this native is unsociable and ungrateful, overbearing and selfish with little regard for others. Otherwise, this is a practical person with the ability to work hard and accomplish much.

MARS IN SAGITTARIUS

Mars in Sagittarius and you are youthfully boisterous and energetic, mentally and physically. The fiery planet in this Fire sign makes you open and free, generous and enthusiastic, ambitious but impulsive. With your love of freedom, you are uncontainable and balk at discipline forever seeking the future and what it will bring. Your energies flow into physical channels, and this vital position of Mars, grants you an athletic ability. You can also be studious and prefer generalizations to details. You are charmingly witty and humorous with an original and independent outlook on life. You are brave, daring and love a good adventure, full of excitement. Then too, you can be inspirational and prophetic with strong intuitive abilities which may develop into metaphysical interests. You are the seeker of quests, or the questioner of fate. Your ideas and antics can be outrageous, regardless of the opinions of others. If Mars is afflicted, it signals danger through travel, risk, or miscalculations. You are the dreamer of dreams forever peering into the clouds.

MARS IN CAPRICORN

Mars in Capricorn begets a person who puts raw energy to work with sustained efficiency. Mars is in exaltation in Saturn-ruled Capricorn, joining the drive of Mars with the organization of Saturn. Your energy is controlled through containment and compression making you ambitious, enterprising, industrious and intent on acquisition. You direct your energies toward your objectives in life. You are courageous, brave, bold, self-reliant, self-assured and are not opposed to adventure or excitement. Danger is an afterthought for you, which at times means unforeseen accidents. However, your practical self-control shows in your speech and actions. You are as comfortable with details as generalizations, and you exhibit executive and leadership abilities. You are proud but tactful, subtle but intuitive, and have a love for duty and responsibilities. If Mars is afflicted, it indicates conflicts with authority figures and friends, a quick temper and irritability. This is a favorable position for Mars for financial success.

Mars in Aquarius

Mars in Aquarius and you spend your energy freely, independently and inventively. You are the reasoner looking for a unique and original point of view. You are impulsive but determined, whether idealistically or in personal pursuits. You are forceful and convincing in speech, arriving at conclusions and summations quickly. You have a strong intellect, a quirky sense of humor, and a scientific bend to your mind. You can be impulsive, rash, head strong and abrupt, but you are an humanitarian at heart. You make friends easily, are faithful in love, and most capable of quick decisions in emergencies. There is a tendency for you to become set in your ways, and you must guard against becoming introverted, preferring your own thoughts to the ways of the world. Then too, you can just as easily become the humanitarian leader of social revolution and change. If a writer, this produces an interest in expressing socially significant messages. If Mars is afflicted, this native is too independent, rash, abrupt, and outspoken; indicates separation from friends. You are ambitious, enterprising, and fixed in opinion but capable of abrupt changes. Gain is seen through your career.

Mars in Pisces

Mars in Pisces and your energy is diffused in numerous directions. This can leave you feeling either tired or emotionally drained. Your emotional desire is so strong, and you are so generous, you are capable of great sacrifices for others. At the same time, cautious in financial affairs, you strive to accumulate money. You can be timid or bold, cautious or outspoken, but you are easily influenced by others. There is a tendency for you to deflect the vital forces inward, to worry yourself into becoming indolent and moody. This location of Mars leads one to be either sensual, temperamental, and pleasure-seeking, or, when self-control is exhibited, passionately focused on a purpose. If Mars is afflicted, the native sees misfortunes and difficulties, suffering from theft, scandal, slander, and false accusation. Your nature is sympathetic, affectionate, and sensitive. At times, you must slow your pace so as not to lose your energy.

JUPITER

Rules: SAGITTARIUS

KEYWORDS: Good luck, knowledge, philosophy, faith, religion, justice, law, wealth, opportunity, expansion, speculation, understanding, higher education and universities, compassion, congenial, growth, optimism, jovial, enthusiasm, new experiences, wisdom, legal affairs, long distance travel, foreigners and foreign countries, cultural institutions, abstract mental processes, ethics, social order, overconfidence, conceit, indulgence, freedom-loving, resentful of restrictions. Jupiter rules Sagittarius; is exalted in Cancer; is in detriment in Gemini; is in fall in Capricorn.

Jupiter, named for the Greek god Zues or the Roman god Jove, is the planet that represents opportunity and your responses and reactions to it. Jupiter is associated with the characteristics of joy, friendliness, hope, benevolence, compassion, justice, honesty, spirituality, and calculations. Jupiter is referred to as the greater fortune, and it is often associated with expansion, growth, abundance, wisdom, luck, optimism, success and generosity.

In mythology, Jupiter or Zeus, the ruler of the gods, was as a child nurtured on the milk of a goat whose horns overflowed with food and drink. The planet of Jupiter pours outs it gifts through the opportunity of experience. Jupiter can be thought of as coordinating the personal experiences of the Moon and Venus.

If Jupiter is in the same sign as your Sun or your Moon sign, it grants a direct and effective response to opportunity and is at its most fortunate or luckiest. If Jupiter is in the same sign with Mercury, you perceive opportunity optimistically, but with some degree of stubbornness. If Jupiter is in the same sign with Venus, you perceive emotions in a way that allows you to turn them to your advantage, harmoniously. In the same sign with Mars, your energy, drive and courage are directed toward opportunity and you aren't above taking a chance in life.

Jupiter indicates whether you are sociable and friendly or not, how you will respond to opportunities in life, and what career choices are best for you. Jupiter represents that aspect of life in which you are the luckiest, or most fortunate, or where you find the most opportunity, and it is that stroke of luck that arrives when you most need it. Jupiter is warm, moist, sanguine, temperate, social, expansive, masculine and moderate.

If well-aspected, Jupiter grants a logical mind, confidence, and a self-assured determination. If Jupiter is afflicted, it can indicate restlessness, uncertainty, misjudgment, unfortunate investments and speculations, and a tendency toward extravagance, overspending for luxury items, and an overly optimistic outlook. In regards to health, Jupiter rules the thighs, blood, liver, veins, the pituitary gland and arteries.

451

JUPITER IN ARIES

Jupiter in Aries makes you progressive, ambitious, and aspiring with an urge to expand that inspires direct and forceful action. You possess grand ideas and the enthusiasm to carry them out. Opportunity becomes personal and ego driven. Jupiter adds fire to a self-assured person or self-assurance to one who is not as outgoing. You have the ability to be responsibility and to handle situations of authority well. You prefer to be in a leadership position or working for yourself. Either way, you like to be the person making the plans. You may find yourself changing your career, following different objectives, or having two occupations in life. You have a strong intellect and are attracted to science, literature, philosophy, travel, sports, and nature. Success may be realized through personal merits, domestic relationship, social standing or influential friends. You find yourself naturally attracted to work that is satisfying to you, but you must watch against being rash, impulsive and over-optimistic. You possess an ability to exert yourself and the courage of your convictions.

JUPITER IN TAURUS

Jupiter in Taurus grants a love of justice, and to you, opportunity and security are perceived as one in the same thing. The chances are, you hold back from taking a chance, preferring to protect your security. Your tendencies toward expansionism is related to utilitarian endeavors in that you understand the value of money. At the same time, you are affectionate, generous, peaceful, reserved and firm in your opinions. You have a strong love for your home, and not being restless, you have little interest in change. With Taurus being the sign of material possession and Jupiter the sign of abundance, you may do well in careers related to finance and investments, minerals and oil, ranching, banking, construction, and merchandising. You find that you benefit through the opposite sex, society, the church, philosophy, your intellectual endeavors, gifts, investments, speculation, and inheritance. If afflicted, you suffer through the same aspects. You are most likely a person who believes that positive thinking brings profitable results. Not a gambler, you take life seriously and consider opportunities cautiously.

JUPITER IN GEMINI

Jupiter in Gemini and you are a person who is versatile and open minded with an adventurous attitude toward opportunity. Sympathetic and benevolent with humanitarian tendencies, you are friendly and well mannered with a love for novel situations, traveling and intellectual pursuits. You may find the most opportunity in exciting adventures in far away places, and others may think you impractical at times. Although clever, your interests may be scattered. You are more than willing to try anything once, and opportunities seem to come to you through social contacts and friends. Sometimes restless and changeable, you want to see and experience life, to travel, and to meet other people. You may find opportunities in the fields of math, communications, literature, education, law, diplomatic positions, consulting, inventions, and the travel industry. If afflicted, there are problems in marriage, some difficulties with adversaries, an unprofitable profession, separation from relatives, and problems associated with writings. You may find your fortune success by accident while you're not even looking for it.

JUPITER IN CANCER

Jupiter is exalted in Cancer making you a kind, generous person filled with good humor. You are ambitious, enterprising, popular and sociable with a friendly disposition. You tend to see opportunity along lines that promote security and prosperity. You aren't grasping, but you have a tendency to hold on to your money and to strive to satisfy your wants. You have a close association with your mother, but you yearn to travel and to improve you insight and knowledge of cultures and places. You are intellectual, intuitive, and imaginative with an appreciation for the arts. You are patriotic and possess an interest in public welfare and an insatiable curiosity about psychic matters. You do well in investments, real estate, inheritances, public work, or gains through marriage. The chances are you will travel far from where you began. To you, home, family, spouse, children and friends are important, and you strive to maintain your security in life. You follow traditions and find comfort in attending religious services. Your knowledge of life develops out of a sympathetic response to feelings and emotions.

JUPITER IN LEO

Jupiter in Leo grants you public appeal. You are good-natured, magnanimous, loyal, courteous, generous and compassionate. More than likely you see opportunity as a chance to show your virtues and abilities and to expand results, preferably on a large scale. Intelligent and ambitious, you have a love of display with a flair for the dramatic. The expansion of Jupiter working through this sign of self-expression enlarges the ego, making you dream of conquering the heights of success. Your emotions are deep, sincere and honest, and you are endowed with your own special wisdom, judgment, and strong will power. Capable, honest and trustable, you do well in positions of responsibility, and you enjoy honors and recognition. Intuitive, at times inspiring and diplomatic, you do well in acting, politics, advertising, public relations, government, and positions of prominence. You benefit through investment, speculations, travel, sports, education or diplomatic positions. Guard against easy success making you boastful or power hungry. You are most satisfied when others are aware of your success.

JUPITER IN VIRGO

Jupiter in Virgo makes you kind and conscientious but also skeptical and with a factual, sometimes critical, outlook. Jupiter is in detriment in Virgo making you intellectual but overly concerned with details. You can systematically accumulate knowledge and perceive progress in material aspects rather than as an expansion of consciousness. Chances are, you are cautious, prudent, discreet, and discriminating with a tendency to put all of your efforts into one endeavor, and find success by building on that endeavor, however humble your beginning. Practical minded, you are also analytical, persevering, and endowed with common sense. You probably prefer ethics to theology. You may find success in literature, investment, commercial and speculative dealings. You have the ability to live by your wits, but others trust your judgment and will probably back your business interests. If afflicted, there is seen loss of benefits, illness, and a tendency not to apply yourself through lack of concentration. Not rash or impulsive, you gain through your own endeavors.

JUPITER IN LIBRA

Jupiter in Libra makes you kind, charming, magnetic, sympathetic, and hospitable with an artistic flair. Well mannered and sincere, you enjoy being conscientious, compassionate, imaginative, and perceptive with a judicial outlook of acceptance and harmony. You gain much wisdom through an understanding of relationships, but at times you are easily influenced. And while you may be talented in a number of areas, you may find yourself pursuing a course that isn't what you're best suited for, or which was suggested by someone else. You love to entertain and to attend to the needs of others, and being diplomatic, you like to inspire and encourage others. You do well in art, music, business, commerce, law, science, medicine, or public institutions. Jupiter influences your ability to plan functions and grants you social consciousness with a capacity to interact with others. This is also a good location for marriage. If afflicted, there are legal problems, problems through friends, laziness, self-indulgence and conceit. You must become firm to find success in any one area and worry less about the opinions of others.

JUPITER IN SCORPIO

Jupiter in Scorpio effects personal growth and transformation, and grants you a strong and powerful will power, deep emotions, enthusiasm and perseverance. You are ambitious, generous, proud, aggressive, and self-confident without being ego driven. Opportunity to you is associated with deep personal needs, and you follow instinctively that which satisfies these needs. You have an active and analytical mind and an intense desire to live life fully. You have a flair for business, finance, and positions requiring locating information such as investigative work or research positions. Opportunities may come from associations with the opposite sex, and gains from litigation and investments. You travel, experience strange adventures, and meet questionable people. If afflicted, you have jealous friends, loss through speculation, danger through travel and social or political associations, and if Mars overrules Jupiter's restrictions, you seek sensations through pleasures and experiences. You can be forceful, farseeing, and driven to complete your tasks, possessing a sublime intuition for finding the right information and making the right choice. You are ardent in life.

JUPITER IN SAGITTARIUS

Jupiter in Sagittarius brings a wide range of interests and generally good fortune in financial matters. You are attracted to opportunities related to ideals, knowledge, philosophy, and adventure. You are courteous, friendly, tolerant and accepting of others, kind, and generous. Your mind is liberal, progressive, and compassionate. You are the sincere humanitarian wanting what is best for all. You may well find that you are successful in your endeavors, receive honors, and become a leader in your field. You prefer to live well and to spend freely, turning your ideas into profit. You find success in sports, literature, law, government, politics, scientific, or spiritual matters. You may gain through speculation, marriage, inheritance and travel. If afflicted, you experience problems with social affairs, sports or loss by speculation. You can be prophetic and inspirational and often impress others. Not particularly materialistic, you find success when it relates to an ideal such as duty or security. You prefer to please the crowd, and must guard against this desire for popularity.

JUPITER IN CAPRICORN

Jupiter in Capricorn and you are prudent and conscientious with a deliberate, thoughtful, ingenious, serious and well-organized mind. You seek opportunity for positions of authority and dignity. You are the perfect mixture of daring and caution but with your strong will power and ambition you are unafraid of hard work. You can be either economical or frugal, and this doesn't slow you down in the least. You gain success in positions of authority, exhibiting natural leadership abilities. You may have an interest in philosophy, politics, science, or theology, and do well in government service, business, finance, trading, mining, construction, real estate and development, or the petroleum industry. You gain by commercial or foreign affairs, and an inheritance. There is indication for travel, a marriage affected by family, and a concern for others. If afflicted, there is an unorthodox attitude, career difficulties, and public discredit. You must account for all that you do. But for you opportunity is seen practically, with no inclination toward speculation, and you abide by traditions and well-tried practices.

JUPITER IN AQUARIUS

Jupiter in Aquarius grants you the ability to win friends and to realize opportunities through social, artistic, or political matters. However, you are as content to be a drifter as a success story along as you have your principles and other people to keep you company. Naturally cheerful and good humored, you are compassionate and sympathetic with a giving and congenial manner. You strongly dislike discord or disharmony in your affairs. You possess a love for the ideal and may idealize love in an impersonal manner. You envision expansive dreams that may be realized or may just be fanciful thinking. You prefer careers having a higher goal than simply making money, and you seem to bring luck to others. You are intuitive about human nature and prefer to consider new concepts of social, spiritual or humanitarian causes. Careers that attract you include the media, computers, electronics, aviation and the space industry, and you have an interest in science, literature, music and the arts. Gain is seen through the career and perhaps pertaining to the government, and expect travel and unusual experiences. Nonmaterialistic, you view money as a means of doing what you want in life.

JUPITER IN PISCES

Jupiter in Pisces grants compassion, benevolence, and good humor with strong ideals and an interest in charitable organizations. You prefer to expand consciousness by broadening relationships, seeing opportunity in how it relates to your private dream of self-justification. Chances are, you will pass up financial gain if it is associated with unworthy causes, having a personal code by which you judge all things. Your are attracted to unusual interests including the mystical. Original, independent and progressive in your thinking, you prefer professions in which you deal personally with others such as social work, counseling, teaching, politics or government services. You also like nature and do well in careers dealing with animals and wildlife. If afflicted there is seen loss through speculation and deception, and an attitude that is unambitious and pleasure seeking. You may find success in your secret ambition and will always find that you attract popularity through your personality.

SATURN

Rules: CAPRICORN

KEYWORDS: **D**iscipline, restrictions, responsibil-ities, limitations, patience, long term relationships, authority, leadership, career plans, older people, groups, influential relationships, public reputation, social standing, political outlook, ambitions, serious social affliations, government, legalities, math, science, time, separations, difficulties, obstacles, constriction, sorrow, delay, self-discipline to overcome problems, wisdom through effort and experience, crystallization, caution, perseverance, endurance, stability, reserved, dignity, contraction, organization, seriousness, duty, obligations, prudent, economical, suppression, suspicion, pessimism, selfishness, indifference. Saturn rules Capricorn; is exalted in Libra; is in detriment in Cancer; is in fall in Aries.

Saturn represents limitations, self-preservation, hard work, and the burden of responsibility and duty. It is basically a protective influence providing growth and survival through restriction. Saturn provides us with the lessons in life, the trials and tribulations, and the training needed to become self-disciplined. Saturn is exacting, but once a person has endured the hardships, it can be expected that Saturn will then grant acceptance, justice and achievement through personal ambition and aspiration. Mars is referred to as the lesser malefic, and Saturn as the greater malefic with its influence granting patience and a mature stability as seen through realism. Saturn rules the end of life.

Saturn in mythology was Cronus, the father of Jupiter, Neptune, and Pluto; Cronus was dethroned by Zeus. Saturn's symbol is the sickle that Father Time uses to harvest the fruits of a man's life.

Those with a positive Saturn influence are serious, practical, and can be profound thinkers with an economical, prudent, and conservative outlook. The further Saturn is located from your Sun, Moon, or Ascendant, the more objective and extroverted you are. If Saturn is in your Sun or Moon sign, you are defensive and at times prefer to seek isolation. If Saturn is located in the same sign as Mercury, you are a profound thinker with a preference for serious reactions to sensory impressions. With Saturn in the same sign as Venus, you may be cool in emotions and have problems with interpersonal relationships, being luckier in finances than with love. Saturn combined with your Mars sign makes you either defensive, indecisive and aggressive, or if the Sun and Moon are stronger, well-balanced, calm and moderate. With Saturn in the same sign as Jupiter, you take opportunities seriously.

Saturn rules our destiny and fate, deciding the price we pay for what we have received in life. It rules the skin, teeth, bones, gall bladder, spleen, some nerves and joints, and hearing, and is associated with maturity, perseverance, tenacity, inhibitions, and intolerance. Poorly aspected, it produces adversities, delays, disappointments and sorrows. Saturn's nature is cold, dry, melancholy, earthy and masculine. It teaches us not only to respect life, but that through introspection and reviewing our lives, we can see how the lessons learned in life benefit our choices in the future.

Saturn in Aries

Saturn in Aries and you are resolute, determined and ambitious, but this planet spells delays and obstacles in your path that can cause you some confusion. You realize success through hard work and perseverance. You find yourself contemplating your plans with sound thinking, but you are easily angered when opposed and you forcefully assert your control over your situation and over others. Ruled by Mars, you are aggressive, but Saturn provides a restraint that leaves you a disciplinarian of military precision, and this combination of forcefulness and organization dictates limits and restrictions. You can be reserved but are striving to acquire success or possessions. At your best, you are self-reliant, dutiful, and persistent with the strength of character to face hardships and obstacles. In its worst, this location of Saturn influences a person to be narrow-minded, self-centered, stubborn, defensive, and feeling that the world is against him or her. You may experience jealousies in life from a partner or friends, difficulties in marriage, and numerous obstacles and setbacks in your early life. Life becomes more settled as you mature.

Saturn in Taurus

Saturn in Taurus and you are a kind, thoughtful person who is cautious and prudent, but at times easy to anger, stubborn, resentful and unforgiving. You take responsibilities and duties seriously, working tenaciously with capable and determined effort. Your self-preservation instinct is satisfied by security and material possessions, but you aren't necessarily selfish or materialistic as much as striving for a sense of well being and security. Once you have acquired enough in life to make you feel secure, you become generous with others. You can be either purposeful or obstinate, but you have a strength of character and morals that see you through most situations. Economical and thrifty, you are not one to speculate on the future, but choose to follow a conservative path, working hard and gaining through your own merits. You may experience loss and sorrows associated with relatives, but gain through savings and investments. With a strong love of nature, you prefer to abide by nature's laws.

Saturn in Gemini

Saturn functions in Gemini to concentrate the mind on facts, organizing your energies constructively. This is considered one of the best locations for Saturn, granting you an ingenious and observant nature with a mastery of mind and perhaps of life. You have intellectual abilities and an interest in scientific subjects, research, education, literature, or math. You possess a shrewd business mind, and justify your actions forcefully and articulately. You can be versatile, adaptable, and resourceful with a steady, impartial mind, cautious reasoning, and profound insights. Unfortunately, Saturn and Gemini can combine to produce a person who is controlling, cynical, stubborn and pessimistic who doesn't see through obstacles to the future. A realist, this person becomes overly concerned with the present and is at times gloomy and depressed. You prefer travel associated with your career rather than for pleasure alone, may experience problems legal affairs, accusations, and problems which develop into restrictions and limitations with relatives and friends. You exhibit an interest in innovative thought and intellectual pursuits.

Saturn in Cancer

Saturn in Cancer finds a person whose practical concerns for security restrict emotional responses. You are shrewd, ambitious and tenacious, make a reliable partner, but may be emotionally dependent on others. Saturn is in detriment in Cancer which can make you somewhat changeable, fretful, discontented or jealous. You may worry yourself into being introverted, or on the other hand use your insecurities to force yourself into the world. If afflicted, this native becomes defensive, builds protective emotional walls, and turns irritable and self-absorbed. The challenge here is to learn to use the lessons learned from Saturn's discipline and Cancer's naturally protective instinct to overcome any obstacles. And your obstacles may be many including domestic problems, sorrows with parents and friends, and worries with home and children. You develop an interest in psychic affairs, prefer hobbies and subjects related to the home, and are very concerned with social issues. Take the intuitive to overcome obstacles in preparation for maturity.

Saturn in Leo

Saturn in Leo grants you powerful characteristics. You are determined, ambitious, strong-willed and bold, but quick tempered. You are self-assured, well organized, and authoritative. Dramatic, you excel when in the public eye, finding justification but perhaps not much fun. This love for attention predominates your life, whether successful or not. Saturn's restrictions and Leo's expansive nature aren't necessarily in harmony. You may find problems expressing your emotions and troubles in relationships of love. And your authoritative nature may make you appear cool, haughty and controlling. Your strength is solving problems, organizing, and establishing order, and you may do well in government, politics, or leadership positions. Rigid and conservative, your sense of personal responsibility oversees your life, and at times you prefer this to more pleasurable past times or relationships. Your challenge is to learn to be more accepting of others and less suspicious of the good will of others. You experience sorrows and obstacles, and may attain success in your career, but must watch for reversals.

Saturn in Virgo

Saturn in Virgo is advantageous and compatible. The earthy, practical nature of Virgo does well under the limitations placed by Saturn. You are reserved, discreet, and cautious with a preference for sound methods, rules and regulations, precision, and good judgment. You are found to be most conscientious and responsible, finding expression and a sense of worth in work and duty. You are most happy when things are going well in your career, but you must guard against stress and depression associated with over working. You realize gains through investments, but encounter obstacles in marriage and partnerships particularly in the early adult years. If afflicted, this person is stubborn, intolerant, and too detail-oriented. You possess the ability to work well by yourself, and no doubt will find success in your career. However, in order to find harmony in your personal life, you must develop an understanding and acceptance of other people whose methods and opinions differ from yours. Real vision in life is found when one pulls all the details in life together to find a larger picture.

Saturn in Libra

Saturn is favorably placed in Libra making you kind, pleasant, lovable, and well-adjusted. You are patient with a spiritual nature and a reasonable perspective on life whose balanced judgment inspires others to trust you. You possess refined tastes, an interest in scientific subjects, and a good intellect with a tendency to play the advocate, loving a good discussion on controversial topics. Your nature inclines you to be faithful in love and marriage, honest in your transactions, and reliable in your friendships. You are responsible, flexible, diplomatic and know when to be assertive, and you naturally make a good impression on others with little effort. Saturn is exalted in Libra, allowing you to seek harmony and balance in life and relationships. If afflicted, this person becomes intolerant, insincere and impractical, becoming lonely and depressed. Obstacles in life may include sorrow and separations, delays in marriage, domestic problems, and reversals in the career which are unfortunate. With your grace, tact and charm you develop an overpowering interest in the world at large and other people.

Saturn in Scorpio

Saturn in Scorpio and you are a passionate and complex person, subtle, forceful, independent, willful, inquisitive, but somewhat reserved and at times secretive, jealous, and resourcefully cautious. Your shrewd mind combined with the seriousness of Saturn results in executive ability and business sense. You are capable of making sudden resolutions, having deep feelings, being masterful and difficult to fathom. It is almost like, at times, your primal instincts and urges are driving you, rather than conscious thought. You have a great sense of purpose and strong reserves. At times you are inflexible and have a tendency to be moody or to brood over circumstances. Your rather dry humor can turn everyday situations into insightful ones. Excellent detectives or secret agents, persons with Saturn in Scorpio prefer to work secretively, even deviously, rather than taking a straightforward path. Cautious, this person doesn't avert danger. You may experience sorrow through love, secret alliances or intrigues, or difficulties in marriage. Persistent effort against obstacles produces success.

Saturn in Sagittarius

Sagittarius warms the austerity of Saturn, and Saturn influences this native to be serious about goals and objectives, bringing into reality abstract ideas and plans. You are candid, show little fear, and are kind, obliging and somewhat philosophical. You are self-reliant and confident in your abilities, but your aim in life is to master it not merely to acquire position, success, or material possessions. You are dignified and can be grave, even at times moralizing, with an intuitive perception and insight into social welfare and scientific innovations. Strongly motivated, you excel at directing others and do well in administrative positions. You can be thrown off course by a sensitivity to criticism or opposition, but otherwise you gain through your own merit and hard work. If afflicted, this person can be ostentatious, cynical, harsh, and insincere. Problems are indicated from public, political or government affairs which may harm your reputation. You may find that you have more than one career, and you realize gains from investments. Guard against not watching your health, worrying too much, and nervousness. You develop intellectually and spiritually finding success in leadership positions.

Saturn in Capricorn

Saturn in Capricorn influences this person to be self-disciplined, practical and persevering. You are serious and at times become melancholy, apprehensive or suspicious. You are ambitious, and your persistent diplomacy and tact allows you to succeed in your career. You are more than willing to start at the bottom if it offers an opportunity for advancement. You possess the ability to turn abstract concepts into concrete terms. This position of Saturn allows a person to attain achievement or defeat, depending on personal actions in that he or she follows a path to its conclusion. You most desire success either financially, materially or through fame. If afflicted, this person is pessimistic, miserly, selfish, and arrogant. There is a tendency for unreliable friendships, difficulties in marriage, illnesses associated with stress and nerves. Your ambitions are important to you, and you are willing to sacrifice for them, and you prove you are capable of responsibilities. Success is based on your own merit and ability to face obstacles.

463

SATURN IN AQUARIUS

Saturn in Aquarius and this independent, original and inventive person, once a decision is made, sticks to plans and objectives. You are courteous and friendly but somewhat reserved and thoughtful with a humane and serious nature. You have a tendency to ponder and think deeply, and with your penetrating intellect and reasoning ability, your thoughts are insightful. You are an impressive speaker when you care to be, and then too you are deliberate in your actions. When the intellect is developed and refined through study, observations, and experience, this person's inclinations toward humanitarian and scientific subjects produce profound achievements. Success is indicated in a career choice utilizing practical application of knowledge, and you are capable of leadership positions. Guard against your tendency for inhibitions, frustrations and isolation. If afflicted, this person is obstinate, indifferent, cunning, and sly. This person has numerous friends and acquaintances and a lasting romantic relationship. You may find that success is attained during maturity after encountering obstacles in early adulthood and learning to deal with them.

SATURN IN PISCES

Saturn in Pisces and you are imaginative and intuitive, ingenious and aspiring, but sensitive to the disharmony in the world. Saturn's influence forces you to come to terms with your own tendency to brood and give up and to withdraw to safe territory. Only through self-discipline do you gain a spiritual ability and the perseverance to withstand the many obstacles Saturn places in your path. Called to sacrifice for others and to watch less deserving and talented achieve when you don't, it is left up to you to find the courage to utilize your creative abilities and strive for the success which Saturn eventually endows, that is if you don't give up by accepting existing conditions. You are sympathetic, flexible, creative and many times blessed with talent. If afflicted, this individual is moody and hypersensitive, lacks courage, worries excessively, and is sloppy and untidy. Misfortunes and sorrows are experienced, at times caused by the native's own actions, and success is realized only with the development of hope, resolve, and effort.

URANUS

Rules: AQUARIUS

KEYWORDS: Insight, originality, illumination, invention, genius, friends, groups, organizations, sudden events, changes, surprises, sudden destruction, the unexpected, unusual occurrences, revolution, disruptive events, advanced technology, electronics, electricity, independence, personal freedoms and liberties, ideals, humanitarian efforts, astrology, occult, corporate finance, intuition, reforms, ingenuity, eccentricities, rebelliousness, unconventional, new rules, futuristic visions, revelations, aeronautics, aerospace. Uranus rules Aquarius; is exalted in Scorpio; is in detriment in Leo; is in fall in Taurus.

Uranus, the seventh planet from the Sun, is referred to as one of the three modern planets. It was discovered in 1781 by William Herschel, British court astronomer. Uranus rules over sudden or disruptive changes and unpremeditated actions, signifying dramatic flashes of insight and of overcoming barriers. Then too, it influences liberty, equality, curiosity, inventions and investigations, innovations, unexplained occurrences, originality and modern art. Uranus is associated with advanced science, electricity, social and humanitarian changes and movements, and revolutions. This planet signifies the unexpected, upheavals, and the unorthodox: change, new or different, and original. Those people influenced by Uranus are often reformers, pioneers, inventors, geniuses, or are creative and intuitive.

Uranus was named for the Roman god of the sky, Ouranos, the personification of the heavens and ruler of the world. Ouranos was the father of the Titans and of Cronus who dethroned him.

Because of its distance from the Sun, Uranus remains in each Zodiac sign for seven years, taking eighty four years to pass through all twelve signs. The nature of Uranus is considered cold, dry, airy, positive, magnetic, unusual, occult and malefic. It rules the ankles and the intuition, and relates to your inner will and inherent abilities and powers. It is that energy which lends itself to will power and purpose.

In the same sign with Mercury or the Moon, Uranus grants acute awareness, quick reactions to perceptions and experience, and a quick mind. If in the same sign as the Sun, there is found nervous activity, creativity, originality and at times an eccentric nature. In the same sign as Mars, it produces fast actions and fearlessness. In the same sign as Venus, there are found unusual reactions to emotions, and sensual, idealistic, and original perceptions of love and human relations. With Saturn in the same sign, the person must balance both creativity and practical tendencies. In the same sign as Jupiter expect opportunity, inventive, daring and executive skills.

If afflicted, Uranus inclines one to be too forceful, abrupt, erratic, willful, obstinate, sarcastic and overly sensitive. These natives must strive to improve by combining effort, aspiration, and self-control, and by avoiding any risks associated with those things ruled by Uranus.

URANUS IN ARIES

Uranus in Aries and you love independence and freedom and are positive, forceful and at times impulsive with an original, imaginative and inventive mind. You are mentally and physically energetic and resourceful. You prefer to produce your own plans, be in charge of them and take charge of other people involved in your plans, and to receive recognition of your successes. You can be impatient with the ideas of others, preferring to develop your own, and fearless of following through with them. You like innovative new devices either mechanical, electrical or electronic. Travel inspires you and you change locations when your curiosity gets the best of you. If afflicted, this person can be impulsive, tactless, sharp-spoken and blunt with radical ideas and a lack of self-control. Disputes and disagreements are frequent, but your strong will power, self-reliance, and belief in yourself continues to compel you. Forceful and often inspiring, you convince others of the worthiness of your plans.

URANUS IN TAURUS

Uranus in Taurus influences a person to be determined and headstrong with fixed and immovable opinions. You are resourceful and ingenious with a tendency to plow through any obstacles in your way. You strive patiently and with effort to consolidate your work using will power and determination to make plans for future endeavors. You are good humored and friendly and enjoy the companionship of others. You possess a tendency to have an active mind that focuses on wanting newer and different material possessions, and you may come across a particular find that gains in value. You possess an inner drive to be constructive and to achieve through your efforts. You may be lucky in finances and prosperous in marriage. Uranus, however, brings gains and reversals in life, including sudden losses and a domestic difficulty caused by jealousy. You gain through partnerships, marriage, friends and associates, inventions and creative endeavors. You possess a natural intuitive ability that brings insights and inspiration into your pursuits. Tenacity, hard work and the results of your own efforts see you through life.

URANUS IN GEMINI

Uranus in Gemini and you are versatile and inventive with a flair for writing, speaking, invention or scientific skills. You are an original and imaginative thinker whose ingenuity impresses others. You feel drawn to innovative ideas, revolutionary concepts, and unusual subjects. You love ideas and your active mind draws the attention of other people, and you possess the ability to influence the thoughts, opinions and ideas of others. You are humorous and

466

possess an amusing and quick way with words often turning dull phrases and subjects into a light-hearted discussion. You love to create a new and impressive outlook, an original slant, or an insightful perception that you can express in writing or speech. If afflicted, problems with nervousness, estrangement from family, undue criticism, problems with education, tests, letters, and with trips. Your enjoyment of travel and meeting new people brings you exposure to new people and ideas.

Uranus in Cancer

Uranus in Cancer produces a person who possesses a love for home and family. You are highly sensitive to other people and may at times choose to isolate yourself finding comfort in your personal creativity, imagination, art and self-made fantasies. You possess a quick sense of humor often turning ordinary incidences into funny, quirky happenings. You can be unpredictable or at times uncertain, but you are also intuitive and insightful having sudden flashes of inspiring thought which at times borders on mysticism. A bit restless, you love to travel, to be exposed to new places, scenes, and tastes. You have a love for food which at times you find difficult to control. Because you are so sensitive, the opinions and remarks of others offend you, making you sometimes nervous, eccentric, cranky, and impatient with friends and family. Changes occur in the domestic situation, and loss and difficulty may be experienced in regards to possessions and property. Guard against health problems associated with nerves and stomach. Your creative and original nature finds expression through seeking security and comfort in pleasant home situations.

URANUS IN LEO

Uranus in Leo grants this native an industrious and aspiring nature with a forceful personality and strong leadership skills. You like being in charge and take to this position naturally because you dislike taking orders from others. Expect this person to be either independent, arrogant, headstrong, fiery, eccentric or defiant. You can be unconventional and even rebellious and worry little about the opinions of others. You have an interest in electricity, machines, and inventions. When your creative flair exerts itself, you are original in thought and like to see your ideas carried out, with you receiving the deserved recognition. Leo, as usual, stands out in a crowd. At the same time, being daring, you love a good adventure, excitement, and unusual distractions. You may encounter sudden chances through romantic relationships which bring either opportunity, odd experiences, danger or sorrow. If Uranus is well aspected, you achieve a distinctive position in a professional or public career.

URANUS IN VIRGO

Uranus in Virgo and you find that your originality most asserts itself in the areas of methods, organization, routine which allows you to analyze and use facts and figures. Your mind is subtle, independent and original while your nature is somewhat quiet and reserved but at the same time stubborn. You have a general fondness for science and unsolved phenomenon. You can be eccentric in your curiosities and determination. You are concerned with the social welfare of society, but sometimes become bogged down with the details which doesn't allow you to draw a general conclusion. If you are rebellious, it is when your plans, ideas and independence are restricted by others. If afflicted, there are disappointed ambitions, problems with either employment or employees, and a restrictive career. Generally, however, Uranus brings this native gains through opportunities and changes in the career at which time this person must set aside his or her usual caution and accept the change for the better. With your tendency toward weight gain, it is helpful if you become knowledgeable about health and nutrition.

URANUS IN LIBRA

Uranus in Libra inclines this person to be a good reasoner who loves harmonious situations. You find yourself at times restless, and you enjoy the opportunity to travel and meet new people. Being open and tolerant, you are considered somewhat eccentric in your choice of friends and associates. Difficulties can make you quick-tempered, but generally you are ambitious with a creative imagination and insightful intuition. You possess a refined taste and love aesthetically pleasing surroundings and situations. You find opportunities through your associates and friends, and possess a fondness for artistic, literary or judicial careers. Your strong magnetic personality and inventive flair draws the attentions of others. Guard against a hasty marriage which brings separation or divorce. If well aspected, Uranus in this location favors partnerships for Libra natives. If afflicted, there is an indication for an unsympathetic or unaffectionate nature, oppositions, rivalries and criticisms resulting in broken friendships and problems with plans. You are capable of always making a good first impression.

URANUS IN SCORPIO

Uranus in Scorpio makes you an angel or a little devil with the innate ability, on some deep, subconscious level, to use your genius and power for either good or evil. Uranus is exalted in Scorpio granting you a powerful personal magnetism that compels others to your control. You possess a strength of mind, determination, and persistence that drives you through your daily life. You have a strong power of concentration and a will power that is un deterred by opposition. Resistance may leave you unable to express your emotions because your emotions, working under a force of their own, focus on gathering strength and empowering your will power and determination. You can be boldly stubborn and at other times quite reserved, forceful and if necessary sharp-spoken and direct. You can also be shrewd and secretive, but aggressive to the point of being rebellious. If afflicted, there is danger of accidents. You have a mesmerizing quality and a strong magnetic appeal especially to the opposite sex.

Uranus in Sagittarius

Uranus in Sagittarius and expect the scope of your originality to be drawn from pure vision. Uranus increases the already natural imaginative, inventive and creative nature of Sagittarius inclining you toward dreams, insights, intuition, premonitions and travel. The planetary influence of Uranus also increases any rebellious nature leading to recklessness. But generally speaking it drives your freedom-loving nature to pioneer in new endeavors and to risk adventurous schemes. You love all areas of science but have a curious interest in innovations in the travel industry. You are proud and courageous with a seeking, progressive mind. You can be daring and bold, loving excitement, and you are just as enthusiastic in your beliefs and opinions. You are known for being generous, congenial, and well liked among peers and friends. If afflicted, strange occurrences related to adventures, partners, scientific endeavors, foreign affairs or travel. If well aspected, these same circumstances may bring you opportunities and gains. You often know intuitively that moment when something is about to occur, and your prophetic visions serve you well.

Uranus in Capricorn

Uranus in Capricorn grants you leadership abilities and excellent organizational skills, sound reasoning faculties and a penetrating mind with perceptive and profound insights. You are thoughtful with a serious nature that is marked by self-discipline. Your strong will power compels you to positions of authority, and you strive to succeed in all endeavors. Uranus intensifies your already ambitious and persevering nature making you even more independent with a will to be in charge and not under the dictates of others. Uranus influences you toward bold enterprises, radical and innovative changes in methods and procedures, and to take strong initiatives in your efforts. You display foresight, intuition and a propensity for correct hunches and guessing trends. If afflicted, there is an indication for family problems, oppositions from authority figures, reversals in career, and public criticism. Guard against periodic restlessness and feelings of uneasiness.

URANUS IN AQUARIUS

Uranus rules the sign of Aquarius influencing these individuals to be original, ingenious, inventive and independent. You are resourceful as well as intuitive with comprehensive mental abilities and a creative imagination. You are pleasant, friendly and sociable with humanitarian tendencies and a desire for freedom in thought and actions. Your love of people and ability to make friends plus that special stroke of creative genius allows you to sway others. Not tied to present day thinking, your unique outlook jumps light years ahead giving you what others consider an eccentric or different set of beliefs. You are drawn to science, novel subjects, and unusual endeavors not to mention other people with unconventional interests and tastes. You hold firmly to your personal opinions sometimes not listening well to others. You interests may lead you to a successful career in science, mechanical endeavors, with partners, in public life, in transportation fields, or in radio, television, or the computer industry. If afflicted, this person has difficulty through friends, partners and travel. If well aspected, friends and partners bring you luck.

URANUS IN PISCES

Uranus in Pisces can grant an individual an unique idealism with pure visionary insight. You are emotional, sensitive, and subtly insightful with an interest in philosophy, theology, astrology or psychic subjects. At the same time, you are logical and take a realistic viewpoint, and are able to research and investigate the subject matter that interests you. Your creative flair expresses itself in sensual expressions of humanity and the human condition. Being sensitive and perhaps psychic yourself, you may find that you experience strange occurrences or have remarkable dreams and visions. Your intuition leads you to act or begin an endeavor at the most advantageous time, granting you a special luck in opportunities if you listen to your own counsel and follow it. Your visions can bring you insights into the future, but this ability may also tends to dampen your spirits at times. You discover friends who are also gifted with unusual abilities and others who are public figures. If inclined toward a career in science, you may discover an affinity for developing new techniques, treatments or medicines for man's welfare.

471

NEPTUNE

Rules: PISCES

KEYWORDS: Intuition, imagination, sensitivities, psychic abilities, dreams, unreality, shadows, oceans and seas, cosmic consciousness, artistic creativity, sentiments, journeys by water, idealism, past memories, self-sacrifice, sympathy, confusion, illusion, magic, universal love, charity, romance, alcohol, drugs, indulgence, perfumes, oil, airplanes, movies, television, chain stores, business mergers, subliminal thoughts, secrets, hidden thoughts, the subconscious mind, mysticism, the astral plane, confinement, prisons, hospitals, institutions, hallucination, hypnotism, neurosis, psychosis, chemicals, poisons, deceit, self-deceiving, impressionable. Uranus rules Pisces; is exalted in Leo; is in detriment in Virgo; is in fall in Aquarius.

Neptune is indicative of love, beauty and joy found on the subliminal plane of higher consciousness. It is that mysterious and elusive desire to experience what is beyond the confines of man, material possessions and earthly desires. Because most people prefer the distractions of everyday life, few individuals respond to this influence of Neptune, causing it to be diffused, like light passing through the depths of the ocean. Neptune's influence can either be indicative of human compassion or personal confusion, of a spiritual tendency or devilment, insightfulness or a susceptibility to indulgences in alcohol, drugs or sex, and to an optimistic visionary outlook on life or to delusions in life, dreams and visions. Neptune relates to the deepest part of our subconscious, allowing human kind to see pass the everyday delusions in order to contemplate the essence of being.

Neptune, Roman god of the sea and identified with the Greek god Poseidon, ruled over the watery depths of oceans, seas, rivers, streams and fountains. The planet was discovered in 1846 and spends approximately fourteen years in each sign, resulting in it producing strong generational effects. Under the auspices of Neptune, the planet of idealism and spirituality, man is entranced by the mysteries of phenomenon. It rules over the subconscious awareness of memory, intuition and visions, and represents inspiration, spirituality, inner feelings and artistic imagination. It rules over drama, theater, dance, poetry, and religious inspiration; hospitals and anesthetics; maritime endeavors, institutions, prisons, gases, poison, and drugs; and the nervous system, mental processes, and the thalamus. Its negative influence leads to pessimism, apathy, carelessness, and to impractical worries and weaknesses that can develop into tendencies to lie, steal or to commit fraud or scams.

Neptune in the same sign with the Sun or Moon, relates to intuition and insights, or delusions, and to a need to stay grounded in reality. In the same sign as Mercury, there is creativity with a sensitive mind which responds with intensity to sensory impressions. Located with Venus, this idealistic person is romantic and sentimental or overly fond of exotic pleasures. In the same sign as Mars, your energy and intuition work harmoniously. With Jupiter, Neptune influences intuitive, practical responses to opportunity which produces security. Located with

472

Saturn, either your intuitive self-defenses protect you or you suffer from delusions and unhappiness.

NEPTUNE IN ARIES

Neptune was last in Aries from 1861 to 1874/05 and will reenter this sign in 2014 to 2028. Neptune influences the fiery energy of Aries with leadership qualities and an introspective intellect. Neptune intensifies the emotions and sensitivities, elevating the nature of this person to be inclined toward sympathy and benevolence with a spiritual perception and attuned inner understanding. Aries innovates his or her personal ideas and plans and this will be noted in the areas of science, medicine, social institutions, international affairs, and political traditions. You have a strong imagination, creativity and self-awareness combined with a desire to travel and see the world. Your impulses lead you to improve and reform with opportunity seen in a public career in business, the media, politics, institutions, science or medicine. If afflicted, this individual distrusts his or her own abilities, seeks self-gratification and pleasures, promotes personal ideas and plans out of egotism, and experiences unusual occurences and notoriety. Your strong will power and inexhaustible energies will see you through the completion of your plans.

NEPTUNE IN TAURUS

Neptune was last in Taurus from 1874 to 1887/89 and will reenter this sign in 2028. Taurus feels most secure with the acquisition of material possessions, and Neptune influences those born during this period to reevaluate the value of life. You are inclined toward artistic, musical and spiritual endeavors with a progressive outlook regarding the natural sciences and the arts. This is a good position for Neptune for financial profits, perhaps through speculation, and in business endeavors. You have an appreciation for history, antiques, and the legends and traditions of the past. You possess an aesthetic appreciation for beauty and nature, and enjoy travel and sight seeing. You are enthsiastic, patient, compatible, soft-hearted, and fun loving with a good sense of humor. This location of Neptune favors love and marriage. If afflicted, the individual over indulges in fun, pleasure and materialism. You are professional in business and social in your private life, preferring to simplify methods and procedures

NEPTUNE IN GEMINI
(1887/89--1901/02)

Neptune in Gemini and you are inclined toward innovations and novel subjects. You are intuitive, sensitive, imaginative and creative with a taste for music, drama, or poetry and an inclination for prophetic dreams. You have a personal magnetism that is expressed in your speech and communications. And you have an aptitude for science, math, inventions or mechanical skills. You are sympathetic and congenial with quick perceptions. You are resourceful, flexible, and versatile with a tolerant attitude toward others. If afflicted, the individual can be somewhat flighty, irresponsible, overly friendly and interested in the opposite sex, preoccupied with worries, restless and changeable; experiences difficulties with relatives, friends, associates, and with deceptions, and broken promises. Under affliction this native can become narrow minded, gossipy, and lack vision. This was a period of time of invention, development and change requiring individuals to adjust to new lifestyles and changing trends.

NEPTUNE IN CANCER
(1901/02--1914/16)

Neptune in Cancer and you discover that your formative years at home deeply influenced your perceptions, morals, ethics, and sense of responsibility. You Possess an inner strength and spiritualism that is refined and idealistic. You have a strong imagination, powerful impressions, and intense emotions with a love for outdoors and the grandeur of nature. Sensitive, compassionate, and congenial, you are fond of sports, social activities, and the arts. You possess the ability to escape the everyday world with the imaginative world you create through dance, music, theater, and art. Your are fond of travel, science, and new and innovative ideas, gadgets, inventions, and other items that add to the home life. You my feel that you have experienced unusual or strange occurrences in your life as well as psychic phenomenon. If afflicted, the individual is overly sensitive and impressionable, discontent, worried, and restless with a desire for change. You love harmonious settings and feel most secure when settled in your home.

NEPTUNE IN LEO
(1914/15--1928/29)

Neptune, exalted in Leo, and you are ambitious but reserved and dignified, benevolent and warm-hearted with courage and leadership abilities. You possess intuitive insight and are sympathetic, charitable and generous. There is an idealistic and creative artistic ability and high aspirations for bringing dreams and innovations into reality. You are sensitive to human emotions which is expressed in your spirituality, making you conscientious, dutiful, and responsible. You possess a love for sports, the companionship of others, social gatherings, literature, music and art. You are receptive and responsive to your inner feelings and perceptions and openly tolerant of change and unconventional ideals. If afflicted, you are drawn to pleasure and your emotions are easily swayed, you are impulsive and restlessly seek change, you can overly generous and spend too freely on luxury items. You have a love for glamour, innovative schemes, and self-expression of freedom and ideals.

NEPTUNE IN VIRGO
(1928/29--1942/43)

Neptune in Virgo and you may find that you have a tendency to be discerning, questioning conventional and accepted thoughts, principles, and institutions. Practical and capable, you have a concern for the welfare of humanity. Your nature is gentle and patient, and you are reserved with an inclination toward science, math, and a curiosity about psychic phenomenon. You have a tendency to develop your own thoughts and ideals about lifestyles, change, and innovations. Your analytical nature compels you to critically observe and this may deter you from your powerfully inspirational and idealistic tendencies. You possess a drive to serve, and being creative, this is expressed either in art, music, or public endeavors. In some aspects, these individuals appeared to have been born with a special wisdom, taken for granted, which granted a direct and warm-hearted nature and concern for others. If afflicted, the person is selfish, deceitful, confused, and prone to addictions. Your intuitive insights are more powerful than you accept.

NEPTUNE IN LIBRA
(1942/43--1955/57)

Neptune in Libra grants a compassionate and caring nature while intensifying the imagination in literature, music and art. You are easy-going, preferring to be pleasant, congenial and to relate well to others. You are strongly and prophetically idealistic particularly about issues related to social welfare, humanity, war and peace. Neptune in the sign of love, beauty and balance of Libra predisposes a strenuous striving for establishing harmonious institutions and personal situations. You find yourself offended by injustices and inequities against people, humanitarian efforts, nature, the environment and social institutions. Along with your idealism, you possess strong powers of influence and persuasion, and your patience allows you to wait for the results. If afflicted, this person is overly sympathetic and emotional with a strong attraction to the opposite sex. You experience the mystery of meeting new, different and eccentric individuals who expose you to unique thoughts, perceptions and occurrences.

NEPTUNE IN SCORPIO
(1955/57--1970/01)

Neptune in Scorpio intensifies the emotions inclining an individual to be either subtle or sensational. You find yourself fascinated by innovation, change, advanced technology and science, and are particularly interested in unlocking the mysteries of the universe. You can be persistent in your efforts, possessing a secretive nature that can be reserved but that at times flairs in anger. You have a love for the unknown whether it be unsolved phenomenon or delving into the secret lives and unsavory deals of public officials and celebrities. You are somewhat skeptical of accepted practices and policies, questioning the soundness of decisions being made by politicians and business interests. You have a strong attraction toward sexual relationships and this is reflected in your tastes in movies and entertainment. If afflicted, the individual is drawn to sensational activities, luxury, pleasures, drugs, alcohol and is given to lies, business deceptions, and an unscrupulous nature. You have a strong interest in what is unanswered.

Neptune in Sagittarius
(1970/01--1984/05)

Sagittarius in Neptune influences natives who are open-minded, direct and idealistic to seek higher spiritual and philosophical values. Freedom loving Sagittarius, you possess an inherent reverence, sound reasoning ability, determination and ambition. Left to your own desires, you would prefer to travel seeking knowledge and insights. You are farsighted and inspired by your dreams and visions. You prefer to explore the powers of the intellect, revising laws and mores, and searching for a truer and more meaningful outlook on life. You are curious and insightful regarding business affairs, art, science, theology, international affairs, literature, politics, and education. If afflicted, this individual is vague, indefinite, distrustful, overly sensitive, and restless seeking aimless change and travel; experiences unusual dreams, problems in travels, discord through religion, politics, or following the wrong cause and ideas. Your strong ideals, high purpose, and humane nature leads you to possess an utopian outlook on life.

Neptune in Capricorn
(1984/05--1998)

Neptune in Capricorn makes for a well-disciplined, practical outlook on life with an inclination for turning ideas into real achievements. You possess a strong faith in your sound reasoning ability and can be cautious and prudent but decisive. You are meticulously thorough in your effort to carry through in your endeavors, exhibiting strengths of courage and fortitude and the ability to see your plans through to completion. You find yourself questioning outdated practices, methods and accepted social institutions. You are insightful in professional endeavors and discover gain through the areas of art, music, large businesses, science, chemistry, medicine, and institutions both public and private. If afflicted, the individual is indefinite, secretive, and scheming, and experiences family difficulties, and numerous discords and complications in business affairs. You turn ideas and inspiration into standards and practices.

NEPTUNE IN AQUARIUS
(1998--2012)

Neptune in Aquarius enhances the intuition and innate perceptual abilities. Humanitarian Aquarius under the influence of Neptune is idealistic and desires social fairness. You possess an appreciation for nature, wildlife, and the environment which you would like to see preserved and protected for future generations. You are friendly and sociable while accepting others and being tolerant of different lifestyles and circumstances. You would like to see society protect and benefit the less fortunate. You have an independent outlook on life, not accepting conventional ideas and practices. You are creative and would prefer to build a better tomorrow than to destroy what exists today. If afflicted, the individual is overly independent to the point of being eccentric, suffers from problems in love and marriage, and is involved in endless problems with friends. Your ideas are progressively humanitarian and sympathetic with an interest in social, philosophical and political policies.

NEPTUNE IN PISCES
(2012--2026)

Neptune rules Pisces and, if well aspected, it lends dignity to these inspirational, spiritual, sensitive and even prophetic individuals. You are creative but with a serious, contemplative outlook on life that lends itself to profound thought and perceptions. You are accepting, sympathetic, and charitable, benefitting through giving to and receiving from others. You would love to see the world, and you are inclined to travel, seeking exposure to different cultures and practices. And through travel you seek to experience and to gain insight from the various and different auras found in natural settings throughout the world. You are creatively talented in music, art, drama, science and medicine and insightful in business endeavors. If afflicted, this individual suffers from personal psychic experences, and endures loss and misfortune in plans and endeavors. You are an understanding person who is not necessarily materialistic, and you may well lead the way in new cultural concepts.

PLUTO

Rules: SCORPIO

KEYWORDS: Change, mutation, transformation, regeneration, reproduction, death, catastrophes, dictators, death, endings, resourcefulness, creativity and acceptance of change, enforced changes; a curiosity regarding the unknown; the unconscious/subconscious, abnormalities, unnatural events, natural disasters, the underworld, Hades, the Mafia, clairvoyancy, advanced science and technology, atomic energy, corporate enterprises, insurance, taxes, alimony, funerals, secrecy, mysteries, espionage, cruelty, sadism. It rules Scorpio; is in detriment in Taurus.

Pluto, the farthest planet from the Sun, was discovered in 1930 by Clyde W. Tombaugh at the Lowell Observatory, and was named by a young British girl whose letter was the first to arrive at the Observatory. Unlike the other planets, Pluto's orbit tilts, bringing it at times closer to the Earth than Neptune, and its complete orbit is larger and therefore slower than the other planets. It requires approximately two hundred and forty-eight years for Pluto to travel through the Zodiac, staying in each sign for somewhere between twelve to thirty-two years. Pluto has a generational influence as well as an influence on personal horoscopes.

Pluto was the Roman god that ruled the underworld and Hades, overseeing the spirits of the dead. The planet Pluto rules the subconscious workings of the body, change and transformation and regeneration. It represents both the reforming and the destructive forces on Earth. It is associated with the creative and regenerative influences, the reproductive system of the body, volcanoes, earthquakes, big business, mass media and communication, world finances, and the beginning phase of life as well as the last phase of life. The positive aspects of Pluto include the ability to make a new beginning under unfavorable circumstances and an understanding and ability in big business. It grants an analytical intellect and financial security. It influences the discover of mistakes and detection of wrong doings. Pluto instills new life into ideas and ideologies. If afflicted, the negative traits include a troubled subconscious, low morality, indecency, secretiveness, criminal tendencies, treacherousness and cruelty. Pluto, it is felt, represents the highest and lowest of which man is capable.

Pluto influences the dramatic changes that takes place in the lives of people, either as a group influence or as experienced by individuals. Sudden changes or shifts in location of groups of people, for example, or the sudden relocation of an individual. Upheavals, revolutions, and revelations are influenced by this sign as are the personal plans of an individual that get off to a quick start or are suddenly disrupted and brought to an end.

Pluto may well be that influence that bridges the material and spiritual world, but it will require more time for astrologers to fully understand the influence of this planet.

479

Pluto in Aries

Pluto in Aries indicates exploration, reformation and a drive for power or, if adversely affected, revenge. These individuals possess much daring, energy, and drive. Changes in political, social, scientific and economic situations are indicated with revolutionary and innovative ideas marking this period of endeavor. The individual possesses courage, will power, a strong self-reliance, individuality, and a powerful belief in one's ideas and abilities. Energetic and driven to succeed, this individual is imaginative and resourceful. Pioneering new thoughts, innovations and directions will be undertaken with foresight and an energetic drive to succeed. This person will find it necessary to strive to develop a self-discipline in order not to diffuse the natural energies and strengths. The individual is expansive, progressive and broad-minded, striving for a leadership position in all endeavors.

Pluto in Taurus

Pluto was last in Taurus from 1851 to 1883. Pluto in Taurus grants endurance, perseverance, sensuality, and an obstinate stubbornness. This individual sticks to his or her goals and objectives seeking completion of the tasks at hand. There is an over powering need for stability, permanence and security as realized through material gain and possessions. In historical times, it was noted that the influence of Pluto lead the wealthy to exploit and take advantage of the working poor. Pluto is in detriment in Taurus, and while Pluto in Aries brought pioneers and adventurers, Pluto in Taurus promoted industrialists, investors and financiers who built complicated and complex social and political institutions. Pluto located in Taurus grants determination, drive, and the endurance to succeed at all endeavors, but it influences extremes in ideas and emotions, promoting either wealth or poverty, success or failure. Taurus is steady and tenacious, but Pluto indicates changes and abrupt starts and endings to plans, endeavors, relationships, and encounters. Taurus brings a desire for permanency and lasting values and relationships, but these are gained only through hard work and great effort.

PLUTO IN GEMINI
(1882/84--1912/14)

Pluto was last in Gemini from 1882/84 to 1912/13 seeing a need for change, and indeed change was noted in many aspects of life including communication, transportation, and technologies. The Air sign of Gemini saw the realization of mass communication through newspapers, radio, telegraph and the telephone. New ideas and ideologies were promoted, and old ideas, customs and habits were put aside. Pluto grants Gemini natives a depth of character but a restless, seeking and curious nature which wants to experience and to explore. And Gemini individuals influenced by Pluto want the freedom to express their ideas and thoughts. This person loves family and friends, but can be changeable and restless, seeking new experiences and forms of expressions. There is a desire to expand the intellect and to feed the mind. This is a sensual person who appreciates the beauty found in nature, and is forever pulled to see and meet new people, and to experience new places and different settings.

PLUTO IN CANCER
(1912/14--1937/39)

Pluto was last in Cancer from approximately 1912 to 1939. Cancer possesses a love for home and family, and this period saw a drastic rise in the world population as well as the drastic changes brought about by a sudden relocation of people from country to cities. This individual possess a need for security through home, family and through personal and supportive friends and neighbors. There is indicated a strong social awareness, an appreciation for wildlife and nature, and a fondness for artistic pursuits and creative past times. Cancer is instinctive, intuitive, and highly creative and imaginative. This native is also intensely emotionally and craves the attention and recognition of friends and family. If afflicted, this person tends to isolation, pride, selfishness, overly sensitive, and is jealous of the success, possessions or attentions of others. Persons born during Pluto in Cancer are bound to effect traditions, society, and social institutions preferring conservative politics that favor the home and family. Warm-hearted with a quick sense of humor, this native creates a home atmosphere that pleases.

PLUTO IN LEO
(1937/39--1956/58)

Pluto in the forceful sign of Leo saw WWII and its after effects. There was an unprecedented number of rise and falls of governments throughout the world. The formation of the United Nations brought about an institution that allowed a forum for the discussion of ideas, social order and the development of third world countries. This native is self-confident, authoritative and possesses a good business ability, but loves power, prestige and leadership positions. The native has a strong sense of personal pride as well as a pride in his or her country and beliefs. The domineering ego of Leo brings austerity to the drive for success and completion of endeavors. If afflicted, the individual can be selfish, arrogant, prideful, ego-driven and pleasure seeking with an obstinate and over bearing nature. Persons born during this period have experienced many changes, successes, and reversals in their lives both personally, socially and economically. Pleasures, enjoying life, and making heroes out of personalities marks the influence of persons born during this period. It can also be said that this generation produced any number of important leaders who influenced the world.

PLUTO IN VIRGO
(1956/58--1971/72)

Pluto in Virgo influences the individual to be analytical, inventive, technical, and detail-oriented. You are practical in the sense that you acquire all the details necessary to complete your projects. You possess an interest in matters related to science, medicine, mental and physical health, diet, and the upkeep of the body. You posses the ability to bring order to a situation. There is a tendency to over analyze and to be critical and discerning. Afflictions bring dependency on alcohol and illicit drugs, a self centered outlook on life, concern for self coming first above all others, a suspicious and selfishness nature, fault-finding and critical, and pleasure seeking to a destructive degree. You most seek perfection in all that you do and prefer that sensible ideas also be reflected in society, institutions and in government and politics. Your obstacle overcoming an overly cautious, detail-oriented nature that may prevent you seeing the bigger picture and from sharing in life with others.

PLUTO IN LIBRA
(1971/72--1983/84)

Libra seeks balance and harmony, and Pluto in this sign sees persons who are strongly aware of injustices and inequalities. These individuals prefers that people are treated as equals, including themselves. You want laws, rules and regulations to be fair, and not misused, and you find that many laws actually limit the freedoms of individuals. You exhibit empathy and concern for other people and for groups of people and abhor the misuse of power and laws for personal gain and to restrain others. You strive for new approaches to relationships, justice, prison reforms, politics, and especially to international relationships. You are indeed adaptable and flexible with an appreciation for beauty and harmony that transcends into art and music. You prefer to be direct and honest in relationships and expect the same from others. Becoming upset when you discover dishonesty, you are capable of leaving and seeking harmony elsewhere. You are also capable of ignoring the harsher, more distasteful aspects of life, preferring to shut them out of your life and to avoid stressful and painful situations. You discover that the greatest challenge in your life is resolving conflicts in your personal relationships.

PLUTO IN SCORPIO
(1983/84--1995)

Pluto rules Scorpio and moves rather rapidly through this sign in only eleven to twelve years as compared to up to thirty years in other signs. In fact, for a period of time in 1989, Pluto, in its tilted orbit, came closer to the Earth than Neptune. The Pluto/Scorpio influence grants an individual strong will power and a curious, penetrating intellect. Your relationships are intense, sensual, and passionate, and you are not sexually inhibited. The conflict in your life centers around jealousies, and rivalries, and you have a tendency to be private even to the point of being secretive. Your curious, fact finding nature leads you to want to uncover the truths in situations, politics, and institutions. You are imaginative and insightful and may discover that you have some psychic abilities. You possess a strong interest in the environment and appreciate the beauty of nature. You can be aggressive when necessary, and will push forward your ideas and objectives forcefully even ruthlessly at times. Life to you is a mystery, and you feel that mystery must be examined and understood.

PLUTO IN SAGITTARIUS
(1995--2008)

Pluto in Sagittarius finds a person who loves his or her personal freedom and wants to preserve it. It is expected in this period, that individuals will strive for new ideals, new philosophies, and new ways of dealing with laws, rules and regulations that would enhance the freedom and independence to think and to move about freely. You are humane, expansive, friendly and open to new ideas and innovations. There is found a spiritual inclination to your nature, and you seek a greater awareness of being. You are energetic, enthusiastic, flexible, versatile, and tolerant of different ideas and lifestyles. The negative aspect is the tendency to become eccentric in ideas and lifestyle, to follow an idea or thought to extremes, and to be indecisive in judgments. You may possess revolutionary, new ideas, but must guard that your wanderlust doesn't deter from the implementation of your ideas.

PLUTO IN CAPRICORN
(2008--2024)

Pluto in Capricorn finds a person who is persevering, ambitious, efficient, and who seeks to establish order by organizing and managing well. Capricorn finds security through establishing order, by attempting to preserve systems that work well, and by innovating new systems to replace outdated ones. Capricorn seeks to protect and even to insulate or isolate in self-defense. You possess a conservative tendency and indeed would like to conserve energies, preferring to utilize what is necessary to produce the best end results. You are materialistic in the sense that you want a secure home, financial security, and possessions to enhance your personal situation. You also possess a strong spiritual nature, preferring traditional and sensible religions and doctrines.

PLUTO IN AQUARIUS
(2023--2044)

Pluto was last in Aquarius from 1778 to 1798, and this period saw the American Revolution, the French Revolution, and the revolution of new ideas which produced the Constitution and the many French writings which called for instilling freedoms into everyday lives, a casting off of the old ways and an inaugurating of new ways. You are the intellectual who seeks to understand and to instill new humanitarian means and methods into our daily lives which promote freedom, understanding and acceptance. You are unconventional, ingenious, and you love your personal freedom. You are capable of inspiring others to great thoughts, and when called upon, you become a great leader yourself.

PLUTO IN PISCES
(2043--2068)

Pluto was last in Pisces from 1798 to 1823, which was the Romantic period in art and literature. This is a compassionate and caring person who is willing to sacrifice for the good of others. You are intuitive, creative and imaginative, and if left to your own tendencies will produce even more innovative changes in art, music, literature and the philosophies of this period of time. You are adaptable, flexible and tolerant of the ideas, thoughts and lifestyles of others. You adapt easily to new situations and new people, and have a strong desire to meet new people and to make friends. You must guard against be easily impressed, influenced and led by others. Intuitive and introspective, you must also guard against procrastination and living much of your life in the fantasy world of your mind. You are a spiritual, insightful person who may discover great gifts of psychic and prophetic abilities.

485

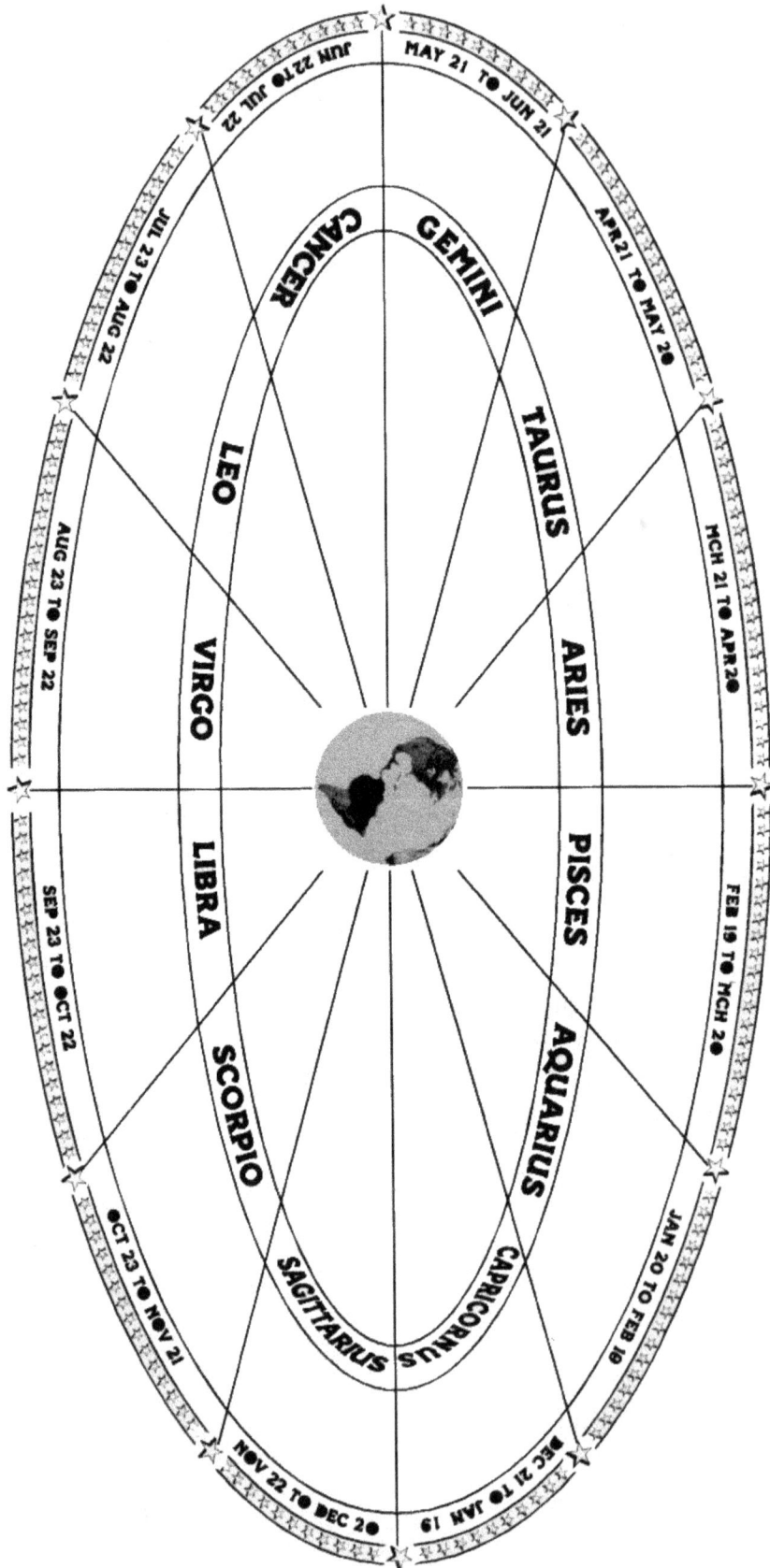

THE MOON SIGNS

The Moon reflects the light of the Sun, and in your horoscope it reflects your inner feelings and urges. The Moon sign is considered the second most important aspect of the horoscope next to the Sun sign. The Moon influences the individual's habits, reactions, emotions, moods, instincts, and the subconscious. Your hunches and intuitions come from the influence of the Moon. The waxing and waning Moon represents duality and change as in the ebb and flow of the waters of the Earth which produces two tides a day in the oceans. It exerts a strong influence over the daily and ordinary affairs of life as well as the cyclical nature of life.

In ancient times, the Moon was called Isis, Esses, Luna, Eleusis and the Virgin Nere. While the Sun remains unchanging, the Moon is constantly changing but is predictable in its orbit. The Moon completes its transition through the Zodiac faster than any of the other Celestial bodies, making a complete cycle in twenty-seven days, seven hours and forty-three minutes, staying in each sign for two to three days. As it orbits the Earth, the Moon's appearance changes, and in astrology the New Moon is in conjunction with the Sun, the First Quarter is ninety degrees of the Sun, the Half Moon is illuminated, the Full Moon is in opposition to the Sun, and the Third Quarter is ninety degrees west of the Sun.

The Moon is receptive, sensitive, passive, and feminine, representing women, mother, and child birth. It is nocturnal, cold, moist, phlegmatic and fruitful and rules the digestive system, stomach, sympathetic nervous system, breasts, and the left eye of a male and the right eye of a female. The Moon rules the public, commodities, liquids, nutrition, the home, family, ancestors, responses, and the memory.

Your Moon sign indicates where the Moon falls on the date of your birth, and the Moon sign indicates your instinctive behavior. The positive Moon traits include being passive, patient, tenacious, imaginative, sensitive, and protectively maternal, while being sympathetic and receptive but shrewd in business and possessing a good memory. The negative Moon traits shows an inclination to be moody, overly sensitive, stand-offish, changeable, exhibiting a poor reasoning ability, unreliable, gullible, narrow minded, and unforgiving.

Your inner self, your dreams, fantasies and private feelings are all indicated by your Moon sign.

MOON IN ARIES

The Moon in Aries influences an individual to have an instinctive and noticeable "me first" tendency. The quick temper can be erratic and fluctuating with an irritable and irascible nature. While Aries is fiery and energetically active, the Moon is passive and cool, resulting in nervous tendencies. There is found, however, a strong imagination and a nature which is positive, masterful, independent, and self-reliant. You can be courageous, practical, and sincerely enthusiastic in your endeavors, but there is a tendency to be restless and changeable with an unwillingness to take direction from others.

This individual possesses a strong inclination to be aggressively persistent, but at the same time can be impulsive, occasionally making rash decisions. Your impatience marks many of your decisions, and rather than being tied down with considering details, you will follow your own ideas and impulses. Your energy and independent nature leads you to attempt at all cost to achieve through action. You are known for being enterprising, original and inventive. Your plans are no one else's but your own, and you pursue them with all the energy and drive you possess. At the same time you are implementing your own ideas, you strive to be in charge, and will relentlessly take charge of whatever you become involved in. You can be head strong in this manner, and you have a tendency not to listen to the advice of others.

You are vigorous and direct in your methods, protecting what is yours, especially your emotions. You love travel, meeting new people and becoming involved in new plans, many of which are of your own design. You move through people collecting friendships and relationships as are necessary to augment your plans, your ego, and your feelings. In a relationship, the other person must reflect what you most admire and desire, and that is making a lasting impression on others. It would appear that you use other people in your attempt to complete your plans, but it may well be that you simply see your plans as all important to the situation at hand.

If well-aspected, the individual is energetic, enterprising, optimistic, open to new ideas, and possesses strong values and ideals; will attempt to succeed at his or her own ideas and will attain a leadership position. If afflicted, this individual is rash, opinionated, domineering, impatient and egotistical; encounters danger through travel and water, problems with the opposite sex, and numerous changes in his or her career. The nervous disposition can bring on health problems related to headaches, indigestion, and blood pressure. Physically active, the native can suffer from accidents.

You are socially uninhibited, and possess a strong preference for being in the middle of a social scene, being noticed and admired. Outgoing, decisive and self-confident, you can delight and inspire others. Socially, you are congenial, generous, witty and humorous, well-informed, entertaining and more than likely you stand out in a crowd. You have a great love of adventure and for personal freedom, and you desire new beginnings, new experiences, and new endeavors.

MOON IN TAURUS

The Moon in Taurus indicates a person who is sensual but possessive, loyal and determined, and obstinate with a strong need for security. Your emotional security depends upon possessing and protecting that which you value whether it be material possessions, home, or ideals. You are courteous and sociable with a strong preference for friends and family, love and marriage. You have a strong determination and prefer not to be undermined in your efforts to achieve your goals. You are probably conservative, and if not you still hold strongly to your own ideas and concepts and strongly resist any obstacles or forced attempts to change your mind. Ambitious and determined, you aspire most to excel at your endeavors. This is a stable position for the Moon, and the ever changing Moon influence becomes more stable and reliant, lead the native to be persistence rather than impulsive. You outlook on life is positive, energetic and upbeat. And the Moon in this sign influences the native to be financially successful.

You possess a strong self-image and project it to others. This native can be either enterprising or lazy, and either way, the person thinks well of himself or herself. Friends and companions are easily made because the native is as accepting of others as he or she is of self. You are considered sympathetic and good hearted with a sincere concern for others. You possess a strong appreciation for pleasure, luxury, music, art, and enjoying life.

Not always a self-starter, once this native begins on a path, the natural tenacity of Taurus takes over and this individual becomes determined to follow through to the end of the endeavor. You are intuitive and generally speaking, you exhibit sound judgment making reasonable and sensible decisions. However, not being easily influenced, you are known for your stubbornness, and you face down any opposition fearlessly.

The Moon in Taurus influences the native to be concerned with family and home, and there is often found a strong interest in relatives, ancestors and the family history. You also possess a strong business sense, and you make, save and invest money purposefully and sensibly. You appear to possess a rather special intuition in business being able to judge and to perceive coming trends and fashions.

If well aspect, this individual is caring and compassionate and will succeed in endeavors connected to nature and related products, chemistry, business, water-related industry, speaking or singing careers, real estate, and the food industry, and there is some indication for gains through a relationship with the opposite sex. If afflicted, the native is overly possessive, stingy, selfish, lazy and concerned with self-indulgence and earthly pleasures. There is some indication for health problems related to the throat.

The Moon sign of Taurus indicates a person who is trustworthy, devoted and tenaciously determined. You are known for being warm and affectionate with a strong appreciation for nature and the beauty found in art and music.

MOON IN GEMINI

The Moon in Gemini signifies a strong urge for this native to strive to communicate effectively. You are energetic with a creative and imaginative intellect, and a tendency to be restless and to seek change. You are best known for being agreeable, sociable, sympathetic and warm-hearted with a caring and humane nature. You can be reserved at times, but you are a progressive, ingenious and innovative thinker who has a well-developed intellect and who is well informed. You love information, literature and science and seek out new information from books, the Internet, or other sources. The duality of your nature is expressed in your changing interests and preferences.

Your great need for variety and your curiosity leads you on any number of adventures, some daring and some simply complying with your natural love of other people, places and lifestyles. Your quick responses to ideas adds to the variety in your life, making you flexible, ever changing, and fluctuating in your ideas and activities. You are seemingly most capable of reflecting any number of ideas with the same enthusiasm and intensity. You respond intimately to the moment at hand, but you possess a strong desire for the novel and new situation, losing interest in situations requiring any depth of emotion, long-sustained feelings or undivided loyalties. While you exude a fantastically warm personality, you can appear at times insensitive or uncaring.

At the same time, you are perceptive, and you know from experience that your perceptions and intuitions are often correct. You innately respond to situations and to people impersonally through your intellect rather than through your emotions. You accurately and rapidly size up situations, people and ideas, and with a critical and analytical perception, you determine for yourself which direction or decision is best suited for you. Your ability to analyze and your curiosity leads you to self-examination, and you make every attempt to understand your actions and your thoughts. The Moon in Gemini produces excellent writers, psychologists, artists, or other professionals and tends toward the fields of communication.

You are a free spirit in your relationships as well as in your intellectual pursuits. You have a strong desire to maintain your freedom of movement and thought. And your outgoing and personable energies propel you into ever new and changing situations. You generally prefer discussions to quarrels and upsetting situations.

If well aspected, this native is an amusingly witty, charming, lively and entertaining conversationalist with a curious and strong intellect and the ability to succeed in his or her career. If afflicted the native is overly indecisive, changeable and restless, disorganized, inconsistent, superficial, cunning, manipulative, not cautious, and has a tendency to be drawn into questionable situations.

The Moon in Gemini inclines you to numerous changes and frequent travel, and your dual nature leads you to be involved in more than one endeavor at a time. This strong preference for being involved in numerous activities should be accepted as it is a part of your nature. You are a caring and warm individual who responds well to your immediate family and you possess a love and affinity for nature and for children. You appreciate others who are intellectually challenging.

MOON IN CANCER

The Moon rules Cancer granting the individual strong maternal feelings and a sympathetic nature. Passive, affectionate, gentle, and peaceful, you are a romantic at heart, preferring good feelings to the harsh realities of life. You are conscientious, humane and emotionally sensitive. You can be at times too passive, preferring to follow the path of least resistance, and there are times when you naively trust your own feelings and judgments rather than following the advice of others. You have a strong need to cherish and protect what is yours whether it be family, home or possession. You have a strongly developed domestic urge and prefer the stability and security of the home. At the same time you love to travel, to visit and see new places and peoples.

You possess an innately strong desire for supportive friendships and relationships, and become devoted to friends, associates and to family members. Being sensitive, you are often defensive and have little appreciation for criticism no matter how constructive. To you, being admired is to be loved and appreciated, and that is what you seek in life. While you are strongly devoted and supportive, you can become dependent on the other people in your life--needing others in order to feel emotionally secure and whole. You can be somewhat territorial, building walls of defenses and protecting your personal space from outside invasion. You appear to need your private space which you withdraw to for your own personal time.

Your mind is meditative, and you feel that need for your own place to think. Also, you are creatively imaginative and your personal place is where you prefer to dream away your own time in the fantasy world of your own creation--safe from the intrusions of the harsh and demanding world. Intuitive and sensitive, you pick up negative feelings as if from the air, and can become moody. Along with this strong intuitive ability, you also possess psychic abilities which you may or may not choose to develop.

The Moon in Cancer favors occupations that deal with the public, science fields, the food industry, shipping, antiques, art, music and acting. If well aspected, the native is creatively imaginative, sympathetic, protective, tenacious, loyal and devoted. If afflicted, the native is overly sensitive, emotionally unstable, critical, selfish, possessive, moody, and overly self-pitying with a tendency to nag others.

With the Moon in Cancer, you perceive your surroundings and other people through your emotions rather than your intellect. Romantic, intuitive Cancer is in harmony with the sensuous and receptive qualities of the Moon, making you a gentle, devoted and loving individual.

491

MOON IN LEO

The Moon in Leo and you are ambitious, self-confident, and with your naturally good disposition, you reflect with radiance the attentions of others. You are exuberant, energetic, and self-reliant with a strong tendency to be loyal, trustworthy and honorable. You call attention to yourself through your personal creativity and your magnanimous personality. You are open-minded and warm-hearted with a generous and caring nature, but you have a tendency to be most concerned with those matters which directly apply to your life and well being.

You have a dramatic flair and stand out in a crowd, loving to attract attention and to be the center of attention. You excel in the adoration of others. You have a love of pleasurable situations but also an inherent need to control your personal situation. You are persevering with a lively and penetrating intellect. You possess strong leadership abilities and the capacity to organizing and to apply sensible methods to your endeavors. You make quick, accurate and intuitive judgments regarding other people and their motives.

Adventuresome and daring, you have a natural appeal with the opposite sex and enjoy much attention, praise and adoration from others. In love, you are sincere, loyal and devoted, generous and affectionate, but there is a tendency to hold your emotions in check and you may find it difficult to express your emotions well. And when you feel unappreciated by your loved one, you will stray. You are known for being particular in dress and style, preferring a tasteful and fashionable appearance. You have a fun-loving nature with a preference for sports, social gatherings, pleasure, music, and art.

If well aspected, the influence of the Moon grants you trust, respect and a responsible nature that does well in leadership positions. If afflicted, the native is ostentatious, domineering, self-indulgent, self-centered, and conceited. Generally speaking, the Moon in Leo brings positions of authority and responsibility which you handle seriously.

MOON IN VIRGO

The Moon in Virgo enhances the native's intellectual abilities, and the steadiness and practicality of Virgo stabilizes the Moon's changeable nature. The Moon influences Virgo to be more flexible, and these natives use their natural resources to produce better and more efficient results. You are receptive of new information, careful of details, and possess a good memory. You are analytical and discriminating with a strong preference for arranging your life the way you want it, generally neat and orderly. You prefer to put to good use the knowledge you acquire through your intellectual, critical, and analytical process, but you may have a tendency to worry needlessly.

You are not the ostentatious center of attention, but rather the reserved, unpretentious individual who strives ambitiously to achieve on your own merits and talents through hard work. You do respond to appreciation and praise for your responsible and sensible work methods. Your executive abilities make you a natural manager of your career, business or home life. You are steady, reliable and ingenious with an innate interest in diverse aspects of life such as science, nature, politics and world affairs.

Although reserved, you like other people and are generous with your time and attention, wanting to help others as best you can. You love to talk and to share ideas with others, gather information, and listen to other viewpoints during lively discussions. But you stick steadfastly to your opinions, and at the same time, you apply your detail-oriented outlook to the lives of others and can't quite understand why people don't apply common sense to their lives. You may try to enlighten others to the best way, and can sometimes be insistent that you know what's best. That aside, you collect friends easily, especially of the opposite sex, because other people know you are dependable and can be relied on.

If well aspected, this native is ambitious, intellectual, imaginative, meticulous, responsible, and likes changes, travel, investigating and collecting information. If afflicted, this native becomes obsessed with details, not being able to arrive at a sensible conclusion, is overly critical and fault-finding, argumentative, snobbish and hypochondriac tendencies. There is indicated numerous short trips and changes in the life of the Moon-Virgo native, and proper diet becomes very important to the health.

MOON IN LIBRA

The Moon in Libra favorably influences partnerships and popularity. You possess a charming personality, and you are naturally courteous, congenial and diplomatic with a sincere desire to please and to be accepted by others. The Moon's romantic inclination is enhanced granting you an appreciation for beauty, nature, art, poetry, and literature. You delight and enjoy social gatherings, pleasurable activities, and the companionship of others. You have a tendency to put your best foot forward and win appreciation through your considerate, warm-hearted and affectionate nature. You prefer to be agreeable, easy-going, friendly and kind with a joyful and fun-loving outlook on life.

The most important experiences in life for you are those that are shared with others. The balance and harmony of Libra leads you to be open minded. You attempt to rationalize both sides of a conflict or even a discussion, remaining neutral regarding various opinions, outlooks, or even lifestyles. As far as you are concerned, other people must decide what to do with their lives. You are more than capable of gracefully using tact and diplomacy to maintain a peaceful situation. Accepting and tolerant of others, other people naturally gravitate to you for you are an easily likable person. Your greatest challenge is not to be easy influenced by others or to be susceptible to flattery and praise. You must learn to follow your own direction, and on occasion to say no to others. Your most important challenge is to develop self-reliance and independence. If afflicted, this individual is whimsical, changeable, erratic, flighty, dependent, self-indulgent, indecisive or lethargic and overly critical.

You have a strong inclination toward love and marriage, an appreciation for pleasant surroundings, elegance and refinement, and you like nice things whether it be fashionable clothing or stylish furnishings. You also prefer that a certain amount of convention and formalities are observed in everyday life. You would, in fact, prefer if all the world was a pleasant and congenial place for everyone. That not being the case, you prefer to dwell on the more pleasant aspects of life yourself. You may find that you have a tendency to live for the moment not giving much attention to long range plans and goals. This works for a time, but then you must settle and make decisions. Intellectual, you experience beauty and sensations through the mind, and are capable of evaluating, criticizing, analyzing, or appreciating what you sense.

MOON IN SCORPIO

The Moon is in its fall in Scorpio, and this individual is intensely emotional, imaginative and forceful, but sensuality is sublimated. A reserved and somewhat reticent individual, you have a tendency to hide your deep emotions and feelings, preferring to hold them in check and to control them. While others discuss and display their emotions freely, yours are personal and you keep your innermost thoughts to yourself, even your dreams and fantasies. Then too, you are enterprising, determined, practical and possess a strong will power. Your forcefulness, magnetism and self-confidence allows you to succeed in your endeavors.

You are observant with a keen intellect and perceptive mind which allows you to size-up other people and situations accurately and shrewdly, and to use that information to manipulate or control the situation. Your determination and stubborn persistence makes you a reliable and hard worker who is willing to take on difficult tasks and follow them to completion. You may prefer your private space in which to work, away from the comings and goings of other people. And generally, you aren't easily influenced or swayed by the opinions of others.

You are a highly sexual person with a healthy libido, and this aspect of your life is very important to you. You also appreciate pleasures, fun, comfort, and the companionship of others, and possess the capacity for pure enjoyment of life which only others of a like mind realize. For the most part a positive individual, you don't appreciate opposition from others, and with concise and cutting words can put a contender in his or her place. You have a tendency to be unforgiving and even revengeful, and these become traits which you strive to control throughout life. Energetic, masterful, and aggressive, you are also known for your courage and daring willingness to face adversity. If afflicted, this individual is moody, impatient, jealous, revengeful, secretive, intolerant, obstinate, domineering, self-indulgent, with a weakness for drugs and alcohol; problems are indicated with the opposite sex and in marriage.

You have a strong interest in the mysterious and are adept at locating information. You don't appreciate being inconvenienced, but at the same time you are known for being kind, generous and willing to make sacrifices.

495

MOON IN SAGITTARIUS

The Moon in Sagittarius and there appears to be no boundaries to the heights or realms of your intellectual pursuits. Forever a philosopher, you seek ever more information and will either travel frequently seeking new adventures or experiences, or if tied to one place, your mind will travel great lengths. You are emotionally idealistic and are forever exploring and expanding your wealth of knowledge, experiences or ideas. Accepting and tolerant, you are open and friendly with others, and can merge gregariously within the group, accepting possibilities and knowing few limitations, especially in thought. You are freedom loving, searching, and restless. You are optimistic, cheerful and an inspiring and well informed speaker.

Sociable and kind-hearted, you have a generous nature and a willingness to help a friend in need, no matter the inconvenience to yourself. You are the benevolent humanitarian whose charitable instincts know no limits. Optimistic with a good sense of humor, you can be jovial and exuberant, but are also frank and outspoken. When others attempt to limit your freedom, you become easily angered, but you are quick to forgive. You are an energetic person, either physically or mentally, and this is apparent in your restless mannerisms. You prefer to have some form of physical outlet for your energies and usually have a favorite sport or activity.

You have a love of nature, beauty and harmony, and may find that you prefer the wide open spaces that allow your mind and soul to soar. Your perceptions are clear and concise making you insightful, intuitive, and at times prophetic. You find your strength in your independence, and you want no limitations placed on your freedoms. If afflicted, the individual is careless, reckless, overly restless and changeable, too optimistic and extravagant, irresponsible, and indecisive.

You can be enlightening, informative, persuasive and inspiring, and may be called upon for public leadership or speaking. There is an indication for involvement in spiritual, educational, or political reform, and an inclination to receive benefits from the opposite sex. Your dramatic flair can make you as excellent sales person, speaker or leader. More serious and sensitive than your outgoing nature indicates, you may well possess psychic abilities and premonitions.

MOON IN CAPRICORN

The Moon in Capricorn is in its detriment resulting in the emotions being well disciplined and restrained. You are a reserved, cautious and prudent person who prefers to conduct himself or herself in a dignified manner. You display common sense and practical abilities which are exhibited in your dutiful manner. In fact, your responsiveness is displayed through your responsible nature, and you express your thoughts and ideas clearly and rationally. Poised, charming, and ambitious with strong administrative abilities, you are drawn to positions of leadership and authority and do well in public positions.

Your reserved nature may be a reflection of a certain shyness or reticent nature on your part, but you react quickly to your perceptions and intuitions. Your strength lies in your inherent desire to obtain success through power and leadership positions. Your drive and intent can appear austere, cold and calculating to others, but it is simply a reflection of your inherent nature and abilities. And it may be that your fear of failure drives you to success. At the same time, your ambitious nature is focused through caution and prudence with the security of the home remaining important to you. You marry judiciously preferring a spouse who is ambitious and socially aware, economical, responsible, and who likes a well-run home and family routine. You are not adverse to marrying in order to improve your social status or to benefit your business or career. At times self-doubting, you desire the appreciation and admiration of your family, friends and associates.

If not well-developed, the native's natural ambition is overridden with fears and anxieties which lead to indecisiveness. If afflicted, this person is overly sensitive, antagonistic, fanatical, obsessive, morbid, brooding and melancholy, insecure, cold, austere and unsympathetic; self-indulgence and problems with the opposite sex are noted. Enemies cause problems whether deserved or not. If well aspected, leadership and administrative ability is augmented with the native receiving awards, honors, and positions of prominence. This native achieves either public popularity or public notoriety.

You accept responsibility, apply yourself to your goals, and may earn success through hard work, commitment and persistence. You find that you desire practical knowledge that you can put to use effectively.

497

MOON IN AQUARIUS

The Moon in Aquarius finds a person who can be unconventional and who values personal independence and freedoms. Creative and intuitive, you have unusual, original, and progressive ideas. Sensitive and perceptive, you are a humanitarian with an open and tolerant acceptance of others. You are rational, logical and altruistic in you outlook on life. Now, add to all that your visions, ingenuity, imagination and inventive abilities. Insightful people accept you in spite of your outspoken frankness and any misdeeds or mistakes you've made along the way.

Friendly, sociable, and kind, you can be a witty, charming, and expressive companion who sincerely and genuinely likes other people. Gregarious, your friendships are important to you, but at the same time your sense of security is based on your independence and you can appear emotionally detached. Energetic and active, you divide your time between socializing and spending time by yourself either in contemplation or pursuing one of your many interests. Male or female, a friend is a friend until that person attempts to place limitations or restrictions on your independence, freedom or privacy. Chances are you'll back away from that person for awhile, but will accept him or her back in your life after time has erased the threat of restrictions.

You react almost simultaneously with your intellect and emotions to perceptions and sensory input taking into consideration the human element in a situation. Visionary and future thinking, you gather information to you whether it be scientific, artistic, musical, mathematical, or literary. Your interests appear unlimited. You are also interested in the mysteries of life and more importantly the mystery that encompasses the future. Most of all, you would like to be a beneficial influence on humanitarian or social causes. You are drawn to teaching, social work, counseling, science, inventions, politics, communications, the arts, astronomy and astrology. If afflicted the native can be overly independent leading to loneliness, aloof, indifferent, suffering from nervous tension and depression, opinionated, erratic, unpredictable and tactlessly harsh and outspoken; indicates problems with friends, the opposite sex, and needless wandering.

You are the dreamer of dreams, capable of producing ideas and philosophies, and your success is discovered through your magnetic charm and insight.

MOON IN PISCES

The Moon in Pisces makes you a highly responsive, compassionate and considerate person who responds to the needs of others. Sensitive and intuitive, you respond emotionally to perceptions and may be easily hurt or offended by indifference or insults. A loving person who is loyal to others, you are easily disillusioned when you discover the faults and failings of others. You can be benevolent and quiet or charmingly outgoing and gregarious with a strong appreciation for beauty, comforts, luxury, harmony and change. Your nature is somewhat restless in that you are seeking, but you are not always sure what it is you seek. You appreciate new sights, sounds, experiences, and meeting other people.

You are naturally talented, imaginative and creative with an insightful and intuitive intellect. You enjoy time to yourself to lapse into your creative, fantasy mode, but you are drawn to other people. You are so intuitive and perceptive that you can feel the emotions of others which has a tendency to drain you emotionally. The sometimes cold, objectivity of the human condition also confuses you because you prefer harmony and an easy-going life for one and all rather than difficulties and strife. You are at heart an optimist and romantic.

You can be hard working and industrious or easy going to the point of being lazy and restless. You have an appreciation for beauty, nature, art and music, and your works of self-expressions are prolific. You are not afraid of working diligently for a worthwhile cause or goal, but the outcome or goal must be attainable and in clear sight. You must guard against being easily influenced by other people into changing your direction or leading an unproductive life. If afflicted, this native is indecisive, moody, discontent, easily discouraged, overly sensitive, gullible, pleasure-seeking, self-indulgent, vague, secretive, and easily lead and confused. There is a tendency for sorrow, obstacles and self-undoing brought on by the actions of the native or by indecisiveness or self-doubts. You must guard against allowing the criticism of others to undermine your creative efforts and abilities.

You are inspirational and receptive with a tendency to be gifted with psychic or mediumistic abilities. Utilizing your many talents and creativity is your greatest aspiration.

499

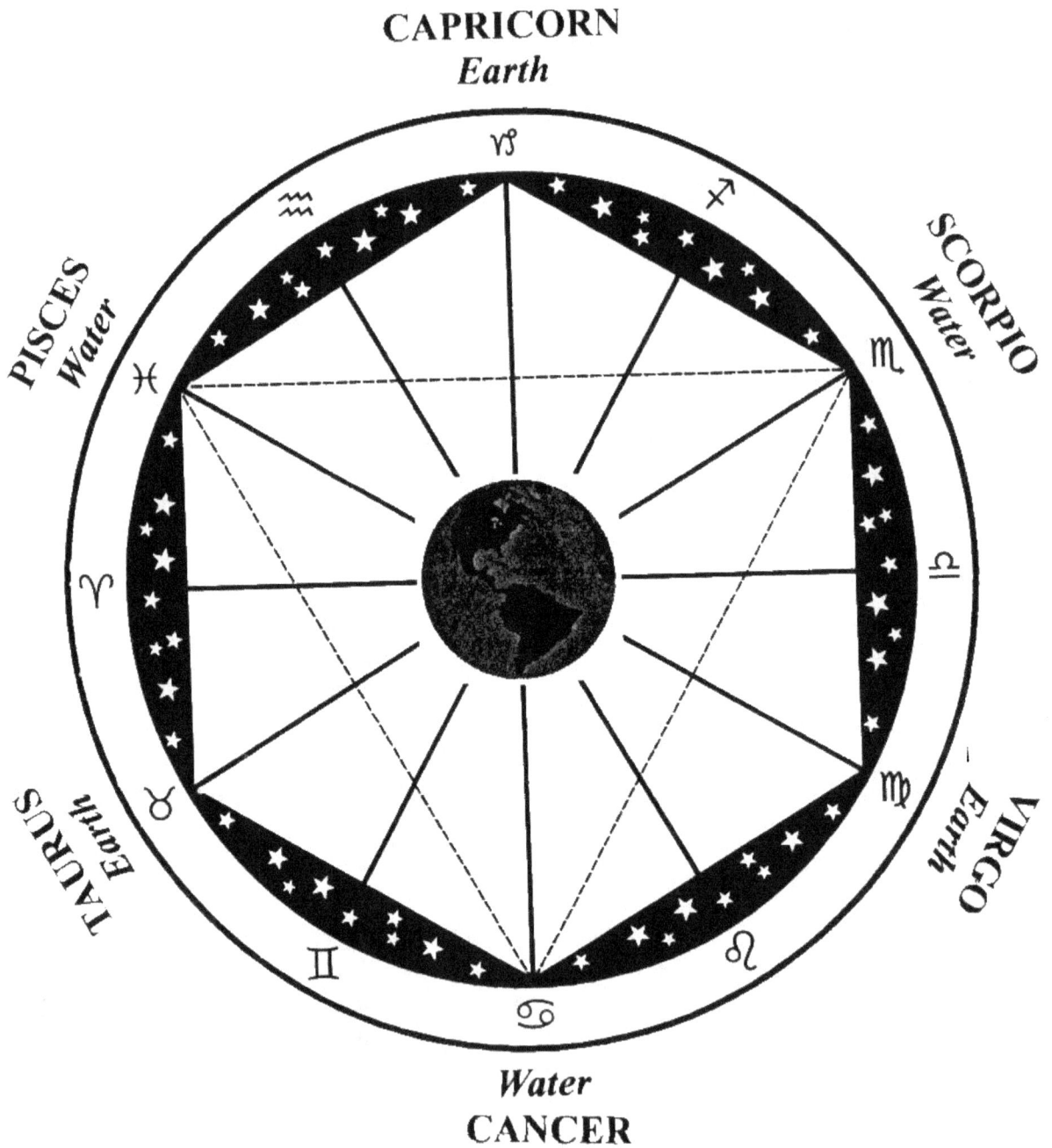

CAPRICORN
Earth

SCORPIO
Water

PISCES
Water

VIRGO
Earth

TAURUS
Earth

Water
CANCER

1900 MOON SIGNS

JAN	FEB	MAR	APR	MAY	JUN
3 AQU	1 PIS	2 ARI	1 TAU	2 CAN	1 LEO
5 PIS	3 ARI	4 TAU	3 GEM	5 LEO	3 VIR
7 ARI	5 TAU	6 GEM	5 CAN	7 VIR	6 LIB
9 TAU	7 GEM	9 CAN	7 LEO	10 LEO	8 SCO
11 GEM	9 CAN	11 LEO	10 VIR	12 SCO	11 SAG
13 CAN	12 LEO	14 VIR	12 LIB	14 SAG	13 CAP
15 LEO	14 VIR	16 LIB	15 SCO	17 CAP	15 AQU
18 VIR	17 LIB	19 SCO	17 SAG	19 AQU	17 PIS
21 LIB	19 SCO	21 SAG	20 CAP	21 PIS	19 ARI
23 SCO	22 SIGT	23 CAP	22 AQU	23 ARI	22 TAU
25 SAG	24 CAP	25 AQU	24 PIS	25 TAU	24 GEM
28 CAP	26 AQU	28 PIS	26 ARI	27 GEM	26 CAN
30 AQU	28 PIS	30 ARI	28 TAU	30 CAN	28 LEO
			30 GEM		

JUL	AUG	SEP	OCT	NOV	DEC
1 VIR	2 SCO	1 SAG	1 CAP	1 SIP	1 ARI
3 LIB	5 SAG	3 CAP	3 AQU	3 ARI	3 TAU
6 SCO	7 CAP	5 AQU	6 PIS	5 TAU	5 GEM
8 SAG	9 AQU	7 PIS	7 ARI	7 GEM	7 CAN
10 CAP	11 PIS	9 ARI	9 TAU	9 CAN	9 LEO
13 AQU	13 ARI	11 TAU	11 GEM	12 LEO	11 VIR
15 PIS	15 TAU	13 GEM	13 CAN	14 VIR	14 LIB`
17 ARI	17 GEM	16 CAN	15 LEO	17 LIB	16 SCO
19 TAU	19 CAN	18 LEO	18 VIR	19 CSO	19 SAG
21 GEM	22 LOE	21 VIR	20 LIB	22 SAG	21 CAP
	24 VIR	23 LIB	23 SCO	24 CAP	24 AQU
26 LEO	27 LIB	26 CSO	25 SIG	26AQU	26 PIS
28 VIR	29 SCO	2SIG	28 CAP	29 PIS	28 ARI
31 LIB			31 AQU		30 TAU

1901 MOON SIGNS

JAN	FEB	MAR	APR	MAY	JUN
1 GEM	2 LEO	1 LEO	2 LIB	2 SCO	1 SIG
3 CAN	4 VIR	3 VIR	5 SCO	5 SIG	3 CAP
5 LEO	7 LIB	6 LIB	7 SIG	7 CAP	6 AQU
8 VIR	9 SCO	8 SCO	10 CAP	9 AQU	8 PIS
10 LIB	12 SIG	11 SIG	12 AQU	12 PIS	10 ARI
13 SCO	12 CAP	13 CAP	14 PIS	14 ARI	12 TAU
15 SIG	16 AQU	16 AQU	16 ARI	16 TAU	14 GEM
18 CAP	18 PIS	18 PIS	18 TAU	18 GEM	16 CAN
20 AQU	20 ARI	20 ARI	20 GEM	20 CAN	18 LEO
22 PIS	22 TAU	22 TAU	22 CAN	22 LEO	21 VIR
24 ARI	25 GEM	24 GEM	25 LEO	24 VIR	23 LIB
26 TAU	27 CAN	26 CAN	27 VIR	27 LIB	26 SCO
28 GEM		28 LEO	29 LIB	29 CSO	28 SIG
31 LEO		31 VIR			

JUL	AUG	SEP	OCT	NOV	DEC
1 CAP	1 PIS	2 TAU	1 GEM	2 LEO	1 VIR
3 AQU	4 ATI	4 GEM	3 CAN	4 VIR	4 LIB
5 PIS	6 TAU	6 CAN	6 LEO	7 LIB	6 SCO
7 ARI	8 GEM	8 LEO	8 VIR	9 SCO	9 SIG
9 TAU	10 CAN	11 VIR	10 LIB	11 SIG	11 CAP
12 GEM	12 LEO	13 LIB	13 CSO	14 CAP	14 AQU
14 CAN	14 VIR	16 SCO	16 SIG	17 AQU	16 PIS
16 LEO	17 LIB	18 SIG	18 CAP	19 PIS	18 ARI
18 VIR	19 CSO	21 CAP	20 AQU	21 ARI	21 TAU
20 LIB	22 SIG	23 AQU	23 PIS	23 TAU	23 GEM
23 SCO	24 CAP	25 PIS	25 ARI	25 GEM	25 CAN
25 SIG	27AQU	27ARI	27 TAU	27 CAN	27 LEO
28 CAP	29 PIS	29 TAU	29 GEM	29 LEO	29 VIR
30 AQU	31 ARI		31 CAN		31 LIB
31 LIB			31 AQU		30 TAU

1902 MOON SIGNS

JAN	FEB	MAR	APR	MAY	JUN
3 SCO	1 SIG	1 SIG	2 AQU	2 PIS	3 TAU
5 SIG	4 CAP	3 CAP	4 PIS	4 ARI	5 GEM
8 CAP	6 AQU	6 AQU	7 ARI	6 TAU	7 CAN
10 AQU	9 PIS	8 PIS	9 TAU	8 GEM	9 LEO
12 PIS	11 ARI	10 ARI	11 GEM	10 CAN	11 VIR
15 ARI	13 TAU	12 TAU	13 CAN	12 LEO	13 LIB
17 TAU	15 GEM	14 GEM	15 LEO	14 VIR	15 SCO
19 GEM	17 CAN	17 CAN	17VIR	17LIB	18 SIG
21 CAN	19 LEO	19 LEO	20 LIB	19 SCO	20 CAP
23 LEO	22 VIR	21 VIR	22 SCO	22 SAG	23 AQU
25 VIR	24 LIB	23 LIB	24 SIG	24 CAP	25 PIS
27 LIB	26 SCO	25 SCO	27 CAP	27 AQU	28 ARI
30SCO		28 SAG	29AQU	29 PIS	30 TAU
		31 CAP		31 ARI	

JUL	AUG	SEP	OCT	NOV	DEC
2 GEM	2 LEO	1 VIR	3 SCO	2 SAG	1 CAP
4 CAN	4 VIR	3 LIB	5 SAG	4 CAP	4 AQU
6 LEO	7 LIB	5 SCO	8 CAP	7 AQU	6 PIS
8 VIR	9 SCO	8 SAG	10 AQU	9 PIS	9 ARI
10 LIB	12 SAG	10 CAP	13 PIS	11 ARI	11 TAU
13 SCO	14 CAP	13 AQU	15 ARI	13 TAU	13 GEM
15 SIG	17 AQU	15 PIS	17 TAU	16 GEM	15 CAN
18 CAP	19 PIS	18 ARI	19 GEM	18 CAN	17 LEO
20 AQU	21 ARI	20 TAU	21 CAN	20 LEO	19 VIR
23 PIS	23 TAU	22 GEM	23 LEO	23 VIR	21 LIB
25ARI	26 GEM	24 CAN	25 VIR	24 LIB	24 SCO
27 TAU	28 CAN	26 LEO	28 LIB	26 SCO	26 SIG
29 GEM	30 LEO	28 VIR	30 SCO	29 SAG	29 CAP
31 CAN		30 LIB			31 AQU

1903 MOON SIGNS

JAN	FEB	MAR	APR	MAY	JUN
3 PIS	1 ARI	3 TAU	1 GEM	1 CAN	1 VIR
5 ARI	4 TAU	5 GEM	3 CAN	3 LEO	3 LIB
7 TAU	6 GEM	7 CAN	5 LEO	5 VIR	6 SCO
9 GEM	8 CAN	9 LEO	8 VIR	7 LIB	8 SAG
11 CAN	10 LEO	11 VIR	10 LIB	9 SCO	10 CAP
13 LEO	12 VIR	13 LIB	12 SCO	12 SIG	13 AQU
15 VIR	14 LIB	16 SCO	14 SAG	14 CAP	15 PIS
18 LIB	16 SCO	18 SAG	17 CAP	17 AQU	18 ARI
20 SCO	19 SAG	20 CAP	19 AQU	19 PIS	20 TAU
22 SAG	21 CAP	23 AQU	22 PIS	22ARI	22 GEM
25 CAP	24 AQU	25 PIS	24 ARI	24 TAU	24 CAN
27 AQU	26 PIS	28 ARI	26 TAU	26 GEM	26 LEO
30 PIS	28 ARI	30 TAU	29 GEM	28 CAN	28 VIR
				30 LEO	

JUL	AUG	SEP	OCT	NOV	DEC
1 LIB	1 SAG	3 AQU	3 PIS	1 ARI	1 TAU
3 SCO	4 CAP	5 PIS	5 ARI	4 TAU	3 GEM
5 SAG	6 AQU	8 ARI	7 TAU	6 GEM	5 CAN
8 CAP	9 PIS	10 TAU	10 GEM	8 CAN	7 LEO
10 AQU	11 ARI	12 GEM	12 CAN	10 LEO	9 VIR
13 PIS	14 TAU	15 CAN	14 LEO	12 VIR	12 LIB
15 ARI	16 GEM	17 LEO	16 VIR	14 LIB	14 CSO
18 TAU	18 CAN	19 VIR	18 LIB	17 SCO	16 SAG
20 GEM	20 LEO	21 LIB	20 SCO	19 SAG	19 CAP
22 CAN	22 VIR	23 SCO	22 SAG	21 CAP	21 AQU
24 LEO	24 LIB	25 SAG	25 CAP	24 AQU	24 PIS
26 VIR	26 SCO	27 CAP	27 AQU	26 PIS	26 ARI
28 LIB	29 SAG	30 AQU	30 PIS	29 ARI	28 TAU
30 SCO	31 CAP				31 GEM

1904 MOON SIGNS

JAN	FEB	MAR	APR	MAY	JUN
2 CAN	2 VIR	1 VIR	1 SCO	1 SAG	2 AQU
4 LEO	4 LIB	3 LIB	3 SAG	3 CAP	4 PIS
6 VIR	6 SCO	4 SCO	6 CAP	5 AQU	7 ARI
8 LIB	9 SAG	7 SAG	8 AQU	8 PIS	9 TAU
10 SCO	11 CAP	9 CAP	11 PIS	10 ARI	12 GEM
12 SAG	14 AQU	12 AQU	13 ARI	13 TAU	14 CAN
15 CAP	16 PIS	14 PIS	16 TAU	15 GEM	16 LEO
17 AQU	19 ARI	17 ARI	18 GEM	17 CAN	18 VIR
20 PIS	21 TAU	19 TAU	20 CAN	20 LOE	20 LIB
22 ARI	23 GEM	22 GEM	22 LEO	22 VIR	22 SCO
25 TAU	26 CAN	24 CAN	24 VIR	24 LIB	24 SIG
27 GEM	28 LEO	26 LEO	27 LIB	26 SCO	27 CAP
29 CAN		28 VIR	29SCO	28 SAG	29 ARI
31 LEO		30 LIB		30 CAP	
JUL	**AUG**	**SEP**	**OCT**	**NOV**	**DEC**
2 PIS	3 TAU	2 GEM	1 CAN	2 LEO	1 LIB
4 ARI	5 GEM	4 CAN	3 LEO	4 LIB	3 SCO
7 TAU	8 CAN	6 LEO	5 VIR	6 SCO	5 SAG
9 LOE	10 LOE	8 VIR	7 LIB	8 SAG	8 CAP
11 CAN	12 VIR	10 LIB	9 SCO	10 CAP	10 AQU
13 LEO	14 LIB	13 SCO	13 SAG	12 AQU	12 PIS
15 VIR	16 SCO	14 SAG	14 CAP	15 PIS	15 ARI
17 LIB	18 SAG	16 CAP	16 AQU	18 ARI	17 TAU
19 SCO	20 CAP	19 AQU	19 PIS	20 TAU	20 GEM
22 SAG	23 AQU	21 PIS	21 ARI	22 GEM	22 CAN
24 CAP	25 PIS	24 RAI	24 TAU	25 CAN	24 LEO
26 ARI	28ARI	26 TAU	26 GEM	27 LEO	26 VIR
29 PIS	30 TAU	29 GEM	28 CAN	29 VIR	28 LIB
31 ARI			31 LEO		31 SCO

1906 MOON SIGNS

JAN	FEB	MAR	APR	MAY	JUN
1 ARI	2 GEM	2 GEM	1 LEO	3 VIR	1 LIB
3 TAU	5 CAN	4 CAN	3 LEO	4 LIB	3 SCO
6 GEM	7 LEO	7 LEO	5 VIR	7 SCO	5 SAG
8 CAN	9 VIR	9 VIR	7 LIB	9 SAG	7 CAP
11 LEO	12 LIB	11 LIB	9 SCO	11 CAP	9 AQU
13 VIR	14 SCO	13 SCO	11 SAG	13 AQU	11 PIS
15 LIB	16 SAG	15 SAG	13 CAP	15 PIS	14 ARI
17 SCO	18 CAP	17 CAP	16 AQU	17 ARI	16 TAU
19 SAG	20 AQU	19 AQU	18 PIS	20 TAU	19 GEM
22 CAP	22 PIS	22 PIS	20 ARI	23 GEM	21 CAN
24 AQU	25 ARI	24 ARI	23 TAU	25 CAN	24 LEO
26 PIS	27 TAU	26 TAU	25 GEM	28 LEO	26 VIR
28 ARI		29 GEM	28 CAN	30 VIR	28 LIB
31 TAU			30 LEO		
JUL	**AUG**	**SEP**	**OCT**	**NOV**	**DEC**
1 SCO	1 CAP	2 PIS	1 ARI	2 GEM	2 CAN
3 SAG	3 AQU	4 ARI	4 TAU	5 CAN	5 LEO
5 CAP	5 PIS	6 TAU	6 GEM	7 LEO	7 VIR
7 AQU	7 ARI	9 GEM	9 CAN	10 VIR	9 LIB
9 PIS	10 TAU	11 CAN	11 LEO	12 LIB	12 SCO
11 ARI	12 GEM	14 LEO	13 VIR	14 SCO	14 SAG
14 TAU	15 CAN	16 VIR	16 LIB	16 SAG	16 CAP
16 GEM	17 LEO	18 LIB	18 SCO	18 CAP	18 AQU
19 CAN	20 VIR	20 SCO	20 SAG	20 AQU	20 PIS
21 LOE	22 LIB	22SAG	22CAP	22PIS	22ARI
23 VIR	24 SCO	24 CAP	24 AQU	25 ARI	24 TAU
26 LIB	26 SAG	27 AQU	26 PIS	27 TAU	27 GEM
28 SCO	28 CAP	29 PIS	28 ARI	30 GEM	29 CAN
30 SAG	30 AQU		31 TAU		

1905 MOON SIGNS

JAN	FEB	MAR	APR	MAY	JUN
2 SAG	3 AQU	2 AQU	1 PIS	3 TAU	2 GEM
4 CAP	4 PIS	4 PIS	3 ARI	4 GEM	4 CAN
6 AQU	8 ARI	7 ARI	6 TAU	8 CAN	6 LEO
9 PIS	10 TAU	9 TAU	8 GEM	10 LEO	8 VIR
11 GEM	13 GEM	12 GEM	10 CAN	12 VIR	11 LIB
14 TAU	15 CAN	14 CAN	13 LEO	14 LIB	13 SAG
16 GEM	17 LEO	16 LEO	15 VIR	16 CSO	15 SAG
18 CAN	19 VIR	19 VIR	17 LIB	18 SAG	17 CAP
21 LEO	21 LIB	21 LIB	19 SCO	20 CAP	19 AQU
23 VIR	23 SCO	23 SCO	21 SAG	23 AQU	21 PIS
25 LIB	25 SAG	25 SAG	23 CAP	25 PIS	24 ARI
27 SCO	27 CAP	27 CAP	25 AQU	28 ARI	26 TAU
29 SAG		29 AQU	28 PIS	30 TAU	29 GEM
31 CAP			30 ARI		
JUL	**AUG**	**SEP**	**OCT**	**NOV**	**DEC**
1 CAN	2 VIR	2 SCO	2 SAG	3 AQU	2 PIS
4 LEO	4 LIB	5 SAG	4 CAP	4 PIS	4 ARI
6 VIR	6 SCO	7 CAP	6 AQU	7 ARI	7 TAU
8 LIB	8 SAG	9 AQU	9 PIS	10 TAU	10 GEM
10 SCO	10 CAP	11 PIS	11 ARI	12 GEM	12 CAN
12 SAG	13 AQU	14 RAI	14 TAU	15 CAN	15 LEO
14 CAP	15 PIS	16 TAU	16 GEM	17 LEO	17 VIR
16 AQU	18 ARI	19 GEM	19 CAN	20 VIR	19 LIB
19 PIS	20 TAU	21 CAN	21 LEO	22 LIB	21 SCO
21 ARI	23 GEM	24 LEO	23 VIR	24 SCO	23 SAG
24 TAU	25 CAN	26 VIR	25 LIB	26 SAG	25 CAP
26 GEM	27 LEO	28 LIB	27 SCO	28 CAP	27 AQU
29 CAN	29 VIR	30 SCO	29 SAG	30 AQU	30 PIS
31 LEO	31 LIB		31 CAP		

1907 MOON SIGNS

JAN	FEB	MAR	APR	MAY	JUN
1 LEO	2 LIB	1 LIB	2 SAG	1 CAP	2 PIS
3 VIR	4 SCO	3 CSO	4 CAP	3 AQU	4 ARI
6 LIB	6 SAG	6 SAG	6 AQU	5 PIS	6 TAU
8 SCO	8 CAP	8 CAP	8 PIS	8 ARI	9 GEM
10 SAG	10 AQU	10 AQU	10 ARI	10 TAU	11 CAN
12 CAP	13 PIS	12 PIS	13 TAU	12 GEM	14 LEO
14 AQU	15 ARI	14 ARI	15 GEM	15 CAN	16 VIR
16 PIS	17 TAU	16 TAU	18 CAN	17 LEO	19 LIB
18 ARI	19 GEM	19 GEM	20 LEO	20 VIR	21 SCO
21 TAU	22 CAN	21 CAN	23 VIR	22 LIB	23 SAG
23 GEM	24 LEO	24 LEO	25 LIB	25 SCO	25 CAP
26 CAN	27 VIR	26 VIR	27 SCO	27 SAG	27 AQU
28 LEO		29 SAG	29 SAG	29 CAP	29 PIS
31 VIR		31 SCO		31 AQU	
JUL	**AUG**	**SEP**	**OCT**	**NOV**	**DEC**
1 ARI	2 GEM	1 CAN	1 LEO	2 LIB	2 SCO
3 TAU	5 CAN	4 LEO	3 VIR	4 SCO	4 SAG
6 GEM	7 LOE	6 VIR	6 LIB	6 SAG	6 CAP
8 CAN	10 VIR	8 LIB	8 SCO	9 CAP	8 AQU
11 LEO	12 LIB	11 SCO	10 SAG	11 AQU	10 PIS
14 VIR	14 SCO	13 SAG	12 CAP	13 PIS	12 ARI
16 LIB	17 SAG	15 CAP	14 AQU	15 ARI	14 TAU
18 SCO	19 CAP	17 AQU	17 PIS	17 TAU	17 GEM
20 SAG	21 AQU	19 PIS	19 ARI	20 GEM	19 CAN
22 CAP	23 PIS	21 ARI	21 TAU	22 CAN	22 LEO
24 AQU	25 ARI	24 TAU	23 GEM	25 LEO	24 VIR
25 PIS	27 TAU	26 GEM	26 CAN	27 VIR	27 LIB
29 ARI	30 GEM	28 CAN	28 LEO	30 LIB	29 SCO
31 TAU			31 VIR		31 SAG

1908 MOON SIGNS

JAN	FEB	MAR	APR	MAY	JUN
2 CAP	1 AQU	1 PIS	2 TAU	1 GEM	3 LEO
4 AQU	3 PIS	3 ARI	4 GEM	4 CAN	5 VIR
6 PIS	5 ARI	5 TAU	6 CAN	6 LEO	8 LIB
8 ARI	7 TAU	8 GEM	9 LOE	9 VIR	10 SCO
11 TAU	9 GEM	10 CAN	11 VIR	11LIB	12 SAG
13 GEM	12 CAN	13 LEO	14 LUIB	14 SCO	14 CAP
16 CAN	14 LEO	15 VIR	16 SCO	16 SAG	16 AQU
18 LEO	17 VIR	18 LIB	19 SAG	18 CAP	18 PIS
21 VIR	19 LIB	20 SCO	21 CAP	20 AQU	21 ARI
23 LIB	22 CSO	22 SAG	23 AQU	22 PIS	23 TAU
26 SCO	24 SAG	24 CAP	25 PIS	24 ARI	25 GEM
28 SAG	26 CAP	27 AQU	27 ARI	27 TAU	26 CAN
30 CAP	28 AQU	29 PIS	29 TAU	29 GEM	30 LEO
31 VIR		31 ARI		31 CAN	

JUL	AUG	SEP	OCT	NOV	DEC
2 VIR	1 SAG	2 SAG	2 CAP	2 PIS	2 ARI
5 LIB	4 SCO	5 CAP	4 AQU	4 ARI	4 TAU
7 SCO	6 SAG	7 AQU	6 PIS	7 TAU	6 GEM
10 SAG	8 CAP	9 PIS	8 ARI	9 GEM	8 CAN
12 CAP	10 AQU	11ARI	10 TAU	11 CAN	11 LEO
14 AQU	12 PIS	13 TAU	12 GEM	13 LEO	13 VIR
16 PIS	14 ARI	15 GEM	15 CAN	16 VIR	16 LIB
18 ARI	16 TAU	17 CAN	17 LEO	18 LIB	18 SCO
20 TAU	19 GEM	20 LEO	20 VIR	21 SCO	21 SAG
22 GEM	21 CAN	22 VIR	22 LIB	23 SAG	23 CAP
25 CAN	23 LEO	25 LIB	24 SCO	25 CAP	25 AQU
27 LOE	26 VIR	27 SCO	27 SAG	27 AQU	27 PIS
30 VIR	28 LIB	30 SAG	29 CAP	30 PIS	29 ARI
	31 SCO		31 AQU		31 TAU

1910 MOON SIGNS

JAN	FEB	MAR	APR	MAY	JUN
2 LIB	1 SCO	3 SAG	1 CAP	1 AQU	2 ARI
4 SCO	3 SAG	5 CAP	4 AQU	3 PIS	4 TAU
7 SAG	6 CAP	7 AQU	6 PIS	5 ARI	6 GEM
9 CAP	8 AQU	9 PIS	8 ARI	7 TAU	8 CAN
11 AQU	10 PIS	11 ARI	10 TAU	9 GEM	10 LEO
14 PIS	12 ARI	13 TAU	12 GEM	11 CAN	12 VIR
16 ARI	14 TAU	16 GEM	14 CAN	14 LEO	15 VIR
18 TAU	16 GEM	18 CAN	16 LEO	16 VIR	17 SCO
20 GEM	18 CAN	20 LEO	19 VIR	18 LIB	20 SAG
22 CAN	21 LEO	22 VIR	21 LIB	21 SCO	22 CAP
24 LEO	23 VIR	25 LIB	24 SCO	23 SAG	24 AQU
27 VIR	25 LIB	27 SCO	26 SAG	26 CAP	27 PIS
29 LIB	28 SCO	30 SAG	29 CAP	28 AQU	29 ARI
				31 PIS	

JUL	AUG	SEP	OCT	NOV	DEC
1 TAU	2 CAN	2 VIR	2 LIB	1 SCO	3 CAP
3 GEM	4 LEO	5 LIB	4 SCO	3 SAG	5 AQU
5 CAN	6 VIR	7 SCO	7 SAG	6 CAP	8 PIS
7 LEO	8 LIB	10 SAG	9 CAP	8 AQU	10 ARI
10 VIR	11 SCO	12 CAP	12 AQU	11 PIS	12 TAU
12 LIB	13 SAG	14 AQU	14 PIS	13 ARI	14 GEM
14 SCO	16 CAP	17 PIS	16ARI	15 TAU	16 CAN
17 SAG	18 AQU	19 ARI	18 TAU	17 GEM	18 LEO
19 CAP	20 PIS	21 TAU	20 GEM	19 CAN	20 VIR
22AQU	22ARI	23 GEM	22 CAN	21 LEO	23 LIB
24 PIS	25 TAU	25 CAN	24 LEO	23 VIR	25 SCO
26 ARI	27 GEM	27 LEO	27 VIR	25 LIB	28 SAG
28 TAU	29 CAN	30 VIR	29 LIB	28 SCO	30 CAP
30 GEM	31 LEO			30 SAG	

1909 MOON SIGNS

JAN	FEB	MAR	APR	MAY	JUN
2 GEM	1 CAN	3 LEO	1 VIR	1 LIB	2 SAG
5 CAN	3 LOE	5 VIR	4 LIB	4 SCO	5 CAP
7 LEO	6 VIR	8 LIB	6 SCO	6 SAG	7 AQU
10 VIR	8 LIB	10 SCO	9 SAG	8 CAP	9 PIS
12 LIB	11 SCO	13 SAG	11 CAP	11 AQU	11 ARI
15 SCO	13 SAG	15 CAP	13 AQU	13 PIS	13 TAU
17 SAG	16 CAP	17 AQU	16 PIS	15 ARI	15 GEM
19 CAP	18 AQU	19 PIS	18 ARI	17 TAU	18 CAN
21 PIS	20 PIS	21 ARI	20 TAU	19 GEM	20 LEO
23 PIS	22 ARI	23 TAU	22 GEM	21 CAN	22 VIR
25 ARI	24 TAU	25 GEM	24 CAN	23 LEO	25 LIB
27 TAU	26 GEM	27 CAN	26 LEO	26 VIR	27 SCO
30 GEM	28 CAN	30 LEO	29 VIR	28 LIB	30 SAG
				31 SCO	

JUL	AUG	SEP	OCT	NOV	DEC
2 CAP	1 AQU	1 ARI	2 GEM	1 CAN	1 LEO
4 AQU	3 PIS	3 TAU	2 CAN	3 LEO	3 VIR
6 PIS	5 ARI	5 GEM	7 LEO	6 VIR	5 LIB
8 ARI	7 TAU	7 CAN	9 VIR	8 LIB	8 SCO
10 TAU	9 GEM	10 LEO	12 LIB	11 SCO	11 SAG
13 CAN	11 CAN	12 VIR	14 SCO	13 SAG	13 CAP
15 CAN	13 LEO	15 LIB	17 SAG	16 CAP	15 AQU
17 LEO	16 VIR	17 SCO	19 CAP	18 AQU	17 PIS
20 VIR	18 LIB	20 SAG	22 AQU	20 PIS	20 ARI
22 LIB	21 SCO	22 CAP	24 PIS	22 ARI	22 TAU
25 SCO	23 SAG	24 AQU	26 ARI	24 TAU	24 GEM
27 SAG	26 CAP	26 PIS	28 TAU	26 GEM	26 CAN
29 CAP	28 AQU	28 ARI	30 GEM	28 CAN	28 LEO
	30 PIS	30 TAU			30 VIR

1911 MOON SIGNS

JAN	FEB	MAR	APR	MAY	JUN
2 AQU	3 ARI	2 ARI	2 GEM	2 CAN	2 VIR
4 PIS	5 TAU	4 TAU	4 CAN	4 LEO	5 LIB
6 ARI	7 GEM	6 GEM	7 LEO	6 VIR	7 SCO
9 TAU	9 CAN	8 CAN	9 VRI	8 LIB	10 SAG
11 GEM	11 LEO	10 LEO	11 LIB	11 SCO	12 CAP
13 CAN	13 VIR	13 VIR	14 SCO	13 SAG	15 AQU
15 LEO	15 LIB	15 LIB	16 SAG	16 CAP	17 PIS
17 VIR	18 SCO	17 SAG	19 CAP	18 AQU	19 ARI
19 LIB	20 SAG	20 SAG	21 AQU	21 PIS	22 TAU
21 SCO	23 CAP	22 CAP	23 PIS	23 ARI	24 GEM
24 SAG	25 AQU	25 AQU	26 ARI	25 TAU	26 CAN
27 CAP	28 PIS	27 PIS	28 TAU	27 GEM	28 LEO
29 AQU		29 ARI	30 GEM	29 CAN	30 VIR
31 PIS		31 TAU		31 LEO	

JUL	AUG	SEP	OCT	NOV	DEC
2 LIB	1 SCO	2 CAP	2 AQU	1 PIS	2 TAU
4 SCO	3 SAG	4 AQU	4 PIS	3 ARI	4 GEM
7 SAG	6 CAP	7 PIS	6 ARI	5 TAU	7 CAN
9 CAP	8 AQU	9 ARI	9 TAU	7 GEM	9 LEO
12 AQU	11 PIS	11 TAU	11 GEM	9 CAN	11 VIR
14 PIS	13 ARI	13 GEM	13 CAN	11 LEO	13 LIB
17 ARI	15 TAU	16 CAN	15 LEO	13 VIR	15 SCO
19 TAU	17 GEM	18 LEO	17 VIR	16 LIB	18 SAG
21 GEM	19 CAN	20 VIR	19 LIB	18 SCO	20 CAP
23 CAN	21 LEO	22 LIB	22 SCO	20 SAG	23 AQU
25 LEO	23 VIR	24 SCO	24 SAG	23 CAP	25 PIS
27 VIR	26 LIB	27 SAG	27 CAP	26 AQU	28 ARI
29 LIB	28 SCO	29 CAP	29 AQU	28 PIS	30 TAU
	30 SAG			30 ARI	

1912 MOON SIGNS

JAN	FEB	MAR	APR	MAY	JUN
1 GEM	1 LEO	2 VIR	3 SCO	2 SAG	1 CAP
3 CAN	3 VIR	4 LIB	5 SAG	5 CAP	3 AQU
5 LEO	6 LIB	6 SCO	7 CAP	7 AQU	6 PIS
7 VIR	8 SCO	8 SAG	10 AQU	10 PIS	8 ARI
9 LIB	10 SAG	11 CAP	12 PIS	12 ARI	11 TAU
11 SCO	13 CAP	13 AQU	15 ARI	14 TAU	13 GEM
14 SAG	15 AQU	16 PIS	17 TAU	17 GEM	15 CAN
16 CAP	18 PIS	18 ARI	19 GEM	19 CAN	19 LEO
19 AQU	20 ARI	21 TAU	21 CAN	21 LEO	19 VIR
21 PIS	22 TAU	23 GEM	23 LOE	23 VIR	21 LIB
24 ARI	25 GEM	25 CAN	26 VIR	25 LIB	23 SCO
26 TAU	27 CAN	27 LEO	28 LIB	27 SCO	26 SAG
28 GEM	29 LEO	28 VIR	30 SCO	30 SAG	28 CAP
30 CAN		31 LIB			

JUL	AUG	SEP	OCT	NOV	DEC
1 AQU	2 ARI	1 TAU	2 CAN	1 LEO	2 LIB
3 PIS	4 TAU	3 GEM	5 LEO	3 VIR	4 SCO
6 ARI	7 GEM	5 CAN	7 VIR	5 LIB	7 SAG
8 TAU	9 CAN	7 LEO	9 LIB	7 SCO	9 CAP
10 GEM	11 LEO	9 VIR	11 SCO	9 SAG	12 AQU
12 CAN	13 VIR	11 LIB	13 SAG	12 CAP	14 PIS
14 LEO	15 LIB	13 SCO	15 CAP	14 AQU	17 ARI
16 VIR	17 SCO	16 SAG	18 AQU	17 PIS	19 TAU
18 LIB	19 SAG	18 CAP	20 PIS	19 ARI	21 GEM
21 SCO	22 CAP	21 AQU	23 ARI	22 TAU	23 CAN
23 SAG	24 AQU	23 PIS	25 TAU	24 GEM	25 LEO
25 CAP	27 PIS	26 ARI	27 GEM	26 CAN	27 VIR
28 AQU	29 ARI	29 TAU	30 CAN	28 LEO	29 LIB
31 PIS		30 GEM		30 VIR	

1914 MOON SIGNS

JAN	FEB	MAR	APR	MAY	JUN
3 ARI	2 TAU	1 TAU	2 CAN	2 LEO	2 LIB
5 TAU	4 GEM	3 GEM	4 LEO	4 VIR	4 SCO
8 GEM	6 CAN	6 CAN	7 VIR	6 LIB	6 SAG
10 CAN	9 LEO	8 LEO	9 LIB	8 SCO	8 CAP
12 LEO	11 VIR	10 VIR	11 SCO	10 SAG	11 AQU
14 VIR	13 LIB	12 LIB	13 SAG	12 CAP	13 PIS
16 LIB	15 SCO	14 SCO	15 CAP	14 AQU	15 ARI
18 SCO	17 SAG	16 SAG	17 AQU	17 PIS	18 TAU
21 SAG	19 CAP	18 CAP	19 PIS	19 ARI	20 GEM
23 CAP	21 AQU	21 AQU	22 ARI	22 TAU	23 CAN
25 AQU	24 PIS	23 PIS	23 TAU	24 GEM	25 LEO
28 PIS	26 ARI	26 ARI	27 CAN	27 CAN	27 VIR
30 ARI		28 TAU	29 CAN	29 LEO	30 LIB
		31 GEM		31 VIR	

JUL	AUG	SEP	OCT	NOV	DEC
2 SCO	2 CAP	1 AQU	3 ARI	1 TAU	1 GEM
4 SAG	4 AQU	3 PIS	5 TAU	4 GEM	4 CAN
6 CAP	7 PIS	5 ARI	8 GEM	6 CAN	6 LEO
8 AQU	9 ARI	8 TAU	10 CAN	9 LEO	8 VIR
10 PIS	12 TAU	10 GEM	13 LEO	11 VIR	11 LIB
13 ARI	14 GEM	13 CAN	15 VIR	13 LIB	13 SCO
15 TAU	17 CAN	15 LEO	17 LIB	15 SCO	15 SAG
18 GEM	19 LEO	17 VIR	19 SCO	17 SAG	17 CAP
20 CAN	21 VIR	19 LIB	21 SAG	19 CAP	19 AQU
22 LEO	23 LIB	21 SCO	23 CAP	21 AQU	21 PIS
25 VIR	25 SCO	23 SAG	25 AQU	24 PIS	25 ARI
27 LIB	27 SAG	26 CAP	27 PIS	26 ARI	26 TAU
29 SCO	29 CAP	28 AQU	30 ARI	29 TAU	29 GEM
31 SAG		30 PIS			31 CAN

1913 MOON SIGNS

JAN	FEB	MAR	APR	MAY	JUN
1 SCO	2 CAP	1 CAP	2 PIS	2 ARI	1 TAU
3 SAG	4 AQU	3 AQU	5 ARI	4 TAU	3 GEM
5 CAP	7 PIS	6 PIS	7 TAU	7 GEM	5 CAN
8 AQU	9 ARI	8 ARI	10 GEM	8 CAN	7 LEO
10 PIS	12 TAU	11 TAU	12 CAN	11 LEO	10 VIR
13 ARI	14 GEM	13 GEM	14 LEO	13 VIR	12 LIB
15 TAU	16 CAN	16 CAN	16 VIR	15 LIB	14 SCO
18 GEM	18 LEO	18 LEO	18 LIB	18 SCO	16 SAG
20 CAN	20 VIR	20 VIR	20 SCO	20 SAG	18 CAP
22 LEO	22 LIB	22 LIB	22 SAG	22 CAP	21 AQU
24 VIR	24 SCO	24 SCO	25 CAP	24 AQU	23 PIS
26 LIB	27 SAG	26 SAG	27 AQU	27 PIS	26 ARI
28 SCO		28 CAP	29 PIS	29 ARI	28 TAU
30 SAG		31 AQU			30 GEM

JUL	AUG	SEP	OCT	NOV	DEC
3 CAN	1 LEO	2 LIB	1 SCO	1 CAP	1 AQU
5 LEO	3 LIB	4 SCO	3 SAG	4 AQU	4 PIS
7 VIR	5 LIB	6 SAG	5 CAP	7 PIS	6 ARI
9 LIB	7 SCO	8 CAP	8 AQU	9 ARI	9 TAU
11 SCO	10 SAG	10 AQU	10 PIS	12 TAU	11 GEM
13 SAG	12 CAP	13 PIS	13 ARI	14 GEM	14 CAM
16 CAP	14 AQU	15 ARI	15 TAU	16 CAN	16 LEO
18 AQU	17 PIS	18 TAU	18 GEM	19 LEO	18 VIR
20 PIS	19 ARI	20 GEM	20 CAN	21 VIR	20 LIB
23 ARI	22 TAU	23 CAN	22 LEO	24 LIB	23 SCO
25 TAU	24 GEM	25 LEO	25 VIR	25 SCO	24 SAG
28 GEM	26 CAN	27 VIR	27 LIB	27 SAG	27 CAP
30 CAN	29 LEO	29 LIB	29 SCO	29 CAP	29 AQU
	31 VIR		31 SAG		31 PIS

1915 MOON SIGNS

JAN	FEB	MAR	APR	MAY	JUN
2 LEO	1 VIR	2 LIB	1 SCO	2 CAP	1 ARI
5 VIR	3 LIB	5 SCO	3 SAG	4 AQU	3 PIS
7 LIB	5 SCO	7 SAG	5 CAP	7 PIS	5 ARI
9 SCO	7 SAG	9 CAP	7 AQU	9 ARI	8 TAU
11 SAG	10 CAP	11 AQU	9 PIS	12 TAU	10 GEM
13 CAP	12 AQU	13 PIS	12 ARI	14 GEM	13 CAN
15 AQU	14 PIS	16 ARI	14 TAU	17 CAN	15 LEO
18 PIS	16 ARI	18 TAU	17 GEM	19 LEO	18 VIR
20 ARI	19 TAU	21 GEM	19 CAN	21 VIR	20 LIB
22 TAU	21 GEM	23 CAN	22 LEO	24 LIB	22 SCO
25 GEM	24 CAN	25 LEO	24 VIR	26 SCO	24 SAG
27 CAN	26 LEO	28 VIR	26 LIB	28 SAG	28 CAP
30 LEO	29 VIR	30 LIB	28 SCO	30 CAP	28 AQU
			30 SAG		30 PIS

JUL	AUG	SEP	OCT	NOV	DEC
3 ARI	1 TAU	3 CAN	3 LEO	1 VIR	1 LIB
5 TAU	4 GEM	5 LEO	5 VRI	4 LIB	3 SCO
8 GEM	6 CAN	8 VIR	7 LIB	6 SCO	5 SAG
10 CAN	9 LEO	10 LIB	9 SCO	8 SAG	7 CAP
13 LEO	11 VIR	13 SCO	11 SAG	10 CAP	9 AQU
15 VIR	13 LIB	14 SAG	13 CAP	12 AQU	11 PIS
17 LIB	16 SCO	16 CAP	16 AQU	14 PIS	14 ARI
19 SCO	18 SAG	18 AQU	18 PIS	19 ARI	16 TAU
22 SAG	20 CAP	20 PIS	20 ARI	19 TAU	18 GEM
24 CAP	22 AQU	23 ARI	22 TAU	21 GEM	21 CAN
26 AQU	24 PIS	25 TAU	25 GEM	24 CAN	23 LEO
28 PIS	26 ARI	28 GEM	27 CAN	26 LEO	26 VIR
30 ARI	29 TAU	30 CAN	30 LEO	29 VIR	28 LIB
	31 GEM				31 SCO

1916 MOON SIGNS

JAN	FEB	MAR	APR	MAY	JUN
2 SAG	2 AQU	3 PIS	1 ARI	1 TAU	2 CAN
4 CAP	4 PIS	5 ARI	3 TAU	3 GEM	4 LEO
6 AQU	6 ARI	7 TAU	6 GEM	5 CAN	7 VIR
8 PIS	9 TAU	9 GEM	8 CAN	8 LEO	9 LIB
10 ARI	11 GEM	12 CAN	11 LEO	11 VIR	11 SCO
12 TAU	14 CAN	14 LEO	13 VIR	13 LIB	14 SAG
15 GEM	16 LEO	17 VIR	15 LIB	15 SCO	16 CAP
17 CAN	18 VIR	19 LIB	18 SCO	17 SAG	18 AQU
20 LEO	21 LIB	21 SCO	20 SAG	19 CAP	20 PIS
22 VIR	23 SCO	24 SAG	22 CAP	21 AQU	22 ARI
25 LIB	25 SAG	26 CAP	24 AQU	23 PIS	24 TAU
27 SCO	27 CAP	28 AQU	26 PIS	26 ARI	27 GEM
29 SAG	29 AQU	30 PIS	28 ARI	28 TAU	29 CAN
31 CAP				30 GEM	

JUL	AUG	SEP	OCT	NOV	DEC
2 LEO	3 LIB	1 SCO	1 SAG	1 AQU	1 PIS
4 VIR	5 SCO	4 SAG	3 CAP	3 PIS	3 ARI
7 LIB	7 SAG	6 CAP	5 AQU	6 ARI	5 TAU
9 SCO	9 CAP	8 AQU	7 PIS	8 TAU	7 GEM
11 SAG	11 AQU	10 PIS	9 ARI	10 GEM	10 CAN
13 CAP	13 PIS	12 ARI	11 TAU	13 CAN	12 LEO
15 AQU	16 ARI	14 TAU	14 GEM	15 LEO	15 VIR
17 PIS	18 TAU	16 GEM	16 CAN	18 VIR	17 LIB
19 ARI	20 GEM	19 CAN	19 LEO	20 LIB	20 SCO
21 TAU	23 CAN	21 LEO	21 VIR	22 SCO	22 SAG
24 GEM	25 LEO	24 VIR	24 LIB	24 SAG	24 CAP
26 CAN	28 VIR	26 SCO	26 SCO	27 CAP	26 AQU
29 LEO	30 LIB	29 SCO	28 SAG	29 AQU	28 PIS
31 VIR			30 CAP		30 ARI

1917 MOON SIGNS

JAN	FEB	MAR	APR	MAY	JUN
1 TAU	2 CAN	2 CAN	3 VIR	3 LIB	2 SCO
4 GEM	5 LEO	4 LEO	5 LIB	5 SCO	4 SAG
6 CAN	7 VIR	7 VIR	8 SCO	7 SAG	6 CAP
9 LEO	10 LIB	9 LIB	10 SAG	10 CAP	8 AQU
11 VIR	12 SCO	12 SCO	12 CAP	12 AQU	10 PIS
14 LIB	15 SAG	14 SAG	15 AQU	14 PIS	12 ARI
16 SCO	17 CAP	16 CAP	17 PIS	16 ARI	14 TAU
18 SAG	19 AQU	18 AQU	19 ARI	18 TAU	17 GEM
20 CAP	21 PIS	20 PIS	21 TAU	20 GEM	19 CAN
22 AQU	23 ARI	22 ARI	23 GEM	23 CAN	21 LEO
24 PIS	25 TAU	24 TAU	25 CAN	25 LEO	24 VIR
26 ARI	27 GEM	27 GEM	28 LEO	28 VIR	27 LIB
29 GEM		29 CAN	30 VIR	30 LIB	29 SCO
31 GEM		31 LEO			

JUL	AUG	SEP	OCT	NOV	DEC
1 SAG	2 AQU	2 ARI	2 TAU	2 CAN	2 LEO
3 CAP	4 PIS	4 TAU	4 GEM	5 LEO	5 VIR
5 AQU	6 ARI	6 GEM	6 CAN	7 VIR	7 LIB
7 PIS	8 TAU	9 CAN	9 LEO	10 LIB	10 SCO
9 ARI	10 GEM	11 LEO	11 VIR	12 SCO	12 SAG
12 TAU	13 CAN	14 VIR	14 LIB	15 SAG	14 CAP
14 GEM	15 LEO	16 LIB	16 SCO	17 CAP	16 AQU
16 CAN	18 VIR	19 SCO	18 SAG	19 AQU	19 PIS
19 LEO	20 LIB	21 SAG	21 CAP	21 PIS	21 ARI
21 VIR	23 SCO	23 CAP	23 AQU	23 ARI	23 TAU
24 LIB	25 SAG	26 AQU	25 PIS	25 TAU	25 GEM
26 SCO	27 CAP	28 PIS	27 ARI	28 GEM	27 CAN
29 SAG	29 AQU	30 ARI	29 TAU	30 CAN	30 LEO
31 CAP	31 PIS		31 GEM		

1918 MOON SIGNS

JAN	FEB	MAR	APR	MAY	JUN
1 VIR	2 SCO	2 SCO	3 CAP	2 AQU	1 PIS
4 LIB	5 SAG	4 SAG	5 AQU	4 PIS	3 ARI
6 SCO	7 CAP	7 CAP	7 PIS	7 ARI	5 TAU
8 SAG	9 AQU	9 AQU	9 ARI	9 TAU	7 GEM
11 CAP	11 PIS	11 PIS	11 TAU	11 GEM	9 CAN
13 AQU	13 ARI	13 ARI	13 GEM	13 CAN	11 LEO
15 PIS	15 TAU	15 TAU	15 CAN	15 LEO	14 VIR
17 ARI	17 GEM	17 GEM	18 LEO	17 VIR	16 LIB
19 TAU	20 CAN	19 CAN	20 VIR	20 LIB	19 SCO
21 GEM	22 LEO	21 LEO	23 LIB	22 SCO	21 SAG
24 CAN	25 VIR	24 VIR	25 SCO	25 SAG	24 CAP
26 LEO	27 LIB	26 LIB	28 SAG	27 CAP	26 AQU
28 VIR		29 SCO	30 CAP	30 AQU	28 PIS
31 LIB		31 SAG			30 ARI

JUL	AUG	SEP	OCT	NOV	DEC
2 TAU	1 GEM	1 LEO	1 VIR	2 SCO	2 SAG
4 GEM	3 CAN	4 VIR	3 LIB	5 SAG	4 CAP
6 CAN	5 LEO	6 LIB	6 SCO	7 CAP	7 AQU
9 LEO	7 VIR	9 SCO	9 SAG	10 AQU	9 PIS
11 VIR	10 LIB	11 SAG	11 CAP	12 PIS	11 ARI
14 LIB	12 SCO	14 CAP	13 AQU	14 ARI	13 TAU
16 SCO	15 SAG	16 AQU	15 PIS	16 TAU	15 GEM
19 SAG	17 CAP	18 PIS	18 ARI	18 GEM	17 CAN
21 CAP	20 AQU	20 ARI	20 TAU	20 CAN	20 LEO
23 AQU	22 PIS	22 TAU	22 GEM	22 LEO	22 VIR
25 PIS	24 ARI	24 GEM	24 CAN	25 VIR	24 LIB
27 ARI	26 TAU	26 CAN	26 LEO	27 LIB	27 SCO
29 TAU	28 GEM	29 LEO	28 VIR	30 SCO	29 SAG
	30 CAN		31 LIB		

1919 MOON SIGNS

JAN	FEB	MAR	APR	MAY	JUN
1 CAP	2 PIS	1 PIS	1 TAU	1 GEM	1 LEO
3 AQU	4 ARI	3 ARI	3 GEM	3 CAN	4 VIR
5 PIS	6 TAU	5 TAU	6 CAN	5 LEO	6 LIB
7 ARI	8 GEM	7 GEM	8 LEO	7 VIR	9 SCO
10 TAU	10 CAN	9 CAN	10 VIR	10 LIB	11 SAG
12 GEM	12 LEO	12 LEO	13 LIB	12 SCO	14 CAP
14 CAN	15 VIR	14 VIR	15 SCO	15 SAG	16 AQU
16 LEO	17 LIB	16 LIB	18 SAG	17 CAP	18 PIS
18 VIR	20 SCO	19 SCO	20 CAP	20 AQU	21 ARI
21 LIB	22 SAG	21 SAG	23 AQU	22 PIS	23 TAU
23 SCO	25 CAP	24 CAP	25 PIS	24 ARI	25 GEM
26 SAG	27 AQU	26 AQU	27 ARI	26 TAU	27 CAN
28 CAP		28 PIS	29 TAU	28 GEM	29 LEO
30 AQU		30 ARI		30 CAN	

JUL	AUG	SEP	OCT	NOV	DEC
1 VIR	2 SCO	1 SAG	1 CAP	2 PIS	2 ARI
3 LIB	4 SAG	4 CAP	3 AQU	4 ARI	4 TAU
6 SCO	7 CAP	6 AQU	6 PIS	6 TAU	6 GEM
8 SAG	10 AQU	8 PIS	8 ARI	8 GEM	8 CAN
11 CAP	12 PIS	10 ARI	10 TAU	10 CAN	10 LEO
13 AQU	14 ARI	12 TAU	12 GEM	12 LEO	12 VIR
16 PIS	16 ATU	15 GEM	14 CAN	15 VIR	14 LIB
18 ARI	18 GEM	17 CAN	16 LEO	17 LIB	17 SCO
20 TAU	20 CAN	19 LEO	18 VIR	19 SCO	19 SAG
22 GEM	23 LEO	21 VIR	21 LIB	22 SAG	22 CAP
24 CAN	25 VIR	23 LIB	23 SCO	25 CAP	24 AQU
26 LEO	27 LIB	26 SCO	26 SAG	27 AQU	27 PIS
28 VIR	30 SCO	28 SAG	28 CAP	29 PIS	29 ARI
31 LIB			31 AQU		31 TAU

1920 MOON SIGNS

JAN	FEB	MAR	APR	MAY	JUN
2 GEM	1 CAN	1 LEO	2 LIB	1 SCO	3 CAP
4 CAN	3 LEO	3 VIR	4 SCO	4 SAG	5 AQU
6 LEO	5 VIR	5 LIB	7 SAG	6 CAP	8 PIS
8 VIR	7 LIB	8 SAG	9 CAP	9 AQU	10 ARI
11 LIB	9 SCO	10 SAG	12 AQU	11 PIS	12 TAU
13 SCO	12 SAG	13 CAP	14 PIS	14 ARI	14 GEM
16 SAG	14 CAP	15 AQU	16 ARI	16 TAU	16 CAN
18 CAP	17 AQU	18 PIS	18 TAU	18 GEM	18 LEO
21 AQU	19 PIS	20 ARI	20 GEM	20 CAN	20 VIR
23 PIS	21 ARI	22 TAU	22 CAN	22 LEO	22 LIB
25 ARI	24 TAU	24 GEM	24 LEO	24 VIR	25 SCO
27 VIR	26 GEM	26 CAN	27 VIR	26 LIB	27 SAG
30 GEM	28 CAN	28 LEO	29 LIB	29 SCO	30 CAP
		30 VIR		31 SAG	

JUL	AUG	SEP	OCT	NOV	DEC
2 AQU	1 PIS	2 TAU	1 GEM	2 LEO	1 VIR
5 PIS	3 ARI	4 GEM	4 CAN	4 VIR	3 LIB
7 ARI	6 TAU	6 CAN	6 LEO	6 LIB	6 CSO
9 TAU	8 GEM	8 LEO	8 VIR	9 SCO	8 SAG
12 GEM	10 CAN	10 VIR	10 LIB	11 SAG	11 CAP
14 CAN	12 LEO	13 LIB	12 SCO	13 CAP	13 AQU
16 LEO	14 VIR	15 SCO	15 SAG	16 AQU	16 PIS
18 VIR	16 LIB	17 SAG	17 CAP	18 PIS	18 ARI
20 LIB	18 SCO	20 CAP	20 ARI	21 ARI	20 TAU
22 SCO	21 SAG	22 AQU	22 PIS	23 TAU	23 GEM
25 SAG	23 CAP	25 PIS	24 ARI	25 GEM	25 CAN
27 CAP	26 AQU	27 ARI	27 TAU	27 CAN	27 LEO
30 AQU	28 PIS	29 TAU	29 GEM	29 LEO	29 VIR
	31 ARI		31 CAN		31 LIB

1921 MOON SIGNS

JAN	FEB	MAR	APR	MAY	JUN
2 SCO	1 SAG	2 CAP	1 AQU	1 PIS	2 TAU
4 SAG	3 CAP	5 AQU	4 PIS	4 ARI	5 GEM
7 CAP	6 AQU	8 PIS	6 ARI	6 TAU	7 CAN
9 AQU	8 PIS	10 ARI	9 TAU	8 GEM	9 LEO
12 PIS	11 ARI	12 TAU	11 GEM	11 CAN	11 VIR
14 ARI	13 TAU	15 GEM	13 CAN	12 LEO	13 LIB
17 TAU	15 GEM	17 CAN	15 LEO	14 VIR	15 SCO
19 GEM	17 CAN	19 LEO	17 VIR	17 LIB	17 SCO
21 CAN	19 LEO	21 VIR	19 LIB	19 SCO	20 CAP
23 LEO	21 VIR	23 LIB	21 SCO	21 SAG	22 AQU
25 VIR	24 LIB	25 SCO	24 SAG	24 CAP	25 PIS
27 LIB	26 SCO	27 SAG	26 CAP	26 AQU	27 ARI
29 SCO	28 SAG	30 CAP	29 AQU	29 PIS	30 TAU
				31 ARI	

JUL	AUG	SEP	OCT	NOV	DEC
2 GEM	2 LEO	1 VIR	2 SCO	1 SAG	1 CAP
4 CAN	4 VIR	3 LIB	5 SAG	3 CAP	3 AQU
6 LEO	6 LIB	5 SCO	7 CAP	6 AQU	6 PIS
8 VIR	9 SCO	7 SAG	9 AQU	8 PIS	8 ARI
10 LIB	11 SAG	10 CAP	12 PIS	11 ARI	11 TAU
12 SCO	13 CAP	12 AQU	14 ARI	13 TAU	13 GEM
15 SAG	16 AQU	15 PIS	17 TAU	15 GEM	15 CAN
17 CAP	18 PIS	17 ARI	19 GEM	18 CAN	17 LEO
20 AQU	21 ARI	20 TAU	21 CAN	10 LEO	19 VIR
22 PIS	23 TAU	22 GEM	23 LEO	22 VIR	21 LIB
25 ARI	26 GEM	24 CAN	26 VIR	24 LIB	23 SCO
27 TAU	28 CAN	26 LEO	28 LIB	26 SCO	26 SAG
29 GEM	30 LEO	28 VIR	30 SCO	28 SAG	28 CAP
31 CAN		30 LIB			30 AQU

1922 MOON SIGNS

JAN	FEB	MAR	APR	MAY	JUN
2 PIS	1 ARI	2 TAU	1 GEM	1 CAN	1 VIR
4 ARI	4 TAU	5 GEM	3 CAN	3 LEO	3 LIB
7 TAU	6 GEM	7 CAN	6 LEO	5 VIR	5 SCO
9 GEM	8 CAN	9 LEO	8 VIR	7 LIB	8 SAG
11 CAN	10 LEO	11 VIR	10 LIB	9 SCO	10 CAP
13 LEO	12 VIR	13 LIB	12 SCO	11 SAG	12 AQU
15 VIR	14 LIB	15 SCO	14AG	13 CAP	15 PIS
17 LIB	16 SCO	17 SAG	16 CAP	16 AQU	17 ARI
20 SCO	18 SAG	20 CAP	18 AQU	18 PIS	20 TAU
22 SAG	20 CAP	22 AQU	21 PIS	21 ARI	22 GEM
24 CAP	23 AQU	25 PIS	24 ARI	23 TAU	24 CAN
27 AQU	25 PIS	27 ARI	26 TAU	26 GEM	26 LEO
29 PIS	28 ARI	30 TAU	28 GEM	28 CAN	
			30 LEO		

JUL	AUG	SEP	OCT	NOV	DEC
1 LIB	1 SAG	2 AQU	2 PIS	1 ARI	3 GEM
3 SCO	3 CAP	5 PIS	4 ARI	3 TAU	5 CAN
5 SAG	6 AQU	7 ARI	7 TAU	6 GEM	7 LEO
7 CAP	8 PIS	10 TAU	9 GEM	8 CAN	10 VIR
10 AQU	11 ARI	12 GEM	12 CAN	10 LEO	12 LIB
12 PIS	13 TAU	14 CAN	14 LEO	12 VIR	14 SCO
14 ARI	16 GEM	17 LEO	16 VIR	15 LIB	16 SAG
17 TAU	20 LEO	19 VIR	18 LIB	17 SCO	18 CAP
19 GEM	22 VIR	21 LIB	20 SCO	19 SAG	20 AQU
22 CAN	24 LIB	23 SCO	22 SGA	21 CAP	23 PIS
24 LEO	26 SAG	25 SAG	24 CAP	23 AQU	25 ARI
26 VRI	28 SAG	27 CAP	27 AQU	25 PIS	28 TAU
28 LIB	31 CAP	29 AQU	29 PIS	28ARI	30 GEM
30 SCO				30 TAU	

1923 MOON SIGNS

JAN	FEB	MAR	APR	MAY	JUN
2 CAN	2 VIR	2 VIR	2 SCO	2 SAG	2 AQU
4 LEO	4 LIB	4 LIB	4 SAG	4 CAP	4 PIS
6 VIR	6 SCO	6 SCO	6 CAP	6 AQU	7 ARI
8 LIB	9 SAG	8 SAG	8 AQU	8 PIS	9 TAU
10 SCO	11 CAP	10 CAP	11 PIS	11 ARI	12 GEM
12 SAG	13 AQU	12 AQU	13 ARI	13 TAU	14 CAN
14 CAP	15 PIS	15 PIS	16 TAU	16 GEM	17 LEO
17 AQU	18 ARI	17 ARI	18 GEM	18 CAN	19 VIR
19 PIS	20 TAU	20 TAU	21 CAN	21 LEO	21 LIB
22 ARI	23 GEM	22 GEM	23 LEO	23 VIR	23 SCO
24 TAU	25 CAN	25 CAN	25 VIR	25 LIB	25 SAG
27 GEM	28 LEO	27 LEO	28 LIB	27 SCO	27 CAP
29 CAN		29 VIR	30 SCO	29 SAG	30 AQU
31 LEO		31 LIB		31 CAP	

JUL	AUG	SEP	OCT	NOV	DEC
2 PIS	1 ARI	2 GEM	2 CAN	1 LEO	2 LIB
4 ARI	3 TAU	4 CAN	4 LEO	3 VIR	4 SCO
7 TAU	6 GEM	7 LEO	6 VIR	5 LIB	6 SCO
9 GEM	8 CAN	9 VIR	8 LIB	7 SCO	8 CAP
12 CAN	10 LEO	11 LIB	10 SCO	9 SAG	10 AQU
14 LEO	13 VIR	13 SCO	12 SAG	11 CAP	13 PIS
16 VIR	15 LIB	15 SAG	15 CAP	13 AQU	15 ARI
18 LIB	17 SCO	17 CAP	17 AQU	15 PIS	18 TAU
21 SCO	19 SAG	19 AQU	19 PIS	18 ARI	20 GEM
23 SAG	21 CAP	22 PIS	22 ARI	20 TAU	23 CAN
25 CAP	23 AQU	24 ARI	24 TAU	23 GEM	25 LEO
27 AQU	26 PIS	27 TAU	27 GEM	25 CAN	27 VIR
29 PIS	28 ARI	29 GEM	29 CAN	28 LEO	30 LIB
	30 TAU			30 VIR	

1924 MOON SIGNS

JAN	FEB	MAR	APR	MAY	JUN
1 SCO	1 CAP	2 AQU	2 ARI	2 TAU	1 GEM
3 SAG	3 AQU	4 PIS	5 TAU	5 GEM	3 CAN
5 CAP	5 PIS	6 ARI	7 GEM	7 CAN	6 LEO
7 AQU	8 ARI	9 TAU	10 CAN	10 LEO	8 VIR
9 PIS	10 TAU	11 GEM	12 LEO	12 VIR	11 LIB
11 ARI	13 GEM	14 CAN	15 VIR	14 LIB	13 SCO
14 TAU	15 CAN	16 LEO	17 LIB	16 SCO	15 SAG
16 GEM	18 LEO	18 VIR	19 SCO	18 SAG	17 CAP
19 CAN	20 VIR	20 LIB	21 SAG	20 CAP	19 AQU
21 LEO	22 LIB	23 SCO	23 CAP	23 AQU	21 PIS
24 VIR	24 SCO	25 SAG	25 AQU	25 PIS	23 ARI
26 LIB	26 SAG	27 CAP	27 PIS	27 ARI	26 TAU
28 SCO	28 CAP	29 AQU	30 ARI	29 TAU	28 GEM
30 SAG		31 PIS			

JUL	AUG	SEP	OCT	NOV	DEC
1 CAN	2 VIR	3 SCO	2 SAG	2 AQU	2 PIS
3 LEO	4 LIB	5 SAG	4 CAP	5 PIS	4 ARI
6 VIR	6 SCO	7 CAP	6 AQU	7 ARI	7 TAU
8 LIB	8 SAG	9 AQU	8 PIS	9 TAU	9 GEM
10 SCO	11 CAP	11 PIS	11 ARI	12 GEM	12 CAN
12 SAG	13 AQU	13 ARI	13 TAU	14 CAN	14 LEO
14 CAP	15 PIS	16 TAU	15 GEM	17 LEO	17 VIR
16 AQU	17 ARI	18 GEM	18 CAN	19 VIR	19 LIB
18 PIS	19 TAU	21 CAN	20 LEO	22 LIB	21 SCO
21 ARI	22 GEM	23 LEO	23 VIR	24 SCO	24 SAG
23 TAU	24 CAN	26 VIR	25 LIB	26 SAG	25 CAP
25 GEM	27 LEO	28 LIB	27 SCO	27 CAP	27 AQU
28 CAN	29 VIR	30 SCO	29 SAG	30 AQU	29 PIS
30 LEO	31 LIB		31 CAP		31 ARI

1926 MOON SIGNS

JAN	FEB	MAR	APR	MAY	JUN
3 VIR	2 LIB	1 LIB	2 SAG	1 CAP	2 PIS
5 LIB	4 SCO	3 SCO	4 CAP	3 AQU	4 ARI
8 SCO	6 SAG	6 SAG	6 AQU	6 PIS	6 TAU
10 SAG	8 CAP	8 CAP	8 PIS	8 ARI	8 GEM
12 CAP	10 AQU	10 AQU	10 ARI	10 TAU	11 CAN
14 AQU	12 PIS	12 PIS	12 TAU	12 GEM	13 LEO
16 PIS	14 ARI	14 ARI	15 GEM	14 CAN	16 VIR
18 ARI	17 TAU	16 TAU	17 CAN	17 LEO	18 LIB
20 TAU	19 GEM	18 GEM	19 LEO	19 VIR	20 SCO
23 GEM	21 CAN	21 CAN	22 VIR	22 LIB	23 SAG
25 CAN	24 LEO	23 LEO	24 LIB	24 SCO	25 CAP
27 LEO	26 VIR	26 VIR	27 SCO	26 SAG	27 AQU
30 VIR		28 LIB	29 SAG	29 CAP	29 PIS
		30 SCO		31 AQU	

JUL	AUG	SEP	OCT	NOV	DEC
1 ARI	2 GEM	3 LEO	3 VIR	1 LIB	1 SCO
3 TAU	4 CAN	5 VIR	5 LIB	4 SCO	4 SAG
6 GEM	7 LEO	8 LIB	8 SCO	6 SCO	6 CAP
8 CAN	9 VIR	10 SCO	10 SAG	8 CAP	8 AQU
10 LEO	12 LIB	13 SAG	12 CAP	11 AQU	10 PIS
13 VIR	14 SCO	15 CAP	15 AQU	13 PIS	12 ARI
15 LIB	17 SAG	17 AQU	17 PIS	17 ARI	14 TAU
18 SCO	19 CAP	19 PIS	19 ARI	17 TAU	17 GEM
20 SAG	21 AQU	21 ARI	21 TAU	19 GEM	19 CAN
22 CAP	23 PIS	23 TAU	23 GEM	21 CAN	21 LEO
24 AQU	25 ARI	25 GEM	25 CAN	24 LEO	24 VIR
26 PIS	27 TAU	28 CAN	27 LEO	26 VIR	26 LIB
28 ARI	29 GEM	30 LEO	30 VIR	29 LIB	29 SCO
31 TAU	31 CAN				31 SAG

1925 MOON SIGNS

JAN	FEB	MAR	APR	MAY	JUN
3 TAU	2 GEM	1 GEM	2 LEO	2 VIR	1 LIB
5 GEM	4 CAN	3 CAN	5 VIR	4 LIB	3 SCO
8 CAN	7 LEO	6 LEO	7 LIB	7 SCO	5 SAG
10 LEO	9 VIR	8 VIR	9 SCO	9 SAG	7 CAP
13 VIR	11 LIB	11 LIB	11 SAG	11 CAP	9 AQU
15 LIB	14 SCO	13 SCO	13 CAP	13 AQU	11 PIS
17 SCO	16 SAG	15 SAG	16 AQU	15 PIS	13 ARI
20 SAG	18 CAP	17 CAP	18 PIS	17 ARI	16 TAU
22 CAP	20 AQU	19 AQU	20 ARI	19 TAU	18 GEM
24 AQU	22 PIS	21 PIS	22 TAU	22 GEM	21 CAN
26 PIS	24 ARI	24 ARI	25 GEM	24 CAN	23 LEO
28 ARI	26 TAU	26 TAU	27 CAN	27 LEO	26 VIR
30 TAU		28 GEM	30 LEO	29 VIR	28 LIB
		31 CAN			31 SCO

JUL	AUG	SEP	OCT	NOV	DEC
3 SAG	1 CAP	1 PIS	1 ARI	2 GEM	1 CAN
5 CAP	3 AQU	4 ARI	3 TAU	4 CAN	4 LEO
7 AQU	5 PIS	6 TAU	5 GEM	7 LEO	6 VIR
9 PIS	7 ARI	8 GEM	8 CAN	9 VIR	9 LIB
11 ARI	9 TAU	10 CAN	10 LEO	12 LIB	11 SCO
13 TAU	12 GEM	13 LEO	13 VIR	14 SCO	13 SAG
15 GEM	14 CAN	15 VIR	15 LIB	16 SAG	16 CAP
18 CAN	17 LEO	18 LIB	18 SCO	18 CAP	18 AQU
20 LEO	19 VIR	20 SCO	20 SAG	20 AQU	20 PIS
23 VIR	22 LIB	22 SAG	22 CAP	22 PIS	22 ARI
25 LIB	24 SCO	25 CAP	24 AQU	25 ARI	24 TAU
28 SCO	26 SAG	27 AQU	26 PIS	27 TAU	26 GEM
30 SAG	28 CAP	29 PIS	28 ARI	29 GEM	29 CAN
	30 AQU		30 TAU		31 LEO

1927 MOON SIGNS

JAN	FEB	MAR	APR	MAY	JUN
2 CAP	1 AQU	2 PIS	1 ARI	2 GEM	1 CAN
4 AQU	3 PIS	4 ARI	3 TAU	4 CAN	3 LEO
6 PIS	5 ARI	6 TAU	5 GEM	7 LEO	5 VIR
9 ARI	7 TAU	8 GEM	7 CAN	9 VIR	8 LIB
11 TAU	9 GEM	11 CAN	9 LEO	13 LIB	10 CSO
13 GEM	11 CAN	13 LEO	12 VIR	16 SCO	14 SCO
15 CAN	14 LEO	15 VIR	14 LIB	18 SAG	15 CAP
17 LEO	16 VIR	18 LIB	17 SCO	21 CAP	17 ARI
20 VIR	19 LIB	21 SAG	19 SAG	23 PIS	10 LIB
22 LIB	21 SCO	23 SAG	22 CAP	25 ARI	22 ARI
25 SCO	24 SAG	25 CAP	24 AQU	28 TAU	24 TAU
27 SAG	26 CAP	28 AQU	26 PIS	30 GEM	26 GEM
30 CAP	28 AQU	30 PIS	28 ARI		28 CAN
			30 TAU		30 LEO

JUL	AUG	SEP	OCT	NOV	DEC
3 VIR	1 LIB	3 SAG	3 CAP	1 AQU	1 PIS
5 LIB	4 SCO	5 CAP	5 AQU	3 PIS	3 ARI
8 SCO	7 SAG	8 AQU	7 PIS	6 ARI	5 TAU
10 SAG	9 CAP	10 PIS	9 ARI	8 TAU	7 GEM
13 CAP	11 AQU	12 ARI	11 TAU	10 GEM	9 CAN
15 AQU	13 PIS	14 TAU	13 GEM	12 CAN	11 LEO
17 PIS	15 ARI	16 GEM	15 CAN	14 LEO	13 VIR
19 ARI	17 TAU	18 CAN	17 LEO	16 VIR	16 LIB
21 TAU	19 GEM	20 LEO	20 VIR	19 LIB	18 SCO
23 GEM	22 CAN	23 VIR	22 LIB	21 SCO	21 SAG
21 CAN	24 LEO	25 LIB	25 SCO	24 SAG	23 CAP
28 LEO	26 VIR	28 SCO	27 SAG	26 CAP	26 AQU
30 VIR	29 LIB	30 SAG	30 CAP	28 AQU	28 PIS
31 SCO					30 ARI

1928 MOON SIGNS

JAN	FEB	MAR	APR	MAY	JUN
1 TAU	2 CAN	2 LEO	1 VIR	3 SCO	2 SAG
2 GEM	4 LEO	5 VIR	3 LIB	5 SAG	4 CAP
5 CAN	6 VIR	7 LIB	6 SCO	8 CAP	7 AQU
8 LEO	9 LIB	9 SCO	8 SAG	10 AQU	9 PIS
10 VIR	11 SCO	12 SCO	11 CAP	13 PIS	11 ARI
12 LIB	14 SAG	14 CAP	13 AQU	15 ARI	13 TAU
15 SCO	16 CAP	17 AQU	15 PIS	17 TAU	15 GEM
17 SAG	18 AQU	19 PIS	18 ARI	19 GEM	17 CAN
20 CAP	21 PIS	21 ARI	20 TAU	21 CAN	19 LEO
22 AQU	23 ARI	23 TAU	22 GEM	23 LEO	22 VIR
24 PIS	25 TAU	25 GEM	24 CAN	25 VIR	24 LIB
26 ARI	27 GEM	27 CAN	26 LEO	28 LIB	26 SCO
28 TAU	29 CAN	29 LEO	28 VIR	30 SCO	29 SAG
31 GEM			30 LIB		

JUL	AUG	SEP	OCT	NOV	DEC
2 CAP	3 PIS	1 ARI	3 GEM	1 CAN	3 VIR
4 AQU	5 ARI	3 TAU	5 CAN	3 LEO	5 LIB
6 PIS	7 TAU	5 GEM	7 LEO	5 VIR	7 SCO
9 ARI	9 GEM	7 CAN	9 VIR	8 LIB	10 SAG
11 TAU	11 CAN	10 LEO	11 LIB	10 SCO	12 CAP
13 GEM	13 LEO	12 VIR	13 SCO	13 SAG	15 AQU
15 CAN	15 VIR	14 LIB	16 SAG	15 CAP	17 PIS
17 LEO	18 LIB	16 SCO	18 CAP	18 AQU	20 ARI
19 VIR	20 SCO	19 SAG	21 AQU	20 PIS	22 TAU
21 LIB	23 SAG	22 CAP	24 PIS	22 ARI	24 GEM
24 SCO	25 CAP	24 AQU	26 ARI	24 TAU	26 CAN
26 SAG	28 AQU	26 PIS	28 TAU	26 GEM	28 LEO
29 CAN	30 PIS	28 ARI	30 GEM	28 CAN	30 VIR
31 AQU		30 TAU		30 LEO	

1929 MOON SIGNS

JAN	FEB	MAR	APR	MAY	JUN
1 LIB	2 SAG	2 SAG	1 CAP	3 PIS	2 ARI
4 SCO	5 CAP	4 CAP	3 AQU	5 ARI	4 TAU
6 SAG	7 AQU	7 AQU	5 PIS	7 TAU	6 GEM
9 CAP	10 PIS	9 PIS	8 ARI	9 GEM	8 CAN
11 AQU	12 ARI	11 ARI	10 TAU	11 CAN	10 LEO
14 PIS	14 TAU	14 TAU	12 GEM	13 LEO	12 VIR
16 ARI	16 GEM	16 GEM	14 CAN	16 VIR	14 LIB
18 TAU	19 CAN	18 CAN	16 LEO	18 LIB	16 SCO
20 GEM	21 LEO	20 LEO	18 VIR	20 SCO	19 SAG
22 CAN	23 VIR	22 VIR	21 LIB	23 SAG	21 CAP
24 LEO	25 LIB	24 LIB	23 SCO	25 CAP	24 AQU
26 VIR	27 SCO	27 SCO	25 SAG	28 AQU	26 PIS
29 LIB		29 SAG	28 CAP	30 PIS	29 ARI
31 SCO			30 AQU		

JUL	AUG	SEP	OCT	NOV	DEC
1 TAU	2 CAN	2 VIR	2 LIB	2 SAG	2 CAP
3 GEM	4 LEO	4 LIB	4 SCO	5 CAP	5 AQU
5 CAN	6 VIR	6 SCO	6 SAG	7 AQU	7 PIS
7 LEO	8 LIB	9 SAG	9 CAP	10 PIS	10 ARI
9 VIR	10 SCO	11 CAP	11 AQU	12 ARI	12 TAU
11 LIB	12 SAG	14 AQU	14 PIS	15 TAU	14 GEM
14 SCO	15 CAP	16 PIS	16 ARI	17 GEM	16 CAN
16 SAG	17 AQU	19 ARI	18 TAU	19 CAN	18 LEO
19 CAP	20 PIS	21 TAU	20 GEM	21 LEO	20 VIR
21 AQU	22 ARI	23 GEM	22 CAN	23 VIR	22 LIB
24 PIS	25 TAU	25 CAN	25 LEO	25 LIB	25 SCO
26 ARI	27 GEM	27 LEO	27 VIR	27 SCO	27 SAG
28 TAU	29 CAN	29 VIR	29 LIB	30 SAG	30 CAP
31 GEM	31 LEO		31 SCO		

1930 MOON SIGNS

JAN	FEB	MAR	APR	MAY	JUN
1 AQU	2 ARI	2 ARI	2 GEM	2 CAN	2 VIR
4 PIS	5 TAU	4 TAU	5 CAN	4 LEO	4 LIB
6 ARI	7 GEM	6 GEM	7 LEO	6 VIR	7 SCO
8 ATU	9 CAN	8 CAN	9 VIR	8 LIB	9 SAG
11 GEM	11 LEO	10 LEO	11 LIB	10 SCO	11 CAP
13 CAN	13 VIR	12 VIR	13 SCO	13 SAG	14 AQU
15 LEO	15 LIB	15 LIB	15 SAG	15 CAP	16 PIS
17 VIR	17 SCO	17 SCO	18 CAP	18 AQU	19 ARI
19 LIB	20 SAG	19 SAG	20 AQU	20 PIS	21 TAU
21 SCO	22 CAP	21 CAP	23 PIS	23 ARI	24 GEM
23 SAG	25 AQU	24 AQU	25 ARI	25 TAU	26 CAN
26 CAP	27 PIS	26 PIS	28 TAU	28 GEM	28 LEO
28 AQU		29 ARI	30 GEM	29 CAN	30 VIR
31 PIS		31 TAU		31 LEO	

JUL	AUG	SEP	OCT	NOV	DEC
2 LIB	2 SAG	1 CAP	1 AQU	2 ARI	2 TAU
4 SCO	5 CAP	4 AQU	3 PIS	5 TAU	4 GEM
6 SAG	7 AQU	6 PIS	6 ARI	7 GEM	7 CAN
8 CAP	10 PIS	8 ARI	8 TAU	8 CAN	9 LEO
11 AQU	12 ARI	11 TAU	11 GEM	11 LEO	11 VIR
14 PIS	15 TAU	14 GEM	13 CAN	13 VIR	13 LIB
16 ARI	17 GEM	16 CAN	15 LEO	16 LIB	15 SCO
19 TAU	19 CAN	18 LEO	17 VIR	18 SCO	17 SAG
21 GEM	21 LEO	20 VIR	19 LIB	20 SAG	20 CAP
23 CAN	23 VIR	22 LIB	21 SCO	22 CAP	22 AQU
25 LEO	25 LIB	24 SCO	24 SAG	25 AQU	24 PIS
27 VIR	28 SCO	26 SAG	26 CAP	27 PIS	27 ARI
29 LIB	30 SAG	28 CAP	28 AQU	30 ARI	29 TAU
31 SCO			31 PIS		

1931 MOON SIGNS

JAN	FEB	MAR	APR	MAY	JUN
1 GEM	1 LEO	1 LEO	1 LIB	1 SCO	1 CAP
3 CAN	3 VIR	3 VIR	3 SCO	3 SAG	4 AQU
5 LEO	5 LIB	5 LIB	5 SAG	5 CAP	6 PIS
7 VIR	8 SCO	7 SCO	8 CAP	7 AQU	9 ARI
9 LIB	10 SAG	9 SAG	10 AQU	10 PIS	11 TAU
11 SCO	12 CAP	11 CAP	13 PIS	12 ARI	14 GEM
13 SAG	15 AQU	14 AQU	15 ARI	15 TAU	16 CAN
16 CAP	17 PIS	16 PIS	18 TAU	17 GEM	18 LEO
18 AQU	20 ARI	19 ARI	20 GEM	20 CAN	20 VIR
21 PIS	22 TAU	21 TAU	22 CAN	22 LEO	22 LIB
23 ARI	25 GEM	24 GEM	25 LEO	24 VIR	24 SCO
26 TAU	27 CAN	26 CAN	27 VIR	26 LIB	27 SAG
28 GEM		28 LEO	29 LIB	28 SCO	29 CAP
30 CAN		30 VIR		30 SAG	

JUL	AUG	SEP	OCT	NOV	DEC
1 AQU	2 ARI	1 TAU	1 GEM	2 LEO	1 VIR
4 PIS	5 TAU	4 GEM	3 CAN	4 VIR	3 LIB
6 ARI	7 GEM	6 CAN	6 LEO	6 LIB	6 SCO
9 TAU	10 CAN	8 LEO	8 VIR	8 SCO	8 SAG
11 GEM	12 LEO	10 VIR	10 LIB	10 SAG	10 CAP
13 CAN	14 VIR	12 LIB	12 SCO	12 CAP	12 AQU
15 LEO	16 LIB	14 SCO	14 SAG	14 AQU	14 PIS
17 VIR	18 SCO	16 SAG	16 CAP	17 PIS	17 ARI
20 LIB	20 SAG	19 CAP	18 AQU	19 ARI	19 TAU
22 SCO	22 CAP	21 AQU	21 PIS	22 TAU	22 GEM
24 SAG	25 AQU	23 PIS	23 ARI	24 GEM	24 CAN
26 CAP	27 PIS	26 ARI	26 TAU	27 CAN	26 LEO
28 AQU	30 ARI	28 TAU	28 GEM	29 LEO	29 VIR
31 PIS			31 CAN		31 LIB

1932 MOON SIGNS

JAN	FEB	MAR	APR	MAY	JUN
2 SCO	2 CAP	1 CAP	2 PIS	1 ARI	2 GEM
4 SAG	5 AQU	3 AQU	4 ARI	4 TAU	5 CAN
6 CAP	7 PIS	5 PIS	7 TAU	6 GEM	7 LEO
8 AQU	9 ARI	8 ARI	9 GEM	9 CAN	10 VIR
11 PIS	12 TAU	10 TAU	12 CAN	11 LEO	12 LIB
13 ARI	14 GEM	13 GEM	14 LEO	13 VIR	14 SCO
16 TAU	17 CAN	15 CAN	16 VIR	16 LIB	16 SAG
18 GEM	19 LEO	18 LEO	18 LIB	18 SCO	18 CAP
20 CAN	21 VIR	20 VIR	20 SCO	20 SAG	20 AQU
23 LEO	23 LIB	22 LIB	22 SAG	22 CAP	22 PIS
25 VIR	25 SCO	24 SCO	24 CAP	24 AQU	25 ARI
27 LIB	27 SAG	26 SAG	26 AQU	26 PIS	27 TAU
29 SCO		28 CAP	29 PIS	29 ARI	30 GEM
31 SAG		30 AQU		31 TAU	

JUL	AUG	SEP	OCT	NOV	DEC
2 CAN	1 LEO	2 LIB	1 SCO	2 CAP	1 AQU
5 LEO	3 VIR	4 SCO	3 SAG	4 AQU	3 PIS
7 VIR	5 LIB	6 SAG	5 CAP	6 PIS	6 ARI
9 LIB	7 SCO	8 CAP	7 AQU	8 ARI	8 TAU
11 SCO	10 SAG	10 AQU	10 PIS	11 TAU	11 GEM
13 SAG	12 CAP	12 PIS	12 ARI	13 GEM	13 CAN
15 CAP	14 AQU	15 ARI	15 TAU	16 CAN	16 LEO
18 AQU	16 PIS	17 TAU	17 GEM	18 LEO	18 VIR
20 PIS	19 ARI	20 GEM	20 CAN	21 VIR	20 LIB
22 ARI	21 TAU	22 CAN	22 LOE	23 LIB	22 SCO
25 TAU	24 GEM	25 LEO	24 VIR	25 SCO	24 SAG
27 GEM	26 CAN	27 VIR	27 LIB	27 SAG	26 CAN
30 CAN	28 LEO	29 LIB	29 SCO	29 CAP	28 AQU
	31 VIR		31 SAG		31 PIS

1933 MOON SIGNS

JAN	FEB	MAR	APR	MAY	JUN
2 ARI	1 TAU	3 GEM	1 CAN	1 LEO	2 LIB
4 TAU	3 GEM	5 CAN	4 LEO	4 VIR	4 SCO
7 GEM	6 CAN	8 LEO	6 VIR	6 LIB	6 SAG
9 CAN	8 LEO	10 VIR	8 LIB	8 SCO	8 CAP
12 LEO	10 VIR	12 LIB	11 SCO	10 SAG	10 AQU
14 VIR	13 LIB	14 SCO	13 SAG	14 CAP	14 PIS
16 LIB	15 SCO	16 SAG	15 CAP	14 AQU	15 ARI
19 SCO	17 SAG	18 CAP	17 AQU	16 PIS	17 TAU
21 SAG	19 CAP	20 AQU	19 PIS	19 ARI	20 GEM
23 CAP	21 AQU	23 PIS	21 ARI	21 TAU	22 CAN
25 AQU	23 PIS	25 ARI	24 TAU	23 GEM	25 LEO
27 PIS	26 ARI	27 TAU	26 GEM	26 CAN	27 VIR
29 ARI	28 TAU	30 GEM	29 CAN	29 LEO	30 LIB
				31 VIR	

JUL	AUG	SEP	OCT	NOV	DEC
2 SCO	2 CAP	1 AQU	2 ARI	1 TAU	1 GEM
4 SAG	4 AQU	3 PIS	5 TAU	3 GEM	3 CAN
6 CAP	6 PIS	5 ARI	7 GEM	6 CAN	6 LEO
8 AQU	8 ARI	7 TAU	9 CAN	8 LEO	8 VIR
10 PIS	11 TAU	10 GEM	12 LEO	11 VIR	11 LIB
12 ARI	13 GEM	12 CAN	14 VIR	13 LIB	13 SCO
14 TAU	16 CAN	15 LEO	17 LIB	15 SCO	15 SAG
17 GEM	18 LEO	17 VIR	19 SCO	17 SAG	17 CAP
20 CAN	21 VIR	19 LIB	21 SAG	19 CAP	19 AQU
22 LEO	23 LIB	21 SCO	23 CAP	21 AQU	21 PIS
24 VIR	25 SCO	24 SAG	25 AQU	23 PIS	23 ARI
27 LIB	27 SAG	26 CAP	27 PIS	26 ARI	25 TAU
29 SCO	29 CAP	28 AQU	30 ARI	28 TAU	28 GEM
31 SAG		30 PIS			

1934 MOON SIGNS

JAN	FEB	MAR	APR	MAY	JUN
2 LEO	1 VIR	2 LIB	1 SCO	2 CAP	1 AQU
4 VIR	3 LIB	5 SCO	3 SAG	5 AQU	3 PIS
7 LIB	5 SCO	7 SAG	5 CAP	7 PIS	5 ARI
9 SCO	8 SAG	8 CAP	7 AQU	9 ARI	7 TAU
11 SAG	10 CAP	11 AQU	9 PIS	11 TAU	10 GEM
13 CAP	12 AQU	13 PIS	12 ARI	13 GEM	12 CAN
15 AQU	14 PIS	15 ARI	14 TAU	16 CAN	15 LEO
17 PIS	16 ARI	17 TAU	16 GEM	18 LEO	17 VIR
19 ARI	18 TAU	20 GEM	19 CAN	21 VIR	20 LIB
22 TAU	20 GEM	22 CAN	21 LEO	23 LIB	22 SCO
24 GEM	23 CAN	25 LEO	24 VIR	26 SCO	24 SAG
27 CAN	25 LEO	27 VIR	26 LIB	28 SAG	26 AQU
29 LEO	28 VIR	30 LIB	28 SCO	30 CAP	28 AQU
			30 SAG		30 PIS

JUL	AUG	SEP	OCT	NOV	DEC
2 ARI	1 TAU	2 CAN	2 LEO	1 VRI	3 SCO
5 TAU	3 GEM	4 LEO	4 VIR	3 LIB	5 SAG
7 GEM	6 CAN	7 VIR	7 LIB	5 SCO	7 CAP
9 CAN	8 LEO	9 LIB	9 SCO	8 SAG	8 AQU
12 LEO	11 VIR	12 SCO	11 SAG	10 CAP	11 PIS
15 VIR	13 LIB	14 SAG	14 CAP	12 AQU	13 ARI
17 LIB	16 SCO	16 CAP	16 AQU	14 PIS	16 TAU
19 SCO	18 SAG	18 AQU	18 PIS	16 ARI	18 GEM
22 SAG	20 CAP	20 PIS	20 ARI	18 TAU	20 CAN
24 CAP	22 AQU	23 ARI	22 TAU	21 GEM	23 LEO
26 AQU	24 PIS	25 TAU	24 GEM	23 CAN	25 VIR
28 PIS	26 ARI	27 GEM	27 CAN	25 LEO	28 LIB
30 ARI	28 TAU	29 CAN	29 LEO	28 VIR	30 SCO
	30 GEM			30 LIB	

1935 MOON SIGNS

JAN	FEB	MAR	APR	MAY	JUN
1 SAG	2 AQU	2 AQU	2 ARI	1 TAU	2 CAN
4 CAP	4 PIS	4 PIS	4 TAU	4 GEM	5 CAN
6 AQU	6 ARI	6 ARI	6 GEM	6 CAN	7 VIR
8 PIS	8 TAU	8 TAU	8 CAN	8 LEO	10 LIB
10 ARI	10 GEM	10 GEM	11 LEO	11 VIR	12 SCO
12 TAU	13 CAN	12 CAN	13 VIR	13 LIB	14 SAG
14 GEM	15 LEO	15 LEO	16 LIB	16 SCO	17 CAP
17 CAN	18 VIR	17 VIR	18 SCO	18 SCO	19 AQU
19 LEO	20 LIB	29 LIB	21 SAG	20 CAP	21 PIS
22 VIR	23 SCO	22 SCO	23 CAP	22 AQU	23 ARI
24 LIB	25 SAG	24 SAG	25 AQU	24 PIS	25 TAU
27 SCO	27 CAP	27 CAP	27 PIS	27 ARI	27 GEM
29 SAG		29 AQU	29 ARI	29 TAU	29 CAN
31 CAP		31 PIS		31 GEM	

JUL	AUG	SEP	OCT	NOV	DEC
2 LEO	1 VIR	2 SCO	2 SAG	2 AQU	2 PIS
4 VIR	3 LIB	4 SAG	4 CAP	5 PIS	4 ARI
7 LIB	6 SCO	7 CAP	6 AQU	7 ARI	6 TAU
9 SCO	8 SAG	9 AQU	8 PIS	9 TAU	8 GEM
12 SAG	10 CAP	11 PIS	10 ARI	11 GEM	10 CAN
14 CAP	12 AQU	13 ARI	12 TAU	13 CAN	13 LOE
16 AQU	14 PIS	15 TAU	14 GEM	15 LEO	15 VIR
18 PIS	16 ARI	17 GEM	17 CAN	18 VIR	18 LIB
20 ARI	18 TAU	19 CAN	19 LEO	20 LIB	20 SCO
22 TAU	21 GEM	22 LEO	21 VIR	23 SCO	23 SAG
24 GEM	23 CAN	24 VIR	24 LIB	25 SAG	25 CAP
27 CAN	25 LEO	27 LIB	26 SCO	27 CAP	26 AQU
29 LEO	28 VIR	29 SCO	29 SAG	30 AQU	29 PIS
	30 LIB		31 CAP		31 ARI

1936 MOON SIGNS

JAN	FEB	MAR	APR	MAY	JUN
2 TAU	1 GEM	1 CAN	2 VIR	2 LIB	1 SCO
5 GEM	3 CAN	4 LEO	5 LIB	5 SCO	3 SAG
7 CAN	5 LEO	6 VIR	7 SCO	7 SAG	6 CAP
9 LEO	8 VIR	9 LIB	10 SAG	9 CAP	8 AQU
11 VIR	10 LIB	11 SCO	12 CAP	12 AQU	10 PIS
14 LIB	13 SCO	14 SAG	15 AQU	14 PIS	12 ARI
16 SCO	15 SAG	16 CAP	17 PIS	16 ARI	14 TAU
19 SAG	18 CAP	18 AQU	19 ARI	18 TAU	17 GEM
21 CAP	20 AQU	20 PIS	21 TAU	20 GEM	19 CAN
23 AQU	22 PIS	22 ARI	23 GEM	22 CAN	21 LEO
25 PIS	24 ARI	24 TAU	25 CAN	24 LEO	23 VIR
27 ARI	26 TAU	26 GEM	27 LEO	27 VIR	26 LIB
30 TAU	28 GEM	28 CAN	30 VIR	29 LIB	28 SCO
		31 LEO			

JUL	AUG	SEP	OCT	NOV	DEC
1 SCO	2 AQU	2 ARI	2 TAU	2 CAN	2 LEO
3 CAP	4 PIS	4 TAU	4 GEM	4 LEO	4 VIR
5 AQU	6 ARI	6 GEM	6 CAN	7 VIR	6 LIB
8 PIS	8 TAU	9 CAN	8 LEO	9 LIB	9 SCO
10 ARI	10 GEM	11 LEO	10 VIR	12 SCO	11 SAG
12 TAU	12 CAN	13 VIR	13 LIB	14 SAG	14 CAP
14 GEM	15 LEO	15 LIB	15 SCO	17 CAP	16 AQU
16 CAN	17 VIR	18 SCO	18 SAG	19 AQU	19 PIS
18 LEO	19 LIB	21 SAG	20 CAP	21 PIS	21 ARI
21 VIR	22 SCO	23 CAP	23 AQU	24 ARI	23 TAU
23 LIB	24 SAG	25 AQU	25 PIS	26 TAU	25 GEM
26 SCO	27 CAP	28 PIS	27 ARI	28 GEM	27 CAN
28 SAG	29 AQU	30 ARI	29 TAU	30 CAN	29 LEO
30 CAP	31 PIS		31 GEM		31 VIR

1938 MOON SIGNS

JAN	FEB	MAR	APR	MAY	JUN
3 AQU	1 PIS	1 PIS	1 TAU	1 GEM	1 LEO
5 PIS	4 ARI	3 ARI	4 GEM	3 CAN	3 VIR
7 ARI	6 TAU	5 TAU	6 CAN	5 LEO	6 LIB
10 TAU	8 GEM	7 GEM	8 LEO	7 VIR	8 SCO
12 GEM	10 CAN	9 CAN	10 VIR	9 LIB	10 SAG
14 CAN	12 LOE	12 LEO	12 LIB	12 SCO	13 CAP
16 LEO	14 VIR	14 VIR	15 SCO	14 SAG	16 AQU
18 VIR	16 LIB	16 LIB	17 SAG	17 CAP	18 PIS
20 LIB	19 SCO	18 SCO	19 CAP	19 AQU	20 ARI
22 SCO	21 SAG	21 SAG	22 AQU	22 PIS	23 TAU
25 SAG	24 CAP	23 CAP	24 PIS	24 ARI	25 GEM
27 CAP	26 AQU	26 AQU	27 ARI	26 TAU	27 CAN
30 AQU		28 PIS	29 TAU	28 GEM	29 LEO
		30 ARI		30 CAN	

JUL	AUG	SEP	OCT	NOV	DEC
1 VIR	2 SCO	3 CAP	3 AQU	2 PIS	1 ARI
3 LIB	4 SAG	5 AQU	5 PIS	4 ARI	4 TAU
5 SCO	7 CAP	8 PIS	8 ARI	6 TAU	6 GEM
8 SAG	9 AQU	10 ARI	10 TAU	8 GEM	8 CAN
10 CAP	12 PIS	12 TAU	12 GEM	10 CAN	10 LEO
13 AQU	14 ARI	15 GEM	14 CAN	12 LEO	12 VIR
15 PIS	16 TAU	17 CAN	16 LEO	15VIR	14 LIB
18 ARI	18 GEM	19 LEO	18 VIR	17 LIB	16 SCO
20 TAU	21 CAN	21 VIR	20 LIB	19 SCO	19 SAG
22 GEM	23 LEO	23 LIB	23 SCO	21 SAG	21 CAP
24 CAN	25 VIR	25 SCO	25 SAG	24 CAP	24 AQU
26 LEO	27 LIB	28 SAG	27 CAP	26 AQU	26 PIS
28 VIR	29 SCO	30 CAP	30 AQU	29 PIS	29 ARI
30 LIB	31 SAG				31 TAU

1937 MOON SIGNS

JAN	FEB	MAR	APR	MAY	JUN
3 LIB	2 SCO	1 SCO	2 CAP	2 AQU	1 PIS
5 SCO	4 SAG	3 SAG	5 AQU	4 PIS	3 ARI
8 SAG	7 CAP	6 CAP	7 PIS	7 ARI	5 TAU
10 CAP	9 AQU	8 AQU	9 ARI	9 TAU	7 GEM
13 AQU	11 PIS	11 PIS	11 TAU	11 GEM	9 CAN
15 PIS	13 ARI	13 ARI	13 GEM	13 CAN	11 LEO
17 ARI	15 TAU	15 TAU	15 CAN	15 LEO	13 VIR
19 TAU	18 GEM	17 GEM	17 LEO	17 VIR	16 LIB
21 GEM	20 CAN	19 CAN	20 VIR	19 LIB	18 SCO
23 CAN	22 LEO	21 LEO	22 LIB	22 SCO	21 SAG
26 LEO	24 VIR	23 VIR	25 SCO	24 SAG	23 CAP
28 VIR	26 LIB	26 LIB	27 SAG	27 CAP	26 AQU
28 LIB		28 SCO	30 CAP	29 AQU	28 PIS
		31 SAG			30 ARI

JUL	AUG	SEP	OCT	NOV	DEC
2 TAU	1 GEM	1 LEO	1 VIR	2 SCO	1 SAG
4 GEM	3 CAN	3 VIR	3 LIB	4 SAG	4 CAP
6 CAN	5 LEO	6 LIB	5 SCO	7 CAP	6 AQU
8 LEO	7 VIR	8 SCO	8 SAG	9 AQU	9 PIS
11 VIR	9 LIB	11 SAG	10 CAP	12 PIS	11 ARI
13 LIB	12 SCO	13 CAP	13 AQU	14 ARI	13 TAU
15 SCO	14 SAG	15 AQU	15 PIS	16 TAU	15 GEM
18 SAG	17 CAP	18 PIS	17 ARI	18 GEM	17 CAN
20 CAP	19 AQU	20 ARI	19 TAU	20 CAN	19 LEO
23 AQU	21 PIS	22 TAU	21 GEM	22 LEO	21 VIR
25 LIS	24 ARI	24 GEM	24 CAN	24 VIR	24 LIB
27 ARI	26 TAU	26 CAN	26 LEO	26 LIB	26 SCO
30 TAU	28 GEM	28 LEO	28 VIR	29 SCO	29 SAG
	30 CAN		30 LIB		31 CAP

1939 MOON SIGNS

JAN	FEB	MAR	APR	MAY	JUN
2 GEM	1 CAN	2 LEO	3 LIB	2 SCO	1 SAG
4 CAN	3 LEO	4 VIR	5 SCO	4 SAG	3 CAP
6 LEO	5 VIR	6 LIB	7 SAG	7 CAP	7 AQU
8 VIR	7 LIB	8 SCO	9 CAP	9 AQU	8 PIS
10 LIB	9 SCO	10 SAG	12 AQU	12 PIS	10 ARI
12 SCO	11 SAG	13 CAP	14 PIS	14 ARI	13 TAU
15 SAG	14 CAP	15 AQU	17 ARI	16 TAU	15 GEM
17 CAP	16 AQU	18 PIS	19 TAU	19 GEM	17 CAN
20 AQU	19 PIS	20 ARI	21 GEM	21 CAN	19 LEO
22 PIS	21 ARI	23 TAU	24 CAN	23 LEO	21 VIR
25 ARI	24 TAU	25 GEM	26 LEO	25 VIR	23 LIB
27 TAU	26 GEM	27 CAN	28 VIR	27 LIB	26 SCO
30 GEM	28 CAN	29 LEO	30 LIB	29 SCO	28 SAG
		31 VIR			30 CAP

JUL	AUG	SEP	OCT	NOV	DEC
3 AQU	1 PIS	2 TAU	2 GEM	1 CAN	2 VIR
5 PIS	4 ARI	5 GEM	5 CAN	3 LEO	5 LIB
8 ARI	6 TAU	7 CAN	7 LEO	5 VIR	7 SCO
10 TAU	9 GEM	9 LEO	9 VIR	7 LIB	9 SAG
12 GEM	11 CAN	11 VIR	11 LIB	9 SCO	11 CAP
15 CAN	13 LEO	13 LIB	13 SCO	11 SAG	13 AQU
17 LEO	15 VIR	15 SCO	15 SAG	14 CAP	16 PIS
19 VIR	17 LIB	18 SAG	17 CAP	16 AQU	19 ARI
21 LIB	19 SCO	20 CAP	20 AQU	19 PIS	21 TAU
23 SCO	21 SAG	22 AQU	22 PIS	21 ARI	23 GEM
25 SAG	24 CAP	25 PIS	25 ARI	24 TAU	26 CAN
27 CAP	26 AQU	28 ARI	27 TAU	26 GEM	28 LEO
30 AQU	29 PIS	30 TAU	30 GEM	28 CAN	30 VIR
	31 ARI			30 LEO	

1940 MOON SIGNS

JAN	FEB	MAR	APR	MAY	JUN
1 LIB	1 SAG	2 CAP	1 AQU	3 ARI	2 TAU
3 SCO	4 CAP	4 AQU	3 PIS	5 TAU	4 GEM
5 SAG	6 AQU	7 PIS	6 ARI	8 GEM	6 CAN
7 CAP	9 PIS	9 ARI	8 TAU	10 CAN	9 LEO
10 AQU	11 ARI	12 TAU	11 GEM	12 LEO	12 VIR
12 LIS	14 TAU	14 GEM	13 CAN	15 VIR	13 LIB
15 ARI	16 GEM	17 CAN	15 LEO	17 LIB	15 SCO
17 TAU	18 CAN	19 LEO	17 VIR	19 SCO	17 SAG
20 GEM	20 LEO	21 VIR	19 LIB	21 SAG	19 CAP
22 CAN	22 VIR	23 LIB	21 SCO	23 CAP	22 AQU
24 LEO	24 LIB	25 SCO	23 SAG	25 AQU	24 PIS
26 VIR	26 SCO	27 SAG	26 CAP	28 PIS	27 ARI
28 LIB	29 SAG	29 CAP	28 AQU	30 ARI	28 TAU
30 SCO			30 PIS		
JUL	**AUG**	**SEP**	**OCT**	**NOV**	**DEC**
2 GEM	2 LEO	1 VIR	2 SCO	1 SAG	2 AQU
4 CAN	4 VIR	3 LIB	4 SAG	3 CAP	5 PIS
6 LEO	6 LIB	5 SCO	6 CAP	5 AQU	7 ARI
8 VIR	9 SCO	7 SAG	9 AQU	7 PIS	10 TAU
10 LIB	11 SAG	9 CAP	11 PIS	10 ARI	12 GEM
12 SCO	13 CAP	11 AQU	14 ARI	13 TAU	15 CAN
14 SAG	15 AQU	14 PIS	16 TAU	15 GEM	17 LEO
17 CAP	18 PIS	16 ARI	19 GEM	17 CAN	19 VIR
19 AQU	20 ARI	19 TAU	21 CAN	20 LEO	21 LIB
21 PIS	23 TAU	22 GEM	23 LEO	22 VIR	23 SCO
24 ARI	25 GEM	24 CAN	26 VIR	24 LIB	26 SAG
26 TAU	28 CAN	26 LEO	28 LIB	26 SCO	28 CAP
29 GEM	30 LEO	28 VIR	30 SCO	28 SAG	30 AQU
31 CAN		30 LIB		30 CAP	

1941 MOON SIGNS

JAN	FEB	MAR	APR	MAY	JUN
1 PIS	2 TAU	2 TAU	1 GEM	3 LEO	1 VIR
4 ARI	5 GEM	4 GEM	3 CAN	5 VIR	4 LIB
6 TAU	7 CAN	7 CAN	5 LEO	7 LIB	6 SCO
9 GEM	10 LEO	9 LEO	8 VIR	9 SCO	8 SAG
11 CAN	12 VIR	11 VIR	10 LIB	11 SAG	10 CAP
13 LEO	14 LIB	13 LIB	12 SCO	13 CAP	12 AQU
15 VIR	16 SCO	15 SCO	14 SAG	15 AQU	14 PIS
18 LIB	18 SAG	17 SAG	16 CAP	18 PIS	16 ARI
20 SCO	20 CAP	19 CAP	18 AQU	20 ARI	19 TAU
22 SAG	23 AQU	22 AQU	20 PIS	23 TAU	21 GEM
24 CAP	25 PIS	24 PIS	23 ARI	25 GEM	24 CAN
26 AQU	27 ARI	27 ARI	25 TAU	28 CAN	26 LEO
29 PIS		29 TAU	28 GEM	30 LEO	29 VIR
31 ARI			30 CAN		
JUL	**AUG**	**SEP**	**OCT**	**NOV**	**DEC**
1 LIB	1 SAG	2 AQU	1 PIS	2 TAU	2 GEM
3 SCO	3 CAP	4 PIS	4 ARI	5 GEM	5 CAN
5 SAG	5 AQU	6 ARI	6 TAU	7 CAN	7 LEO
7 CAP	8 PIS	9 TAU	9 GEM	10 LEO	10 VIR
9 AQU	10 ARI	11 GEM	11 CAN	12 VIR	12 LIB
11 PIS	13 TAU	14 CAN	14 LEO	15 LIB	14 SCO
14 ARI	15 GEM	16 LEO	16 VIR	17 SCO	16 SAG
16 TAU	18 CAN	19 VIR	18 LIB	19 SAG	18 CAP
19 GEM	20 LEO	21 LIB	20 SCO	21 CAP	20 AQU
21 CAN	22 VIR	23 SCO	22 SAG	23 AQU	22 PIS
24 LEO	24 LIB	25 SAG	24 CAP	25 PIS	24 ARI
26 VIR	26 SCO	27 CAP	26 AQU	27 ARI	27 TAU
28 LIB	28 SAG	29 AQU	29 PIS	30 TAU	29 GEM
30 SCO	31 CAP		31 ARI		

1942 MOON SIGNS

JAN	FEB	MAR	APR	MAY	JUN
1 CAN	2 VIR	1 VIR	2 SCO	2 SAG	2 AQU
3 LEO	4 LIB	4 LIB	4 SAG	4 CAP	4 PIS
6 VIR	7 SCO	6 SCO	6 CAP	6 AQU	6 ARI
8 LIB	9 SAG	8 SAG	8 AQU	8 PIS	9 TAU
10 SCO	11 CAP	10 CAP	11 PIS	10 ARI	11 GEM
12 SAG	13 AQU	12 AQU	13 ARI	13 TAU	14 CAN
14 CAP	15 PIS	14 PIS	15 TAU	15 GEM	16 LEO
16 AQU	17 ARI	17 ARI	18 GEM	18 CAN	19 VIR
20 PIS	20 TAU	19 TAU	20 CAN	20 LEO	21 LIB
21 ARI	22 GEM	21 GEM	23 LEO	23 VIR	23SCO
23 TAU	25 CAN	24 CAM	25 VIR	25 LIB	25 SAG
26 GEM	27 LEO	26 LEO	27 LIB	27 SCO	27 CAP
28 CAN		29 VIR	30 SCO	29 SAG	29 AQU
31 LEO		31 LIB		31 CAP	
JUL	**AUG**	**SEP**	**OCT**	**NOV**	**DEC**
1 PIS	2 TAU	1 GEM	1 CAN	2 VIR	2 LIB
4 ARI	5 GEM	4 CAN	4 LEO	5 LIB	4 SCO
6 TAU	7 CAN	6 LEO	6 VIR	7 SCO	6 SAG
9 GEM	10 LEO	9 VIR	8 LIB	9 SAG	8 CAP
11 CAN	12 VIR	11 LIB	10 SCO	11 CAP	10 AQU
14 LEO	15 LIB	13 SCO	13 SAG	13 AQU	12 PIS
16 VIR	17 SCO	15 SAG	15 CAP	15 PIS	15 ARI
18 LIB	19 SAG	17 CAP	17 AQU	17 ARI	17 TAU
21 SCO	21 CAP	20 AQU	19 PIS	20 TAU	19 GEM
23 SAG	23 AQU	22 PIS	21 ARI	22 GEM	22 CAN
25 CAP	25 PIS	24 ARI	23 TAU	25 CAN	24 LEO
27 AQU	27 ARI	26 TAU	26 GEM	27 LEO	27 VIR
29 PIS	30 TAU	29 GEM	28 CAN	30 VIR	29 LIB
31 ARI			31 LEO		

1943 MOON SIGNS

JAN	FEB	MAR	APR	MAY	JUN
1 SCO	1 CAP	1 CAP	1 PIS	3 TAU	1 GEM
3 SAG	3 AQU	3 AQU	3 ARI	5 GEM	4 CAN
5 CAP	5 PIS	5 PIS	5 TAU	7 CAN	6 LEO
7 AQU	7 ARI	7 ARI	8 GEM	10 LEO	9 VIR
9 PIS	10 TAU	9 TAU	10 CAN	12 VIR	11 LIB
11 ARI	1 GEM	11 GEM	13 LEO	15 LIB	14 SCO
13 TAU	14 CAN	14 CAN	15 VIR	17 SCO	16 SAG
16 GEM	17 LEO	16 LEO	18 LIB	19 SAG	18 CAP
18 CAN	19 VIR	19 VIR	20 SCO	21 CAP	20 AQU
21 LEO	22 LIB	21 LIB	22 SAG	23 AQU	22 PIS
23 VIR	24 SCO	23 SCO	24 CAP	26 PIS	24 ARI
26 LIB	26 SAG	26 SAG	26 AQU	28 ARI	26 TAU
28 SCO		28 CAP	28 PIS	30 TAU	29 GEM
30 SAG		30 AQU	30 ARI		
JUL	**AUG**	**SEP**	**OCT**	**NOV**	**DEC**
1 CAN	2 VIR	1 LIB	1 SCO	1 CAP	1 AQU
4 LEO	5 LIB	3 SCO	3 SAG	4 AQU	3 PIS
6 VIR	7 SCO	6 SAG	5 CAP	6 PIS	5 ARI
9 LIB	10 SAG	8 CAP	7 AQU	8 ARI	7 TAU
11 SCO	12 CAP	10 AQU	9 PIS	10 TAU	10 GEM
13 SAG	14 AQU	12 PIS	12 ARI	12 GEM	12 CAN
15 CAP	16 PIS	14 ARI	14 TAU	15 CAN	14 LEO
17 AQU	18 ARI	16 TAU	16 GEM	17 LEO	17 VIR
19 PIS	20 TAU	18 GEM	18 CAN	20 VIR	19 LIB
21 ARI	22 GEM	21 CAN	21 LEO	22 LIB	22 SCO
23 TAU	25 CAN	23 LEO	23 VIR	24 SCO	24 SAG
26 GEM	27 LEO	26 VIR	25 LIB	27 SAG	27 CAP
28 CAN	30 VIR	28 LIB	28 SCO	28 CAP	29 AQU
31 LEO			30 SAG		30 PIS

511

1944 MOON SIGNS

JAN	FEB	MAR	APR	MAY	JUN
1 ARI	2 GEM	3 CAN	1 LEO	1 VIR	3 SCO
3 TAU	4 CAN	5 LEO	4 VIR	4 LIB	5 SAG
6 GEM	7 LEO	8 VIR	6 LIB	6 SCO	7 CAP
8 CAN	9 VIR	10 LIB	9 SCO	9 SAG	9 AQU
11 LEO	12 LIB	13 SCO	11 SAG	11 CAP	11 PIS
13 VIR	14 SCO	15 SAG	14 CAP	13 AQU	13 ARI
16 LIB	17 SAG	17 CAP	16 AQU	15 PIS	16 TAU
18 SCO	19 CAP	19 AQU	18 PIS	17 ARI	18 GEM
20 SAG	21 AQU	22 PIS	20 ARI	19 TAU	20 CAN
23 CAP	23 PIS	24 ARI	22 TAU	21 GEM	22 LEO
25 AQU	25 ARI	26 TAU	24 GEM	24 CAN	25 VIR
27 PIS	27 TAU	28 GEM	26 CAN	26 LEO	27 LIB
29 ARI	29 GEM	30 CAN	29 LEO	29 VIR	30 SCO
31 TAU				31 LIB	

JUL	AUG	SEP	OCT	NOV	DEC
2 SAG	1 CAP	1 PIS	1 ARI	1 GEM	1 CAN
4 CAP	3 AQU	3 ARI	3 TAU	4 CAN	3 LEO
7 AQU	5 PIS	5 TAU	5 GEM	6 LEO	6 VIR
9 PIS	7 ARI	8 GEM	7 CAN	8 VIR	8 LIB
11 ARI	9 TAU	10 CAN	10 LEO	11 LIB	11 SCO
13 TAU	11 GEM	12 LEO	12 VIR	13 SCO	13 SAG
15 GEM	14 CAN	15 VIR	15 LIB	16 SAG	15 CAP
17 CAN	16 LEO	17 LIB	17 SCO	18 CAP	18 AQU
20 LEO	18 VI	20 SCO	19 SAG	20 AQU	20 PIS
22 VIR	21 LIB	22 SAG	22 CAP	23 PIS	22 ARI
25 LIB	24 SCO	25 CAP	24 AQU	25 ARI	24 TAU
27 SCO	26 SAG	27 AQU	26 PIS	27 TAU	26 CAN
30 SAG	28 CAP	29 PIS	28 ARI	29 GEM	28 CAN
	30 AQU		30 TAU		31 LEO

1946 MOON SIGNS

JAN	FEB	MAR	APR	MAY	JUN
2 CAP	1 AQU	2 PIS	1 ARI	2 GEM	1 CAN
4 AQU	3 PIS	4 ARI	3 TAU	4 CAN	3 LEO
6 PIS	5 ARI	6 TAU	5 GEM	6 LEO	5 VIR
9 ARI	7 TAU	8 GEM	7 CAN	6 VIR	7 LIB
11 TAU	9 GEM	11 CAN	9 LEO	11 LIB	10 SCO
13 GEM	11 CAN	13 LEO	11 VIR	13 SCO	12 SAG
15 CAN	13 LEO	15 VIR	14 LIB	16 SAG	15 CAP
17 LEO	16 VIR	17 LIB	16 SCO	18 CAP	17 AQU
19 VIR	18 LIB	20 SCO	19 SAG	21 AQU	20 PIS
22 LIB	20 SCO	22 SAG	21 CAP	23 PIS	22 ARI
24 SCO	23 SAG	25 CAP	24 AQU	26 ARI	24 TAU
27 SAG	26 CAP	27 AQU	26 PIS	28 TAU	26 GEM
29 CAP	28 AQU	30 PIS	28 ARI	30 GEM	28 CAN
			30 TAU		30 LEO

JUL	AUG	SEP	OCT	NOV	DEC
2 VIR	1 LIB	2 SAG	2 CAP	1 AQU	3 ARI
4 LIB	3 SCO	5 CAP	4 AQU	3 PIS	5 TAU
7 SCO	6 SCO	7 AQU	7 PIS	5 ARI	7 GEM
9 SAG	8 CAP	9 PIS	9 ARI	7 TAU	9 CAN
12 CAP	11 CAP	12 ARI	11 TAU	10 GEM	11 LEO
14 AQU	13 PIS	14 TAU	13 GEM	12 CAN	13 VIR
17 PIS	15 ARI	16 GEM	15 CAN	14 LEO	15 LIB
19 ARI	17 TAU	18 CAN	17 LEO	16 VIR	18 SCO
21 TAU	20 GEM	20 LEO	20 VIR	18 LIB	20 SAG
23 GEM	22 CAN	22 VIR	22 LIB	20 SCO	23 CAP
25 CAN	24 LEO	25 LIB	24 SCO	23 SAG	25 AQU
27 LEO	26 VIR	27 SCO	27 SAG	25 CAP	28 PIS
30 VIR	28 LIB	29 CAP	29 CAP	28 AQU	30 ARI
31 SCO				30 PIS	

1945 MOON SIGNS

JAN	FEB	MAR	APR	MAY	JUN
2 VIR	1 LIB	3 SCO	1 SAG	1 CAP	2 PIS
4 LIB	3 SCO	5 SAG	4 CAP	3 AQU	4 ARI
7 SCO	6 SAG	8 CAP	6 AQU	6 PIS	6 TAU
9 SAG	8 CAP	10 AQU	8 PIS	8 ARI	8 GEM
12 CAP	10 AQU	12 PIS	10 ARI	10 TAU	10 CAN
14 AQU	12 PIS	14 ARI	12 ATU	12 GEM	12 LEO
16 PIS	14 ARI	16 TAU	14 GEM	14 CAN	15 VIR
18 ARI	17 TAU	18 GEM	16 CAN	16 LEO	17 LIB
20 GEM	19 GEM	20 CAN	19 LEO	18 VIR	20 SCO
22 GEM	21 CAN	22 LEO	21 VIR	21 LIB	22 SAG
25 CAN	23 LEO	25 VIR	24 LIB	23 SCO	25 CAP
27 LEO	26 VIR	27 LIB	26 SCO	26 SAG	27 AQU
29 VIR	28 LIB	30 SCO	29 SAG	29 CAP	29 PIS
				31 AQU	

JUL	AUG	SEP	OCT	NOV	DEC
1 ARI	2 GEM	2 LEO	2 VIR	1 LIB	3 SAG
3 TAU	4 CAN	5 VIR	4 LIB	3 SCO	6 CAP
6 GEM	6 LEO	7 LIB	7 SCO	6 SAG	8 AQU
8 CAN	8 VIR	10 SCO	10 SAG	8 CAP	10 PIS
10 LEO	11 LIB	12 SAG	12 CAP	11 AQU	12 ARI
12 VIR	13 SCO	15 CAP	14 AQU	13 PIS	15 TAU
15 LIB	16 SAG	17 AQU	17 PIS	15 ARI	17 GEM
17 SCO	18 CAP	19 PIS	19 ARI	17 TAU	19 CAN
20 SAG	21 AQU	21 ARI	21 TAU	19 GEM	21 LEO
22 CAP	23 PIS	23 TAU	23 GEM	21 CAN	23 VIR
24 AQU	25 ARI	25 GEM	25 CAN	23 LEO	25 LIB
26 PIS	27 TAU	27 CAN	27 LEO	26 VIR	28 SCO
29 ARI	29 GEM	30 LEO	29 VIR	28 LIB	30 SAG
31 TAU	31 CAN			30 SCO	

1947 MOON SIGNS

JAN	FEB	MAR	APR	MAY	JUN
1 TAU	2 CAN	1 CAN	2 VIR	1 LIB	2 SAG
3 GEM	4 LEO	3 LEO	4 LIB	3 SCO	5 CAP
5 CAN	6 VIR	5 VIR	6 SCO	6 SAG	7 AQU
7 LEO	8 LIB	7 LIB	8 SAG	8 CAP	10 PIS
9 VIR	10 SCO	10 SCO	11 CAP	11 AQU	12 ARI
12 LIB	13 SAG	12 SAG	13 AQU	13 PIS	14 TAU
14 SCO	15 CAP	15 CAP	16 PIS	16 ARI	16 GEM
16 SAG	18 AQU	17 AQU	18 ARI	18 TAU	18 CAN
19 CAP	20 PIS	20 PIS	20 TAU	20 GEM	20 LEO
22 AQU	23 ARI	22 ARI	23 GEM	22 CAN	22 VIR
22 PIS	25 TAU	24 TAU	25 CAN	24 LEO	25 LIB
26 ARI	27 GEM	26 GEM	27 LEO	26 VIR	27 SCO
29 TAU		28 CAN	29 VIR	28 LIB	29 SAG
31 GEM		31 LEO		31 SCO	

JUL	AUG	SEP	OCT	NOV	DEC
2 CAP	1 AQU	2 ARI	1 TAU	2 CAN	1 LOE
4 AQU	3 PIS	4 TAU	4 GEM	4 LEO	3 VIR
7 PIS	6 ARI	6 GEM	6 CAN	6 VI	6 LIB
9 ARI	8 TAU	9 CAN	8 LEO	8 LIB	8 SCO
12 TAU	10 GEM	11 LEO	10 VIR	11 SCO	10 SAG
14 GEM	12 CAN	13 VIR	12 LIB	13 SAG	13 CAP
16 CAN	14 LEO	15 LIB	14 SCO	15 CAP	15 AQU
18 LEO	16 VIR	17 SCO	17 SAG	18 AQU	18 PIS
20 VIR	18 LIB	19 SAG	19 CAP	20 PIS	20 ARI
20 LIB	20 SCO	22 CAP	22 AQU	23 ARI	23 TAU
24 SCO	23 SAG	24 AQU	24 PIS	25 TAU	25 GEM
27 SAG	25 CAP	27 PIS	26 ARI	27 GEM	27 CAN
29 CAP	28 AQU	29 ARI	29 TAU	29 CAN	29 LEO
	30 PIS		31 GEM		31 VIR

1948 MOON SIGNS

JAN	FEB	MAR	APR	MAY	JUN
2 LIB	3 SAG	1 SAG	2 AQU	2 PIS	1 ARI
4 SCO	5 CAP	3 CAP	5 PIS	5 ARI	3 TAU
6 SAG	8 AQU	6 AQU	7 ARI	7 TAU	6 GEM
9 CAP	10 PIS	8 PIS	10 TAU	9 GEM	8 CAN
11 AQU	13 ARI	11 ARI	12 GEM	11 CAN	10 LEO
14 PIS	15 TAU	13 TAU	14 CAN	14 LEO	12 VIR
16 ARI	17 GEM	16 GEM	16 LEO	16 VIR	14 LIB
19 TAU	20 CAN	18 CAN	18 VIR	18 LIB	16 SCO
21 GEM	22 LEO	20 LEO	21 LIB	20 SCO	18 SAG
23 CAN	24 VIR	22 VIR	23 SCO	22 SAG	21 CAP
25 LEO	26 LIB	24 LIB	25 SAG	25 CAP	23 AQU
27 VIR	28 SCO	26 SCO	27 CAP	27 AQU	26 PIS
29 LIB		28 SAG	30 AQU	29 PIS	28 PRI
31 SCO		31 CAP			

JUL	AUG	SEP	OCT	NOV	DEC
1 TAU	2 CAN	2 VIR	1 LIB	2 SAG	2 CAP
3 GEM	4 LEO	4 LIB	3 SCO	4 CAP	4 AQU
5 CAN	6 VIR	6 SCO	6 SAG	7 AQU	6 PIS
7 LEO	8 LIB	8 SAG	8 CAP	9 PIS	9 ARI
9 VIR	10 SCO	11 CAP	10 AQU	12 AQU	12 ARI
11 LIB	12 SAG	13 AQU	13 PIS	14 TAU	14 GEM
13 SCO	14 CAP	16 PIS	15 ARI	17 GEM	16 CAN
16 SAG	17 AQU	18 ARI	18 TAU	19 CAN	18 LEO
18 CAP	19 PIS	21 TAU	20 GEM	21 LEO	20 VIR
21 AQU	22 ARI	23 GEM	23 CAN	23 VIR	22 LIB
23 PIS	24 TAU	25 CAN	25 LEO	25 LIB	25 SCO
26 ARI	27 GEM	27 LEO	27 VIR	27 SCO	27 CAP
28 TAU	29 CAN	29 VIR	29 LIB	29 SAG	29 CAP
30 GEM	31 LEO		31 SCO		31 AQU

1949 MOON SIGNS

JAN	FEB	MAR	APR	MAY	JUN
3 PIS	2 ARI	1 ARI	2 GEM	2 CAN	2 VIR
5 ARI	4 TAU	3 TAU	5 CAN	4 LEO	5 LIB
8 TAU	7 GEM	6 GEM	7 LEO	6 VIR	7 SCO
10 GEM	9 CAN	8 CAN	9 VIR	8 LIB	9 SAG
12 CAN	11 LEO	10 LEO	11 LIB	10 SCO	11 CAP
15 LEO	13 VIR	13 VIR	13 SCO	12 SAG	13 AQU
17 VIR	15 LIB	15 LIB	15 SAG	15 CAP	16 PIS
19 LIB	17 SCO	17 SCO	17 CAP	17 AQU	18 ARI
21 SCO	19 SAG	19 SAG	19 AQU	20 PIS	21 TAU
23 SAG	22 CAP	21 CAP	22 PIS	22 ARI	23 GEM
25 CAP	24 AQU	23 AQU	24 ARI	24 TAU	25 CAN
28 AQU	26 PIS	26 PIS	27 TAU	27 GEM	28 LEO
30 PIS		28 ARI	29 GEM	29 CAN	30 VIR
		31 TAU		31 LEO	

JUL	AUG	SEP	OCT	NOV	DEC
2 LIB	2 SAG	1 CAP	3 PIS	2 ARI	1 TAU
4 SCO	5 CAP	3 AQU	5 ARI	4 TAU	4 GEM
6 SAG	7 AQU	6 PIS	8 TAU	7 GEM	6 CAN
8 CAP	9 PIS	8 ARI	10 GEM	9 CAN	9 LEO
11 AQU	12 ARI	11 TAU	13 CAN	11 LEO	11 VIR
13 PIS	14 TAU	13 GEM	15 LEO	14 VIR	13 LIB
15 ARI	17 GEM	15 CAN	17 VIR	16 LIB	15 SCO
18 TAU	19 CAN	18 LEO	19 LIB	18 SCO	17 SAG
20 GEM	21 LEO	20 VIR	21 SCO	20 SAG	19 CAP
23 CAN	23 VIR	22 LIB	23 SAG	22 CAP	21 AQU
25 LEO	25 LIB	24 SCO	25 CAP	24 AQU	23 SCO
27 VIR	27 SCO	26 SAG	28 AQU	26 PIS	25 SAG
29 LIB	30 SAG	28 CAP	30 PIS	29 ARI	29 TAU
31 SCO		30 AQU			31 GEM

1950 MOON SIGNS

JAN	FEB	MAR	APR	MAY	JUN
3 CAN	1 LEO	1 LEO	1 LIB	1 SCO	1 CAP
5 LEO	3 VIR	3 VIR	3 SCO	3 SAG	3 AQU
7 VIR	6 LIB	5 LIB	5 SAG	5 CAP	5 PIS
9 LIB	8 SCO	7 SCO	7 CAP	7 AQU	8 ARI
11 SCO	10 SAG	8 SAG	10 AQU	9 PIS	10 TAU
14 SAG	12 CAP	11 CAP	12 PIS	12 ARI	13 GEM
16 CAP	14 AQU	13 AQU	14 ARI	14 TAU	15 CAN
18 AQU	16 PIS	16 PIS	17 TAU	17 GEM	18 LEO
20 PIS	19 ARI	18 ARI	19 GEM	19 CAN	20 VIR
22 ARI	21 TAU	21 TAU	22 CAN	22 LEO	22 LIB
25 TAU	24 GEM	23 GEM	24 LEO	24 VIR	25 SCO
28 GEM	26 CAN	26 CAN	27 VIR	26 LIB	27 CAP
30 CAN		28 LEO	29 LIB	28 SCO	29 CAP
		30 VIR		30 SAG	

JUL	AUG	SEP	OCT	NOV	DEC
1 AQU	1 ARI	3 GEM	3 CAN	2 LEO	1 VIR
3 PIS	4 TAU	5 CAN	5 LEO	4 VIR	3 LIB
5 ARI	7 GEM	8 LEO	7 VIR	6 LIB	6 SCO
8 TAU	9 CAN	10 VIR	10 LIB	8 SCO	8 SAG
10 GEM	11 LEO	12 LIB	12 SCO	10 SCO	10 CAP
13 CAN	14 VIR	14 SCO	14 SAG	12 CAP	12 AQU
15 ELO	16 LIB	16 SAG	16 CAP	14 AQU	14 PIS
17 VIR	18 SCO	18 CAP	18 AQU	16 PIS	16 ARI
20 LIB	20 SAG	21 AQU	20 PIS	19 ARI	19 TAU
22 SCO	22 CAP	23 PIS	23 ARI	21 TAU	21 GEM
24 SAG	24 AQU	25 ARI	25 TAU	24 GEM	24 CAN
26 CAP	27 PIS	28 TAU	28 GEM	26 CAN	26 LEO
28 AQU	29 ARI	30 GEM	30 CAN	29 LEO	28 VIR
30 PIS	31 TAU				31 LIB

1951 MOON SIGNS

JAN	FEB	MAR	APR	MAY	JUN
2 SCO	2 CAP	2 CAP	2 PIS	2 ARI	3 GEM
4 SAG	4 AQU	4 AQU	5 ARI	4 TAU	5 CAN
6 CAP	7 PIS	6 PIS	7 TAU	7 GEM	8 LEO
8 AQU	9 ARI	8 ARI	9 GEM	9 CAN	10 VIR
10 PIS	11 TAU	11 TAU	12 CAN	12 LEO	13 LIB
12 ARI	14 GEM	13 GEM	14 LEO	14 VIR	15 SCO
15 TAU	16 CAN	16 CAN	17 VIR	16 LIB	17 SAG
17 GEM	19 LEO	18 LEO	19 LIB	19 SCO	19 CAP
20 CAN	21 VIR	20 VIR	21 SCO	21 SAG	21 AQU
22 LEO	23 LIB	23 LIB	23 SAG	23 CAP	23 PIS
25 VIR	25 SCO	25 SCO	25 CAP	25 AQU	25 ARI
27 LIB	28 SAG	27 SAG	27 AQU	27 PIS	28 TAU
29 SCO		29 CAP	29 PIS	29 ARI	30 GEM
31 SAG		31 AQU		31 TAU	

JUL	AUG	SEP	OCT	NOV	DEC
3 CAN	1 LEO	3 LIB	2 SCO	1 SAG	2 AQU
5 LEO	4 VIR	5 SCO	4 SAG	3 CAP	4 PIS
8 VIR	6 LIB	7 SAG	6 CAP	5 AQU	6 ARI
10 LIB	9 SCO	9 CAP	8 AQU	7 PIS	9 TAU
12 SCO	11 SAG	11 AQU	11 PIS	9 ARI	11 GEM
14 SAG	13 CAP	13 PIS	13 ARI	11 TAU	13 CAN
16 CAP	15 AQU	15 ARI	15 TAU	14 GEM	16 LEO
18 AQU	17 PIS	18 TAU	17 GEM	16 CAN	19 VIR
20 PIS	19 ARI	20 GEM	20 CAN	19 LEO	21 LIB
23 ARI	21 TAU	23 CAN	22 LEO	21 VIR	23 SCO
25 TAU	24 GEM	25 LEO	25 VIR	24 LIB	25 SAG
27 GEM	26 CAN	28 VIR	27 LIB	26 SCO	27 CAP
30 CAN	29 LEO	30 LIB	29 SCO	28 SAG	29 AQU
	31 VIR			30 CAP	31 PIS

513

1952 MOON SIGNS

JAN	FEB	MAR	APR	MAY	JUN
3 ARI	1 TAU	2 GEM	1 CAN	3 VIR	2 LIB
5 TAU	3 GEM	4 CAN	3 LEO	5 LIB	4 SCO
7 GEM	6 CAN	7 LEO	6 VIR	8 SCO	6 SAG
10 CAN	9 LEO	9 VIR	8 LIB	10 SAG	8 CAP
12 LEO	11 VIR	12 LIB	10 SCO	12 CAP	10 AQU
15 VIR	14 LIB	14 SCO	13 SAG	14 AQU	12 PIS
17 LIB	16 SCO	16 SAG	15 CAP	16 PIS	15 ARI
20 SCO	18 SAG	19 CAP	17 AQU	18 ARI	17 TAU
22 SAG	20 CAP	21 AQU	19 PIS	21 TAU	19 GEM
24 CAP	22 AQU	23 PIS	21 ARI	23 GEM	22 CAN
26 AQU	24 PIS	25 ARI	23 TAU	25 CAN	24 LEO
28 PIS	26 ARI	27 TAU	26 GEM	28 LEO	27 VIR
30 ARI	29 TAU	29 GEM	28 CAN	30 VIR	29 LIB
			30 LEO		

JUL	AUG	SEP	OCT	NOV	DEC
2 SCO	2 CAP	1 AQU	2 ARI	1 TAU	2 CAN
4 SAG	4 AQU	3 PIS	4 TAU	3 GEM	5 LEO
6 CAN	6 PIS	5 ARI	6 GEM	5 CAN	7 VIR
8 AQU	8 ARI	7 TAU	9 CAN	7 LEO	10 LIB
10 PIS	10 TAU	9 GEM	11 LEO	10 VIR	12 SCO
12 ARI	13 GEM	11 CAN	14 VIR	13 LIB	15 SAG
14 TAU	15 CAN	14 LEO	16 LIB	15 SCO	17 CAP
16 CAN	18 LEO	16 VIR	19 SCO	17 SAG	19 AQU
19 CAN	20 VIR	19 LIB	21 SAG	19 CAP	21 PIS
21 LEO	23 LIB	21 SCO	23 CAP	21 AQU	23 ARI
24 VIR	25 SCO	24 SAG	25 AQU	24 PIS	25 TAU
26 LIB	27 SAG	26 CAP	26 PIS	26 ARI	27 GEM
29 SCO	30 CAP	28 AQU	29 ARI	28 TAU	30 CAN
31 SAG		30 PIS		30 GEM	

1953 MOON SIGNS

JAN	FEB	MAR	APR	MAY	JUN
1 LEO	3 LIB	2 LIB	1 SCO	2 CAP	1 AQU
4 VIR	5 SCO	4 SCO	3 SAG	5 AQU	3 PIS
6 LIB	7 SAG	7 SAG	5 CAP	7 PIS	5 ARI
9 SCO	10 CAP	9 CAP	7 AQU	9 ARI	7 TAU
11 SAG	12 AQU	11 AQU	10 PIS	11 TAU	9 GEM
13 CAP	14 PIS	13 PIS	12 ARI	13 GEM	12 CAN
15 AQU	16 ARI	15 ARI	14 TAU	15 CAN	14 LEO
17 PIS	18 TAU	17 TAU	16 GEM	18 LEO	16 VIR
19 ARI	20 GEM	19 GEM	18 CAN	20 VIR	19 LIB
21 TAU	22 CAN	22 CAN	20 LEO	23 LIB	21 SCO
24 GEM	25 LEO	24 LEO	23 VIR	25 SCO	24 SAG
26 CAN	27 VIR	27 VIR	25 LIB	27 SAG	26 CAP
28 LEO		29 LIB	26 SCO	30 CAP	28 AQU
31 VIR			30 SAG		30 PIS

JUL	AUG	SEP	OCT	NOV	DEC
2 ARI	1 TAU	1 CAN	1 LEO	2 LIB	2 SCO
5 TAU	3 GEM	4 LEO	4 VIR	5 SCO	5 SAG
7 GEM	5 CAN	6 VIR	6 LIB	7 SAG	7 CAP
9 CAN	8 LEO	9 LIB	9 SCO	10 CAP	9 AQU
11 LEO	10 VIR	11 SCO	11 SAG	12 AQU	11 PIS
14 VIR	13 LIB	14 SAG	13 CAP	14 PIS	14 ARI
16 LIB	15 SCO	16 CAP	16 AQU	16 ARI	16 TAU
19 SCO	18 SAG	18 AQU	18 PIS	18 TAU	18 GEM
21 SAG	20 CAP	21 PIS	20 ARI	20 GEM	20 CAN
23 CAP	22 AQU	23 ARI	22 TAU	22 CAN	20 CAN
26 AQU	24 PIS	25 TAU	24 GEM	25 LEO	25 VIR
28 PIS	26 ARI	27 GEM	26 CAN	27 VIR	27 LIB
30 ARI	28 TAU	29 CAN	28 LEO	30 LIB	30 SCO
	30 GEM		31 VIR		

1954 MOON SIGNS

JAN	FEB	MAR	APR	MAY	JUN
1 SAG	2 AQU	1 AQU	2 ARI	1 TAU	2 CAN
3 CAP	4 ARI	3 SAG	4 TAU	3 GEM	4 LEO
6 AQU	6 ARI	5 ARI	6 GEM	5 CAN	6 VIR
8 PIS	8 TAU	7 TAU	8 CAN	8 LEO	9 LIB
10 ARI	10 GEM	10 GEM	10 LEO	10 VIR	11 SCO
12 TAU	13 CAN	12 CAN	13 VIR	12 LIB	14 SAG
14 GEM	15 LEO	14 LEO	15 LIB	15 SCO	16 CAP
16 CAN	17 VIR	16 VIR	18 SCO	17 SAG	19 AQU
19 LIB	20 LIB	19 LIB	20 SAG	20 CAP	21 PIS
21 VIR	22 SCO	21 SCO	23 CAP	22 AQU	23 ARI
23 LIB	25 SAG	24 SAG	25 AQU	25 PIS	25 TAU
26 SCO	27 CAP	26 CAP	27 PIS	27 ARI	27 GEM
28 SAG		29 AQU	29 ARI	29 TAU	29 CAN
31 CAP		31 PIS		31 GEM	

JUL	AUG	SEP	OCT	NOV	DEC
1 LEO	2 LIB	1 SCO	1 SAG	2 AQU	2 PIS
4 VIR	5 SCO	5 SAG	4 CAP	5 PIS	4 ARI
6 LIB	7 SAG	6 CAP	6 AQU	7 ARI	6 TAU
9 SCO	10 CAP	9 AQU	9 PIS	9 TAU	8 GEM
10 SAG	12 AQU	11 PIS	10 ARI	11 GEM	10 CAN
14 CAN	14 PIS	13 ARI	12 TAU	13 CAN	12 LEO
16 AQU	16 ARI	15 TAU	14 GEM	15 LEO	14 VIR
18 PIS	19 TAU	17 GEM	16 CAN	17 VIR	17 LIB
20 ARI	21 GEM	19 CAN	19 LEO	20 LIB	19 SCO
22 TAU	23 CAN	21 LEO	21 VIR	22 SCO	22 SAG
24 GEM	25 LEO	24 VIR	23 LIB	25 SAG	24 CAP
27 CAN	27 VIR	26 LIB	26 SCO	27 CAP	27 AQU
29 LEO	30 LIB	29 SCO	28 SAG	30 AQU	29 PIS
31 VIR			31 CAP		31 ARI

1955 MOON SIGNS

JAN	FEB	MAR	APR	MAY	JUN
3 TAU	1 GEM	2 CAN	1 LEO	2 LIB	1 SCO
5 GEM	3 CAN	4 LEO	3 VIR	5 SCO	4 SAG
7 CAN	5 LEO	7 VIR	5 LIB	7 SAG	6 CAP
9 LEO	7 VIR	9 LIB	8 SCO	10 CAP	9 AQU
11 VIR	10 LIB	11 SCO	10 SAG	12 AQU	11 PIS
13 LIB	12 SCO	14 SAG	13 CAP	15 PIS	13 ARI
16 SCO	17 SAG	16 CAP	15 AQU	17 ARI	16 TAU
18 SAG	17 CAP	19 AQU	18 P[IS	19 TAU	18 GEM
21 CAP	19 AQU	21 PIS	20 ARI	21 GEM	20 CAN
23 AQU	22 PIS	23 ARI	22 TAU	23 CAN	22 LEO
25 PIS	24 ARI	25 TAU	24 GEM	25 LEO	24 VIR
28 ARI	26 TAU	27 GEM	26 CAN	27 VIR	26 LIB
30 TAU	28 GEM	29 CAN	28 LEO	30 LIB	28 SCO
			30 VIR		

JUL	AUG	SEP	OCT	NOV	DEC
1 SAG	2 AQU	1 PIS	1 ARI	1 GEM	5 CAN
3 CAP	5 PIS	3 ARI	3 TAU	3 CAN	3 LEO
6 AQU	7 ARI	5 TAU	5 GEM	5 LEO	5 VIR
8 PIS	9 TAU	8 GEM	7 CAN	7 VIR	7 LEB
11 ARI	11 GEM	10 CAN	9 LEO	10 LIB	9 SCO
13 TAU	13 CAN	12 LEO	11 VIR	12 SCO	12 SAG
15 GEM	15 LEO	14 VIR	13 LIB	15 SAG	14 CAP
17 CAN	18 VIRF	16 LIB	16 SCO	17 CAP	17 AQU
19 LEO	20 LIB	18 SCO	18 SAG	20 AQU	19 PIS
21 VIR	22 SCO	21 SAG	21 CAP	22 PIS	22 ARI
23 LIB	25 SAG	23 CAP	23 AQU	24 ARI	24 TAU
26 SCO	27 CAP	26 AQU	26 PUIS	27 TAU	26 GEM
28 SAG	30 AQU	28 PIS	28 ARI	29 GEM	28 CAN
31 CAP			30 TAU		30 LEO

514

1956 MOON SIGNS

AN	FEB	MAR	APR	MAY	JUN
1 VIR	2 SCO	3 SAG	1 CAP	1 AQU	3 ARI
3 LIB	4 SAG	5 CAP	4 AQU	4 PIS	5 TAU
6 SCO	7 CAP	8 AQU	6 PIS	6 ARI	7 GEM
8 SAG	9 AQU	10 PIS	8 ARI	8 TAU	9 CAP
11 CAP	12 PIS	12 ARI	11 TAU	11 GEM	11 LEO
13 AQU	14 ARI	15 TAU	13 GEM	13 CAN	13 VIR
16 PIS	16 TAU	17 GEM	15 CAN	15 LEO	15 LIB
18 ARI	19 GEM	19 CAN	17 LEO	17 VIR	18 SCO
20 TAU	21 CAN	21 LEO	20 VIR	19 LIB	20 SAG
22 GEM	23 LEO	23 VIR	22 LIB	21 SCO	22 CAP
24 CAN	25 VIR	25 LIB	24 SCO	24 SAG	25 AQU
26 LEO	27 LIB	28 SCO	26 SAG	26 CAP	27 PIS
28 VIR	29 SCO	30 SAG	29 CAP	29 AQU	30 ARI
31 LIB					31 PIS

JUL	AUG	SEP	OCT	NOV	DEC
2 TAU	1 GEM	1 LEO	1 VIR	1 SCO	1 SAG
4 GEM	3 CAN	3 VIR	3 LIB	3 SAG	3 CAP
6 CAN	5 LEO	5 LIB	5 SCO	6 CAP	6 AQU
8 LEO	7 VIR	7 SCO	7 SAG	8 AQU	8 PIS
10 VIR	9 LIB	10 SAG	10 CAP	11 PIS	11 ARI
12 LIB	11 SCO	12 CAP	12 AQU	13 ARI	13 TAU
15 SCO	13 SAG	15 AQU	15 PIS	16 TAU	15 GEM
17 SAG	16 CAP	17 PIS	17 ARI	18 GEM	17 CAN
20 CAP	18 AQU	20 ARI	19 TAU	20 CAN	19 LEO
22 AQU	21 PIS	22 TAU	22 GEM	22 LEO	21 VIR
25 PIS	23 ARI	24 GEM	24 CAN	24 VIR	24 LIB
27 ARI	26 TAU	26 CAN	26 LEO	26 LIB	26 SCO
30 TAU	28 GEM	29 LEO	28 VIR	29 SCO	28 SAG
	30 CAN		30 LIB		31 CAP

1957 MOON SIGNS

JAN	FEB	MAR	APR	MAY	JUN
2 AQU	1 PIS	3 ARI	1 TAU	1 GEM	1 LEO
5 PIS	3 ARI	5 TAU	4 GEM	3 CAN	4 VIR
7 ARI	6 TAU	7 GEM	6 CAN	5 LEO	6 LIB
9 TAU	8 GEM	10 CAN	8 LEO	7 VIR	8 SCO
12 GEM	10 CAN	12 LEO	10 VIR	9 LIB	10 SAG
14 CAN	12 LEO	14 VIR	12 LIB	12 SCO	12 CAP
16 LEO	14 VIR	16 LIB	14 SCO	14 SAG	15 AQU
18 VIR	16 LIB	18 SCO	16 SAG	16 CAP	17 PIS
20 LIB	18 SCO	20 SAG	19 CAP	18 AQU	20 ARI
22 SCO	21 SAG	22 CAP	21 AQU	21 PIS	22 TAU
24 SAG	23 CAP	25 AQU	24 PIS	23 ARI	25 GEM
27 CAP	26 AQU	27 PIS	26 ARI	26 TAU	27 CAN
29 AQU	28 PIS	30 ARI	29 TAU	28 GEM	29 LEO
				30 CAN	

JUL	AUG	SEP	OCT	NOV	DEC
1 VIR	1 SCO	2 CAP	2 AQU	1 PIS	1 ARI
3 LIB	4 SAG	5 AQU	4 PIS	3 ARI	3 TAU
5 SCO	6 CAP	7 PIS	7 ARI	6 TAU	5 GEM
7 SAG	8 AQU	10 ARI	9 TAU	8 GEM	8 CAN
10 CAP	11 PIS	12 TAU	12 GEM	10 CAN	10 LEO
12 AQU	13 ARI	15 GEM	14 CAN	13 LEO	12 VIR
15 PIS	16 TAU	17 CAN	16 LEO	15 VIR	14 LIB
17 ARI	18 GEM	19 LEO	18 VIR	17 LIB	16 SCO
20 TAU	21 CAN	21 VIR	21 LIB	19 SCO	18 SAG
22 GEM	23 LEO	23 LIB	23 SCO	21 SAG	21 CAP
24 CAN	25 VIR	25 SCO	25 SAG	23 CAP	23 AQU
26 LEO	27 LIB	27 SAG	27 CAP	26 AQU	25 PIS
28 VIR	29 SCO	29 CAP	29 AQU	28 PIS	28 ARI
30 LIB	31 SAG				30 TAU

1958 MOON SIGNS

JAN	FEB	MAR	APR	MAY	JUN
2 GEM	3 LEO	2 LEO	1 VIR	2 SCO	3 CAP
4 CAN	5 VIR	4 VIR	3 LIB	4 SAG	5 AQU
6 LEO	7 LIB	6 LIB	5 SCO	6 CAP	7 PIS
8 VIR	9 SCO	8 SCO	7 SAG	8 AQU	10 ARI
10 LIB	11 SAG	10 SAG	9 CAP	11 PIS	12 TAU
12 SCO	13 CAP	12 CAP	11 AQU	13 ARI	15 GEM
15 SAG	16 AQU	15 AQU	13 PIS	16 TAU	17 CAN
17 CAP	18 PIS	17 PIS	16 ARI	18 GEM	19 LEO
19 AQU	21 ARI	20 ARI	19 TAU	21 CAN	21 VIR
22 PIS	23 TAU	22 TAU	21 GEM	23 LEO	24 LIB
24 ARI	26 GEM	25 GEM	23 CAN	25 VIR	26 SCO
27 TAU	28 CAN	27 CAN	26 LEO	27 LIB	28 SAG
29 GEM		29 LEO	28 VIR	29 SCO	30 CAP
31 CAN			30 LIB	31 SAG	

JUL	AUG	SEP	OCT	NOV	DEC
2 AQU	1 PIS	2 TAU	2 GEM	1 CAN	3 VIR
4 PIS	3 ARI	5 GEM	4 CAN	3 LEO	5 LIB
7 ARI	6 TAU	7 CAN	7 LEO	5 VIR	7 SCO
9 TAU	8 GEM	9 LEO	9 VIR	7 LIB	9 SAG
12 GEM	11 CAN	11 VIR	11 LIB	9 SCO	11 CAP
14 CAN	13 LEO	13 LIB	13 SCO	11 SAG	13 AQU
17 LEO	15 VIR	15 SCO	15 SAG	13 CAP	15 PIS
19 VIR	17 LIB	18 SAG	17 CAP	16 AQU	18 ARI
21 LIB	19 SCO	20 CAP	19 AQU	18 PIS	20 TAU
23 SCO	21 SAG	22 AQU	22 PIS	20 ARI	23 GEM
25 SAG	23 CAP	24 PIS	24 ARI	23 TAU	25 CAN
27 CAP	26 AQU	27 ARI	27 TAU	25 GEM	27 LEO
29 AQU	28 PIS	29 TAU	29 GEM	28 CAN	30 VIR
	31 ARI			30 LEO	

1959 MOON SIGNS

JAN	FEB	MAR	APR	MAY	JUN
1 LIB	1 SAG	1 SAG	1 AQU	1 PIS	2 TAU
3 SCO	4 CAP	3 CAP	4 PIS	3 ARI	5 GEM
5 SAG	6 AQU	5 AQU	6 ARI	6 TAU	7 CAN
7 CAP	8 PIS	7 PIS	8 TAU	8 GEM	9 LEO
9 AQU	10 ARI	10 ARI	11 GEM	11 CAN	12 VIR
12 PIS	13 TAU	12 TAU	14 CAN	13 LEO	14 LIB
14 ARI	15 GEM	15 GEM	16 LEO	16 VIR	16 SCO
17 TAU	18 CAN	17 CAN	18 VIR	18 LIB	18 SAG
19 GEM	20 LEO	20 LEO	20 LIB	20 SCO	20 CAP
21 CAN	22 VIR	22 VIR	22 SCO	22 SAG	22 AQU
24 LEO	24 LIB	24 LIB	24 SAG	24 CAP	24 PIS
26 VIR	27 SCO	26 SCO	26 CAP	26 AQU	27 ARI
28 LIB		28 SAG	28 AQU	28 PIS	29 TAU
30 SCO		30 CAP		30 ARI	

JUL	AUG	SEP	OCT	NOV	DEC
2 GEM	1 CAN	2 VIR	1 LIB	2 SAG	1 CAP
4 CAN	3 LEO	4 LIB	3 SCO	4 CAP	3 AQU
7 LEO	5 VIR	6 SCO	5 SAG	6 AQU	5 PIS
9 VIR	8 LIB	8 SAG	7 CAP	8 PIS	8 ARI
11 LIB	10 SCO	10 CAP	10 AQU	10 ARI	10 TAU
13 SCO	12 SAG	12 AQU	12 PIS	13 TAU	13 GEM
16 SAG	14 CAP	15 PIS	14 ARI	15 GEM	15 CAN
18 CAP	16 AQU	17 ARI	17 TAU	18 CAN	18 LEO
20 AQU	18 PIS	19 TAU	19 GEM	20 LEO	20 VIR
22 PIS	20 ARI	22 GEM	22 CAN	23 VIR	22 LIB
24 ARI	23 TAU	24 CAN	24 LEO	25 LIB	25 SCO
27 TAU	25 GEM	27 LEO	26 VIR	27 SCO	27 SAG
29 GEM	28 CAN	29 VIR	29 LIB	29 SAG	29 CAP
30 LEO			31 SCO		31 AQU

1960 MOON SIGNS

JAN	FEB	MAR	APR	MAY	JUN
2 PIS	3 TAU	1 TAU	2 CAN	2 LEO	1 VIR
4 ARI	5 GEM	4 GEM	5 LEO	5 VIR	3 LIB
6 TAU	8 CAN	6 CAN	7 VIR	7 LIB	6 SCO
9 GEM	10 LEO	9 LEO	10 LIB	9 SCO	8 SAG
11 CAN	13 VIR	11 VIR	12 SCO	11 SAG	10 CAP
14 LEO	15 LIB	13 LIB	14 SAG	13 CAP	12 AQU
16 VIR	17 SCO	15 SCO	16 CAP	15 AQU	14 PIS
19 LIB	19 SAG	17 SAG	18 AQU	17 PIS	16 ARI
21 SCO	21 CAP	20 CAP	20 PIS	20 ARI	18 TAU
23 SAG	23 AQU	22 AQU	22 ARI	22 TAU	21 GEM
25 CAP	26 PIS	24 PIS	25 TAU	24 GEM	23 CAN
27 AQU	28 ARI	26 ARI	27 GEM	27 CAN	26 LEO
29 PIS		28 TAU	30 CAN	29 LEO	28 VIR
31 ARI		31 GEM			

JUL	AUG	SEP	OCT	NOV	DEC
1 LIB	1 SAG	2 AQU	1 PIS	2 TAU	2 GEM
3 SCO	3 CAP	4 PIS	3 ARI	4 GEM	4 CAN
5 SAG	5 AQU	6 ARI	6 TAU	7 CAN	7 LEO
7 CAP	7 PIS	8 TAU	8 GEM	9 LEO	9 VIR
9 AQU	10 ARI	11 GEM	10 CAN	12 VIR	12 LIB
11 PIS	12 TAU	13 CAN	13 LEO	14 LIB	14 SCO
13 ARI	14 GEM	16 LEO	15 VIR	16 SCO	16 SAG
15 TAU	17 CAN	18 VIR	18 LIB	19 SAG	18 CAP
18 GEM	19 LEO	20 LIB	20 SCO	21 CAP	20 AQU
20 CAN	22 VIR	23 SCO	22 SAG	23 AQU	22 PIS
23 LEO	24 LIB	25 SAG	24 CAP	25 PIS	24 ARI
25 VIR	26 SCO	27 CAP	26 AQU	27 ARI	26 TAU
28 LIB	29 SAG	29 AQU	28 PIS	29 TAU	29 GEM
30 SCO	31 CAP		31 ARI		31 CAN

1961 MOON SIGNS

JAN	FEB	MAR	APR	MAY	JUN
3 LEO	2 VIR	1 VIR	2 SCO	2 SAG	2 AQU
5 VIR	4 LIB	3 LIB	4 SAG	4 CAP	4 PIS
8 LIB	6 SCO	6 SCO	6 CAP	6 AQU	6 ARI
10 SCO	9 SAG	8 SAG	9 AQU	8 PIS	8 TAU
12 SAG	11 CAP	10 CAP	11 PIS	10 ARI	11 GEM
14 CAP	13 AQU	12 AQU	13 ARI	12 TAU	13 CAN
16 AQU	15 PIS	14 PIS	15 TAU	14 GEM	16 LEO
18 PIS	17 ARI	16 ARI	17 GEM	17 CAN	18 VIR
20 ARI	19 TAU	18 TAU	19 CAN	19 LEO	21 LIB
23 TAU	21 GEM	21 GEM	22 LEO	22 VIR	23 SCO
25 GEM	24 CAN	23 CAN	25 VIR	24 LIB	25 SAG
28 CAN	26 LEO	26 LEO	27 LIB	27 SCO	27 CAP
30 LEO		28 VIR	29 SCO	29 SAG	29 AQU
		31 LIB		31 CAP	

JUL	AUG	SEP	OCT	NOV	DEC
1 PIS	2 TAU	1 GEM	3 LEO	2 VIR	1 LIB
4 ARI	4 GEM	3 CAN	5 VIR	4 LIB	4 SCO
6 TAU	7 CAN	5 LEO	8 LIB	6 SCO	6 SAG
8 GAM	9 LEO	8 VIR	10 SCO	9 SAG	9 CAP
10 CAN	12 VIR	10 LIB	13 SAG	11 CAP	10 AQU
13 LEO	14 LIB	13 SCO	15 CAP	13 AQU	13 PIS
15 VIR	17 SCO	15 SAG	17 AQU	15 PIS	15 ARI
18 LIB	19 SAG	18 CAP	19 PIS	17 ARI	17 TAU
20 SCO	21 CAP	20 AQU	21 ARI	20 TAU	19 GEM
23 SAG	23 AQU	22 PIS	23 TAU	22 GEM	21 CAN
25 CAP	25 PIS	24 ARI	25 GEM	24 CAN	24 LEO
27 AQU	27 ARI	26 TAU	28 CAN	26 LEO	26 VIR
29 PIS	29 TAU	28 GEM	30 LEO	29 VIR	29 LIB
31 ARI		30 CAN			31 SCO

1962 MOON SIGNS

JAN	FEB	MAR	APR	MAY	JUN
3 SAG	1 CAP	1 CAP	1 PIS	1 ARI	1 GEM
5 CAP	3 AQU	3 AQU	3 ARI	3 TAU	3 CAN
7 AQU	5 PIS	5 PIS	5 TAU	5 GEM	6 LEO
9 PIS	7 ARI	7 ARI	7 GEM	7 CAN	8 VIR
11 ARI	9 TAU	9 TAU	9 CAN	9 LEO	10 LIB
13 TAU	12 GEM	11 GEM	12 LEO	12 VIR	13 SCO
15 GEM	14 CAN	13 CAN	14 VIR	14 LIB	15 SAG
18 CAN	16 LEO	16 LEO	17 LIB	17 SCO	18 CAP
20 LEO	19 VIR	18 VIR	19 SCO	19 SAG	20 AQU
23 VIR	21 LIB	21 LIB	22 SAG	21 CAP	22 PIS
25 LIB	24 SCO	23 SCO	24 CAP	24 AQU	24 ARI
28 SCO	26 SAG	26 SAG	26 AQU	26 PIS	26 TAU
30 SAG		28 CAP	298 PIS	28 ARI	28 GEM
		30 AQU		30 TAU	

JUL	AUG	SEP	OCT	NOV	DEC
1 CAN	2 VIR	3 SCO	3 SAG	1 CAP	1 AQU
3 LEO	4 LIB	5 SAG	5 CAP	4 AQU	3 PIS
5 VIR	7 SCO	8 CAP	7 AQU	6 PIS	5 ARI
8 LIB	9 SAG	10 AQU	10 PIS	8 ARI	7 TAU
10 SCO	11 CAP	12 PIS	12 ARI	10 TAU	9 GEM
13 SAG	14 AQU	14 ARI	14 TAU	12 GEM	11 CAN
15 CAP	16 PIS	16 TAU	16 GEM	14 CAN	14 LEO
17 AQU	18 ARI	18 GEM	18 CAN	16 LEO	16 VIR
19 PIS	20 TAU	20 CAN	20 LEO	19 VIR	19 LIB
21 ARI	22 GEM	23 LEO	22 VIR	21 LIB	21 SCO
23 TAU	24 CAN	25 VIR	25 LIB	24 SCO	24 SAG
26 GEM	26 LEO	28 LIB	27 SCO	26 SAG	26 CAP
28 CAN	29 VIR	30 SCO	30 SAG	29 CAP	28 AQU
30 LEO	31 LIB				30 PIS

1963 MOON SIGNS

JAN	FEB	MAR	APR	MAY	JUN
1 ARI	2 GEM	1 GEM	2 LEO	2 VIR	3 SCO
4 TAU	4 CAN	3 CAN	4 VIR	4 LIB	5 SAG
6 GEM	6 LEO	6 LEO	7 LIB	7 SCO	8 CAP
8 CAN	9 VIR	8 VIR	9 SCO	9 SAG	10 AQU
10 LEO	11 LIB	11 LIB	12 CAP	12 PIS	12 VIR
12 VIR	14 SCO	13 SCO	14 AQU	14 AQU	15 ARI
15 LIB	16 SAG	16 SAG	17 AQU	16 PIS	17 TAU
17 SCO	19 CAP	18 CAP	19 PIS	18 ARI	19 GEM
20 SAG	21 AQU	20 AQU	21 ARI	20 TAU	21 LEO
22 CAP	23 PIS	23 PIS	23 TAU	22 GEM	23 LEO
25 AQU	25 ARI	25 ARI	25 GEM	24 CAN	25 VIR
27 PIS	27 TAU	27 TAU	27 CAN	27 LEO	28 LIB
29 ARI		29 GEM	29 LEO	29 VIR	30 SCO
31 TAU		31 CAN		31 LIB	

JUL	AUG	SEP	OCT	NOV	DEC
3 SCO	1 CAP	2 PIS	2 ARI	2 GEM	2 CAN
5 CAP	4 AQU	4 ARI	4 TAU	4 CAN	4 LEO
7 AQU	6 PIS	7 TAU	6 GEM	6 LEO	6 VIR
10 PIS	8 ARI	9 GEM	8 CAN	9 VIR	8 LIB
12 ARI	10 TAU	11 CAN	10 LEO	11 LIB	11 SCO
14 TAU	12 GEM	13 LEO	12 VIR	14 SCO	13 SAG
16 GEM	14 CAN	15 VIR	15 LIB	16 SAG	16 CAP
18 CAN	17 LEO	18 LIB	17 SCO	19 CAP	18 AQU
20 LEO	19 VIR	20 SCO	20 SAG	21 AQU	21 PIS
23 VIR	21 LIB	23 SAG	22 CAP	24 PIS	23 ARI
25 LIB	24 SCO	25 CAP	25 AQU	26 ARI	25 TAU
27 SCO	26 SAG	28 AQU	27 PIS	28 TAU	27 GEM
30 SAG	29 CAP	30 PIS	29 ARI	30 GEM	29 CAN
	31 AQU		31 TAU		31 LEO

1964 MOON SIGNS

JAN	FEB	MAR	APR	MAY	JUN
2 VIR	1 LIB	2 SCO	1 SAG	1 CAP	2 PIS
5 LIB	4 SCO	4 SAG	3 CAP	3 AQU	4 ARI
7 SCO	6 SAG	7 CAP	6 AQU	5 PIS	6 TAU
10 SAG	9 CAP	9 AQU	8 PIS	8 ARI	8 GEM
12 CAP	11 AQI	12 PIS	10 ARI	10 TAU	10 CAN
15 AQU	13 PIS	14 ARI	12 TAU	12 GEM	12 LEO
17 PIS	16 ARI	16 TAU	14 GEM	14 CAN	14 VIR
19 ARI	18 TAU	18 GEM	16 CAN	16 LEO	17 LIB
21 TAU	20 GEM	20 CAN	19 LEO	18 VIR	19 SAG
24 GEM	22 CAN	22 LEO	21 VIR	20 LIB	20 SAG
26 CAN	24 LEO	25 VIR	23 LIB	23 SCO	24 CAP
28 LEO	26 VIR	27 LIB	26 SCO	25 SAG	27 AQU
30 VIR	28 LIB	29 SCO	28 SAG	28 CAP	29 PIS
				30 AQU	
JUL	AUG	SEP	OCT	NOV	DEC
1 ARI	2 GEM	2 LEO	2 VIR	3 SCO	2 SAG
4 TAU	4 CAN	5 VIR	4 LIB	5 SAG	5 CAP
6 GEM	6 LEO	7 LIB	6 SCO	8 CAP	7 AQU
8 CAN	8 VIR	9 SCO	9 SAG	10 AQU	10 PIS
10 LEO	10 LIB	11 SAG	11 CAP	13 PIS	12 ARI
12 VIR	13 SCO	14 CAP	14 AQU	15 ARI	15 TAU
14 LIB	15 SAG	16 AQU	16 PIS	17 TAU	17 GEM
16 SCO	18 CAP	19 PIS	19 ARI	19 GEM	19 CAN
19 SAG	20 AQU	21 ARI	21 TAU	21 CAN	21 LEO
21 CAP	23 PIS	23 TAU	23 GEM	23 LEO	23 VIR
24 AQU	25 ARI	25 GEM	25 CAN	25 VIR	25 LIB
26 PIS	27 TAU	28 CAN	27 LEO	28 LIB	27 SCO
29 ARI	29 GEM	30 LEO	29 VIR	30 SCO	30 SAG
31 TAU	31 CAN		31 LIB		

1965 MOON SIGNS

JAN	FEB	MAR	APR	MAY	JUN
1 CAP	2 PIS	2 PIS	3 TAU	2 GEM	1 CAN
4 AQU	5 ARI	4 ARI	5 GEM	4 CAN	3 LEO
6 PIS	7 TAU	6 TAU	7 CAN	6 LEO	5 VIR
9 ARI	9 GEM	9 GEM	9 LEO	8 VIR	7 LIB
11 TAU	11 CAN	11 CAN	11 VIR	11 LIB	9 SCO
13 GEM	13 LEO	13 LEO	13 LIB	13 SCO	12 SAG
15 CAN	16 VIR	15 VIR	16 SCO	15 SAG	14 CAP
17 LEO	18 LIB	17 LIB	18 SAG	18 CAP	16 AQU
19 VIR	20 SCO	19 SCO	20 CAP	20 AQU	19 PIS
21 LIB	22 SAG	22 SAG	23 AQU	23 PIS	21 ARI
23 SCO	25 CAP	24 CAP	25 PIS	25 ARI	24 TAU
26 SAG	27 AQU	27 AQU	28 ARI	27 TAU	26 GEM
28 CAP		29 PIS	30 TAU	30 GEM	28 CAN
31 AQU		31 ARI			30 LEO
JUL	AUG	SEP	OCT	NOV	DEC
2 VIR	3 SCO	1 SAG	1 CAP	2 PIS	2 ARI
4 LIB	5 SAG	4 CAP	4 AQU	5 ARI	5 TAU
6 SCO	7 CAP	6 AQU	6 PIS	7 TAU	7 GEM
9 SAG	10 AQU	9 PIS	9 ARI	9 GEM	9 CAN
11 CAP	12 PIS	11 ARI	11 TAU	12 CAN	11 LEO
14 AQU	15 ARI	14 TAU	13 GEM	14 LEO	13 VIR
16 PIS	17 TAU	16 GEM	15 CAN	16 VIR	15 LIB
19 ARI	20 GEM	18 CAN	17 LEO	18 LIB	17 SCO
21 TAU	22 CAN	20 LEO	20 VIR	20 SCO	20 SAG
23 GEM	24 LEO	22 VIR	22 LIB	22 SAG	22 CAP
25 CAN	26 VIR	24 LIB	24 SCO	25 CAP	25 AQU
27 LEO	28 LIB	26 SCO	26 SAG	27 AQU	27 PIS
29 VIR	30 SCO	29 SAG	28 CAP	30 PIS	30 ARI
31 LIB			31 AQU		

1966 MOON SIGNS

JAN	FEB	MAR	APR	MAY	JUN
1 TAU	2 CAN	1 CAN	2 VIR	1 LIB	2 SAG
3 GEM	4 LEO	3 LEO	4 LIB	3 SCO	4 CAP
5 CAN	6 VIR	5 VIR	6 SCO	5 SCO	6 AQU
7 LEO	8 LIB	7 LIB	8 SAG	8 CAP	8 PIS
9 VIR	10 SCO	9 SCO	10 CAP	10 AQU	11 ARI
11 LIB	12 SAG	12 SAG	13 AQU	12 PIS	14 TAU
14 SCO	15 CAP	14 CAP	15 PIS	15 ARI	16 GEM
16 SAG	17 AQU	16 AQU	18 ARI	17 TAU	18 CAN
18 CAP	20 PIS	19 PIS	20 TAU	20 GEM	20 LEO
21 AQU	22 ARI	21 ARI	22 GEM	22 CAN	23 VIR
23 PIS	25 TAU	24 TAU	25 CAN	24 LEO	25 LIB
26 ARI	27 GEM	26 GEM	27 LEO	26 VIR	27 SCO
28 TAU		29 CAN	29 VIR	28 LIB	29 SAG
31 GEM		31 LEO		31 SCO	
JUL	AUG	SEP	OCT	NOV	DEC
1 CAP	2 PIS	1 ARI	1 TAU	2 CAN	2 LEO
4 AQU	5 ARI	4 TAU	3 GEM	4 LEO	4 VIR
6 PIS	7 TAU	6 GEM	6 CAN	6 VIR	6 LIB
9 ARI	10 GEM	9 CAN	8 LEO	8 LIB	8 SCO
11 TAU	12 CAN	11 LEO	10 VIR	11 SCO	10 SAG
14 GEM	14 LEO	13 VIR	12 LIB	13 SAG	12 CAP
14 CAN	16 VIR	15 LIB	14 SCO	15 CAP	14 AQU
18 LEO	18 LIB	17 SCO	16 SAG	17 AQU	17 PIS
20 VIR	20 SCO	19 SAG	18 CAP	20 PIS	19 ARI
22 LIB	22 SAG	21 CAP	21 AQU	22 ARI	22 TAU
24 SCO	25 CAP	23 AQU	23 PIS	25 TAU	24 GEM
26 SAG	27 AQU	26 PIS	26 ARI	28 GEM	27 CAN
29 CAP	30 PIS	28 ARI	28 TAU	29 CAN	29 LEO
31 AQU			31 GEM		31 VIR

1967 MOON SIGNS

JAN	FEB	MAR	APR	MAY	JUN
2 LIB	3 SAG	2 SAG	3 AQU	2 PIS	1 ARI
4 SCO	5 CAP	4 CAP	5 PIS	5 ARI	4 TAU
6 SAG	7 AQU	6 AQU	8 ARI	7 TAU	6 GEM
9 CAP	10 PIS	9 PIS	10 TAU	10 GEM	9 CAN
11 AQU	12 ARI	11 ARI	13 GEM	12 CAN	11 LEO
13 PIS	15 TAU	14 TAU	15 CAN	15 LEO	13 VIR
16 ARI	17 GEM	16 GEM	17 LEO	17 VIR	15 LIB
18 TAU	19 CAN	19 CAN	20 VIR	19 LIB	17 SCO
21 GEM	22 LEO	21 LEO	22 LIB	21 SCO	19 SAG
23 CAN	24 VIR	23 VIR	24 SAG	23 SAG	21 CAP
25 LEO	26 LIB	25 LIB	26 SAG	25 CAP	24 AQU
27 VIR	28 SCO	27 SCO	29 CAP	27 AQU	26 PIS
29 LIB		29 SAG	30 AQU	30 PIS	28 ARI
31 SCO		31 CAP			
JUL	AUG	SEP	OCT	NOV	DEC
1 TAU	2 CAN	1 LEO	2 LIB	1 SCO	2 CAP
3 GEM	4 LEO	3 VIR	4 SCO	3 SAG	4 AQU
6 CAN	7 VIR	5 LIB	6 SAG	5 CAP	7 PIS
8 LEO	9 LIB	7 SCO	9 CAP	7 AQU	9 ARI
10 VIR	11 SCO	9 SAG	11 AQU	9 PIS	12 TAU
12 LIB	13 SAG	11 CAP	13 PIS	12 ARI	14 GEM
15 SCO	15 CAP	14 AQU	16 ARI	14 TAU	17 CAN
17 SAG	17 AQU	16 PIS	18 TAU	17 GEM	19 LEO
19 CAP	20 PIS	18 ARI	21 GEM	19 CAN	21 VIR
21 AQU	22 ARI	21 TAU	23 CAB	22 LEO	24 LIB
23 PIS	25 TAU	23 GEM	26 LEO	2 VIR	26 SCO
26 ARI	27 GEM	26 CAN	28 VIR	26 LIB	28 SAG
28 TAU	30 CAN	28 LEO	30 LIB	28 SCO	30 CAP
31 GEM		30 VIR		30 SAG	

517

1968 MOON SIGNS

JAN	FEB	MAR	APR	MAY	JUN
1 AQU	2 ARI	3 TAU	2 GEM	1 CAN	2 VIR
3 PIS	4 TAU	5 GEM	4 CAN	4 LEO	5 LIB
6 ARI	7 GEM	8 CAN	7 LEO	6 VIR	7 SCO
8 TAU	9 CAN	10 LEO	9 VIR	8 LIB	9 SAG
11 GEM	12 LEO	12 VIR	11 LIB	10 SCO	11 CAP
13 CAN	14 VIR	14 LIB	13 SCO	12 SAG	13 AQU
15 LEO	16 LIB	17 SCO	15 SAG	14 CAP	15 PIS
18 VIR	18 SCO	19 SAG	17 CAP	16 AQU	17 ARI
20 LIB	20 SAG	21 CAP	19 AQU	19 PIS	20 TAU
22 SCO	22 CAP	23 AQU	21 PIS	21 ARI	22 GEM
24 SAG	25 AQU	25 PIS	24 ARI	24 TAU	24 CAN
26 CAP	27 PIS	28 ARI	26 TAU	26 GEM	27 LEO
28 AQU	29 ARI	30 TAU	29 GEM	29 CAN	30 VIR
31 PIS				31 LEO	
JUL	AUG	SEP	OCT	NOV	DEC
2 LIB	3 SAG	1 CAP	2 PIS	1 ARI	1 TAU
4 SCO	5 CAP	3 AQU	5 ARI	3 TAU	3 GEM
6 SAG	7 AQU	5 PIS	7 TAU	6 GEM	6 CAN
8 CAP	9 PIS	7 ARI	10 GEM	8 CAN	8 LEO
10 AQU	11 ARI	10 TAU	12 CAN	11 LEO	11 VIR
12 PIS	13 TAU	13 GEM	15 LEO	13 VIR	13 LIB
15 ARI	16 GEM	15 CAN	17 VIR	16 LIB	15 SCO
17 TAU	18 CAN	17 LEO	19 LIB	18 SCO	17 SAG
20 GEM	21 LEO	20 VIR	21 SCO	20 SAG	19 CAP
22 CAN	23 VIR	22 LIB	23 SAG	22 CAP	21 AQU
25 LEO	25 LIB	24 SCO	25 CAP	24 AQU	23 PIS
27 VIR	28 SCO	26 SAG	27 AQU	26 PIS	26 ARI
29 LIB	30 SAG	28 CAP	30 PIS	28 ARI	28 TAU
31 SCO		30 AQU			30 GEM

1969 MOON SIGNS

JAN	FEB	MAR	APR	MAY	JUN
2 CAN	1 LEO	2 VIR	1 LIB	1 SCO	1 CAP
4 LEO	3 VIR	5 LIB	3 SCO	3 SAG	3 AQU
7 VIR	6 LIB	7 SCO	5 SAG	5 CAP	5 PIS
9 LIB	8 SCO	9 SAG	8 CAP	7 AQU	7 ARI
12 SCO	10 SAG	11 CAP	10 AQU	9 PIS	10 TAU
14 SAG	12 CAP	13 ARU	12 PIS	11 ARI	12 GEM
16 CAP	14 AQU	16 PIS	14 ARI	14 TAU	15 CAN
18 AQU	16 PIS	18 ARI	16 TAU	16 GEM	17 LEO
20 PIS	18 ARI	20 TAU	19 GEM	19 CAN	20 VIR
22 ARI	21 TAU	22 GEM	21 CAN	21 LEO	22 LIB
24 TAU	23 GEM	25 CAN	24 LEO	23 VIR	25 SCO
27 GEM	26 CAN	27 LEO	26 VIR	26 LIB	27 SAG
29 CAN	28 LEO	30 VIR	29 LIB	28 SCO	29 CAP
				30 SAG	
JUL	AUG	SEP	OCT	NOV	DEC
1 AQU	1 ARI	2 GEM	2 CAN	1 LEO	1 VIR
3 PIS	3 TAU	5 CAN	4 LEO	3 VIR	3 LIB
5 ARI	6 GEM	7 LEO	7 VIR	6 LIB	5 SCO
7 TAU	8 CAN	10 VIR	9 LIB	8 SCO	8 SAG
10 GEM	11 LEO	12 LIB	12 SCO	10 SAG	10 CAP
12 CAN	13 VIR	14 SCO	14 SAG	12 CAP	12 AQU
15 LEO	16 LIB	17 SAG	16 CAP	14 AQU	14 PIS
17 VIR	18 SCO	19 CAP	18 AQU	16 PIS	16 ARI
20 LIB	20 SAG	21 AQU	20 PIS	19 ARI	18 TAU
22 SCO	22 CAP	23 PIS	22 ARI	21 TAU	20 GEM
24 SAG	24 AQU	25 ARI	25 TAU	23 GEM	23 CAN
26 CAP	26 PIS	27 TAU	27 GEM	26 CAN	25 LEO
28 AQU	29 ARI	28 GEM	29 CAN	28 LEO	28 VIR
30 PIS	31 TAU				30 LIB

1970 MOON SIGNS

JAN	FEB	MAR	APR	MAY	JUN
2 SCO	2 CAP	2 CAP	2 PIS	2 ARI	2 GEM
4 SAG	4 AQU	4 AQU	4 ARI	4 TAU	5 GEM
6 CAP	6 PIS	6 PIS	6 TAU	6 GEM	7 LEO
8 AQU	8 ARI	8 ARI	9 GEM	8 CAN	10 VIR
10 PIS	11 TAU	10 TAU	11 CAN	11 LEO	12 LIB
12 ARI	13 GEM	12 GEM	14 LEO	13 VIR	15 SCO
14 TAU	15 CAN	15 CAN	16 VIR	16 LIB	17 SAG
17 GEM	18 LEO	17 LEO	19 LIB	18 SCO	19 CAP
19 CAN	20 VIR	20 VIR	21 SCO	20 SCG	21 AQU
22 LEO	23 LIB	22 LIB	23 SAG	23 CAP	23 PIS
24 VIR	25 SCO	25 SCO	25 CAP	25 AQU	25 ARI
27 LIB	28 SAG	27 SAG	27 AQU	27 PIS	27 TAU
29 SCO		29 CAP	30 PIS	29 ARI	30 GEM
31 SAG		31 AQU		31 TAU	
JUL	AUG	SEP	OCT	NOV	DEC
2 CAN	1 LEO	2 LIB	2 SCO	3 CAP	2 AQU
4 LEO	3 VIR	5 SCO	4 SAG	5 AQU	4 PIS
7 VIR	6 LIB	7 SAG	6 CAP	6 PIS	6 ARI
10 LIB	8 SCO	9 CAP	9 AQU	9 ARI	8 TAU
12 SCO	11 SAG	11 AQU	11 PIS	11 TAU	11 GEM
14 SAG	13 CAP	13 PIS	13 ARI	13 GEM	13 CAN
16 CAP	15 AQU	15 ARI	15 TAU	16 CAN	15 LEO
18 AQU	17 PIS	17 TAU	17 GEM	18 LEO	18 VIR
20 PIS	19 ARI	19 GEM	19 CAN	20 VIR	20 LIB
22 ARI	21 TAU	22 CAN	22 LEO	23 LIB	23 SCO
25 TAU	23 GEM	24 LEO	24 VIR	25 SCO	25 SAG
27 GEM	26 CAN	27 VIR	26 LIB	28 SAG	27 CAP
29 CAN	28 LEO	28 LIB	29 SCO	30 CAP	29 AQU
	31 VIR		31 SAG		31 PIS

1971 MOON SIGNS

JAN	FEB	MAR	APR	MAY	JUN
3 ARI	1 TAU	2 GEM	1 CAN	1 LEO	2 LIB
5 TAU	3 GEM	5 CAN	3 LEO	3 VIR	5 SCO
7 GEM	5 CAN	7 LEO	6 VIR	6 LIB	7 SAG
9 CAN	8 LEO	10 VIR	8 LIB	8 SCO	9 CAP
12 LEO	10 VIR	12 LIB	11 SCO	11 SAG	11 AQU
14 VIR	13 LIB	15 SCO	13 SAG	13 CAP	14 PIS
17 LIB	15 SCO	17 SAG	16 CAP	15 AQU	16 ARI
19 SCO	18 SAG	19 CAP	18 AQU	17 PIS	18 TAU
22 SAG	20 CAP	22 AQU	20 PIS	20 ARI	20 GEM
24 CAP	22 AQU	24 PIS	22 ARI	22 TAU	22 CAN
26 AQU	24 PIS	26 ARI	24 TAU	24 GEM	24 LEO
28 PIS	26 ARI	28 TAU	26 GEM	26 CAN	27 VIR
30 ARI	28 TAU	30 GEM	28 CAN	28 LEO	29 LIB
				30 VIR	
JUL	AUG	SEP	OCT	NOV	DEC
2 SCO	1 SAG	2 AQU	1 PIS	2 TAU	1 GEM
4 SAG	3 CAP	4 PIS	3 ARI	4 GEM	3 CAN
7 CAP	5 AQU	6 ARI	5 TAU	6 CAN	5 LEO
9 AQU	7 PIS	8 TAU	7 GEM	8 LEO	8 VIR
11 PIS	9 ARI	10 GEM	9 CAN	10 VIR	10 LIB
13 ARI	11 TAU	12 CAN	12 L;EO	13 LIB	13 SCO
15 TAU	13 GEM	14 LEO	14 VIR	15 SCO	15 SAG
17 GEM	16 CAN	17 VIR	16 LIB	18 SAG	17 CAP
19 CAN	18 LEO	19 LIB	19 SCO	20 CAP	20 AQU
22 LEO	20 VIR	22 SCO	22 SAG	23 AQU	22 PIS
24 VIR	23 LIB	24 SAG	24 CAP	25 PIS	24 ARI
27 L;IB	26 SCO	27 CAP	26 AQU	27 ARI	25 TAU
29 SCO	28 SAG	29 AQU	29 PIS	29 TAU	28 GEM
	30 CAP		31 ARI		30 CAN

1972 MOON SIGNS

JAN	FEB	MAR	APR	MAY	JUN
2 LEO	3 LIB	1 LIB	2 SAG	2 CAP	1 AQU
4 VIR	5 SCO	5 SCO	5 CAP	6 AQU	3 PIS
6 LIB	8 SAG	6 SAG	7 AQU	7 PIS	5 ARI
9 SCO	10 CAP	9 CAP	10 PIS	9 ARI	7 TAU
11 SAG	12 AQU	11 AQU	12 ARI	11 TAU	9 GEM
14 CAP	15 ARI	13 PIS	14 ATU	13 GEM	11 CAN
16 AQU	17 ARI	15 ARI	16 GEM	15 CAN	14 LEO
18 PIS	19 TAU	17 TAU	18 CAN	17 LEO	16 VIR
20 ARI	21 GEM	19 GEM	20 LEO	19 VIR	18 LIB
23 TAU	23 CAN	21 CAN	22 VIR	22 LIB	21 SCO
25 GEM	25 LEO	24 LEO	25 LIB	24 SCO	23 SAG
27 CAN	28 VIR	26 VIR	27 SCO	27 SAG	26 CAP
27 LEO		28 LIB	30 SAG	29 CAP	28 AQU
31 VIR		31 SCO			30 PIS

JUL	AUG	SEP	OCT	NOV	DEC
3 ARI	1 TAU	1 CAN	1 LEO	2 LIB	1 CAO
5 TAU	3 GEM	4 LEO	3 VIR	4 SCO	4 SAG
7 GEM	5 CAN	6 VIR	5 LIB	7 SAG	7 CAP
9 CAN	7 LEO	8 LIB	8 SCO	9 CAP	9 AQU
11 LEO	10 VIR	11 SCO	10 SAG	12 AQU	11 PIS
13 VIR	12 LIB	13 SAG	13 CAP	14 PIS	14 ARI
15 LIB	14 SCO	16 CAP	15 AQU	16 ARI	16 TAU
18 SCO	17 SAG	18 AQU	18 PIS	18 TAU	18 GEM
20 SAG	19 CAP	20 PIS	20 ARI	20 GEM	20 CAN
23 CAP	22 AQU	22 ARI	22 TAU	22 CAN	22 LEO
25 AQU	24 PIS	24 TAU	24 GEM	24 LEO	24 VIR
28 PIS	26 ARI	27 GEM	26 CAN	27 VIR	26 LIB
30 ARI	28 TAU	29 CAN	28 LEO	29 LIB	29 SCO
	30 GEM		30 VIR		31 SAG

1973 MOON SIGNS

JAN	FEB	MAR	APR	MAY	JUN
3 CAP	2 AQU	1 AQU	2 ARI	1 TAU	2 CAN
5 AQU	4 PIS	3 PIS	4 TAU	3 GEM	4 LEO
8 PIS	6 ARI	5 ARI	6 GEM	5 CAN	6 VIR
10 ARI	8 TAU	8 TAU	8 CAN	7 LEO	8 LIB
12 TAU	10 GEM	10 GEM	10 LEO	10 VIR	11 SCO
14 GEM	13 CAN	12 CAN	12 VIR	12 LIB	13 SAG
16 CAN	15 LEO	14 LEO	15 LIB	14 SCO	16 CAP
18 LEO	17 VIR	16 VIR	17 SCO	17 SAG	18 AQU
20 VIR	19 LIB	19 LIB	20 SAG	19 CAP	21 PIS
23 LIB	21 SCO	21 SCO	22 CAP	22 AQU	23 ARI
25 SCO	24 SAG	23 SAG	25 AQU	24 PIS	25 TAU
28 SAG	26 CAP	26 CAP	27 PIS	27 ARI	27 GEM
30 CAP		28 AQU	29 ARI	29 TAU	29 CAN
		31 PIS		31 GEM	

JUL	AUG	SEP	OCT	NOV	DEC
1 LEO	2 LIB	1 SCO	3 CAP	2 AQU	1 PIS
3 VIR	4 SCO	3 SAG	5 AQU	4 PIS	4 ARI
5 LIB	7 SAG	5 CAP	8 PIS	6 ARI	6 TAU
8 SCO	9 CAP	8 AQU	10 ARI	9 TAU	8 GEM
10 SAG	12 AQU	10 PIS	12 TAU	11 GEM	10 CAN
13 CAP	14 PIS	13 ARI	14 GEM	13 CAN	12 LEO
15 AQU	16 ARI	15 TAU	16 CAN	15 LEO	14 VIR
18 PIS	19 TAU	17 GEM	19 LEO	17 VIR	16 LIB
20 ARI	21 GEM	19 CAN	21 VIR	19 LIB	19 SCO
22 TAU	23 CAN	21 LEO	23 LIB	22 SCO	21 SAG
25 GEM	25 LEO	23 VIR	25 SCO	24 SAG	24 CAP
27 CAN	27 VIR	26 LIB	28 SAG	26 CAP	26 AQU
29 LEO	29 LIB	28 SCO	30 CAP	29 AQU	29 PIS
31 VIR		30 SAG			31 ARI

1974 MOON SIGNS

JAN	FEB	MAR	APR	MAY	JUN
2 TAU	1 GEM	2 CAN	1 LEO	2 LIB	1 SCO
4 GEM	3 CAN	4 LEO	3 VIR	4 SCO	3 SAG
7 CAN	5 LEO	7 VIR	5 LIB	7 SAG	6 CAP
9 LEO	7 VIR	9 LIB	7 SCO	9 CAP	8 AQU
11 VIR	9 LIB	11 SCO	9 SAG	12 AQU	11 PIS
13 LIB	11 SCO	13 SAG	12 CAP	14 PIS	13 ARI
15 SCO	14 AG	16 CAP	14 AQU	17 ARI	15 TAU
17 SAG	16 CAP	18 AQU	17 PIS	19 TAU	18 GEM
20 CAP	19 AQU	21 PIS	19 ARI	21 GEM	20 CAN
22 AQU	21 PIS	23 ARI	22 TAU	23 CAN	22 LEO
25 PIS	24 ARI	25 TAU	24 GEM	25 LEO	24 VIR
27 ARI	26 TAU	27 GEM	26 CAN	27 VIR	26 LIB
30 TAU	28 GEM	30 CAN	28 LEO	30 LIB	28 SCO
			30 VIR		30 SAG

JUL	AUG	SEP	OCT	NOV	DEC
3 CAP	2 AQU	3 ARI	2 TAU	1 GEM	1 CAN
5 AQU	4 PIS	5 TAU	5 GEM	3 CAN	3 LEO
8 PIS	7 ARI	8 GEM	7 CAN	5 LEO	5 VIR
10 ARI	9 TAU	10 CAN	9 LEO	8 VIR	7 LIB
13 TAU	11 GEM	12 LEO	11 VIR	10 LIB	9 SCO
15 GEM	13 CAN	14 VIR	13 LIB	12 SCO	11 SAG
17 CAN	15 LEO	16 LIB	15 SCO	14 SAG	14 CAP
19 LEO	17 VIR	18 SCO	18 SAG	16 CAP	16 AQU
21 VIR	20 LIB	20 SAG	20 CAP	19 AQU	19 PIS
23 LIB	22 SCO	23 CAP	22 AQU	21 PIS	21 ARI
25 SCO	24 SAG	25 AQU	25 PIS	24 ARI	24 TAU
28 SAG	26 CAP	28 PIS	28 ARI	26 TAU	26 GEM
30 CAP	29 AQU	30 ARI	30 TAU	28 GEM	28 CAN
	31 PIS				30 LEO

1975 MOON SIGNS

JAN	FEB	MAR	APR	MAY	JUN
1 VIR	2 SCO	1 SCO	2 CAP	2 AQU	3 ARI
3 LIB	4 SAG	3 SAG	4 AQU	4 PIS	5 TAU
5 SCO	6 CAP	5 CSP	7 PIS	7 ARI	8 GEM
8 SAG	9 AQU	8 AQU	9 ARI	9 TAU	10 CAN
10 CAP	11 PIS	10 PIS	12 TAU	11 GEM	12 LEO
12 AQU	14 ARI	13 ARI	14 GEM	14 CAN	14 VIR
15 PIS	16 TAU	15 TAU	16 CAN	16 LEO	16 LIB
17 ARI	19 GEM	18 GEM	19 LEO	18 VIR	18 SCO
20 TAU	21 CAN	20 CAN	21 VIR	20 LIB	21 SAG
22 GEM	23 LEO	22 LEO	21 LIB	22 SCO	23 CAP
24 CAN	25 VIR	24 VIR	SCO	24 SAG	25 AQU
26 LEO	27 LIB	26 LIB	27 SAG	27 CAP	28 PIS
28 VIR		28 SCO	29 CAP	29 AQU	30 ARI
30 LIB		30 SAG		31 PIS	

JUL	AUG	SEP	OCT	NOV	DEC
3 TAU	1 GEM	2 LEO	2 VIR	2 SCO	2 SAG
5 GEM	4 CAN	4 VIR	4 LIB	4 SAG	4 CAP
7 CAN	6 LEO	6 LIB	6 SCO	6 CAP	6 AQU
9 LEO	8 VIR	8 SCO	8 SAG	9 AQU	8 PIS
11 VIR	10 LIB	10 SAG	10 CAP	11 PIS	11 ARI
14 LIB	12 SCO	13 CAP	12 AQU	14 ARI	13 TAU
16 SCO	14 SAG	15 AQU	15 PIS	16 TAU	16 GEM
18 SAG	16 CAP	18 PIS	17 ARI	19 GEM	18 CAN
20 CAP	19 AQU	20 ARI	20 TAU	21 CAN	20 LEO
23 AQU	21 PIS	23 TAU	22 GEM	23 LEO	23 VIR
25 PIS	24 ARI	25 GEM	25 CAN	25 VIR	25 LIB
28 ARI	26 TAU	27 CAN	27 LEO	27 LIB	27 SCO
30 TAU	29 GEM	30 LEO	29 VIR	30 SCO	29 SAG
	31 CAN		31 LIB		31 CAP

1976 MOON SIGNS

JAN	FEB	MAR	APR	MAY	JUN
2 AQU	1 PIS	2 ARI	1 TAU	3 CAN	1 LEO
5 PIS	4 ARI	4 TAU	3 GEM	5 LEO	4 VIR
7 ARI	6 TAU	7 GEM	6 CAN	7 VIR	6 LIB
10 TAU	9 GEM	9 CAN	8 LEO	10 LIB	8 SCO
12 GEM	11 CAN	12 LEO	10 VIR	12 SCO	10 SAG
15 CAN	13 LEO	14 VIR	12 LIB	14 SAG	12 CAP
17 LEO	15 VIR	16 LIB	14 SCO	16 CAP	14 AQU
19 VIR	17 LIB	18 SCO	16 SAG	18 AQU	17 PIS
21 LIB	19 SCO	20 SAG	18 CAP	20 PIS	19 ARI
23 SCO	21 SAG	22 CAP	20 AQU	23 ARI	22 TAU
25 SAG	24 CAP	24 AQU	23 PIS	25 TAU	24 GEM
27 CAP	26 AQU	27 PIS	25 ARI	28 GEM	26 CAN
30 AQU	28 PIS	29 ARI	28 TAU	30 CAN	29 LEO
			30 GEM		

JUL	AUG	SEP	OCT	NOV	DEC
1 VIR	1 SCO	2 CAP	1 AQU	2 ARI	2 TAU
3 LIB	4 SAG	4 AQU	4 PIS	5 TAU	5 GEM
5 SCO	6 CAP	7 PIS	6 ARI	8 GEM	7 CAN
7 SAG	8 AQU	9 ARI	9 TAU	10 CAN	10 LEO
9 CAP	10 PIS	11 TAU	11 GEM	12 LEO	12 VIR
12 AQU	13 ARI	14 GEM	14 CAN	15 VIR	14 LIB
14 PIS	15 TAU	17 CAN	16 LEO	17 LIB	16 SCO
16 ARI	18 GEM	19 LEO	18 VIR	19 SCO	18 SAG
19 TAU	20 CAN	21 VIR	21 LIB	21 SAG	20 CAP
21 GEM	22 LEO	23 LIB	23 SCO	23 CAP	22 AQU
24 CAN	25 VIR	25 SCO	25 SAG	25 AQU	25 PIS
26 LEO	27 LIB	27 SAG	27 CAP	27 PIS	27 ARI
28 VIR	29 SCO	29 CAP	29 AQU	30 ARI	30 TAU
30 LIB	31 SAG		31 PIS		

1977 MOON SIGNS

JAN	FEB	MAR	APR	MAY	JUN
1 GEM	2 LEO	2 LEO	2 LIB	2 SCO	2 CAP
4 CAN	5 VIR	4 VIR	5 SCO	4 SAG	4 AQU
6 LEO	7 LIB	6 LIB	7 SAG	6 CAP	7 PIS
8 VIR	9 SCO	8 SCO	8 CAP	8 AQU	9 ARI
10 LIB	11 SAG	10 SAG	11 AQU	10 PIS	11 TAU
13 SCO	13 CAP	12 CAP	13 PIS	13 ARI	14 GEM
15 SAG	15 AQU	15 AQU	15 ARI	15 TAU	16 CAN
17 CAP	17 PIS	17 PIS	18 TAU	18 GEM	19 LEO
19 AQU	20 ARI	19 ARI	20 GEM	20 CAN	21 VIR
21 PIS	22 TAU	22 TAU	23 CAN	23 LEO	24 LIB
23 ARI	25 GEM	24 GEM	25 LEO	25 VIR	26 SCO
26 TAU	27 CAN	27 CAN	28 VIR	27 LIB	28 SAG
28 GEM		29 LEO	30 LIB	29 SCO	30 CAP
31 CAN		31 VIR		31 SAG	

JUL	AUG	SEP	OCT	NOV	DEC
2 AQU	3 ARI	1 TAU	1 GEM	3 LEO	2 VIR
4 PIS	5 TAU	4 GEM	4 CAN	5 VIR	5 LIB
6 ARI	7 GEM	6 CAN	6 LEO	7 LIB	7 SCO
9 TAU	10 CAN	9 LEO	9 VIR	9 SCO	9 SAG
11 GEM	12 LEO	11 VIR	11 LIB	11 SAG	11 CAP
14 CAN	15 VIR	13 LIB	13 SCO	13 CAP	13 AQU
16 LEO	17 LIB	16 SCO	15 SAG	15 AQU	15 PIS
19 VIR	19 SCO	18 SAG	17 CAP	18 PIS	17 ARI
21 LIB	21 SAG	20 CAP	19 AQU	20 ARI	19 TAU
23 SCO	24 CAP	22 AQU	21 PIS	22 TAU	22 CAM
25 SAG	26 AQU	24 PIS	24 ARI	25 GEM	25 CAN
27 CAP	28 PIS	26 ARI	26 TAU	27 CAN	27 LEO
29 AQU	30 ARI	28 TAU	28 GEM	30 LEO	30 VIR
31 PIS			31 CAN		

1978 MOON SIGNS

JAN	FEB	MAR	APR	MAY	JUN
1 LIB	2 SAG	1 SAG	1 AQU	1 PIS	1 TAU
3 SCO	4 CAP	3 CAP	3 PIS	3 ARI	4 GEM
5 SAG	6 AQU	5 AQU	6 ARI	5 TAU	6 CAN
7 CAP	8 PIS	7 PIS	8 TAU	8 GEM	9 LEO
9 AQU	10 ARI	9 ARI	10 GEM	10 CAN	11 VIR
11 PIS	12 TAU	12 TAU	13 CAN	13 LEO	14 LIB
13 ARI	15 GEM	14 GEM	15 LEO	15 VIR	16 SCO
16 TAU	17 CAN	16 CAN	18 VIR	17 LIB	18 SAG
18 GEM	20 LEO	19 LEO	20 LIB	20 SCO	20 CAP
21 CAN	22 VIR	21 VIR	22 SCO	22 SAG	22 AQU
23 LEO	24 LIB	24 LIB	24 SAG	24 CAP	24 PIS
26 VIR	27 SCO	26 SCO	26 CAP	26 AQU	26 ARI
28 LIB		28 SAG	29 AQU	28 PIS	29 TAU
30 SCO		30 CAP		30 ARI	

JUL	AUG	SEP	OCT	NOV	DEC
1 GEM	2 LEO	1 VIR	1 LIB	2 SAG	1 CAP
4 CAN	5 VIR	4 LIB	3 SCO	4 CAP	3 AQU
6 LEO	7 LIB	6 SCO	5 SAG	6 AQU	5 PIS
9 VIR	10 SCO	8 SAG	8 CAP	8 PIS	7 ARI
11 LIB	12 SAG	10 CAP	10 AQU	10 ARI	10 TAU
13 SCO	14 CAP	12 AQU	12 PIS	12 TAU	12 GEM
16 SAG	16 AQU	14 PIS	14 ARI	15 GEM	14 CAN
18 CAP	18 PIS	17 ARI	16 TAU	17 CAN	17 LEO
20 AQU	20 ARI	19 TAU	18 GEM	20 LEO	19 VIR
22 PIS	22 TAU	21 GEM	21 CAN	22 VIR	22 LIB
24 ARI	25 GEM	23 CAN	23 LEO	25 LIB	24 SCO
26 TAU	27 CAN	26 LEO	26 VIR	27 SCO	27 CAP
28 GEM	30 LEO	28 VIR	28 LIB	29 SAG	29 CAP
31 CAN			31 SCO		31 AQU

1979 MOON SIGNS

JAN	FEB	MAR	APR	MAY	JUN
2 PIS	2 TAU	2 TAU	3 CAN	2 LEO	1 VIR
4 ARI	5 GEM	4 GEM	5 LEO	5 VIR	4 LIB
6 TAU	7 CAN	6 CAN	8 VIR	7 LIB	6 SCO
8 GEM	9 LEO	9 LEO	10 LIB	10 SCO	8 SAG
11 CAN	12 VIR	11 VIR	12 SCO	12 SAG	11 CAP
13 LEO	15 LIB	14 LIB	15 SAG	14 CAP	13 AQU
16 VIR	17 SCO	16 SCO	17 CAP	16 AQU	15 PIS
18 LIB	19 SAG	19 SAG	19 AQU	18 PIS	17 ARI
21 SCO	21 CAP	21 CAP	21 PIS	21 ARI	19 TAU
23 SAG	24 AQU	23 AQU	23 ARI	23 TAU	21 GEM
25 CAP	26 PIS	25 PIS	25 TAU	25 GEM	24 CAN
27 AQU	28 ARI	27 ARI	28 GEM	27 CAN	26 LEO
29 PIS		29 TAU	30 CAN	30 LEO	29 VIR
31 ARI		31 GEM			

JUL	AUG	SEP	OCT	NOV	DEC
1 LIB	2 SAG	1 CAP	2 PIS	1 ARI	2 GEM
4 SCO	4 CAP	3 AQU	4 ARI	3 TAU	4 CAN
6 SAG	6 AQU	5 PIS	6 TAU	5 GEM	7 LEO
8 CAP	8 PIS	7 ARI	8 GEM	7 CAN	9 VIR
10 AQU	10 ARI	9 TAU	11 CAN	9 LEO	12 LIB
12 PIS	13 TAU	11 GEM	13 LEO	12 VIR	14 SCO
14 ARI	15 GEM	13 CAN	16 VIR	14 LIB	17 SAG
16 TAU	17 CAN	16 LEO	18 LIB	17 SCO	19 CAP
19 GEM	20 LEO	18 VIR	21 SCO	19 SAG	21 AQU
21 CAN	22 VIR	21 LIB	23 SAG	22 CAP	23 PIS
23 LEO	25 LIB	23 SCO	25 CAP	24 AQU	25 ARI
26 VIR	27 SCO	26 SAG	28 AQU	26 PIS	27 TAU
28 LIB	30 SAG	28 CAP	30 PIS	28 ARI	30 GEM
31 SCO		30 AQU		30 TAU	

1980 MOON SIGNS

JAN	FEB	MAR	APR	MAY	JUN
1 CAN	2 VRI	3 LIB	2 SCO	1 SAG	2 AQU
3 LEO	4 LIB	5 SCO	4 SAG	4 CAP	4 PIS
6 VIR	7 SCO	8 SAG	6 CAP	6 AQU	6 ARI
8 LIB	9 SAG	10 CAP	9 AQU	8 PIS	9 TAU
11 SCO	12 CAP	12 AQU	11 PIS	10 ARI	11 GEM
13 SAG	14 AQU	14 PIS	13 ARI	12 TAU	13 CAN
15 CAP	16 PIS	16 ARI	15 TAU	14 GEM	15 LEO
17 AQU	18 ARI	18 TAU	17 GEM	16 CAN	17 VIR
19 PIS	20 TAU	20 GEM	19 CAN	19 LEO	20 LIB
21 ARI	22 GEM	23 CAN	21 LEO	21 VIR	22 SCO
24 TAU	24 CAN	25 LEO	24 VIR	24 LIB	25 SAG
26 GEM	27 LEO	27 VIR	26 LIB	26 SCO	27 CAP
28 CAN	29 VIR	30 LIB	29 SCO	29 SAG	29 AQU
30 LEO				31 CAP	

JUL	AUG	SEP	OCT	NOV	DEC
2 PIS	2 TAU	3 CAN	2 LEO	1 VIR	1 LIB
4 ARI	4 GEM	5 LEO	5 VIR	3 LIB	3 SCO
6 TAU	6 CAN	7 VIR	7 LIB	6 SCO	6 SAG
8 GEM	9 LEO	10 LIB	10 SCO	8 SAG	8 CAP
10 CAN	11 VIR	12 SCO	12 SAG	11 CAP	10 AQU
12 LEO	14 LIB	15 SAG	15 CAP	13 AQU	13 PIS
15 VIR	16 SCO	17 CAP	17 AQU	15 PIS	15 ARI
17 LIB	19 SAG	20 AQU	19 PIS	18 ARI	17 TAU
20 SCO	21 CAP	22 PIS	21 ARI	20 TAU	19 GEM
22 SAG	23 AQU	24 ARI	23 TAU	22 GEM	21 CAN
25 CAP	25 PIS	26 TAU	25 GEM	24 CAN	23 LEO
27 AQU	27 ARI	28 GEM	27 CAN	26 LEO	25 VIR
29 PIS	29 TAU	30 CAN	29 LEO	28 VIR	28 LIB
31 ARI	31 GEM				30 SCO

1982 MOON SIGNS

JAN	FEB	MAR	APR	MAY	JUN
2 ARI	3 GEM	1 GEM	2 LEO	1 VIR	2 SCO
4 TAU	4 CAN	3 CAN	4 VIR	4 LIB	5 SAG
6 GEM	6 LEO	6 LEO	6 LIB	6 SCO	7 CAP
8 CAN	8 VIR	8 VIR	9 SCO	8 SAG	10 AQU
10 LEO	11 LIB	10 LIB	11 SAG	11 CAP	12 PIS
12 VIR	13 SCO	12 SCO	14 CAP	13 AQU	15 ARI
14 LIB	15 SAG	15 SAG	16 AQU	16 PIS	17 TAU
17 SCO	18 CAP	17 CAP	19 PIS	18 ARI	19 GEM
19 SAG	20 AQU	20 AQU	21 ARI	20 TAU	21 CAN
22 CAP	23 PIS	22 PIS	23 TAU	22 GEM	23 LEO
24 AQU	25 ARI	24 ARI	25 GEM	24 CAN	25 VIR
26 PIS	27 TAU	27 TAU	27 CAN	26 LEO	27 LIB
29 ARI		29 GEM	29 LEO	29 VIR	29 SCO
31 TAU		31 CAN		31 LIB	

JUL	AUG	SEP	OCT	NOV	DEC
2 SAG	1 CAP	2 PIS	2 ARI	2 GEM	2 CAN
4 CAP	3 AQU	4 ARI	4 TAU	4 CAN	4 LEO
7 AQU	6 PIS	7 TAU	6 GEM	6 LEO	6 VIR
9 PIS	8 ARI	9 GEM	8 CAN	9 VIR	8 PIB
12 ARI	10 TAU	11 CAN	10 LEO	11 LIB	10 SCO
14 TAU	13 GEM	13 LEO	12 VIR	13 SCO	13 SAG
16 GEM	16 CAN	15 VIR	15 LIB	15 SAG	15 CAN
18 CAN	17 LEO	17 LIB	17 SCO	18 CAP	18 AQU
20 LEO	19 VIR	19 SCO	19 SAG	21 AQU	20 PIS
22 VIR	21 LIB	22 SAG	22 CAP	23 PIS	23 ARI
24 LIB	23 SCO	24 CAP	24 AQU	24 ARI	25 TAU
27 SCO	25 SAG	27 AQU	27 PIS	28 TAU	27 GEM
29 SAG	28 CAP	29 PIS	29 ARI	30 GEM	29 CAN
	31 AQU		31 TAU		31 LEO

1981 MOON SIGNS

JAN	FEB	MAR	APR	MAY	JUN
2 SAG	1 CAP	2 AQU	1 PIS	1 ARI	1 GEM
4 CAP	3 AQU	5 PIS	3 ARI	3 TAU	3 CAN
7 AQU	5 PIS	7 ARI	5 TAU	5 GEM	5 LEO
9 PIS	7 ARI	9 TAU	7 GEM	7 CAN	7 VIR
11 ARI	9 TAU	11 GEM	9 CAN	9 LEO	10 LIB
13 TAU	12 GEM	13 CAN	11 LEO	11 VIR	12 SCO
15 GEM	14 CAN	15 LEO	14 VIR	13 LIB	15 SAG
17 CAN	16 LEO	18 VIR	16 LIB	16 SCO	17 CAP
20 LEO	18 VIR	20 LIB	19 SCO	18 SAG	20 AQU
22 VIR	21 LIB	22 SCO	21 SAG	21 CAP	22 PIS
24 LIB	23 SCO	25 SAG	24 CAP	23 AQU	24 ARI
27 SCO	26 SAG	27 CAP	26 AQU	26 PIS	26 TAU
29 SAG	28 CAP	30 AQU	28 PIS	28 ARI	28 GEM
				30 TAU	30 CAN

JUL	AUG	SEP	OCT	NOV	DEC
2 LEO	1 VIR	2 SCO	2 SAG	1 CAP	1 AQU
5 VIR	3 LIB	5 SAG	5 CAP	3 AQU	3 PIS
7 LIB	6 SCO	7 CAP	7 AQU	6 PIS	5 ARI
10 SCO	8 SAG	10 AQU	9 PIS	8 ARI	7 TAU
12 SAG	11 CAP	12 PIS	11 ARI	10 TAU	9 GEM
15 CAP	13 AQU	14 ARI	13 TAU	12 GEM	11 CAN
17 AQU	16 PIS	16 TAU	15 GEM	14 CAN	13 LEO
19 PIS	18 ARI	18 GEM	18 CAN	16 LEO	16 VIR
21 ARI	20 TAU	20 CAN	20 LEO	18 VIR	18 LIB
24 TAU	22 GEM	22 LEO	22 VIR	21 LIB	20 SCO
26 GEM	24 CAN	25 VIR	24 LIB	23 SCO	23 SAG
28 CAN	26 LEO	27 LIB	27 SCO	26 SAG	25 CAP
30 LEO	28 VIR	29 SCO	29 SAG	28 CAP	28 AQU
	31 LIB				30 PIS

1983 MOON SIGNS

JAN	FEB	MAR	APR	MAY	JUN
2 VIR	1 LIB	2 SCO	1 SAG	1 CAP	2 PIS
4 LIB	3 SCO	5 SAG	3 CAP	3 AQU	5 ARI
7 SCO	5 SAG	7 CAP	6 AQU	6 PIS	7 TAU
9 SAG	8 CAP	10 AQU	8 PIS	8 ARI	9 GEM
12 CAP	12 AQU	12 PIS	11 ARI	11 TAU	11 CAN
14 AQU	13 PIS	15 ARI	13 TAU	13 GEM	13 LEO
17 PIS	15 ARI	15 TAU	15 GEM	15 CAN	15 VIR
19 ARI	18 TAU	19 GEM	18 CAN	17 LEO	17 LIB
21 TAU	20 GEM	21 CAN	20 LEO	19 VIR	20 SCO
24 GEM	22 CAN	23 LEO	22 VIR	21 LIB	22 SAG
26 CAN	24 LEO	26 VIR	24 LIB	23 SCO	24 CAP
28 LEO	26 VIR	28 LIB	26 SCO	26 SAG	26 AQU
30 VIR	28 LIB	30 SCO	28 SAG	28 CAP	29 PIS
				31 AQU	

JUL	AUG	SEP	OCT	NOV	DEC
2 ARI	1 TAU	1 CAN	1 LEO	1 LIB	1 SCO
4 TAU	3 GEM	3 LEO	3 VIR	3 SCO	3 SAG
7 GEM	5 CAN	5 VIR	5 LIB	6 SAG	5 CAP
9 CAN	7 LEO	7 LIUB	7 SCO	8 CAP	8 AQU
11 LEO	9 LOIB	10 SCO	9 SAG	10 AQU	10 PIS
13 VIR	11 VIR	12 SAG	11 CAP	`13 PIS	13 ARI
15 LIB	13 SCO	14 CAP	14 AQU	15 ARI	15 TAU
17 SCO	15 SAG	17 AQU	16 PIS	18 TAU	17 GEM
19 SAG	18 CAP	19 PIS	19 ARI	20 GEM	20 CAN
22 CAP	20 AQU	22 ARI	21 TAU	22 CAN	22 LEO
24 AQU	23 PIS	24 TAU	24 GEM	24 LEO	24 VIR
27 PIS	27 ARI	26 GEM	26 CAN	26 VIR	26 LIB
29 ARI	28 TAU	29 CAN	28 LEO	29 LIB	28 SCO
	30 GEM		30 VIR		30 SAG

521

1984 MOON SIGNS

JAN	FEB	MAR	APR	MAY	JUN
2 CAP	3 PIS	1 PIS	2 TAU	2 GEM	1 CAN
4 AQU	5 ARI	4 ARI	5 GEM	4 CAN	3 LEO
6 PIS	8 TAU	6 TAU	7 CAN	6 LEO	5 VIR
9 ARI	10 GEM	8 GEM	9 LEO	9 VIR	7 LIB
11 TAU	12 CAN	11 CAN	11 VIR	11 LIB	9 SCO
14 GEM	15 LEO	13 LEO	13 LIB	13 SCO	13 SAG
16 CAN	17 VIR	15 VIR	15 SCO	15 SAG	13 CAP
18 LEO	19 LIB	17 LIB	17 SAG	17 CAP	16 AQU
20 VIR	21 SCO	19 SCO	20 CAP	19 AQU	18 PIS
22 LIB	23 SAG	21 SAG	22 AQU	22 PIS	21 ARI
24 SCO	25 CAP	23 CAP	25 PIS	24 ARI	23 TAU
26 SAG	28 AQU	26 AQU	27 ARI	27 TAU	26 GEM
29 CAP		28 PIS	30 TAU	29 GEM	28 CAN
31 AQU		31 ARI			30 LEO

JUL	AUG	SEP	OCT	NOV	DEC
2 VIR	3 SCO	1 SAG	1 CAP	2 PIS	1 ARI
4 LIB	5 SAG	3 CAP	3 AQU	4 ARI	4 TAU
6 SCO	7 CAP	6 AQU	5 PIS	7 TAU	6 GEM
9 SAG	9 AQU	9 PIS	8 ARI	9 GEM	9 CAN
11 CAP	12 PIS	11 ARI	10 TAU	12 CAN	11 LEO
13 AQU	14 ARI	13 TAU	13 GEM	14 LEO	13 VIR
16 PIS	17 TAU	16 GEM	15 CAN	16 VIR	15 LIB
18 ARI	19 GEM	18 CAN	18 LEO	18 LIB	17 SCO
21 TAU	22 CAN	20 LEO	20 VIR	20 SCO	20 SCO
23 GEM	24 LEO	22 VIR	22 LIB	22 SAG	22 CAP
25 CAN	26 VIR	24 LIB	24 SCO	24 CAP	24 AQU
27 LEO	28 LIB	26 SCO	26 SAG	27 AQU	26 PIS
29 VIR	30 SCO	28 SAG	28 CAP	29 PIS	29 ARI
31 LIB			30 AQU		31 TAU

1985 MOON SIGNS

JAN	FEB	MAR	APR	MAY	JUN
3 GEM	2 CAN	1 CAN	2 VIR	1 LIB	2 SAG
5 CAN	4 LEO	3 LIB	4 LIB	3 SCO	4 CAP
7 LOE	6 VIR	5 LIB	6 SCO	5 SAG	6 AQU
9 VIR	8 LIB	7 LIB	8 SAG	7 CAP	8 PIS
12 LIB	10 SCO	9 SCO	10 CAP	9 AQU	11 ARI
14 SCO	12 SAG	11 SAG	12 AQU	12 PIS	13 TAU
16 SAG	14 CAP	14 CAP	14 PIS	14 ARI	16 GEM
18 CAP	17 AQU	16 AQU	17 ARI	17 TAU	18 CAN
20 AQU	19 PIS	18 PIS	20 TAU	19 GEM	20 LEO
22 PIS	21 ARI	21 ARI	22 GEM	22 CAN	23 VIR
25 ARI	24 TAU	23 TAU	25 CAN	24 LEO	25 LIB
28 TAU	27 GEM	26 GEM	27 LEO	26 VIR	27 SCO
30 GEM		28 CAN	29 VIR	29 LIB	29 SAG
		31 LEO		31 SCO	

JUL	AUG	SEP	OCT	NOV	DEC
1 CAP	2 PIS	1 ARI	3 GEM	2 CAN	1 LEO
3 AQU	4 ARI	3 TAU	5 CAN	4 LEO	4 VIR
5 PIS	7 TAU	6 GEM	8 LEO	6 VIR	6 LIB
8 ARI	9 GEM	8 CAN	10 VIR	9 LIB	8 SCO
10 TAU	12 CAN	10 LEO	12 LIB	11 SCO	10 SAG
13 GEM	14 LEO	13 VIR	14 SCO	13 SAG	12 CAP
15 CAN	16 VIR	15 LIB	16 SAG	15 CAP	14 AQU
18 LEO	18 LIB	17 SCO	18 CAP	17 AQU	16 PIS
20 VIR	20 SCO	19 SAG	20 AQU	19 PIS	19 ARI
22 LIB	22 SAG	21 CAP	23 PIS	21 ARI	21 TAU
24 SCO	25 CAP	23 AQU	25 ARI	24 TAU	24 GEM
26 SAG	27 AQU	25 PIS	28 TAU	26 GEM	26 CAN
28 CAP	29 PIS	28 ARI	30 GEM	29 CAN	29 LEO
31 AQU		30 TAU			31 VIR

1986 MOON SIGNS

JAN	FEB	MAR	APR	MAY	JUN
2 LIB	1 SCO	2 SAG	2 AQU	2 PIS	3 TAU
4 SCO	3 SAG	4 CAP	5 PIS	4 ARI	5 GEM
6 SAG	5 CAP	6 AQU	7 ARI	7 TAU	8 CAN
8 CAP	7 AQU	8 PIS	9 TAU	9 GEM	11 LEO
11 AQU	9 PIS	11 ARI	12 GEM	12 CAN	13 VIR
13 PIS	11 ARI	13 TAU	14 CAN	13 LEO	15 LIB
15 ARI	14 TAU	16 GEM	17 LEO	17 VIR	17 SCO
17 TAU	16 GEM	18 CAN	19 VIR	19 LIB	19 SAG
20 GEM	19 CAN	21 LEO	21 LIB	21 SCO	21 CAP
22 CAN	21 LEO	23 VIR	24 SCO	23 SAG	23 AQU
25 LEO	243 VIR	25 SAG	26 SAG	25 CAP	26 PIS
27 VIR	26 LIB	27 SCO	28 CAP	27 AQU	28 ARI
29 LIB	28 SCO	29 SAG	30 AQU	29 PIS	30 TAU
	31 CAP			31 ARI	

JUL	AUG	SEP	OCT	NOV	DEC
3 GEM	2 CAN	3 VIR	2 LIB	1 SCO	2 CAP
5 CAN	4 LEO	5 LIB	4 SCO	3 SAG	4 AQU
8 LEO	6 VIR	7 SCO	7 SAG	5 CAP	6 PIS
10 VIR	8 LIB	9 SAG	9 CAP	7 AQU	9 ARI
12 LIB	11 SCO	11 CAP	11 AQU	9 PIS	11 LEO
15 SCO	13 SAG	14 AQU	13 PIS	11 ARI	14 GEM
17 SAG	15 CAP	16 PIS	15 ARI	14 TAU	16 CAN
19 CAP	17 AQU	18 ARI	18 TAU	16 GEM	19 LEO
21 AQU	19 PIS	20 TAU	20 GEM	19 CAN	21 VIR
23 PIS	22 ARI	23 GEM	23 CAN	21 LEO	24 LIB
25 ARI	24 TAU	25 CAN	25 LEO	24 VIR	26 SCO
28 TAU	26 GEM	28 LEO	27 VIR	26 LIB	28 SCO
30 GEM	29 CAN	30 VIR	30 LIB	28 SCO	30 CAP
	30 LEO			30 SAG	

1987 MOON SIGNS

JAN	FEB	MAR	APR	MAY	JUN
1 AQU	1 ARI	1 ARI	2 GEM	2 CAN	3 VIR
3 PIS	4 TAU	3 TAU	4 CAN	4 LEO	5 LIB
5 ARU	6 GEM	5 GEM	7 LEO	7 VIR	8 SCO
7 TAU	9 CAN	8 CAN	8 VIR	9 LIB	10 SAG
10 GEM	11 LEO	10 LEO	12 LIB	11 SCO	12 CAP
12 CAN	14 VIR	13 VIR	14 SCO	13 SAG	14 AQU
15 LEO	16 LIB	15 LIB	16 SAG	15 CAP	16 PIS
17 VIR	18 SCO	18 SCO	18 CAP	17 AQU	18 ARI
20 LIB	21 SAG	20 SAG	20 AQU	20 PIS	20 TAU
22 SCO	23 CAP	22 CAP	22 PIS	22 ARI	23 GEM
24 SAG	25 AQU	24 AQU	25 ARI	24 TAU	25 CAN
26 CAP	27 PIS	26 PIS	27 TAU	26 GEM	28 LEO
28 AQU		28 ARI	29 GEM	29 CAN	30 VIR
30 PIS		30 TAU		31 LEO	

JUL	AUG	SEP	OCT	NOV	DEC
3 LIB	1 SCO	1 CAP	1 AQU	2 ARI	1 TAU
5 SCO	4 SAG	4 AQU	3 PIS	4 TAU	4 GEM
7 SAG	6 CAP	6 PUIS	6 ARI	6 GEM	6 CAN
9 CAP	8 AQU	8 ARI	8 TAU	9 CAN	8 LEO
11 AQU	10 PIS	10 TAU	10 GEM	11 LEO	11 VIR
13 PIS	12 ARI	13 GEM	12 CAN	14 VIR	14 L;IB
15 ARI	14 TAU	15 CAN	15 LEO	16 LIB	16 SCO
18 TAU	16 GEM	17 LEO	17 VIR	18 SCO	18 SAG
20 GEM	19 CAN	20 VIR	20 LIB	21 SAG	20 CAP
22 CAN	21 LEO	22 LIB	22 SCO	23 CAP	22 AQU
25 LEO	24 VIR	25 SCO	24 SAG	25 AQU	24 PIS
27 VIR	26 LIB	27 SAG	26 CAP	27 PIS	26 ARI
30 LIB	29 SCO	29 CAP	29 AQU	29 ARI	29 TAU
	31 SAG		31 PIS		31 GEM

1988 MOON SIGNS

JAN	FEB	MAR	APR	MAY	JUN
2 CAN	1 LEO	2 VIR	1 LIB	3 SAG	1 CAP
5 LEO	4 VIR	4 LIB	3 SCO	5 CAP	3 AQU
7 VIR	6 LIB	7 SCO	5 SAG	7 AQU	5 PIS
10 LIB	9 SCO	9 SAG	8 CAP	9 PIS	8 ARI
12 SCO	11 SAG	11 CAP	10 AQU	11 ARI	10 TAU
15 SAG	13 CAP	14 AQU	12 PIS	13 TAU	12 GEM
17 CAP	15 AQU	16 PIS	14 ARI	16 GEM	14 CAN
19 AQU	17 PIS	18 ARI	16 TAU	18 CAN	17 LEO
21 PIS	19 ARI	20 TAU	18 GEM	20 LEO	19 VIR
23 ARI	21 TAU	22 GEM	20 CAN	23 VIR	22 LIB
25 TAU	23 GEM	24 CAN	23 LEO	25 LIB	24 SCO
27 GEM	26 CAN	27 LEO	25 VIR	28 SCO	26 SAG
30 CAN	28 LEO	29 VIR	28 LIB	30 SAG	29 CAP
			30 SCO		

JUL	AUG	SEP	OCT	NOV	DEC
1 AQU	1 ARI	2 GEM	1 CAN	2 VIR	2 LIB
3 PIS	3 TAU	4 CAN	4 LEO	5 LIB	5 SCO
5 ARI	5 GEM	6 LEO	6 VIR	7 SCO	7 SAG
7 TAU	8 CAN	9 VIR	9 LIB	10 SAG	9 CAP
9 GEM	10 LEO	11 LIB	11 SCO	12 CAP	12 AQU
11 CAN	13 VIR	14 SCO	14 SAG	14 AQU	14 PIS
14 LEO	15 LIB	16 SAG	16 CAP	17 PIS	16 ARI
16 VIR	18 SCO	19 CAP	18 AQU	19 ARI	18 TAU
19 LIB	20 SAG	21 AQU	20 PIS	21 TAU	20 GEM
21 SCO	22 CAP	23 PIS	22 ARI	23 GEM	22 CAN
24 SAG	24 AQU	25 ARI	24 TAU	25 CAN	25 LEO
26 CAP	26 PIS	27 TAU	26 GEM	27 LEO	27 VIR
28 AQU	28 ARI	29 GEM	29 CAN	30 VIR	30 LIB
30 PIS	30 TAU		31 LEO		

1989 MOON SIGNS

JAN	FEB	MAR	APR	MAY	JUN
1 SCO	2 CAP	2 CAP	2 PIS	2 ARI	2 GEM
4 SAG	4 AQU	4 AQU	4 ARI	4 TAU	4 CAN
6 CAP	6 PIS	6 PIS	6 TAU	6 GEM	7 LEO
8 AQU	8 ARI	8 ARI	8 GEM	8 CAN	9 VIR
10 PIS	11 TAU	10 TAU	11 CAN	10 LEO	11 LIB
12 ARI	13 GEM	12 GEM	13 LEO	13 VIR	14 SCO
14 TAU	15 CAN	14 CAN	15 VIR	15 LIB	16 SAG
16 GEM	17 LEO	17 LEO	18 LIB	18 SCO	19 CAP
19 CAN	20 VIR`	19 VIR	20 SCO	20 SAG	21 AQU
21 LEO	22 LIB	22 LIB	23 SAG	22 CAP	23 PIS
23 VIR	25 SCO	24 SCO	25 CAP	23 AQU	25 ARI
26 LIB	27 SAG	27 SAG	28 AQU	27 PIS	27 TAU
29 SCO		29 CAP	30 PIS	29 ARI	30 GEM
31 SAG		31 AQU		31 TAU	

JUL	AUG	SEP	OCT	NOV	DEC
2 CAN	3 VIR	1 LIB	1 SCO	2 CAP	2 AQU
4 LEO	5 LIB	4 SCO	4 SAG	5 AQU	4 PIS
6 VIR	8 SCO	6 SAG	6 CAP	7 PIS	7 ARI
9 LIB	10 SAG	9 CAP	9 AQU	9 ARI	9 TAU
11 SCO	12 CAP	11 AQU	11 PIS	11 TAU	11 GEM
14 SAG	15 AQU	13 PIS	13 ARI	13 GEM	13 CAN
16 CAP	17 PIS	15 ARI	15 TAU	15 CAN	15 LEO
18 AQU	19 ARI	17 TAU	17 GEM	17 LEO	17 VIR
20 PIS	21 TAU	19 GEM	19 CAN	20 VIR	19 LIB
23 ARI	23 GEM	21 CAN	21 LEO	22 LIB	22 SCO
25 TAU	25 CAN	25 LEO	23 VIR	25 SCO	24 SAG
27 GEM	28 LEO	26 VIR	26 LIB	27 SAG	27 CAP
29 CAN	30 VIR	29 LIB	28 SCO	30 CAP	29 AQU
31 LEO			31 SAG		

1990 MOON SIGNS

JAN	FEB	MAR	APR	MAY	JUN
1 PIS	1 TAU	2 GEM	1 CAN	3 VIR	1 LIB
3 ARI	3 GEM	5 CAN	3 LEO	5 LIB	4 SCO
5 TAU	5 CAN	7 LEO	5 VIR	8 SCO	6 SAG
7 GEM	8 LEO	9 VIR	8 LIB	10 SAG	9 CAP
9 CAN	10 VIR	12 LIB	10 SCO	13 CAP	11 AQU
11 LEO	12 LIB	14 SCO	13 SAG	15 AQU	14 PIS
13 VIR	15 SCO	16 SAG	15 CAP	17 PIS	16 ARI
16 LIB	17 SAG	19 CAP	18 AQU	20 ARI	18 TAU
18 SCO	20 CAP	21 AQU	20 PIS	22 TAU	20 GEM
21 SAG	22 AQU	24 PIS	22 ARI	24 GEM	22 CAN
23 CAP	24 PIS	26 ARI	24 TAU	26 CAN	24 LEO
26 AQU	26 ARI	28 TAU	26 GEM	28 LEO	26 VIR
28 PIS	28 TAU	30 GEM	28 CAN	30 VIR	29 LIB
30 ARI			30 LEO		

JUL	AUG	SEP	OCT	NOV	DEC
1 SCO	2 CAP	1 AQU	1 PIS	2 TAU	1 GEM
4 SAG	5 AQU	3 PIS	3 ARI	4 GEM	3 CAN
6 CAP	7 PIS	6 ARI	5 TAU	6 CAN	5 LEO
9 ARQ	9 ARI	8 TAU	7 GEM	8 LEO	7 VIR
11 PIS	12 TAU	10 GEM	9 CAN	10 VIR	9 LIB
13 ARI	14 GEM	12 CAN	11 LEO	12 LIB	12 SAG
15 TAU	16 CAN	14 LEO	14 VIR	15 SCO	14 SAG
17 GEM	18 LEO	16 VIR	16 LIB	17 SAG	17 CAP
19 CAN	20 VIR	19 LIB	18 SCO	20 CAP	19 AQU
21 LEO	22 LIB	21 SCO	21 SAG	22 AQU	22 PIS
24 VIR	25 SCO	24 SAG	23 CAP	25 PIS	24 ARI
26 LIB	27 SAG	26 CAP	26 AQU	27 ARI	26 TAU
28 SCO	30 CAP	29 AQU	28 PIS	29 TAU	28 GEM
31 SAG			30 ARI		30 CAN

1991 MOON SIGNS

JAN	FEB	MAR	APR	MAY	JUN
1 LEO	2 LIB	2 LIB	3 SAG	2 CAP	1 AQU
4 VIR	4 SCO	4 SCO	5 CAP	5 AQU	4 PIS
6 LIB	7 SAG	6 SAG	8 AQU	7 PIS	6 ARI
8 SCO	9 CAP	9 CAP	10 PIS	10 ARI	8 TAU
11 SAG	12 AQU	11 AQU	12 ARI	12 TAU	10 GEM
13 CAP	14 PIS	14 PIS	15 TAU	14 GEM	12 CAN
16 AQU	17 ARI	16 ARI	17 GAM	16 CAN	14 LEO
18 PIS	19 TAU	18 TAU	19 CAN	18 LEO	16 VIR
20 ARI	21 GEM	20 GEM	21 LEO	20 VIR	19 LIB
23 TAU	23 CAN	22 CAN	23 VIR	22 LIB	21 SCO
25 GEM	25 LEO	25 LEO	25 LIB	25 SCO	23 SAG
27 CAN	27 VIR	27 VIR	28 SCO	27 SAG	26 CAP
29 LEO		29 LIB	30 SAG	30 CAP	29 AQU
31 VIR		31 SCO			

JUL	AUG	SEP	OCT	NOV	DEC
1 PIS	2 TAU	3 CAN	2 LEO	2 LIB	2 SCO
3 ARI	4 GEM	5 LEO	4 VIR	5 SCO	4 SAG
6 TAU	6 CAN	7 VIR	6 LIB	7 SAG	7 CAN
8 GEM	8 LEO	9 LIB	8 SCO	10 CAP	9 AQU
10 CAN	10 VIR	11 SCO	11 SAG	12 AQU	12 PIS
12 LEO	12 LIB	13 SAG	13 CAP	15 PIS	14 ARI
14 VIR	15 SCO	16 CAP	16 AQU	17 ARI	17 TAU
16 LIB	17 SAG	18 AQU	18 PIS	19 TAU	19 GEM
18 SCO	20 CAP	21 PIS	21 ARI	21 GEM	21 CAN
21 SAG	22 AQU	23 ARI	23 TAU	23 CAN	23 LEO
23 CAP	25 PIS	25 TAU	25 GEM	25 LEO	25 VIR
26 AQU	27 ARI	28 GEM	27 CAN	28 VIR	27 LIB
28 PIS	29 TAU	30 CAN	29 LEO	30 LIB	29 SCO
31 ARI	31 GEM		31 VIR		

1992 MOON SIGNS

JAN	FEB	MAR	APR	MAY	JUN
1 SAG	2 AQU	3 PIS	1 ARI	1 TAU	2 CAN
3 CAP	4 PIS	5 ARI	4 TAU	3 GEM	4 LEO
6 AQU	7 ARI	8 TAU	6 GEM	5 CAN	6 VIR
8 PIS	9 TAU	10 GEM	8 CAN	8 LEO	8 LIB
11 ARI	12 GEM	12 CAN	10 LEO	10 VIR	10 SCO
13 TAU	14 CAN	14 CAN	12 VIR	12 LIB	13 SAG
15 GEM	16 LEO	16 VIR	15 LIB	14 SCO	15 CAP
17 CAN	18 VIR	18 LIB	17 SCO	16 SAG	18 AQU
19 LEO	20 LIB	20 SCO	19 SAG	19 CAP	20 PIS
21 VIR	22 SCO	23 SAG	21 CAP	21 AQU	22 ARI
23 LIB	24 SAG	25 CAP	24 AQU	24 PIS	24 TAU
25 SCO	27 CAP	27 AQU	26 PIS	26 ARI	27 GEM
28 SAG	29 AQU	30 PIS	29 ARI	28 TAU	29 CAN
30 CAP				31 GEM	

JUL	AUG	SEP	OCT	NOV	DEC
1 LEO	2 LOB	2 SAG	2 CAP	1 AQU	1 PIS
3 VIR	4 SCO	5 CAP	5 AQU	3 PIS	3 ARI
5 LIB	6 SAG	7 AQU	7 PIS	6 ARI	6 TAU
7 SCO	8 CAP	10 PIS	10 ARI	8 TAU	8 GEM
10 SAG	11 AQU	12 ARI	12 TAU	11 GEM	10 CAN
12 CAP	13 PIS	15 TAU	14 GEM	13 CAN	12 LEO
15 AQU	16 ARI	17 GEM	17 CAN	15 LEO	14 VIR
17 PIS	18 TAU	19 CAN	19 LEO	17 VIR	16 LIB
20 ARI	21 GEM	21 LEO	21 VIR	19 LIB	19 SCO
22 TAU	23 CAN	24 VIR	23 LIB	21 SCO	21 SAG
24 GEM	25 LEO	26 LIB	25 SCO	24 SAG	23 CAP
27 CAN	27 VIR	28 SCO	27 SAG	26 CAP	26 AQU
29 LEO	29 LIB	30 SAG	29 CAP	28 AQU	28 PIS
31 VIR	31 SCO				31 ARI

1994 MOON SIGNS

JAN	FEB	MAR	APR	MAY	JUN
1 VIR	2 SCO	1 SCO	1 CAP	1 AQU	2 ARI
3 LIB	4 SAG	3 SAG	4 AQU	3 PIS	5 TAU
5 SCO	6 CAP	5 CAP	6 PIS	6 ARI	7 GEM
8 SAG	8 AQU	7 AQU	9 ARI	8 TAU	10 CAN
10 CAP	11 PIS	10 PIS	11 TAU	11 GEM	12 LEO
12 AQU	13 ARI	12 ARI	14 GEM	13 CAN	14 VIR
14 PIS	16 TAU	15 TAU	16 CAN	16 LEO	16 LIB
17 ARI	18 GEM	17 GEM	18 LEO	18 VIR	19 SCO
19 TAU	20 CAN	20 CAN	21 VIR	20 LIB	21 SAG
22 GEM	23 LEO	22 LEO	23 LIB	22 SCO	23 CAP
24 CAN	25 VIR	24 VIR	25 SCO	24 SAG	25 AQU
26 LEO	27 LIB	26 LIB	27 SAG	26 CAP	27 PIS
28 VIR		28 SCO	29 CAP	28 AQU	29 ARI
31 LIB		30 SAG		31 PIS	

JUL	AUG	SEP	OCT	NOV	DEC
2 TAU	1 GEM	2 LEO	2 VIR	2 SCO	2 SAG
4 GEM	3 CAN	4 VIR	4 LIB	4 SAG	4 CAP
7 CAN	6 LEO	6 LIB	6 SCO	6 CAP	6 AQU
9 LEO	8 VIR	8 SCO	8 SAG	8 AQU	8 PIS
11 VIR	10 LIB	10 SAG	10 CAP	11 PIS	10 ARI
14 LIB	12 SCO	13 CAP	12 AQU	13 ARI	13 TAU
16 SCO	14 SAG	15 AQU	14 PIS	15 TAU	15 GEM
18 SAG	16 CAP	17 PIS	17 ARI	18 GEM	18 CAN
20 CAP	18 AQU	19 ARI	19 TAU	20 CAN	20 LEO
22 AQU	21 PIS	22 TAU	22 GEM	23 LEO	23 VIR
24 PIS	23 ARI	24 GEM	24 CAN	25 VIR	25 LIB
27 ARI	26 TAU	27 CAN	27 LEO	28 LIB	27 SCO
29 TAU	28 GEM	29 LEO	29 VIR	30 SCO	29 SAG
	31 CAN		31 LIB		31 CAP

1993 MOON SIGNS

JAN	FEB	MAR	APR	MAY	JUN
2 TAU	1 GEM	2 CAN	1 LEO	2 LIB	1 SCO
4 GEM	3 CAN	5 LEO	1 VIR	4 SCO	3 SAG
7 CAN	5 LEO	7 VIR	5 LIB	6 SAG	5 CAP
9 LEO	7 VIR	9 LIB	7 SCO	9 CAP	7 AQU
11 VIR	9 LIB	11 SCO	9 SAG	11 AQU	10 PIS
13 LIB	11 SCO	13 SAG	13 CAP	13 PIS	12 ARI
15 SCO	13 SAG	15 CAP	14 AQU	16 ARI	15 TAU
17 SAG	16 CAP	17 AQU	16 PIS	18 TAU	17 GEM
19 CAP	18 AQU	20 PIOS	19 ARI	21 GEM	19 CAN
22 AQU	21 PIS	22 ARI	21 TAU	23 CAN	22 LEO
24 PIS	23 ARI	25 TAU	24 GEM	25 LEO	24 VIR
27 ARI	26 TAU	27 GEM	26 CAN	28 VIR	26 LIB
29 TAU	28 GEM	30 CAN	28 LEO	30 LIB	28 SCO
			30 VIR		30 SAG

JUL	AUG	SEP	OCT	NOV	DEC
2 CAP	1 AQU	2 ARI	2 TAU	1 GEM	3 LEO
5 AQU	3 PIS	5 TAU	4 GEM	3 CAN	5 VIR
7 PIS	6 ARI	7 GEM	7 CAN	5 LEO	7 LIB
10 ARI	8 TAU	10 CAN	9 LEO	8 VIR	9 SCO
12 TAU	11 GEM	12 LEO	11 VIR	10 LIB	11 SAG
15 GEM	13 CAN	14 VIR	13 LIB	12 SCO	13 CAP
17 CAN	15 LEO	16 LIB	15 SCO	14 SAG	15 AQU
19 LEO	17 VIR	18 SCO	17 SAG	16 CAP	18 PIS
21 VIR	19 LIB	20 SAG	19 CAP	18 AQU	20 ARI
23 LIB	21 SCO	22 CAP	22 AQU	20 PIS	23 TAU
25 SCO	24 SAG	24 AQU	24 PIS	23 ARI	25 GEM
27 SAG	26 CAP	27 PIS	27 ARI	26 TAU	28 CAN
30 CAP	28 AQU	29 ARI	29 TAU	28 GEM	30 LEO
	31 PIS			30 CAN	

1995 MOON SIGNS

JAN	FEB	MAR	APR	MAY	JUN
2 AQU	1 PIS	2 ARI	1 TAI	1 GEM	2 LEO
4 PIS	3 ARI	5 TAU	3 GEM	3 CAN	5 VIR
7 ARI	5 TAU	7 GEM	6 CAN	6 LEO	7 LIB
9 TAU	8 GEM	10 CAN	9 LEO	8 VIR	9 SCO
12 GEM	10 CAN	12 LEO	11 VIR	10 LIB	11 SAG
14 CAN	13 LEO	14 VIR	13 LIB	13 SCO	13 CAP
16 LEO	15 VIR	17 LIB	15 SCO	15 SAG	15 AQU
19 VIR	17 LIB	19 SCO	17 SAG	17 CAP	17 PIS
21 LIB	19 SCO	21 SAG	19 CAP	19 AQU	19 ARI
23 SCO	22 SAG	23 CAP	21 AQU	21 PIS	22 TAU
25 SAG	24 CAP	25 AQU	24 PIS	23 ARI	24 GEM
27 CAP	26 AQU	27 PIS	26 ARI	26 TAU	27 CAN
30 AQU	28 PIS	30 ARI	28 TAU	28 GEM	29 LEO
				31 CAN	

JUL	AUG	SEP	OCT	NOV	DEC
2 VIR	3 SCO	1 SAG	2 AQU	1 PIS	3 TAU
4 LIB	5 SAG	3 CAP	5 PIS	3 ARI	5 GEM
6 SCO	7 CAP	5 AQU	7 ARI	5 TAU	8 CAP
8 SAG	9 AQU	7 PIS	9 TAU	8 GEM	10 LEO
10 CAP	11 PIS	9 ARI	12 GEM	10 CAN	13 VIR
12 AQU	13 ARI	12 TAU	14 CAN	13 LEO	15 LIB
14 PIS	15 TAU	14 GEM	17 LEO	15 VIR	17 SCO
17 ARI	18 GEM	17 CAN	19 VIR	18 LIB	19 SAG
19 TAU	20 CAN	19 LEO	21 LIB	20 SCO	21 CAP
22 GEM	23 LEO	22 VIR	23 SCO	22 SAG	23 AQU
24 CAN	25 VIR	24 LIB	26 SAG	24 CAP	25 PIS
27 LEO	28 LIB	26 SCO	28 CAP	26 AQU	28 ARI
29 VIR	30 SCO	28 SAG	30 AQU	28 PIS	30 TAU
31 LIB		30 CAP		30 ARI	

1996 MOON SIGNS

JAN	FEB	MAR	APR	MAY	JUN
1 GEM	3 LEO	1 LEO	2 LIB	2 SCO	2 CAP
4 CAN	5 VIR	3 VIR	4 SCO	4 SAG	4 AQU
6 LEO	8 LIB	6 LIB	7 SAG	6 CAP	6 PIS
9 VIR	10 SCO	8 SCO	9 CAP	8 AQU	9 ARI
11 LIB	12 SAG	10 SAG	11 AQU	10 PIS	11 TAU
14 SCO	14 CAP	13 CAP	13 PIS	12 ARI	13 GEM
16 SAG	16 AQU	15 AQU	15 ARI	15 TAU	16 CAN
18 CAP	18 PIS	17 PIS	17 TAU	17 GEM	18 LEO
20 AQU	20 ARI	19 ARI	20 GEM	19 CAN	21 VIR
22 PIS	23 TAU	21 TAU	22 CAN	22 LEO	23 LIB
24 ARI	25 GEM	23 GEM	25 LEO	25 VIR	26 SCO
26 TAU	27 CAN	26 CAN	27 VIR	27 LIB	28 SAG
29 GEM		28 LEO	30 LIB	29 SCO	30 CAP
31 CAN		31 VIR		31 SAG	

JUL	AUG	SEP	OCT	NOV	DEC
2 AQU	2 ARI	1 TAU	3 CAN	2 LEO	2 VIR
4 PIS	2 TAU	3 GEM	5 LEO	4 VIR	4 LIB
6 ARI	7 GEM	6 CAN	8 VIR	7 LIB	6 SCO
8 TAU	9 CAN	8 LEO	10 LIB	9 SCO	9 SAG
11 GEM	12 LEO	11 VIR	13 SCO	11 SAG	11 CAP
13 CAN	14 VIR	13 LIB	15 SAG	13 CAP	13 AQU
16 LEO	17 LIB	15 SCO	17 CAP	16 AQU	15 PIS
18 VIR	19 SCO	18 SAG	19 AQU	18 PIS	17 ARI
21 LIB	21 SAG	20 CAP	21 PIS	20 ARI	19 TAU
23 SCO	24 CAP	22 AQU	23 ARI	22 TAU	22 GEM
25 SAG	26 AQU	24 PIS	26 TAU	24 GEM	24 CAN
27 CAP	28 PIS	26 ARI	28 GEM	27 CAN	26 LEO
29 AQU	30 ARI	28 TAU	30 CAN	29 LEO	29 VIR
31 PIS		30 GEM			31 LIB

1997 MOON SIGNS

JAN	FEB	MAR	APR	MAY	JUN
3 SCO	1 SAG	1 SAG	1 AQU	1 PIS	1 TAU
5 SAG	4 CAP	3 CAP	4 PIS	3 ARI	4 GEM
7 CAP	6 AQU	5 AQU	6 ARI	5 TAU	6 CAN
9 AQU	8 PIS	7 PIS	8 TAU	9 GEM	8 LEO
11 PIS	10 ARI	9 ARI	10 GEM	9 CAN	11 VIR
13 ARI	12 TAU	11 TAU	12 CAN	12 LEO	13 LIB
15 TAU	14 GEM	13 GEM	14 LEO	14 VIR	16 SCO
18 GEM	16 CAN	16 CAN	17 VIR	17 LIB	18 SAG
20 CAN	19 LEO	18 LEO	19 LIB	19 SCO	20 CAP
23 LEO	21 VIR	21 VIR	22 SCO	22 SAG	22 AQU
25 VIR	24 LIB	23 LIB	24 SAG	24 CAP	24 PIS
28 LIB	26 SCO	26 SCO	27 CAP	26 AQU	26 ARI
30 SCO		28 SAG	29 AQU	28 PIS	29 TAU
		30 CAP		30 ARI	

JUL	AUG	SEP	OCT	NOV	DEC
1 GEM	2 LEO	3 LIB	3 SCO	1 SAG	1 CAP
3 CAN	4 VIR	6 SCO	5 SAG	4 CAP	3 AQU
5 LEO	7 LIB	8 SAG	8 CAP	6 AQU	5 PIS
8 VIR	9 SCO	10 CAP	10 AQU	8 PIS	8 ARI
10 LIB	12 SAG	12 AQU	12 PIS	10 ARI	10 TAU
13 SCO	14 CAP	15 PIS	14 ARI	12 TAU	12 GEM
15 SCG	16 AQU	17 ARI	16 TAI	14 GEM	14 CAN
18 CAP	18 PIS	19 TAU	18 GEM	17 CAN	16 LEO
20 AQU	20 ARI	21 GEM	20 CAN	19 LEO	19 VIR
22 PIS	22 TAU	23 CAN	23 LEO	21 VIR	21 LIB
24 ARI	24 GEM	25 LEO	25 VIR	24 LIB	26 SAG
26 TAU	27 CAN	28 VIR	28 LIB	26 SCO	26 SAG
28 GEM	29 LEO	30 LIB	30 SCO	29 SAG	28 CAP
30 CAN	31 VIR				31 AQU

1998 MOON SIGNS

JAN	FEB	MAR	APR	MAY	JUN
2 PIS	2 TAU	2 CAN	2 CAN	2 LEO	3 LIB
4 ARI	4 GEM	4 GEM	4 LEO	4 VIR	5 SCO
6 TAU	7 CAN	6 CAN	7 VIR	7 LIB	8 SAG
8 GEM	9 LEO	8 LEO	9 LIB	9 SCO	10 CAP
10 CAN	11 VIR	11 VIR	12 SCO	12 SAG	13 AQU
13 LEO	14 LIB	13 LIB	14 SAG	14 CAP	15 PIS
15 VIR	16 SCO	16 SCO	17 CAP	16 AQU	17 ARI
18 LIB	19 SAG	18 SAG	19 AQU	19 PIS	19 TAU
20 SCO	21 CAP	21 CAP	21 PIS	21 ARI	21 GEM
23 SAG	23 AQU	23 AQU	23 ARI	23 TAU	23 CAN
25 CAP	25 PIS	25 PIS	25 TAU	25 GEM	25 LEO
27 AQU	27 ARI	27 ARI	27 GEM	27 CAN	28 VIR
29 PIS		29 TAU	29 CAN	29 LEO	30 LIB
31 ARI		31 GEM		31 VIR	

JUL	AUG	SEP	OCT	NOV	DEC
3 SCO	2 SAG	3 AQU	2 PIS	1 ARI	2 GEM
5 SAG	4 CAP	5 PIS	4 ARI	3 TAU	4 CAN
8 CAP	6 AQU	7 ARI	6 TAU	5 GEM	6 LEO
10 AQU	8 PIS	9 TAU	8 GEM	7 CAN	9 VIR
12 PIS	11 ARI	11 GEM	10 CAN	9 LEO	11 LIB
14 ARI	13 TAU	13 CAN	13 LEO	11 VIR	14 SCO
16 TAU	15 GEM	15 LEO	15 VIR	14 LIB	16 SAG
18 GEM	17 CAN	18 VIR	17 LIB	16 SCO	19 CAP
21 CAN	19 LEO	20 LIB	20 SCO	19 SAG	21 AQU
23 LEO	21 VIR	23 SCO	23 SAG	21 CAP	23 PIS
25 VIR	24 LIB	25 SAG	25 CAP	24 AQU	25 ARI
28 LIB	26 SCO	28 CAP	27 AQU	26 PIS	28 TAU
30 SCO	29 SAG	30 AQU	30 PIS	28 ARI	30 GEM
	31 CAP			30 TAU	

1999 MOON SIGNS

JAN	FEB	MAR	APR	MAY	JUN
1 CAN	1 VIR	1 VIR	2 SCO	2 SAG	3 AQU
3 LEO	4 LIB	3 LIB	4 SAG	4 CAP	5 PIS
5 VIR	6 SCO	6 SCO	7 CAP	7 AQU	8 ARI
7 LIB	9 SAG	8 SAG	9 AQU	9 PIS	10 TAU
10 SCO	11 CAP	11 CAP	12 PIS	11 ARI	12 GEM
12 SAG	14 AQU	13 AQU	14 ARI	13 TAU	14 CAN
15 CAP	16 PIS	15 PIS	16 TAU	15 GEM	16 LEO
17 LEO	18 ARI	17 ARI	18 GEM	17 CAN	18 VIR
19 PIS	20 TAU	19 TAU	20 CAN	19 LEO	20 LIB
22 ARI	22 GEM	21 GEM	22 LEO	21 VIR	23 SCO
24 TAU	24 CAN	23 CAN	24 VIR	24 LIB	25 SAG
26 GEM	26 LEO	26 LEO	27 LIB	26 SCO	28 CAP
28 CAN		28 VIR	29 SCO	29 SAG	30 AQU
30 LEO		30 LIB	31 CAP		

JUL	AUG	SEP	OCT	NOV	DEC
2 PIS	1 ARI	2 GEM	1 CAN	1 VIR	1 LIB
5 ARI	3 TAU	4 CAN	3 LEO	4 LIB	3 SCO
7 TAU	5 GEM	6 LEO	5 VIR	6 SCO	6 SAG
9 GEM	7 CAN	8 VIR	8 LIB	9 SAG	8 CAP
11 CAN	9 LEO	10 LIB	10 SCO	11 CAP	11 AQU
13 LEO	12 VIR	13 SCO	12 SAG	14 AQU	13 PIS
15 VIR	14 LIB	15 SAG	15 CAP	16 PIS	16 ARI
17 LIB	16 SCO	18 CAP	17 CAP	18 ARI	18 TAU
20 SCO	19 SAG	20 AQU	20 PIS	21 TAU	20 GEM
22 SAG	21 CAP	22 PIS	22 ARI	23 GEM	22 CAN
25 CAP	24 AQU	25 ARI	24 TAU	25 CAN	24 LEO
27 AQU	26 PIS	27 TAU	26 GEM	27 LEO	26 VIR
30 PIS	28 ARI	29 GEM	28 CAN	29 VIR	28 LIB
	30 TAU		30 LEO		31 SCO

2000 MOON SIGNS

JAN	FEB	MAR	APR	MAY	JUN
3 SAG	1 CAP	2 AQU	1 PIS	3 TAU	1 GEM
3 CAP	4 AQU	4 PIS	3 ARI	5 GEM	3 CAN
7 AQU	6 PIS	7 ARI	5 TAU	7 CAN	5 LEI
10 PIS	8 ARI	9 TAU	7 GEM	9 LEO	7 VIR
12 ARI	11 TAU	11 GEM	9 CAN	11 VIR	9 LIB
14 TAU	13 GEM	13 CAN	11 LEO	13 LIB	12 SCO
16 GEM	15 CAN	15 LEO	14 VIR	15 SCO	14 SAG
18 CAN	17 LEO	17 VIR	16 LIB	18 SAG	17 CAP
20 LEO	19 VIR	20 LIB	18 SCO	20 CAP	19 AQU
23 VIR	21 LIB	22 SCO	21 SAG	23 AQU	22 PIS
25 LIB	23 SCO	24 SAG	23 CAP	25 PIS	24 ARI
27 SCO	26 SAG	27 CAP	26 AQU	28 ARI	26 TAU
29 TAU	28 CAP	29 AQU	28 PIS	30 TAU	28 GEM
			30 ARI		30 CAN

JUL	AUG	SEP	OCT	NOV	DEC
2 LEO	1 VIR	2 SCO	1 SAG	3 AQU	2 PIS
4 VIR	3 LIB	4 SAG	4 CAP	5 PIS	5 ARI
7 LIB	5 SCO	6 CAP	6 AQU	8 ARI	7 TAU
9 SCO	8 SAG	9 AQU	9 PIS	10 TAU	9 GEM
11 SAG	10 CAP	11 PIS	11 ARI	12 GEM	11 CAN
14 CAP	13 AQU	14 ARI	13 TAU	14 CAN	13 LEO
16 AQU	15 PIS	16 TAU	16 GEM	16 LEO	15 VIR
19 PIS	18 ARI	18 GEM	18 CAN	18 VIR	18 LIB
21 ARI	20 TAU	20 CAN	20 LEO	20 LIB	20 SCO
24 TAU	22 GEM	23 LEO	22 VIR	23 SCO	22 SAG
26 GEM	24 CAN	25 VIR	24 LIB	25 SAG	25 CAP
28 CAN	26 LEO	27 LIB	26 SCO	27 CAP	27 AQU
30 LEO	28 VIR	29 SCO	29 SAG	30 AQU	30 PIS
	30 LIB		31 CAP		

2001 MOON SIGNS

JAN	FEB	MAR	APR	MAY	JUN
1 ARI	2 GEM	1 GEM	2 LEO	1 VIR	2 SCO
4 TAU	4 CAN	4 CAN	4 VIR	3 LIB	4 SAG
6 GEM	6 LEO	6 LEO	6 LIB	6 SCO	7 CAP
8 CAN	8 VIR	8 VIR	8 SCO	8 SAG	9 AQO
10 LEO	10 LIB	10 LIB	10 SAG	10 CAP	10 PIS
12 VIR	12 SCO	12 SCO	13 CAP	13 AQU	14 ARI
14 LIB	15 SAG	14 SAG	15 AQU	15 PIS	16 TAU
16 SCO	17 CAP	16 CAP	18 PIS	18 ARI	19 GEM
19 SAG	20 AQU	19 AQU	20 ARI	20 TAU	21 CAN
21 CAP	22 PIS	22 PIS	23 TAU	22 GEM	23 LEO
23 AQU	25 ARI	24 ARI	25 GEM	24 CAN	25 VIR
26 PIS	27 TAU	26 TAU	27 CAN	27 LEO	27 LIB
28 ARI		29 GEM	29 LEO	29 VIR	29 SCO
31 TAU		31 CAN		31 LIB	

JUL	AUG	SEP	OCT	NOV	DEC
1 SAG	3 AQU	1 PIS	1 ARI	2 GEM	2 CAN
4 CAP	5 PIS	4 ARI	4 TAU	4 CAN	4 LEO
6 AQU	8 ARI	6 TAU	6 GEM	7 LEO	6 VIR
8 PIS	10 TAU	9 GEM	8 CAN	9 VIR	8 LIB
11 ARI	12 GEM	11 CAN	10 LEO	11 LIB	10 SCO
14 TAU	15 CAN	13 LEO	13 VIR	13 SCO	12 SAG
16 GEM	17 LEO	15 VIR	15 LIB	15 SAG	15 CAP
18 CAN	19 VIR	17 LIB	17 SCO	17 CAP	17 AQU
20 LEO	21 LIB	19 SCO	19 SAG	20 AQU	20 PIS
22 VIR	23 SCO	21 SAG	21 CAP	21 PIS	22 ARI
24 LIB	25 SAG	24 CAP	23 AQU	25 ARI	25 TAU
26 SCO	27 CAP	26 AQU	26 PIS	27 TAU	27 GEM
29 SAG	30 AQU	29 PIS	28 ARI	30 GEM	29 CAN
31 CAP			31 TAU		31 LEO

2002 MOON SIGNS

JAN	FEB	MAR	APR	MAY	JUN
2 VIR	1 LIB	2 SCO	1 SAG	2 AQU	1 PIS
4 LIB	3 SCO	4 SAG	3 CAP	5 PIS	4 ARI
6 SCO	5 SAG	6 CAP	5 AQU	7 ARI	6 TAU
9 SAG	7 CAP	9 ARI	8 PIS	9 TAU	9 GEM
11 CAP	10 AQU	11 PIS	10 ARI	12 GEM	11 CAN
13 AQU	12 PIS	14 ARI	13 TAU	15 CAN	13 LEO
16 PIS	15 ARI	16 TAU	15 GEM	17 LEO	15 VIR
18 ARI	17 TAU	19 GEM	18 CAN	19 VIR	18 LIB
21 TAU	20 GEM	21 CAN	20 LEO	21 LIB	20 SCO
23 GEM	22 CAN	24 LEO	22 VIR	23 SCO	23 SAG
26 CAN	24 LEO	26 VIR	24 LIB	25 SAG	24 CAP
28 LEO	26 VIR	28 LIB	26 SCO	28 CAP	26 AQU
30 VIR	28 LIB	30 SCO	28 SAG	30 AQU	29 PIS
			30 CAP		

JUL	AUG	SEP	OCT	NOV	DEC
1 ARI	2 GEM	1 CAN	1 LEO	1 LIB	1 SCO
4 TAU	5 CAN	3 LEO	3 VIR	3 SCO	3 SAG
6 GEM	7 LEO	5 VIR	5 LIB	5 SAG	5 CAP
8 CAN	9 VIR	7 LIB	7 SCO	7 CAP	7 AQU
11 LEO	11 LIB	9 SCO	9 SCO	10 AQU	9 PIS
13 VIR	13 SCO	12 SAG	11 CAP	12 PIS	12 ARI
15 LIB	15 SAG	14 CAP	13 AQU	15 ARI	14 TAU
17 SCO	18 CAP	16 AQU	16 PIS	17 TAU	17 GEM
19 SAG	20 AQU	19 PIS	18 ARI	20 GEM	19 CAN
21 CAP	22 PIS	21 ARI	21 TAU	22 CAN	22 LEO
24 AQU	25 ARI	24 TAU	23 GEM	24 LEO	24 VIR
26 PIS	27 TAU	26 GEM	26 CAN	27 VIR	26 LIB
28 ARI	30 GEM	29 CAN	28 LEO	29 LIB	28 SCO
31 TAU			30 VIR		30 SAG

2003 MOON SIGNS

JAN	FEB	MAR	APR	MAY	JUN
1 CAP	2 PIS	1 PIS	3 TAU	2 GEM	1 CAN
3 AQU	5 ARI	4 ARI	5 GEM	5 CAN	4 LEO
6 PIS	7 TAU	6 TAU	8 CAN	7 LEO	6 VIR
8 ARI	10 GEM	9 GEM	10 LEO	10 VIR	8 LIB
11 TAU	11 CAN	11 CAN	12 VIR	12 LIB	10 SCO
13 GEM	14 LEO	14 LEO	14 LIB	14 SCO	12 SAG
16 CAN	16 VIR	16 VIR	16 SCO	16 SAG	14 CAP
18 LEO	18 LIB	18 LIB	18 SAG	18 CAP	16 AQU
20 VIR	21 SCO	20 SCO	20 CAP	20 AQU	19 PIS
22 LIB	23 SAG	22 SAG	23 AQU	22 PIS	21 ARI
24 SCO	25 CAP	24 CAP	25 PIS	25 ARI	23 TAU
26 SAG	27 AQU	26 AQU	27 ARI	27 TAU	26 GEM
29 CAP		29 PIS	30 TAU	30 GEM	28 CAN
31 AQU		31 ARI			

JUL	AUG	SEP	OCT	NOV	DEC
1 LEO	2 LIB	2 SAG	1 CAP	2 PIS	2 ARI
3 VIR	4 SCO	4 CAP	4 AQU	5 ARI	4 TAU
5 LIB	6 SAG	6 AQU	6 PIS	7 TAU	7 GEM
7 SCO	8 CAP	9 PIS	8 ARI	10 GEM	9 CAN
10 SAG	10 AQU	11 ARI	11 TAU	12 CAN	12 LEO
12 CAP	12 PIS	13 TAU	13 GEM	15 LEO	14 VIR
14 AQU	15 ARI	16 GEM	16 CAN	17 VIR	16 LIB
16 PIS	17 TAU	18 CAN	18 LEO	19 LIB	19 SCO
18 ARI	20 GEM	21 LEO	21 VIR	21 SCO	21 SAG
21 TAU	22 CAN	23 VIR	23 LIB	23 SAG	23 CAP
23 GEM	24 LEO	25 LIB	25 SCO	25 CAP	25 AQU
26 CAN	27 VIR	27 SCO	27 SAG	27 AQU	27 PIS
28 LEO	29 LIB	29 SAG	29 CAP	29 PIS	29 ARI
30 VIR	31 SCO		31 AQU		

2004 MOON SIGNS

JAN	FEB	MAR	APR	MAY	JUN
1 TAU	2 CAN	3 LEO	1 VIR	1 LIB	2 SAG
3 GEM	4 LEO	4 VIR	4 LIB	3 SCO	4 CAP
6 CAN	76 VIR	7 LIB	6 SCO	5 SAG	6 AQU
8 LEO	9 LIB	9 SCO	8 SAG	7 CAP	8 PIS
10 VIR	11 SCO	12 SAG	10 CAP	9 AQU	10 ARI
13 LIB	13 SAG	14 CAP	12 ARI	11 PIS	12 TAU
15 SCO	15 CAP	16 AQU	14 PIS	14 ARI	15 GEM
17 SAG	17 AQU	18 PIS	16 ARI	16 TAU	17 CAN
19 CAP	20 PIS	20 ARI	19 TAU	19 GEM	20 LEO
21 ARI	22 ARI	23 TAU	21 GEM	21 CAN	22 VIR
23 PIS	24 TAU	25 GEM	24 CAN	24 LEO	24 LIB
25 ARI	27 GEM	28 CAN	26 LEO	26 VIR	27 SCO
28 TAU	29 CAN	30 LEO	29 VIR	28 LIB	29 SAG
30 GEM				31 SCO	

JUL	AUG	SEP	OCT	NOV	DEC
1 CAP	1 PIS	2 TAU	2 GEM	1 CAN	1 LEO
3 AQU	4 ARI	5 GEM	5 CAN	3 LEO	3 VIR
5 PIS	6 TAU	7 CAN	7 LEO	6 VIR	6 LIB
7 ARI	8 GEM	10 LEO	10 VIR	8 LIB	8 SCO
10 TAU	11 CAN	12 VIR	12 LIB	10 SCO	10 SAG
12 GEM	13 LEO	14 LIB	14 SCO	13 SAG	12 CAP
15 CAN	16 VIR	17 SCO	16 SAG	15 CAP	14 AQU
17 LEO	18 LIB	19 SAG	18 CAP	17 AQU	16 PIS
20 VIR	20 SCO	21 CAP	20 AQU	19 PIS	18 ARI
22 LIB	23 SAG	23 AQU	23 PIS	21 ARI	21 TAU
24 SAO	25 CAP	25 PIS	25 ARI	23 TAU	23 GEM
26 SCO	27 AQU	27 ARI	27 TAU	26 GEM	25 CAN
28 CAP	29 PIS	30 TAU	29 GEM	28 CAN	28 LEO
30 AQU	31 ARI				31 VIR

2005 MOON SIGNS

JAN	FEB	MAR	APR	MAY	JUN
2 LIB	1 SCO	2 SAG	3 AQU	2 PIS	3 TAU
4 SCO	3 SAG	4 CAP	5 PIS	4 ARI	5 GEM
6 SAG	5 CAP	6 AQU	7 ARI	6 TAU	7 CAN
8 CAP	7 AQU	8 PIS	9 TAU	9 GEM	10 LEO
10 AQU	10 PIS	10 ARI	11 GEM	11 CAN	12 VIR
12 PIS	11 ARI	13 TAU	14 CAN	14 LEO	15 LIB
15 ARI	13 TAU	15 GEM	16 LEO	16 VIR	17 SCO
17 TAU	16 GEM	17 CAN	19 VIR	18 LIB	19 SAG
19 GEM	18 CAN	20 LEO	21 LIB	21 SCO	21 CAP
22 CAN	21 LEO	22 VIR	23 SCO	23 SCO	23 AQU
24 LEO	23 VIR	25 LIB	26 SAG	25 CAP	25 PIS
27 VIR	25 LIB	27 SCO	28 CAP	27 AQU	28 ARI
29 LIB	28 SCO	29 SAG	30 AQU	29 PIS	30 TAU
		31 CAP		31 ARI	

JUL	AUG	SEP	OCT	NOV	DEC
2 GEM	1 CAN	2 VIR	2 LIB	1 SCO	2 CAP
5 CAN	3 LEO	5 LIB	4 SCO	3 SCG	4 AQU
7 LEO	6 VIR	7 SCO	7 SAG	5 CAP	7 PIS
10 VIR	8 LIB	9 SAG	9 CAP	7 AQU	9 ARI
12 LIB	11 SCO	12 CAP	11 AQU	9 PIS	11 TAU
15 SCO	13 SAG	14 AQU	13 PIS	11 ARI	13 GEM
17 SAG	15 CAP	16 PIS	15 ARI	14 TAU	15 CAN
19 CAP	17 AQU	18 ARI	17 TAU	16 GEM	18 LEO
21 AQU	19 PIS	20 TAU	19 GEM	18 CAN	20 VIR
23 PIS	21 ARI	22 GEM	22 CAN	21 LEO	23 LIB
25 ARI	23 TAU	24 CAN	24 LEO	24 LEO	23 VIR
27 TAU	26 GEM	27 LEO	27 VIR	26 LIB	28 SAG
29 GEM	28 CAN	29 VIR	29 LIB	28 SCO	30 CAP
	31 LEO			30 SAG	

2006 MOON SIGNS

JAN	FEB	MAR	APR	MAY	JUN
1 AQU	1 ARI	1 ARI	1 GEM	1 CAN	2 VIR
3 PIS	3 TAU	3 TAU	4 CAN	3 LEO	5 LIB
5 ARI	6 GEM	5 GEM	6 LEO	6 VIR	7 SCO
7 TAU	8 CAN	7 CAN	9 VIR	8 LIB	10 SAG
9 GEM	10 LEO	10 LEO	11 LIB	11 SCO	12 CAP
12 CAN	13 VIR	12 VIR	14 SCO	13 SAG	14 AQU
14 LEO	16 LIB	15 LIB	16 SAG	15 CAP	16 PIS
17 VIR	18 SCO	17 SCO	18 CAP	18 AQU	18 ARI
19 LIB	20 SAG	20 SAG	20 AQU	20 PIS	20 TAU
22 SCO	23 CAP	22 CAP	22 PIS	22 ARI	22 GEM
24 SAG	25 AQU	24 AQU	25 ARI	24 TAU	25 CAN
26 CAP	27 PIS	26 PIS	27 TAU	26 GEM	27 LEO
28 AQU		28 ARI	29 GEM	28 CAN	29 VIR
30 PIS		30 TAU		31 LEO	

JUL	AUG	SEP	OCT	NOV	DEC
2 LIB	1 SCO	2 CAP	1 AQU	2 ARI	1 TAU
5 SCO	3 SAG	4 AQU	4 PIS	4 TAU	3 GEM
7 SAG	6 CAP	6 PIS	6 ARI	6 GEM	6 CAN
9 CAP	8 AQU	8 ARI	8 TAU	8 CAN	8 LEO
11 AQU	10 PIS	10 TAU	10 GEM	10 LEO	10 VIR
13 PIS	12 ARI	12 GEM	12 CAN	13 VIR	13 LIB
15 ARI	14 TAU	14 CAN	14 LEO	15 LIB	15 SCO
17 TAU	16 GEM	17 LEO	17 VIR	18 SCO	18 SAG
20 GEM	18 CAN	19 VIR	19 LIB	20 SAG	20 CAP
22 CAN	21 LEO	22 LIB	22 SCO	23 CAP	23 AQU
24 LEO	23 VIR	24 SCO	24 SAG	25 AQU	24 PIS
27 VIR	26 LIB	27 SAG	26 CAP	27 PIS	27 ARI
29 LIB	28 SCO	29 CAP	29 AQU	29 ARI	29 TAU
	31 SAG		31 PIS		31 GEM

2007 MOON SIGNS

JAN	FEB	MAR	APR	MAY	JUN
2 CAN	1 LEO	2 VIR	1 LIB	1 SCO	1 CAP
4 LEO	3 VIR	5 LIB	3 SCO	3 SAG	4 AQU
7 VIR	5 LIB	7 SCO	6 SAG	6 CAP	6 PIS
7 LIB	8 SCO	10 SAG	8 CAP	8 AQU	9 ARI
12 SCO	10 SAG	12 CAP	11 AQU	10 PIS	11 TAU
14 SAG	13 CAP	14 AQU	13 PIS	12 ARI	13 GEM
16 CAP	15 AQU	17 PIS	13 ARI	12 TAU	13 CAN
19 AQU	17 PIS	19 ARI	17 TAU	16 GEM	17 LEO
21 PIS	19 ARI	21 TAU	19 GEM	18 CAN	19 VIR
23 ARI	21 TAU	23 GEM	21 CAN	21 LEO	22 LIB
25 TAU	23 GEM	25 CAN	23 LEO	23 VIR	24 SCO
27 GEM	25 CAN	27 LEO	26 VIR	25 LIB	27 SAG
29 CAN	28 LEO	29 VIR	28 LIB	28 SCO	29 CAP
				31 SAG	

JUL	AUG	SEP	OCT	NOV	DEC
2 AQU	2 ARI	1 CAN	2 CAN	3 VIR	3 LIB
4 PIS	4 TAU	3 GEM	4 LEO	5 LIB	5 SCO
6 ARI	6 GEM	5 CAN	7 VIR	8 SCO	8 SAG
8 TAU	9 CAN	7 LEO	9 LIB	10 SAG	10 CAP
10 GEM	11 LEO	9 VIR	12 SCO	13 CAP	13 AQU
12 CAN	13 VIR	12 LIB	14 SAG	15 AQU	15 PIS
14 LEO	15 LIB	14 SCO	17 CAP	18 PIS	17 ARI
17 VIR	18 SCO	17 SAG	19 AQU	20 ARI	19 TAU
17 LIB	20 SAG	19 CAP	21 PIS	22 TAU	21 GEM
22 SCO	23 CAP	22 AQU	23 ARI	24 GEM	23 CAN
24 SAG	25 AQU	24 PIS	25 TAU	26 CAN	25 LEO
27 CAP	27 PIS	26 ARI	27 GEM	28 LEO	27 VIR
29 AQU	29 ARI	28 TAU	29 CAN	30 VIR	30 LIB
31 PIS		30 GEM	31 LEO		

2008 MOON SIGNS

JAN	FEB	MAR	APR	MAY	JUN
1 SCO	3 CAP	1 CAP	2 PIS	2 ARI	2 GEM
4 SAG	5 AQU	3 AQU	4 ARI	4 TAU	4 CAN
6 CAP	7 PIS	6 PIS	6 TAU	6 GEM	6 LEO
9 AQU	10 ARI	8 ARI	8 GEM	8 CAN	8 VIR
11 PIS	12 TAU	10 TAU	10 CAN	10 LEO	11 LIB
13 ARI	14 GEM	12 GEM	13 LEO	12 VIR	13 SCO
15 TAU	16 CAN	14 CAN	15 VIR	14 LIB	16 SAG
18 GEM	18 LEO	16 LEO	17 LIB	17 SCO	18 CAP
20 CAN	20 VIR	19 VIR	20 SCO	19 SAG	21 AQU
22 LEO	23 LIB	21 LIB	22 SAG	22 CAP	23 PIS
24 VIR	25 SCO	23 SCO	25 CAP	24 AQU	25 ARI
26 LIB	28 SCO	26 SAG	27 AQU	27 PIS	28 TAU
29 SCO		28 CAP	30 PIS	29 ARI	30 GEM
31 SAG		31 AQU		31 TAU	

JUL	AUG	SEP	OCT	NOV	DEC
2 CAN	2 VIR	1 LIB	3 SAG	2 CAP	2 AQU
4 LEO	4 LIB	3 SCO	5 CAP	4 AQU	4 PIS
6 VIR	7 SCO	6 SAG	8 AQU	7 PIS	6 ARI
8 LIB	9 SAG	8 CAP	10 PIS	9 ARI	9 TAU
10 SCO	12 CAP	11 AQU	13 ARI	11 TAU	11 GEM
13 SAG	14 AQU	13 PIS	15 TAU	13 GEM	13 CAN
15 CAP	17 PIS	15 ARI	17 GEM	15 CAN	15 LEO
18 AQU	19 ARI	17 TAU	19 CAN	17 LEO	17 VIR
20 PIS	21 TAU	19 GEM	21 LEO	19 VIR	19 LIB
23 ARI	23 GEM	22 CAN	23 VIR	22 LIB	21 SCO
25 TAU	25 CAN	24 LEO	25 LIB	24 SCO	24 SAG
27 GEM	27 LEO	26 VIR	28 SCO	27 SAG	26 CAP
29 CAN	30 VIR	28 LIB	30 SAG	29 CAP	29 AQU
31 LEO		30 SCO			31 PIS

2009 MOON SIGNS

JAN	FEB	MAR	APR	MAY	JUN
3 ARI	1 TAU	3 GEM	1 CAN	2 VIR	1 LIB
5 TAU	3 GEM	5 CAN	3 LEO	5 LIB	3 SCO
7 GEM	5 CAN	7 LEO	5 VIR	7 SCO	6 SAG
9 CAN	7 LEO	9 VIR	7 LIB	9 SAG	8 CAP
11 LEO	10 VIR	11 LIB	10 SCO	12 CAP	11 AQU
13 VIR	12 LIB	13 CSO	12 SAG	14 AQU	13 PIS
15 LIB	14 SCO	16 SAG	15 CAP	17 PIS	16 ARI
18 SCO	16 SAG	18 CAP	17 AQU	19 ARI	18 TAU
20 SAG	19 CAP	21 AQU	20 PIS	21 TAU	20 GEM
23 CAP	21 AQU	23 PIS	22 ARI	24 GEM	22 CAN
25 AQU	24 PIS	26 ARI	24 TAU	26 CAN	24 LEO
28 PIS	26 ARI	28 TAU	26 GEM	28 LEO	26 VIR
30 ARI	28 TAU	30 GEM	28 CAN	30 VIR	28 LIB
			30 LEO		30 SCO

JUL	AUG	SEP	OCT	NOV	DEC
3 SAG	2 CAP	3 PIS	3 ARI	1 TAU	1 GEM
5 CAP	4 AQU	5 ARI	5 TAU	4 GEM	3 CAN
8 AQU	7 PIS	8 TAU	7 GEM	6 CAN	5 LEO
10 PIS	9 ARI	10 GEM	9 CAN	8 LEO	7 VIR
13 ARI	11 TAU	12 CAN	12 LEO	10 VIR	9 LIB
15 TAU	14 GEM	14 LEO	14 VIR	12 LIB	11 SCO
17 GEM	16 CAN	16 VIR	16 LIB	14 SCO	14 SAG
19 CAN	18 LEO	18 LIB	18 SCO	17 SAG	16 CAP
21 LEO	20 VIR	20 SCO	20 SAG	19 CAP	19 AQU
23 VIR	22 LIB	23 SAG	23 CAP	21 AQU	21 PIS
26 LIB	24 SCO	25 CAP	25 AQU	24 PIS	24 ARI
28 SCO	26 SAG	28 AQU	28 PIS	26 ARI	26 TAU
30 SAG	29 CAP	30 PIS	30 ARI	29 TAU	29 GEM
	31 AQU				30 CAN

2010 MOON SIGNS

JAN	FEB	MAR	APR	MAY	JUN
1 LEO	2 LIB	1 LIB	2 SAG	2 CAP	1 AQU
3 VIR	4 SCO	3 SCO	4 CAP	4 AQU	3 PIS
6 LIB	6 SAG	6 SAG	7 AQU	7 PIS	6 ARI
8 SCO	9 CAP	8 CAP	9 PIS	9 ARI	8 TAU
10 SAG	11 AQU	11 AQU	12 ARI	12 TAU	10 GEM
13 CAP	14 PIS	13 PIS	14 TAU	14 GEM	12 CAN
15 AQU	16 ARI	16 ARI	17 GEM	16 CAN	14 LEO
18 PIS	19 TAU	18 TAU	19 CAN	18 LEO	17 VIR
20 ARI	21 GEM	20 GEM	21 LEO	20 VIR	19 LIB
22 TAU	23 CAN	23 CAN	23 VIR	22 LIB	21 SCO
25 GEM	25 LEO	25 LEO	25 LIB	25 SCO	23 SAG
27 CAN	27 VIR	27 VIR	27 SCO	27 SAG	25 CAP
29 LEO		28 LIB	29 SAG	29 CAP	28 AQU
31 VIR		31 SCO			30 PIS

JUL	AUG	SEP	OCT	NOV	DEC
3 ARI	2 TAU	3 CAN	2 LEO	3 LIB	2 SCO
5 TAU	4 GEM	5 LEO	4 VIR	5 SCO	4 SAG
8 GEM	6 CAN	7 VIR	6 LIB	7 SAG	6 CAP
10 CAN	8 LEO	9 LIB	8 SCO	9 CAP	9 AQU
12 LEO	10 VIR	11 SCO	10 SAG	11 AQU	11 PIS
14 VIR	12 LIB	13 SAG	12 CAP	14 PIS	14 ARI
16 LIB	14 SCO	15 CAP	15 AQU	16 ARI	16 TAU
18 SCO	17 SAG	18 AQU	17 PIS	19 TAU	18 GEM
20 SAG	19 CAP	20 PIS	20 ARI	21 GEM	21 CAN
23 CAP	21 AQU	23 ARI	22 TAU	23 CAN	23 LEO
25 AQU	24 PIS	25 TAU	25 GEM	26 LEO	25 VIR
28 PIS	26 ARI	28 GEM	27 CAN	28 VIR	27 LIB
30 ARI	29 TAU	30 CAN	29 LEO	30 LIB	29 SCO
	31 GEM		31 VIR		31 SAG

2011 MOON SIGNS

JAN	FEB	MAR	APR	MAY	JUN
3 CAP	1 AQU	1 AQU	2 ARI	2 TAU	3 CAN
5 AQU	4 PIS	3 PIS	4 TAU	4 GEM	5 LEO
7 PIS	6 ARI	6 ARI	7 GEM	6 CAN	7 VIR
10 ARI	9 TAU	8 TAU	9 CAN	9 LEO	9 LIB
12 TAU	11 GEM	11 GEM	11 LEO	11 VIR	11 SCO
15 GEM	14 CAN	13 CAN	14 VIR	13 LIB	13 SAG
17 CAN	16 LEO	15 LEO	16 LIB	15 SCO	16 CAP
19 LEO	18 VIR	17 VIR	18 SCO	17 SAG	18 AQU
21 VIR	20 LIB	19 LIB	20 SAG	19 CAP	20 PIS
23 LIB	22 SCO	21 SCO	22 CAP	21 AQU	23 ARI
25 SCO	24 SAG	23 SAG	24 AQU	24 PIS	25 TAU
28 SAG	26 CAP	25 CAP	27 PIS	26 ARI	28 GEM
30 CAP		28 AQU	29 ARI	29 TAU	30 CAN
		30 PIS		31 GEM	

JUL	AUG	SEP	OCT	NOV	DEC
2 LEO	1 VIR	1 SCO	1 SAG	1 AQU	1 PIS
4 VIR	3 LIB	3 SAG	3 CAP	4 PIS	3 ARI
6 LIB	5 SCO	5 CAP	5 AQU	6 ARI	6 TAU
9 SCO	7 SAG	8 AQU	7 PIS	9 TAU	8 GEM
11 SAG	9 CAP	10 PIS	10 ARI	11 GEM	11 CAN
13 CAP	11 AQU	13 ARI	12 TAU	14 CAN	13 LEO
15 AQU	14 PIS	15 TAU	15 GEM	16 LEO	15 VIR
18 PIS	16 ARI	18 GEM	17 CAN	18 VIR	18 LIB
20 ARI	19 TAU	20 CAN	20 LEO	20 LIB	20 SCO
23 TAU	21 GEM	22 LEO	22 VIR	22 SCO	22 SAG
25 GEM	24 CAN	24 VIR	24 LIB	24 SAG	24 CAP
27 CAN	26 LEO	27 LIB	26 SCO	26 CAP	26 AQU
30 LEO	28 VIR	29 SCO	28 SAG	29 AQU	28 PIS
	30 LIB		30 CAP		31 ARI

2012 MOON SIGNS

JAN	FEB	MAR	APR	MAY	JUN
2 TAU	1 GEM	2 CAN	1 LEO	2 LIB	1 SCO
5 GEM	4 CAN	4 LEO	3 VIR	4 SCO	3 SAG
7 CAN	6 LEO	6 VIR	5 LIB	6 SAG	5 CAP
9 LEO	8 VIR	8 LIB	7 SCO	8 CAP	7 AQU
12 VIR	10 LIB	11 SCO	9 SAG	11 AQU	9 PIS
14 LIB	12 SCO	13 SAG	11 CAP	13 PIS	11 ARI
16 SCO	14 SAG	15 CAP	13 AQU	15 ARI	14 TAU
18 SAG	17 CAP	17 AQU	16 PIS	18 TAU	17 GEM
20 CAP	19 AQU	19 PIS	18 ARI	20 GEM	19 CAN
22 AQU	21 PIS	22 ARI	20 TAU	23 CAN	21 LEO
25 PIS	23 ARI	24 TAU	23 GEM	25 LEO	24 VIR
27 ARI	26 TAU	27 GEM	26 CAN	28 VIR	26 LIB
30 TAU	28 GEM	29 CAN	28 LEO	30 LIB	28 SCO
			30 VIR		30 SAG

JUL	AUG	SEP	OCT	NOV	DEC
2 CAP	1 AQU	2 ARI	1 TAU	1 CAN	2 LEO
4 AQU	3 PIS	4 TAU	4 GEM	5 LEO	5 VIR
6 PIS	5 ARI	6 GEM	6 CAN	7 VIR	7 LIB
9 ARI	8 TAU	9 CAN	9 LEO	10 LIB	9 SCO
11 TAU	10 GEM	11 LEO	11 VIR	12 SCO	11 SAG
14 GEM	13 CAN	14 VIR	13 LIB	14 SAG	13 CAP
16 CAN	15 LEO	16 LIB	15 SCO	16 CAP	15 AQU
19 LEO	17 VIR	18 SCO	17 SAG	18 AQU	17 PIS
21 VIR	19 LIB	20 SAG	19 CAP	20 PIS	20 ARI
23 LIB	22 SCO	22 CAP	22 AQU	22 ARI	22 TAU
25 SCO	24 SAG	24 AQU	24 PIS	25 TAU	25 GEM
28 SAG	26 CAP	27 PIS	26 ARI	27 GEM	27 CAN
30 CAP	28 AQU	29 ARI	28 TAU	30 TAU	30 LEO
	30 PIS		31 GEM		

2013 MOON SIGNS

JAN	FEB	MAR	APR	MAY	JUN
1 VIR	2 SCO	1 SCO	2 CAP	1 AQU	2 ARI
3 LIB	4 SAG	3 SAG	4 AQU	3 PIS	4 TAU
6 SCO	6 CAP	5 CAP	6 PIS	5 ARI	6 GEM
8 SAG	8 AQU	7 AQU	8 ARI	8 TAU	9 CAN
10 CAP	10 PIS	10 PIS	10 TAU	10 GEM	12 LEO
12 AQU	12 ARI	12 ARI	13 GEM	13 CAN	13 VIR
14 PIS	15 TAU	14 TAU	15 CAN	15 LEO	16 LIB
16 ARI	17 GEM	17 GEM	18 LEO	18 VIR	18 SCO
18 TAU	20 CAN	19 CAN	20 VIR	20 LIB	21 SAG
21 GEM	22 LEO	22 LEO	23 LIB	22 SCO	23 CAP
23 CAN	25 VIR	24 VIR	25 SCO	24 SAG	25 AQU
26 LEO	27 LIB	26 LIB	27 SAG	26 CAP	27 PIS
28 VIR		28 SCO	29 CAP	28 AQU	29 ARI
31 LIB		30 SAG		30 PIS	

JUL	AUG	SEP	OCT	NOV	DEC
1 TAU	2 CAN	1 LEO	1 VIR	2 SCO	2 SAG
4 GEM	5 LEO	4 VIR	3 LIB	4 SAG	4 CAP
6 CAN	7 VIR	6 LIB	6 SCO	6 CAP	6 AQU
9 LEO	10 LIB	8 SCO	8 SAG	8 AQU	8 PIS
11 VIR	12 SCO	11 SAG	10 CAP	10 PIS	10 ARI
14 LIB	14 SAG	13 CAP	12 AQU	12 ARI	12 TAU
16 SCO	16 CAP	15 AQU	14 PIS	15 TAU	15 GEM
18 SAG	18 AQU	17 PIS	16 ARI	18 GEM	17 CAN
20 CAP	20 PIS	19 ARI	19 TAU	20 CAN	20 LEO
22 AQU	23 ARI	21 TAU	21 GEM	22 LEO	22 VIR
24 PIS	25 TAU	24 GEM	23 CAN	25 VIR	25 LIB
26 ARI	27 GEM	26 CAN	26 LEO	27 LIB	27 SCO
28 TAU	30 CAN	29 LEO	28 VIR	29 SCO	29 SAG
31 GEM			31 LIB		31 CAP

2014 MOON SIGNS

JAN	FEB	MAR	APR	MAY	JUN
2 AQU	1 PIS	2 ARI	1 TAU	3 CAN	1 LEO
4 PIS	3 ARI	4 TAU	3 GEM	5 LEO	4 VIR
6 ARI	5 TAU	6 GEM	5 CAN	8 VIR	6 LIB
8 TAU	7 GEM	9 CAN	8 LEO	10 LIB	9 SCO
11 GEM	10 CAN	11 LEO	10 VIR	12 SCO	11 SAG
13 CAN	12 LEO	14 VIR	13 LIB	15 SAG	13 CAP
16 LEO	15 VIR	16 LIB	15 SCO	17 CAP	15 AQU
18 VIR	17 LIB	19 SCO	17 SAG	19 AQU	17 PIS
21 LIB	19 SCO	21 SAG	19 CAP	21 PIS	19 ARI
23 SCO	22 SAG	23 CAP	21 AQU	23 ARI	21 TAU
25 SAG	24 CAP	25 AQU	24 PIS	25 TAU	24 GEM
28 CAP	26 AQU	27 PIS	26 ARI	27 GEM	26 CAN
30 AQU	28 PIS	29 ARI	29 TAU	30 CAN	29 LEO
			30 GEM		

JUL	AUG	SEP	OCT	NOV	DEC
1 VIR	2 SCO	1 SAG	3 AQU	1 PIS	3 TAU
4 LIB	5 SAG	3 CAP	5 PIS	3 ARI	5 GEM
6 SCO	7 CAP	5 AQU	7 ARI	5 TAU	7 CAN
8 SAG	9 AQU	7 PIS	9 TAU	7 GEM	9 LEO
10 CAP	11 PIS	9 ARI	11 GEM	10 CAN	12 VIR
12 AQU	13 ARI	11 TAU	13 CAN	12 LEO	14 LIB
14 PIS	15 TAU	14 GEM	16 LEO	15 VIR	17 SCO
16 ARI	17 GEM	16 CAN	18 VIR	17 LIB	19 SAG
19 TAU	20 CAN	18 LEO	21 LIB	20 SCO	21 CAP
21 GEM	22 LEO	21 VIR	23 SCO	22 SAG	23 AQU
23 CAN	25 VIR	23 LIB	25 SAG	24 CAP	25 PIS
26 LEO	27 LIB	26 SCO	28 CAP	26 AQU	28 ARI
28 VIR	30 SCO	28 SAG	30 AQU	28 PIS	30 TAU
31 LIB		30 CAP		30 ARI	

2015 MOON SIGNS

JAN	FEB	MAR	APR	MAY	JUN
1 GEM	2 LEO	1 LEO	2 LIB	2 SCO	1 SAG
3 CAN	5 VIR	4 VIR	5 SCO	5 SAG	3 CAP
6 LEO	7 LIB	6 LIB	8 SAG	7 CAP	6 AQU
8 VIR	10 SCO	9 SCO	10 CAP	9 AQU	8 PIS
11 LIB	12 SAG	11 SAG	12 AQU	11 PIS	11 ARI
13 SCO	14 CAP	14 CAP	14 PIS	14 ARI	13 TAU
16 SAG	16 AQU	16 AQU	16 ARI	16 TAU	14 GEM
18 CAP	18 PIS	18 PIS	18 TAU	18 GEM	16 CAN
20 AQU	20 ARI	20 ARI	20 GEM	20 CAN	19 LEO
22 PIS	22 TAU	22 TAU	22 CAN	22 LEO	21 VIR
24 ARI	25 GEM	24 GEM	25 LEO	25 VIR	24 LIB
26 TAU	27 CAN	26 CAN	27 VIR	27 LIB	26 SCO
28 GEM		29 LEO	30 LIB	30 SCO	28 SAG
31 CAN		31 VIR			

JUL	AUG	SEP	OCT	NOV	DEC
1 CAP	1 PIS	2 TAU	1 GEM	2 LEO	2 VIR
3 AQU	3 ARI	4 GEM	3 CAN	4 VIR	4 LIB
5 PIS	5 TAU	6 CAN	6 LEO	7 LIB	7 SCO
7 ARI	8 GEM	8 LEO	8 VIR	9 SCO	9 SAG
9 TAU	10 CAN	11 VIR	11 LIB	12 SAG	12 CAP
11 GEM	12 LEO	13 LIB	13 SCO	14 CAP	14 AQU
14 CAN	15 VIR	16 SCO	16 SAG	17 AQU	16 PIS
16 LEO	17 LIB	18 SAG	18 CAP	19 PIS	18 ARI
18 VIR	20 SCO	21 CAP	20 AQU	21 ARI	20 TAU
21 LIB	22 SAG	23 AQU	23 PIS	23 TAU	22 GEM
23 SCO	24 CAP	25 PIS	25 ARI	25 GEM	25 CAN
26 SAG	27 AQU	27 ARI	27 TAU	27 CAN	27 LEO
28 CAP	29 PIS	29 TAU	29 GEM	30 LEO	29 VIR
30 AQU	31 ARI		31 CAN		

2016 MOON SIGNS

JAN	FEB	MAR	APR	MAY	JUN
1 LIB	2 SAG	3 CAP	1 AQU	1 PIS	1 TAU
3 SCO	4 CAP	5 AQU	4 PIS	3 ARI	3 GEM
6 SAG	7 AQU	7 PIS	6 ARI	5 TAU	5 CAN
8 CAP	9 PIS	9 ARI	8 TAU	7 GEM	8 LEO
10 AQU	11 ARI	11 TAU	10 GEM	9 CAN	10 VIR
12 PIS	13 TAU	13 GEM	12 CAN	11 LEO	12 LIB
14 ARI	15 GEM	15 CAN	14 LEO	14 VIR	15 SCO
17 TAU	17 CAN	18 LEO	16 VIR	16 LIB	17 SAG
19 GEM	19 LEO	20 VIR	19 LIB	19 SCO	20 CAP
21 CAN	22 VIR	23 LIB	21 SCO	21 SAG	22 AQU
23 LEO	24 LIB	25 SAG	24 SAG	24 CAP	24 PIS
25 VIR	27 SCO	28 SAG	26 CAP	26 AQU	27 ARI
28 LIB	29 SAG	30 CAP	29 AQU	28 PIS	29 TAU
30 SCO				30 ARI	

JUL	AUG	SEP	OCT	NOV	DEC
1 GEM	1 LEO	2 LIB	2 SCO	1 SAG	1 CAP
3 CAN	4 VIR	5 SCO	5 SAG	3 CAP	3 AQU
5 LEO	6 LIB	7 SAG	7 CAP	6 AQU	5 PIS
7 VIR	9 SCO	10 CAP	10 AQU	8 PIS	8 ARI
10 LIB	11 SAG	12 AQU	12 PIS	10 ARI	10 TAU
12 SCO	13 CAP	14 PIS	14 ARI	12 TAU	12 GEM
15 SAG	16 AQU	16 ARI	16 TAU	14 GEM	14 CAN
17 CAP	18 PIS	19 TAU	18 GEM	16 CAN	16 LEO
19 AQU	20 ARI	21 GEM	20 CAN	18 LEO	18 VIR
22 PIS	22 TAU	23 CAN	22 LEO	21 VIR	20 LIB
24 ARI	24 GEM	25 LEO	24 VIR	23 LIB	23 SCO
26 TAU	26 CAN	27 VIR	27 LIB	26 SCO	25 SAG
28 GEM	29 LEO	30 PIB	29 SCO	28 SAG	29 CAP
30 CAN	31 VIR				30 AQU

2017 MOON SIGNS

JAN	FEB	MAR	APR	MAY	JUN
2 PIS	2 TAU	2 TAU	2 CAN	1 LEO	2 LIB
4 ARI	4 GEM	4 GEM	4 LEO	4 VIR	5 SCO
6 TAU	7 CAN	6 CAN	6 VIR	6 LIB	7 SAG
8 GEM	9 LEO	8 LEO	9 LIB	9 SCO	10 CAP
10 CAN	11 VIR	10 VIR	11 SCO	11 SAG	12 AQU
12 LEO	13 LIB	13 LIB	14 SAG	14 CAP	15 PIS
14 VIR	16 SCO	15 SCO	16 CAP	16 AQU	17 ARI
17 LIB	18 SAG	17 SAG	19 AQU	18 PIS	19 TAU
19 SCO	21 CAP	20 CAP	21 PIS	21 ARI	21 GEM
22 SAG	23 AQU	22 AQU	23 ARI	23 TAU	23 GEM
24 CAP	25 PIS	25 PIS	25 TAU	25 GEM	25 LEO
27 CAP	28 ARI	27 ARI	27 GEM	27 CAN	27 VIR
29 PIS		29 TAU	29 CAN	29 LEO	30 LIB
31 ARI		31 GEM		31 VIR	

JUL	AUG	SEP	OCT	NOV	DEC
2 SCO	1 SAG	2 AQU	2 PIS	1 ARI	2 GEM
5 SAG	3 CAP	5 PIS	4 ARI	3 TAU	4 CAN
7 CAP	6 TAU	7 ARI	6 TAU	5 GEM	6 LEO
10 AQU	8 PIS	9 TAU	8 GEM	7 CAN	8 VIR
12 PIS	11 ARI	11 GEM	10 CAN	9 LEO	11 LIB
14 ARI	13 TAU	13 CAN	13 LEO	11 VIR	13 SCO
17 TAU	15 GEM	15 LEO	15 VIR	13 LIB	15 SAG
19 GEM	17 CAN	18 VIR	17 LIB	16 SAC	18 CAP
21 CAN	19 LEO	20 LIB	19 SCO	18 SAG	20 AQU
23 LEO	21 VIR	22 SCO	22 SAG	21 CAP	23 PIS
25 VIR	23 LIB	24 SAG	24 CAP	23 AQU	25 ARI
27 LIB	26 SCO	27 CAP	27 AQU	26 PIS	28 TAU
29 SCO	28 SAG	29 AQU	29 PIS	28 ARI	30 GEM
	31 CAP			30 TAU	

2018 MOON SIGNS

JAN	FEB	MAR	APR	MAY	JUN
1 CAN	1 VIR	1 VIR	1 SCO	1 SAG	2 AQU
3 LEO	3 LIB	3 LIB	4 SAG	3 CAP	5 PIS
5 VIR	5 SCO	5 SCO	6 CAP	6 AQU	7 ARI
7 LIB	8 SAG	7 SAG	9 AQU	8 PIS	9 TAI
9 SCO	10 CAP	10 CAP	11 PIS	11 ARI	12 GEM
12 SAG	13 AQU	12 AQU	13 ARI	13 TAU	14 CAN
14 CAP	15 PIS	15 PIS	16 TAU	15 GEM	16 LEO
17 AQU	18 ARI	17 ARI	18 GEM	17 CAN	18 VIR
19 PIS	20 TAU	19 TAU	20 CAN	19 LEO	20 LIB
22 ARI	22 GEM	22 GEM	22 LEO	21 VIR	22 SCO
24 TAU	24 CAN	24 CAN	24 VIR	24 LIB	24 SAG
26 GEM	26 LEO	26 LEO	26 LIB	26 SCO	27 CAP
28 CAN		28 VIR	29 SCO	28 SAG	29 AQU
30 LEO		30 LIB		31 CAP	

JUL	AUG	SEP	OCT	NOV	DEC
2 PIS	1 ARI	2 GEM	1 CAN	2 VIR	1 LIB
4 ARI	3 TAU	4 CAN	3 LEO	4 LIB	3 SCO
7 TAU	5 GEM	6 LEO	5 VIR	6 SCO	5 SAG
9 GEM	7 CAN	8 VIR	7 LIB	8 SAG	8 CAP
11 CAN	9 LEO	10 LIB	9 SCO	10 CAP	10 AQU
13 LEO	11 VIR	12 SCO	12 SAG	13 AQU	13 PIS
15 VIR	14 LIB	14 SAG	14 CAP	15 PIS	15 ARI
17 LIB	16 SCO	17 CAP	17 AQU	18 ARI	18 TAU
19 SCO	18 SAG	19 AQU	19 PIS	20 TAU	20 GEM
22 SAG	20 CAP	22 PIS	22 ARI	22 GEM	22 CAN
24 CAN	23 AQU	24 ARI	24 TAU	25 CAN	24 LEO
27 AQU	26 PIS	27 TAU	26 GEM	27 LEO	26 VIR
29 PIS	28 ARI	29 GEM	28 CAN	29 VIR	28 LIB
	30 TAU		30 LEO		30 SCO

2019 MOON SIGNS

JAN	FEB	MAR	APR	MAY	JUN
2 SAG	3 AQU	2 AQU	1 PIS	1 ARI	2 GEM
4 CAP	5 PIS	5 PIS	3 ARI	3 TAU	4 CAN
7 AQU	8 ARI	7 ARI	6 TAU	5 GEM	6 LEO
9 PIS	10 TAU	10 TAU	8 GEM	8 CAN	8 VIR
12 ARI	13 GEM	12 GEM	10 CAN	10 LEO	10 LIB
14 TAU	15 CAN	14 CAN	13 LEO	12 VIR	12 VIR
16 GEM	17 LEO	16 LEO	15 VIR	14 LIB	15 SAG
18 CAN	19 VIR	18 VIR	17 LIB	16 SCO	17 CAP
20 LEO	21 LIB	20 LIB	19 SCO	18 SAG	19 AQU
22 VIR	23 SCO	22 SCO	21 SAG	21 CAP	22 PIS
24 LIB	25 SAG	25 SAG	23 CAP	23 AQU	24 ARI
27 SCO	28 CAP	27 CAP	26 AQU	26 PIS	27 TAU
29 SAG		29 AQU	28 PIS	28 ARI	29 GEM
31 CAP				30 TAU	

JUL	AUG	SEP	OCT	NOV	DEC
1 CAN	2 VIR	2 SCO	3 SAG	3 AQU	3 PIS
3 LEO	4 LIB	4 SAG	4 CAP	5 PIS	5 ARI
5 VIR	6 SCO	7 CAP	6 AQU	8 ARI	8 TAU
8 LIB	8 SAG	9 AQU	9 PIS	10 TAU	10 GEM
10 SCO	11 CAP	12 PIS	11 ARI	13 GEM	12 CAN
12 SAG	13 AQU	14 ARI	14 TAU	15 CAN	14 LEO
14 CAP	15 PIS	17 TAU	16 GEM	17 LEO	17 VIR
17 AQU	18 ARI	19 GEM	19 CAN	19 VIR	19 LIB
19 PIS	20 TAU	22 CAN	21 LEO	21 LIB	21 SCO
22 ARI	23 GEM	24 LEO	23 VIR	24 SCO	23 SAG
24 TAU	25 CAN	26 VIR	25 LIB	26 SAG	25 CAP
27 GEM	27 LEO	28 LIB	27 SCO	28 CAP	28 AQU
29 CAN	29 VIR	30 SCO	29 SAG	30 AQU	30 PIS
31 LEO	31 LIB		31 CAP		

530

2020 MOON SIGNS

JAN	FEB	MAR	APR	MAY	JUN
1 ARI	3 GEM	1 GEM	2 LEO	2 VIR	2 SCO
4 TAU	5 CAN	3 CAN	4 VIR	4 LIB	4 SAG
6 GEM	7 LEO	6 LEO	6 LIB	6 SCO	6 CAP
9 CAN	9 VIR	8 VIR	8 SCO	8 SAG	8 AQU
11 LEO	11 LIB	10 LIB	10 SAG	10 CAP	11 PIS
13 VIR	13 SCO	12 SCO	12 CAP	12 AQU	13 ARI
15 LIB	15 SAG	14 SAG	15 AQU	14 PIS	16 TAU
17 SCO	18 CAP	16 CAP	17 PIS	17 ARI	18 GEM
19 SAG	20 AQU	18 AQU	20 ARI	19 TAU	21 CAN
22 CAP	23 PIS	21 PIS	22 TAU	22 GEM	23 LEO
24 AQU	25 ARI	23 ARI	25 GEM	24 CAN	25 VIR
26 PIS	28 TAU	26 TAU	27 CAN	27 LEO	27 LIB
29 ARI		28 GEM	29 LEO	29 VIR	29 SCO
31 TAU		31 CAN		31 LIB	

JUL	AUG	SEP	OCT	NOV	DEC
1 SAG	2 ARI	1 PIS	3 TAU	2 GEM	1 CAN
3 CAP	4 PIS	3 ARI	5 GEM	4 CAN	4 LEO
6 AQU	7 ARI	6 TAU	8 CAN	7 LEO	6 VIR
8 PIS	9 TAU	8 GEM	10 LEO	9 VIR	8 LIB
11 ARI	12 GEM	11 CAN	13 VIR	11 LIB	10 SCO
13 TAU	14 CAN	13 LEO	15 LIB	13 SCO	12 SAG
16 GEM	17 LEO	15 VIR	17 SCO	15 SAG	14 CAP
18 CAN	19 VIR	17 LIB	19 SAG	17 CAP	17 AQU
20 LEO	21 LIB	19 SCO	21 CAP	19 AQU	19 PIS
22 VIR	23 SCO	21 SAG	23 AQU	21 PIS	21 ARI
24 LIB	25 SAG	23 CAP	25 PIS	24 ARI	24 TAU
26 SCO	27 CAP	26 AQU	28 ARI	26 TAU	26 GEM
29 SAG	29 AQU	28 PIS	30 TAU	29 GEM	29 CAN
31 CAP		30 ARI			31 LEO

2021 MOON SIGNS

JAN	FEB	MAR	APR	MAY	JUN
2 VIR	1 LIB	2 SCO	1 SAG	2 AQU	1 PIS
5 LIB	3 SCO	4 SAG	3 CAP	4 PIS	3 ARI
7 SCO	5 SAG	6 CAP	5 AQU	7 ARI	6 TAU
9 SAG	7 CAP	9 AQU	7 PIS	9 TAU	8 GEM
11 CAP	9 AQU	11 PIS	10 ARI	12 GEM	11 CAN
13 AQU	12 PIS	13 ARI	12 TAU	14 CAN	13 LEO
15 PIS	14 ARI	16 TAU	15 GEM	17 LEO	15 VIR
18 ARI	16 TAU	18 GEM	17 CAN	19 VIR	18 LIB
20 TAU	19 GEM	21 CAN	20 LEO	21 LIB	20 SCO
23 GEM	21 CAN	23 LEO	22 VIR	23 SCO	22 SAG
25 CAN	24 LEO	25 VIR	24 LIB	25 SAG	24 CAP
27 LEO	26 VIR	28 LIB	26 SCO	27 CAP	26 AQU
30 VIR	28 LIB	30 SCO	28 SAG	29 AQU	28 PIS
			30 CAP		30 ARI

JUL	AUG	SEP	OCT	NOV	DEC
3 TAU	2 GEM	1 CAN	3 VIR	1 LIB	1 SCO
5 GEM	4 CAN	3 LEO	5 LIB	3 SCO	3 SAG
8 CAN	7 LEO	5 VIR	7 SCO	5 SAG	5 CAP
10 LEO	9 VIR	7 LIB	9 SAG	7 CAP	7 AQU
13 VIR	11 LIB	10 SCO	11 CAP	9 AQU	9 PIS
15 LIB	13 SCO	12 SAG	13 AQU	12 PIS	11 ARI
17 SCO	15 SAG	14 CAP	15 PIS	14 ARI	14 TAU
19 SAG	18 CAP	16 AQU	18 ARI	16 TAU	16 GEM
21 CAP	20 AQU	18 PIS	20 TAU	19 GEM	19 CAN
23 AQU	22 PIS	20 ARI	23 GEM	21 CAN	21 LEO
25 PIS	24 ARI	23 TAU	25 CAN	24 LEO	24 VIR
28 ARI	26 TAU	25 GEM	28 LEO	26 VIR	26 LIB
30 TAU	29 GEM	28 CAN	30 VIR	29 LIB	28 SCO
		30 LEO			30 SAG

2022 MOON SIGNS

JAN	FEB	MAR	APR	MAY	JUN
1 CAP	1 PIS	1 PIS	2 TAU	2 GEM	1 CAN
3 AQU	4 ARI	3 ARI	4 GEM	4 CAN	3 LEO
5 PIS	6 TAU	6 TAU	7 CAN	7 LEO	6 VIR
8 ARI	9 GEM	8 GEM	9 LEO	9 VIR	8 LIB
10 TAU	11 CAN	11 CAN	12 VIR	12 LIB	10 SCO
12 GEM	14 LEO	13 LEO	14 LIB	14 SCO	12 SAG
15 CAN	16 VIR	16 VIR	16 SCO	16 SAG	14 CAP
17 LEO	18 LIB	18 LIB	18 SAG	18 CAP	16 AQU
20 VIR	21 SCO	20 SCO	20 CAP	20 AQU	18 PIS
22 LIB	23 SAG	22 SAG	23 AQU	22 PIS	20 ARI
24 SCO	25 CAP	24 CAP	25 PIS	24 ARI	23 TAU
27 SAG	27 AQU	27 AQU	27 ARI	27 TAU	25 GEM
29 CAP		28 PIS	29 TAU	29 GEM	29 CAN
31 AQU		31 ARI			30 LEO

JUL	AUG	SEP	OCT	NOV	DEC
3 VIR	1 LIB	2 SAG	2 CAP	2 PIS	1 ARI
5 LIB	4 SCO	4 CAP	4 AQU	4 ARI	4 TAU
8 SCO	6 SAG	6 AQU	6 PIS	7 TAU	6 GEM
10 SAG	8 CAP	8 PIS	8 ARI	9 GEM	9 CAN
12 CAP	10 AQU	11 ARI	10 TAU	11 CAN	11 LEO
14 AQU	12 PIS	13 TAU	13 GEM	14 LEO	14 VIR
16 PIS	14 ARI	15 GEM	15 CAN	16 VIR	16 LIB
18 ARI	16 TAU	18 CAN	17 LEO	19 LIB	18 SCO
20 TAU	19 GEM	20 LEO	20 VIR	21 SCO	21 SAG
23 GEM	21 CAN	23 VIR	22 LIB	23 SAG	23 CAP
25 CAN	24 LEO	25 LIB	25 SCO	25 CAP	25 AQU
28 LEO	26 VIR	27 SCO	27 SAG	27 AQU	27 PIS
30 VIR	29 LIB	29 SAG	29 CAP	29 PIS	29 ARI
	31 AQU		31 AQU		31 TAU

2023 MOON SIGNS

JAN	FEB	MAR	APR	MAY	JUN
2 GEM	1 CAN	3 LEO	2 VIR	2 LIB	3 SAG
5 CAN	4 LEO	5 VIR	4 LIB	4 SCO	5 CAP
7 LEO	6 VIR	8 LIB	7 SCO	6 SAG	7 AQU
10 VIR	9 LIB	10 SCO	9 SAG	8 CAP	9 PIS
12 LIB	11 SCO	13 SAG	11 CAP	10 AQU	11 ARI
15 SCO	13 SAG	15 CAP	13 AQU	12 PIS	13 TAU
17 SAG	16 CAP	17 AQU	15 PIS	15 ARI	15 GEM
19 CAP	18 AQU	19 PIS	17 ARI	17 TAU	18 CAN
21 AQU	20 PIS	21 ARI	19 TAU	19 GEM	20 LEO
23 PIS	22 ARI	23 TAU	22 GEM	21 CAN	23 VIR
25 ARI	24 TAU	25 GEM	24 CAN	24 LEO	25 LIB
27 TAU	26 GEM	28 CAN	27 LEO	26 VIR	28 SCO
30 GEM	28 CAN	30 LEO	29 VIR	29 LIB	30 SAG
				31 SCO	

JUL	AUG	SEP	OCT	NOV	DEC
2 CAP	2 PIS	1 ARI	3 GEM	1 CAN	1 LEO
4 AQU	4 ARI	3 TAU	5 CAN	4 LEO	3 VIR
6 PIS	7 TAU	5 GEM	7 LEO	6 VIR	6 LIB
8 ARI	9 GEM	8 CAN	10 VIR	9 LIB	8 SCO
10 TAU	11 CAN	10 LEO	12 LIB	11 SCO	11 SAG
13 GEM	14 LEO	13 VIR	15 SCO	13 SAG	13 CAP
15 CAN	16 VIR	15 LIB	17 SAG	16 CAP	15 AQU
17 LEO	19 LIB	18 SCO	19 CAP	18 AQU	17 PIS
20 VIR	21 SCO	20 SAG	22 AQU	20 PIS	19 ARI
23 LIB	24 SAG	22 CAP	24 PIS	22 ARI	21 TAU
25 SCO	26 CAP	24 AQU	26 ARI	24 TAU	24 GEM
27 SAG	28 AQU	26 PIS	28 TAU	26 GEM	26 CAN
29 CAP	30 PIS	28 ARI	30 GEM	29 CAN	28 LEO
31 AQU		30 TAU			31 VIR

2024 MOON SIGNS

JAN	FEB	MAR	APR	MAY	JUN
2 LIB	1 SCO	2 SAG	3 AQU	2 PIS	3 TAU
5 SCO	4 SAG	4 CAP	5 PIS	4 ARI	5 GEM
7 SAG	6 CAP	6 AQU	7 ARI	6 TAU	7 CAN
9 CAP	8 AQU	8 PIS	9 TAU	8 GEM	9 LEO
11 AQU	10 PIS	10 ARI	11 GEM	10 CAN	12 VIR
13 PIS	12 AQU	12 TAU	13 CAN	13 LEO	14 LIB
16 ARI	14 TAU	14 GEM	15 LEO	15 VIR	17 SCO
18 TAU	16 GEM	17 CAN	18 VIR	18 LIB	19 SAG
20 GEM	18 CAN	19 LEO	20 LIB	20 SCO	21 CAP
22 CAN	21 LEO	22 VIR	23 SCO	23 SAG	23 AQU
25 LEO	23 VIR	24 LIB	25 SAG	25 CAP	26 PIS
27 VIR	26 LIB	27 SCO	28 CAP	27 AQU	27 ARI
30 LIB	28 SCO	29 SAG	30 AQU	29 PIS	30 TAU
		31 CAP		31 ARI	

JUL	AUG	SEP	OCT	NOV	DEC
2 GEM	3 LEO	1 VIR	1 LIB	3 SAG	2 CAP
2 CAN	5 VIR	4 LIB	4 SCO	5 CAP	4 AQU
6 LEO	8 LIB	7 SCO	6 SAG	7 AQU	7 PIS
9 VIR	10 SCO	9 SAG	9 CAP	9 PIS	9 ARI
11 LIB	13 SAG	11 CAP	11 AQU	12 ARI	11 TAU
14 SCO	15 CAP	14 AQU	13 PIS	14 TAU	13 GEM
16 SAG	17 AQU	16 PIS	15 ARI	16 GEM	16 CAN
19 CAP	19 PIS	18 ARI	17 TAU	18 CAN	17 LEO
21 AQU	21 ARI	20 TAU	19 GEM	20 LEO	20 VIR
23 PIS	23 TAU	22 GEM	21 CAN	22 VIR	22 LIB
25 ARI	25 GEM	24 CAN	24 LEO	25 LIB	25 SCO
27 TAU	28 CAN	26 LEO	26 VIR	27 SCO	27 SAG
29 GEM	30 LEO	29 VIR	28 LIB	30 SAG	29 CAP
31 CAN			31 SCO		

2025 MOON SIGNS

JAN	FEB	MAR	APR	MAY	JUN
1 AQU	1 ARI	1 ARI	1 GEM	1 CAN	1 VIR
3 PIS	3 TAU	3 TAU	3 CAN	3 LEO	4 LIB
5 ARI	6 GEM	5 GEM	5 LEO	5 VIR	6 SCO
7 TAU	8 CAN	7 CAN	8 VIR	8 LIB	9 SAG
9 GEM	10 LEO	9 LEO	10 LIB	10 SCO	11 CAP
11 CAN	12 VIR	12 VIR	13 SCO	13 SAG	14 AQU
14 LEO	15 LIB	14 LIB	15 SAG	15 CAP	16 PIS
16 VIR	17 SCO	17 SCO	18 CAP	18 AQU	18 ARI
18 LIB	20 SAG	19 SAG	20 AQU	20 PIS	20 TAU
21 SCO	22 CAP	22 CAP	23 PIS	22 ARI	22 GEM
23 SAG	25 AQU	24 AQU	25 ARI	24 TAU	24 CAN
26 CAP	27 PIS	26 PIS	27 TAU	26 GEM	27 LEO
28 AQU		28 ARI	29 GEM	28 CAN	29 VIR
30 PIS		30 TAU		30 LEO	

JUL	AUG	SEP	OCT	NOV	DEC
1 LEO	3 SAG	1 CAP	1 AQU	2 ARI	1 TAU
4 SCO	5 CAP	4 AQU	3 PIS	4 TAU	3 GEM
6 SAG	7 AQU	6 PIS	6 ARI	6 GEM	5 CAN
9 CAP	10 PIS	8 ARI	8 TAU	8 CAN	7 LEO
11 AQU	12 ARI	10 TAU	10 GEM	10 LEO	10 VIR
13 PIS	14 TAU	12 GEM	12 CAN	12 VIR	12 LIB
15 ARI	16 GEM	14 CAN	14 LEO	15 LIB	14 SCO
18 TAU	18 CAN	17 LEO	16 VIR	17 SCO	17 SAG
20 GEM	20 LEO	19 VIR	18 LIB	20 SAG	20 CAP
22 CAN	23 VIR	21 LIB	21 SCO	22 CAP	22 AQU
24 LEO	25 LIB	24 SCO	23 SAG	25 AQU	24 PIS
26 VIR	27 SCO	26 SAG	26 CAP	27 PIS	27 ARI
29 LIB	30 SAG	29 CAP	28 AQU	29 ARI	29 TAU
31 SCO			31 PIS		31 GEM

Numerology - What Do Numbers Tell About You?

There are certain vibrations in the letters of your name and in the date of birth, which could influence you life and destiny. First, let's find the' numerical sign'. The science of numbers is the oldest magic science in the world. Next, you have a table with the numerical values from the mathematician and philosopher Pythagoras. Here is how you can find your number!.

1	2	3	4	5	6	7	8	9
A	B	C	D	E	F	G	H	I
J	K	L	M	N	O	P	Q	R
S	T	U	V	W	X	Y	Z	

Let's suppose that your name is LOREDANA ELENA BALU and that you were born in **11/27/1972**. Write the corresponding numbers under your name, that is: **36954151 53551 2133**. Add up all these numbers. The result is **62**. Then you add up **6 + 2 = 8**. If this sum is also a two digit number, add these two digits together. You were born under this number. If you are married you can use that name also. Use the name that you feel closer to.

Let's see where your destiny leads you! Using your date of birth you can determine your destiny or, in other words, your life partner. Using the example above (**11/27/1972**), add up all these numbers - **1 + 1 + 2 + 7 + 7 + 2 = 30**. Since **3 + 0 = 3**, your destiny is number **3**.

One - The Leader

This number has the following symbols: the Sun and the Sword. Number one means first. You are a leader, or you consider yourself a leader. You think you are in the center of the Universe. You are strong, and you can influence everybody around you. You have the talent to lead. You are ambitious, authoritarian, and always in a hurry. Sometimes you make decisions too fast, and as a result, you might make mistakes. If you make mistakes, you push things to their limits just to show that you are right. You are stubborn, and you never give in. You have to win. You are aggressive; you are the warrior type. It's good for you to be busy in a sport. You have to select a career or position in life that brings you satisfaction with the responsibility and authority that you have. Your destiny is to be a leader, but if you are obliged to be a subordinate you will become bitter and rude, and you will not collaborate with the others. You may also win a great deal of money, but you will spend it fast. You try to do your best in understanding other people socially and romantically. You can get along with number 3, who is charming; with number 6, who is obedient; and with number 9, who loves you. Be careful, don't be too bossy!

Your Road leads you toward the top of the mountain; once there, you should stay there. Never give up! This road requires ambition, strong will, and determination!

Two - Good and Quiet

This number has the following symbols: The Book and the Moon. This number is characterized by good balance and good health. It can also be a sign of poverty and death. You are generous and a diplomat. Your mind is very clear and bright. You are such an optimist that you forget your own interest and so generous that you might lose everything. But this doesn't bother you much. You are attracted to people who have problems. You love to give an good advice. Tolerant and understanding, you forgive a lot. Some people will take advantage of you. You are very friendly, full of imagination, and you love peace. Sometimes you are lazy; you accept undesirable conditions without complaining. You adapt to any situation. You don't seek power. In a difficult situation you can become a dreamer, looking for shelter in the misty world of imagination. You never aim very high. Two is an emotional number. Your partners should not hurt your feelings. You will get along well with the numbers 4, 7, and 8. Be careful about the numbers 6 and 9, who are also emotional. If you run into these numbers, the journey is not going to be very pleasant.

Your Road winds smoothly along the green meadows without ups and downs. This number is well balanced and quiet, never pushing himself ahead of others.

Three - Smart

This number has the following symbols: the Triangle and Mars. The past, present, and future play an important role in your life. You are sociable, attractive, convincing, charming, and have influence upon the people around you. You adapt easily to any situation because you have a quick mind, you are intuitive, and you are a native psychologist. In any situation, you choose the best way to solve the problem. You have talent, and you are gifted in any field of work you choose. You struggle to satisfy everybody around you; you do your best to entertain others, and it's hard for you to break relationships. Number 3 lives in the present, never regretting the past and never thinking about the future. You have a tendency to buy on credit and to spend beyond your means. You are an optimist; you know how to take advantage of any opportunity. You are inpatient, and you cannot stand dealing with the every day troubles of life. You cannot be careless about your duties. You are very independent, and you have a lot of ideas. It is hard for you to be obedient. You can become too proud and without scruples. The number 3 has to make some efforts to understand the emotional signs. You get along well with numbers 1, 5, 6, and 9.

YOUR ROAD is well built running here and there, going round obstacles, and adapting to certain situations. You are clever and flexible.

Four - Solidarity

This number has the following symbols: the Square and Mercury, and represents the four seasons and the four elements. This is the number of solidarity. You are honest and loyal. Anybody can count on you, but you are not very happy. Entertainment and leisure is not for you. You take life very seriously, and you are attracted by convention. You are conservative, and you enjoy family life, being faithful to its obligations and duties. You don't really enjoy new ideas without studying them for awhile. You are methodical, spending a lot of time before deciding what to do, and your plans are very detailed. You appreciate receiving high honors, and they make you very happy. You appreciate stability and security in life. Sometimes you underestimate yourself. Number 4 can also become the symbol of poverty and defeat. You always fear the future, and you hate gambling and taking risks - unless you are well rewarded. You have no one particular talent, and that's why you have to work hard to succeed. You are good in any activity that requires precession, method, and observation. Number 4 is a rational number, and he gets along well with numbers 2, 7, and 8.

YOUR ROAD is the main road. It is straight; it has many traffic signs and speed restrictions. It is the road of hard work and duty. It does not lead to danger and misfortune.

Five - Adventure

All risks are for number 5, regardless of the game. You are an adventurer; you love any unexpected change in your life; you love new experiences and the unknown. You are right most of the time, and you are annoyingly lucky. You are a revolutionary under the sign of Jupiter. You take advantage of all opportunities. You feel at home everywhere, and you have a real talent for foreign languages. You hate to be bored, so you look for obstacles and dangers. You are independent, very active, and practical. You are not very educated, but you have a lot of life experiences. You love to live your life fully with your friends, and you can do a lot for them. However, you do not accept their advice; it is too boring for you. Nothing is monotonous around you; you always look for excitement in a variety of directions. Nothing scares you. You can count on your luck no matter what happens. Sometimes you get very angry, and you might even become dangerous to the people around you. You succeed in any job that implies risk. Banks fascinate you. You are intuitive and will yield to the emotional signs in order to get along with them. Number 5 will associate with the following numbers: 1, 3, 6, and 9, but they should be careful because you will quickly get tired of them. To maintain the relationship, they will have to surprise you frequently.

Your Road is abrupt and has ups and downs. It is full of surprises, and of course, it is not boring at all. You need a lot of good luck to pass all dangers and barriers.

Six - Good Heart

This number has the following symbols: the 6 colors of the rainbow and Venus. This sign means attraction, harmony, and trust. You like nice things because you are sensitive. You are also a little shy and naive. You love children, animals, nature, flowers, and birds. You are always happy, nice, open, and always changing your ideas. You love to be appreciated, and you also love receiving honors - even if they are minor. You hate to argue when your friend's opinion is different from yours. You are easily influenced by someone else, and you have a hard time making up your own mind. Only the people closest to you might be right, everybody else is wrong. People might think you are hypocritical. Sometimes you are; you agree in order to avoid arguing. This diplomacy might be due to fear. You are very sensitive; you hurt many times; and you might cry. You will succeed in life because you are an artist, but if you aren't lucky, it means that you lack ambition. You may be lucky in politics because you are very conventional. Your closest friends are numbers: 1, 3, 5, and 9.

Your Road is a smooth, winding path along a quiet river with plenty of resting places. You are happy and patient. This is the path of duty and altruism.

SEVEN - MYSTERY

There are 7 Cardinal points, 7 planets and 7 days of the week. The number 7 is a magical number. It is the number of poetry and mystery. It is under the influence of Saturn, and it means knowledge and meditation. You have a universal intelligence, an exceptional intuition, and an active imagination that can lead you to success. You are not open, you don't say much. You like to be by yourself. You hate mediocrity and take offense to your partners' vulgarity and bad actions. You want to be above everybody else. Material issues are not a problem for you. You will be good as a monk or philosopher. If you reach the top, you will be isolated. You have good intuition and clairvoyance, but you lack tact. This might bring you trouble. You should have no connection with 2, 6, or 9, but you can get along fine with 1, 3, 4, and 8.

YOUR ROAD is scattered with crosses and cannibalistic signs. It is up to you to interpret all these. The road goes through thick forests, and there are many places good for meditation.

EIGHT - MONEY

This number is under the influence of Uranus. You never change direction, you are straight in your thoughts and actions, and nobody can stop you. If you come to a wall that you cannot climb, you break it down. You are strong, and you know how to make people love you. You have an excellent memory, and you are highly resilient. You don't have patience for vague ideas. You have a tendency of taking advantage of your friends. Sometimes they take advantage of you as well. You have magic in yourself in making money. You have to be careful, though, or you might go to jail. Your best companion is number 2 because he or she brings you balance. You also feel secure with number 4 and number 7.

YOUR ROAD is wide and functional. Walking on it, you should be careful. You are efficient and willing to keep on going. Your fate will pay you for your effort.

NINE - GENIUS

This number is under the influence of Neptune. The symbol is the vast sea. You are strong, and you have a strong personality. You have genius, intelligence, and a great energy for creation. You will get anything you wish for, and you will always want more because you are ambitious. You are honest, good, generous, and optimistic. You are also wise, and this will keep you away from troubles and extremes. You might become very proud, arrogant, and preoccupied

537

with yourself. Stop admiring and thinking of yourself so highly while ignoring others. You can do well in art, industry, or science. People tend to admire you and appreciate you, attributing to you qualities that you might not in reality have. You are like a magnet; you are controlled by the stars. Avoid number 2, who is very emotional, and number 6, who likes your spirit and flexibility. Number 9s will get along very well with number 1, will love number 3's charm, and will become number 5's accomplice.

YOUR ROAD is privileged and protected and has lots of priorities. It leads you everywhere - though fields and oceans, seas and mountains - and nothing stops it. This is truly the successful road.

LIGIA BALU

www.ligiabalu.com

ASTROLOGICAL BOOKS:

A COMPLETE COMPILATION of ancient and modern reflections

on the individual zodiac signs. Learn how to chart your **PERSONAL DESTINY**, understand your **SEXUALITY**, discover your **COMPATIBILITY WITH YOUR SOUL-MATE**, determine the **DESTINY OF YOUR SOUL-MATE**, find your **STARS**, and gain other information about your **FUTURE**. **Complete astrological information on Love Signs, Sun Signs, Moon Signs, Planets, Houses, Numerology**, as well as the complete **Astrological Tables for the Years from 1900 to 2025 and instruction on how to cast your very own Chart.**

Order the book for your specific Zodiac sign or the COMPLETE ASTROLOGY book series which contains information on *ALL TWELVE SIGNS* - from **ARIES** to **PISCES**. Each book contain over 550 pages.

INDIVIDUAL ZODIAC BOOKS

Individual Love Signs, Sun Signs, Moon Signs, Planets, Houses, Astrological Tables, Numerology, Relationships With Other Signs and a lot more in each book.

ASTROLOGY - ARIES

HOW TO FIND YOUR SOUL-MATE, STARS AND DESTINY
ISBN: 0-9651186-2-2   Price: $49.95

ASTROLOGY - TAURUS

HOW TO FIND YOUR SOUL-MATE, STARS AND DESTINY
ISBN: 0-9651186-3-0   Price: $49.95

Astrology - Gemini

HOW TO FIND YOUR SOUL-MATE, STARS AND DESTINY
ISBN: 0-9651186-4-9   Price: $49.95

Astrology - Cancer

HOW TO FIND YOUR SOUL-MATE, STARS AND DESTINY
ISBN: 0-9651186-5-7   Price: $49.95

Astrology - Leo

HOW TO FIND YOUR SOUL-MATE, STARS AND DESTINY
ISBN: 0-9651186-6-5   Price: $49.95

Astrology - Virgo

HOW TO FIND YOUR SOUL-MATE, STARS AND DESTINY
ISBN: 0-9651186-7-3   Price: $49.95

Astrology - Libra

HOW TO FIND YOUR SOUL-MATE, STARS AND DESTINY
ISBN: 0-9651186-8-1   Price: $49.95

Astrology - Scorpio

HOW TO FIND YOUR SOUL-MATE, STARS AND DESTINY
ISBN: 0-9651186-9-X   Price: $49.95

Astrology - Sagittarius

HOW TO FIND YOUR SOUL-MATE, STARS AND DESTINY
ISBN: 1-892530-00-7   Price: $49.95

Astrology - Capricorn

HOW TO FIND YOUR SOUL-MATE, STARS AND DESTINY
ISBN: 1-892530-02-3 Price: $49.95

Astrology - Aquarius

HOW TO FIND YOUR SOUL-MATE, STARS AND DESTINY
ISBN: 1-892530-01-5 Price: $49.95

Astrology - Pisces

HOW TO FIND YOUR SOUL-MATE, STARS AND DESTINY
ISBN: 1-892530-03-1 Price: $49.95

True - Stories:

Believe In Your Dreams, Not In Your Fears

Is the inspiring and unforgettable story of a young girl who possessed an **INDOMITABLE SPIRIT** that r5efused to give up no matter what life gave her. I*n her own brutally honest words, **Ligia Balu** paints a haunting picture of her life. She tells how she survived not only the **ABUSE** of her family, but also a man who took **ADVANTAGE** of her, and finally a government that wanted to **IMPRISION** her. **RISKING HER LIFE**, she **ESCAPED** two communist countries and finally found freedom for herself and her daughters in America. "Running from the **WOLVES** and finding the **BIG BAD BEARS**"
ISBN: 0-9651186-0-6

American Dream Made Me Cry and Scream

Is Ligia Balu's INCREDIBLE TRUE STORY of arriving in America and finding the AMERICAN DREAM THAT MADE HER CRY and SCREAM? Once in America, Ligia became ENTRAPPED and VICTIMIZED by the POWERFULL BUREAUCRACY that RAPED, BETRAYED. EXTORTED, and ROBBED.. She was abused by the greed fro money of the BUREAUCRACTIC JUNGLE. She was DISCRIMINATED against, and her CHARACTER was ASSASSINATED. The PAIN, SUFFERING, MANIPULATION, DISAPPOINTMENT, and ISOLATION inflicted upon her by the justice system and her legal advisors were unbelievable. She found that only those who have the power have the rights and the freedom. What kind of system would robe her DREAM and make her CRY and SCREAM? You have to read the book to believe it.\
ISBN: 1-892530-04-X

Adult Romantic Fiction:

Talk Dirty To Me is a collection of light-hearted adult SATRICAL FANTASIES of MODER **N SEXUALITY. Each story is filled with WILD, UNIHIBITED, and INTIMATE SEXUAL DISIRES and PLEAURES.**
ISBN: 1-892530-05-8 Price: $39.99

Order Online

To order or learn more about Ligia Balu's books, visit
www.ligiabalu.com